CLYMER®

HARLEY-DAVIDSON

FLS/FXS TWIN CAM 88B • 2000-2003

MAR – – 2005

The world's finest publisher of mechanical how-to manuals

PRIMEDIA
Business Magazines & Media

P.O. Box 12901, Overland Park, Kansas 66282-2901

Copyright ©2003 PRIMEDIA Business Magazines & Media Inc.

FIRST EDITION
First Printing October, 2003

Printed in U.S.A.

CLYMER and colophon are registered trademarks of PRIMEDIA Business Magazines & Media Inc.

ISBN: 0-89287-865-7

Library of Congress: 2003095966

AUTHOR: Ed Scott.

TECHNICAL PHOTOGRAPHY: Ed Scott, with technical assistance from Jordan Engineering, Oceanside, CA. Motorcycles courtesy of San Diego Harley-Davidson at www.sandiegoharley.com.

TECHNICAL ILLUSTRATIONS: Errol McCarthy.

WIRING DIAGRAMS: Bob Meyer.

EDITOR: James Grooms.

PRODUCTION: Sarah Van Goethen.

TOOLS AND EQUIPMENT: K & L Supply at www.klsupply.com. Engine and transmission special tools provided by JIMS Tools at www.jimsusa.com.

COVER: Mark Clifford Photography at www.markclifford.com. Motorcycle courtesy of Michael Jones, Thousand Oaks, CA.

CONTENTS

QUICK REFERENCE DATA

MOTORCYCLE INFORMATION

MODEL:_____ YEAR:_____

VIN NUMBER:_____

ENGINE SERIAL NUMBER:_____

CARBURETOR SERIAL NUMBER OR I.D. MARK:_____

TIRE INFLATION PRESSURE (COLD)*

Model	kPa	PSI
Front wheels		
Rider only	207	30
Rider and passenger	207	30
Rear wheels		
Rider only	248	36
Rider and passenger	275	40

*Tire pressure for original equipment tires. Aftermarket tires may require different inflation pressure.

ENGINE OIL SPECIFICATIONS

Type	HD rating	Viscosity	Ambient operating temperature
HD Multi-grade	HD360	SAE 10W/40	Below 40° F
HD Multi-grade	HD360	SAE 20W/50	Above 40° F
HD Regular heavy	HD360	SAE 50	Above 60° F
HD Extra heavy	HD360	SAE 60	Above 80° F

ENGINE AND PRIMARY DRIVE/TRANMSSION OIL CAPACITIES

Oil tank refill with filter capacity	3.5 U.S. qts. (3.3 L)
Primary chaincase	26 U.S. oz. (768 ml)
Transmission	
Oil change	20-24 U.S. oz. (591-709 ml)
Rebuild (dry)	24 U.S. oz. (709 ml)

RECOMMENDED LUBRICANTS AND FLUIDS

Brake fluid	DOT 5 silicone
Front fork oil	HD Type E or an equivalent
Fuel	91 pump octane or higher leaded or unleaded
Transmission	HD Transmission Lubricant or an equivalent
Primary chaincase	HD Primary Chaincase Lubricant or an equivalent

MAINTENANCE AND TUNE-UP TORQUE SPECIFICATIONS

Item	Ft.-lb.	in.-lb.	N.m
Air filter			
Torx screws	–	20-40	2-4
Cover screw*	–	36-60	4-7
Clutch adjusting screw			
locknut	–	72-120	8-14
Clutch inspection cover			
screws	–	84-108	9.5-12
Crankcase oil plug	–	120-144	14-16
Front axle nut			
FXST, FLSTC, FLSTF,			
FXSTB, FXSTD	50-55	–	68-75
FLSTS, FXSTS	60-65	–	81-88
Front fork			
Fork tube cap	40-60	–	54-81
Drain screw			
FXSTD	–	12-18	1.4-2.0
All models except FXSTD	52-78	–	6-9
Jiffy stand leg			
stop bolt	–	144-180	16-20
Primary chaincase			
inspection cover screws	–	84-108	9.5-12.2
Chain adjuster shoe nut	21-29	–	29-39
Oil tank drain plug			
on frame rail	14-21	–	19-29
Rear axle nut	60-65	–	81-88
Spark plug	11-18	–	15-24
Transmission drain plug	14-21	–	19-28

*Apply threadlocking compound

FRONT FORK OIL CAPACITY

Model	Capacity (each fork leg)
FLSTF, FLSTC, FXST	12.9 U.S. oz. (382 cc)
FXSTB	12.0 U.S. oz. (356 cc)
FXSTD	11.6 U.S. oz. (343 cc)

MAINTENANCE AND TUNE-UP SPECIFICATIONS

Item	Specification
Engine compression	90 psi (620 kPa)
Spark plugs	HD No. 6R12*
Gap	0.038-0.043 in. (0.97-1.09 mm)
Idle speed	
Carbureted	950-1050 rpm
EFI	Non-adjustable
Ignition timing	Non-adjustable
Drive belt deflection	5/16-3/8 in. (8-10 mm)
Brake pad minimum thickness	
FLSTS & FXSTS	1/16 in. (1.6 mm)
All other models	0.04 in. (1.02 mm)
Clutch cable free play	1/16-1/8 in. (1.6-3.2 mm)

* Harley-Davidson recommends that no other type of spark plug be substituted for the recommended H-D type.

CHAPTER ONE

GENERAL INFORMATION

This detailed and comprehensive manual covers the Harley-Davidson FLST and FXST Softail Series of motorcycles equipped with the Twin Cam 88B engine.

The text provides complete information on maintenance, tune-up, repair and overhaul. Hundreds of original photographs and illustrations created during the complete disassembly of the motorcycle guide the reader through every job. All procedures are in step-by-step form and designed for the reader who may be working on the motorcycle for the first time.

MANUAL ORGANIZATION

A shop manual is a tool and as in all Clymer manuals, the chapters are thumb tabbed for easy reference. Main headings are listed in the table of contents and the index. Frequently used specifications and capacities from the tables at the end of each individual chapter are listed in the *Quick Reference Data* section at the front of the manual. Specifications and capacities are provided in U.S. standard and metric units of measure.

During some of the procedures there will be references to headings in other chapters or sections of the manual. When a specific heading is called out it in a step it will

be *italicized* as it appears in the manual. If a sub-heading is indicated as being "in this section" it is located within the same main heading. For example, the sub-heading *Handling Gasoline Safely* is located within the main heading *SAFETY.*

This chapter provides general information on shop safety, tools and their usage, service fundamentals and shop supplies. **Tables 1-12**, at the end of the chapter, list the following:

Table 1 lists model designation.

Table 2 lists general dimensions.

Table 3 lists motorcycle weight.

Table 4 lists motorcycle weight ratings.

Table 5 lists fuel tank capacity.

Table 6 lists decimal and metric equivalents.

Table 7 lists general torque specifications.

Table 8 lists conversion formulas.

Table 9 lists technical abbreviations.

Table 10 lists American tap and drill sizes.

Table 11 lists Metric tap and drill sizes.

Table 12 lists special tools and their part numbers.

Chapter Two provides methods for quick and accurate diagnosis of problems. Troubleshooting procedures present typical symptoms and logical methods to pinpoint and repair the problem.

Chapter Three explains all routine maintenance necessary to keep the motorcycle running well. Chapter Three also includes recommended tune-up procedures, eliminating the need to constantly consult other chapters on the various assemblies.

Subsequent chapters describe specific systems such as engine, transmission, clutch, drive system, fuel and exhaust systems, suspension and brakes. Each disassembly, repair and assembly procedure is given in step-by-step form.

WARNINGS, CAUTIONS AND NOTES

The terms, WARNING, CAUTION and NOTE have specific meanings in this manual.

A WARNING emphasizes areas where injury or even death could result from negligence. Mechanical damage may also occur. WARNINGS *are to be taken seriously.*

A CAUTION emphasizes areas where equipment damage could occur. Disregarding a CAUTION could cause permanent mechanical damage, though injury is unlikely.

A NOTE provides additional information to make a step or procedure easier or clearer. Disregarding a NOTE could cause inconvenience, but would not cause equipment damage or personal injury.

SAFETY

Professional mechanics can work for years and never sustain a serious injury or mishap. Follow these guidelines and practice common sense to safely service the motorcycle.

1. Do not operate the motorcycle in an enclosed area. The exhaust gasses contain carbon monoxide, an odorless, colorless and tasteless poisonous gas. Carbon monoxide levels build quickly in small enclosed areas and can cause unconsciousness and death in a short time. Make sure the work area is properly ventilated or operate the motorcycle outside.

2. *Never* use gasoline or extremely flammable liquid to clean parts. Refer to *Cleaning Parts* and *Handling Gasoline Safely* in this chapter.

3. *Never* smoke or use a torch in the vicinity of flammable liquids, such as gasoline or cleaning solvent.

4. Before welding or brazing on the motorcycle, remove the fuel tank, carburetor and shocks to a safe distance at least 50 ft. (15 m) away.

5. Use the correct type and size of tools to avoid damaging fasteners.

6. Keep tools clean and in good condition. Replace or repair worn or damaged equipment.

7. When loosening a tight fastener, be guided by what would happen if the tool slips.

8. When replacing fasteners, make sure the new fasteners are the same size and strength as the original ones.

9. Keep the work area clean and organized.

10. Wear eye protection *anytime* the safety of the eyes is in question. This includes procedures involving drilling, grinding, hammering, compressed air and chemicals.

11. Wear the correct clothing for the job. Tie up or cover long hair so it can not get caught in moving equipment.

12. Do not carry sharp tools in clothing pockets.

13. Always have an approved fire extinguisher available. Make sure it is rated for gasoline (Class B) and electrical (Class C) fires.

14. Do not use compressed air to clean clothes, the motorcycle or the work area. Debris may be blown into the eyes or skin. *Never* direct compressed air at anyone. Do not allow children to use or play with any compressed air equipment.

15. When using compressed air to dry rotating parts, hold the part so it cannot rotate. Do not allow the force of the air to spin the part. The air jet is capable of rotating parts at extreme speed. The part may be damaged or disintegrate and cause serious injury.

16. Do not inhale the dust created by brake pad and clutch wear. These particles may contain asbestos. In addition, some types of insulating materials and gaskets may contain asbestos. Inhaling asbestos particles is hazardous to health.

17. Never work on the motorcycle while someone is working under it.

18. When placing the motorcycle on a stand, make sure it is secure before walking away.

Handling Gasoline Safely

Gasoline is a volatile flammable liquid and is one of the most dangerous items in the shop. Because gasoline is used so often, many people forget that it is hazardous. Only use gasoline as fuel for gasoline internal combustion engines. When working on a motorcycle, keep in mind that gasoline is always present in the fuel tank, fuel line and carburetor. To avoid a disastrous accident when working around the fuel system, carefully observe the following precautions:

1. *Never* use gasoline to clean parts. See *Parts Cleaning* in this section.

2. When working on the fuel system, work outside or in a well-ventilated area.

3. Do not add fuel to the fuel tank or service the fuel system while the motorcycle is near open flames, sparks or where someone is smoking. Gasoline vapor is heavier than air, it collects in low areas and is more easily ignited than liquid gasoline.

4. Allow the engine to cool completely before working on any fuel system component.

5. When draining the carburetor, catch the fuel in a plastic container and pour it into an approved gasoline storage devise.

6. Do not store gasoline in glass containers. If the glass breaks, a serious explosion or fire may occur.

7. Immediately wipe up spilled gasoline with rags. Store the rags in a metal container with a lid until they can be properly disposed of, or place them outside in a safe place for the fuel to evaporate.

8. Do not pour water onto a gasoline fire. Water spreads the fire and makes it more difficult to put out. Use a class B, BC or ABC fire extinguisher to extinguish the fire.

9. Always turn off the engine before refueling. Do not spill fuel onto the engine or exhaust system. Do not overfill the fuel tank. Leave an air space at the top of the tank to allow room for the fuel to expand due to temperature fluctuations.

Parts Cleaning

Cleaning parts is one of the more tedious and difficult service jobs performed in the home garage. There are many types of chemical cleaners and solvents available for shop use. Most are poisonous and extremely flammable. To prevent chemical exposure, vapor buildup, fire and serious injury, note the following:

1. Read and observe the entire product label before using any chemical. Always know what type of chemical is being used and whether it is poisonous and/or flammable.

2. Do not use more than one type of cleaning solvent at a time. When mixing chemicals, measure the proper amounts according to the manufacturer.

3. Work in a well-ventilated area.

4. Wear chemical-resistant gloves.

5. Wear safety glasses.

6. Wear a vapor respirator if the instructions call for it.

7. Wash hands and arms thoroughly after cleaning parts.

8. Keep chemical products away from children and pets.

9. Thoroughly clean all oil, grease and cleaner residue from any part that must be heated.

10. Use a nylon brush when cleaning parts. Metal brushes may cause a spark.

11. When using a parts washer, only use the solvent recommended by the manufacturer. Make sure the parts washer is equipped with a metal lid that will lower in case of fire.

Warning Labels

Most manufacturers attach information and warning labels to the motorcycle. These labels contain instructions that are important to personal safety when operating, servicing, transporting and storing the motorcycle. Refer to the owner's manual for the description and location of labels. Order replacement labels from the manufacturer if they are missing or damaged.

SERIAL NUMBERS

Serial numbers are stamped on various locations on the frame, engine, transmission and carburetor. Record these numbers in the *Quick Reference Data* section in the front of the manual. Have these numbers available when ordering parts.

The frame serial number (**Figure 1**) is stamped on the right side of the frame down tube.

The VIN number label (**Figure 2**) is located just below the frame number on the right side frame down tube.

The engine serial number is stamped on a pad on the left side of the crankcase (**Figure 3**) and the right side of the crankcase (**Figure 4**).

The transmission serial number (**Figure 5**) is stamped on a pad on the right side of the transmission case next to the side door.

The carburetor serial number (**Figure 6**) is located on the side of the carburetor body next to the accelerator pump linkage. There is no serial number for the fuel injection module.

Table 1 lists model designation.

FASTENERS

Proper fastener selection and installation is important to ensure the motorcycle operates as designed and can be serviced efficiently. The choice of original equipment fasteners is not arrived at by chance. Make sure that replacement fasteners meet all the same requirements as the originals.

Threaded Fasteners

Threaded fasteners secure most of the components on the motorcycle. Most are tightened by turning them clockwise (right-hand threads). If the normal rotation of the component being tightened would loosen the fastener, it may have left-hand threads. If a left-hand threaded fastener is used, it is noted in the text.

Two dimensions are required to match the threads of the fastener: the number of threads in a given distance and the outside diameter of the threads.

CAUTION
There are a variety of Metric and American fasteners used on the engine and chassis. Do not interchange fasteners of the incorrect type as the component along with the fastener may be damaged.

Two systems are currently used to specify threaded fastener dimensions: the U.S. Standard system and the metric system (**Figure 7**). Pay particular attention when working with unidentified fasteners; mismatching thread types can damage threads.

NOTE
To ensure the fastener threads are not mismatched or cross-threaded, start all fasteners by hand. If a fastener is hard to start or turn, determine the cause before tightening with a wrench.

The length (L, **Figure 8**), diameter (D) and distance between thread crests (pitch) (T) classify metric screws and bolts. A typical bolt may be identified by the numbers, 8—1.25 × 130. This indicates the bolt has diameter of 8 mm, the distance between thread crests is 1.25 mm and the length is 130 mm. Always measure bolt length as shown in **Figure 8** to avoid purchasing replacements of the wrong length.

If a number is located on the top of the fastener, (**Figure 8**) this indicates the strength of the fastener. The higher the number, the stronger the fastener. Generally, unnumbered fasteners are the weakest.

Many screws, bolts and studs are combined with nuts to secure particular components. To indicate the size of a

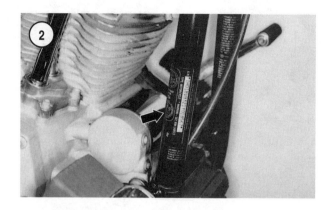

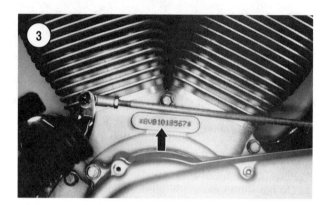

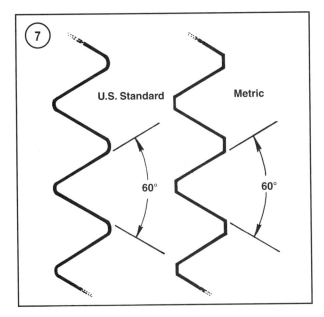

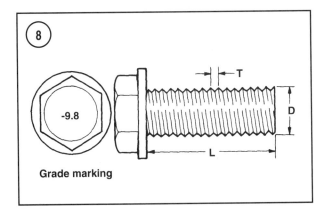

Grade marking

nut, manufacturers specify the internal diameter and the thread pitch.

The measurement across two flats on a nut or bolt indicates the wrench size.

WARNING
Do not install fasteners with a strength classification lower than what was originally installed by the manufacturer. Doing so may cause equipment failure and/or damage.

Torque Specifications

The materials used in the manufacture of the motorcycle may be subjected to uneven stresses if the fasteners of the various subassemblies are not installed and tightened correctly. Fasteners that are improperly installed or work loose can cause extensive damage. It is essential to use an accurate torque wrench, described in this chapter, with the torque specifications in this manual.

Specifications for torque are provided in Newton-meters (N•m), foot-pounds (ft.-lb.) and inch-pounds (in.-lb.). Refer to **Table 7** for general torque specifications. To use **Table 7**, first determine the size of the fastener as described in *Threaded Fasteners* in this section. Torque specifications for specific components are at the end of the appropriate chapters. Torque wrenches are covered in the *Basic Tools* section.

Self-Locking Fasteners

Several types of bolts, screws and nuts incorporate a system that creates interference between the two fasteners. Interference is achieved in various ways. The most common type is the nylon insert nut and a dry adhesive coating on the threads of a bolt.

Self-locking fasteners offer greater holding strength than standard fasteners, which improves their resistance to vibration. Most self-locking fasteners cannot be reused. The materials used to form the lock become distorted after the initial installation and removal. It is a good practice to discard and replace self-locking fasteners after their removal. Do not replace self-locking fasteners with standard fasteners.

Washers

There are two basic types of washers: flat washers and lockwashers. Flat washers are simple discs with a hole to fit a screw or bolt. Lockwashers are used to prevent a fastener from working loose. Washers can be used as spacers and seals, or to help distribute fastener load and to prevent the fastener from damaging the component.

As with fasteners, when replacing washers, make sure the replacement washers are of the same design and quality.

Cotter Pins

A cotter pin is a split metal pin inserted into a hole or slot to prevent a fastener from loosening. In certain applications, such as the rear axle on an ATV or motorcycle, the fastener must be secured in this way. For these applications, a cotter pin and castellated (slotted) nut is used.

To use a cotter pin, first make sure the diameter is correct for the hole in the fastener. After correctly tightening the fastener and aligning the holes, insert the cotter pin through the hole and bend the ends over the fastener (**Figure 9**). Unless instructed to do so, never loosen a torqued fastener to align the holes. If the holes do not align, tighten the fastener just enough to achieve alignment.

Cotter pins are available in various diameters and lengths. Measure length from the bottom of the head to the tip of the shortest pin.

Snap Rings and E-clips

Snap rings (**Figure 10**) are circular-shaped metal retaining clips. They are required to secure parts and gears in place on parts such as shafts, pins or rods. External type snap rings are used to retain items on shafts. Internal type snap rings secure parts within housing bores. In some applications, in addition to securing the component(s), snap rings of varying thickness also determine endplay. These are usually called selective snap rings.

Two basic types of snap rings are used: machined and stamped snap rings. Machined snap rings (**Figure 11**) can be installed in either direction, since both faces have sharp edges. Stamped snap rings (**Figure 12**) are manufactured with a sharp edge and a round edge. When installing a stamped snap ring in a thrust application, install the sharp edge facing away from the part producing the thrust.

Remove E-clips with a flat blade screwdriver by prying between the shaft and E-clip. To install an E-clip, center it over the shaft groove and push or tap it into place.

Observe the following when installing snap rings:

1. Remove and install snap rings with snap ring pliers. See *Snap Ring Pliers* in this chapter.

2. In some applications, it may be necessary to replace snap rings after removing them.

3. Compress or expand snap rings only enough to install them. If overly expanded, they lose their retaining ability.

4. After installing a snap ring, make sure it seats completely.

5. Wear eye protection when removing and installing snap rings.

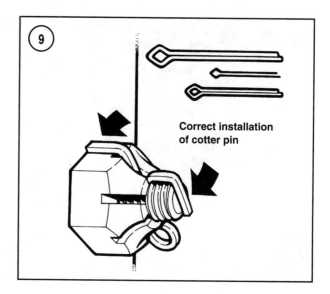

Correct installation of cotter pin

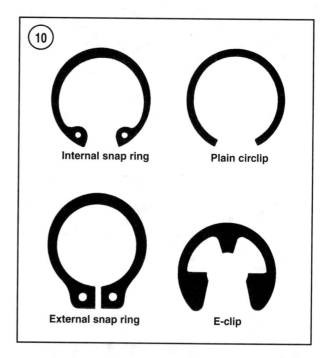

Internal snap ring   Plain circlip

External snap ring   E-clip

SHOP SUPPLIES

Lubricants and Fluids

Periodic lubrication helps ensure a long service life for any type of equipment. Using the correct type of lubricant is as important as performing the lubrication service, although in an emergency the wrong type is better than none. The following section describes the types of lubricants most often required. Make sure to follow the manufacturer's recommendations for lubricant types.

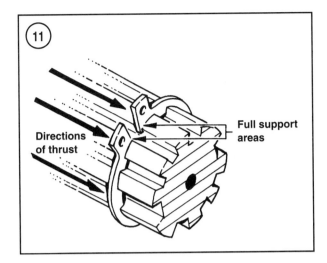

Directions of thrust

Full support areas

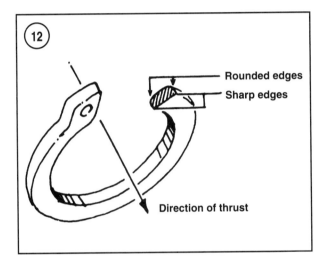

Rounded edges

Sharp edges

Direction of thrust

Viscosity is an indication of the oil's thickness. Thin oils have a lower number while thick oils have a higher number. Engine oils fall into the 5- to 50-weight range for single-grade oils.

Most manufacturers recommend multigrade oil. These oils perform efficiently across a wide range of operating conditions. Multigrade oils are identified by a (*W*) after the first number, which indicates the low-temperature viscosity.

Engine oils are most commonly mineral (petroleum) based; however, synthetic and semi-synthetic types are used more frequently. When selecting engine oil, follow the manufacturer's recommendation for type, classification and viscosity.

Greases

Grease is lubricating oil with thickening agents added to it. The National Lubricating Grease Institute (NLGI) grades grease. Grades range from No. 000 to No. 6, with No. 6 being the thickest. Typical multipurpose grease is NLGI No. 2. For specific applications, manufacturers may recommend water-resistant type grease or one with an additive such as molybdenum disulfide (MoS_2).

Brake fluid

Brake fluid is the hydraulic fluid used to transmit hydraulic pressure (force) to the wheel brakes. Brake fluid is classified by the Department of Transportation (DOT). Current designations for brake fluid are DOT 3, DOT 4 and DOT 5. This classification appears on the fluid container.

Each type of brake fluid has its own definite characteristics. The Harley-Davidson Softail uses the silicone based DOT 5 brake fluid. Do not intermix DOT 3 or DOT 4 with DOT 5 type brake fluid as this may cause brake system failure since the DOT 5 brake fluid is not compatible with other brake fluids. When adding brake fluid, *only* use the fluid recommended by the manufacturer.

Brake fluid will damage any plastic, painted or plated surface it contacts. Use extreme care when working with brake fluid and clean up spills immediately with soap and water.

Hydraulic brake systems require clean and moisture-free brake fluid. Never reuse brake fluid. Keep containers and reservoirs properly sealed.

> *WARNING*
> *Never put a mineral-based (petroleum) oil into the brake system. Mineral oil will cause rubber parts in the system to swell and*

Engine oils

Engine oil is classified by two standards: the American Petroleum Institute (API) service classification and the Society of Automotive Engineers (SAE) viscosity rating. This information is on the oil container label. Two letters indicate the API service classification. The number or sequence of numbers and letter (10W-40 for example) is the oil's viscosity rating. The API service classification and the SAE viscosity index are not indications of oil quality.

The service classification indicates that the oil meets specific lubrication standards. The first letter in the classification (*S*) indicates that the oil is for gasoline engines. The second letter indicates the standard the oil satisfies.

Always use an oil with a classification recommended by the manufacturer. Using an oil with a different classification can cause engine damage.

break apart, resulting in complete brake failure.

Cleaners, Degreasers and Solvents

Many chemicals are available to remove oil, grease and other residue from the motorcycle. Before using cleaning solvents, consider how they will be used and disposed of, particularly if they are not water-soluble. Local ordinances may require special procedures for the disposal of many types of cleaning chemicals. Refer to *Safety* and *Parts Cleaning* in this chapter for more information on their use.

To clean brake system components, use brake parts cleaner. Petroleum-based products will damage brake system seals. Brake parts cleaner leaves no residue. Use electrical contact cleaner to clean electrical connections and components without leaving any residue. Carburetor cleaner is a powerful solvent used to remove fuel deposits and varnish from fuel system components. Use this cleaner carefully, as it may damage finishes.

Generally, degreasers are strong cleaners used to remove heavy accumulations of grease from engine and frame components.

Most solvents are designed to be used in a parts washing cabinet for individual component cleaning. For safety, use only nonflammable or high flash point solvents.

Gasket Sealant

Sealants are used with a gasket or seal and are occasionally used alone. Follow the manufacturer's recommendation when using sealants. Use extreme care when choosing a sealant different from the type originally recommended. Choose sealants based on their resistance to heat and various fluids, and their sealing capabilities.

One of the most common sealants is RTV, or room temperature vulcanizing sealant. This sealant cures at room temperature over a specific time period. This allows the repositioning of components without damaging gaskets.

Moisture in the air causes the RTV sealant to cure. Always install the tube cap as soon as possible after applying RTV sealant. RTV sealant has a limited shelf life and will not cure properly if the shelf life has expired. Keep partial tubes sealed and discard them if they have surpassed the expiration date.

Applying RTV sealant

Clean all old gasket residue from the mating surfaces. Remove all gasket material from blind threaded holes; it

can cause inaccurate bolt torque. Spray the mating surfaces with aerosol parts cleaner and wipe with a lint-free cloth. The area must be clean for the sealant to adhere.

Apply RTV sealant in a continuous bead 2-3 mm (0.08-0.12 in.) thick. Circle all the fastener holes unless otherwise specified. Do not allow any sealant to enter these holes. Assemble and tighten the fasteners to the specified torque within the time frame recommended by the RTV sealant manufacturer.

Gasket Remover

Aerosol gasket remover can help remove stubborn gaskets. This product can speed up the removal process and prevent damage to the mating surface that may be caused by using a scraping tool. Most of these types of products are very caustic. Follow the gasket remover manufacturer's instructions for use.

Threadlocking Compound

A threadlocking compound is a fluid applied to the threads of fasteners. After the fastener is tightened, the fluid dries and becomes a solid filler between the threads. This makes it difficult for the fastener to work loose from vibration, or heat expansion and contraction. Some threadlocking compounds also provide a seal against fluid leakage.

Before applying threadlocking compound, remove any old compound from both thread areas and clean them with aerosol parts cleaner. Use the compound sparingly. Excess fluid can run into adjoining parts.

Threadlocking compounds are available in different strengths. Follow the particular manufacturer's recommendations regarding compound selection. A number of manufacturers offer a wide range of threadlocking compounds for various strength, temperature and repair applications.

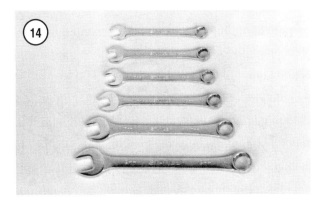

BASIC TOOLS

Most of the procedures in this manual can be carried out with simple hand tools and test equipment familiar to the home mechanic. Always use the correct tools for the job at hand. Keep tools organized and clean. Store them in a tool chest with related tools organized together.

Some of the procedures in this manual specify special tools. In most cases, the tool is illustrated in use. Well-equipped mechanics may be able to substitute similar tools or fabricate a suitable replacement. In some cases, specialized equipment or expertise may make it impractical for the home mechanic to attempt the procedure. Such operations are identified in the text with the recommendation to have a dealership or specialist perform the task. It may be less expensive to have a professional perform these jobs, especially when considering the cost of the equipment.

Quality tools are essential. The best are constructed of high-strength alloy steel. These tools are light, easy to use and resistant to wear. Their working surface is devoid of sharp edges and the tool is carefully polished. They have an easy-to-clean finish and are comfortable to use. Quality tools are a good investment.

When purchasing tools to perform the procedures covered in this manual, consider the tool's potential frequency of use. If starting a tool kit, consider purchasing a basic tool set (**Figure 13**) from a large tool supplier. These sets are available in many tool combinations and offer substantial savings when compared to individually purchased tools. As work experience grows and tasks become more complicated, specialized tools can be added.

The models covered in this manual use both U.S. Standard and metric fasteners. Make sure the correct type of tool is used.

Screwdrivers

Screwdrivers of various lengths and types are mandatory for the simplest tool kit. The two basic types are the slotted tip (flat blade) and the Phillips tip. These are available in sets that often include an assortment of tip sizes and shaft lengths.

As with all tools, use a screwdriver designed for the job. Make sure the size of the tip conforms to the size and shape of the fastener. Use them only for driving screws. Never use a screwdriver for prying or chiseling metal. Repair or replace worn or damaged screwdrivers. A worn tip may damage the fastener, making it difficult to remove.

Torx Drivers

Many of the components on the Harley-Davidson models covered in this manual are secured with internal Torx fasteners. These fasteners require specific Torx drivers for removal and installation. These fasteners reduce cam-out and fastener damage, and allow high torque transmission due to the complete enclosure of the driver within the fastener.

Torx screwdrivers in individual sizes, or screwdrivers that accept various bit sizes are available. However, the most practical application is a Torx bit set that accepts various drive types and sizes. A typical set contains T-10 through T40 bits that accept 1/4 and 3/8 in. drive attachments.

Wrenches

Open-end, box-end and combination wrenches (**Figure 14**) are available in a variety of types and sizes.

The number stamped on the wrench refers to the distance between the work areas. This size must match the size of the fastener head.

The box-end wrench is an excellent tool because it grips the fastener on all sides. This reduces the chance of the tool slipping. The box-end wrench is designed with either a 6- or 12-point opening. For stubborn or damaged fasteners, the 6-point provides superior holding ability by contacting the fastener across a wider area at all six edges. For general use, the 12-point works well. It allows the wrench to be removed and reinstalled without moving the handle over such a wide arc.

An open-end wrench is fast and works best in areas with limited overhead access. It contacts the fastener at only two points, and is subject to slipping under heavy force, or if the tool or fastener is worn. A box-end wrench is preferred in most instances, especially when breaking a fastener loose and applying the final tightness to a fastener.

The combination wrench has a box-end on one end and an open-end on the other. This combination makes it a very convenient tool.

Adjustable Wrenches

An adjustable wrench or Crescent wrench (**Figure 15**) can fit nearly any nut or bolt head that has clear access around its entire perimeter. Adjustable wrenches are best used as a backup wrench to keep a large nut or bolt from turning while the other end is being loosened or tightened with a box-end or socket wrench.

Adjustable wrenches contact the fastener at only two points, which makes them more subject to slipping off the fastener. The fact that one jaw is adjustable and may loosen only aggravates this shortcoming. Make certain the solid jaw is the one transmitting the force.

Socket Wrenches, Ratchets and Handles

Sockets that attach to a ratchet handle (**Figure 16**) are available with 6-point (A, **Figure 17**) or 12-point (B) openings and different drive sizes. The drive size indicates the size of the square hole that accepts the ratchet handle. The number stamped on the socket is the size of the work area and must match the fastener head.

As with wrenches, a 6-point socket provides superior holding ability, while a 12-point socket needs to be moved only half as far to reposition it on the fastener.

Sockets are designated for either hand or impact use. Impact sockets are made of thicker material for more durability. Compare the size and wall thickness of a 19-mm hand socket (A, **Figure 18**) and the 19-mm impact socket (B). Use impact sockets when using an impact driver or air tools. Use hand sockets with hand-driven attachments.

> *WARNING*
> *Do not use hand sockets with air or impact tools as they may shatter and cause injury. Always wear eye protection when using impact or air tools.*

Various handles are available for sockets. The speed handle is used for fast operation. Flexible ratchet heads in varying lengths allow the socket to be turned with varying force, and at odd angles. Extension bars allow the socket setup to reach difficult areas. The ratchet is the most versatile. It allows the user to install or remove the nut without removing the socket.

Sockets combined with any number of drivers make them undoubtedly the fastest, safest and most convenient tool for fastener removal and installation.

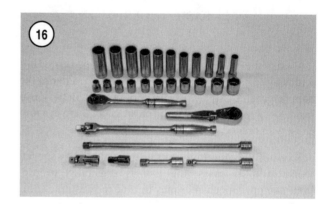

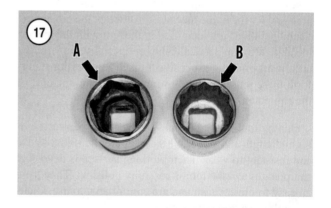

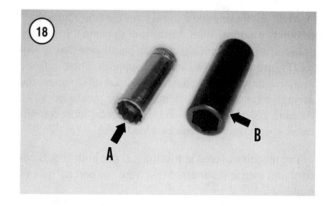

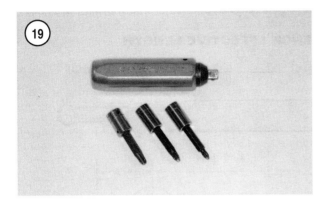

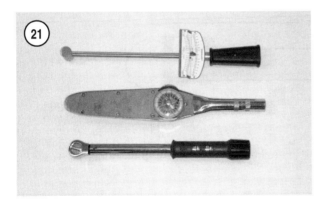

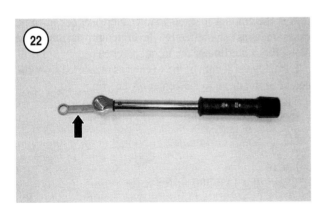

Impact Driver

An impact driver provides extra force for removing fasteners by converting the impact of a hammer into a turning motion. This makes it possible to remove stubborn fasteners without damaging them. Impact drivers and interchangeable bits (**Figure 19**) are available from most tool suppliers. When using a socket with an impact driver, make sure the socket is designed for impact use. Refer to *Socket Wrenches, Ratchets and Handles* in this section.

WARNING
Do not use hand sockets with air or impact tools as they may shatter and cause injury. Always wear eye protection when using impact or air tools.

Allen Wrenches

Allen or setscrew wrenches (**Figure 20**) are used on fasteners with hexagonal recesses in the fastener head. These wrenches are available in L-shaped bar, socket and T-handle types. Most motorcycles are equipped with metric fasteners. Allen bolts are sometimes called socket bolts.

Torque Wrenches

A torque wrench (**Figure 21**) is used with a socket, torque adapter or similar extension to tighten a fastener to a measured torque. Torque wrenches come in several drive sizes (1/4, 3/8, ½ and 3/4) and have various methods of reading the torque value. The drive size indicates the size of the square drive that accepts the socket, adapter or extension. Common methods of reading the torque value are the deflecting beam, the dial indicator and the audible click .

When choosing a torque wrench, consider the torque range, drive size and accuracy. The torque specifications in this manual indicate the range required.

A torque wrench is a precision tool that must be properly cared for to remain accurate. Store torque wrenches in cases or separate padded drawers within a toolbox. Follow the manufacturer's instructions for their care and calibration.

Torque Adapters

Torque adapters or extensions extend or reduce the reach of a torque wrench. The torque adapter shown in **Figure 22** is used to tighten a fastener that cannot be reached due to the size of the torque wrench head, drive and socket. If a torque adapter changes the effective lever length (**Figure 23**), the torque reading on the wrench will not equal the actual torque applied to the fastener. It is nec-

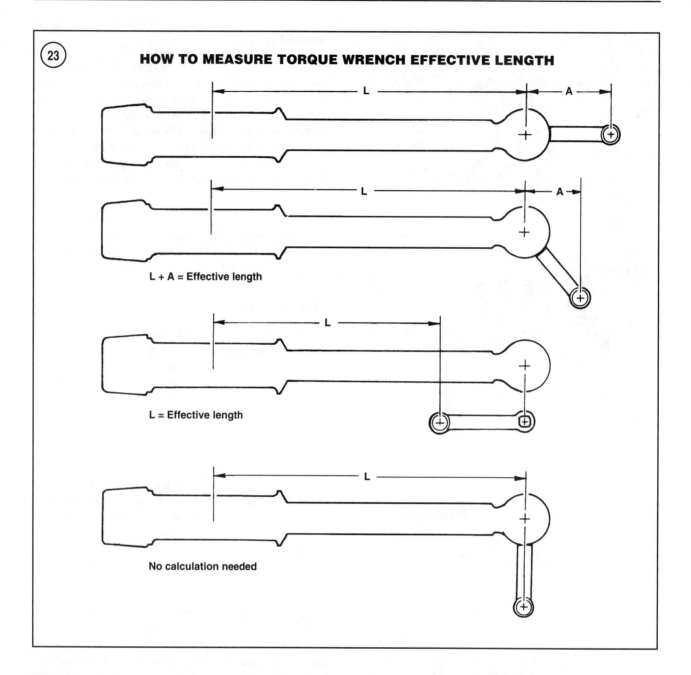

HOW TO MEASURE TORQUE WRENCH EFFECTIVE LENGTH

L + A = Effective length

L = Effective length

No calculation needed

essary to recalibrate the torque setting on the wrench to compensate for the change of lever length. When a torque adapter is used at a right angle to the drive head, calibration is not required since the effective length has not changed.

To recalculate a torque reading when using a torque adapter, use the following formula and refer to **Figure 23**.

$$TW = \frac{TA \times L}{L + A}$$

TW is the torque setting or dial reading on the wrench.

TA is the torque specification and the actual amount of torque that will be applied to the fastener.

A is the amount that the adapter increases (or in some cases reduces) the effective lever length as measured along the centerline of the torque wrench.

L is the lever length of the wrench as measured from the center of the drive to the center of the grip.

The effective length is the sum of L and A.

Example:

TA = 20 ft.-lb.

A = 3 in.

L = 14 in.

$$TW = \frac{20 \times 14}{14 + 3} = \frac{280}{17} = 16.5 \text{ ft. lb.}$$

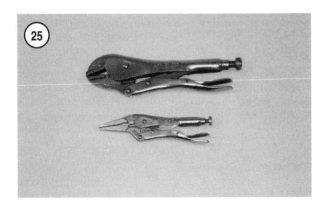

In this example, the torque wrench would be set to the recalculated torque value (TW = 16.5 ft.-lb.) . When using a beam-type wrench, tighten the fastener until the pointer aligns with 16.5 ft.-lb. In this example, although the torque wrench is pre-set to 16.5 ft.-lb., the actual torque is 20 ft.-lb.

Pliers

Pliers come in a wide range of types and sizes. Pliers are useful for holding, cutting, bending and crimping. Do not use them to turn fasteners. **Figure 24** show several types of useful pliers. Each design has a specialized function. Slip-joint pliers are general-purpose pliers used for gripping and bending. Diagonal cutting pliers are needed to cut wire and can be used to remove cotter pins. Needlenose pliers are used to hold or bend small objects. Locking pliers (**Figure 25**), sometimes called Vise-grips, are used to hold objects very tightly. They have many uses ranging from holding two parts together, to gripping the end of a broken stud. Use caution when using locking pliers, as the sharp jaws will damage the objects they hold.

Snap Ring Pliers

Snap ring pliers are specialized pliers with tips that fit into the ends of snap rings to remove and install them.

Snap ring pliers are available with a fixed action (either internal or external) or convertible (one tool works on both internal and external snap rings). They may have fixed tips or interchangeable ones of various sizes and angles. For general use, select a convertible type pliers with interchangeable tips.

> *WARNING*
> *Snap rings can slip and fly off when they are being removed and installed. Also, the snap ring pliers tips may break. Always wear eye protection when using snap ring pliers.*

Hammers

Various types of hammers (**Figure 26**) are available to fit a number of applications. A ball-peen hammer is used to strike another tool, such as a punch or chisel. Soft-faced hammers are required when a metal object must be struck without damaging it. *Never* use a metal-faced hammer on engine and suspension components, as damage will occur in most cases.

Always wear eye protection when using hammers. Make sure the hammer face is in good condition and the handle is not cracked. Select the correct hammer for the job and make sure to strike the object squarely. Do not use the handle or the side of the hammer to strike an object.

SPECIAL TOOLS

Many of the procedures in this manual require special tools. These are described in the appropriate chapter and are available from either the manufacturer or a tool supplier. See **Table 12**.

In many cases, an acceptable substitute may be found in an existing tool kit. Another alternative is to make the tool. Many schools with a machine shop curriculum welcome outside work that can be used as practical shop applications for students.

PRECISION MEASURING TOOLS

The ability to accurately measure components is essential to successful service and repair. Equipment is manufactured to close tolerances, and obtaining consistently accurate measurements is essential to determining which components require replacement or further service.

Each type of measuring instrument is designed to measure a dimension with a certain degree of accuracy and within a certain range. When selecting the measuring tool, make sure it is applicable to the task.

As with all tools, measuring tools provide the best results if cared for properly. Improper use can damage the tool and result in inaccurate results. If any measurement is questionable, verify the measurement using another tool. A standard gauge is usually provided with measuring tools to check accuracy and calibrate the tool if necessary.

Precision measurements can vary according to the experience of the person performing the procedure. Accurate results are only possible if the mechanic possesses a feel for using the tool. Heavy-handed use of measuring tools will produce less accurate results. Hold the tool gently by the fingertips so the point at which the tool contacts the object is easily felt. This feel for the equipment will produce more accurate measurements and reduce the risk of damaging the tool or component. Refer to the following sections for specific measuring tools.

Feeler Gauge

The feeler or thickness gauge (**Figure 27**) is used for measuring the distance between two surfaces.

A feeler gauge set consists of an assortment of steel strips of graduated thickness. Each blade is marked with its thickness. Blades can be of various lengths and angles for different procedures.

A common use for a feeler gauge is to measure valve clearance. Wire (round) type gauges are used to measure spark plug gap.

Calipers

Calipers (**Figure 28**) are excellent tools for obtaining inside, outside and depth measurements. Although not as precise as a micrometer, they allow reasonable precision, typically to within 0.05 mm (0.001 in.). Most calipers have a range up to 150 mm (6 in.).

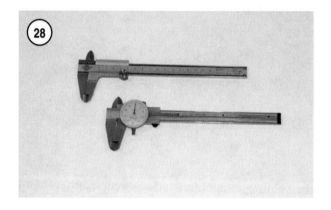

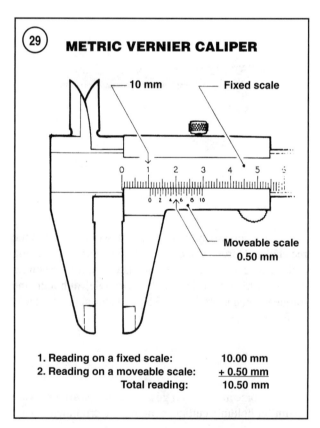

METRIC VERNIER CALIPER

10 mm
Fixed scale

0 1 2 3 4 5

Moveable scale
0.50 mm

1. Reading on a fixed scale:	10.00 mm
2. Reading on a moveable scale:	+ 0.50 mm
Total reading:	10.50 mm

DECIMAL PLACE VALUES*	
0.1	Indicates 1/10 (one tenth of an inch or millimeter)
0.010	Indicates 1/100 (one one-hundreth of an inch or millimeter)
0.001	Indicates 1/1,000 (one one-thousandth of an inch or millimeter)

*This chart represents the values of figures placed to the right of the decimal point. Use it when reading decimals from one-tenth to one one-thousandth of an inch or millimeter. It is not a conversion chart (for example: 0.001 in. is not equal to 0.001 mm).

Calipers are available in dial, vernier or digital versions. Dial calipers have a dial readout that provides convenient reading. Vernier calipers have marked scales that must be compared to determine the measurement. The digital caliper uses an LCD to show the measurement.

Properly maintain the measuring surfaces of the caliper. There must not be any dirt or burrs between the tool and the object being measured. Never force the caliper closed around an object; close the caliper around the highest point so it can be removed with a slight drag. Some calipers require calibration. Always refer to the manufacturer's instructions when using a new or unfamiliar caliper.

To read a vernier caliper, refer to **Figure 29**. The fixed scale is marked in 1.0 mm increments. Ten individual lines on the fixed scale equal 1 cm. The moveable scale is marked in 0.05 mm (hundredth) increments. To obtain a reading, establish the first number by the location of the 0 line on the movable scale in relation to the first line to the left on the fixed scale. In this example, the number is 10 mm. To determine the next number, note which of the lines on the movable scale align with a mark on the fixed scale. A number of lines will seem close, but only one will

align exactly. In this case, 0.50 mm is the reading to add to the first number. The result of adding 10 mm and 0.50 mm is a measurement of 10.50 mm.

Micrometers

A micrometer is an instrument designed for linear measurement using the decimal divisions of the inch or meter (**Figure 30**). While there are many types and styles of micrometers, most of the procedures in this manual call for an outside micrometer. The outside micrometer is used to measure the outside diameter of cylindrical forms and the thickness of materials.

A micrometer's size indicates the minimum and maximum size of a part that it can measure. The usual sizes (**Figure 31**) are 0-1 in. (0-25 mm), 1-2 in. (25-50 mm), 2-3 in. (50-75 mm) and 3-4 in. (75-100 mm).

Micrometers that cover a wider range of measurements are available. These use a large frame with interchangeable anvils of various lengths. This type of micrometer offers a cost savings, however, its overall size may make it less convenient.

Reading a Micrometer

When reading a micrometer, numbers are taken from different scales and added together. The following sections describe how to read the measurements of various types of outside micrometers.

For accurate results, properly maintain the measuring surfaces of the micrometer. There cannot be any dirt or burrs between the tool and the measured object. Never force the micrometer closed around an object. Close the micrometer around the highest point so it can be removed with a slight drag. **Figure 32** shows the markings and parts

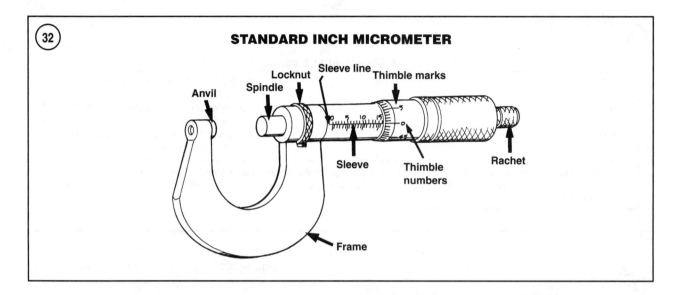

of a standard inch micrometer. Be familiar with these terms before using a micrometer in the follow sections.

Standard inch micrometer

The standard inch micrometer is accurate to one-thousandth of an inch or 0.001. The sleeve is marked in 0.025 in. increments. Every fourth sleeve mark is numbered 1, 2, 3, 4, 5, 6, 7, 8, 9. These numbers indicate 0.100, 0.200, 0.300, and so on.

The tapered end of the thimble has 25 lines marked around it. Each mark equals 0.001 in. One complete turn of the thimble will align its zero mark with the first mark on the sleeve or 0.025 in.

To read a standard inch micrometer, perform the following steps and refer to **Figure 33**.

1. Read the sleeve and find the largest number visible. Each sleeve number equals 0.100 in.

2. Count the number of lines between the numbered sleeve mark and the edge of the thimble. Each sleeve mark equals 0.025 in.

3. Read the thimble mark that aligns with the sleeve line. Each thimble mark equals 0.001 in.

NOTE
If a thimble mark does not align exactly with the sleeve line, estimate the amount between the lines. For accurate readings in ten-thousandths of an inch (0.0001 in.), use a vernier inch micrometer.

4. Add the readings from Steps 1-3.

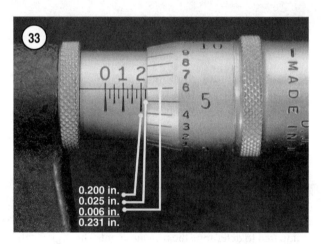

Metric micrometer

The standard metric micrometer (**Figure 34**) is accurate to one one-hundredth of a millimeter (0.01-mm). The sleeve line is graduated in millimeter and half millimeter increments. The marks on the upper half of the sleeve line equal 1.00 mm. Every fifth mark above the sleeve line is identified with a number. The number sequence depends on the size of the micrometer. A 0-25 mm micrometer, for example, will have sleeve marks numbered 0 through 25 in 5 mm increments. This numbering sequence continues with larger micrometers. On all metric micrometers, each mark on the lower half of the sleeve equals 0.50 mm.

The tapered end of the thimble has 50 lines marked around it. Each mark equals 0.01 mm. One complete turn of the thimble aligns its 0 mark with the first line on the lower half of the sleeve line or 0.50 mm.

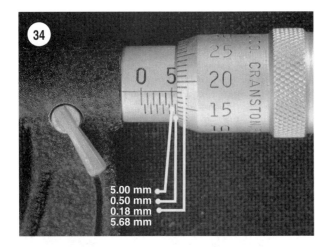

5.00 mm
0.50 mm
0.18 mm
5.68 mm

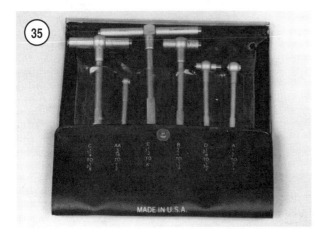

MADE IN U.S.A.

To read a metric micrometer, add the number of millimeters and half-millimeters on the sleeve line to the number of one one-hundredth millimeters on the thimble. Perform the following steps and refer to **Figure 34**.

1. Read the upper half of the sleeve line and count the number of lines visible. Each upper line equals 1 mm.

2. See if the half-millimeter line is visible on the lower sleeve line. If so, add 0.50 mm to the reading from Step 1.

3. Read the thimble mark that aligns with the sleeve line. Each thimble mark equals 0.01 mm.

NOTE
If a thimble mark does not align exactly with the sleeve line, estimate the amount between the lines. For accurate readings in two-thousandths of a millimeter (0.002 mm), use a metric vernier micrometer.

4. Add the readings from Steps 1-3.

Micrometer Adjustment

Before using a micrometer, check its adjustment as follows.
1. Clean the anvil and spindle faces.
2A. To check a 0-1 in. or 0-25 mm micrometer:
    a. Turn the thimble until the spindle contacts the anvil. If the micrometer has a ratchet stop, use it to ensure the proper amount of pressure is applied.
    b. If the adjustment is correct, the 0 mark on the thimble will align exactly with the 0 mark on the sleeve line. If the marks do not align, the micrometer is out of adjustment.
    c. Follow the manufacturer's instructions to adjust the micrometer.
2B. To check a micrometer larger than 1 in. or 25 mm, use the standard gauge supplied by the manufacturer. A standard gauge is a steel block, disc or rod that is machined to an exact size.
    a. Place the standard gauge between the spindle and anvil, and measure its outside diameter or length. If the micrometer has a ratchet stop, use it to ensure the proper amount of pressure is applied.
    b. If the adjustment is correct, the 0 mark on the thimble will align exactly with the 0 mark on the sleeve line. If the marks do not align, the micrometer is out of adjustment.
    c. Follow the manufacturer's instructions to adjust the micrometer.

Micrometer Care

Micrometers are precision instruments. They must be used and maintained with great care. Note the following:
1. Store micrometers in protective cases or separate padded drawers in a toolbox.
2. When in storage, make sure the spindle and anvil faces do not contact each other or an other object. If they do, temperature changes and corrosion may damage the contact faces.
3. Do not clean a micrometer with compressed air. Dirt forced into the tool will cause wear.
4. Lubricate micrometers with WD-40 to prevent corrosion.

Telescoping and Small Bore Gauges

Use telescoping gauges (**Figure 35**) and small hole gauges (**Figure 36**) to measure bores. Neither gauge has a scale for direct readings. An outside micrometer must be used to determine the reading.

To use a telescoping gauge, select the correct size gauge for the bore. Compress the movable post and carefully insert the gauge into the bore. Carefully move the gauge in the bore to make sure it is centered. Tighten the knurled end of the gauge to hold the movable post in position. Remove the gauge and measure the length of the posts. Telescoping gauges are typically used to measure cylinder bores.

To use a small-bore gauge, select the correct size gauge for the bore. Carefully insert the gauge into the bore. Tighten the knurled end of the gauge to carefully expand the gauge fingers to the limit within the bore. Do not overtighten the gauge, as there is no built-in release. Excessive tightening can damage the bore surface and damage the tool. Remove the gauge and measure the outside dimension (**Figure 37**). Small hole gauges are typically used to measure valve guides.

Dial Indicator

A dial indicator (**Figure 38**) is a gauge with a dial face and needle used to measure variations in dimensions and movements. Measuring brake rotor runout is a typical use for a dial indicator.

Dial indicators are available in various ranges and graduations, and with three basic types of mounting bases: magnetic, clamp, or screw-in stud. When purchasing a dial indicator, select the magnetic stand type with a continuous dial.

Cylinder Bore Gauge

A cylinder bore gauge is similar to a dial indicator. The gauge set shown in **Figure 39** consists of a dial indicator, handle and different length adapters (anvils) to fit the gauge to various bore sizes. The bore gauge is used to measure bore size, taper and out-of-round. When using a bore gauge, follow the manufacturer's instructions.

Compression Gauge

A compression gauge (**Figure 40**) measures combustion chamber (cylinder) pressure, usually in psi or kg/cm^2. The gauge adapter is either inserted or screwed into the spark plug hole to obtain the reading. Disable the engine so it will not start and hold the throttle in the wide-open position when performing a compression test. An engine that does not have adequate compression cannot be properly tuned. See Chapter Three.

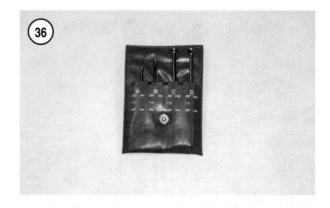

Multimeter

A multimeter (**Figure 41**) is an essential tool for electrical system diagnosis. The voltage function indicates the voltage applied or available to various electrical components. The ohmmeter function tests circuits for continuity, or lack of continuity, and measures the resistance of a circuit.

Some manufacturers' specifications for electrical components are based on results using a specific test meter. Results may vary if using a meter not recommend by the

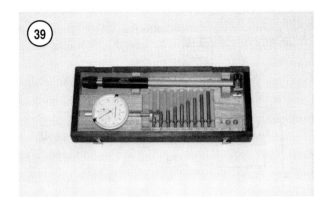

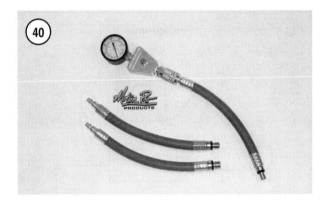

manufacturer is used. Such requirements are noted when applicable.

Ohmmeter (analog) calibration

Each time an analog ohmmeter is used or if the scale is changed, the ohmmeter must be calibrated. Digital ohmmeters do not require calibration.

1. Make sure the meter battery is in good condition.

2. Make sure the meter probes are in good condition.

3. Touch the two probes together and watch the needle location on the ohms scale. The needle must align with the 0 mark to obtain accurate measurements.

4. If necessary, rotate the meter ohms adjust knob until the needle and 0 mark align.

ELECTRICAL SYSTEM FUNDAMENTALS

A thorough study of the many types of electrical systems used in today's motorcycles is beyond the scope of this manual. However, an understanding of electrical basics is necessary to perform simple diagnostic tests.

Voltage

Voltage is the electrical potential or pressure in an electrical circuit and is expressed in volts. The more pressure (voltage) in a circuit, the more work can be performed.

Direct current (DC) voltage means the electricity flows in one direction. All circuits powered by a battery are DC circuits.

Alternating current (AC) means the electricity flows in one direction momentarily then switches to the opposite direction. Alternator output is an example of AC voltage. This voltage must be changed or rectified to direct current to operate in a battery powered system.

Measuring voltage

Unless otherwise specified, perform all voltage tests with the electrical connectors attached. When measuring voltage, select the meter range that is one scale higher than the expected voltage of the circuit to prevent damage to the meter. To determine the actual voltage in a circuit, use a voltmeter. To simply check if voltage is present, use a test light.

> *NOTE*
> *When using a test light, either lead can be attached to ground.*

1. Attach the negative meter test lead to a good ground (bare metal). Make sure the ground is not insulated with a rubber gasket or grommet.

2. Attach the positive meter test lead to the point being checked for voltage (**Figure 42**).

3. Turn on the ignition switch. The test light should light or the meter should display a reading. The reading should be within one volt of battery voltage. If the voltage is less, there is a problem in the circuit.

Voltage drop test

Resistance causes voltage to drop. This resistance can be measured in an active circuit by using a voltmeter to perform a voltage drop test. A voltage drop test compares the difference between the voltage available at the start of a circuit to the voltage at the end of the circuit while the circuit is operational. If the circuit has no resistance, there will be no voltage drop. The greater the resistance, the greater the voltage drop will be. A voltage drop of one volt or more indicates excessive resistance in the circuit.

1. Connect the positive meter test lead to the electrical source (where electricity is coming from).

2. Connect the negative meter test lead to the electrical load (where electricity is going). See **Figure 43.**

3. If necessary, activate the component(s) in the circuit.

4. A voltage reading of 1 volt or more indicates excessive resistance in the circuit. A reading equal to battery voltage indicates an open circuit.

Resistance

Resistance is the opposition to the flow of electricity within a circuit or component and is measured in ohms. Resistance causes a reduction in available current and voltage.

Resistance is measured in an *inactive* circuit with an ohmmeter. The ohmmeter sends a small amount of current into the circuit and measures how difficult it is to push the current through the circuit.

An ohmmeter, although useful, is not always a good indicator of a circuit's actual ability under *operating* conditions. This is due to the low voltage (6-9 volts) that the meter uses to test the circuit. The voltage in an ignition coil secondary winding can be several thousand volts. Such high voltage can cause the coil to malfunction, even though it tests acceptable during a resistance test.

Resistance generally increases with temperature. Perform all testing with the component or circuit at room temperature. Resistance tests performed at high temperatures may indicate high resistance readings and result in the unnecessary replacement of a component.

Measuring resistance and continuity testing

> *CAUTION*
> *Only use an ohmmeter on a circuit that has no voltage present. The meter will be damaged if it is connected to a live circuit. An analog meter must be calibrated each time it is used or the scale is changed. See **Multimeter** in this chapter.*

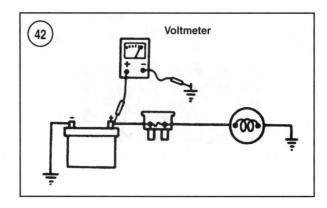

42 Voltmeter

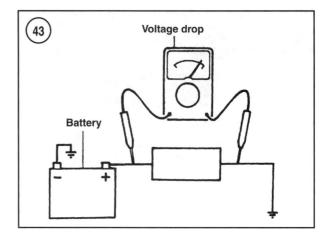

43 Voltage drop

Battery

A continuity test can determine if the circuit is complete. This type of test is performed with an ohmmeter or a self-powered test lamp.

1. Disconnect the negative battery cable.

2. Attach one test lead (ohmmeter or test light) to one end of the component or circuit.

3. Attach the other test lead to the opposite end of the component or circuit (**Figure 44**).

4. A self-powered test light will come on if the circuit has continuity or is complete. An ohmmeter will indicate either low or no resistance if the circuit has continuity. An open circuit is indicated if the meter displays infinite resistance.

Amperage

Amperage is the unit of measurement for the amount of current within a circuit. Current is the actual flow of electricity. The higher the current, the more work that can be performed up to a given point. If the current flow exceeds the circuit or component capacity, the system will be damaged.

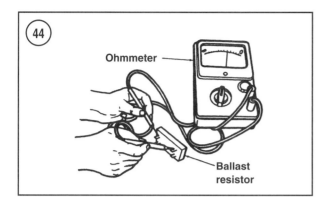

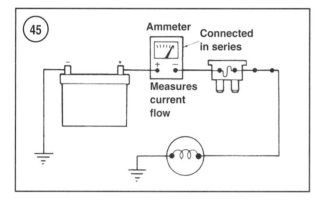

Measuring amps

An ammeter measures the current flow or amps of a circuit (**Figure 45**). Amperage measurement requires that the circuit be disconnected and the ammeter be connected in series to the circuit. Always use an ammeter that can read higher than the anticipated current flow to prevent damage to the meter. Connect the red test lead to the electrical source and the black test lead to the electrical load.

BASIC SERVICE METHODS

Most of the procedures in this manual are straightforward and can be performed by anyone reasonably competent with tools. However, consider personal capabilities carefully before attempting any operation involving major disassembly of the engine.

1. Front, in this manual, refers to the front of the motorcycle. The front of any component is the end closest to the front of the motorcycle. The left and right sides refer to the position of the parts as viewed by the rider sitting on the seat facing forward.

2. Whenever servicing an engine or suspension component, secure the motorcycle in a safe manner.

3. Tag all similar parts for location and mark all mating parts for position. Record the number and thickness of shims as they are removed. Identify parts by placing them in sealed and labeled plastic sandwich bags.

4. Tag disconnected wires and connectors with masking tape and a marking pen. Do not rely on memory alone.

5. Protect finished surfaces from physical damage or corrosion. Keep gasoline and other chemicals off painted surfaces.

6. Use penetrating oil on frozen or tight bolts. Avoid using heat where possible. Heat can warp, melt or affect the temper of parts. Heat also damages the finish of paint and plastics.

7. When a part is a press fit or requires a special tool for removal, the information or type of tool is identified in the text. Otherwise, if a part is difficult to remove or install, determine the cause before proceeding.

8. To prevent objects or debris from falling into the engine, cover all openings.

9. Read each procedure thoroughly and compare the illustrations to the actual components before starting the procedure. Perform the procedure in sequence.

10. Recommendations are occasionally made to refer service to a dealership or specialist. In these cases, the work can be performed more economically by the specialist than by a home mechanic.

11. The term *replace* means to discard a defective part and replace it with a new part. *Overhaul* means to remove, disassemble, inspect, measure, repair and/or replace parts as required to recondition an assembly.

12. Some operations require the use of a hydraulic press. If a press is not available, have these operations performed by a shop equipped with the necessary equipment. Do not use makeshift equipment that may damage the motorcycle.

13. Repairs are much faster and easier if the motorcycle is clean before starting work. Degrease the motorcycle with a commercial degreaser; follow the directions on the container for the best results. Clean all parts with cleaning solvent as they are removed.

CAUTION
Do not direct high-pressure water at steering bearings, carburetor hoses, wheel bearings, and suspension and electrical components. The water will force the grease out of the bearings and possibly damage the seals.

14. If special tools are required, have them available before starting the procedure. When special tools are required, they will be described at the beginning of the procedure.

15. Make diagrams of similar-appearing parts. For instance, crankcase bolts are often not the same lengths. Do not rely on memory alone. It is possible that carefully laid out parts will become disturbed, making it difficult to reassemble the components correctly without a diagram.

16. Make sure all shims and washers are reinstalled in the same location and position.

17. Whenever rotating parts contact a stationary part, look for a shim or washer.

18. Use new gaskets if there is any doubt about the condition of old ones.

19. If self-locking fasteners are used, replace them with new ones. Do not install standard fasteners in place of self-locking ones.

20. Use grease to hold small parts in place if they tend to fall out during assembly. Do not apply grease to electrical or brake components.

Removing Frozen Fasteners

If a fastener cannot be removed, several methods may be used to loosen it. First, apply penetrating oil such as Liquid Wrench or WD-40. Apply it liberally and let it penetrate for 10-15 minutes. Rap the fastener several times with a small hammer. Do not hit it hard enough to cause damage. Reapply the penetrating oil if necessary.

For frozen screws, apply penetrating oil as described, then insert a screwdriver in the slot and rap the top of the screwdriver with a hammer. This loosens the rust so the screw can be removed in the normal way. If the screw head is too damaged to use this method, grip the head with locking pliers and twist the screw out.

Avoid applying heat unless specifically instructed, as it may melt, warp or remove the temper from parts.

Removing Broken Fasteners

If the head breaks off a screw or bolt, several methods are available for removing the remaining portion. If a large portion of the remainder projects out, try gripping it with locking pliers. If the projecting portion is too small, file it to fit a wrench or cut a slot in it to fit a screwdriver (**Figure 46**).

If the head breaks off flush, use a screw extractor. To do this, centerpunch the exact center of the remaining portion of the screw or bolt. Drill a small hole in the screw and tap the extractor into the hole. Back the screw out with a wrench on the extractor (**Figure 47**).

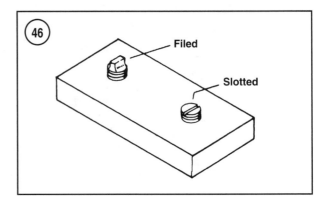

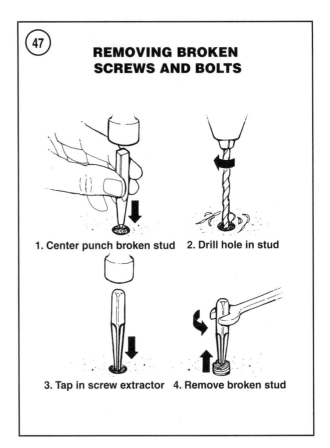

Repairing Damaged Threads

Occasionally, threads are stripped through carelessness or impact damage. Often the threads can be repaired by running a tap (for internal threads on nuts) or die (for external threads on bolts) through the threads. To clean or repair spark plug threads, use a spark plug tap.

If an internal thread is damaged, it may be necessary to install a Helicoil or some other type of thread insert. Follow the manufacturer's instructions when installing their insert.

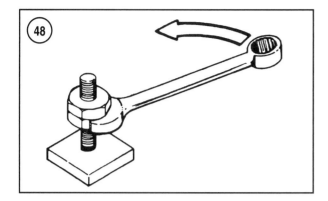

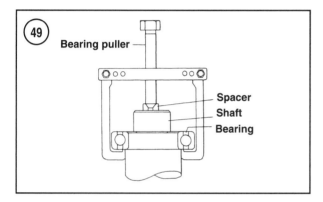

If it is necessary to drill and tap a hole, refer to **Table 10** and **Table 11** for tap and drill sizes.

Stud Removal/Installation

A stud removal tool is available from most tool suppliers. This tool makes the removal and installation of studs easier. If one is not available, thread two nuts onto the stud and tighten them against each other. Remove the stud by turning the lower nut (**Figure 48**).

1. Measure the height of the stud above the surface.

2. Thread the stud removal tool onto the stud and tighten it, or thread two nuts onto the stud.

3. Remove the stud by turning the stud remover or the lower nut.

4. Remove any threadlocking compound from the threaded hole. Clean the threads with an aerosol parts cleaner.

5. Install the stud removal tool onto the new stud or thread two nuts onto the stud.

6. Apply threadlocking compound to the threads of the stud.

7. Install the stud and tighten with the stud removal tool or the top nut.

8. Install the stud to the height noted in Step 1 or its torque specification.

9. Remove the stud removal tool or the two nuts.

Removing Hoses

When removing stubborn hoses, do not exert excessive force on the hose or fitting. Remove the hose clamp and carefully insert a small screwdriver or pick tool between the fitting and hose. Apply a spray lubricant under the hose and carefully twist the hose off the fitting. Clean the fitting of any corrosion or rubber hose material with a wire brush. Clean the inside of the hose thoroughly. Do not use any lubricant when installing the hose (new or old). The lubricant may allow the hose to come off the fitting, even with the clamp secure.

Bearings

Bearings are used in the engine and transmission assembly to reduce power loss, heat and noise caused by friction. Because bearings are precision parts, they must be maintained by proper lubrication and maintenance. If a bearing is damaged, replace it immediately. When installing a new bearing, take care to prevent damaging it. Bearing replacement procedures are included in the individual chapters where applicable; however, use the following sections as a guideline.

NOTE
Unless otherwise specified, install bearings with the manufacturer's mark or number facing outward.

Removal

While bearings are normally removed only when damaged, there may be times when it is necessary to remove a bearing that is in good condition. Improper bearing removal will damage the bearing and maybe the shaft or case half. Note the following when removing bearings.

1. When using a puller to remove a bearing from a shaft, take care that the shaft is not damaged. Always place a piece of metal between the end of the shaft and the puller screw. In addition, place the puller arms next to the inner bearing race. See **Figure 49**.

2. When using a hammer to remove a bearing from a shaft, do not strike the hammer directly against the shaft. Instead, use a brass or aluminum spacer between the hammer and shaft (**Figure 50**) and make sure to support both bearing races with wooden blocks as shown.

3. The ideal method of bearing removal is with a hydraulic press. Note the following when using a press:

    a. Always support the inner and outer bearing races with a suitable size wooden or aluminum ring (**Figure 51**). If only the outer race is supported, pressure applied against the balls and/or the inner race will damage them.

    b. Always make sure the press arm (**Figure 51**) aligns with the center of the shaft. If the arm is not centered, it may damage the bearing and/or shaft.

    c. The moment the shaft is free of the bearing, it will drop to the floor. Secure or hold the shaft to prevent it from falling.

Installation

1. When installing a bearing in a housing, apply pressure to the *outer* bearing race (**Figure 52**). When installing a bearing on a shaft, apply pressure to the *inner* bearing race (**Figure 53**).

2. To install a bearing as described in Step 1, some type of driver is required. Never strike the bearing directly with a hammer or the bearing will be damaged. When installing a bearing, use a piece of pipe or a driver with a diameter that matches the bearing inner race. **Figure 54** shows the correct way to use a driver and hammer to install a bearing.

3. Step 1 describes how to install a bearing in a case half or over a shaft. However, to install a bearing over a shaft and into a housing at the same time, a tight fit will be required for both outer and inner bearing races. In this situation, install a spacer underneath the driver tool so that pressure is applied evenly across both races. See **Figure 55**. If the outer race is not supported as shown in **Figure 55**, the balls will push against the outer bearing race and damage it.

Interference fit

1. Follow this procedure to install a bearing over a shaft. When a tight fit is required, the bearing inside diameter will be smaller than the shaft. In this case, driving the bearing on the shaft using normal methods may cause bearing damage. Instead, heat the bearing before installation. Note the following:

    a. Secure the shaft so it is ready for bearing installation.

    b. Clean all residues from the bearing surface of the shaft. Remove burrs with a file or sandpaper.

    c. Fill a suitable pot or beaker with clean mineral oil. Place a thermometer rated above 120° C (248° F) in the oil. Support the thermometer so that it does not rest on the bottom or side of the pot.

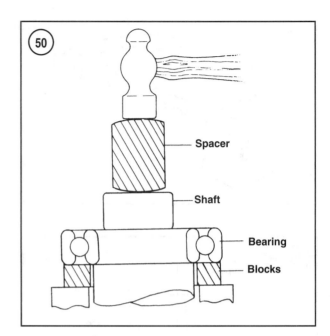

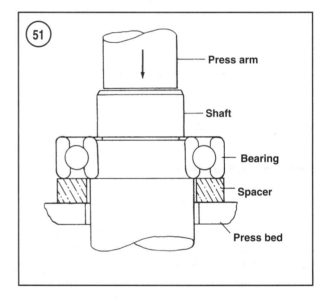

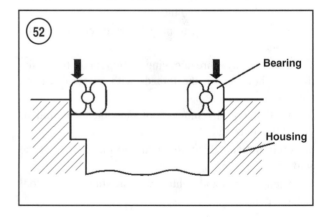

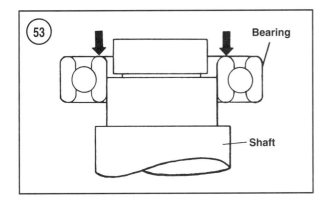

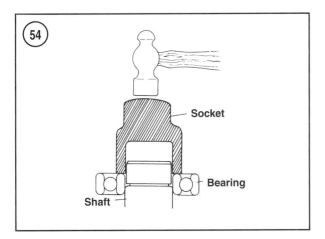

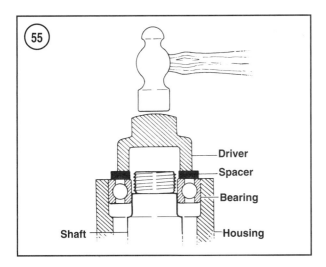

120° C (248° F), remove the bearing from the pot and quickly install it. If necessary, place a socket on the inner bearing race and tap the bearing into place. As the bearing chills, it will tighten on the shaft, so installation must be done quickly. Make sure the bearing is installed completely.

2. Follow this step to install a bearing in a housing. Bearings are generally installed in a housing with a slight interference fit. Driving the bearing into the housing using normal methods may damage the housing or cause bearing damage. Instead, heat the housing before the bearing is installed. Note the following:

CAUTION
Before heating the housing in this procedure, wash the housing thoroughly with detergent and water. Rinse and rewash the cases as required to remove all traces of oil and other chemical deposits.

a. Heat the housing to approximately 100° C (212° F) in an oven or on a hot plate. An easy way to check that it is the proper temperature is to place tiny drops of water on the housing; if they sizzle and evaporate immediately, the temperature is correct. Heat only one housing at a time.

CAUTION
Do not heat the housing with a propane or acetylene torch. Never bring a flame into contact with the bearing or housing. The direct heat will destroy the case hardening of the bearing and will likely warp the housing.

b. Remove the housing from the oven or hot plate, and hold onto the housing with a kitchen potholder, heavy gloves or heavy shop cloth. It is hot!

NOTE
Remove and install the bearings with a suitable size socket and extension.

c. Hold the housing with the bearing side down and tap the bearing out. Repeat for all bearings in the housing.

d. Before heating the bearing housing, place the new bearing in a freezer if possible. Chilling a bearing slightly reduces its outside diameter while the heated bearing housing assembly is slightly larger due to heat expansion. This will make bearing installation easier.

NOTE
Always install bearings with the manufacturer's mark or number facing outward.

d. Remove the bearing from its wrapper and secure it with a piece of heavy wire bent to hold it in the pot. Hang the bearing in the pot so it does not touch the bottom or sides of the pot.

e. Turn the heat on and monitor the thermometer. When the oil temperature rises to approximately

e. While the housing is still hot, install the new bearing(s) into the housing. Install the bearings by hand, if possible. If necessary, lightly tap the bearing(s) into the housing with a socket placed on the outer bearing race (**Figure 53**). Do not install new bearings by driving on the inner-bearing race. Install the bearing(s) until it seats completely.

Seal Replacement

Seals (**Figure 56**) are used to contain oil, water, grease or combustion gasses in a housing or shaft. Improper removal of a seal can damage the housing or shaft. Improper installation of the seal can damage the seal. Note the following:

1. Prying is generally the easiest and most effective method of removing a seal from a housing. However, always place a rag underneath the pry tool (**Figure 57**) to prevent damage to the housing.

2. Pack waterproof grease in the seal lips before the seal is installed.

3. In most cases, install seals with the manufacturer's numbers or marks face out.

4. Install seals with a socket placed on the outside of the seal as shown in **Figure 58**. Drive the seal squarely into the housing. Never install a seal by hitting against the top of the seal with a hammer.

STORAGE

Several months of non-use can cause a general deterioration of the motorcycle. This is especially true in areas of extreme temperature variations. This deterioration can be minimized with careful preparation for storage. A properly stored motorcycle will be much easier to return to service.

Storage Area Selection

When selecting a storage area, consider the following:

1. The storage area must be dry. A heated area is best, but not necessary. It should be insulated to minimize extreme temperature variations.

2. If the building has large window areas, mask them to keep sunlight off the motorcycle.

3. Avoid buildings in industrial areas where corrosive emissions may be present. Avoid areas close to saltwater.

4. Consider the area's risk of fire, theft or vandalism. Check with an insurer regarding motorcycle coverage while in storage.

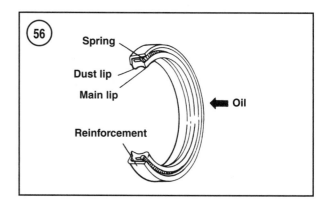

Preparing the Motorcycle for Storage

The amount of preparation a motorcycle should undergo before storage depends on the expected length of non-use, storage area conditions and personal preference. Consider the following list the minimum requirement:

1. Wash the motorcycle thoroughly. Make sure all dirt, mud and road debris are removed.

2. Start the engine and allow it to reach operating temperature. Drain the engine oil and transmission oil, regardless of the riding time since the last service. Fill the engine and transmission with the recommended type of oil.

3. Drain all fuel from the fuel tank, run the engine until all the fuel is consumed from the lines and carburetor or fuel injection module.

4. Remove the spark plugs and pour a teaspoon of engine oil into the cylinders. Place a rag over the openings and slowly turn the engine over to distribute the oil. Reinstall the spark plugs.

5. Remove the battery. Store the battery in a cool and dry location.

6. Cover the exhaust and intake openings.

7. Reduce the normal tire pressure by 20 percent.

8. Apply a protective substance to the plastic and rubber components, including the tires. Make sure to follow the manufacturer's instructions for each type of product being used.

9. Place the motorcycle on a stand or wooden blocks, so the wheels are off the ground. If this is not possible, place a piece of plywood between the tires and the ground. In-flate the tires to the recommended pressure if the motorcycle can not be elevated.

10. Cover the motorcycle with old bed sheets or something similar. Do not cover it with plastic material that will trap moisture.

Returning the Motorcycle to Service

The amount of service required when returning a motorcycle to service after storage depends on the length of non-use and storage conditions. In addition to performing the reverse of the above procedure, make sure the brakes, clutch, throttle and engine stop switch work properly before operating the motorcycle. Refer to Chapter Three and evaluate the service intervals to determine which areas require service.

Table 1 MODEL DESIGNATION

FLSTC/FLSTCI* Heritage Classic
FLSTF/FLSTFI* Fat Boy
FLSTS/FLSTSI* Heritage Springer
FXST/FXSTI* Softail Standard
FXSTB/FXSTBI* Night Train
FXSTS/FXSTSI* Springer Softail
FXSTD/FXSTDI* Softail Deuce
*The I designation indicates models equipped with fuel injection from 2001-on.

Table 2 GENERAL DIMENSIONS

Item/model	in.	mm
Wheel base		
FLSTC/FLSTCI*	64.5	1638.3
FLSTF/FLSTFI*	64.5	1638.3
FLSTS/FLSTSI*	64.2	1630.7
FXST/FXSTI*	66.9	1699.3
FXSTB/FXSTBI*	66.9	1699.3
FXSTS/FXSTSI*	65.4	1661.2
FXSTD/FXSTDI*	66.6	1691.6
Overall length		
FLSTC/FLSTCI*	94.5	2400.3
FLSTF/FLSTFI*	94.5	2400.3
FLSTS/FLSTSI*	94.1	2390.1
FXST/FXSTI*	95.0	2413.0
FXSTB/FXSTBI*	95.0	2413.0
FXSTS/FXSTSI*	93.5	2374.9
FXSTD/FXSTDI*	95.4	2423.2
	(continued)	

Table 2 GENERAL DIMENSIONS (continued)

Item/model	in.	mm
Overall width		
FLSTC/FLSTCI*	37.5	952.5
FLSTF/FLSTFI*	40.2	1021.1
FLSTS/FLSTSI*	35.0	889.0
FXST/FXSTI*	37.9	962.66
FXSTB/FXSTBI*	30.9	784.9
FXSTS/FXSTSI*	32.6	828.0
FXSTD/FXSTDI*	35.9	911.9
Road clearance		
FLSTC/FLSTCI*	5.1	129.5
FLSTF/FLSTFI*	5.1	129.5
FLSTS/FLSTSI*	4.9	124.5
FXST/FXSTI*	5.6	142.2
FXSTB/FXSTBI*	5.6	142.2
FXSTS/FXSTSI*	5.4	137.2
FXSTD/FXSTDI*	5.6	142.2
Overall height		
FLSTC/FLSTCI*	57.8	1468.1
FLSTF/FLSTFI*	44.5	1130.3
FLSTS/FLSTSI*	46.0	1168.4
FXST/FXSTI*	46.4	1178.0
FXSTB/FXSTBI*	44.9	1140.0
FXSTS/FXSTSI*	47.3	1201.4
FXSTD/FXSTDI*	46.4	1178.0
Saddle height		
FLSTC/FLSTCI*	25.4	645.2
FLSTF/FLSTFI*	25.5	647.7
FLSTS/FLSTSI*	25.9	657.9
FXST/FXSTI*	26.1	662.9
FXSTB/FXSTBI*	25.2	640.1
FXSTS/FXSTSI*	25.9	657.9
FXSTD/FXSTDI*	26.0	660.4

*The I designation indicates models equipped with fuel injection from 2001-on.

Table 3 MOTORCYCLE WEIGHT (DRY)

Model	lbs.	kg
FLSTC/FLSTCI*	695.6	315.5
FLSTF/FLSTFI*	665	301.6
FLSTS/FLSTSI*	716.6	325
FXST/FXSTI*	628.6	285.1
FXSTB/FXSTBI*	629.6	285.6
FXSTS/FXSTSI*	652.6	296
FXSTD/FXSTDI*	644.6	292.4

*The I designation indicates models equipped with fuel injection from 2001-on.

Table 4 GROSS VEHICLE WEIGHT RATINGS

Model	lbs.	kg
Gross vehicle weight rating (GVWR)[1]		
FLSTC/FLSTCI[2]	1160	526.1
FLSTF/FLSTFI[2]	1160	526.1
FLSTS/FLSTSI[2]	1175	532.09
All FXST models	1125	510.3

(continued)

Table 4 GROSS VEHICLE WEIGHT RATINGS (continued)

Model	lbs.	kg
Gross axle weight rating (GAWR)		
Front axle		
All FLST models	430	195
All FXST models	415	188.2
Rear axle		
FLSTC/FLSTCI[2]	730	331.1
FLSTF/FLSTFI[2]	730	331.1
FLSTS/FLSTSI[2]	745	337.9
All FXST models	710	322.1

1. GVWR is the maximum allowable vehicle weight. This includes combined vehicle, rider(s) and accessory weight.
2. The I designation indicates models equipped with fuel injection from 2001-on.

Table 5 FUEL TANK CAPACITY

Model	U.S. gal	Liters
Total		
FXSTD/FXDT	4.9	18.55
All other models	5.0	18.9
Reserve	0.9	3.4

Table 6 DECIMAL AND METRIC EQUIVALENTS

Fractions	Decimal in.	Metric mm	Fractions	Decimal in.	Metric mm
1/64	0.015625	0.39688	33/64	0.515625	13.09687
1/32	0.03125	0.79375	17/32	0.53125	13.49375
3/64	0.046875	1.19062	35/64	0.546875	13.89062
1/16	0.0625	1.58750	9/16	0.5625	14.28750
5/64	0.078125	1.98437	37/64	0.578125	14.68437
3/32	0.09375	2.38125	19/32	0.59375	15.08125
7/64	0.109375	2.77812	39/64	0.609375	15.47812
1/8	0.125	3.1750	5/8	0.625	15.87500
9/64	0.140625	3.57187	41/64	0.640625	16.27187
5/32	0.15625	3.96875	21/32	0.65625	16.66875
11/64	0.171875	4.36562	43/64	0.671875	17.06562
3/16	0.1875	4.76250	11/16	0.6875	17.46250
13/64	0.203125	5.15937	45/64	0.703125	17.85937
7/32	0.21875	5.55625	23/32	0.71875	18.25625
15/64	0.234375	5.95312	47/64	0.734375	18.65312
1/4	0.250	6.35000	3/4	0.750	19.05000
17/64	0.265625	6.74687	49/64	0.765625	19.44687
9/32	0.28125	7.14375	25/32	0.78125	19.84375
19/64	0.296875	7.54062	51/64	0.796875	20.24062
5/16	0.3125	7.93750	13/16	0.8125	20.63750
21/64	0.328125	8.33437	53/64	0.828125	21.03437
11/32	0.34375	8.73125	27/32	0.84375	21.43125
23/64	0.359375	9.12812	55/64	0.859375	22.82812
3/8	0.375	9.52500	7/8	0.875	22.22500
25/64	0.390625	9.92187	57/64	0.890625	22.62187
13/32	0.40625	10.31875	29/32	0.90625	23.01875
27/64	0.421875	10.71562	59/64	0.921875	23.41562
7/16	0.4375	11.11250	15/16	0.9375	23.81250
29/64	0.453125	11.50937	61/64	0.953125	24.20937
15/32	0.46875	11.90625	31/32	0.96875	24.60625
31/64	0.484375	12.30312	63/64	0.984375	25.00312
1/2	0.500	12.70000	1	1.00	25.40000

Table 7 GENERAL TORQUE SPECIFICATIONS

Type[2]	1/4	5/16	3/8	7/16	1/2	9/16	5/8	3/4	7/8	1
SAE 2	6	12	20	32	47	69	96	155	206	310
SAE 5	10	19	33	54	78	114	154	257	382	587
SAE 7	13	25	44	71	110	154	215	360	570	840
SAE 8	14	29	47	78	119	169	230	380	600	700

1. Convert ft.-lb. specification to N•m by multiplying by 1.3558.
2. Fastener strength of SAE bolts can be determined by the bolt head grade markings. Unmarked bolt heads and cap screws are usually mild steel. More grade markings indicate higher fastener quality.

SAE 2   SAE 5   SAE 7   SAE 8

Table 8 CONVERSION FORMULAS

Multiply:	By:	To get the equivalent of:
Length		
Inches	25.4	Millimeter
Inches	2.54	Centimeter
Miles	1.609	Kilometer
Feet	0.3048	Meter
Millimeter	0.03937	Inches
Centimeter	0.3937	Inches
Kilometer	0.6214	Mile
Meter	3.281	Mile
Fluid volume		
U.S. quarts	0.9463	Liters
U.S. gallons	3.785	Liters
U.S. ounces	29.573529	Milliliters
Imperial gallons	4.54609	Liters
Imperial quarts	1.1365	Liters
Liters	0.2641721	U.S. gallons
Liters	1.0566882	U.S. quarts
Liters	33.814023	U.S. ounces
Liters	0.22	Imperial gallons
Liters	0.8799	Imperial quarts
Milliliters	0.033814	U.S. ounces
Milliliters	1.0	Cubic centimeters
Milliliters	0.001	Liters
Torque		
Foot-pounds	1.3558	Newton-meters
Foot-pounds	0.138255	Meters-kilograms
Inch-pounds	0.11299	Newton-meters
Newton-meters	0.7375622	Foot-pounds
Newton-meters	8.8507	Inch-pounds
Meters-kilograms	7.2330139	Foot-pounds
Volume		
Cubic inches	16.387064	Cubic centimeters
Cubic centimeters	0.0610237	Cubic inches

(continued)

Table 8 CONVERSION FORMULAS (continued)

Multiply:	By:	To get the equivalent of:
Temperature		
Fahrenheit	$(F - 32°) \times 0.556$	Centigrade
Centigrade	$(C \times 1.8) + 32$	Fahrenheit
Weight		
Ounces	28.3495	Grams
Pounds	0.4535924	Kilograms
Grams	0.035274	Ounces
Kilograms	2.2046224	Pounds
Pressure		
Pounds per square inch	0.070307	Kilograms per square centimeter
Kilograms per square centimeter	14.223343	Pounds per square inch
Kilopascals	0.1450	Pounds per square inch
Pounds per square inch	6.895	Kilopascals
Speed		
Miles per hour	1.609344	Kilometers per hour
Kilometers per hour	0.6213712	Miles per hour

Table 9 TECHNICAL ABBREVIATIONS

ABDC	After bottom dead center
ATDC	After top dead center
BBDC	Before bottom dead center
BDC	Bottom dead center
BTDC	Before top dead center
BAS	Bank angle sensor
C	Celsius (centigrade)
cc	Cubic centimeters
cid	Cubic inch displacement
CKP	Crankshaft position sensor
CDI	Capacitor discharge ignition
CMP	Camshaft position sensor
cu. in.	Cubic inches
ECM	Electronic control module
ET	Engine temperature sensor
F	Fahrenheit
ft.	Feet
ft.-lb.	Foot-pounds
gal.	Gallons
H/A	High altitude
HDI	Harley-Davidson International
IAC	Idle air control
IAT	Intake air temperature sensor
hp	Horsepower
in.	Inches
in.-lb.	Inch-pounds
I.D.	Inside diameter
kg	Kilograms
kgm	Kilogram meters
km	Kilometer
kPa	Kilopascals
L	Liter
m	Meter
MAG	Magneto
MAP	Manifold absolute pressure sensor

(continued)

Table 9 TECHNICAL ABBREVIATIONS (continued)

ml	Milliliter
mm	Millimeter
N•m	Newton-meters
O.D.	Outside diameter
oz.	Ounces
psi	Pounds per square inch
PTO	Power take off
pt.	Pint
qt.	Quart
rpm	Revolutions per minute
TP	Throttle position sensor
TSM	Turn signal module
TSSM	Turn signal security module

Table 10 AMERICAN TAP AND DRILL SIZES

Tap thread	Drill size	Tap thread	Drill size
#0-80	3/64	1/4-28	No. 3
#1-64	No. 53	5/16-18	F
#1-72	No. 53	5/16-24	I
#2-56	No. 51	3/8-16	5/16
#2-64	No. 50	3/8-24	Q
#3-48	5/64	7/16-14	U
#3-56	No. 46	7/16-20	W
#4-40	No. 43	1/2-13	27/64
#4-48	No. 42	1/2-20	29/64
#5-40	No. 39	9/16-12	31/64
#5-44	No. 37	9/16-18	33/64
#6-32	No. 36	5/8-11	17/32
#6-40	No. 33	5/18-18	37/64
#8-32	No. 29	3/4-10	21/32
#8-36	No. 29	3/4-16	11/16
#10-24	No. 25	7/8-9	49/64
#10-32	No. 21	7/8-14	13/16
#12-24	No. 17	1-8	7/8
#12-28	No. 15	1-14	15/16
1/4-20	No. 8		

Table 11 METRIC TAP AND DRILL SIZES

Metric size	Drill equivalent	Decimal fraction	Nearest fraction
3 × 0.50	No. 39	0.0995	3/32
3 × 0.60	3/32	0.0937	3/32
4 × 0.70	No. 30	0.1285	1/8
4 × 0.75	1/8	0.125	1/8
5 × 0.80	No. 19	0.166	11/64
5 × 0.90	No. 20	0.161	5/32
6 × 1.00	No. 9	0.196	13/64
7 × 1.00	16/64	0.234	15/64
8 × 1.00	J	0.277	9/32
8 × 1.25	17/64	0.265	17/64
9 × 1.00	5/16	0.3125	5/16
9 × 1.25	5/16	0.3125	5/16

(continued)

Table 11 METRIC TAP AND DRILL SIZES (continued)

Metric size	Drill equivalent	Decimal fraction	Nearest fraction
10 × 1.25	11/32	0.3437	11/32
10 × 1.50	R	0.339	11/32
11 × 1.50	3/8	0.375	3/8
12 × 1.50	13/32	0.406	13/32
12 × 1.75	13/32	0.406	13/32

Table 12 SPECIAL TOOLS

Tool description	Part No.	Manufacturer
Balancer shaft alignment tool	1166	JIMS
Balancer shaft bearing remove and install	1167	JIMS
Balancer shaft retaining pins	1725	JIMS
Balancer shaft retaining pins	HD-44062	H-D
Balancer sprocket alignment tool	1166	JIMS
Balancer sprocket alignment tool	HD-44064	H-D
Belt tension gauge	HD-355381	H-D
Camshaft bearing puller	1280	JIMS
Camshaft remove and installer	1277	JIMS
Camshaft chain tensioner tool	1283	JIMS
Camshaft inner bearing installer	1278	JIMS
Camshaft inner bearing remover tool	1279	JIMS
Camshaft/crankshaft sprocket lock tool	1285	JIMS
Connecting rod bushing tool	1051	JIMS
Connecting rod holding tool	1284	JIMS
Connecting rod clamping tool	HD-95952-33B	H-D
Connecting rod bushing hone	HD-422569	H-D
Crankcase bearing snap ring remover and installer	1710	JIMS
Crankshaft assembly removing tool	1047-TP	JIMS
Crankshaft bearing remover and installer	1146	JIMS
Crankshaft bushing tool	1281	JIMS
Crankshaft roller bearing pilot/driver	HD-997225-55B	H-D
Crankshaft roller bearing support tube	HD-42720-5	H-D
Crankshaft seal installation tool	39361-69	JIMS
Crankshaft guide	1288	JIMS
Crankshaft hard cap	1048	JIMS
Crankcase stud installer	08-0148	Motion Pro
Cylinder chamfering cone	2078	JIMS
Cylinder torque plates	1287	JIMS
Cylinder head stand	HD-39782	H-D
Driver handle and remover	HD-34740	H-D
Drive sprocket lock	2260	JIMS
Engine stand/Twin Cam 88B		
Base stand	1138	JIMS
Engine stand	1142	JIMS
Fork seal/cap installer	2046	JIMS
Fork oil level gauge	8-0121	Motion Pro
Hose clamp pliers	HD-97087-65B	H-D
Hydraulic brake bleeder	Mityvac	
Hydraulic tensioner compression tool	HD-44063	H-D
Hydraulic tensioner retainer	HD-44408	H-D
Mainshaft bearing race puller and installer	34902-84	JIMS
Motor sprocket shaft seal installer tool	39361-69	JIMS
Oil line remover and replacement tool	HD-4445	H-D
Primary drive locking tool	2234	JIMS
Retaining ring pliers	J-5586	H-D

(continued)

Table 12 SPECIAL TOOLS (continued)

Tool description	Part No.	Manufacturer
Rocker arm bushing retainer	94804-57	JIMS
Rocker arm shaft reamer	94804-57	JIMS
Spark tester	08-0122	Motion Pro
Sprocket shaft bearing cone installer	HD-997225-55B	H-D
Sprocket shaft bearing installation tool	97225-55	JIMS
Sprocket shaft bearing race tool set	94547-80A	JIMS
Springer fork spring tool	08-0144	Motion Pro
Snap ring remover and installer	1710	JIMS
Steering head bearing race installer	1725	JIMS
Timken bearing race installer	2246	JIMS
Transmission bearing and race installer tool handle	33416-80	JIMS
Transmission main drive gear tool set	35316-80	JIMS
Transmission main drive gear bearing tool	37842-91	JIMS
Transmission main bearing remover set	1720	JIMS
Vacuum hose identifier kit	74600	Lisle
Valve cutter set Neway	HD-35758A	H-D
Valve guide brush	HD-34751	H-D
Valve guide driver	HD-34740	H-D
Valve guide installation sleeve	HD-34731	H-D
Valve guide reamer	HD-39932	H-D
Valve guide reamer T-handle	HD-39847	H-D
Valve guide reamer and honing lubricant	HD-39064	H-D
Valve guide hone	HD-34723	H-D
Valve seat installation tool	HD-34643A	H-D
Valve seat driver handle	HD-34740	H-D
Wheel bearing race remover and installer	33461	JIMS
Wrist pin bushing reamer tool	1726	JIMS

CHAPTER TWO

TROUBLESHOOTING

The troubleshooting procedures described in this chapter provide typical symptoms and logical methods for isolating the cause(s). There may be several ways to solve a problem, but only a systematic approach will be successful in avoiding wasted time and possibly unnecessary parts replacement.

Gather as much information as possible to aid in diagnosis. Never assume anything and do not overlook the obvious. Make sure there is fuel in the tank. On carbureted models, make sure the fuel shutoff valve is in the on position. If the motorcycle has been sitting for any length of time, fuel deposits may have gummed up the carburetor jets or plugged the injector nozzles on fuel injected models. Gasoline loses its volatility after standing for long periods and water condensation may have diluted it. Drain the old gas and start with a new tank full. Make sure the engine stop switch is in the run position. Make sure the spark plug wires are attached to the spark plugs.

If a quick check does not reveal the problem, proceed with one of the troubleshooting procedures described in this chapter. After defining the symptoms, follow the procedure that most closely relates to the condition(s).

In most cases, expensive and complicated test equipment is not needed to determine whether repairs can be performed at home. A few simple checks could prevent an unnecessary repair charge and lost time while the motorcycle is at a dealership's service department. On the other hand, be realistic and do not attempt repairs beyond personal capabilities. Many service departments will not take work that involves the reassembly of damaged or abused equipment. If they do, expect the cost to be high.

If the motorcycle does require the attention of a professional, describe the symptoms, conditions and previous repair attempts accurately and fully. The more information a technician has available, the easier it will be to diagnose.

By following the lubrication and maintenance schedule described in Chapter Three, the need for troubleshooting can be reduced by eliminating potential problems before they occur. However, even with the best of care the motorcycle may require troubleshooting.

Refer to **Tables 1-3**, at the end of this chapter, for electrical specifications and diagnostic trouble codes.

OPERATING REQUIREMENTS

An engine needs three basics to run properly: correct air/fuel mixture, compression and a spark at the right time.

If one basic requirement is missing, the engine will not run. Refer to **Figure 1** for four-stroke engine operating principles.

STARTING THE ENGINE

NOTE
*On fuel injected models, do **not** open the throttle when starting either a cold or warm engine. The electronic control module automatically adjusts the fuel mixture to the conditions.*

Engine Fails to Start (Spark Test)

Perform the following spark test to determine if the ignition system is operating properly:

CAUTION
Before removing the spark plugs in Step 1, clean all dirt and debris away from the plug base. Dirt that falls into the cylinder causes rapid engine wear.

1. Disconnect the spark plug wire and remove the spark plug as described in Chapter Three.

NOTE
*A spark tester is a useful tool for testing spark output. **Figure 2** shows the Motion Pro Ignition System Tester (part No. 08-0122). This tool is inserted in the spark plug cap and its base is grounded against the cylinder head. The tool's air gap is adjustable, and it allows the visual inspection of the spark while testing the intensity of the spark. This tool is available through motorcycle repair shops.*

2. Cover the spark plug hole with a clean shop cloth to reduce the chance of gasoline vapors being emitted from the hole.
3. Insert the spark plug (**Figure 3**), or spark tester (**Figure 4**), into its plug cap and ground the spark plug base against the cylinder head. Position the spark plug so the electrode is visible.

WARNING
Mount the spark plug, or tester, away from the spark plug hole in the cylinder so that the spark plug or tester cannot ignite the gasoline vapors in the cylinder. If the engine is flooded, do not perform this test. The firing of the spark plug can ignite fuel that is ejected through the spark plug hole.

NOTE
If a spark plug is used, perform this test with a new spark plug.

4. Turn the ignition switch to the ON position.

WARNING
*Do **not** hold the spark plug, wire or connector, or a serious electrical shock may result.*

5. Turn the engine over with the electric starter. A crisp blue spark should be evident across the spark plug electrode or spark tester terminals. If there is strong sunlight on the plug, shade the plug by hand to better see the spark.
6. If the spark is good, check for one or more of the following possible malfunctions:
   a. Obstructed fuel line or fuel filter.
   b. Malfunctioning fuel pump (EFI models).
   c. Low compression or engine damage.
   d. Flooded engine.
   e. Incorrect ignition timing.

NOTE
*If the engine backfires during starting, the ignition timing may be incorrect due to a defective ignition component. Refer to **Ignition Timing** in Chapter Three for more information.*

7. If the spark is weak or if there is no spark, refer to *Engine is Difficult to Start* in this section.

Engine is Difficult to Start

Check for one or more of the following possible malfunctions:
1. Fouled spark plug(s).
2. Improperly adjusted enrichment valve (carbureted models).
3. Intake manifold air leak.
4. A plugged fuel tank filler cap.
5. Clogged fuel line.
6. Contaminated fuel system.
7. An improperly adjusted carburetor.
8. Malfunctioning fuel pump (EFI models).
9. A defective ignition module.
10. A defective ignition coil.
11. Damaged ignition coil primary and/or secondary wires.
12. Incorrect ignition timing.
13. Low engine compression.
14. Engine oil too heavy (winter temperatures).
15. Discharged battery.
16. A defective starter motor.

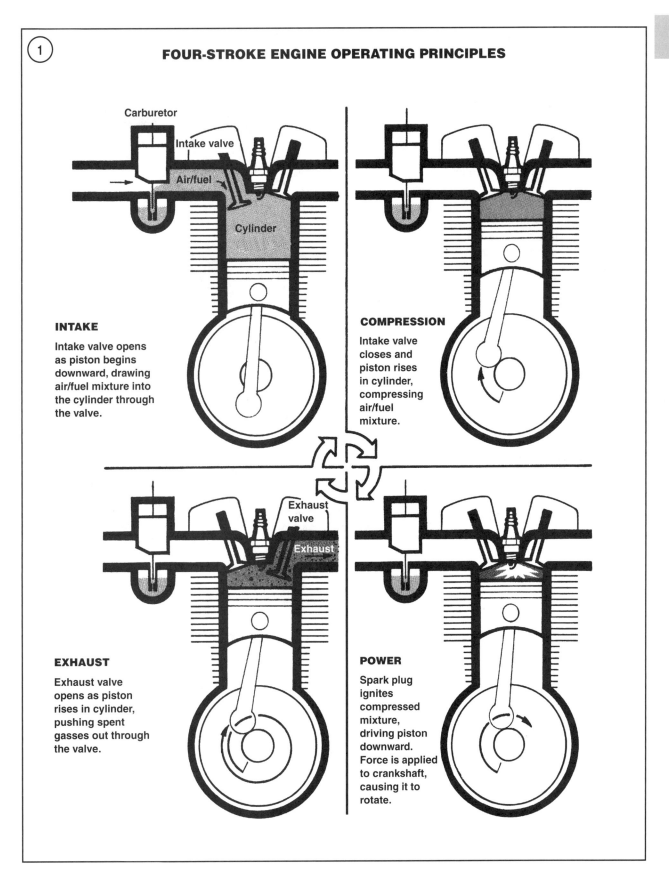

① **FOUR-STROKE ENGINE OPERATING PRINCIPLES**

Carburetor

Intake valve

Air/fuel

Cylinder

INTAKE

Intake valve opens
as piston begins
downward, drawing
air/fuel mixture into
the cylinder through
the valve.

COMPRESSION

Intake valve
closes and
piston rises
in cylinder,
compressing
air/fuel
mixture.

Exhaust
valve

Exhaust

EXHAUST

Exhaust valve
opens as piston
rises in cylinder,
pushing spent
gasses out through
the valve.

POWER

Spark plug
ignites
compressed
mixture,
driving piston
downward.
Force is applied
to crankshaft,
causing it to
rotate.

17. Loose or corroded starter and/or battery cables.
18. A loose ignition sensor and module electrical connector.
19. Incorrect pushrod length (intake and exhaust valve pushrods interchanged).

Engine Will Not Crank

Check for one or more of the following possible malfunctions:
1. Ignition switch turned off.
2. A faulty ignition switch.
3. Engine run switch in off position.
4. A defective engine run switch.
5. Loose or corroded starter and battery cables (solenoid chatters).
6. A discharged or defective battery.
7. A defective starter motor.
8. A defective starter solenoid.
9. A defective starter shaft pinion gear.
10. Slipping overrunning clutch assembly.
11. A seized piston(s).
12. Seized crankshaft bearings.
13. A broken connecting rod.

ENGINE PERFORMANCE

The following check lists assume the engine runs, but is not operating at peak performance. This will serve as a starting point from which to isolate a performance malfunction.

Spark Plugs Fouled

If the spark plugs continually foul, check for the following:
1. Severely contaminated air filter element.
2. Incorrect spark plug heat range. See Chapter Three.
3. Rich fuel mixture.
4. Worn or damaged piston rings.
5. Worn or damaged valve guide oil seals.
6. Excessive valve stem-to-guide clearance.
7. Incorrect carburetor float level.

Engine Runs but Misfires

1. Fouled or improperly gapped spark plugs.
2. Damaged spark plug cables.
3. Incorrect ignition timing.
4. Defective ignition components.

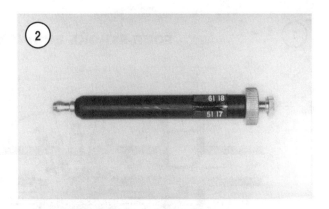

5. An obstructed fuel line or fuel shutoff valve (carbureted models).
6. Obstructed fuel filter.
7. Clogged carburetor jets.
8. Malfunctioning fuel pump (fuel injected models).
9. Loose battery connection.
10. Wiring or connector damage.
11. Water or other contaminates in the fuel.
12. Weak or damaged valve springs.
13. Incorrect camshaft/valve timing.
14. A damaged valve(s).

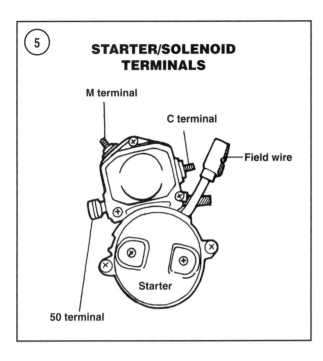

STARTER/SOLENOID TERMINALS

(5)

M terminal

C terminal

Field wire

Starter

50 terminal

15. Dirty electrical connections.
16. Intake manifold or carburetor air leak.
17. Induction module air leak (fuel-injected models).
18. A plugged carburetor vent hose.
19. Plugged fuel tank vent system.

Engine Overheating

1. Incorrect carburetor adjustment or jet selection.
2. Incorrect ignition timing or defective ignition system components.
3. Improper spark plug heat range.
4. Damaged or blocked cooling fins.
5. Low oil level.
6. Oil not circulating properly.
7. Leaking valves.
8. Heavy engine carbon deposits.

Engine Runs Rough with Excessive Exhaust Smoke

1. Clogged air filter element.
2. Rich carburetor adjustment.
3. Choke not operating correctly (carbureted models).
4. Water or other fuel contaminants.
5. Clogged fuel line and/or filter.
6. Spark plug(s) fouled.
7. A defective ignition coil.
8. A defective ignition module or sensor(s).
9. Loose or defective ignition circuit wire.
10. Short circuits from damaged wire insulation.

11. Loose battery cable connections.
12. Incorrect camshaft/valve timing.
13. Intake manifold or air filter air leak (carbureted models).
14. Induction module or air filter air leak (fuel injected models).

Engine Loses Power

1. Incorrect carburetor adjustment.
2. Engine overheating.
3. Incorrect ignition timing.
4. Incorrectly gapped spark plugs.
5. An obstructed muffler(s).
6. Dragging brake(s).

Engine Lacks Acceleration

1. Incorrect carburetor adjustment.
2. Clogged fuel line.
3. Incorrect ignition timing.
4. Dragging brake(s).

Valve Train Noise

1. A bent pushrod(s).
2. A defective hydraulic lifter(s).
3. A bent valve(s).
4. Rocker arm seizure or damage (binding on shaft).
5. Worn or damaged camshaft gear bushing(s).
6. Worn or damaged camshaft gear(s).
7. Worn or damaged camshaft drive chain(s).

STARTING SYSTEM

The starting system consists of the battery, starter, starter relay, solenoid, start button, starter mechanism and related wiring.

When the ignition switch is turned on and the start button is pushed in, current is transmitted from the battery to the starter relay. When the relay is activated, it activates the starter solenoid that mechanically engages the starter with the engine.

Starting system problems are most often related to a loose or corroded electrical connection.

Refer to **Figure 5** for starter and solenoid terminal identification.

Troubleshooting Preparation

Before troubleshooting the starting system, check for the following:

1. The battery is fully charged.

2. Battery cables are the proper size and length. Replace damaged or undersized cables.

3. All electrical connections are clean and tight. High resistance caused from dirty or loose connectors can affect voltage and current levels.

4. The wiring harness is in good condition, with no worn or frayed insulation or loose harness sockets.

5. The fuel tank is filled with an adequate supply of fresh gasoline.

6. The spark plugs are in good condition and properly gapped.

7. The ignition system is working correctly.

Voltage Drop Test

Before performing the steps listed under *Starter Testing*, perform this voltage drop test. These steps check the entire starting circuit to find weak or damaged electrical components that may be causing the starting system problem. A voltmeter is required to test voltage drop.

1. To check voltage drop in the solenoid circuit, connect the positive voltmeter lead to the positive battery terminal. Connect the negative voltmeter lead to the solenoid (**Figure 6**).

> *NOTE*
> *The voltmeter lead must not touch the starter-to-solenoid terminal.* **Figure 7** *shows the solenoid terminal with the starter/solenoid removed to better illustrate the step.*

2. Turn the ignition switch ON and push the starter button while reading the voltmeter scale. Note the following:

   a. The circuit is operating correctly if the voltmeter reading is 2 volts or less. A voltmeter reading of 12 volts indicates an open circuit.

   b. A voltage drop of more than 2 volts shows a problem in the solenoid circuit.

   c. If the voltage drop reading is correct, continue with Step 3.

3. To check the starter motor ground circuit, connect the negative voltmeter lead to the negative battery terminal. Connect the positive voltmeter lead to the starter motor housing (**Figure 8**).

4. Turn the ignition switch ON and push the starter button while reading the voltmeter scale. The voltage drop must

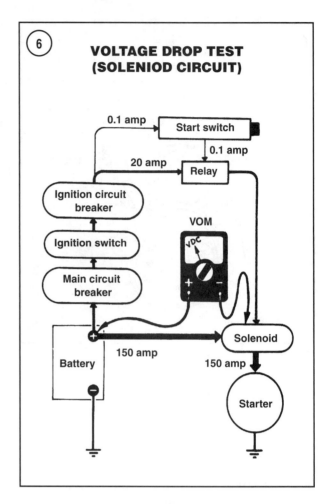

VOLTAGE DROP TEST (SOLENIOD CIRCUIT)

not exceed 0.2 volts. If it does, check the ground connections between the meter leads.

5. If the problem is not found, refer to *Starter Testing* in this section.

> *NOTE*
> *Steps 3 and 4 check the voltage drop across the starter ground circuit. To check any*

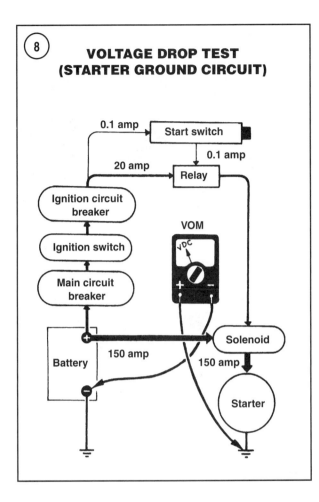

(8) VOLTAGE DROP TEST (STARTER GROUND CIRCUIT)

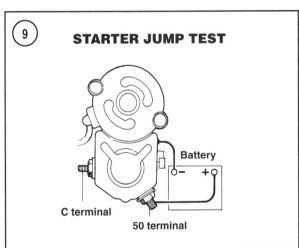

(9) STARTER JUMP TEST

ground circuit in the starting circuit, repeat this test and leave the negative voltmeter lead connected to the battery and connect the positive voltmeter lead to the ground in question.

Starter Testing

The basic starter-related troubles are:

1. Starter does not spin.
2. Starter spins but does not engage.
3. The starter will not disengage after the start button is released.
4. Loud grinding noises when starter turns.
5. Starter stalls or spins too slowly.

> *CAUTION*
> *Never operate the starter for more than 30 seconds at a time. Allow the starter to cool before reusing it. Failing to allow the starter to cool after continuous starting attempts can damage the starter.*

Starter does not spin

1. Turn the ignition switch ON and push the starter button while listening for a click at the starter relay in the electrical panel. Turn the ignition switch OFF and note the following:
   a. If the starter relay clicks, test the starter relay as described in this section. If the starter relay test readings are correct, continue with Step 2.
   b. If the solenoid clicks, go to Step 3.
   c. If there was no click, go to Step 6.
2. Check the wiring connectors between the starter relay and solenoid. Note the following:
   a. Repair any dirty, loose fitting or damaged connectors or wiring.
   b. If the wiring is in good condition, remove the starter motor as described in Chapter Eight. Perform the solenoid and starter motor bench tests described in this section.
3. Perform a voltage drop test between the battery and solenoid terminals as described under *Voltage Drop Test* in this section. The normal voltage drop is less than 2 volts. Note the following:
   a. If the voltage drop is less than 2 volts, perform Step 4.
   b. If the voltage drop is more than 2 volts, check the solenoid and battery wires and connections for dirty or loose fitting terminals; clean and repair as required.
4. Remove the starter as described in Chapter Eight. Momentarily connect a fully charged 12-volt battery to the starter as shown in **Figure 9**. If the starter is operational, it will turn when connected to the battery. Disconnect the battery and note the following:

a. If the starter turns, perform the solenoid pull-in and hold-in tests as described under *Solenoid Testing (Bench Tests)* in this section.

b. If the starter does not turn, disassemble the starter as described in Chapter Eight, and check it for opens, shorts and grounds.

5. If the problem is not evident after performing Steps 3 and 4, check the starter shaft to see if it is binding at the jackshaft. Check the jackshaft for binding or damage. Refer to *Starter Jackshaft* in Chapter Five.

6. If there is no click when performing Step 1, measure voltage between the starter button and the starter relay. The voltmeter must read battery voltage. Note the following:

a. If battery voltage is noted, continue with Step 7.

b. If there is no voltage, go to Step 8.

7. Check for voltage at the starter button. Note the following:

a. If there is voltage at the starter button, test the starter relay as described in this section.

b. If there is no voltage at the starter button, check continuity across the starter button. If there is voltage leading to the starter button but no voltage leaving the starter button, replace the button switch and retest. If there is no voltage leading to the starter button, check the starter button wiring for dirty or loose-fitting terminals or damaged wiring; clean and/or repair as required.

Starter spins but does not engage

If the starter spins but the pinion gear does not engage the clutch shell ring gear, perform the following:

1. Remove the outer primary cover as described in Chapter Five.

2. Check the pinion gear (A, **Figure 10**) mounted on the end of the jackshaft. If the teeth are chipped or worn, inspect the clutch shell ring gear (B, **Figure 10**) for the same problems. Note the following:

a. If the pinion gear and ring gears are damaged, service these parts as described in Chapter Five.

b. If the pinion gear and clutch shell ring gears are not damaged, continue with Step 3.

3. Remove and disassemble the starter as described in Chapter Eight. Then check the overrunning clutch assembly (**Figure 11**) for the following:

a. Roller damage (**Figure 12**).

b. Compression spring damage (A, **Figure 13**).

c. Excessively worn or damaged pinion teeth.

d. Pinion does not run in overrunning direction.

e. Damaged clutch shaft splines (B, **Figure 13**).

f. Damaged overrunning clutch assembly (**Figure 14**).

4. Replace worn or damaged parts as required.

Starter will not disengage after the start button is released

1. A sticking solenoid, caused by a worn solenoid compression spring (A, **Figure 13**), can cause this problem. Replace the solenoid if damaged.

2. On high-mileage motorcycles, the pinion gear (A, **Figure 10**) can jam on a worn clutch ring gear (B). Unable to return, the starter will continue to run. This condition usually requires ring gear replacement.

3. Check the start button switch and starter relay for internal damage. Test the start switch as described under

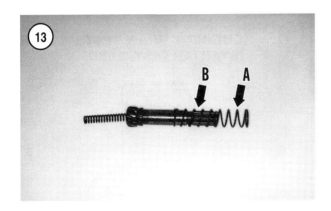

Switches in Chapter Eight. Test the starter relay as described in this chapter.

Loud grinding noises when the starter turns

Incorrect pinion gear and clutch shell ring gear engagement (B, **Figure10**) or a broken overrunning clutch mechanism (**Figure 14**) can cause this problem. Remove and inspect the starter as described in Chapter Eight.

Starter stalls or spins too slowly

1. Perform a voltage drop test between the battery and solenoid terminals as described under *Voltage Drop Test* in this section. The normal voltage drop is less than 2 volts. Note the following:
   a. If the voltage drop is less than 2 volts, continue with Step 2.
   b. If the voltage drop exceeds 2 volts, check the solenoid and battery wires and connections for dirty or loose-fitting terminals; clean and repair as required.
2. Perform a voltage drop test between the solenoid terminals and the starter. The normal voltage drop is less than 2 volts. Note the following:

a. If the voltage drop is less than 2 volts, continue with Step 3.
b. If the voltage drop exceeds 2 volts, check the solenoid and starter wires and connections for dirty or loose-fitting terminals; clean and repair as required.
3. Perform a voltage drop test between the battery ground wire and the starter as described under *Voltage Drop Tests* in this section. The normal voltage drop is less than 0.2 volts. Note the following:
   a. If the voltage drop is less than 0.2 volts, continue with Step 4.
   b. If the voltage drop exceeds 0.2 volts, check the battery ground wire connections for dirty or loose-fitting terminals; clean and repair as required.
4. Refer to *Starter Current Draw Tests* in this section and perform the first test. Note the following:
   a. If the current draw is excessive, check for a damaged starter or starter drive assembly. Remove the starter as described in Chapter Eight and perform the second test.
   b. If the current draw reading is correct, continue with Step 5.
5. Remove the outer primary cover as described in Chapter Five. Check the pinion gear (A, **Figure 10**). If the teeth are chipped or worn, inspect the clutch ring gear (B, **Figure 10**) for the same problem.
   a. If the pinion gear and ring gears are damaged, service these parts as described in Chapter Five.
   b. If the pinion gear and ring gears are not damaged, continue with Step 6.
6. Remove and disassemble the starter as described in Chapter Eight. Check the disassembled starter for opens, shorts and grounds.

Starter Current Draw Tests

The following current draw test measures the current (amperage) the starter circuit requires to crank over the engine. Refer to **Table 1** for current draw specifications.

A short circuit in the starter or a damaged pinion gear assembly can cause excessive current draw. If the current draw is low, suspect an undercharged battery or an open circuit in the starting circuit.

Current draw test (starter installed)

NOTE
This test requires a fully charged battery and an inductive ammeter.

1. Shift the transmission into NEUTRAL.

2. Disconnect the two spark plug caps from the spark plugs. Then ground the plug caps with two extra spark plugs. Do *not* remove the spark plugs from the cylinder heads.

3. Connect an inductive ammeter between the starter motor terminal and positive battery terminal (**Figure 15**). Connect a jumper cable from the negative battery terminal to ground (**Figure 15**).

4. Turn the ignition switch ON and press the start button for approximately ten seconds. Note the ammeter reading.

NOTE
The current draw is high when the start button is first pressed, then it will drop and stabilize at a lower reading. Refer to the lower stabilized reading during this test.

5. If the current draw exceeds the specification in **Table 1**, check for a defective starter or starter drive mechanism. Remove and service these components as described in Chapter Eight.

6. Disconnect the ammeter and jumper cables.

Current draw test (starter removed)

This test requires a fully charged 12-volt battery, an inductive ammeter, a jumper wire (14 gauge minimum) and three jumper cables (6-gauge minimum).

Refer to Figure 16.

1. Remove the starter as described in Chapter Eight.

NOTE
The solenoid must be installed on the starter during the following tests.

2. Mount the starter in a vise with soft jaws.

3. Connect the 14-gauge jumper cable between the positive battery terminal and the solenoid 50 terminal.

4. Connect a jumper cable (6-gauge minimum) between the positive battery terminal and the ammeter.

5. Connect the second jumper cable between the ammeter and the M terminal on the starter solenoid.

6. Connect the third jumper cable between the battery ground terminal and the starter motor mounting flange.

7. Read the ammeter; the no-load current specification is 90 amps. A damaged pinion gear assembly will cause an excessively high current draw reading. If the current draw reading is low, check for an undercharged battery, or an open field winding or armature in the starter.

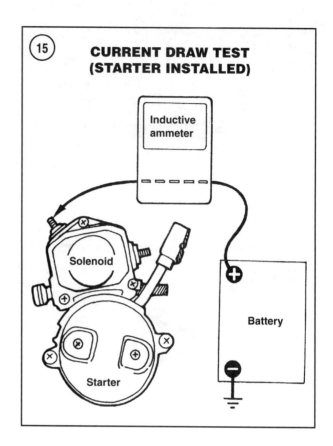

15 **CURRENT DRAW TEST (STARTER INSTALLED)**

Inductive ammeter

Solenoid

Battery

Starter

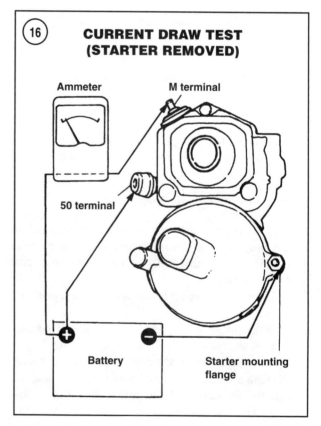

16 **CURRENT DRAW TEST (STARTER REMOVED)**

Ammeter

M terminal

50 terminal

Battery

Starter mounting flange

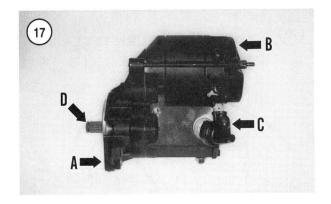

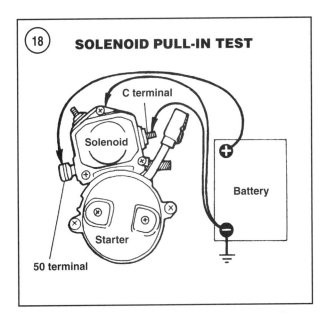

SOLENOID PULL-IN TEST

C terminal

Solenoid

Starter

Battery

50 terminal

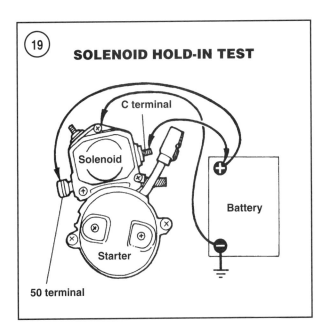

SOLENOID HOLD-IN TEST

C terminal

Solenoid

Starter

Battery

50 terminal

Solenoid Testing (Bench Tests)

This test requires a fully charged 12-volt battery and three jumper wires.

1. Remove the starter (A, **Figure 17**) as described in Chapter Eight.

NOTE
*The solenoid (B, **Figure 17**) must be installed on the starter during the following tests.*

2. Disconnect the C field wire terminal (C, **Figure 17**) from the solenoid before performing the following tests. Insulate the end of the wire terminal so that it cannot short out on any of the test connectors.

CAUTION
Because battery voltage is being applied directly to the solenoid and starter in the following tests, do not leave the jumper cables connected to the solenoid for more than three-five seconds; otherwise, the voltage will damage the solenoid.

NOTE
Thoroughly read the following procedure to become familiar with and understand the procedures and test connections, then perform the tests in the order listed and without interruption.

3. Perform the solenoid pull-in test as follows:
   a. Connect one jumper wire from the negative battery terminal to the solenoid C terminal (**Figure 18**).
   b. Connect one jumper wire from the negative battery terminal to the solenoid housing (ground) (**Figure 18**).
   c. Touch a jumper wire from the positive battery terminal to the starter 50 terminal (**Figure 18**). The pinion shaft (D, **Figure 17**) should pull into the housing.
   d. Leave the jumper wires connected and continue with Step 4.

4. To perform the solenoid hold-in test, perform the following:
   a. With the pinion shaft pulled in (Step 3), disconnect the C terminal jumper wire from the negative battery terminal and connect it to the positive battery terminal (**Figure 19**). The pinion shaft should remain in the housing. If the pinion shaft returns to its original position, replace the solenoid.
   b. Leave the jumper wires connected and continue with Step 5.

5. To perform the solenoid return test, perform the following:

   a. Disconnect the jumper wire from the starter 50 terminal (**Figure 20**); the pinion shaft should return to its original position.

   b. Disconnect all of the jumper wires from the solenoid and battery.

6. Replace the solenoid if the starter shaft failed to operate as described in Steps 3-5. See *Solenoid Replacement* in Chapter Eight.

Starter Relay Removal/Testing/Installation

Check the starter relay operation with an ohmmeter, jumper wires and a fully charged 12-volt battery.

1. Remove the seat as described in Chapter Fourteen.

2. Disconnect the negative battery cable as described in Chapter Eight.

3. Carefully pull the top cover (**Figure 21**) from the fuse block.

4. Pull straight up and remove the starter relay (**Figure 22**) from the fuse block.

> *CAUTION*
> *The battery negative lead must be connected to the relay terminal No. 85 to avoid internal diode damage.*

5. Connect an ohmmeter and 12-volt battery between the relay terminals shown in **Figure 23**. This setup will energize the relay for testing.

6. Check for continuity through the relay contacts using an ohmmeter while the relay coil is energized. The correct reading is 0 ohm. If resistance is excessive or if there is no continuity, replace the relay.

7. If the starter relay passes this test, reconnect the relay.

8. Install the starter relay (**Figure 22**) into the fuse block. Press it in until it bottoms.

9. Install the top cover onto the fuse block and press it on until it latches correctly.

10. Connect the negative battery cable as described in Chapter Eight.

11. Install the seat as described in Chapter Fourteen.

CHARGING SYSTEM

The charging system consists of the battery, alternator and a solid state voltage regulator/rectifier.

The alternator generates alternating current (AC) which the rectifier converts to direct current (DC). The regulator maintains the voltage to the battery and load (lights, igni-

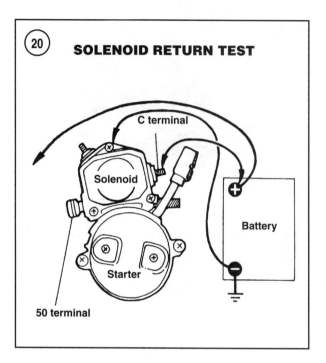

SOLENOID RETURN TEST

tion and accessories) at a constant voltage despite variations in engine speed and load.

A malfunction in the charging system generally causes the battery to remain undercharged.

Service Precautions

Before servicing the charging system, observe the following precautions to prevent damage to any charging system component:

1. Never reverse battery connections.

2. Do not short across any connection.

3. Never start the engine with the alternator disconnected from the voltage regulator/rectifier unless instructed to do so during testing.

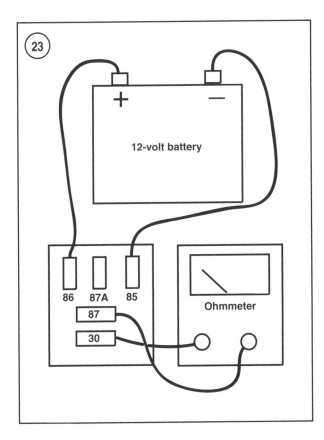

2

4. Never attempt to start or run the engine with the battery disconnected.

5. Never attempt to use a high-output battery charger to help start the engine.

6. Before charging the battery, remove it from the motorcycle as described in Chapter Eight.

7. Never disconnect the voltage regulator/rectifier connector with the engine running. The voltage regulator/rectifier (**Figure 24**) is mounted on the front frame cross member.

8. Do not mount the voltage regulator/rectifier unit in another location.

9. Make sure the negative battery terminal is connected to the engine and frame.

Troubleshooting Sequence

If the battery is discharged, perform the following procedures as listed:

1. Test the battery as described in Chapter Eight. Charge the battery if necessary. If the battery will hold a charge while riding, perform the *Charging System Output Test*.

2. If the charging system output is with specification, determine the total amount of current demand by the electrical system and all accessories as described under *Electrical System Current Load Test*.

3. If the charging system output exceeds the current demand and the battery continues to not hold a charge, perform the *Battery Current Draw Test*.

4. If the charging system output is not within specification, test the stator and voltage regulator as described in this section.

Charging System Output Test

This test requires a load tester.

1. To perform this test, the battery must be fully charged.

> *NOTE*
> *When using a load tester, refer to the manufacturer's instructions. To prevent tester damage caused by overheating, do not leave the load switch ON for more than 20 seconds at a time.*

2. Connect the load tester negative and positive leads to the battery terminals. Then place the load tester's induction pickup over the circuit breaker to voltage regulator wire (**Figure 25**).

3. Start the engine and slowly bring the speed up to 3000 rpm while reading the load tester scale. With the engine running at 3000 rpm, operate the load tester switch until

the voltage scale reads 13.0 volts. The tester should show a regulated (DC) current output reading as follows:

    a. Carbureted models: 34-40 amps.

    b. Fuel-injected models: 41-48 amps.

4. With the engine still running at 3000 rpm, turn the load off and read the load tester voltage scale. Battery voltage should not exceed 15 volts. Turn the engine off and disconnect the load tester from the motorcycle.

5. Perform the *Stator Test* described in this section. If the stator tests acceptable, a defective voltage regulator/rectifier or a wiring short circuit is indicated.

Make sure to eliminate the possibility of a poor connection or damaged wiring before replacing the voltage regulator/rectifier.

Electrical System Current Load Test

This test, requiring a load tester, measures the total current load of the electrical system and any additional accessories while the engine is running. Perform this test if the battery keeps being discharged, yet the charging system output is within specifications.

If aftermarket electrical components have been added to the motorcycle, the increased current demand may exceed the charging systems capacity and result in a discharged battery.

NOTE
When using a load tester, refer to the manufacturer's instructions. To prevent tester damage caused by overheating, do not leave the load switch ON for more than 20 seconds at a time.

1. Connect a load tester to the battery as shown in **Figure 26**.

2. Turn the ignition switch ON but do not start the engine. Then turn on *all* electrical accessories and switch the headlight beam to HIGH.

3. Read the ampere reading (current draw) on the load tester and compare it to the test results obtained in the *Charging System Output Test* in this section. The charging system output test results (current reading) must exceed the electrical system current load by 3.5 amps for the battery to remain sufficiently charged.

4. If aftermarket accessories have been added to the motorcycle, disconnect them and repeat Step 3. If the electrical system current load is now within the specification, the problem is with the additional accessories.

5. If no accessories have been added to the motorcycle, a short circuit may be causing the battery to discharge.

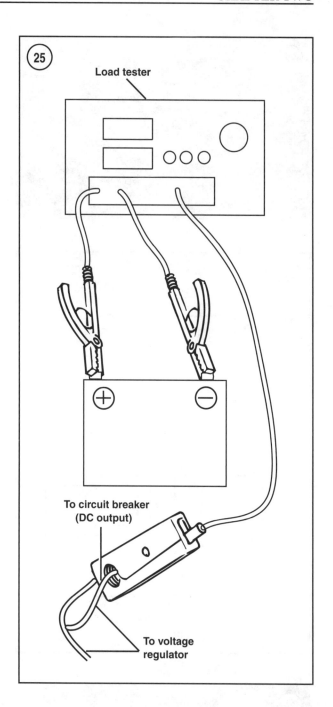

Stator Test

1. With the ignition switch turned OFF, disconnect the regulator/rectifier connector (**Figure 27**) below the mounting bracket.

2. Switch an ohmmeter to its R × 1 scale. Then connect it between either stator socket and ground. The correct ohmmeter reading is infinity. Any other reading indicates a grounded stator. Repeat this test for the other stator socket.

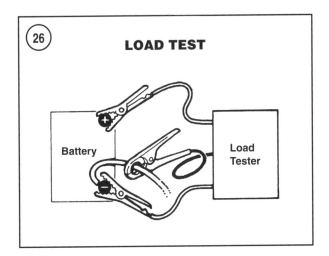

LOAD TEST

Battery

Load Tester

3. Switch an ohmmeter to its R × 1 scale. Then connect it between both stator sockets at the crankcase. The correct ohmmeter reading should be less than 0.5 ohm. If the resistance is not as specified, replace the stator.

4. Check stator AC voltage output as follows:

   a. Connect an AC voltmeter across the stator pins.

   b. Start the engine and slowly increase engine speed to 2000 rpm. The AC output on carbureted models is

16-20 VAC per 1000 rpm. The AC output on fuel injected models is 19-26 VAC per 1000 rpm.

   c. If the AC voltage output reading is below the specified range, the problem is probably a defective stator or rotor. If these parts are not damaged, perform the *Charging System Output Test* in this section.

5. Reconnect the regulator/rectifier connector.

Voltage Regulator Ground Test

The voltage regulator must be grounded to the mounting bracket and the frame for proper operation as shown in **Figure 28**.

1. Switch an ohmmeter to the R × 1 scale.

2. Connect one ohmmeter lead to a good engine or frame ground and the other ohmmeter lead to the regulator base. Read the ohmmeter scale. The correct reading is 0 ohm. Note the following:

   a. If there is low resistance (0 ohm), the voltage regulator is properly grounded.

   b. If there is high resistance, remove the voltage regulator and clean its frame mounting points.

3. Check the voltage regulator connector (**Figure 27**) and make sure it is clean and tightly connected.

Voltage Regulator Bleed Test

1. Disconnect the voltage regulator connector (**Figure 27**).

NOTE
Do not disconnect the wire from the voltage regulator to the circuit breaker.

2. Connect one probe of a 12-volt test lamp to a good frame or engine ground.

3. Connect the other test lamp probe to one of the voltage regulator pins, then to the other pin.

4. If the test lamp lights, replace the voltage regulator.

5. If the voltage regulator passes this test, reconnect the voltage regulator connector at the engine crankcase.

Battery Current Draw Test

This test measures the current draw or drain on the battery when all electrical systems and accessories are off. Perform this test if the battery will not hold a charge when the motorcycle is not being used. A current draw that exceeds 5.5 mA will discharge the battery. The ECM (1 mA), voltage regulator (0.5 mA), TSM (0.5 mA), TSSM disarmed (0.5 mA) and TSSM armed (3.0 mA) account for a 5.0 mA current draw. The battery must be fully charged to perform this test.

1. Disconnect the negative battery cable as described in Chapter Eight.

2. Connect an ammeter between the negative battery terminal and the battery ground cable as shown in **Figure 29**.

3. With the ignition switch, lights and all accessories turned off, read the ammeter. If the current drain exceeds 5.5 mA, continue with Step 4.

4. Refer to the wiring diagrams at the end of the manual for the necessary model. Check the charging system wires and connectors for shorts or other damage.

5. Unplug each electrical connector separately and check for a reduction in the current draw. If the meter reading changes after a connector is disconnected, the source of the current draw has been found. Check the electrical connectors carefully before testing the individual component.

6. After completing the test, disconnect the ammeter and reconnect the negative battery cable.

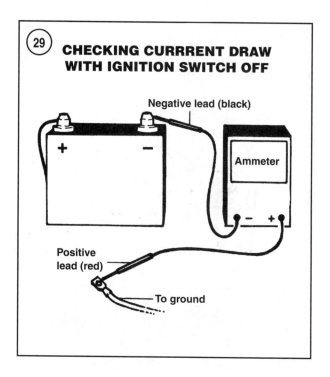

IGNITION SYSTEM

All models are equipped with a transistorized ignition system. This solid-state system uses no contact breaker points to trigger the ignition. Refer to the wiring diagrams at the end of this manual for the necessary model and year.

Because of the solid-state design, problems with the transistorized system are rare. If a problem occurs, it generally causes a weak spark or no spark at all. An ignition system with a weak spark or no spark is relatively easy to troubleshoot. It is difficult, however, to troubleshoot an ignition system that only malfunctions when the engine is hot or under load.

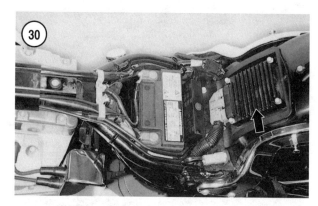

Ignition System Precautions

The following measures must be taken to protect the ignition system:

1. Never disconnect any of the electrical connectors while the engine is running.

2. Apply dielectric grease to all electrical connectors prior to reconnecting them. This will help seal out moisture.

3. Make sure all electrical connectors are free of corrosion and are completely coupled to each other.

4. The ignition module, or electronic control module must always be mounted securely to the mounting bracket under the seat (**Figure 30**, typical).

Troubleshooting Preparation

1. Refer to the wiring diagrams at the end of this manual for the specific model.

2. Check the wiring harness for visible signs of damage.

3. Make sure all connectors are properly attached to each other and locked in place.

4. Check all electrical components for a good ground to the engine.

5. Check all wiring for short circuits or open circuits.

6. Remove the rear fender inner panel as described in Chapter Fourteen.

7. Check for a damaged ignition circuit breaker (**Figure 31**) located on the electrical panel forward of the rear wheel.

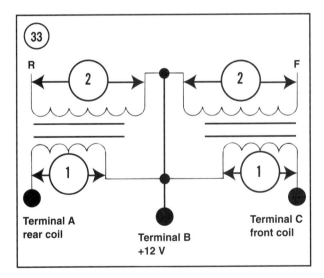

Terminal A
rear coil

Terminal B
+12 V

Terminal C
front coil

8. Make sure the fuel tank has an adequate supply of fresh gasoline.

9. Check the spark plug cable routing and the connections at the spark plugs. If there is no spark or only a weak one, repeat the test with new spark plugs. If the condition remains the same with new spark plugs and if all external wiring connections are good, the problem is most likely in

the ignition system. If a strong spark is present, the problem is probably not in the ignition system. Check the fuel system.

10. Remove the spark plugs and examine them as described in Chapter Three.

Ignition Module or Electronic Control Module Testing and Replacement

If the ignition module, or electronic control module, is suspected of being defective, have it tested by a Harley-Davidson dealership before purchasing a replacement. The cost of the test will not exceed the cost of replacing an ignition module, or electronic control module, that may not repair the problem. Most parts suppliers will not accept returns on electrical components.

Ignition Coil Testing

Use an ohmmeter to check the ignition coil secondary and primary resistance. Test the coil twice: first when it is cold (room temperature), then at normal operating temperature. If the engine will not start, heat the coil with a hair dryer, then test with the ohmmeter.

1. Remove the seat as described in Chapter Fourteen.

2. Remove the fuel tank as described in Chapter Seven.

3. Remove the cover from the ignition coil.

4. Disconnect the secondary wires and the primary wire connector (**Figure 32**) from the ignition coil.

NOTE
When switching between ohmmeter scales in the following tests, always cross the test leads and zero the needle to assure a correct reading (analog meter only).

5. Set an ohmmeter on R × 1. Measure the ignition coil primary resistance between the primary coil terminals. Refer to **Figure 33** for carbureted models or **Figure 34** for fuel-injected models. Compare the reading to the specification in **Table 2**. Replace the ignition coil if the reading is not within specification.

6. Set the ohmmeter on its highest scale. Measure the resistance between the secondary terminals. Refer to **Figure 33** for carbureted models or **Figure 34** for fuel injected models. Compare the reading to the specification in **Table 2**. Replace the ignition coil if the reading is not within specification.

Spark Plug Cable and Cap Inspection

All models are equipped with resistor- or suppression-type spark plug cables (**Figure 35**). These cables reduce radio interference. The cable's conductor consists of a carbon-impregnated fabric core material instead of solid wire.

If a plug cable becomes damaged, due to either corrosion or conductor breaks, its resistance increases. Excessive cable resistance will cause engine misfire and other ignition or driveability problems.

When troubleshooting the ignition system, inspect the spark plug cables (**Figure 36**, typical) for:

1. Corroded or damaged connector ends.
2. Breaks in the cable insulation that could allow arcing.
3. Split or damaged plug caps that could allow arcing to the cylinder heads.
4. Replace damaged or questionable spark plug cables.

ENGINE MANAGEMENT SYSTEM DIAGNOSTIC CODES

All models covered in this manual are equipped with an on-board diagnostic system that identifies and stores faults as a two-digit diagnostic code. The retrieved code(s) indicate in which system a fault(s) has occurred.

Troubleshooting is limited to code retrieval. Further diagnosis and clearing of codes requires specific Harley-Davidson test equipment that is *only* available to dealership personnel.

If a diagnostic code has been set, the check-engine light will be activated. During normal operation, the check-engine light illuminates for approximately four seconds when the ignition is turned on. The check-engine light then turns off and remains off. If a diagnostic code(s) has been set, the check-engine light turns on for four seconds, turns off, then turns back on for eight seconds or longer.

Diagnostic codes are by counting the number of times the check-engine light flashes.

Carbureted Models

Diagnostic codes retrieval

> NOTE
> *Diagnostic codes can only be cleared by a Harley-Davidson dealership.*

Diagnostic trouble codes are displayed as a series of flashes at the check engine light on the speedometer face. To retrieve the stored codes, a jumper wire made of 18-gauge

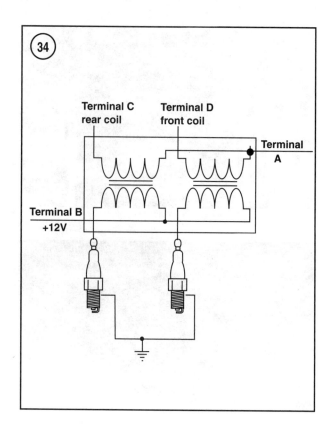

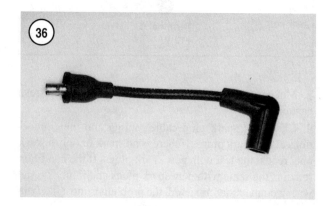

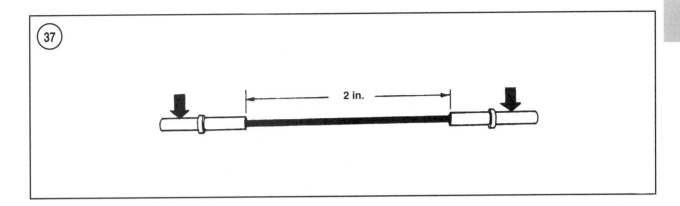

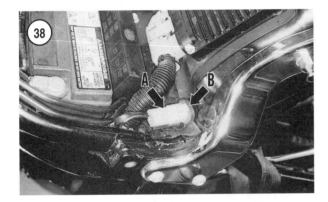

wire and two Deutsch sockets (H-D part No. 72191-94), shown in **Figure 37**, are required.

To retrieve the diagnostic code(s), perform the following:

1. Remove the seat as described in Chapter Fourteen.

2. Lift the data link connector up and off the mounting bracket.

3. Remove the protective cover from the data link connector.

4. Install the jumper wire onto pins No. 1 (light green/red) and No. 2 (black) on the data link connector.

5. Turn the ignition/light key switch to the IGNITION position. After approximately eight seconds, the different systems enter the diagnostic codes:

   a. The check engine light begins with a ready signal, which is a series of six rapid flashes, approximately three per second. The ready signal indicates the check engine light is ready to flash a diagnostic code.

   b. The ready signal is followed by a two-second pause.

   c. Then the system flashes the first digit of the stored diagnostic code. The check engine light will illuminate for one second then turn off for one second. Record the number of flashes. For example, two flashes indicate the first digit is two.

   d. The system pauses for two seconds then flashes the second digit of the diagnostic code. record the number of flashes. For example, five flashes indicate the second digit is five. In this example, the first code is 25, or a problem with the rear cylinder ignition coil.

   e. If more than one code is present, the system will pause for two seconds then flash the ready signal, which is a series of six rapid flashes.

   f. The system pauses for two seconds, then flashes the first digit of the next diagnostic code, followed by the second digit.

6. The system displays the stored codes sequentially until each diagnostic code has been displayed. Then the system repeats the codes. The check-engine light repeats the stored codes until the jumper wire is disconnected. When the codes repeat, all stored codes have been displayed. Turn the ignition switch to the OFF position and remove the jumper wire from the data link connector.

7. Refer to diagnostic codes in **Table 3** to locate the problem.

8. Install the protective cover onto the data link connector and fit the data link connector onto the mounting bracket.

9. Install the seat as described in Chapter Fourteen.

Fuel Injected Models

Diagnostic codes retrieval

NOTE
Diagnostic codes can only be cleared by a Harley-Davidson dealership.

1. Remove the seat as described in Chapter Fourteen.

2. Lift the data link connector (A, **Figure 38**) up and off the mounting bracket.

3. Remove the protective cover (B, **Figure 38**) from the data link connector.

4. Install the jumper wire onto pins No. 1 (light green/red) and No. 2 (black) on the data link connector (**Figure 39**).

5. Turn the ignition/light key switch to the ON position. After approximately nine seconds (four seconds lamp is on, then five seconds lamp is off), the different systems enter the diagnostic codes:

    a. Then the system flashes the first digit of the stored diagnostic code. The check engine light will illuminate for about 1/2 second then turn off for one second. Record the number of flashes. For example, two flashes indicate the first digit is two.

    b. The system pauses for approximately one second then flashes the second digit of the diagnostic code. Record the number of flashes. For example, five flashes indicate the second digit is five. In this example, the first code is 25, or a problem with the rear cylinder ignition coil.

    c. If more than one code is present, the system will pause for three seconds in which the lamp is off.

    d. The system then flashes the first digit of the next diagnostic code, followed by the second digit.

6. The system displays the stored codes sequentially until each diagnostic code has been displayed. Then the system repeats the codes until the ignition/light key switch is turned to the off position.

7. Refer to diagnostic codes in **Table 3** to locate the problem.

8. Install the protective cover onto the data link connector (B, **Figure 38**) and fit the data link connector onto the mounting bracket.

9. Install the seat as described in Chapter Fourteen.

FUEL SYSTEM (CARBURETED MODELS)

Begin fuel system troubleshooting with the fuel tank and work through the system, reserving the carburetor as the final point. Most fuel system problems result from an empty fuel tank, a plugged fuel filter or fuel valve, sour fuel, a dirty air filter or clogged carburetor jets. Do not assume the carburetor is the problem. Unnecessary carburetor adjustment can compound the problem.

Identifying Carburetor Conditions

Refer to the following conditions to identify whether the engine is running lean or rich.

Rich

1. Fouled spark plugs.

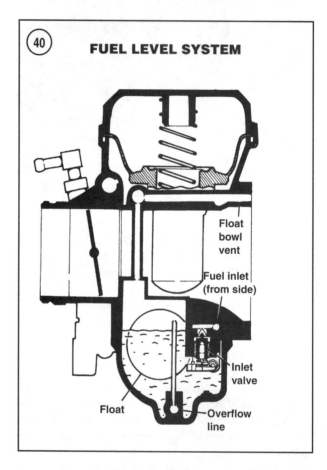

FUEL LEVEL SYSTEM

Float bowl vent

Fuel inlet (from side)

Inlet valve

Float

Overflow line

2. Engine misfires and runs rough under load.

3. Excessive exhaust smoke as the throttle is increased.

4. An extreme rich condition causes a choked or dull sound from the exhaust and an inability to clear the exhaust with the throttle held wide open.

Lean

1. Blistered or very white spark plug electrodes.

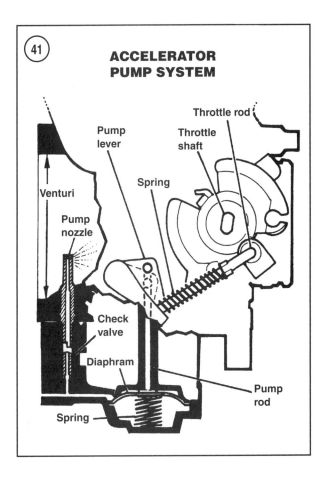

ACCELERATOR PUMP SYSTEM

2. Engine overheats.
3. Slow acceleration and engine power is reduced.
4. Flat spots on acceleration that are similar in feel to when the engine starts to run out of gas.
5. Engine speed fluctuates at full throttle.

Troubleshooting

Isolate fuel system problems to the fuel tank, fuel shut-off valve and filter, fuel hoses, external fuel filter (if used) or carburetor. In the following procedures, it is assumed that the ignition system is working properly and is correctly adjusted.

Fuel level system

The fuel level system is shown in **Figure 40**. Proper carburetor operation depends on a constant and correct carburetor fuel level. As fuel is drawn from the float bowl during engine operation, the float level in the bowl drops. As the float drops, the fuel valve moves from its seat and allows fuel to flow through the seat into the float bowl. Fuel entering the float bowl causes the float to rise and

push against the fuel valve. When the fuel level reaches a predetermined level, the fuel valve is pushed against the seat to prevent the float bowl from overfilling.

If the fuel valve fails to close, the engine will run too rich or flood with fuel. Symptoms of this problem are rough running, excessive black smoke and poor acceleration. This condition will sometimes clear up when the engine is run at wide-open throttle and the fuel is being drawn into the engine before the float bowl can overfill. However, as the engine speed is reduced, the rich running condition returns.

Several things can cause fuel overflow. In most instances, a small piece of dirt is trapped between the fuel valve and seat, or the float level is incorrect. If fuel is flowing out of the overflow tube connected to the bottom of the float bowl, the fuel valve inside the carburetor is being held open. First check the position of the fuel shutoff valve lever. Turn the fuel shutoff valve lever OFF. Then lightly tap on the carburetor float bowl and turn the fuel shutoff valve lever ON. If the fuel flow stops running out of the overflow tube, whatever was holding the fuel valve off of its seat has been dislodged. If fuel continues to flow from the overflow tube, remove and service the carburetor. See Chapter Seven.

NOTE
Fuel will not flow from the vacuum-operated fuel shutoff valve until the engine is running.

Starting enrichment (choke) system

A cold engine requires a rich mixture to start and run properly. On all models, a cable-actuated starter enrichment valve is used for cold starting.

If the engine is difficult to start when cold, check the starting enrichment (choke) cable adjustment described in Chapter Three.

Accelerator pump system

During sudden acceleration, the diaphragm type accelerator pump system (**Figure 41**) provides additional fuel to the engine. Without this system, the carburetor would not be able to provide a sufficient amount of fuel.

The system consists of a spring loaded neoprene diaphragm that is compressed by the pump lever during sudden acceleration. This causes the diaphragm to force fuel from the pump chamber, through a check valve and into the carburetor venturi. The diaphragm spring returns the diaphragm to the uncompressed position, which allows the chamber to refill with fuel.

If the engine hesitates during sudden acceleration, check the operation of the accelerator pump system. Carburetor service is covered in Chapter Seven.

Vacuum-operated fuel shutoff valve testing

All models are equipped with a vacuum-operated fuel shutoff valve. A vacuum hose is connected between the fuel shutoff valve diaphragm and the carburetor. When the engine is running, vacuum is applied to the fuel shutoff valve through this hose. For fuel to flow through the fuel valve, a vacuum must be present with the fuel shutoff valve handle in the ON or RES position. The following steps troubleshoot the fuel shutoff valve by applying a vacuum from a separate source. A Miti-Vac hand-operated vacuum pump (**Figure 42**), gas can, drain hose that is long enough to reach from the fuel valve to the gas can, and hose clamp are required for this test.

> *WARNING*
> *Gasoline is highly flammable. When servicing the fuel system in the following sections, work in a well-ventilated area. Do not expose gasoline and gasoline vapors to sparks or other ignition sources.*

1. Disconnect the negative battery cable as described in Chapter Eight.
2. Visually check the amount of fuel in the tank. Add fuel if necessary.
3. Turn the fuel shutoff valve (A, **Figure 43**) to the OFF position and disconnect the fuel hose (B) from the fuel shutoff valve. Plug the open end of the hose.
4. Connect the drain hose to the fuel shutoff valve and secure it with a hose clamp. Insert the end of the drain hose into a gas can.
5. Disconnect the vacuum hose from the fuel shutoff valve.
6. Connect a hand-operated vacuum pump to the fuel shutoff valve vacuum hose nozzle.
7. Turn the fuel shutoff valve lever to the ON position.

> *CAUTION*
> *In Step 8, do not apply more than 25 in. (635 mm) Hg vacuum or the fuel shutoff valve diaphragm will be damaged.*

8. Apply 25 in. (635 mm) Hg of vacuum to the valve. Fuel should flow through the fuel shutoff valve when the vacuum is applied.
9. With the vacuum still applied, turn the fuel shutoff valve lever to the RES position. Fuel should continue to flow through the valve.

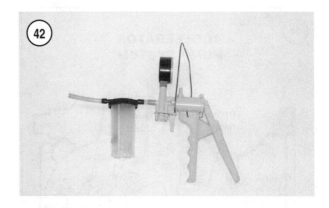

10. Release the vacuum and make sure the fuel flow stops.
11. Repeat Steps 8-10 five times. Fuel should flow with vacuum applied and stop flowing when the vacuum is released.
12. Turn the fuel shutoff valve OFF. Disconnect the vacuum pump and drain hoses.
13. Reconnect the fuel hose (B, **Figure 43**) to the fuel shutoff valve.
14. If the fuel valve failed this test, replace the fuel shutoff valve as described in Chapter Seven.

FUEL SYSTEM (FUEL-INJECTION MODELS)

The fuel injection system is controlled by the engine management system and by the ignition control module. Troubleshooting this system, due to the specialized equipment required, must be performed by a Harley-Davidson dealership.

However, most fuel system problems result from an empty tank, a plugged filter, fuel pump failure, contaminated fuel or a restricted air filter element. Begin any fuel system troubleshooting with these items first. Refer to the *Engine Starting* and *Engine Performance* procedures in this chapter.

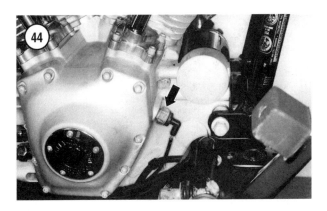

ENGINE NOISES

1. Knocking or pinging during acceleration can be caused by using a lower octane fuel than recommended or a poor grade of fuel. Incorrect carburetor jetting (carbureted models) and an incorrect spark plug heat range (too hot) can cause pinging. Refer to *Spark Plug Heat Range* in Chapter Three. Check also for excessive carbon buildup in the combustion chamber or a defective ignition module.

2. Slapping or rattling noise at low speed or during acceleration can be caused by excessive piston-to-cylinder wall clearance. Also check also for a bent connecting rod(s) or worn piston pin and/or piston pin hole in the piston(s).

3. Knocking or rapping during deceleration is usually caused by excessive rod bearing clearance.

4. Persistent knocking and vibration or other noises are usually caused by worn main bearings. If the main bearings are in good condition, consider the following:

    a. Loose engine mounts.
    b. Cracked frame.
    c. Leaking cylinder head gasket(s).
    d. Exhaust pipe leakage at cylinder head(s).
    e. Stuck piston ring(s).
    f. Broken piston ring(s).
    g. Partial engine seizure.
    h. Excessive connecting rod bearing clearance.
    i. Excessive connecting rod side clearance.
    j. Excessive crankshaft runout.

5. Rapid on-off squeal indicates a compression leak around the cylinder head gasket or spark plug.

6. For valve train noise, check for the following:

    a. Bent pushrod(s).
    b. Defective lifter(s).
    c. Valve sticking in guide.
    d. Worn cam gears and/or cam.
    e. Damaged rocker arm or shaft. Rocker arm may be binding on shaft.

ENGINE LUBRICATION

An improperly operating engine lubrication system will quickly lead to serious engine damage. Check the engine oil level as described in Chapter Three weekly. Oil pump service is covered in Chapter Four.

Low Oil Warning Light

The low oil warning light, mounted on the indicator light panel, should come on when the ignition switch is turned on before the engine is started. After the engine is started, the oil light should turn off when the engine speed is above idle.

If the low oil warning light does not come on when the ignition switch is turned to on and the engine is not running, check for a defective light bulb as described in Chapter Eight. If the bulb is working, check the oil pressure switch (**Figure 44**) as described in Chapter Eight.

If the oil light remains on when the engine speed is above idle, turn the engine off and check the oil level in the oil tank. If the oil level is correct, oil may not be returning to the oil tank from the return line. Check for a clogged or damaged return line or a damaged oil pump. If the motorcycle is being operated in conditions where the ambient temperature is below freezing, ice and sludge may be blocking the oil feed pipe.

Oil Consumption High or Engine Smokes Excessively

1. Worn valve guides.
2. Worn valve guide seals.
3. Worn or damaged piston rings.
4. Oil tank overfilled.
5. Oil filter restricted.
6. Leaking cylinder head surfaces.

Oil Fails to Return to Oil Tank

1. Oil lines or fittings restricted or damaged.
2. Oil pump damaged or operating incorrectly.
3. Oil tank empty.
4. Oil filter restricted.
5. Damaged oil feed pump.

Engine Oil Leaks

1. Clogged air filter breather hose.
2. Restricted or damaged oil return line (A, **Figure 45**) and/or vent line (B) to oil tank.
3. Loose engine parts.

4. Damaged gasket sealing surfaces.
5. Oil tank overfilled.
6. Restricted oil filter.
7. Plugged air filter-to-breather system hose.

CLUTCH

Clutch diagnosis, except adjustment, requires partial clutch disassembly to identify and correct the problem. Refer to Chapter Five for clutch service procedures.

Clutch Chatter or Noise

Clutch chatter or noise is usually caused by worn or warped clutch plates.

Clutch Slippage

1. Incorrect clutch adjustment.
2. Worn friction plates.
3. Weak or damaged diaphragm spring.
4. Damaged pressure plate.

Clutch Dragging

1. Incorrect clutch adjustment.
2. Warped clutch plates.
3. Worn or damaged clutch shell or clutch hub.
4. Worn or incorrectly assembled clutch ball and ramp mechanism.
5. Incorrect primary chain alignment.
6. Weak or damaged diaphragm spring.

TRANSMISSION

Transmission symptoms are sometimes hard to distinguish from clutch symptoms. Refer to Chapter Six for transmission service procedures.

Gears Will Not Stay Engaged

1. Worn or damaged shifter parts.
2. Incorrect shifter rod adjustment.
3. Incorrect shifter drum adjustment.
4. Severely worn or damaged gears and/or shift forks.

Difficult Shifting

1. Worn or damaged shift forks.
2. Worn or damaged shifter clutch dogs.

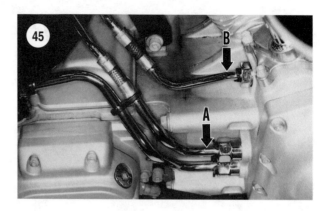

3. Weak or damaged shifter return spring.
4. Clutch drag.

Excessive Gear Noise

1. Worn or damaged bearings.
2. Worn or damaged gears.
3. Excessive gear backlash.

LIGHTING SYSTEM

If bulbs burn out frequently, check for excessive vibration, loose connections that permit sudden current surges, or the installation of the wrong type of bulb.

Most light and ignition problems are caused by loose or corroded ground connections. Check these prior to replacing a bulb or electrical component.

EXCESSIVE VIBRATION

Excessive vibration is usually caused by loose engine mounting hardware. A bent wheel axle shaft(s) or loose suspension component causes high-speed vibration problems. Vibration can also be caused by the following conditions:
1. Balancer system out of alignment or component damaged.
2. Cracked or broken frame.
3. Severely worn primary chain.
4. Tight primary chain links.
5. Loose, worn or damaged engine stabilizer link.
6. Improperly balanced wheel(s).
7. Defective or damaged wheel(s).
8. Defective or damaged tire(s).
9. Internal engine wear or damage.
10. Loose or worn steering head bearings.
11. Loose swing arm pivot shaft nut.

FRONT SUSPENSION AND STEERING

Poor handling may be caused by improper tire inflation pressure, a damaged or bent frame or front steering components, worn wheel bearings, or dragging brakes. Possible causes for suspension and steering malfunctions are listed below.

Irregular or Wobbly Steering

1. Loose wheel axle nut(s).
2. Loose or worn steering head bearings.
3. Excessive wheel bearing play.
4. Damaged cast wheel.
5. Laced wheel out of alignment.
6. Unbalanced wheel assembly.
7. Incorrect wheel alignment.
8. Bent or damaged steering stem or frame at steering neck.
9. Tire incorrectly seated on rim.
10. Excessive front end load from nonstandard equipment.

Stiff Steering

1. Low front tire air pressure.
2. Bent or damaged steering stem or frame.
3. Loose or worn steering head bearings.

Stiff or Heavy Fork Operation (Non-Springer Front Fork)

1. Incorrect fork springs.
2. Incorrect fork oil viscosity.
3. Excessive amount of fork oil.
4. Bent fork tubes.

Poor Fork Operation (Non-Springer Front Fork)

1. Worn or bent fork tubes.
2. Leaking fork seals.
3. Contaminated fork oil.
4. Incorrect fork springs.
5. Excessive front end load from nonstandard equipment.

Poor Fork Operation (Springer Front Fork)

1. Worn or bent rigid or spring fork legs.
2. Leaking or damaged shock absorber.

3. Incorrect tightened rebound springs.
4. Fork rocker spherical bearings out of adjustment or lack of lubrication.
5. Excessive front end load from nonstandard equipment.

Poor Rear Shock Absorber Operation

1. Damper unit leaking.
2. Rear shocks adjusted incorrectly.
3. Loose mounting hardware.
4. Excessive rear end load from nonstandard equipment.
5. Incorrect loading.

BRAKE PROBLEMS

All models are equipped with front and rear disc brakes. Good brakes are vital to the safe operation of any motorcycle. Perform the maintenance procedures in Chapter Three to minimize brake system problems. Brake system service is covered in Chapter Thirteen. To refill the front and rear master cylinders, only use DOT 5 silicone-based brake fluid.

Insufficient Braking Power

Worn brake pads or discs, air in the hydraulic system, glazed or contaminated pads, low brake fluid level, or a leaking brake line or hose can cause this problem. Visually check for leaks. Check for worn brake pads. Also check for a leaking or damaged primary cup seal in the master cylinder. Bleed and adjust the brakes. Rebuild a leaking master cylinder or brake caliper. Brake drag causes excessive heat and brake fade. See *Brake Drag* in this section.

Spongy Brake Feel

Spongy brake feel is generally caused by air in the hydraulic system. Bleed and adjust the brakes as described in Chapter Thirteen.

Brake Drag

Check the brake adjustment, while checking for insufficient brake pedal and/or hand lever free play. Also check for worn, loose or missing parts in the brake calipers. Check the brake disc for excessive runout.

Brakes Squeal or Chatter

Check brake pad thickness and disc condition. Make sure the caliper anti-rattle springs are properly installed and in good condition. Clean off any dirt on the pads. Loose components can also cause this problem. Check for:

1. Warped brake disc.
2. Loose brake disc.
3. Loose caliper mounting bolts.
4. Loose front axle nut.
5. Worn wheel bearings.
6. Damaged hub.

Table 1 STARTER SPECIFICATIONS

Minimum no-load speed @ 11.5 volts	3000 rpm
Maximum no-load current @ 11.5 volts	90 amps (max)
Current draw	
Normal	160-180 amps
Maximum	200 amps
Brush length (minimum)	0.433 in. (11.0 mm)
Commutator diameter (minimum)	1.141 in. (28.981 mm)

Table 2 ELECTRICAL SPECIFICATIONS

Item	Specification
Battery capacity	12 volts, 19 amp hour/270 CCA*
Maximum current draw	5.5 mA
Alternator	
AC voltage output	
Carbureted	16-20 volts per 1000 rpm
EFI	19-26 VAC per 1000 rpm
Stator coil resistance	0.1-0.3 ohm
Voltage regulator	
Voltage output @ 3600 rpm	14.3-14.7 @ 75° F (24° C)
Amps @ 3000 rpm	
Carbureted	34-40 amps
EFI	41-48 amps
Ignition coil	
Primary resistance	0.5-0.7 ohm
Secondary resistance	5500-7500 ohms
Spark plug cable resistance	
Short cable (7.25 in./184 mm)	1812-4375 ohms
Long cable (19.0 in./483 mm)	4750-11,230 ohms
Circuit breaker	30 amp
Fuses	
Ignition	15 amp
Lighting	15 amp
Accessory	15 amp
Instrument	15 amp
Security	15 amp
Fuel pump (EFI)	15 amp
Electronic control module (EFI)	15 amp
*CCA (Cold cranking amperage)	

Table 3 ENGINE MANAGEMENT DIAGNOSTIC TROUBLE CODES

Diagnostic code No.	Fault condition
11	Throttle position sensor (EFI)
12	MAP sensor (carburetted)
13	Barometric pressure sensor (EFI)
14	Engine temperature sensor (EFI)
15	Intake air temperature sensor (EFI)
16	Battery positive voltage
23	Front cylinder fuel injector (EFI)
24	Front cylinder ignition coil
25	Rear cylinder ignition coil
32	Rear cylinder fuel injector (EFI)
33	Fuel pump relay (EFI)
34	Loss of idle speed control
41	Crankshaft position sensor
43	VSS sensor low
44	Bank angle sensor
52	RAM error or failure
53	ROM error or failure
54	EPROM error or failure
55	Ignition module failure
56	Camshaft position sensor and crankshaft position sensor timing or signal error

CHAPTER THREE

LUBRICATION, MAINTENANCE AND TUNE-UP

This chapter covers lubrication, maintenance and tune-up procedures. If a procedure requires more than minor disassembly, reference to the appropriate chapter is listed. Maintenance intervals, capacities, recommendations and specification are in **Tables 1-10** at the end of this chapter.

To maximize the service life of the motorcycle, and gain maximum safety and performance, it is necessary to perform periodic inspections and maintenance. Minor problems found during routine service can be corrected before they develop into major ones.

Consider the maintenance schedule a guide. Harder than normal use and exposure to mud, water or high humidity indicates the need for more frequent servicing to most maintenance items. Record all service and repairs in the maintenance log at the back of this manual. A running record will make it easier to evaluate future maintenance requirements and maintain the motorcycle in top condition.

ROUTINE SAFETY CHECKS

Pre-ride Inspection

1. Check wheel and tire condition. Check tire pressure. Refer to *Tires and Wheels* in this chapter.

2. Make sure all lights work. Refer to *Lights and Horn* in this chapter.

3. Check engine, transmission and primary drive chaincase for oil leakage. If necessary, add oil as described in this chapter.

4. Check brake fluid level and condition. If necessary, add fluid as described in this chapter.

5. Check the operation of the front and rear brakes.

6. Check clutch operation. If necessary, adjust the clutch as described in this chapter.

7. Check the throttle operation. The throttle should move smoothly and return quickly when released. If necessary, adjust throttle free play as described in this chapter.

8. Inspect the front and rear suspension. They should have a solid feel with no looseness.

9. Check the exhaust system for leakage or damage.

10. Inspect the fuel system for leakage.

11. Check the fuel level in fuel tank.

12. Check drive belt tension as described in this chapter.

CAUTION
When checking the tightness of the exposed fasteners, do not check the cylinder head bolts without following the procedure described in Chapter Four.

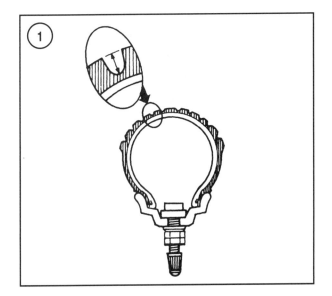

Lights and Horn

Turn the ignition switch ON, and check the following:
1. Pull the front brake lever and make sure the brake light works.
2. Push the rear brake pedal down and check that the brake light comes on soon after the pedal has been depressed.
3. Make sure the headlight and taillight work.
4. Move the dimmer switch between the HIGH and LOW positions, and make sure both headlight elements are working.
5. Push the turn signal switch to the left and right positions, and make sure all four turn signal lights are working.
6. Make sure all accessory lights work properly, if so equipped.
7. Check the horn button operation.
8. If the horn or any light fails to work properly, refer to Chapter Eight.

TIRES AND WHEELS

Tire Pressure

Check the tire pressure often to maintain tire profile, traction and handling, and to get the maximum life out of the tire. Carry a tire gauge in the motorcycle's tool kit. **Table 2** lists the cold tire pressures for the original equipment tires.

> *NOTE*
> *After checking and adjusting the air pressure, reinstall the air valve caps. These caps prevent debris from collecting in the valve stems and causing air leakage or incorrect tire pressure readings.*

Tire Inspection

Inspect the tires periodically for excessive wear, deep cuts and imbedded objects such as stones or nails. If a nail or other object is found in a tire, mark its location with a light crayon prior to removing it. This will help locate the hole for repair.

Measure the depth (**Figure 1**) with a tread depth gauge or a small ruler. As a guideline, replace tires when the tread depth is 5/16 in. (8. 0 mm.) or less. Refer to Chapter Nine for tire changing and repair information.

Laced Wheel Spoke Tension

On models with laced wheels, check for loose or damaged spokes. Refer to Chapter Nine for spoke service.

Rim Inspection

Check the wheel rims for cracks and other damage. If they are damaged, a rim can make the motorcycle handle poorly. Refer to Chapter Nine for wheel service.

PERIODIC LUBRICATION

Oil Tank Inspection

Before inspecting the oil level, inspect the oil tank for cracks or other damage. If oil seepage is evident on or near the oil tank, locate and repair the problem. Check the oil tank mounting bolts for loose or missing fasteners; replace or tighten all fasteners. Check all oil line connections on the tank (**Figure 2** and **Figure 3**) and the engine crankcase (**Figure 4**). Each oil line is connected with a

3

special connector assembly. Replace damaged oil lines immediately as described under *Oil Tank* in Chapter Four.

Engine Oil Level Check

Check the engine oil level with the dipstick/oil filler cap (**Figure 5**) on the right side of the oil tank.

1. Start and run the engine for approximately ten minutes or until the engine has reached normal operating temperature. Then turn the engine off and allow the oil to settle in the oil tank.

2. Place the motorcycle on a level surface and park it on its jiffy stand.

> *CAUTION*
> *Holding the motorcycle straight up will result in an incorrect oil level reading.*

3. Wipe the area around the oil filler cap with a clean rag. Then pull the oil filler cap (**Figure 5**) out of the oil tank. Wipe the dipstick with a clean rag and reinsert the filler cap all the way into the oil tank until it bottoms. Withdraw the filler cap and check the oil level on the dipstick. The oil level should be at the upper groove mark on the dipstick (**Figure 6**). If the oil level is even with or below the ADD QUART mark, continue with Step 4. If the oil level is correct, go to Step 5.

4. Add the recommended engine oil listed in **Table 3**.

> *CAUTION*
> *Do not overfill the oil level in the oil tank or the oil filler cap will pop out when the oil gets hot.*

5. Check the oil filler cap O-ring (**Figure 7**) for cracks or other damage. Replace the O-ring if necessary.

6. Reinstall the oil filler cap and push it down until it bottoms.

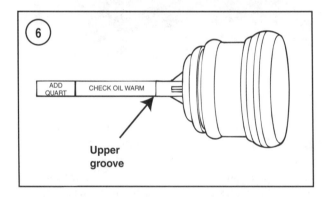

ADD QUART | CHECK OIL WARM

Upper groove

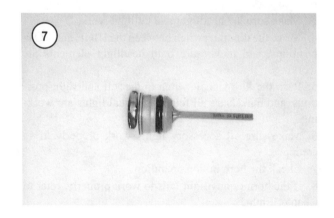

3

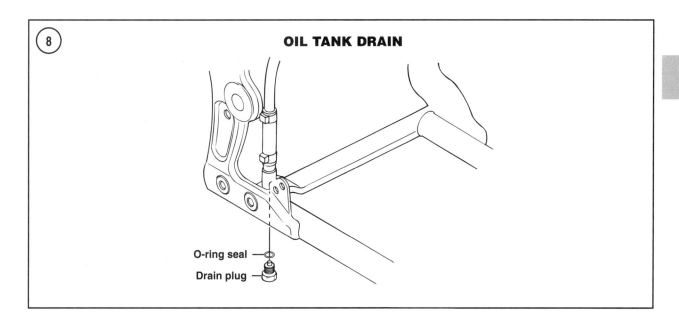

(8)   **OIL TANK DRAIN**

O-ring seal
Drain plug

Engine Oil and Filter Change

Regular oil and filter changes contribute more to engine longevity than any other maintenance performed. **Table 1** lists the recommended oil and filter change intervals for motorcycles operated in moderate climates. If the motorcycle is operated under dusty conditions, the oil becomes contaminated more quickly and should be changed more frequently than recommended.

Use a motorcycle oil with an API classification of *SF* or *SG*. The classification is printed on the container. Always use the same brand of oil at each change. Refer to **Table 3** for correct oil viscosity to use under anticipated ambient temperatures, not engine oil temperature. Using oil additives is not recommended as they may cause clutch slippage.

All Softail models are equipped with a premium 10 micron synthetic media oil filter. This is the only type of oil filter recommended by Harley-Davidson.

WARNING
Contact with oil may cause skin cancer. Wash oil from hands with soap and water as soon as possible after handling engine oil.

CAUTION
Do not use the current SH and SJ rated automotive oils in motorcycle engines. The SH and SJ rated oils contain friction modifiers that reduce frictional losses on engine components. Specifically designed for automotive engines, these oils can damage motorcycle engines and clutches.

NOTE
Never dispose of motor oil in the trash, on the ground or down a storm drain. Many service stations and oil retailers accept used oil for recycling. Do not combine other fluids with motor oil to be recycled. To locate a recycler, contact the American Petroleum Institute (API) at www.recycleoil.org.

1. Start and run the engine for approximately ten minutes or until the engine has reached normal operating temperature. Turn the engine off and allow the oil to settle in the oil tank. Support the motorcycle so that the oil can drain completely.

CAUTION
Before removing the oil filler cap, clean off all dirt and debris around it.

2. Remove the oil filler cap (**Figure 5**) to speed up the flow of oil.

CAUTION
To avoid burning hands and arms, work quickly and carefully when removing the oil tank plug.

NOTE
*The oil tank is equipped with an oil drain line and hose that is connected to a fitting on the rear right side of the frame (**Figure 8**).*

3. Place a drain pan underneath the oil tank drain line (**Figure 9**) drain plug, and remove the engine oil drain plug and O-ring (**Figure 10**).

4. Allow the oil to drain completely.

5. To replace the oil filter (**Figure 11**), perform the following:

   a. Temporarily install the drain bolt and O-ring, and tighten the bolt finger-tight. Then move the drain pan underneath the front portion of the crankcase and the oil filter.

   b. At the front left side of the engine, install a socket type oil filter wrench (**Figure 12**) squarely over the oil filter and loosen it *counterclockwise*. Quickly remove the oil filter as oil will begin to run out of it.

   c. Hold the filter over the drain pan and pour out the remaining oil. Place the filter in a plastic bag, seal the bag and dispose of it properly.

   d. Thoroughly wipe off all oil that drained onto the top surface of the left crankcase half. Clean with a contact cleaner to eliminate all oil residue from the engine prior to installing the new oil filter.

   e. Coat the gasket on the new filter with clean oil.

CAUTION
Tighten the oil filter by hand. Do not overtighten.

   f. Screw the oil filter onto its mount by hand and tighten it until the filter gasket touches the sealing surface, then tighten the filter by hand an additional 1/2 to 3/4 turn.

6. Remove the oil tank drain plug and gasket. Wipe the drain plug sealing surface on the frame rail pan with a clean, lint-free cloth.

7. Replace the engine oil tank drain plug O-ring (**Figure 13**) if it is leaking or damaged.

8. Lubricate the O-ring with clean engine oil before installing it. Then screw in the drain plug and O-ring, and tighten to 14-21 ft.-lb. (19-29 N•m).

CAUTION
Do not overfill the engine in Step 9. If too much oil is added, the filler cap will be forced out of the oil tank case when the oil gets hot.

9. Add the correct viscosity (**Table 3**) and quantity (**Table 4**) of oil to the oil tank case. Insert the oil filler cap into the case and push it down until it bottoms.

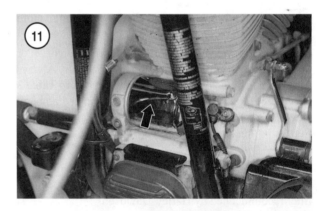

NOTE
*After oil has been added, the oil level will register above the upper groove dipstick mark (**Figure 6**) until the engine runs and the filter fills with oil. To obtain a correct reading after adding oil and installing a new oil filter, follow the procedure in Step 10.*

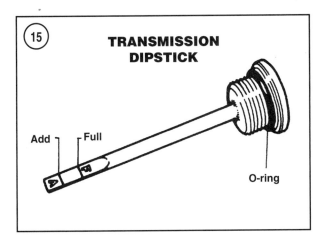

**TRANSMISSION
DIPSTICK**

Add ⌐ Full

O-ring

10. After changing the engine oil and filter, check the oil level as follows:

   a. Start and run the engine for one minute, then shut it off.

   b. Check the oil level on the dipstick as described in this chapter.

   c. If the oil level is correct, it will register in the dipstick's safe operating level range. If so, *do not* top off or add oil to bring it to the upper groove level on the dipstick.

11. Check the oil filter and drain plug for leaks.

12. Dispose the used oil properly.

Transmission Oil Level Check

   Table 1 lists the recommended transmission oil inspection intervals. When checking the transmission oil level, do not allow any dirt or debris to enter the transmission case opening.

WARNING
Contact with oil may cause skin cancer. Wash oil from hands with soap and water as soon as possible after handling engine oil.

NOTE
The transmission oil level dipstick is on the forward portion of the clutch release cover.

1. Ride the motorcycle for approximately ten minutes and shift through all five gears until the transmission oil has reached normal operating temperature. Turn the engine off and allow the oil to settle in the case. Park the motorcycle on a level surface and have an assistant support it so that it is standing straight up.

CAUTION
Do not check the oil level with the motorcycle supported on its jiffy stand or the reading will be incorrect.

2. Clean the area around the transmission filler cap/dipstick (**Figure 14**) and unscrew it.

3. Wipe the dipstick and reinsert it into the clutch release cover housing. Do not screw the cap/dipstick into place. Rest it on the housing top thread, then withdraw it. The oil level is correct when it registers between the two dipstick marks (**Figure 15**).

CAUTION
*Do not add engine oil. Add only the recommended transmission oil listed in **Table 5**.*

4. If the oil level is low, add the recommended type of transmission oil listed in **Table 5**. Do not overfill.

5. Inspect the filler cap O-ring. Replace it if it is worn or damaged.

6. Install the oil filler cap/dipstick and tighten it securely.

7. Wipe any spilled oil off the clutch release cover housing.

Transmission Oil Change

   Table 1 lists the recommended transmission oil change intervals.

1. Ride the motorcycle for approximately ten minutes and shift through all five gears until the transmission oil has reached normal operating temperature. Turn off the engine and allow the oil to settle in the case. Park the motorcycle on a level surface and have an assistant support it so that it is standing straight up.

2. Clean the area around the transmission filler cap/dipstick (**Figure 14**). Unscrew and remove the filler cap/dipstick.

NOTE
*The transmission drain plug is located on the underside of the transmission case between the shock absorbers. A, **Figure 16** indicates the location of the drain plug but the plug is not visible.*

3. Place a drain pan underneath the transmission case and remove the transmission oil drain plug and O-ring (A, **Figure 16**).

4. Check the drain plug O-ring for damage and replace it if necessary.

5. The drain plug is magnetic. Check the plug for metal debris that may indicate transmission damage, then wipe the plug off. Replace the plug if it is damaged.

6. Install the transmission drain plug and O-ring and tighten to 14-21 ft.-lb. (19-29 N•m).

CAUTION
*Do not add engine oil. Only add the recommended transmission oil in **Table 5**. Make sure to add the oil to the correct oil filler hole.*

7. Refill the transmission through the filler cap/dipstick hole with the recommended quantity (**Table 4**) and type (**Table 5**) of transmission oil.

8. Install the transmission filler cap/dipstick cap and O-ring (A, **Figure 16**), and tighten securely.

9. Remove the oil drain pan and dispose of the oil as outlined under *Engine Oil and Filter Change* in this chapter.

10. Ride the motorcycle until the transmission oil reaches normal operating temperature. Then shut the engine off.

11. Check the transmission drain plug for leaks.

12. Check the transmission oil level as described in this chapter. Readjust the level if necessary.

Primary Chaincase Oil Level Check

The primary chaincase oil lubricates the clutch, primary chain and sprockets. **Table 1** lists the intervals for checking the chaincase oil level. When checking the primary

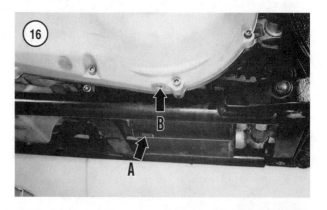

chaincase oil level, do not allow any dirt or debris to enter the housing.

1. Park the motorcycle on a level surface and support it so that it is standing straight up. Do not support it on the jiffy stand.

CAUTION
Do not check the oil level with the motorcycle supported on its jiffy stand or the reading will be incorrect.

2. Remove the screws securing the clutch inspection cover and quad ring (**Figure 17**). Remove the cover.

3. The oil level is correct when it is even with the bottom of the clutch opening or at the bottom of the clutch diaphragm spring (**Figure 18**).

CAUTION
*Do not add engine oil. Only add the recommended primary chaincase lubricant listed in **Table 5**.*

4. If necessary, add the recommended type of primary chaincase lubricant listed in **Table 5** through the opening to correct the level.

5. Install the clutch inspection cover quad ring onto the primary chain case cover.

6. Install the clutch inspection cover (**Figure 17**) and tighten the screws to 84-108 in.-lb. (9.5-12 N•m).

Primary Chaincase Oil Change

Table 1 lists the recommended replacement intervals for the primary chaincase lubricant.

1. Ride the motorcycle for approximately ten minutes and shift through all five gears until the primary chaincase oil has reached normal operating temperature. Turn off the engine and allow the oil to settle. Park the motorcycle on a level surface and have an assistant support it so that it is standing straight up. Do not support it with its jiffy stand.

2. Place a drain pan under the chaincase and remove the drain plug (B, **Figure 16**).

3. Allow the oil to drain for at least ten minutes.

4. The drain plug is magnetic. Check the plug for metal debris that may indicate drive component or clutch damage, then wipe the plug off. Replace the plug if it is damaged.

5. Reinstall the drain plug and tighten it securely.

6. Remove the screws securing the clutch inspection cover and quad ring (**Figure 17**). Remove the cover.

CAUTION
Do not add engine oil. Only add the recommended primary chaincase lubricant listed in Table 5.

7. Refill the primary chaincase through the clutch opening with the recommended quantity (**Table 4**) and type (**Table 5**) of primary chaincase oil. Do not overfill. The oil level must be even with the bottom of the clutch opening or at the bottom of the clutch diaphragm spring (**Figure 18**).

8. Install the clutch inspection cover quad ring onto the primary chain case cover.

9. Install the clutch inspection cover (**Figure 17**) and tighten the screws to 84-108 in.-lb. (9.5-12 N•m).

10. Ride the motorcycle until the primary chaincase oil reaches normal operating temperature. Then shut the engine off.

11. Check the primary chaincase drain plug for leaks.

Front Fork Oil Change

This procedure is for a routine fork oil change. If the fork has been disassembled for service, refer to Chapter Ten for fork oil refilling and oil level procedures and specifications.

Table 1 lists the recommended fork oil change intervals.

CAUTION
Use only a 6-point socket to loosen and tighten the fork tube cap to avoid cosmetic damage to the fork tube cap. Using a 12-point socket may round off the corners of the fork tube cap.

NOTE
The fork tube cap is not under fork spring pressure.

1. Remove the fork tube cap, spacer and oil seal (**Figure 19**) from the top of the fork tube plug.

2. Place a drain pan beside one fork tube, then remove the drain screw and washer (**Figure 20**, typical) from the slider.

3. Straddle the motorcycle and apply the front brake lever. Push down on the fork and release. Repeat to force as much oil out of the fork tube and slider as possible.

CAUTION
Do not allow the fork oil to come in contact with the brake components.

4. Replace the drain screw washer if it is damaged.

5. Repeat Steps 1-4 for the opposite fork tube.

6. After the fork oil has thoroughly drained, install the drain screw and washer (**Figure 20**) onto the fork slider. Tighten the drain screw to 52-78 in.-lb. (6-9 N•m). For FXSTD 12-18 in.-lb. (1.4-2.0 N•m).

> *NOTE*
> *Use a plastic tube that is slightly smaller in diameter than the opening in the fork tube plug. This will allow air to exit the fork assembly during the filling procedure.*

7. Insert a clear plastic tube into the fork tube plug opening. Attach a funnel to the plastic tube and refill each fork leg with the correct viscosity and quantity of fork oil. Refer to **Table 7**. Remove the funnel and plastic tube.

8. Repeat Step 7 for the opposite fork tube.

9. Install the fork tube cap, spacer and oil seal (**Figure 21**) onto the top of the fork tube. Tighten the fork tube cap to 40-60 ft.-lb. (54-81 N•m).

10. Road test the motorcycle and check for leaks.

Control Cables (Non-Nylon Lined Cables)

The major cause of cable breakage or cable stiffness is improper lubrication. Maintaining the cables as described in this section will ensure long service life. Lubricate the control cables with a cable lubricant at the intervals in **Table 1**, or when they become stiff or sluggish. When lubricating the control cables, inspect each cable for fraying and cable sheath damage. Replace damaged cables.

> *CAUTION*
> *If the original equipment cables have been replaced with nylon-lined cables, do not lubricate them as described in this procedure. Oil and most cable lubricants will cause the cable liner to expand, pushing the liner against the cable sheath. Nylon-lined cables are normally used dry. When servicing nylon-lined and other aftermarket cables, follow the manufacturer's instructions.*

> *CAUTION*
> *Do not use chain lubricant to lubricate control cables.*

> *CAUTION*
> *On carbureted models, the starting enrichment valve (choke) cable is designed to operate with a certain amount of cable resistance. Do **not** lubricate the enrichment cable or its conduit.*

1A. Disconnect the clutch cable ends as described under *Clutch Cable Replacement* in Chapter Five.

1B. Disconnect both throttle cable ends as described under *Throttle and Idle Cables* in Chapter Seven.

2. Attach a lubricator tool to the cable following the tool manufacturer's instructions. Place a shop cloth at the end of the cable to catch all excess lubricant.

3. Insert the lubricant nozzle tube into the lubricator, press the button on the can and hold it down until the lubricant begins to flow out of the other end of the cable. If the lubricant squirts out from around the lubricator, it is not clamped to the cable properly. Loosen and reposition the cable lubricator.

> *NOTE*
> *If the lubricant does not flow out of the other end of the cable, check the cable for fraying, bending or other damage. Replace damaged cables.*

4. Remove the lubricator tool and wipe off both ends of the cable.

5A. Reconnect the clutch cable ends as described under *Clutch Cable Replacement* in Chapter Five.

5B. Reconnect both throttle cable ends as described under *Throttle and Idle Cable Replacement* in Chapter Seven.

6. Adjust the cables as described in this chapter.

Throttle Control Grip Lubrication

Table 1 lists the recommended throttle control grip lubrication intervals. To remove and install the throttle grip, refer to *Throttle and Idle Cable Replacement* in Chapter Seven. Lubricate the throttle control grip where it contacts the handlebar with graphite.

Steering Head Lubrication

Lubricate the steering head bearings at the intervals in **Table 1**. Wipe off all old grease and debris from the grease fitting on the right side of the steering head. Apply grease to the fitting (**Figure 22**) until the grease begins to flow out of the top and bottom of the steering head. Wipe off all excessive grease from the steering head and the grease fitting.

Rocker Arm Bearing Lubrication and Adjustment (FLSTS and FXSTS)

Clean, lubricate and adjust the rocker arms and spherical bearings at the intervals in **Table 1**. Refer to Chapter Eleven.

Front Brake Lever Pivot Pin Lubrication

Inspect the front brake lever pivot pin for lubricant at the intervals in **Table 1**. If the pin is dry, lubricate it with a light weight oil. To service the pivot pin, refer to *Front Master Cylinder* in Chapter Twelve.

Clutch Lever Pivot Pin Lubrication

Inspect the clutch lever pivot pin at the intervals in **Table 1**. Lubricate the pin with a light weight oil. To service the pivot pin, refer to *Clutch Cable Replacement* in Chapter Five.

Rear Brake Pedal Lubrication

1. Apply waterproof grease to the rear brake pedal fitting (**Figure 23**).
2. Apply the rear brake to ensure the pedal is moving smoothly.

Jiffy Stand Lubrication

1. Support the motorcycle on a stand or floor jack with the rear wheel off the ground. See *Motorcycle Stands* in Chapter Nine.
2. Wipe the pivot area clean of all road debris.
3. Move the jiffy stand (**Figure 24**) back and forth and check for ease of movement.
4. If the leg stop is covered with mud and debris, remove the bolt, lockwasher and washer securing the leg stop to the pivot post. Remove the pivot post, thoroughly clean all parts in solvent and dry.
5. Apply an aerosol Loctite Anti-Seize lubricant, or an equivalent, onto the leg stop and the pivot area. Move the jiffy stand back and forth to work in the lubricant.
6. If removed, position the leg stop with the DOWN mark facing down, then install the washer, lockwasher and bolt. Tighten the bolt to 144-180 in.-lb. (16-20 N•m).
7. Ensure that the jiffy stand operates correctly in both positions prior to riding the motorcycle.
8. Lower the motorcycle to the ground.

PERIODIC MAINTENANCE

This section describes the periodic inspection, adjustment and replacement of various operational items. Perform these procedures at the intervals in **Table 1**, or earlier if necessary.

Primary Chain Adjustment

As the primary chain stretches and wears, its free play movement increases. Excessive free play causes premature chain and sprocket wear and increases chain noise. If the free play is adjusted too tight, the chain wears prematurely.

NOTE
On models equipped with the TSSM security system, always disarm the system prior to disconnecting the battery or the siren will sound.

1. Disconnect the negative battery cable as described in Chapter Eight.
2. Support the motorcycle on a stand or floor jack with the rear wheel off the ground. See *Motorcycle Stands* in Chapter Nine.

NOTE
Note the location of the inspection cover screws. There are two different length screws and they must be reinstalled in the correct location.

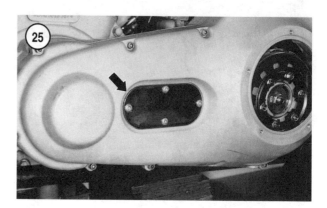

3. Remove the primary chain inspection cover and gasket (**Figure 25**).
4. Turn the primary chain to find the tightest point on the chain. Measure chain free play at this point.

NOTE
***Figure 26** is shown with the primary chain cover removed to better illustrate the steps.*

5. Check primary chain free play at the upper chain run midway between the sprockets (**Figure 26**). If the primary chain free play is incorrect, continue with Step 6. If the free play is correct, go to Step 7. The primary chain free play specifications are:
   a. Cold engine: 5/8 to 7/8 in. (15.9-22. 3 mm).
   b. Hot engine: 3/8 to 5/8 in. (9.5-15.9 mm).

6. To adjust the chain, perform the following:
   a. Loosen the primary chain adjuster shoe nut (**Figure 27**).
   b. Move the shoe assembly up or down to correct free play.
   c. Tighten the primary chain adjuster shoe nut (**Figure 27**) to 21-29 ft.-lb. (29-39 N•m), then recheck free play.
7. Install the primary chain inspection cover (**Figure 25**) and a *new* gasket. Tighten the cover screws to 84-108 in.-lb. (9.5-12.2 N•m).
8. Lower the motorcycle to the ground.

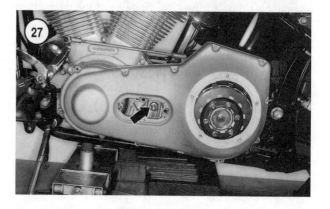

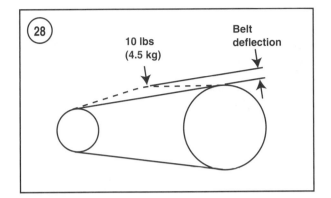

Final Drive Belt Deflection

Inspect drive belt deflection at the intervals in **Table 1**. If the drive belt is severely worn, or if it is wearing incorrectly, refer to Chapter Twelve for inspection and replacement procedures.

NOTE
Check the drive belt deflection when the belt is cold.

1. On models so equipped, remove the left side saddlebag as described in Chapter Fourteen.

2. Remove the bolts and nuts securing the drive chain guard and remove the guard.

3. Support the motorcycle on a stand or floor jack with the rear wheel off the ground. See *Motorcycle Stands* in Chapter Nine.

4. Then turn the rear wheel and check the drive belt for its tightest point. When this point is located, turn the wheel so the belt's tight spot is on the lower belt run, midway between the front and rear sprockets.

5. Lower the motorcycle to the ground.

6. Position the motorcycle so both wheels are on the ground. When checking and adjusting drive belt deflection in the following steps, have an assistant sit on the seat facing forward.

NOTE
Use the Harley-Davidson belt tension gauge (part No. HD-35381) or equivalent to apply pressure against the drive belt in Step 7.

7. Apply a force of 10 lb. (4.5 kg) to the middle of the upper belt strand while measuring the belt's deflection measurement at the same point (**Figure 28**). Compare the correct belt deflection measurement with the specification in **Table 8**. If the deflection measurement is incorrect, adjust the drive belt as follows:

   a. If so equipped, remove the chrome trim cap (**Figure 29**) from each side.

   b. On the left side, remove the spring clip (**Figure 30**) and loosen the rear axle nut (**Figure 31**).

   c. Loosen the jam nut (A, **Figure 32**) on the rear axle adjuster (B) on each side of the swing arm.

   d. Turn both adjusters (B, **Figure 32**), in either direction, an equal number of turns to obtain the correct drive belt deflection.

   e. Recheck the drive belt deflection. Tighten the jam nuts securely.

   f. Check that the rear axle is positioned correctly within the swing arm as described under *Vehicle Alignment* in the following procedure.

8. When the drive belt deflection and axle alignment adjustments are correct, tighten the rear axle nut to 60-65 ft.-lb. (81-88 N•m). Install the spring clip through the axle nut and rear axle (**Figure 30**). If necessary, slightly tighten the rear axle nut to align the axle hole and nut slots in order to install the spring clip.

Vehicle Alignment

There are two different types of vehicle alignment and they should be checked in the following order:
1. Horizontal offset misalignment.
2. Vertical misalignment.

NOTE
Prior to checking for vehicle alignment, the tires and rims must be true and the front wheel must be centered within the front fork and fender bosses.

Horizontal alignment (FXST models)

1. Support the motorcycle on a floor jack with the rear wheel off the ground. Do not use a bike stand as it may interfere with the straightedges.
2. Place a girder-type straightedge tightly against each side of the rear tire (**Figure 33**). Make sure the straightedges are parallel to each other and have an assistant hold them in place.
3. Place the front wheel in the straight ahead position and block it in this position.

NOTE
The following measurements must be equal. If necessary, slightly turn the front wheel to center it.

4. Measure the distance from the straightedge to the left side of the front wheel rim. Take the measurement at the rear (A) and front (B) of the wheel rim. Note the dimensions.
5. Measure the distance from the straightedge to the right side of the front wheel rim. Take the measurement at the rear (C) and front (D) of the wheel rim. Note the dimensions.
6. Subtract the difference from the two sides and compare to the dimensions in **Table 9**. The difference between the two sides should be within 0.250 in. (6.35 mm) of the specified dimension in **Table 9**.
7. If the offset is not within specification, check the following:
   a. On laced wheels, make sure the rim offset dimension is within specification. Refer to **Table 10**. If out

of specification, have the wheel trued by a Harley-Davidson dealership or wheel specialist.
   b. Check that the center of the rear axle is equidistant from the center of the rear swing arm pivot shaft.

Horizontal alignment (FLST models)

1. Support the motorcycle on a floor jack with the rear wheel off the ground. Do not use a bike stand as it may interfere with the straightedges.
2. Place a girder-type straightedge tightly against the *left* side of the rear tire (**Figure 34**). Have an assistant hold the straightedge in place.
3. Place the front wheel in the straight ahead position and block it in this position.

NOTE
The following measurements must be equal. If necessary, slightly turn the front wheel to center it.

4. Measure the distance from the straightedge to the left side of the front wheel rim. Take the measurement at the rear (A) and front (B) of the wheel rim. Note the dimensions.
5. Measure the distance from the straightedge to the left side of the rear wheel rim. Take the measurement at the rear (C) and front (D) of the wheel rim. Note the dimensions.
6. Subtract the rear wheel measurement from the front wheel measurement and compare to the dimensions in **Table 9**. The difference between the two dimensions should be within 0.250 in. (6.35 mm) of the specified dimension in **Table 9**.
7. If the offset is not within specification, check the following:
   a. On laced wheels, make sure the rim offset dimension is within specification. Refer to **Table 10**. If out

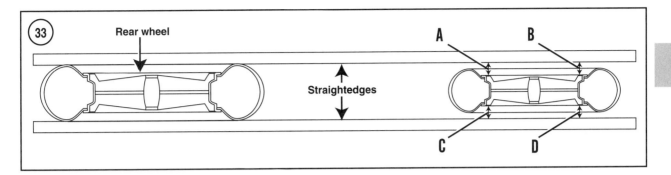

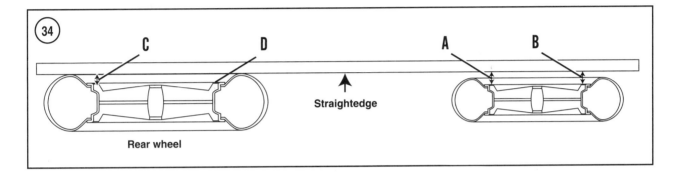

of specification, have the wheel trued by a Harley-Davidson dealership or wheel specialist.

   b. Check that the center of the rear axle is equidistant from the center of the rear swing arm pivot shaft on both sides.

Vertical alignment (all models)

1. Support the motorcycle on a floor jack with the rear wheel off the ground.

2. Place a girder-type straightedge tightly against each side of the rear tire (**Figure 33**). Make sure the straightedges are parallel to each other and have an assistant hold them in place.

3. Place the front wheel in the straight ahead position and block it in this position.

4. Place an inclinometer on the face of the front disc in a true vertical position. Note the reading.

5. Do not allow the motorcycle to move.

6. Place an inclinometer on the face of the rear disc in a true vertical position. Note the reading.

7. Compare the two different readings. If there are more than 0.5 degrees apart, there is a possibility that the frame, fork assembly or swing arm assembly may be bent.

8. Have these chassis components inspected by a Harley-Davidson dealership or frame specialist to confirm the readings.

9. Repair or replace any damaged components.

Brake Pad Inspection

1. Without removing the front (**Figure 35**) or rear (**Figure 36**) brake calipers, inspect the brake pads for damage.

2. Measure the thickness of each brake pad lining (**Figure 37**) with a ruler. Replace the brake pad if its thickness is worn to the minimum thickness in **Table 8**. Replace the brake pads as described in Chapter Thirteen.

Brake Fluid Level

1. To check the front master cylinder, perform the following:

    a. Turn the handlebar straight ahead so the master cylinder is level.

    b. Observe the brake fluid level by looking at the sight glass (**Figure 38**) on the master cylinder reservoir top cover. If the fluid level is correct, the sight glass will be dark purple. If the level is low, the sight glass will have a lightened, clear appearance.

    NOTE
    Access to the rear master cylinder is restricted by the exhaust system. Checking the fluid level and replenishing the fluid is easier with the front cylinder's exhaust pipe removed. Refer to Chapter Seven.

2. To check the rear master cylinder, perform the following:

    a. Support the motorcycle so the rear master cylinder is level.

    b. Observe the brake fluid level by looking at the sight glass (A, **Figure 39**) on the master cylinder reservoir top cover. If the fluid level is correct, the sight glass will be dark purple. If the level is low, the sight glass will have a lightened, clear appearance.

    WARNING
    *Do not use brake fluid labeled **DOT 5.1**. This is a glycol-based fluid that is **not compatible** with silicone based DOT 5. DOT 5 brake fluid is purple while DOT 5.1 is an amber/clear color. Do not intermix these different types of brake fluid, as doing so will lead to brake component damage and possible brake failure.*

    CAUTION
    Be careful when handling brake fluid. Do not spill it on painted or plastic surfaces, as it damages them. Wash the area immediately with soap and water, and thoroughly rinse it.

    NOTE
    To control the flow of brake fluid, punch a small hole in the seal of a new container of brake fluid next to the edge of the pour spout. This helps prevent the fluid spillage, especially while adding fluid to the small reservoir.

3. If the brake fluid level is low, perform the following:

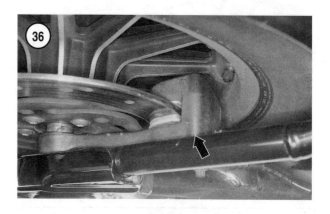

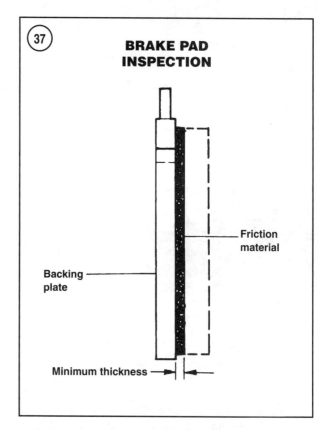

BRAKE PAD INSPECTION

Friction material

Backing plate

Minimum thickness

    a. Clean any dirt from the master cylinder cover prior to removing it.

    b. Remove the top cover (B, **Figure 39**) and lift the diaphragm out of the reservoir.

    c. Add fresh DOT 5 brake fluid to correct the level.

    d. Reinstall the diaphragm and top cover. Tighten the screws securely.

    WARNING
    If the brake fluid level is low enough to allow air in the hydraulic system, bleed the brakes as described in Chapter Thirteen.

Front and Rear Brake Disc Inspection

Visually inspect the front and rear brake discs (**Figure 40**, typical) for scoring, cracks or other damage. Measure the brake disc thickness (**Figure 41**) and, if necessary, service the brake discs as described in Chapter Thirteen.

Brake Lines and Seals

Check the brake lines between each master cylinder and each brake caliper. If there is any leakage, tighten the connections and bleed the brakes as described in Chapter Thirteen.

Brake Fluid Change

Every time the reservoir cover is removed, a small amount of dirt and moisture enters the brake fluid. The same thing happens if there is a leak or if any part of the hydraulic system is loosened or disconnected. Dirt can clog the system and cause unnecessary wear. Water in the fluid vaporizes at high temperatures, impairing the hydraulic action and reducing brake performance.

To change brake fluid, follow the brake bleeding procedure in Chapter Thirteen. Continue adding new fluid to the master cylinder until the fluid leaving the caliper is clean and free of contaminants and air bubbles.

> *WARNING*
> *Do not use brake fluid labeled **DOT 5.1**. This is a glycol-based fluid that is **not compatible** with silicone based DOT 5. DOT 5 brake fluid is purple while DOT 5.1 is an amber/clear color. Do not intermix these different types of brake fluid, as doing so will lead to brake component damage and possible brake failure.*

Front Brake Adjustment

The front brake does not require periodic adjustment.

Rear Brake Adjustment

The rear brake does not require periodic adjustment.

Clutch Adjustment

> *CAUTION*
> *Because the clutch cable adjuster clearance increases with engine temperature, adjust the clutch when the engine is cold. If the*

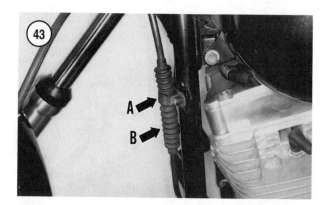

clutch is adjusted when the engine is hot, insufficient pushrod clearance can cause the clutch to slip.

1. Remove the clutch mechanism inspection cover and quad ring (**Figure 42**).

2. Remove the clamp (A, **Figure 43**) and slide the rubber boot (B) off the clutch in-line cable adjuster.

3. Loosen the adjuster locknut (A, **Figure 44**) and turn the adjuster (B) to provide maximum cable slack.

4. Make sure the clutch cable seats squarely in its perch (**Figure 45**) at the handlebar.

5. At the clutch mechanism, loosen the clutch adjusting screw locknut (A, **Figure 46**) and turn the adjusting screw (B) *clockwise* until it is lightly seated.

6. Squeeze the clutch lever three times to verify the clutch balls are seated in the ramp release mechanism located behind the transmission side cover.

7. Back out the adjusting screw (B, **Figure 46**) *counterclockwise* 1/2 to 1 turn. Then hold the adjusting screw (B, **Figure 46**) and tighten the locknut (A) to 72-120 in.-lb. (8-14 N•m).

8. Once again, squeeze the clutch lever to its maximum limit three times to set the clutch ball and ramp release mechanism.

9. Check the free play as follows:

   a. At the in-line cable adjuster, turn the adjuster away from the locknut until slack is eliminated at the clutch hand lever.

   b. Pull the clutch cable sheath away from the clutch lever, then turn the clutch cable adjuster to obtain the clearance gap (**Figure 47**) in **Table 8**.

   c. When the adjustment is correct, tighten the clutch in-line cable locknut and slide the rubber boot over the cable adjuster.

10. Install the clutch inspection cover quad ring onto the primary chain case cover.

11. Install the clutch inspection cover (**Figure 42**) and tighten the screws to 84-108 in.-lb. (9.5-12 N•m).

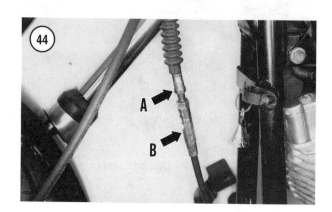

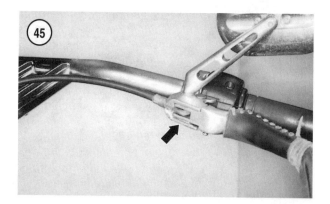

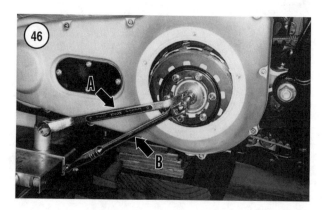

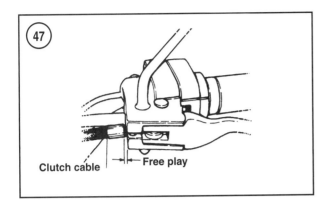

Clutch cable — Free play

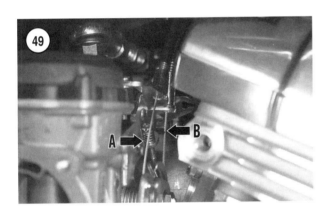

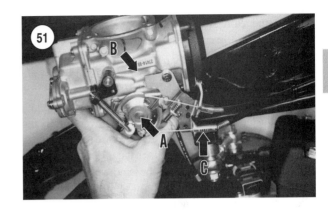

Throttle Cables Inspection

Inspect the throttle cables from the grip to the carburetor or the fuel injector module. Make sure they are not kinked or chafed. Replace them if necessary as described in Chapter Seven.

Make sure the throttle grip rotates smoothly from fully closed to fully open. Check with the handlebar at the center, full left and full right positions.

Throttle Cables Adjustment

There are two different throttle cables. At the throttle grip, the front cable is the throttle control cable (A, **Figure 48**) and the rear cable is the idle control cable (B).

The outboard cable is the throttle control cable (A, **Figure 49**) and the inboard cable is the idle control cable (B).

1. Remove the air filter and backing plate as described in Chapter Seven.

2. Roll the rubber boots (**Figure 50**) off the adjusters.

3. At the handlebar, loosen both control cable adjuster locknuts, then turn the cable adjusters (C, **Figure 48**) *clockwise* as far as possible to increase cable slack.

4. Turn the handlebars so the front wheel points straight ahead. Then turn the throttle grip to open the throttle completely and hold it in this position.

NOTE
Figure 51 is shown with the carburetor body removed to better illustrate the steps.

5A. On carbureted models, at the handlebar, turn the throttle control cable adjuster (C, **Figure 48**) *counterclockwise* until the throttle cam (A, **Figure 51**) stop just touches the stop boss (B) on the carburetor body. Then tighten the throttle cable adjuster locknut and release the throttle grip.

5B. On fuel injected models, at the handlebar, turn the throttle control cable adjuster (C, **Figure 48**) *counterclockwise* until the throttle cam (A, **Figure 52**) stop just touches the cam stop (B) on the throttle body. Then tighten the throttle cable adjuster locknut and release the throttle grip.

6. Turn the front wheel all the way to the full right lock position and hold it there.

7A. On carbureted models, at the handlebar, turn the idle cable adjuster (C, **Figure 48**) until the lower end of the idle control cable just contacts the spring in the carburetor cable guide (C, **Figure 51**). Tighten the idle cable locknut.

7B. On fuel injected models, at the handlebar, turn the idle cable adjuster (C, **Figure 48**) until the lower end of the idle control cable housing just contacts the spring in the cable support sleeve (C, **Figure 52**). Tighten the idle cable locknut.

8. Install the backing plate and the air filter as described in Chapter Seven.

9. Shift the transmission into NEUTRAL and start the engine.

10. Increase engine speed several times. Release the throttle and make sure the engine speed returns to idle. If the engine speed does not return to idle, at the handlebar, loosen the idle control cable adjuster locknut and turn the cable adjuster *clockwise* as required. Tighten the idle control cable adjuster locknut.

11. Allow the engine to idle in NEUTRAL. Then turn the handlebar from side to side. Do not operate the throttle. If the engine speed increases when the handlebar assembly is turned, the throttle cables are routed incorrectly or damaged. Turn off the engine. Recheck cable routing and adjustment.

12. Roll the rubber boots (**Figure 50**) back onto the adjusters.

> *WARNING*
> *Do not ride the motorcycle until the throttle cables are properly adjusted. Also, the cables must not catch or pull when the handlebar is turned from side to side. Improper cable routing and adjustment can cause the throttle to stick open. This could cause loss of control and a possible crash. Recheck this adjustment before riding the motorcycle.*

Starting Enrichment Valve (Choke) Cable Adjustment (Carburetted Models)

The starting enrichment (choke) knob should move from fully open to fully closed position without any sign of binding. The knob should also stay in its fully closed or fully open position without creeping. If the knob does not stay in position, adjust tension on the cable by turning the plastic knurled nut behind the knob as follows:

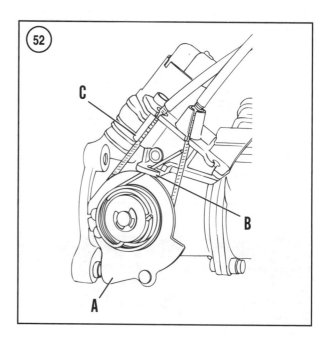

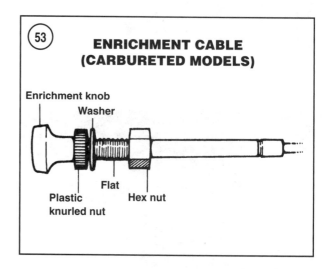

ENRICHMENT CABLE (CARBURETED MODELS)

Enrichment knob
Washer
Plastic knurled nut
Flat
Hex nut

> *CAUTION*
> *The starting enrichment (choke) cable must have sufficient cable resistance to work properly. Do not lubricate the enrichment cable or its conduit.*

1. Loosen the hex nut behind the mounting bracket. Then move the cable to free it from its mounting bracket slot.

2. Hold the cable across its flats with a wrench and turn the knurled plastic nut *counterclockwise* to reduce cable resistance. The knob must slide inward freely.

3. Turn the knurled plastic nut (**Figure 53**) *clockwise* to increase cable resistance. Continue adjustment until the

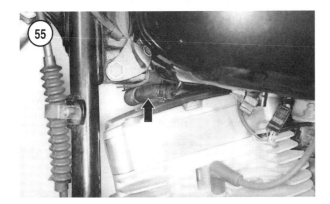

knob remains stationary when it is pulled all the way out. The knob must move without any roughness or binding.

4. Reinstall the cable into the slot in its mounting bracket with the star washer located between the bracket and hex nut. Tighten the hex nut securely.

5. Recheck the knob movement and readjust if necessary.

Fuel Line Inspection

Inspect the fuel line(s) (**Figure 54**) from the fuel tank to the carburetor or fuel injection module. Check the fuel tank crossover fuel line (**Figure 55**). Replace leaking or damaged fuel lines. Make sure the hose clamps are in place and holding securely. Check the hose fittings for looseness.

> *WARNING*
> *A damaged or deteriorated fuel line can cause a fire or explosion if fuel spills onto a hot engine or exhaust pipe.*

Exhaust System

Check all fittings for exhaust leakage. On models so equipped, do not forget the crossover pipe or intercon-

necting tube connections. Tighten all bolts and nuts. Replace gaskets as necessary. See Chapter Seven for removal and installation procedures.

Steering Play

Check the steering head play (Chapter Ten) at the intervals in **Table 1**.

Rear Swing Arm Pivot Bolt

Check the rear swing arm pivot bolt tightness (Chapter Eleven) at the intervals specified in **Table 1**.

Rear Shock Absorbers

Check the rear shock absorbers for oil leakage or damaged bushings. Check the shock absorber mounting bolts and nuts for tightness. Refer to *Shock Absorbers* in Chapter Twelve for procedures.

Engine Mounting Hardware

Check the engine and frame mounts for loose or damaged parts. Refer to Chapter Four for procedures.

Fasteners

> *CAUTION*
> *Special procedures must be used to tighten the cylinder head mounting bolts. To accurately check these bolts for tightness, refer to* **Cylinder Head Installation** *in Chapter Four. Tightening these bolts incorrectly can cause an oil leak or cylinder head warp.*

Constant vibration can loosen many fasteners on a motorcycle. Check the tightness of all fasteners, especially those on:

1. Engine mounting hardware.
2. Engine and primary covers.
3. Handlebar and front fork.
4. Gearshift lever.
5. Sprocket bolts and nuts.
6. Brake lever and pedal.
7. Exhaust system.
8. Lighting equipment.

3

Electrical Equipment and Switches

Check all of the electrical equipment and switches for proper operation. Refer to Chapter Eight.

TUNE-UP

The following section describes tune-up procedures. Perform the tasks at the intervals listed in **Table 1**. Perform a complete tune-up in the following order:
1. Clean or replace the air filter element.
2. Check engine compression.
3. Check or replace the spark plugs.
4. On carbureted models, adjust the idle speed.

Air Filter Element Removal/Installation

Remove and inspect the air filter at the interval in **Table 1**. If necessary, clean the element. Replace the element if it is damaged or starting to deteriorate.

The air filter removes dust and abrasive particles before the air enters the carburetor, or fuel-injection module and the engine. Without the air filter, very fine particles will enter the engine and cause rapid wear of the piston rings, cylinder bores and bearings. Particles also might clog small passages in the carburetor. Never run the motorcycle without the element installed.

Refer to **Figure 56** or **Figure 57**.
1. Remove the air filter cover screw (A, **Figure 58**) and remove the cover (B).
2. Remove the Torx screws and bracket (**Figure 59**) from the air filter element.
3. Gently pull the air filter element from the backplate and disconnect the two breather hoses (A, **Figure 60**) from the breather hollow bolts on the backplate. Remove the air filter element (B, **Figure 60**).
4. Clean the air filter as described in the following procedure.
5. Inspect the gasket (A, **Figure 61**) for damage. Replace it if necessary.
6. Inspect the breather hoses (B, **Figure 61**) for tears or deterioration. Replace them if necessary.

NOTE
Figure 62 is shown with the air filter backplate removed to better illustrate the step.

7. On California models, make sure the trap door swings freely (**Figure 62**).
8. If they were removed, install a new gasket (A, **Figure 61**) and breather hoses (B).

9. Position the element with the flat side facing down and attach the breather hoses (**Figure 63**) to the backside of the element.

NOTE
If an aftermarket air filter element is being installed, position it onto the backplate following the manufacturer's instructions.

10. Move the element into position (B, **Figure 61**) and install the mounting bracket (**Figure 59**) and the Torx screws. Tighten the screws to 20-40 in.-lb. (2-4 N•m).
11. Inspect the seal ring (**Figure 64**) on the air filter cover for hardness or deterioration. Replace it if necessary.
12. Apply a drop of ThreeBond TB1342 (blue) or an equivalent threadlocking compound to the cover screw prior to installation.
13. Install the air filter cover (B, **Figure 58**) and the screw (A). Tighten the screw to 36-60 in.-lb. (4-7 N•m).

Air Filter Element Cleaning

The air filter element is a paper/wire type (**Figure 63**). If an aftermarket element is installed, refer to the manufacturer's cleaning instructions.
1. Remove the air filter element as described in this chapter.
2. Replace the air filter if damaged.

WARNING
Do not clean the air filter in solvent. Never clean the air filter element in gasoline or low flash point solvent. The residual solvent or vapors may cause a fire or explosion after the filter is reinstalled.

CAUTION
Do not tap or strike the air filter element on a hard surface to dislodge dirt. Doing so will damage the element.

3. Place the air filter in a pan filled with lukewarm water and mild detergent. Move the air filter element back and forth to help dislodge trapped dirt. Thoroughly rinse it in clean water to remove all detergent residue.
4. Hold the air filter up to a strong light. Check the filter pores for dirt and oil. Repeat Step 3 until there is no dirt and oil in the filter pores. If the air filter cannot be cleaned, or if the filter is saturated with oil or other chemicals, replace it.

CAUTION
Do not use high air pressure to dry the filter, as this will damage it.

3

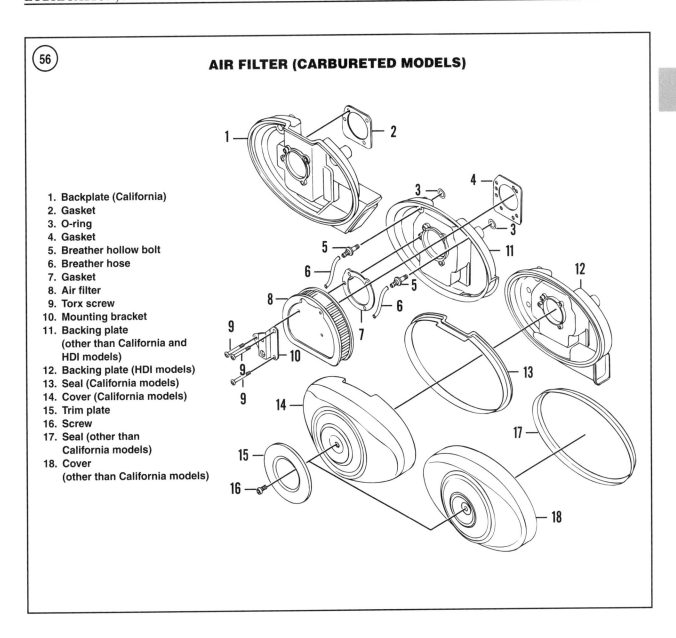

(56)

AIR FILTER (CARBURETED MODELS)

1. Backplate (California)
2. Gasket
3. O-ring
4. Gasket
5. Breather hollow bolt
6. Breather hose
7. Gasket
8. Air filter
9. Torx screw
10. Mounting bracket
11. Backing plate
    (other than California and
    HDI models)
12. Backing plate (HDI models)
13. Seal (California models)
14. Cover (California models)
15. Trim plate
16. Screw
17. Seal (other than
    California models)
18. Cover
    (other than California models)

CAUTION
In the next step, do not blow compressed air through the outer surface of the air filter element. Doing so can force dirt trapped on the outer filter surface deeper into the air filter element, restricting airflow and damaging the air filter element.

5. Gently apply compressed air through the inside surface of the air filter element to remove loosened dirt and dust trapped in the filter.

6. Inspect the air filter element. Replace it if it is torn or damaged. Do not ride the motorcycle with a damaged air filter element as it will allow dirt to enter the engine.

7. Clean the breather hoses in the same lukewarm water and mild detergent. Make sure both hoses are clean and clear. Clean them out with a pipe cleaner if necessary.

8. Wipe the inside of the cover and backplate with a clean damp shop rag.

CAUTION
Air will not pass through a wet or damp filter. Make sure the filter is dry before installing it.

9. Allow the filter to dry completely, then reinstall it as described in this chapter.

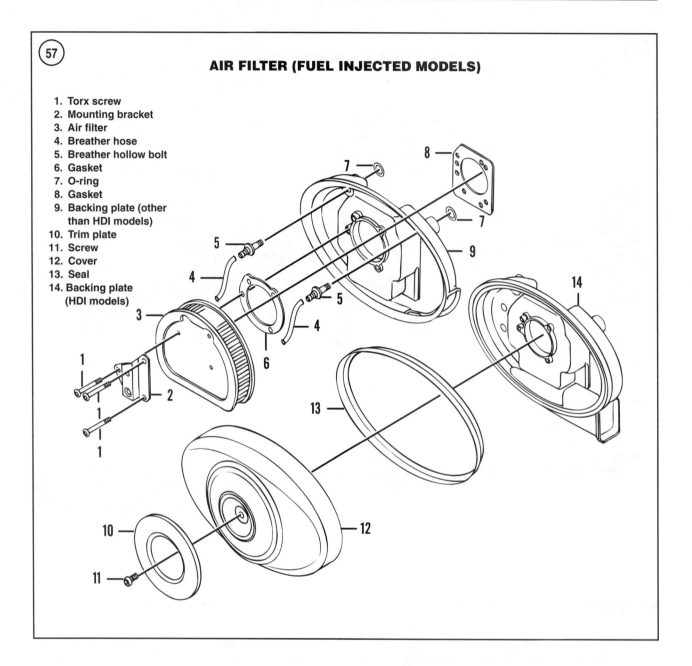

(57) **AIR FILTER (FUEL INJECTED MODELS)**

1. Torx screw
2. Mounting bracket
3. Air filter
4. Breather hose
5. Breather hollow bolt
6. Gasket
7. O-ring
8. Gasket
9. Backing plate (other than HDI models)
10. Trim plate
11. Screw
12. Cover
13. Seal
14. Backing plate (HDI models)

Compression Test

A compression check is one of the most effective ways to check the condition of the engine. If possible, check the compression at each tune-up, and record the results in the maintenance log at the end of this manual. Subsequent results can then be compared to earlier ones to help evaluate any developing engine problems.

1. Prior to starting the compression test, check the following:

    a. Make sure the cylinder head bolts are tightened as specified in Chapter Four.

    b. Make sure the battery is fully charged to ensure proper engine cranking speed.

2. Warm the engine to normal operating temperature. Shut off the engine.

3. Remove the spark plugs and reinstall them in their caps. Place the spark plugs against the cylinder heads to ground them.

4. Connect the compression tester (**Figure 65**) to one cylinder following its manufacturer's instructions.

5. Place the throttle in the wide-open position.

6. On carbureted models, make sure the starting enrichment (choke) knob is pushed in to the fully OFF position.

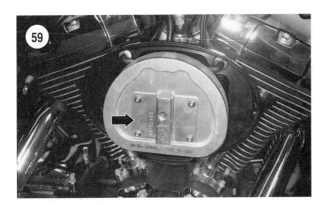

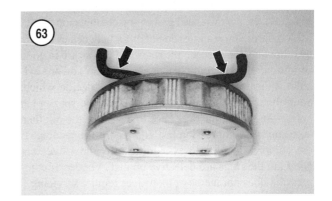

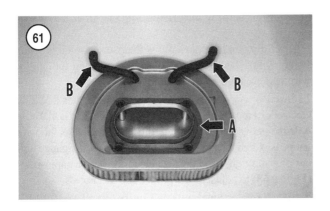

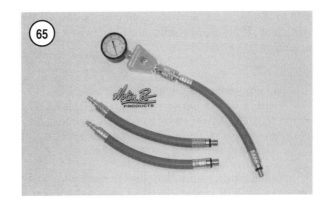

7. Crank the engine over until there is no further rise in pressure.

8. Record the reading and remove the tester.

9. Repeat Steps 4-8 for the other cylinder.

10. Reinstall the spark plugs and reconnect their caps.

Results

When interpreting the results, actual readings are not as important as the difference between the readings. **Table 8** lists the standard engine compression reading. Pressure must not vary between the cylinders by more than ten percent. Greater differences indicate worn or broken rings, leaky or sticky valves, a blown head gasket or a combination of all.

If compression readings do not differ between cylinders by more than ten percent, the rings and valves are in good condition. A low reading (ten percent or more) on one cylinder indicates valve or ring trouble. To decide which, pour about a teaspoon of engine oil into the spark plug hole. Turn the engine over once to distribute the oil, then take another compression test and record the reading. If the compression increases significantly, the valves are good but the rings are defective on that cylinder. If compression does not increase, the valves require servicing.

NOTE
An engine cannot be tuned to maximum performance with low compression.

Spark Plug Removal

CAUTION
Whenever the spark plug is removed, dirt around it can fall into the plug hole. This can cause serious engine damage.

1. Blow away loose dirt or debris that may have accumulated around the base of the spark plug and could fall into the cylinder head.

2. Grasp the spark plug lead (**Figure 66**) and twist it from side to side to break the seal. Then pull the cap off the spark plug. If the cap is stuck to the plug, twist it slightly to break it loose.

NOTE
Use a special spark plug socket equipped with a rubber insert that holds the spark plug. This type of socket is necessary for both removal and installation since the spark plugs are recessed in the cylinder head.

3. Install the spark plug socket onto the spark plug. Make sure it is correctly seated. Install an open-end wrench or

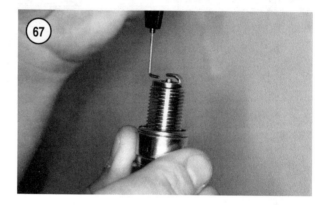

socket handle and remove the spark plug. Mark the spark plug with the cylinder number from which it was removed.

4. Repeat Steps 1-3 for the remaining spark plug.

5. Thoroughly inspect each plug. Look for broken center porcelain, excessively eroded electrodes and excessive carbon or oil fouling.

6. Inspect the spark plug caps and secondary wires for damage or hardness. If any portion is damaged, replace the cap and secondary wire as an assembly. The front and rear cylinder assemblies have different part numbers.

Spark Plug Gaping and Installing

Carefully gap the spark plugs to ensure a reliable, consistent spark. Use a special spark plug gaping tool and a wire feeler gauge.

1. Insert a wire feeler gauge between the center and side electrode of the plug (**Figure 67**). The correct gap is in **Table 8**. If the gap is correct, a slight drag will be felt as the wire gauge is pulled through. If there is no drag, or the gauge will not pass through, bend the side electrode with a gaping tool (**Figure 68**) to adjust to the proper gap in **Table 8**.

2. Install the terminal nut (A, **Figure 69**).

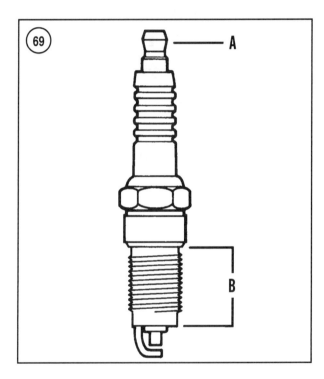

3. Apply a *light coat* of antiseize lubricant on the threads of the spark plug before installing it. Do *not* use engine oil on the plug threads.

CAUTION
The cylinder head is aluminum and the spark plug hole is easily damaged if the spark plug is cross-threaded.

4. Slowly screw the spark plug into the cylinder head by hand until it seats. Very little effort is required. If force is necessary, the plug is cross-threaded; unscrew it and try again.

NOTE
Do not overtighten. This will only distort the gasket and destroy its sealing ability.

5. Hand-tighten the plug until it seats against the cylinder head, then tighten it to 11-18 ft.-lb. (15-24 N•m).

6. Install the spark plug cap and lead to the correct spark plug. Rotate the cap slightly in both directions and make sure it is attached to the spark plug.

7. Repeat for the other spark plug.

Spark Plug Heat Range

Spark plugs are available in various heat ranges that are hotter or colder than the plugs originally installed by the manufacturer.

Select a plug with a heat range designed for the loads and conditions under which the motorcycle will be operated. A plug with an incorrect heat range can foul, overheat and cause piston damage.

In general, use a hot plug for low speeds and low temperatures. Use a cold plug for high speeds, high engine loads and high temperatures. The plug should operate hot enough to burn off unwanted deposits, but not so hot that it is damaged or causes preignition. To determine if plug heat range is correct, remove each spark plug and examine the insulator.

Do not change the spark plug heat range to compensate for adverse engine or air/fuel conditions.

When replacing plugs, make sure the reach or thread length (B, **Figure 69**) is correct. A longer than standard plug could interfere with the piston and cause engine damage.

Refer to **Table 8** for recommended spark plugs.

Spark Plug Reading

Reading the spark plugs can provide information regarding engine performance. Reading plugs that have been in use indicates spark plug operation, air/fuel mixture composition and engine conditions (such as oil consumption or pistons). Before checking the spark plugs, operate the motorcycle under a medium load for approximately 6 miles (10 km). Avoid prolonged idling before shutting off the engine. Remove the spark plugs as described in this chapter. Examine each plug and compare it to those in **Figure 70**. Refer to the following sections to determine the operating conditions.

If the plugs are being inspected to determine if carburetor jetting is correct, start with new plugs and operate the motorcycle at the load that corresponds to the jetting information desired. For example on carbureted models, if the main jet is in question, operate the motorcycle at full throttle, shut the engine off and coast to a stop.

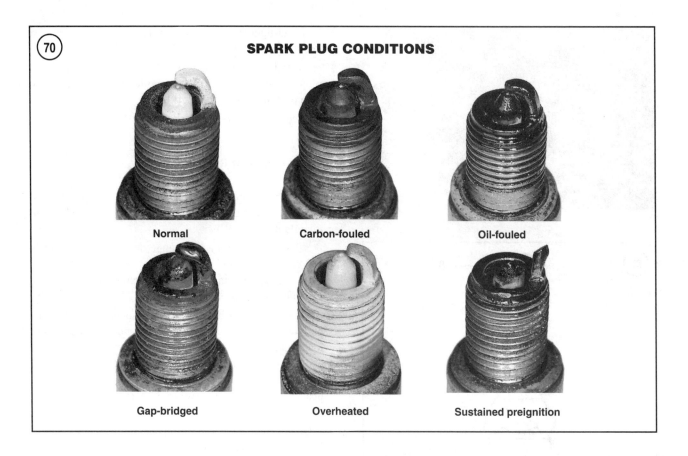

SPARK PLUG CONDITIONS

Normal   Carbon-fouled   Oil-fouled

Gap-bridged   Overheated   Sustained preignition

Normal condition

If the plug has a light tan or gray deposit and no abnormal gap wear or erosion, good engine, air/fuel mixture and ignition conditions are good. The plug in use is of the proper heat range, and may be serviced and returned to use.

Carbon-fouled

Soft, dry, sooty deposits covering the entire firing end of the plug are evidence of incomplete combustion. Even though the firing end of the plug is dry, the plug's insulation decreases when in this condition. An electrical path is formed that bypasses the electrodes and causes in a misfire condition. Carbon fouling can be caused by one or more of the following:
1. Rich fuel mixture.
2. Cold spark plug heat range.
3. Clogged air filter.
4. Improperly operating ignition component.
5. Ignition component failure.
6. Low engine compression.
7. Prolonged idling.

Oil-fouled

The tip of an oil-fouled plug has a black insulator tip, a damp oily film over the firing end and a carbon layer over the entire nose. The electrodes are not worn. Oil-fouled spark plugs may be cleaned in an emergency, but it is better to replace them. Correct the cause of fouling before returning the engine to service. Common causes for this condition are as follows:
1. Incorrect air/fuel mixture.
2. Low idle speed or prolonged idling.
3. Ignition component failure.
4. Cold spark plug heat range.
5. Engine still being broken in.
6. Valve guides worn.
7. Piston rings worn or broken.

Gap bridging

Plugs with gap bridging have gaps shorted out by combustion deposits between the electrodes. If this condition is encountered, check for excessive carbon or oil in the combustion chamber. Be sure to locate and correct the cause of this condition.

Overheating

Badly worn electrodes, premature gap wear and a gray or white blistered porcelain insulator surface are signs of overheating. The most common cause is a spark plug of the wrong heat range (too hot). If spark plug is the correct heat range and is overheated, consider the following causes:

1. Lean air/fuel mixture.
2. Improperly operating ignition component.
3. Engine lubrication system malfunction.
4. Cooling system malfunction.
5. Engine air leak.
6. Improper spark plug installation (over-tightened).
7. No spark plug gasket.

Worn out

Corrosive gases formed by combustion and high voltage sparks have eroded the electrodes. A spark plug in this condition requires more voltage to fire under hard acceleration. Replace it with a new spark plug.

Preignition

If the electrodes are melted, preignition is almost certainly the cause. Check for intake air leaks at the manifold and carburetor, or throttle body, and advanced ignition timing. It is also possible that the plug is the wrong heat range (too hot). Find the cause of the preignition before returning the engine to service. For additional information, refer to *Engine Performance* in Chapter Two.

Ignition Timing

The engine is equipped with a fully transistorized ignition system and is controlled by the ignition module (carbureted models) or electronic control module (fuel injected models). This solid-state system uses no breaker points to trigger the ignition. Problems with the transistorized system are rare and there are no means of adjusting ignition timing. Harley-Davidson does not provide any ignition timing procedures. If an ignition related problem is suspected, inspect the ignition components as described in Chapter Eight.

Incorrect ignition timing can cause a drastic loss of engine performance and efficiency. It may also cause overheating.

IDLE SPEED ADJUSTMENT

Carbureted Models

1. Start the engine and warm it to normal operating temperature. Shut off the engine.
2. Make sure the starting enrichment (choke) valve is pushed all the way to the OFF position.
3. Connect a portable tachometer to the engine following the manufacturer's instructions.

NOTE
Figure 71 is shown with the air filter assembly removed to better illustrate the step.

4. Start the engine and with the engine idling, compare the tachometer reading to the idle speed specification in **Table 8**. If the tachometer reading is incorrect, adjust the idle speed with the carburetor throttle stop screw (**Figure 71**).

NOTE
The idle mixture is set and sealed by the manufacturer and is not adjustable.

5. Accelerate the engine a couple of times and release the throttle. The idle speed should return to the speed set in Step 4. If necessary, readjust the idle speed by turning the throttle stop screw (**Figure 71**). Shut off the engine.
6. Disconnect and remove the portable tachometer.

Fuel Injected Models

Idle speed adjustments on fuel injected models *must* be performed by a Harley-Davidson dealership equipped with a Scanalyzer tool.

Tables 1-10 are on the following pages.

Table 1 MAINTENANCE AND LUBRICATION SCHEDULE[1]

Pre-ride check
  Check tire condition and inflation pressure
  Check wheel rim condition
  Check light and horn operation
  Check engine oil level; add oil if necessary
  Check brake fluid level and condition; add fluid if necessary
  Check the operation of the front and rear brakes
  Check throttle operation
  Check clutch lever operation
  Check fuel level in fuel tank; top off if necessary
  Check fuel system for leaks
Initial 500 miles (800 km)
  Change engine oil and filter
  Check battery condition; clean cable connections if necessary
  Check brake fluid level and condition; add fluid if necessary
  Check front and rear brake pads and discs for wear
  Check tire condition and inflation pressure
  Check primary chain deflection; adjust if necessary
  Check drive belt tension; adjust if necessary
  Change primary chaincase lubricant
  Change transmission lubricant
  Check clutch lever operation; adjust if necessary
  Check drive belt and sprockets condition
  Inspect spark plugs
  Inspect air filter element
  Lubricate front brake and clutch lever pivot pin
  Lubricate clutch cable if necessary
  Check throttle cable operation
  Check enrichener (choke) cable operation (carbureted models)
  Check engine idle speed; adjust if necessary
  Check fuel system for leaks
  Check electrical switches and equipment for proper operation
  Check oil and brake lines for leakage
  Check all fasteners for tightness[2]
  Road test the motorcycle
Every 2500 miles (4000 km)
  Check transmission lubricant level; add lubricant if necessary
  Check drive belt tension; adjust if necessary
  Inspect air filter element; clean or replace if necessary
  Check throttle operation
  Check enrichener (choke) cable operation (carbureted models)
  Check fuel system for leaks
  Check oil and brake lines for leakage
  Check electrical switches and equipment for proper operation
  Road test the motorcycle
Every 5000 miles (8000 km)
  Change engine oil and filter
  Check battery condition; clean cable connections if necessary
  Check brake fluid level and condition; add fluid if necessary
  Check front and rear brake pads and discs for wear
  Check tire condition and inflation pressure
  Check wire wheel spoke nipple tightness; adjust if necessary (models so equipped)
  Check primary chain deflection; adjust if necessary
  Check drive belt tension; adjust if necessary
  Change primary chaincase lubricant
  Change transmission lubricant
  Check clutch lever operation; adjust if necessary
  Check drive belt and sprockets condition
  Check steering head bearing adjustment; adjust if necessary
  Inspect spark plugs

(continued)

Table 1 MAINTENANCE AND LUBRICATION SCHEDULE[1](continued)

Every 5000 miles (8000km) (continued)
  Inspect air filter element; clean or replace if necessary
  Lubricate front brake and clutch lever pivot pin
  Lubricate clutch cable if necessary
  Check throttle cable operation
  Check enrichener (choke) cable operation (carbureted models)
  Check engine idle speed; adjust if necessary (carbureted models)
  Check fuel system for leaks
  Check electrical switches and equipment for proper operation
  Check oil and brake lines for leakage
  Check all fasteners for tightness[2]
  Road test the motorcycle
Every 10,000 miles (16,000 km)
  Replace spark plugs
  Perform a compression test
  Lubricate steering head bearings
  Lubricate rocker arm bearings (FLSTS and FXSTS)
  Lubricate rear swing arm bearings
  Inspect engine mounts for wear or damage; replace if necessary
Every 20,000 miles (32,000 km)
  Change front fork oil
  Inspect fuel tank filter, replace if necessary
  Inspect fuel supply valve filter screen

1. Consider this maintenance schedule a guide to general maintenance and lubrication intervals. Harder than normal use and exposure to mud, water, high humidity indicates more frequent servicing to most of the maintenance items.
2. Except cylinder head bolts. Cylinder head bolts must be tightened following the procedure listed in Chapter Four. Improper tightening of the cylinder head bolts may cause cylinder gasket damage and/or cylinder head leakage.

Table 2 TIRE INFLATION PRESSURE (COLD)*

Model	kPa	PSI
Front wheels		
Rider only	207	30
Rider and passenger	207	30
Rear wheels		
Rider only	248	36
Rider and passenger	275	40

*Tire pressure for original equipment tires. Aftermarket tires may require different inflation pressure.

Table 3 ENGINE OIL SPECIFICATIONS

Type	HD rating	Viscosity	Ambient operating temperature
HD Multi-grade	HD360	SAE 10W/40	Below 40°F
HD Multi-grade	HD360	SAE 20W/50	Above 40°F
HD Regular heavy	HD360	SAE 50	Above 60°F
HD Extra heavy	HD360	SAE 60	Above 80°F

Table 4 ENGINE AND PRIMARY DRIVE/TRANSMISSION OIL CAPACITIES

Oil tank refill with filter capacity	3.5 U.S. qts. (3.3 L)
Primary chaincase	26 U.S. oz. (768 ml)
Transmission	
Oil change	20-24 U.S. oz. (591-709 ml)
Rebuild (dry)	24 U.S. oz. (709 ml)

Table 5 RECOMMENDED LUBRICANTS AND FLUIDS

Brake fluid	DOT 5 silicone
Front fork oil	HD Type E or an equivalent
Fuel	91 pump octane or higher leaded or unleaded
Transmission	HD Transmission Lubricant or an equivalent
Primary chaincase	HD Primary Chaincase Lubricant or an equivalent

Table 6 MAINTENANCE AND TUNE-UP TORQUE SPECIFICATIONS

Item	ft.-lb.	in.-lb.	N•m
Air filter			
Backplate screws	–	20-40	2-4
Cover screw	–	36-60	4-7
Clutch adjusting screw			
locknut	–	72-120	8-14
Clutch inspection cover			
screws	–	84-108	9.5-12
Crankcase oil plug	–	120-144	14-16
Front axle nut			
FXST, FLSTC, FLSTF,			
FXSTB, FXSTD	50-55	–	68-75
FLSTS, FXSTS	60-65	–	81-88
Front fork			
Fork tube cap	40-60	–	54-81
Drain screw			
FXSTD	–	12-18	1.4-2.0
All models except FXSTD	–	52-78	6-9
Jiffy stand leg			
stop bolt	–	144-180	16-20
Primary chaincase			
Inspection cover screws	–	84-108	9.5-12.2
Chain adjuster shoe nut	21-29	–	29-39
Oil tank drain plug			
On frame rail	14-21	–	19-29
Rear axle nut	60-65	–	81-88
Spark plug	11-18	–	15-24
Transmission drain plug	14-21	–	19-28

Table 7 FRONT FORK OIL CAPACITY

Model	Capacity (each fork leg)
FLSTF, FLSTC, FXST	12.9 U.S. oz. (382 cc)
FXSTB	12.0 U.S. oz. (356 cc)
FXSTD	11.6 U.S. oz. (343 cc)

Table 8 MAINTENANCE AND TUNE-UP SPECIFICATIONS

Item	Specification
Engine compression	90 psi (620 kPa)
Spark plugs	HD No. 6R12*
Gap	0.038-0.043 in. (0.97-1.09 mm)
Idle speed	
Carbureted	950-1050 rpm
EFI	Non-adjustable
Ignition timing	Non-adjustable
Drive belt deflection	5/16-3/8 in. (8-10 mm)
Brake pad minimum thickness	
FLSTS & FXSTS	1/16 in. (1.6 mm)
All other models	0.04 in. (1.02 mm)
Clutch cable free play	1/16-1/8 in. (1.6-3.2 mm)

*Harley-Davidson recommends that no other type of spark plug be substituted for the recommended H-D type.

Table 9 VEHICLE ALIGNMENT–HORIZONTAL WHEEL OFFSET

FLSTC, FLSTF	0.359 in. (9.12mm)
FXST, FXSTB, FXSTS	0.526 in. (13.36 mm)
FLSTS	0.320 in. (8.13 mm)
FXSTD	0.154 in. (3.9 mm)

Table 10 VEHICLE ALIGNMENT–LACED WHEEL RADIAL OFFSET

FXSTS	
Front 21 in.	1.440-1.460 in. (36.576-37.084 mm)
Rear 16 in.	1.472-1.492 in. (37.389-37.897 mm)
FXST, FXSTD, FXSTB	
Front 21 in.	1.640-1.660 in. (41.565-42.164 mm)
Rear 16 in.	1.472-1.492 in. (37.389-37.897 mm)

CHAPTER FOUR

ENGINE

This chapter provides complete service and overhaul procedures, including information for disassembly, removal, inspection, service and engine reassembly.

Tables 1-7 at the end of the chapter provide spacer, shim and specification information.

All models covered in this manual are equipped with the Twin Cam 88B engine, an air-cooled four-stroke, overhead-valve V-twin engine. Viewed from the engine's right side, engine rotation is clockwise. A dual counterbalancing system rotates in the opposite direction of the crankshaft to minimize vibration.

Both cylinders fire once in 720° of crankshaft rotation. The rear cylinder fires 315° after the front cylinder. The front cylinder fires again in another 405°. Note one cylinder is always on its exhaust stroke when the other fires on its compression stroke.

SERVICE PRECAUTIONS

Before servicing the engine, note the following:
1. Review the *Basic Service Methods* and *Precision Measuring Tools* sections in Chapter One. Accurate measurements are critical to a successful engine rebuild.

2. Throughout the text there are references to the left and right side of the engine. This refers to the engine as it is mounted in the frame, not how it may sit on the workbench.

3. Always replace worn or damaged fasteners with those of the same size, type and torque requirements. Make sure to identify each bolt before replacing it. Lubricate bolt threads with engine oil, unless otherwise specified, before tightening them. If a specific torque value is not listed in **Table 4**, refer to the general torque specifications in Chapter One.

> *CAUTION*
> *The engine is assembled with hardened fasteners. Do not install fasteners with a lower strength grade classification.*

4. Use special tools where noted. Refer to **Table 12** in Chapter One.

5. Store parts in boxes, plastic bags and containers (**Figure 1**). Use masking tape and a permanent, waterproof marking pen to label parts.

6. Use a box of assorted size and color vacuum hose identifiers, such as those shown in **Figure 2** (Lisle part No.

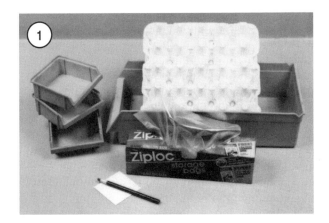

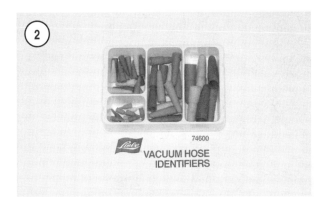

74600

VACUUM HOSE
IDENTIFIERS

74600), to identify hoses and fittings during engine removal and disassembly.

7. Use a vise with protective jaws to hold parts.

8. Use a press or special tools when force is required to remove and install parts. Do not try to pry, hammer or otherwise force them on or off.

9. Replace all O-rings and oil seals during reassembly. Apply a small amount of grease to the inner lips of each new seal to prevent damage when the engine is first started.

10. Record the location, position and thickness of all shims as they are removed.

SPECIAL TOOLS

Engine service requires a number of special tools. These tools and their part numbers are listed with the individual procedures. For a complete list of the special tools mentioned in this manual, refer to **Table 12** in Chapter One. The engine tools used in this chapter are either Harley-Davidson or JIMS special tools. JIMS special tools are available through some Harley-Davidson dealerships or many aftermarket motorcycle suppliers.

When purchasing special tools, make sure to specify that the tools required are for the 2000-on FLST and FXST Softail Twin-Cam 88B models. Many of the tools are specific to this engine. Tools for other engine models may be slightly different.

SERVICING ENGINE IN FRAME

Many components can be serviced while the engine is mounted in the frame:

1. Rocker arm cover and rocker arms.
2. Cylinder heads.
3. Cylinders and pistons.
4. Camshafts.
5. Gearshift mechanism.
6. Clutch and primary drive assembly.
7. Transmission.
8. Carburetor or fuel injection induction module.
9. Starter and gears.
10. Alternator and electrical systems.

ENGINE

Removal

Refer to **Figure 3**.
1. Thoroughly clean the engine of all dirt and debris.
2. Remove the seat as described in Chapter Fourteen.

NOTE
Always disarm the optional TSSM security system prior to disconnecting the battery or the siren will sound.

3. Support the motorcycle on a stand or floor jack. See *Motorcycle Stands* in Chapter Nine and the following:
   a. The motorcycle has almost a 50:50 weight distribution at the center of the engine location on the frame. The jack must be positioned so that the motorcycle is stable after being lifted up off the ground.
   b. The following procedure is shown with a K&L MC450 Center Stand jack as shown in **Figure 4**. The jack's post supports fit onto the frame tubes and help stabilize the jack to the motorcycle.
   c. Use additional wood blocks to ensure that the motorcycle is stabilized.
   d. Also, tie the motorcycle down for additional stability.
4. Remove the fuel tank as described in Chapter Seven.
5. On models so equipped, remove both saddlebags as described in Chapter Fourteen.

4

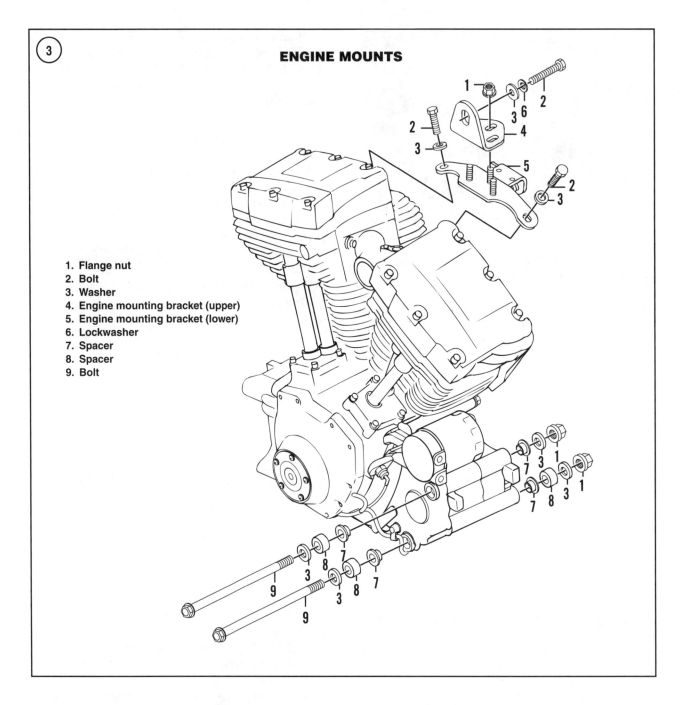

③ ENGINE MOUNTS

1. Flange nut
2. Bolt
3. Washer
4. Engine mounting bracket (upper)
5. Engine mounting bracket (lower)
6. Lockwasher
7. Spacer
8. Spacer
9. Bolt

6. On models so equipped, remove the windshield as described in Chapter Fourteen.

7. Remove the air filter and backing plate as described in Chapter Seven.

8A. On carbureted models, remove the carburetor as described in Chapter Seven.

8B. On fuel injected models, remove the fuel induction module as described in Chapter Seven.

9. Remove the exhaust system as described in Chapter Seven.

10. Remove the rear brake pedal as described in Chapter Twelve.

11. On models so equipped, remove the footboards as described in Chapter Fourteen.

12. Drain the engine oil as described in Chapter Three.

13. Drain the primary chain case as described in Chapter Three.

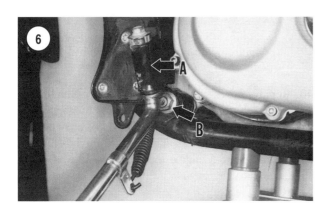

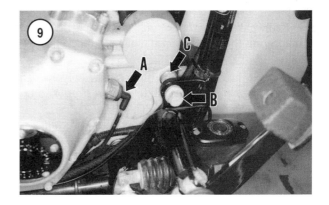

14. To gain access to the electrical panel, remove the rear fender inner panel as described in Chapter Eight.

15. Unplug the speed sensor connector (**Figure 5**) and release the electrical harness from the transmission case.

16. Remove the oil tank as described in this chapter.

17. Remove the bolts securing the drive belt guard and remove the guard.

18. On 2000 models, remove the camshaft position sensor as described in Chapter Eight.

19. Remove the jiffy stand (A, **Figure 6**) as described in Chapter Fourteen.

20. Disconnect the following electrical connectors:

   a. Crankshaft position sensor (A, **Figure 7**).

   b. Alternator stator and voltage regulator (**Figure 8**).

   c. Oil pressure switch (A, **Figure 9**).

   d. Engine temperature sensor (**Figure 10**).

21. Remove the ignition coil and spark plug assembly as described in Chapter Eight.

22. Remove the primary chain case assembly, including the inner housing, as described in Chapter Five.

23. Remove the alternator rotor and stator as described in Chapter Eight.

24. Remove the ignition coil assembly (A, **Figure 11**) as described in Chapter Eight.

25. Remove the voltage regulator from the frame as described in Chapter Eight.

26. Disconnect the hose from the breather cover and move the hose behind the transmission flange.

27. Remove the bolts and washers securing the seat post and remove the seat post.

28. Remove the clutch cable from the lower portion of the crankcase as described under *Clutch Cable Replacement* in Chapter Five.

29. Wrap the frame front down tubes and lower tubes in protective tape to prevent surface damage in the following steps.

30. Remove the transmission case from the engine and frame as described in Chapter Six.

31. On all models except the FLSTS, remove the horn assembly (B, **Figure 11**) as described in Chapter Eight.

NOTE
*Note the location of the ground strap (**Figure 12**) under the bolt on the rear cylinder head.*

32. Remove the bolts and washers (A, **Figure 13**) securing the engine upper mounting bracket to the cylinder heads. Do not forget the ground strap.

33. Remove the bolt, washer and lockwasher (B, **Figure 13**) securing the engine upper mounting bracket to the frame.

34. Support the engine with a floor jack. Apply enough jack pressure on the crankcase to support it prior to removing the engine mounting bolts.

35. On the left side, remove the front upper (B, **Figure 7**) and front lower nuts (B, **Figure 6**) and washers from the engine mounting through bolts.

36. On the right side, slowly withdraw the upper bolt (B, **Figure 9**) and spacer (C). Then remove the lower bolts from the crankcase and frame. Do not lose the outer spacers on the bolts. The shorter top bolt has an outer spacer on the right side only. The longer lower bolt has an outer spacer on both sides.

37. After the bolts have been removed, remove the inner spacers from both sides of the crankcase.

38. Cover both rocker covers with foam padding to protect the finish.

39. Check the engine to make sure all electrical wiring, hoses and other related components have been disconnected from the engine. Make sure nothing will interfere with the removal of the engine from the right side of the frame.

WARNING
Due to the weight of the engine assembly, a minimum of two people are required to safely remove the engine from the frame.

40. Remove the engine from the right side of the frame.

41. If available, mount the engine in the twin cam 88B engine base stand (JIMS part No.1138) and engine stand (JIMS part No.1142) or an equivalent (**Figure 14**).

42. Clean the front engine mount bolts and washers in solvent and dry thoroughly.

43. Replace leaking or damaged oil hoses and fuel lines.

Installation

WARNING
Due to the weight of the engine assembly, a minimum of two people are required to safely install the engine into the frame.

1. Make sure all electrical wiring, hoses and other related components are out of the way and will not interfere with engine installation.

2. Correctly position a floor jack and piece of wood under the frame to support the engine when it is installed into the frame.

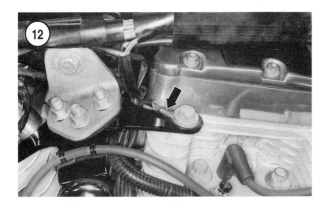

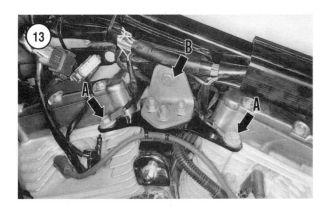

3. Install the engine from the right side of the frame and place it on the piece of wood and floor jack. Apply enough jack pressure on the crankcase to support it prior to installing the engine mounting bolts.

4. Correctly position the engine and align the mounting bolt holes with the frame bolt holes.

5. If removed, install the four inner spacers into the crankcase bolt receptacles. Push them until they bottom.

6. Install the upper (short) bolt as follows:

   a. Install a washer onto the upper bolt and insert it into the frame.

   b. Install the inner spacer onto the upper bolt, then push the upper bolt through the crankcase and inner spacer.

   c. Push the bolt through the frame.

   d. On the left side, install a washer and nut onto the upper bolt. Tighten the nut finger-tight at this time.

7. Install the lower (long) bolt as follows:

   a. Install a washer onto the lower bolt and insert it into the frame.

   b. Install the inner spacer onto the lower bolt, then push the lower bolt through the crankcase, the inner spacer and the outer spacer.

   c. Push the bolt through the frame.

   d. On the left side, install a washer and nut onto the lower bolt. Tighten the nut finger-tight at this time.

8. Install the engine upper mounting bracket onto the cylinder heads and frame. Install the bolts, lockwashers and washers and tighten finger-tight at this time. Do not forget to correctly position the ground strap (**Figure 12**) under the bolt on the rear cylinder head.

9. On all models except the FLSTS, install the horn assembly (B, **Figure 11**) as described in Chapter Eight.

10. Install the transmission case into the frame and engine as described in Chapter Six.

11. Tighten the engine front mounting bolts to 70-80 ft.-lb. (95-108 N•m).

12. Remove the floor jack.

13. Remove the protective tape from the frame front down tubes.

14. Remove the foam padding from the rocker covers.

15. Install the clutch cable onto the lower portion of the crankcase as described under *Clutch Cable Replacement* in Chapter Five.

16. Tighten the engine upper mounting bracket onto the cylinder heads and frame to the specification in **Table 4**.

17. Install the seat post and mounting bolts and tighten securely.

18. Connect the hose onto the transmission breather cover.

19. Install the voltage regulator as described in Chapter Eight.

20. Install the alternator stator and rotor assembly as described in Chapter Eight.

21. Install the primary chain case assembly, including the inner housing, as described in Chapter Five.

22. Install the ignition coil assembly (A, **Figure 11**) as described in Chapter Eight.

23. Connect the following electrical connectors:

   a. Crankshaft position sensor (**Figure 7**).

   b. Alternator stator and voltage regulator (**Figure 8**).

   c. Oil pressure switch (A, **Figure 9**).

   d. Engine temperature sensor (**Figure 10**).

4

ROCKER ARM ASSEMBLY

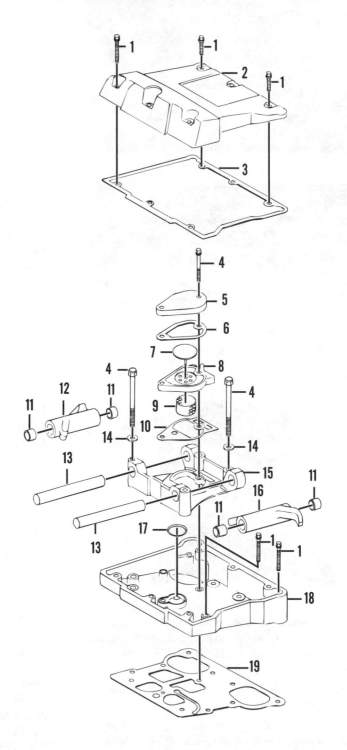

1. Bolt
2. Rocker arm cover
3. Gasket
4. Bolt
5. Breather cover*
6. Gasket*
7. Valve*
8. Breather baffle*
9. Filter element*
10. Gasket*
11. Bushing
12. Rocker arm
   Intake—front cylinder
   Exhaust—rear cylinder
13. Rocker arm shaft
14. Washer
15. Rocker arm support
16. Rocker arm
   Intake—rear cylinder
   Exhaust—front cylinder
17. O-ring seal
18. Rocker arm housing
19. Gasket

*Items 5-10 are combined into an integral unit on 2002-on models.

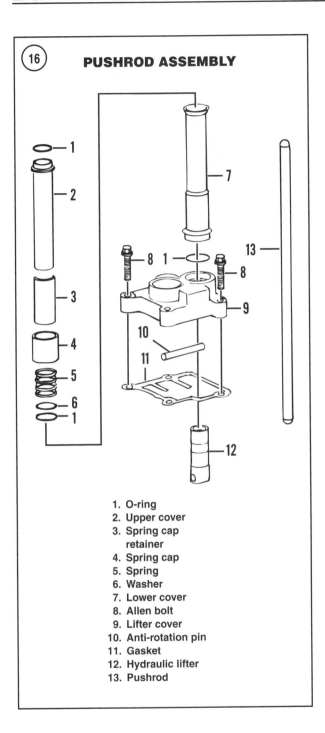

PUSHROD ASSEMBLY

16

1. O-ring
2. Upper cover
3. Spring cap
   retainer
4. Spring cap
5. Spring
6. Washer
7. Lower cover
8. Allen bolt
9. Lifter cover
10. Anti-rotation pin
11. Gasket
12. Hydraulic lifter
13. Pushrod

4

28. Install the rear fender inner panel (to cover the electrical panel) as described in Chapter Eight.

29. Adjust the clutch and primary chain as described in Chapter Three.

30. On models so equipped, install the footboards as described in Chapter Fourteen.

31. Install the exhaust system as described in Chapter Seven.

32. Install the rear brake pedal as described in Chapter Twelve.

33A. On carburetted models, install the carburetor as described in Chapter Seven.

33B. On fuel injected models, install the fuel injection induction module as described in Chapter Seven.

34. Install the air filter backing plate and air filter as described in Chapter Seven.

35. Install the fuel tank as described in Chapter Seven.

36. On models so equipped, install the windshield as described in Chapter Fourteen.

37. On models so equipped, install both saddlebags as described in Chapter Fourteen.

38. Remove the stand from under the motorcycle and place the motorcycle on the jiffy stand.

39. Connect the negative battery cable as described in Chapter Eight.

40. Install the seat.

41. Refill the engine oil as described in Chapter Three.

42. Start the engine and check for leaks.

ROCKER ARMS AND PUSHRODS

Refer to **Figure 15** and **Figure 16**.

The rocker arm and pushrod procedures are shown with the rear cylinder. The same procedures also apply to the front cylinder. Any differences are noted.

The rear cylinder head is closer to the frame backbone than the front cylinder. In some cases it may be possible to completely remove some of the rocker arm mounting bolts on the front cylinder that are not possible to achieve on the rear cylinder.

Removal

1. If the engine is mounted in the frame, perform the following:
   a. Thoroughly clean the engine of all dirt and debris.
   b. Remove the seat as described in Chapter Fourteen.
   c. Remove the fuel tank as described in Chapter Seven.
   d. Remove the air filter and backing plate as described in Chapter Seven.

24. On 2000 models, install the camshaft position sensor as described in Chapter Eight.

25. Install the drive belt guard and tighten the bolts securely.

26. Install the oil tank as described in this chapter.

27. Connect the speed sensor connector (**Figure 5**) and attach the electrical harness to the transmission case.

e. Remove the exhaust system as described in Chapter Seven.

NOTE
Always disarm the optional TSSM security system prior to disconnecting the battery or the siren will sound.

2. Using a crisscross pattern, loosen and remove the rocker arm cover bolts.

3. Remove the rocker arm cover and gasket (**Figure 17**).

4. Remove both spark plugs as described in Chapter Three to make it easier to rotate the engine by hand.

5. Remove the camshaft cover (**Figure 18**) as described under *Camshaft Support Plate Removal* in this chapter.

6. Remove the bolt securing the crankshaft sprocket (**Figure 19**). This is necessary to observe the timing mark on the sprocket.

CAUTION
Do not rotate the engine using the camshaft sprocket mounting bolt. Doing so may break the bolt and damage the camshaft.

CAUTION
The piston must be at top dead center (TDC) to avoid damage to the pushrods and rocker arms in the following steps.

7A. *With the primary chain cover in place,* position the piston for the cylinder being worked on at top dead center (TDC) on the compression stroke as follows:

a. Support the motorcycle on a stand with the rear wheel off the ground. See *Motorcycle Stands* in Chapter Nine.

b. Shift the transmission into fifth gear.

c. Rotate the rear wheel in the direction of normal rotation.

d. Stop rotating the rear wheel when the intake and exhaust valves are closed.

e. The timing mark on the camshaft and crankshaft sprocket must be aligned as shown in **Figure 20** for the front cylinder or **Figure 21** for the rear cylinder.

f. Look into the spark plug hole with a flashlight and verify that the piston is at TDC.

g. Wiggle both rocker arms. There should be free play that indicates that both valves are closed and the piston is at top dead center (TDC) on the compression stroke. Also, the push rods should be in the unloaded position.

h. Reinstall the bolt and washer securing the crankshaft sprocket (**Figure 19**) and tighten to 24 ft.-lb. (33 N•m).

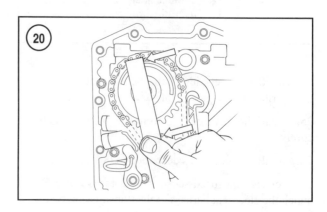

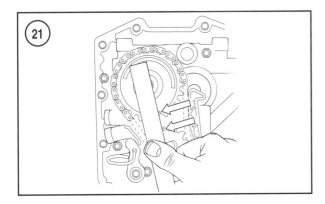

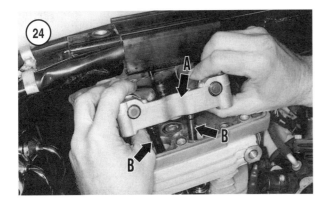

7B. *With the primary chain cover removed,* position the piston for the cylinder being worked on at top dead center (TDC) on the compression stroke as follows:

a. Shift the transmission into NEUTRAL.

b. Install the sprocket shaft nut onto the end of the left side of the crankshaft.

c. Place a socket or wrench on the compensating sprocket shaft nut.

d. Rotate the compensating sprocket shaft *counter-clockwise* until the intake and exhaust valves are closed.

e. The timing mark on the camshaft and crankshaft sprocket must be aligned as shown in **Figure 20** for the front cylinder or **Figure 21** for the rear cylinder.

f. Look into the spark plug hole with a flashlight and verify that the piston is at TDC.

g. Wiggle both rocker arms. There should be free play that indicates both valves are closed and the piston is at top dead center (TDC) on the compression stroke. Also, the push rods should be in the un-loaded position.

h. Reinstall the bolt and washer securing the crankshaft sprocket (**Figure 19**) and tighten to 24 ft.-lb. (33 N•m).

8. Using a crisscross pattern, completely loosen the four bolts (A, **Figure 22**) securing the rocker arm support. The bolts cannot be removed at this time.

9. Completely loosen the bolts securing the breather assembly (B, **Figure 22**).

10. Remove the two right side rocker arm support bolts (A, **Figure 23**) and the right side bolt (B) securing the breather assembly.

NOTE
The left side breather assembly bolt cannot be removed until the rocker arm housing is removed from the cylinder head.

11. Remove the two left side rocker arm support bolts.

12. Lift up on the right side of the rocker arm housing (A, **Figure 24**) sufficiently to clear the push rods (B).

13. Carefully slide the rocker arm support out through the right side and remove it from the cylinder head.

14. Remove the left side bolt and remove the breather assembly.

15. Remove the O-ring seal (**Figure 25**) from the rocker arm housing.

16. Mark each pushrod with its top and bottom position. Then mark its operating position in the cylinder head.

NOTE
When removing the pushrods in the following steps, do not intermix the parts from

each set. When reinstalling the original pushrods, install them so each end faces in its original operating position. The pushrods develop a set wear pattern and installing them upside down may cause rapid wear to the pushrod, lifter and rocker arm.

17. Remove the intake (A, **Figure 26**) (silver) and exhaust (B) (black) pushrods up through the cylinder head.
18. Remove the pushrod covers as follows:
   a. Using a screwdriver, pry the spring cap retainer (**Figure 27**) from between the cylinder head and spring cap.
   b. Slide the upper cover down (A, **Figure 28**) and remove the pushrod cover assembly (B) from the cylinder head and the lifter cover.
   c. Repeat substeps a and b for the opposite pushrod cover.

NOTE
*To clear the cylinder's lower cooling fins, loosen the lifter cover's two inner Allen bolts with a short 90° Allen wrench (**Figure 29**) or a ball-end straight Allen wrench.*

19. Remove the lifter cover mounting bolts (**Figure 30**) and remove the cover.

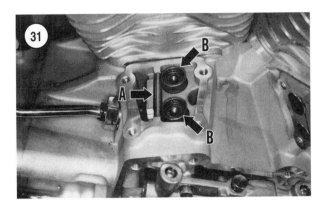

ROCKER ARM HOUSING TORQUE SEQUENCE

20. Remove the lifter cover gasket from the crankcase.

NOTE
Do not intermix the lifters when removing them in Step 21. Mark them so they can be installed in their original positions.

21. Remove the anti-rotation pin (A, **Figure 31**), then remove both hydraulic lifters (B).

22. Cover the crankcase opening with duct tape (**Figure 32**) to prevent the entry of debris.

23. Loosen the rocker housing six bolts 1/8 turn at a time in the pattern shown in **Figure 33**.

24. Tap the rocker arm housing with a rubber mallet to free it, then lift it off the cylinder head.

25. Remove the rocker arm housing gasket.

Installation

NOTE
Figure 34 *and* ***Figure 35*** *are shown with the engine removed from the frame to better illustrate the steps.*

1. Position the *new* rocker arm housing gasket onto the cylinder head so the breather channel (**Figure 34**) is covered and install the gasket (**Figure 35**).

2. Install the rocker arm housing onto the cylinder head.

3. Apply ThreeBond TB1342, or an equivalent, threadlocking compound to the bolt threads. Install the rocker housing six bolts and tighten them 1/8 turn at a time in the pattern shown in **Figure 33**. Tighten them to 120-168 in.-lb. (14-19 N•m).

4. Install a *new* O-ring seal (**Figure 25**) onto the rocker arm housing. Apply a light coat of clean engine oil to the O-ring.

5. Remove the duct tape from the crankcase openings.

6. Install the hydraulic lifters into the correct crankcase receptacles with both flat surfaces (**Figure 36**) facing toward the front and rear of the engine. This is necessary for installation of the anti-rotation pin in the next step.

CAUTION
Failure to install the anti-rotational pin will allow the lifter to rotate off the camshaft lobe and cause severe internal engine damage.

7. Install the anti-rotation pin (**Figure 37**) and make sure it is seated correctly within the crankcase receptacle and against the flats on both hydraulic lifters (A, **Figure 31**).

8. If the engine's position has been disturbed since the rocker arm components have been removed, rotate the engine until both lifters for the cylinder head being serviced seat onto the camshaft's lowest position (base circle). The lifter's top surface will be flush with the top surface of the crankcase surface as shown in **Figure 38**.

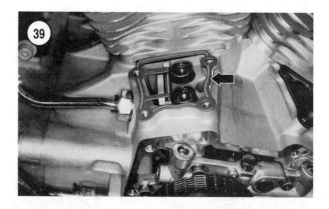

9. Install a *new* lifter cover gasket (**Figure 39**) onto the crankcase.

NOTE
*To clear the cylinder's lower cooling fins, tighten the lifter cover two inner Allen bolts with a short 90 ° Allen wrench (**Figure 29**).*

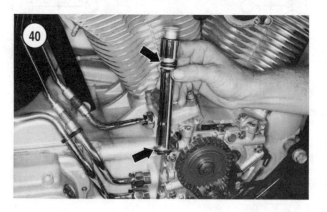

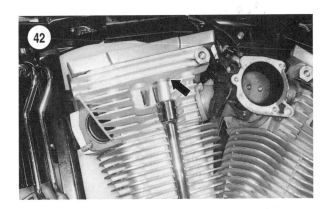

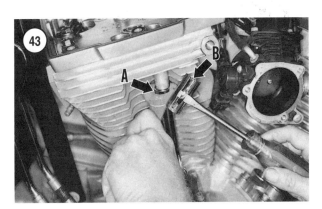

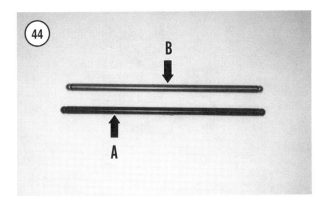

10. Install the lifter cover and the mounting bolts (**Figure 30**). Tighten the bolts to 15-18 ft.-lb. (20-24 N•m).

11. Install *new* O-ring seals (**Figure 40**) onto each end of the pushrod covers. Apply a light coat of clean engine oil to the O-rings.

12. If the pushrod cover assembly was disassembled, re-assemble it as described under *Pushrods* in this chapter.

> *CAUTION*
> *The pushrod covers and the pushrods must be installed in the correct location in the cylinder head and pushrod cover as indicated in **Table 3**.*

13. Install the pushrod cover into the correct location in the crankcase pushrod cover (**Figure 41**).

14. Slide the upper cover (**Figure 42**) up into the cylinder head receptacle.

15. Compress the spring cap with a thin open end wrench (A, **Figure 43**), or an equivalent, onto the spring cap, and install the spring cap retainer (B). Make sure the spring cap retainer is positioned correctly on both the upper cover and the spring cap.

16. Repeat Steps 12-15 for the other pushrod cover.

17. Install the pushrods as follows:

> *CAUTION*
> *Two different length pushrods are used in the Twin Cam 88B engine. The black exhaust pushrods (A, **Figure 44**) are longer than the silver intake pushrods (B).*

  a. When installing the existing pushrods, install each pushrod in its original position and in the correct orientation. Refer to A, **Figure 45** for intake and B, **Figure 45** for exhaust.

> *NOTE*
> *Because new pushrods are symmetrical, they can be installed with either end facing up.*

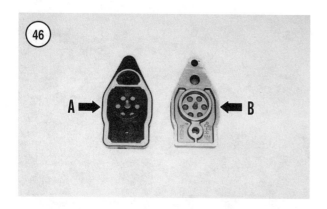

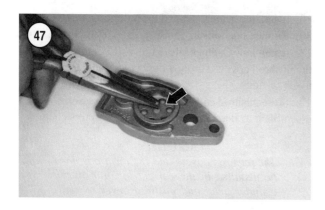

b. Make sure the pushrod is centered into its respective lifter.

NOTE
Step 18A is shown with the engine removed to better illustrate the steps.

NOTE
*The new 2002-on integral breather (A, **Figure 46**) can be installed on 2000-2001 models.*

18A. On 2000-2001 models, if the old breather (B, **Figure 46**) is going to be installed, assemble it as follows:

    a. If removed, install the valve onto the breather baffle and pull the tip through from the other side (**Figure 47**) to seat it.

    b. Install a *new* gasket (**Figure 48**).

    c. Install a *new* filter element.

    d. Hold the filter element in place and install the breather baffle (**Figure 49**).

    e. Install the cover (A, **Figure 50**) and *left side* bolt (B).

18B. On 2002-on models, perform the following:

    a. Install the filter element (**Figure 51**) onto the breather.

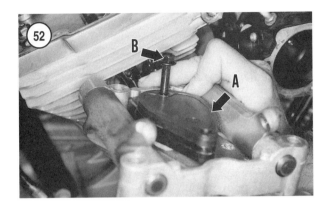

b. Install the breather assembly (A, **Figure 52**) onto the rocker arm support and install the left side bolt (B).

19. From the right side, slide the rocker arm support (A, **Figure 24**) onto the housing, past the pushrods (B). Do not forget to install the breather assembly left side bolt (**Figure 53**). This bolt cannot be installed after the rocker arm support is in place on the cylinder head.

20. Lift up on the left side of the rocker arm support and install the two right side bolts (A, **Figure 23**) and the right side breather assembly bolt (B). Do not tighten at this time.

21. Install the two left side rocker arm support bolts (**Figure 54**).

CAUTION
To avoid damaging a pushrod, rocker arms or valves, tighten the rocker arm support mounting bolts evenly and in a crisscross pattern. When tightening the mounting bolts, spin each pushrod by hand to ensure the rocker arm support is being tightened evenly. If one or both pushrods cannot be rotated, loosen the mounting bolts and determine the cause.

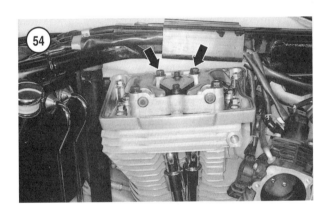

22. Tighten the rocker arm support assembly and bolts evenly in a crisscross pattern to 18-22 ft.-lb. (25-30 N•m).

23. Make sure the pushrod cover O-rings are correctly seated in the cylinder head and lifter cover. Depress the spring cap and install the spring cap retainer. Make sure the spring cap retainer is correctly seated (**Figure 55**). Repeat for the remaining pushrod covers.

24. Install a *new* rocker arm cover gasket (**Figure 56**).

25. Install the rocker arm cover (**Figure 57**).

NOTE
*There are two different length bolts (**Figure 58**) securing the rocker arm cover.*

26. Apply ThreeBond TB1342 (blue) or an equivalent threadlocking compound to the bolt threads. Install the rocker arm cover six bolts and tighten them 1/8 turn at a time in the sequence shown in **Figure 58**. Tighten them to 15-18 ft.-lb. (20-24 N•m).

27. Install the camshaft cover (**Figure 59**) as described under *Camshaft Support Plate Removal* in this chapter.

28. Install both spark plugs as described in Chapter Three.

Rocker Arm Disassembly/Assembly

1. Before removing the rocker arms (**Figure 60**), measure the rocker arm end clearance as follows:
   a. Insert a feeler gauge between the rocker arm and the inside rocker arm cover boss as shown in **Figure 61**. Refer to **Table 2**.
   b. Record the measurement.
   c. Repeat for each rocker arm.
   d. Replace the rocker arm and/or the rocker arm support if necessary.

2. Prior to disassembling the rocker arms, mark each one with an IN (intake) or EX (exhaust) (**Figure 62**) to ensure they are installed in their original positions.

3. Remove the rocker arm shafts (A, **Figure 63**) and remove the rocker arms (B).

4. Clean all parts in solvent. Blow compressed air through all oil passages.

5. Install the rocker arm shaft (A, **Figure 64**) part way into the rocker arm support (B) in its original position.

6. Install a rocker arm (C, **Figure 64**) into its original position and push the shaft part way through the rocker arm.

7. Align the notch in the rocker arm shaft (A, **Figure 65**) with the mating bolt hole (B) in the support and install the shaft all the way. Check for correct alignment (**Figure 66**).

8. Repeat Step 6 and Step 7 for the remaining rocker arm and shaft.

Rocker Arm Component Inspection

When measuring the rocker arm components, compare the actual measurements to the specifications in **Table 2**. Replace any part that is damaged or out of specification as described in this section.

1. Inspect the rocker arm pads and ball sockets (**Figure 67**) for pitting and excessive wear.

2. Examine the rocker arm shaft (**Figure 68**) for scoring, ridge wear or other damage. If these conditions are present, replace the rocker arm shaft. If the shaft does not show any wear or damage, continue with Step 3.

3. Check the rocker arm bushing (**Figure 69**) for wear or scoring.

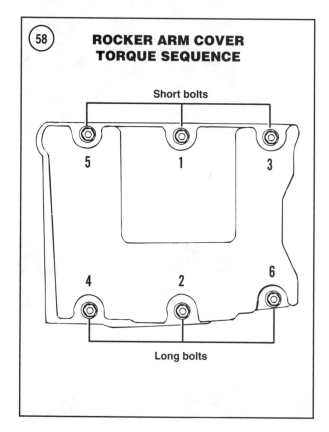

ROCKER ARM COVER TORQUE SEQUENCE

Short bolts

5   1   3

4   2   6

Long bolts

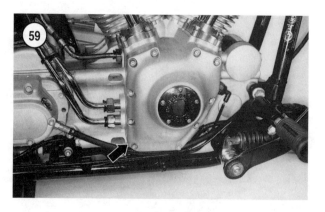

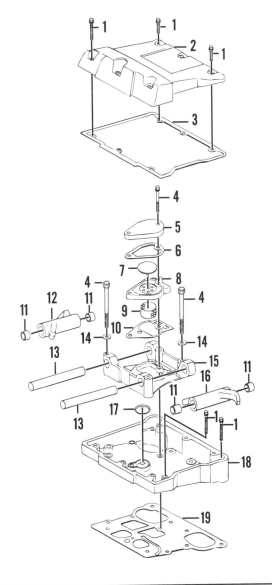

ROCKER ARM ASSEMBLY

1. Bolt
2. Rocker arm cover
3. Gasket
4. Bolt
5. Breather cover*
6. Gasket*
7. Valve*
8. Breather baffle*
9. Filter element*
10. Gasket*
11. Bushing
12. Rocker arm
    Intake—front cylinder
    Exhast—rear cylinder
13. Rocker arm shaft
14. Washer
15. Rocker arm support
16. Rocker arm
    Intake—rear cylinder
    Exhaust—front cylinder
17. O-ring seal
18. Rocker arm housing
19. Gasket

*Items 5-10 are combined into an integral unit on 2002-on models.

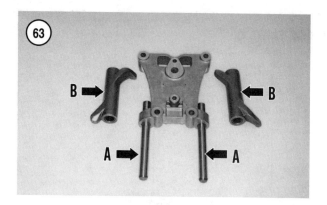

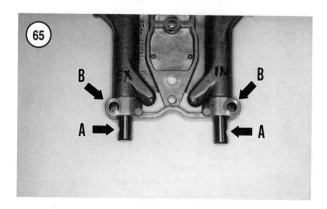

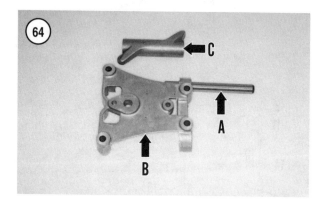

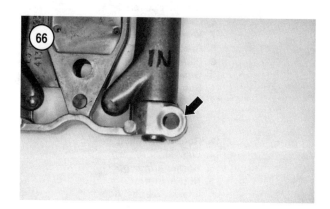

4. Measure the rocker arm shaft diameter (**Figure 70**) where it contacts the rocker arm bushing and rocker arm support. Measure both ends of the shaft. Record each measurement.

5. Measure the rocker arm bushing inside diameter (**Figure 71**) and the rocker arm support (**Figure 72**) inside diameter. Record each measurement.

6. Subtract the measurements taken in Step 4 from those taken in Step 5 to obtain the following rocker arm shaft clearances:

    a. Shaft-to-rocker arm support.

    b. Shaft-to-rocker arm bushing.

7. Replace the rocker arm bushings or the rocker arm support if the clearance exceeds the specifications. Rocker arm bushing replacement is described in this chapter.

8. Inspect the rocker arm shaft contact surfaces in the rocker arm support for wear or elongation.

9. Inspect the gasket surface of the rocker arm cover for damage or warp.

10. Inspect the rocker arm support (**Figure 73**) for damage or warp.

11. Inspect both gasket surfaces of the rocker arm housing for damage or warp.

12. Inspect the lifter cover (**Figure 74**) for cracks or damage.

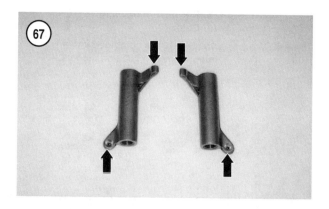

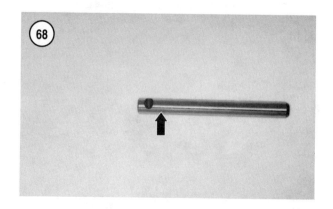

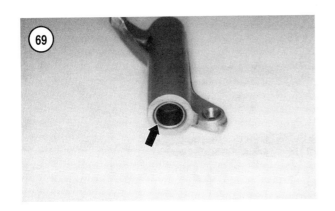

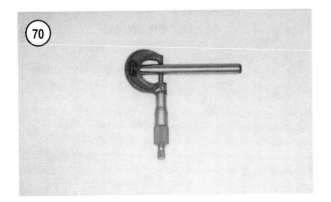

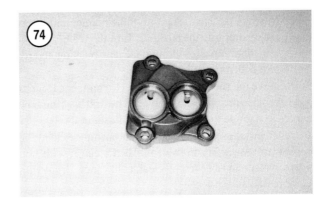

Rocker Arm Bushing Replacement

Each rocker arm is equipped with two bushings (**Figure 69**). Replacement bushings must be reamed after installation. Use the rocker arm bushing line reamer (JIMS part No. 94804-57). If the correct size reamer is unavailable, have the bushings replaced by a Harley-Davidson dealership.

NOTE
Since the new bushings must be reamed, remove one bushing at a time. The opposite bushing is then used as a guide to ream the first bushing.

1. Press one bushing (**Figure 69**) out of the rocker arm. Do not remove the second bushing. If the bushing is difficult to remove, perform the following:
   a. Thread a 9/16 × 18 tap into the bushing.
   b. Support the rocker arm in a press so the tap is at the bottom.
   c. Insert a mandrel through the top of the rocker arm and seat it on top of the tap.
   d. Press on the mandrel to force the bushing and tap out of the rocker arm.
   e. Remove the tap from the bushing and discard the bushing.

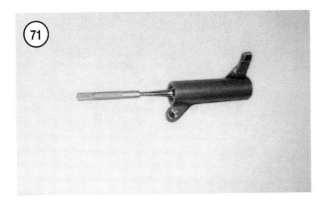

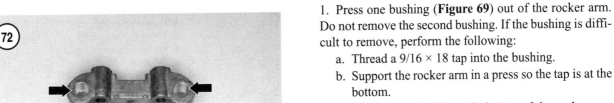

2. Position the new bushing with the split portion facing toward the top of the rocker arm.

3. Press the new bushing into the rocker arm until the bushing's outer surface is flush with the end of rocker arm bore.

4. Ream the new bushing with the bushing line reamer as follows:

  a. Mount the rocker arm in a vise with soft jaws so the new bushing is at the bottom.

CAUTION
Only turn the reamer clockwise. Do not rotate the reamer counterclockwise or the reamer and bushing will be damaged.

  b. Mount a tap handle on top of the reamer and insert the reamer into the bushing. Turn the reamer *clockwise* until it passes through the new bushing and remove it from the bottom side.

5. Remove the rocker arm from the vise and repeat Steps 1-3 to replace the opposite bushing. The first bushing now serves as a guide to ream the second bushing.

6. After installing and reaming both bushings, clean the rocker arm assembly in solvent. Then clean it with hot, soapy water and rinse it with clear, cold water. Dry it with compressed air.

7. Measure the inside diameter of each bushing. When properly reamed, the bushings must provide the shaft clearance listed in **Table 2**.

Pushrod Inspection

1. Clean the pushrods in solvent and dry them with compressed air.

2. Check the pushrods for bending, cracks and worn or damaged ball heads (**Figure 75**).

3. Replace any damaged pushrods.

CYLINDER HEAD

The cylinder head procedures are shown on the rear cylinder (**Figure 76**). The same procedures also relate to the front cylinder. Any differences are noted.

NOTE
The following procedures are shown with the engine removed to better illustrate the steps.

Removal

1. Remove the rocker arm assemblies and pushrods as described in this chapter.

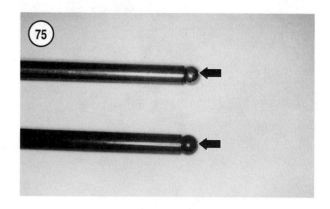

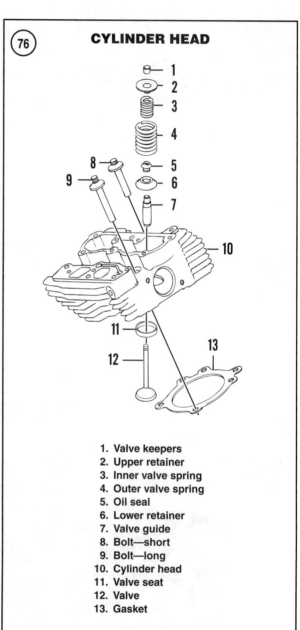

CYLINDER HEAD

1. Valve keepers
2. Upper retainer
3. Inner valve spring
4. Outer valve spring
5. Oil seal
6. Lower retainer
7. Valve guide
8. Bolt—short
9. Bolt—long
10. Cylinder head
11. Valve seat
12. Valve
13. Gasket

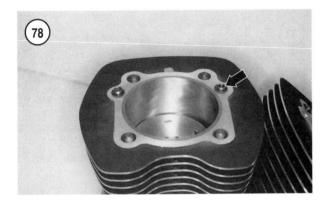

2. Using a crisscross pattern, loosen the four cylinder head bolts (**Figure 77**) 1/8 turn at a time. Remove the four bolts and note the position of the short and long bolts.

3. Tap the cylinder head with a rubber mallet to free it, then lift it off the cylinder.

4. Remove the cylinder head gasket.

5. Remove the two O-rings and the cylinder head dowel pins (**Figure 78**).

6. Repeat these steps to remove the opposite cylinder head.

4

Inspection

1. Thoroughly clean the outside of the cylinder head. Use a stiff brush, soap and water to remove all debris from the cooling fins (**Figure 79**). If necessary, use a piece of wood and scrape away any lodged dirt. Clogged cooling fins can cause overheating and lead to engine damage.

2. *Without removing the valves*, use a wire brush to remove all carbon deposits from the combustion chamber. Use a fine wire brush dipped in solvent or make a scraper from hardwood. Be careful not to damage the head, valves or spark plug threads.

> *CAUTION*
> *Cleaning the combustion chamber with the valves removed can damage the valve seat surfaces. A damaged or even slightly scratched valve seat will cause poor valve seating.*

3. Examine the spark plug threads in the cylinder head for damage. If there is minor damage or if the threads are dirty or clogged with carbon, use a spark plug thread tap (**Figure 80**) to clean the threads following the manufacturer's instructions. If there is severe thread damage, restore the threads by installing a steel thread insert. Purchase thread insert kits at an automotive supply store or have the kits installed by a Harley-Davidson dealership or machine shop.

> *NOTE*
> *When using a tap to clean spark plug threads, coat the tap with an aluminum tap-cutting fluid or kerosene.*

> *NOTE*
> *Aluminum spark plug threads are commonly damaged due to galling, cross-threading and over-tightening. To prevent galling, apply an antiseize compound on the plug threads before installation and do not overtighten.*

4. After all carbon is removed from the combustion chambers and valve ports, and if the spark plug thread

hole has been repaired, clean the entire head in solvent. Dry it with compressed air.

5. Examine the crown on the piston (**Figure 81**). The crown should show no signs of wear or damage. If the crown appears pecked or spongy-looking, also check the spark plug, valves and combustion chamber for aluminum deposits. If these deposits are found, the cylinder has overheated. Check for a lean fuel mixture or other conditions that could cause preignition.

6. Check for cracks in the combustion chamber, the intake port (**Figure 82**) and the exhaust port (**Figure 83**). Replace a cracked head if welding can not repair it.

7. Inspect the exhaust pipe mounting bolts (**Figure 84**) for damage. Repair the threads with a tap if they are damaged.

CAUTION
If the cylinder head is bead-blasted, clean the head thoroughly with solvent, then with hot soapy water. Residual grit seats in small crevices and other areas, and can be hard to get out. Also run a tap through each exposed thread to remove grit from the threads. Residue grit left in the engine will cause premature wear.

8. Thoroughly clean the cylinder head.

9. Measure for warp by placing a straightedge across the gasket surface at several points and attempting to insert a feeler gauge between the straightedge and cylinder head at each location (**Figure 85**). Maximum allowable warp is in **Table 2**. Distortion or nicks in the cylinder head surface could cause an air leak and overheating. If warp exceeds the limit, resurface or replace the cylinder head. Consult a Harley-Davidson dealership or machine shop experienced in this type of work.

10. Check the rocker arm housing mating surfaces for warp (**Figure 86**) using the procedure in Step 9.

11. Make sure the breather channel is clear at each end (**Figure 87**).

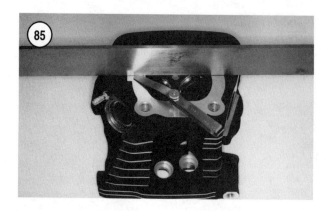

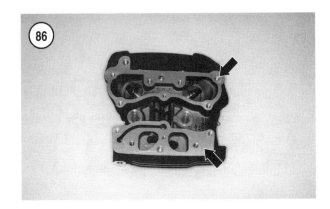

4

12. Check the valves and valve guides as described under *Valves and Valve Components* in this chapter.

Installation

1. If removed, install the piston and cylinder as described in this chapter.

2. Lubricate the cylinder studs and cylinder head bolts as follows:

    a. Clean the cylinder head bolts in solvent and dry with compressed air.

    b. Apply clean engine oil to the cylinder head bolt threads and to the flat shoulder surface on each bolt (**Figure 88**). Wipe excess oil from the bolts, leave only an oil film on these surfaces.

3. Install the two dowel pins (**Figure 78**) into the top of the cylinder.

4. Install a *new* O-ring over each dowel pin. Apply a light coat of clean engine oil to the O-rings.

> *CAUTION*
> *Because the O-rings center the head gasket on the cylinder, install them before installing the head gasket.*

5. Install a *new* cylinder head gasket (**Figure 89**) onto the cylinder.

> *CAUTION*
> *Do not use sealer on the cylinder head gasket. For an aftermarket head gasket, follow the manufacturer's instructions for gasket installation.*

> *NOTE*
> *The cylinder heads are **not** identical. Refer to the FRONT or REAR mark (**Figure 90**) cast into top surface of the cylinder head.*

6. Install the cylinder head (**Figure 91**) onto the cylinder and the dowel pins. Position the head carefully to avoid moving the head gasket out of alignment.

7. Install and finger-tighten the cylinder head bolts. Make sure the short bolts are on the spark plug side.

CAUTION
Failure to follow the torque pattern and sequence in Step 8 may cause cylinder head distortion and gasket leakage.

8. Refer to **Figure 92** for the front and rear cylinder head bolt tightening sequence. Torque the cylinder head bolts as follows:

   a. Starting with bolt No. 1, tighten each bolt in order to 84-97 in.-lb. (9-11 N•m).
   b. Starting with bolt No. 1, tighten each bolt in order to 177-203 in.-lb. (20-23 N•m).
   c. Make a vertical mark with a permanent marker on each bolt head (A, **Figure 93**). Make another mark on the cylinder head (B, **Figure 93**) at a 90° angle, or 1/4 turn from the mark on the bolt head.
   d. Use the marks as a guide and tighten each bolt head 90°, or 1/4 turn, clockwise until the marks are aligned (**Figure 94**).

9. Install the rocker arm assemblies and pushrods as described in this chapter.

VALVES AND VALVE COMPONENTS

Complete valve service requires a number of special tools, including a valve spring compressor to remove and install the valves. The following procedures describe how to check for valve component wear and determine what type of service is required.

Valve Removal

1. Remove the cylinder head as described in this chapter.
2. Install the valve spring compressor (**Figure 95**) squarely over the valve spring upper retainer (**Figure 96**) and against the valve head.

CAUTION
To avoid loss of spring tension, compress the spring only enough to remove the valve keepers.

3. Tighten the valve spring compressor until the valve keepers separate from the valve stem. Lift the valve keepers out through the valve spring compressor with a magnet or needlenose pliers.

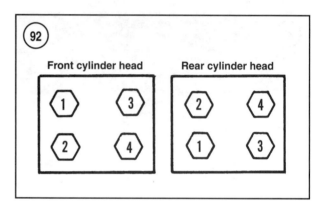

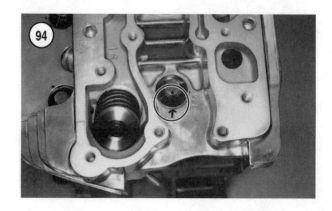

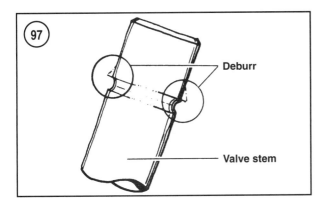

Deburr

Valve stem

4. Gradually loosen the valve spring compressor and re-move it from the cylinder head.

5. Remove the spring retainer and the valve springs.

CAUTION
*Remove any burrs from the valve stem groove before removing the valve (**Figure 97**); otherwise the valve guide will be damaged as the valve stem passes through it.*

6. Remove the valve from the cylinder while rotating it slightly.

7. Remove the valve spring lower retainer.

8. Remove the valve guide oil seal.

CAUTION
Keep the components of each valve assembly together by placing each set in a divided carton, or into separate small boxes or small reclosable plastic bags. Identify the components as either intake or exhaust. If both cylinders are disassembled, also label the components as front and rear. Do not intermix components from the valves or excessive wear may result.

9. Repeat Steps 3-8 to remove the remaining valve.

Valve Inspection

When measuring the valves and valve components in this section, compare the actual measurements to the new and wear limit specifications in **Table 2**. Replace parts that are out of specification or are damaged as described in this section.

1. Clean valves in solvent. Do not gouge or damage the valve seating surface.

2. Inspect the valve face. Minor roughness and pitting (**Figure 98**) can be removed by lapping the valve as described in this chapter. Excessive unevenness to the contact surface indicates the valve is not serviceable.

3. Inspect the valve stem for wear and roughness. Then measure the valve stem outside diameter with a micrometer (**Figure 99**).

4. Remove all carbon and varnish from the valve guides with a stiff spiral wire brush before measuring wear.

5. Measure the valve guide inside diameter with a small hole gauge (**Figure 100**). Measure at the top, center and bottom positions. Then measure the small hole gauge.

6. Determine the valve stem-to-valve guide clearance by subtracting the valve stem outside diameter from the valve guide inner diameter.

7. If a small hole gauge is not available, insert each valve into its guide. Attach a dial indicator to the valve stem

4

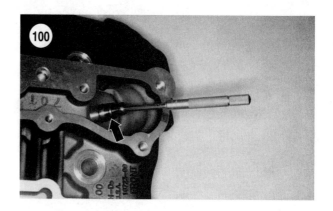

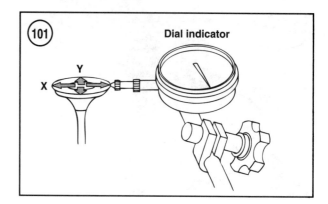

Dial indicator

next to the head (**Figure 101**). Hold the valve slightly off its seat and rock it sideways in both directions 90° to each other. If the valve rocks more than slightly, the guide is probably worn. Take the cylinder head to a Harley-Davidson dealership or machine shop and have the valve guides measured.

8. Check the inner and outer valve springs as follows:

    a. Inspect each of the valve springs (**Figure 102**) for visual damage.

    b. Use a square to visually check the spring for distortion or tilt (**Figure 103**).

    c. Measure the valve spring free length with a vernier caliper (**Figure 104**) and compare it to the specification.

    d. Repeat substeps a-c for each valve spring.

    e. Replace defective springs as a set (inner and outer).

9. Check the valve spring upper and lower retainers seats for cracks or other damage.

10. Check the valve keepers fit on the valve stem end (**Figure 105**). They should index tightly into the valve stem groove.

11. Inspect the valve seats (**Figure 106**) in the cylinder head. If they are worn or burned, they can be reconditioned as described in this chapter. Seats and valves in near-perfect condition can be reconditioned by lapping with fine Carborundum paste.

    a. Clean the valve seat and corresponding valve mating areas with contact cleaner.

    b. Coat the valve seat with layout fluid.

    c. Install the valve into its guide and tap it against its seat. Do not rotate the valve.

    d. Lift the valve out of the guide and measure the seat width at various points around the seat with a vernier caliper.

    e. Compare the seat width with the specification. If the seat width is less than specified or uneven, resurface the seats as described in this chapter.

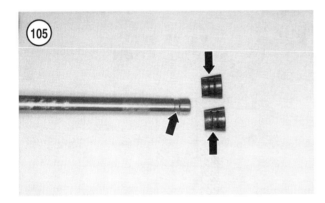

f. Remove all layout fluid residue from the seats and valves.

Valve Installation

1. Clean the end of the valve guide.

2. Install the spring lower retainer (**Figure 107**). Push down until it is seated on the cylinder head surface (**Figure 108**).

3. Coat a valve stem with Torco MPZ, molybdenum disulfide paste or equivalent. Install the valve partway into the guide. Then slowly turn the valve as it enters the oil seal and continue turning it until the valve is installed all the way.

4. Work the valve back and forth in the valve guide to ensure the lubricant is distributed evenly within.

5. Withdraw the valve and apply an additional coat of the lubricant.

6. Reinstall the valve into the valve guide but do not push the valve past the top of the valve guide.

7. Use isopropyl alcohol and thoroughly clean all lubricant from the outer surface of the valve guide.

CAUTION
Do not allow any of the retaining compound to enter the valve guide bore.

8. Apply Loctite Retaining Compound RC/620 or an equivalent to the oil seal seating surface and to the outer surface of the valve guide.

9. Push the valve all the way into the cylinder head until it bottoms (A, **Figure 109**).

CAUTION
The oil seal will be torn as it passes the valve stem keeper groove if the plastic capsule is not installed in Step 10. The capsule is included in the top end gasket set.

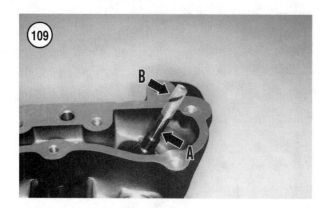

10. Hold the valve in place and install the plastic capsule (B, **Figure 109**) onto the end of the valve stem. Apply a light coat of clean engine oil to the outer surface of the capsule.

11. With the valve held in place, install the oil seal (**Figure 110**) onto the valve stem.

12A. If special tools are used, use the Harley-Davidson valve seal installation tool (part No. HD-34643A) and driver handle (part No. HD-34740) (**Figure 111**) to push the oil seal down until it bottoms on the cylinder head surface.

12B. If special tools are not used, use an appropriate-size deep socket (**Figure 112**) to push the oil seal down until it bottoms on the cylinder head surface.

13. Remove the plastic capsule from the valve stem. Keep the capsule as it will be used on the remaining valves.

14. Install the inner valve spring (**Figure 113**) and make sure it is properly seated on the lower spring retainer.

15. Install the outer valve spring (**Figure 114**) and make sure it is properly seated on the lower spring retainer.

16. Install the upper spring retainer (**Figure 115**) on top of the valve springs.

CAUTION
To avoid loss of spring tension, only compress the springs enough to install the valve keepers.

17. Compress the valve springs with a valve spring compressor (**Figure 95**) and install the valve keepers (**Figure 116**).

18. Make sure both keepers are seated around the valve stem prior to releasing the compressor.

19. Slowly release tension from the compressor and remove it. After removing the compressor, inspect the valve keepers to make sure they are properly seated (**Figure 117**). Tap the end of the valve stem with a *soft-faced* hammer to ensure the keepers are properly seated.

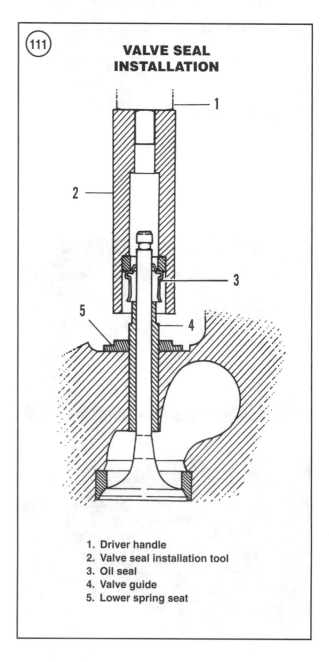

VALVE SEAL INSTALLATION

1. Driver handle
2. Valve seal installation tool
3. Oil seal
4. Valve guide
5. Lower spring seat

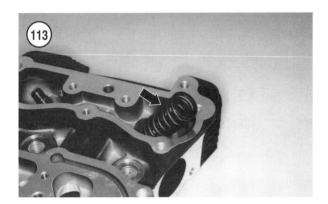

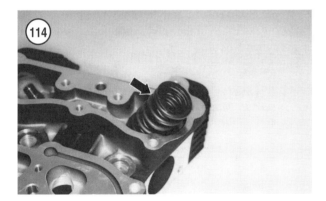

20. Repeat Steps 1-19 for the remaining valves.
21. Install the cylinder head as described in this chapter.

Valve Guide Replacement

Special tools

The following tools or their equivalents are required to replace the valve guides:
1. Driver handle and remover (HD 34740).
2. Valve guide installation sleeve (HD-34741).
3. Valve guide reamer (HD-39932) and T-handle (HD 39847).
4. Valve guide reamer (HD-39964) and honing lubricant.
5. Valve guide hone (HD-34723).
6. Valve guide brush (HD-34751).

Procedure

1. Place the cylinder head on a wooden surface with the combustion chamber side facing down.
2. Shoulderless valve guides (**Figure 118**) are used. Before the valve guides are removed, note and record the shape of the guide that projects into the combustion chamber. If the valve guide installation tool is *not* going to be

used, measure the distance from the face of the guide to the cylinder head surface with a vernier caliper (**Figure 119**). Record the distance for each valve guide. The new valve guides must be installed to this *exact* height dimension.

3. Remove the valve guides as follows:

CAUTION
Use the correct size valve guide removal tool to remove the valve guides or the tool may expand the end of the guide. An expanded guide will widen and damage the guide bore in the cylinder head as it passes through it.

NOTE
The valve guides can either be pressed out or driven out. Pressing the guides out is recommended since it lessens the chance of cylinder head damage.

a. Support the cylinder head so the combustion chamber faces down.

b. To drive the guides out, place the cylinder on a piece of wood.

c. To press the guides out, support the cylinder head in the press with a cylinder head stand (JIMS part No. 39782) so the valve guide is perpendicular to the press table.

d. Insert the driver handle and remover into the top of the valve guide.

e. Press or drive the valve guide out through the combustion chamber.

f. Repeat substeps a-e for the remaining valve guides.

4. Clean the valve guide bores in the cylinder head.

5. Because the valve guide bores in the cylinder head may have enlarged during removal of the old guides, measure each valve guide bore prior to purchasing the new guides. Then purchase the new valve guides to match their respective bore diameters. Determine the bore diameter as follows:

a. Measure the valve guide bore diameter in the cylinder head with a bore gauge or snap gauge. Record the bore diameter.

b. The new valve guide outside diameter must be 0.0020-0.0033 in. (0.050-0.083 mm) larger than the guide bore in the cylinder head. When purchasing new valve guides, measure the new guide's outside diameter with a micrometer. If the new guide's outside diameter is not within this specification, install oversize valve guide(s). See a Harley-Davidson dealership for available sizes and part numbers.

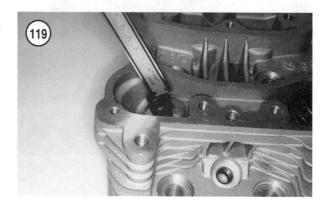

6. Apply a thin coat of molylube or white grease to the entire outer surface of the valve guide before installing it in the cylinder head.

CAUTION
When installing oversize valve guides, make sure to match each guide to its respective bore in the cylinder head.

7. Install the new guide using the driver handle and valve guide installation tools. Press or drive the guide into the cylinder head until the valve guide installation tool bottoms out on the cylinder head surface. When the tool bottoms on the cylinder head surface, the valve guide is installed to the correct height. If the driver handle tool is not used, install the valve guide to the same height recorded prior to removal. Measure the valve guide's installed height using a vernier caliper (**Figure 119**) during installation.

NOTE
Replacement valve guides are sold with a smaller inside diameter than the valve stem. Ream the guide to fit the valve stem.

8. Ream the new valve guide as follows:

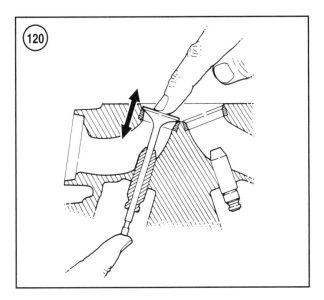

a. Apply a liberal amount of reamer lubricant to the ream bit and to the valve guide bore.

b. Start the reamer straight into the valve guide bore.

CAUTION
Only apply pressure to the end of the drive socket. If pressure is applied to the T-handle, the bore will be uneven, rough cut and tapered.

c. Apply thumb pressure to the end of the drive socket portion of the T-handle while rotating the T-handle *clockwise*. Only *light* pressure is required. Apply additional lubricant to the reamer and into the valve guide while rotating the reamer.

d. Continue to rotate the reamer until the entire bit has traveled through the valve guide and the shank of the reamer rotates freely.

CAUTION
Never back the reamer out through the valve guide as the guide will be damaged.

e. Remove the T-handle from the reamer. Remove the reamer from the combustion chamber side of the cylinder head.

f. Apply low-pressure compressed air to remove the small shavings from the valve guide bore. Then clean the valve guide bore with the small spiral brush.

9. Hone the valve guide as follows:
a. Install the valve guide hone into a high-speed electric drill.
b. Lubricate the valve guide bore and hone stones with the reamer lubricant—*do not use motor oil.*

c. Carefully insert the hone stones into the valve guide bore.
d. Start the drill and move the hone back and forth in the valve guide bore for 10 to 12 complete strokes to obtain a 60° crosshatch pattern.

10. Repeat Steps 8 and 9 for each valve guide.

11. Soak the cylinder head in a container filled with hot, soapy water. Then clean the valve guides with a valve guide brush or an equivalent bristle brush. *Do not use a steel brush.* Do not use cleaning solvent, kerosene or gasoline as these chemicals will not remove all of the abrasive particles produced during the honing operation. Repeat this step until all of the valve guides are thoroughly cleaned. Then rinse the cylinder head and valve guides in clear, cold water and dry them with compressed air.

12. After cleaning and drying the valve guides, apply clean engine oil to the guides to prevent rust.

13. Resurface the valve seats as described in *Valve Seat Reconditioning* in this section.

Valve Seat Inspection

1. Remove all carbon residue from each valve seat. Then clean the cylinder head as described under *Valve Inspection* in this section.

NOTE
Machinist's dye is the most accurate method of checking the valve seat width and position.

2. Check the valve seats in their original locations with machinist's dye as follows:
a. Thoroughly clean the valve face and valve seat with contact cleaner.
b. Spread a thin layer of Prussian blue or machinist's dye evenly on the valve face.
c. Insert the valve into its guide.
d. Support the valve by hand and tap the valve up and down in the cylinder head (**Figure 120**). Do not rotate the valve or the reading will be false.
e. Remove the valve and examine the impression left by the machinist's dye. The impressions on the valve and the seat should be even around their circumferences and the width (**Figure 121**) should be within the specifications in **Table 2**. If the width is beyond the specification or if the impression is uneven, recondition the valve seats.

3. Closely examine the valve seat in the cylinder head (**Figure 106**). It should be smooth and even with a polished seating surface.

4. If the valve seat is in good condition, install the valve as described in this chapter.

5. If the valve seat is not correct, recondition the valve seat as described in this chapter.

Valve Seat Reconditioning

Valve seat reconditioning requires considerable expertise and special tools. In most cases, it is more economical and practical to have these procedures performed by an experienced machinist.

The following procedure is provided for those equipped to perform the task. A valve seat cutter set (HD-35758A) or equivalent is required. Follow the manufacturer's instructions.

Refer to **Figure 122** for valve seat angles. While the valve seat angles for both the intake and exhaust valves are the same, different cutter sizes are required. Also note that a 45° seat angle is specified to grind the seats, while a 46° seat angle is specified to cut the seats.

1. Clean the valve guides as described under *Valve Inspection* in this section.

2. Carefully rotate and insert the solid pilot into the valve guide. Make sure the pilot is correctly seated.

> *CAUTION*
> *Valve seat accuracy depends on a correctly sized and installed pilot.*

3. Using the 45° grinding stone or 46° cutter, descale and clean the valve seat with one or two turns.

> *CAUTION*
> *Measure the valve seat width in the cylinder head (**Figure 121**) after each cut to make sure its size and area are correct. Over-grinding will lower the valves into the cylinder head and of the valve seat will have to be replaced.*

4. If the seat is still pitted or burned, turn the cutter until the surface is clean. Work slowly and carefully to avoid removing too much material from the valve seat.

5. Remove the pilot from the valve guide.

6. Apply a small amount of valve lapping compound to the valve face and install the valve. Rotate the valve against the valve seat using a valve lapping tool. Remove the valve.

7. Measure the valve seat width with a vernier caliper (**Figure 121** and **Figure 122**). Record the measurement to use as a reference point when performing the following steps.

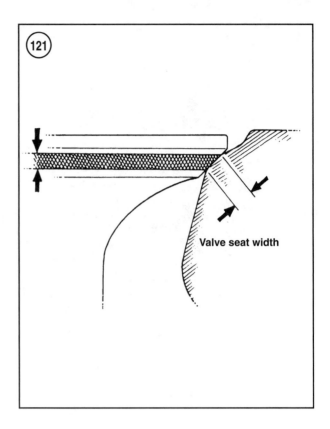

Valve seat width

> *CAUTION*
> *The 31° cutter removes material quickly. Work carefully and check the progress often.*

8. Reinsert the solid pilot into the valve guide. Make sure the pilot is properly seated. Install the 31° cutter onto the solid pilot and lightly cut the seat to remove 1/4 of the existing valve seat.

9. Install the 60° cutter onto the solid pilot and lightly cut the seat to remove the lower 1/4 of the existing valve seat.

10. Measure the valve seat with a vernier caliper. Then fit the 45° grinding stone or 46° cutter onto the solid pilot and cut the valve seat to the specified seat width in **Table 2**.

11. When the valve seat width is correct, check valve seating as follows:

12. Remove the solid pilot from the cylinder head.

13. Inspect the valve seat-to-valve face impression as follows:

  a. Clean the valve seat with contact cleaner.

  b. Spread a thin layer of Prussian Blue or machinist's dye evenly on the valve face.

  c. Insert the valve into its guide.

  d. Support the valve with two fingers and turn it with the valve lapping tool.

  e. Remove the valve and examine the impression left by the Prussian blue or machinist's dye.

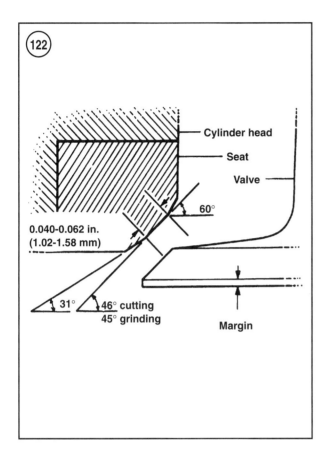

Cylinder head

Seat

Valve

60°

0.040-0.062 in.
(1.02-1.58 mm)

31°   46° cutting
       45° grinding

Margin

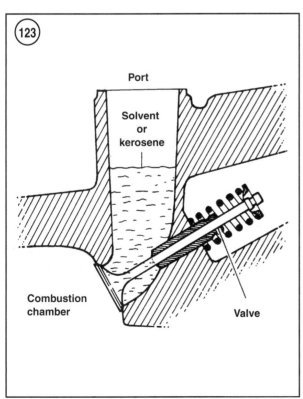

Port

Solvent
or
kerosene

Combustion
chamber

Valve

f. Measure the valve seat width (**Figure 121** and **Figure 122**). Refer to **Table 2** for the correct seat width.

g. The valve seat contact area must be in the center of the valve face area.

14. If the contact area is too high or too wide on the valve, cut the seat with the 31° cutter. This will remove part of the top valve seat area to lower or narrow the contact area.

15. If the contact area is too low or too wide on the valve, use the 60° cutter and remove part of the lower area to raise and widen the contact area.

16. After obtaining the desired valve seat position and angle, use the 45° grinding stone or the 46° cutter and *lightly* clean off any burrs caused by the previous cuts.

17. When the contact area is correct, lap the valve as described in this chapter.

18. Repeat Steps 1-17 for the remaining valve seats.

19. Thoroughly clean the cylinder head and all valve components in solvent, then clean them with detergent and hot water, and rinse in cold water. Dry them with compressed air. Then apply a light coat of engine oil to all non-aluminum surfaces to prevent rust formation.

20. After reconditioning the valve seats, check the valve stem protrusion into the cylinder head as follows:

a. Install the valve into the cylinder head and place a finger on the valve head to keep it seated against the valve seat.

b. Use a vernier caliper and measure the distance from the top of the valve stem to the machined surface of the cylinder head (**Figure 121**).

c. If the protrusion exceeds 2.064 in. (52.43 mm) either the valve seat or valve stem or both are worn. Replace the worn part(s).

CAUTION
Do not grind the end of the valve stem as the hardness of the valve stem will be removed, resulting in premature valve stem wear.

Valve Lapping

If valve wear or distortion is not excessive, attempt to restore the valve seal by lapping the valve to the seat.

After lapping the valves, install the valve assemblies and test each valve seat for a good seal by pouring solvent into the ports (**Figure 123**). If the seal is good, no solvent will leak past the seat surface. If solvent leaks past any seat, the combustion chamber will appear wet. Disassemble the leaking valve and repeat the lapping procedure or recondition the valve as described in this chapter.

1. Smear a light coat of fine grade valve lapping compound on the seating surface of the valve.

2. Insert the valve into the head.

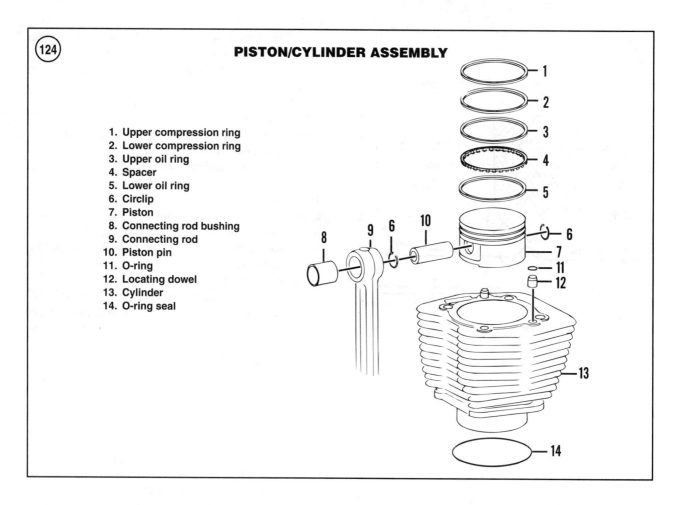

(124)

PISTON/CYLINDER ASSEMBLY

1. Upper compression ring
2. Lower compression ring
3. Upper oil ring
4. Spacer
5. Lower oil ring
6. Circlip
7. Piston
8. Connecting rod bushing
9. Connecting rod
10. Piston pin
11. O-ring
12. Locating dowel
13. Cylinder
14. O-ring seal

3. Wet the suction cup of the lapping tool and stick it onto the head of the valve. Lap the valve to the seat by spinning the tool between both hands while lifting and moving the valve around the seat 1/4 turn at a time.

4. Wipe off the valve and seat frequently to check the progress. Lap only enough to achieve a precise seating ring around the valve head.

5. Closely examine the valve seat in the cylinder head. The seat must be smooth and even with a polished seating ring.

6. Thoroughly clean the valves and cylinder head in solvent to remove all grinding compound residue. Compound left on the valves or the cylinder head will cause rapid engine wear.

7. After installing the valves into the cylinder head, test each valve for proper seating. Pour solvent into the intake and exhaust ports. Solvent should not leak past the valve seats. If the solvent leaks, the combustion chamber will appear wet. If solvent leaks past any of the seats, disassemble that valve assembly and repeat the lapping procedure until there is no leakage.

Valve Seat Replacement

Valve seat replacement requires considerable experience and equipment. Refer this work to a Harley-Davidson dealership or machine shop.

CYLINDER

Refer to **Figure 124**.

Removal

1. Remove the cylinder head as described in this chapter.
2. Remove all dirt and debris from the cylinder base.
3. Remove the two dowel pins and O-rings (**Figure 125**) from the top of the cylinder if they are still in place.
4. Turn the crankshaft until the piston is at bottom dead center (BDC).

NOTE
The front and rear cylinders are identical (same part number). Mark each cylinder so

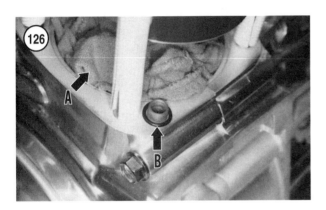

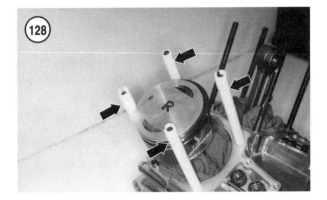

4

they will be reinstalled in their original positions.

5. Pull the cylinder straight up and off the piston and cylinder studs. If necessary, tap around the perimeter of the cylinder with a rubber or plastic mallet.

6. Place clean shop rags (A, **Figure 126**) into the crankcase opening to prevent objects from falling undetected into the crankcase.

7. Remove the O-ring seal (B, **Figure 126**) from the locating dowel. Leave the locating dowels in place unless they are loose.

8. Remove the O-ring (**Figure 127**) from the base of the cylinder.

9. Install a vinyl or rubber hose over each stud (**Figure 128**). This will protect both the piston and the studs from damage.

> *CAUTION*
> *After removing the cylinder, be careful when working around the cylinder studs to avoid bending or damaging them. The slightest bend could cause the stud to fail.*

10. Repeat these steps to remove the other cylinder.

Inspection

To obtain an accurate cylinder bore measurement, the cylinder must be torqued between torque plates (JIMS part No. 1287). Measurements made without the torque plates will be inaccurate and may vary by as much as 0.001 in. (0.025 mm). Refer this procedure to a shop equipped and experienced with this procedure if the tools are not available. The cylinder bore must be thoroughly clean and at room temperature to obtain accurate measurements. Do not measure the cylinder immediately after it has been honed as it will still be warm. Measurements can vary by as much as 0.002 in. (0.051 mm) if the cylinder block is not at room temperature.

1. Thoroughly clean the outside of the cylinder. Use a stiff brush, soap and water to clean all debris from the cooling fins (**Figure 129**). If necessary, use a piece of wood to scrape away lodged dirt. Clogged cooling fins can cause overheating and lead to possible engine damage.

2. Carefully remove all gasket residue from the top and bottom cylinder block gasket surfaces.

3. Thoroughly clean the cylinder with solvent and dry it with compressed air. Lightly oil the cylinder block bore to prevent rust.

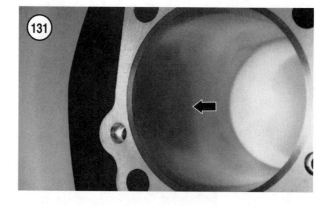

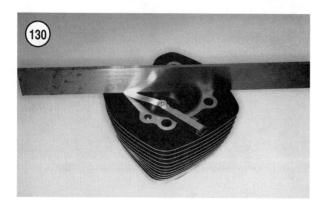

4. Check the top and bottom cylinder gasket surfaces with a straightedge and feeler gauge (**Figure 130**). Replace the cylinder if warp exceeds the limit in **Table 2**.

5. Check the cylinder bore (**Figure 131**) for scuff marks, scratches or other damage.

6. Install the torque plate onto the cylinder (**Figure 132**) following the manufacturer's instructions.

7. Measure the cylinder bore with a bore gauge or inside micrometer at the positions indicated in **Figure 133**. Perform the first measurement 0.500 in. (12.7 mm) below the top of the cylinder (**Figure 134**). Do not measure areas where the rings do not travel.

8. Measure in two axes aligned with the piston pin and at 90 ° to the pin. If the taper or out-of-round measurements exceed the service limits in **Table 2**, bore both cylinders to the next oversize and install oversize pistons and rings. Confirm the accuracy of all measurements and consult with a parts supplier on the availability of replacement parts before having the cylinder serviced.

9. Remove the torque plates.

10. If the cylinders were serviced, wash each cylinder in hot, soapy water to remove the fine grit material left from the boring or honing process. Run a clean white cloth through the cylinder bore. If the cloth shows traces of grit or oil, the bore is not clean. Wash the cylinder until the

cloth passes through cleanly. When the bore is clean, dry it with compressed air, then lubricate it with clean engine oil to prevent the bore from rusting.

> *CAUTION*
> *Only hot, soapy water will completely clean the cylinder bore. Solvent and kerosene cannot wash fine grit out of the cylinder crevices. Abrasive grit left in the cylinder will cause premature engine wear.*

Studs and bolts

The cylinder studs and cylinder head bolts must be in good condition and properly cleaned before the cylinder and cylinder heads are installed. Damaged or dirty studs may cause cylinder head distortion and gasket leaks.

> *CAUTION*
> *The cylinder studs, cylinder head bolts and washers consist of hardened material. Do not substitute them with parts made of a lower grade material. If replacement is required, purchase the parts from the manufacturer.*

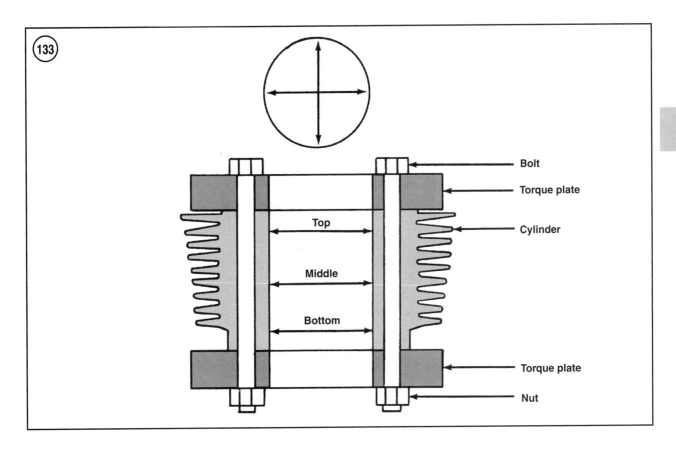

4

1. Inspect the cylinder head bolts. Replace any that are damaged.

2. Examine the cylinder studs for bending, looseness or damage. Replace studs as described under *Cylinder Stud Replacement* in this chapter. If the studs are in good condition, perform Step 3.

3. Cover both crankcase openings with shop rags to prevent debris from falling into the engine.

4. Remove all carbon residue from the cylinder studs and cylinder head bolts as follows:

a. Apply solvent to the cylinder stud and mating cylinder head bolt threads, and thread the bolt onto the stud.

b. Turn the cylinder head bolt back and forth to loosen and remove the carbon residue from the threads. Remove the bolt from the stud. Wipe off the residue with a shop rag moistened in cleaning solvent.

c. Repeat substeps a and b until both thread sets are free of carbon residue.

d. Spray the cylinder stud and cylinder head bolt with an aerosol parts cleaner and allow them to dry.

e. Set the clean bolt aside and install it on the same stud when installing the cylinder head.

5. Repeat Step 4 for each cylinder stud and cylinder head bolt set.

Installation

NOTE
*If a cylinder has been bored oversize, the inner lead-in angle at the base of the bore skirt (**Figure 135**) has been eliminated. This lead-in angle is necessary for the piston rings to safely enter the cylinder bore. If necessary, use a chamfering cone (JIMS*

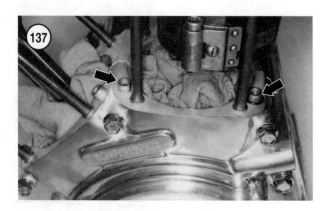

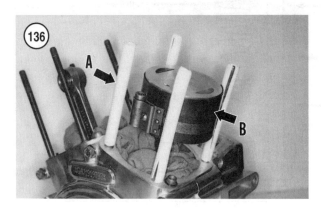

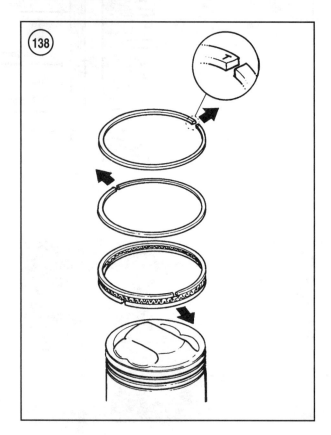

part No. 2078) or a hand grinder with a fine stone to make a new lead-in angle. The finished surface must be smooth so it will not catch and damage the piston rings during installation.

1. If removed, install the pistons and rings as described in this chapter.
2. Remove gasket residue and clean the cylinder as described under *Inspection* in this chapter.
3. Remove the vinyl or rubber hose from each stud (A, **Figure 136**).
4. Install a *new* O-ring onto the base of the cylinder. Apply a light coat of clean engine oil to the O-ring.
5. If removed, install the locating dowels (**Figure 137**) onto the crankcase.
6. Install a *new* O-ring seal (B, **Figure 126**) onto the locating dowel. Apply a light coat of clean engine oil to the O-ring.
7. Turn the crankshaft until the piston is at top dead center (TDC).
8. Lubricate the cylinder bore, piston and piston rings liberally with clean engine oil.
9. Position the top compression ring gap so it is facing the intake port. Then stagger the remaining piston ring end gaps as shown in **Figure 138**.

10. Compress the piston rings with a ring compressor (B, **Figure 136**).

NOTE
Install the cylinder in its original position as noted during removal.

11. Carefully align the cylinder (front facing forward) with the cylinder studs and slide it down until it is over the top of the piston. Continue sliding the cylinder down past the rings. Remove the ring compressor once the piston

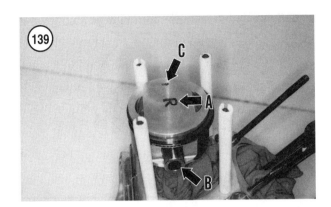

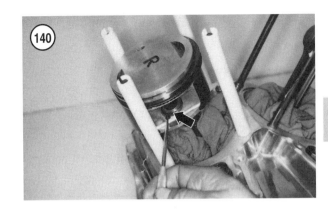

4

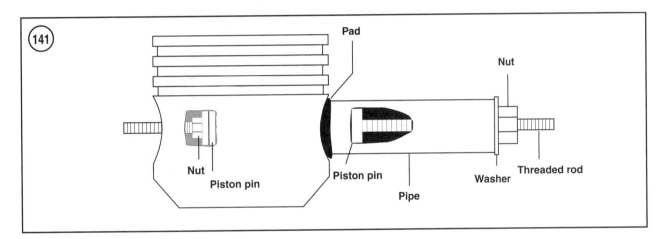

rings enter the cylinder bore. Remove the shop rag from the crankcase opening.

12. Continue to slide the cylinder down until it bottoms out on the crankcase.

13. Repeat Steps 1-12 to install the other cylinder.

14. Install the cylinder heads as described in this chapter.

PISTONS AND PISTON RINGS

Piston and Piston Rings Removal

Refer to **Figure 124**.

1. Remove the cylinder as described in this chapter.

2. Cover the crankcase with clean shop rags.

3. Lightly mark the pistons with F (front) or R (rear) (A, **Figure 139**).

> *WARNING*
> *The piston pin retaining rings may spring out of the piston during removal. Wear safety glasses when removing them in Step 4.*

4. Using an awl, pry the piston pin circlips (**Figure 140**) out of the piston. Place a thumb over the hole to help keep the circlips from flying out during removal.

> *NOTE*
> *Mark the piston pins so they can be reinstalled into their original pistons.*

5. Support the piston and push out the piston pin (B, **Figure 139**). If the piston pin is difficult to remove, use a piston pin removal tool (**Figure 141**).

6. Remove the piston from the connecting rod.

7. Remove the piston rings by using a ring expander tool (**Figure 142**) or spreading them by hand (**Figure 143**).

8. Inspect the pistons, piston pins and pistons rings as described in this chapter.

Piston Inspection

1. If necessary, remove the piston rings as described in this chapter.

2. Carefully clean the carbon from the piston crown (**Figure 144**) with a soft scraper. Large carbon accumulations

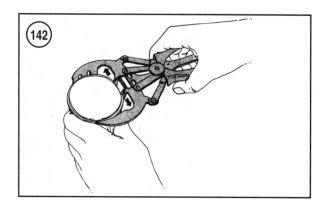

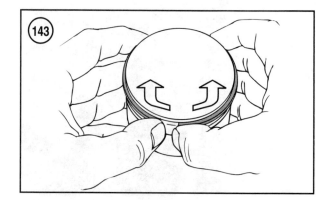

reduce piston cooling and cause detonation and piston damage. Make sure the piston remains properly identified.

> *CAUTION*
> *Be very careful not to gouge or otherwise damage the piston when removing carbon. Never use a wire brush to clean the piston ring grooves. Do not attempt to remove carbon from the sides of the piston above the top ring or from the cylinder bore near the top. Removal of carbon from these two areas may cause increased oil consumption.*

> *CAUTION*
> *The pistons have a special coating on the skirt (**Figure 145**). Do not scrape or use any type of abrasive on this surface as it will be damaged.*

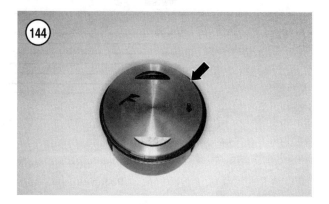

3. After cleaning the piston, examine the crown. The crown should show no signs of wear or damage. If the crown appears pecked or spongy-looking, check the spark plug, valves and combustion chamber for aluminum deposits. If aluminum deposits are found, the engine is overheating.

4. Examine each ring groove for burrs, dented edges or other damage. Pay particular attention to the top compression ring groove as it usually wears more than the others. The oil rings and grooves generally wear less than compression rings and their grooves. If the of oil ring groove is worn or if the oil ring assembly is tight and difficult to remove, the piston skirt may have collapsed due to excessive heat and is permanently deformed. Replace the piston.

5. Check the oil control holes (**Figure 146**) in the piston for carbon or oil sludge buildup. Clean the holes with wire and blow them out with compressed air.

6. Check the piston skirt (**Figure 145**) for cracks or other damage. If a piston shows signs of partial seizure such as aluminum build-up on the piston skirt, replace the piston

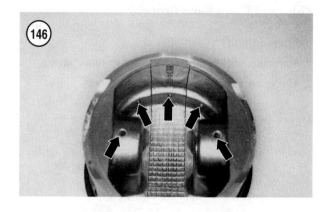

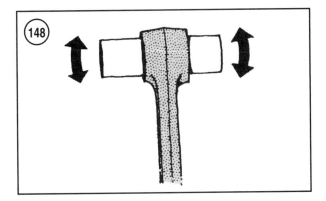

to reduce the possibility of engine noise and further piston seizure.

NOTE
If the piston skirt is worn or scuffed un-evenly from side-to-side, the connecting rod may be bent or twisted.

7. Check the retaining ring groove (**Figure 147**) on each side for wear, cracks or other damage. If the grooves are questionable, check the circlip fit by installing a new circlip into each groove, then attempt to move the circlip from side-to-side. If the circlip has any side play, the groove is worn and the piston must be replaced.

8. Measure piston-to-cylinder clearance as described under *Piston Clearance* in this chapter.

9. If the piston needs to be replaced, select a new piston as described under *Piston Clearance* in this chapter. If the piston, rings and cylinder are not damaged and are dimensionally correct, they can be reused.

Piston Pin Inspection and Clearance

1. Clean the piston pin in solvent and dry it thoroughly.

2. Inspect the piston pin for chrome flaking or cracks. Replace if necessary.

3. Oil the piston pin and install it in the connecting rod (**Figure 148**). Slowly rotate the piston pin and check for radial play.

4. Oil the piston pin and install it in the piston (**Figure 149**). Check the piston pin for excessive play.

5. To measure piston pin-to-piston clearance, perform the following:

    a. Measure the piston pin outer diameter with a micrometer (**Figure 150**).

    b. Measure the inside diameter of the piston pin bore (**Figure 151**) with a telescoping gauge. Measure the telescoping gauge with a micrometer.

c. Subtract the piston pin outer diameter from the piston pin bore to obtain the clearance dimension. Check it against the specification in **Table 2**.

d. If it is out of specification, replace the piston and/or the piston pin.

6. Replace the piston pin and/or piston or connecting rod if necessary.

Piston Clearance

1. Make sure the piston skirt (**Figure 145**) and cylinder bore (**Figure 131**) are clean and dry.

2. Measure the cylinder bore with a bore gauge (**Figure 134**) as described under *Cylinder Inspection* in this chapter.

3. Measure the piston diameter with a micrometer as follows:

a. Hold the micrometer at the bottom of the piston skirt at a right angle to the piston pin bore (**Figure 152**). Adjust the micrometer so the spindle and anvil just touch the skirt.

b. Start below the bottom ring and slowly move the micrometer toward the bottom of the skirt.

c. The micrometer will be loose, then tight at about 0.5 in. (12.7 mm) from the bottom, then loose again.

d. Measure the piston skirt at the tightest point.

4. Subtract the piston diameter from the largest bore diameter; the difference is piston-to-cylinder clearance. If the clearance exceeds the specification in **Table 2**, the pistons should be replaced and the cylinders bored oversize and then honed. Purchase the new pistons first. Measure their diameter and add the specified clearance to determine the proper cylinder bore diameter.

Piston Pin Bushing in Connecting Rod Inspection and Replacement

The piston pin bushings are reamed to provide correct piston pin-to-bushing clearance. This clearance is critical in preventing pin knock and top end damage.

1. Inspect the piston pin bushings (**Figure 153**) for excessive wear or damage such as pit marks, scoring or wear grooves. Then make sure the bushing is not loose. The bushing must be a tight fit in the connecting rods.

2. Measure the piston pin diameter (**Figure 150**) where it contacts the bushing.

3. Measure the piston pin bushing diameter using a snap gauge (**Figure 154**).

4. Subtract the piston pin outer diameter from the bushing inner diameter to determine piston pin-to-connecting rod clearance. Replace the pin and bushing if the clearance exceeds the service limit in **Table 2**.

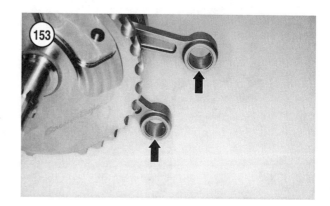

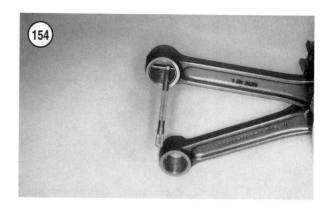

Piston Pin Bushing Replacement

Special tools

The following special tools are required to replace and ream the piston pin bushings. The clamp tool is only required if the bushing is being replaced with the crankcase assembled. If these tools are not available, have a shop with the proper equipment perform the procedure.

1. Connecting rod clamp tool (JIMS part No. 1284) or (HD-95952-33B).

2. Connecting rod bushing tool (JIMS part No. 1051).

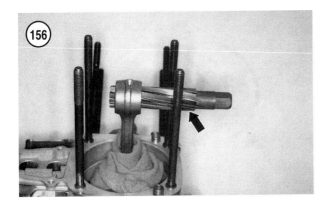

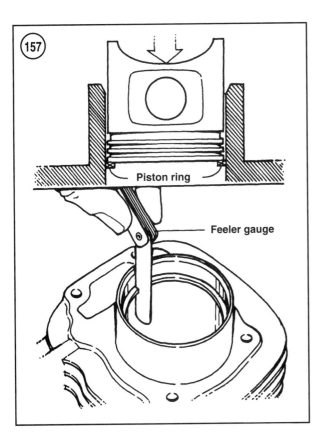

Piston ring

Feeler gauge

3. Bushing reamer tool (JIMS part No. 1726-3).
4. Connecting rod bushing hone (part No. HD-422569).

Procedure

1. Remove two of the plastic hoses protecting the cylinder studs.
2. Install the connecting rod clamping tool as follows:
    a. Install the clamp portion of the connecting rod clamping tool over the connecting rod so the slots engage the cylinder head studs. Do not scratch or bend the studs.
    b. Position the threaded cylinders with the knurled end facing up and install the cylinders onto the studs. Tighten the clamp securely.
    c. Alternately tighten the thumbscrews on the side of the connecting rod. Do not turn only one thumbscrew, as this will move the connecting rod off center and tightening the other thumbscrew will cause the connecting rod to flex or bend.
3. Cover the crankcase opening to keep bushing particles from falling into the engine.

> *NOTE*
> *When installing the new bushing, align the oil slot in the bushing with the oil hole in the connecting rod.*

4. Replace the bushing using the connecting rod bushing tool (**Figure 155**) following the tool manufacturer's instructions. The new bushing must be flush with both sides of the connecting rod.
5. Ream the piston pin with the bushing reamer tool (**Figure 156**) following the manufacturer's instructions.
6. Hone the new bushing to obtain the piston pin clearance in **Table 2**. Use honing oil, not engine oil, when honing the bushing to size.
7. Install the piston pin through the bushing. The pin should move through the bushing smoothly. Confirm pin clearance using a micrometer and bore gauge.
8. Carefully remove all metal debris from the crankcase.

Piston Ring Inspection

1. Clean the piston ring grooves as described under *Piston Inspection*.
2. Inspect the ring grooves for burrs, nicks, or broken or cracked lands. Replace the piston if necessary.
3. Insert one piston ring into the top of its cylinder and push it down approximately 1/2 in. (12.7 mm) using the piston to square it in the bore. Measure the ring end gap with a feeler gauge (**Figure 157**) and compare it with the

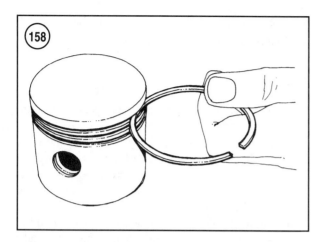

specification in **Table 2**. Replace the piston rings as a set if any one ring end gap measurement is excessive. Repeat Step 3 for each ring.

4. Roll each compression ring around its piston groove as shown in **Figure 158**. The ring should move smoothly with no binding. If a ring binds in its groove, check the groove for damage. Replace the piston if necessary.

Piston Ring Installation

Each piston is equipped with three piston rings: two compression rings (**Figure 159**) and one oil ring assembly (**Figure 160**). The top compression ring is not marked. The lower compression ring is marked with a dot.

Harley-Davidson recommends that *new* piston rings be installed every time the piston is removed. Always lightly hone the cylinder before installing new piston rings.

1. Wash the piston in hot, soapy water. Then rinse it with cold water and dry it with compressed air. Make sure the oil control holes in the lower ring groove are clear.

2. Install the oil ring assembly as follows:

    a. The oil ring consists of three rings: a ribbed spacer ring (A, **Figure 160**) and two steel rings (B).

    b. Install the spacer ring into the lower ring groove. Butt the spacer ring ends together. Do not overlap the ring ends.

    c. Insert one end of the first steel ring into the lower groove so it is below the spacer ring. Then spiral the other end over the piston crown and into the lower groove. To prevent the ring end from scratching the side of the piston, place a piece of shim stock or a thin, flat feeler gauge between the ring and piston.

    d. Repeat substep c to install the other steel ring above the spacer ring.

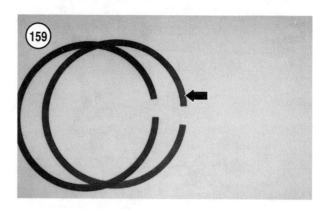

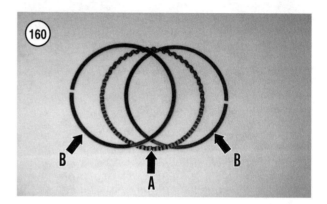

NOTE
*To install the compression rings, use a ring expander as shown in **Figure 142**. Do not expand the rings any more than necessary to install them.*

3. Install the lower compression ring with the dot facing up (**Figure 161**).

4. Install the *new* top compression ring with either side facing up.

5. Check the ring side clearance with a feeler gauge as shown in **Figure 162**. Check the side clearance in several

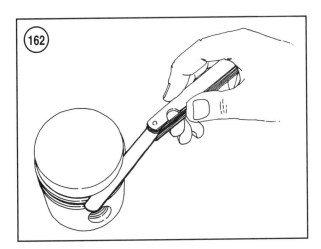

spots around the piston. If the clearance is larger than the service limit in **Table 2**, replace the piston.

6. Stagger the ring gaps around the piston as shown in **Figure 138**.

Piston Installation

1. Cover the crankcase openings to avoid dropping a circlip into the engine.

2. Install a *new* piston pin circlip into one groove in the piston. Make sure the circlip seats in the groove completely.

3. Coat the connecting rod bushing and piston pin with assembly oil.

4. Slide the piston pin into the piston until its end is flush with the piston pin boss (**Figure 163**).

NOTE
The piston markings described in Step 5 are for Harley-Davidson pistons. For aftermarket pistons, follow their manufacturer's directions for piston alignment and installation.

5. Place the piston over the connecting rod with its arrow mark (C, **Figure 139**) facing toward the front of the engine. Install used pistons on their original connecting rods; refer to the marks made on the pistons during removal.

6. Push the piston pin (B, **Figure 139**) through the connecting rod bushing and into the other side of the piston. Push the piston pin in until it bottoms on the circlip.

7. Install the other *new* piston pin circlip (**Figure 164**) into the piston groove. Make sure it seats completely in the piston groove (**Figure 165**).

8. Repeat Steps 1-7 for the other piston.

9. Install the cylinders as described in this chapter.

PUSHRODS

Removal/Installation

Remove and install the pushrods as described under *Rocker Arms And Pushrods* in this chapter.

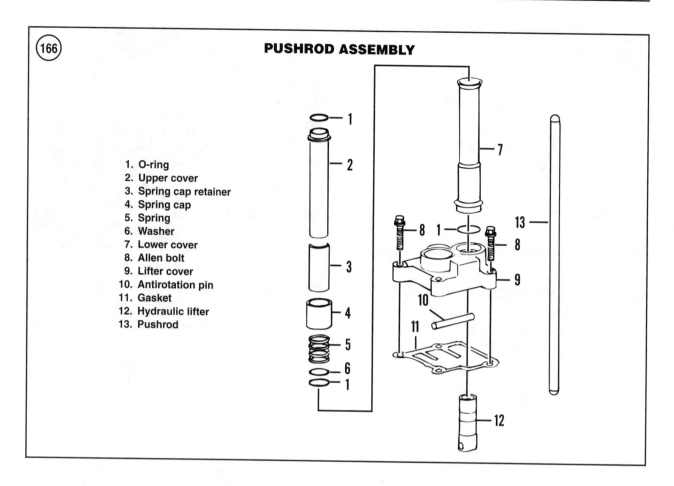

PUSHROD ASSEMBLY

166

1. O-ring
2. Upper cover
3. Spring cap retainer
4. Spring cap
5. Spring
6. Washer
7. Lower cover
8. Allen bolt
9. Lifter cover
10. Antirotation pin
11. Gasket
12. Hydraulic lifter
13. Pushrod

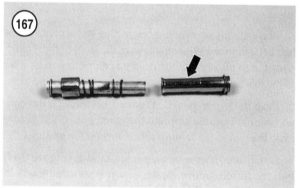

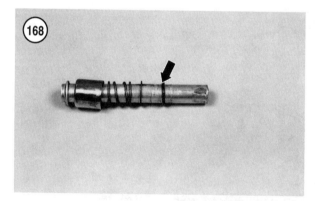

Inspection

1. Disassemble the pushrod assembly (**Figure 166**) as follows:

   a. Remove the lower cover (**Figure 167**).
   b. Remove the O-ring (**Figure 168**).
   c. Remove the washer (**Figure 169**).
   d. Remove the spring (**Figure 170**).
   e. Remove the spring cap (**Figure 171**).

2. Check the upper cover assembly (**Figure 172**) as follows:

   a. Check the spring for sagging or cracking.
   b. Check the spacer for deformation or damage.
   c. Check the pushrod covers for cracking or damage.

3. Check the pushrod ends (**Figure 173**) for wear.

4. Roll the pushrods on a surface plate or plate glass, and check for bending.

5. Replace all worn or damaged parts. Install *new* O-rings.

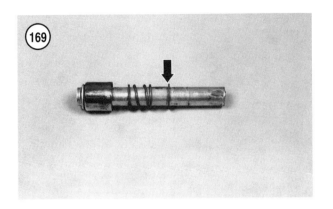

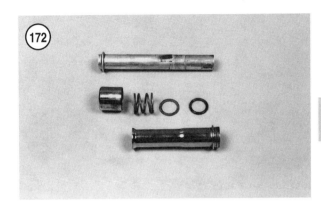

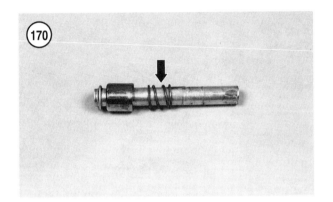

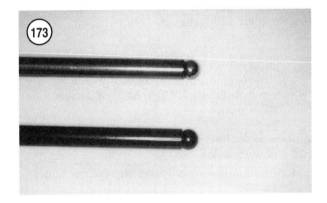

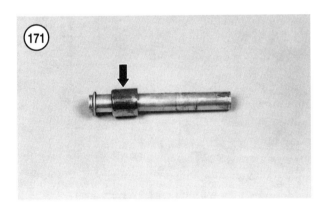

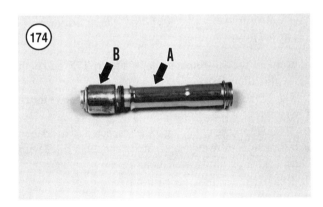

6. Reverse Step 1 to assemble the pushrod assembly. Push the lower cover (A, **Figure 174**) into the spring cap (B) to seat the O-ring.

VALVE LIFTERS

Figure 166 shows a valve lifter in relation to its pushrod and valve lifter cover. The valve lifters and covers are installed on the right side of the engine. During engine operation, the lifters are pumped full of engine oil, thus taking up all play in the valve train. When the engine is turned off, the lifters leak down after a period of time as some of the oil drains out. When the engine is started, the lifters click until they completely refill with oil. The lifters are working properly when they stop clicking after the engine is run for a few minutes. If the clicking persists, there may be a problem with the lifter(s).

Removal

During removal, store lifters in proper sequence so they will be installed in their original position in the crankcase.

1. Remove the pushrods as described under *Rocker Arms And Pushrods* in this chapter.

> *NOTE*
> *In Step 2, loosen the two inner lifter cover Allen bolts with a short 90° Allen wrench, as shown in **Figure 175**, or a ball-end straight Allen wrench.*

2. Remove the lifter cover mounting bolts (**Figure 176**) and remove the cover.

3. Remove the lifter cover gasket from the crankcase.

> *NOTE*
> *Do not intermix the lifters in Step 4. Mark them so they will be installed in their original position.*

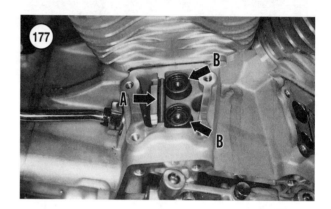

4. Remove the anti-rotation pin (A, **Figure 177**) and both hydraulic lifters (B).

5. Cover the crankcase opening with duct tape (**Figure 178**) to prevent the entry of small parts.

6. If the lifters are not going to be inspected as described in this section, store them upright in a container filled with clean engine oil until installation.

7. Remove the lifter cover gasket.

Inspection

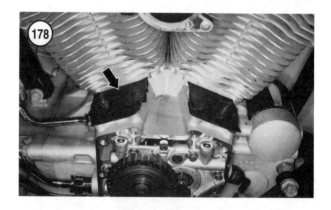

> *NOTE*
> *Place the lifters on a clean, lint-free cloth during inspection. Place inspected lifters in a container of clean engine oil.*

1. Check the pushrod socket (**Figure 179**) in the top of the lifter for wear or damage.

2. Check the lifter roller (**Figure 180**) for pitting, scoring, galling or excessive wear. If the rollers are worn excessively, check the mating cam lobes for the same wear condition.

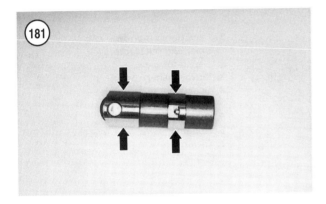

3. Clean the lifter rollers with contact cleaner. Then measure the roller fit and end clearance, and compare them to the specification in **Table 2**. Replace the lifter assembly if either part is worn to the service limit.

4. Determine the lifter-to-crankcase bore clearance as follows:

    a. Measure the lifter bore receptacle in the crankcase and record the measurement.

    b. Measure the lifter outside diameter (**Figure 181**) and record the measurement.

    c. Subtract substep b from substep a to determine the lifter-to-crankcase bore clearance, then compare the measurement to the service limit in **Table 2**. Replace the lifter or crankcase if the clearance is worn to the service limit.

5. If a lifter does not show visual damage, it may be contaminated with dirt or have internal damage. If so, replace it. The lifters are not serviceable and must be replaced as a unit.

6. After inspecting the lifters, store them in a container filled with clean engine oil until installation.

7. If most of the oil has drained out of the lifter, refill it with a pump-type oil can through the oil hole in the side of the lifter.

8. Clean all gasket material from the mating surfaces of the crankcase and the lifter cover.

9. Inspect the lifter cover (**Figure 182**) for cracks or damage.

Installation

1. Remove the duct tape from the crankcase opening (**Figure 178**).

2. Remove two of the lifters from the oil-filled container and keep them vertical.

3. Install the lifters (**Figure 183**) into the crankcase receptacles with the flat surfaces facing toward the front and rear of the engine.

CAUTION
Failure to install the anti-rotation pin will allow the lifter to rotate off the camshaft lobe, and cause severe internal engine damage.

4. Install the anti-rotation pin (**Figure 184**). Make sure it is seated correctly within the crankcase receptacle and against the flats on both hydraulic lifters (B, **Figure 177**).

5. Rotate the engine until both lifters for the cylinder head being serviced seat onto the cam's lowest position (base circle). The lifter's top surface will be flush with the top surface of the crankcase surface as shown in **Figure 185**.

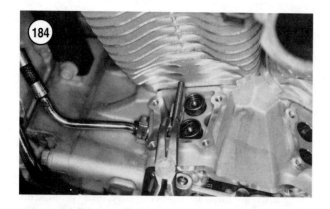

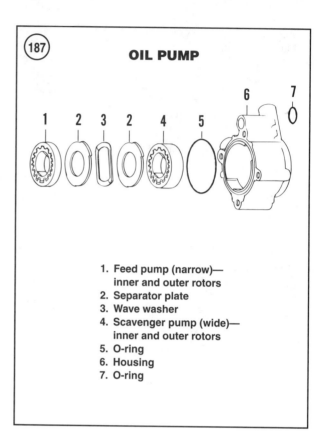

OIL PUMP

1. Feed pump (narrow)—
   inner and outer rotors
2. Separator plate
3. Wave washer
4. Scavenger pump (wide)—
   inner and outer rotors
5. O-ring
6. Housing
7. O-ring

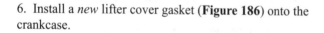

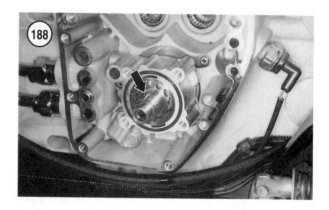

6. Install a *new* lifter cover gasket (**Figure 186**) onto the crankcase.

NOTE
*In Step 2, tighten the two inner lifter cover Allen bolts with a short 90° Allen wrench as shown in **Figure 175**, or ball-end straight Allen wrench.*

7. Install the lifter cover and the mounting bolts (**Figure 176**). Tighten the bolts to the specification in **Table 4**.

8. Repeat Steps 1-7 to install the other set of lifters.

9. Install the pushrods as described under *Rocker Arms And Pushrods* in this chapter.

OIL PUMP

The oil pump is mounted to the right side of the crankcase under the camshaft support plate. The oil pump consists of two sections: a feed pump (narrow rotors) which supplies oil under pressure to the engine components and a scavenger pump (wide rotors) which returns the oil from

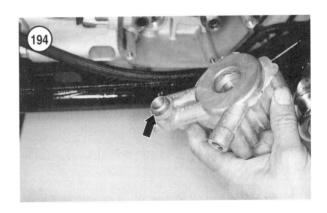

the engine to the oil tank. The oil travels from the engine to the oil tank through two interconnecting hoses.

Disassembly/Removal

The oil pump can be removed with the engine in the frame. Refer to **Figure 187**.

1. Drain the engine oil as described in Chapter Three.

2. Remove the camshaft support plate assembly as described under *Camshaft Support Plate Removal* in this chapter.

3. Remove the feed pump inner and outer rotors (**Figure 188**).

4. Remove the outer separator plate (**Figure 189**), wave washer (**Figure 190**) and the inner separator plate (**Figure 191**).

5. Remove the scavenger pump outer and inner rotors (**Figure 192**).

6. Carefully pull the oil pump body (**Figure 193**) straight off the crankshaft.

7. Remove the O-ring (**Figure 194**) from the backside of the oil pump.

Inspection

1. Clean all parts thoroughly in solvent and place them on a clean, lint-free cloth (**Figure 195**).

2. Inspect both sets of inner and outer rotors (**Figure 196**) for scratches and abrasion.

3. Inspect the oil pump housing for scratches caused by the rotors.

4. Inspect the interior passageways of the oil pump housing (**Figure 197**). Make sure all oil sludge and debris is removed. Blow low-pressure compressed air through all oil pump housing passages.

5. Install the inner rotor into the outer rotor. Check the clearance between the inner tip and outer rotor (**Figure 198**) with a flat feeler gauge. Replace the rotors as a set if the clearance exceeds the dimension in **Table 2**. Also measure the other set of rotors.

6. Measure the thickness of the inner (**Figure 199**) and outer (**Figure 200**) rotors. Both rotors should be the same thickness. If they are not, replace them as a complete set. Also measure the other set of rotors.

4

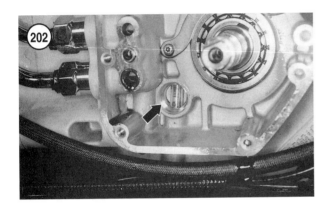

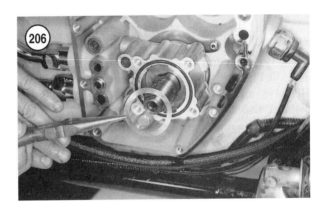

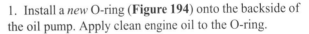

Assembly/Installation

> *NOTE*
> *On oil pumps so equipped, position both in-*
> *ner and outer rotor sets with the punch*
> *marks (**Figure 201**, typical) facing out. If*
> *the rotor set is not marked, position the ro-*
> *tors in either orientation.*

1. Install a *new* O-ring (**Figure 194**) onto the backside of the oil pump. Apply clean engine oil to the O-ring.

2. Carefully push the oil pump body (**Figure 193**) straight onto the crankshaft. Push it on until it bottoms. Make sure the O-ring seats correctly in the crankcase fitting (**Figure 202**).

3. Assemble the scavenge pump outer rotor onto the inner rotor (**Figure 203**).

4. Align the flat on the scavenge inner rotor with the flat on the crankshaft (**Figure 204**) and push the assembly onto the crankshaft and into the oil pump housing (**Figure 192**).

5. Align the tangs (A, **Figure 205**) on the inner separator plate with the oil pump grooves (B) and install the inner separator plate (**Figure 191**).

6. Install the wave washer (**Figure 206**).

7. Align the tangs on the outer separator (A, **Figure 207**) plate with the oil pump grooves (B) and install the outer separator plate (**Figure 189**).

8. Assemble the feed pump outer rotor onto the inner rotor (**Figure 208**).

9. Align the flat on the feed pump inner rotor with the flat on the crankshaft (**Figure 188**) and install the assembly onto the crankshaft and into the oil pump housing.

10. Install the camshaft support plate assembly as described under *Camshaft Support Plate Installation* in this chapter.

11. Refill the engine oil as described in Chapter Three.

OIL TANK AND OIL LINES

The Hose Clamp Pliers (part No. HD 97087-65B) and The Oil Line Remover and Replacement tool (part No. HD-4445) are required to remove and install the oil lines at the oil tank and engine.

There are two sizes of oil line retainers and fittings. Use the correct size tool for all service procedures.

New hose clamps must be used during installation.

Removal/Installation

Refer to **Figure 209**.

1. Remove the seat as described in Chapter Fourteen.

2. Remove the exhaust system as described in Chapter Seven.

3. Remove the battery as described in Chapter Eight.

4. Drain the engine oil as described under *Engine Oil and Filter Change* in Chapter Three.

5. Remove the rear inner fender as described under *Rear Fender Inner Panel Removal/Installation* in Chapter Fourteen.

6. Remove the two bolts (**Figure 210**) securing the electrical panel to the back of the oil tank.

7. Disconnect the oil tank return line and vent line from the oil tank and engine as follows:

> *NOTE*
> *Do not remove the retainer and O-rings from the fitting on the oil tank and crankcase. If the fitting(s) is leaking oil, then the retainer must be removed and repaired.*

   a. At the oil tank, pull the chrome cover (A, **Figure 211**) off the oil line.

   b. Wrap the special tool around the oil line and insert the tool into the retainer (B, **Figure 211**) on the oil tank fitting.

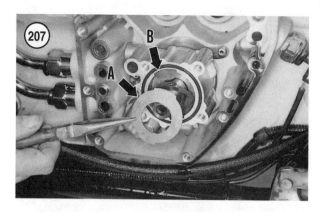

   c. Carefully pull the oil line straight out of the fitting. The retainer must stay within the oil tank fitting.

   d. Repeat substeps b and c for the fittings on the crankcase (**Figure 212**).

8. Remove the two bolts (A, **Figure 213**) behind the fuse block. Lift the fuse block (B) and set it aside.

9. Remove the two bolts and washers (A, **Figure 214**) securing the top bracket.

10. Remove the two screws, washers and flange nuts and remove the battery storage tray (B, **Figure 214**).

11. Remove the clamp securing the drain hose to the frame cross member (**Figure 215**).

12. Remove both clamps securing the oil feed hose (**Figure 216**) and remove the hose from the oil tank.

13. Note the routing of the battery positive cable (C, **Figure 214**) routing behind the oil tank and the frame. It must be installed in the same location during oil tank installation.

14. Carefully remove the oil tank out from the right side of the frame.

15. Install the oil tank by reversing these removal steps. Note the following:

   a. Install *new* clamps on the oil feed hose (**Figure 216**).

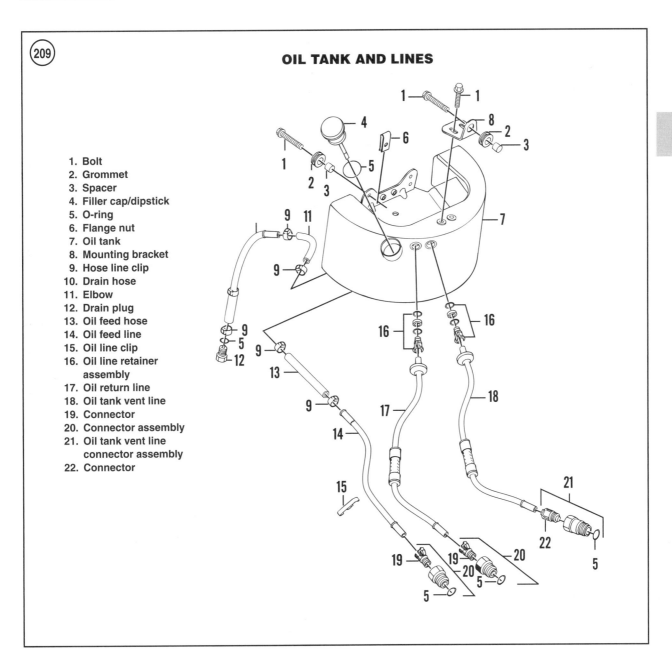

OIL TANK AND LINES

1. Bolt
2. Grommet
3. Spacer
4. Filler cap/dipstick
5. O-ring
6. Flange nut
7. Oil tank
8. Mounting bracket
9. Hose line clip
10. Drain hose
11. Elbow
12. Drain plug
13. Oil feed hose
14. Oil feed line
15. Oil line clip
16. Oil line retainer assembly
17. Oil return line
18. Oil tank vent line
19. Connector
20. Connector assembly
21. Oil tank vent line connector assembly
22. Connector

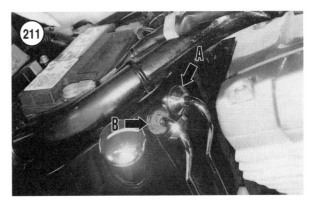

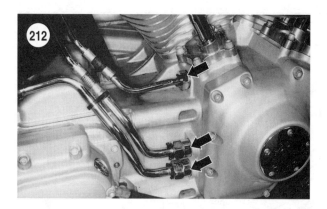

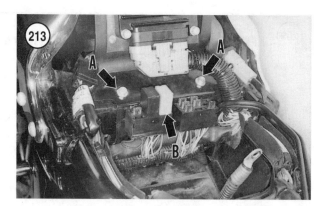

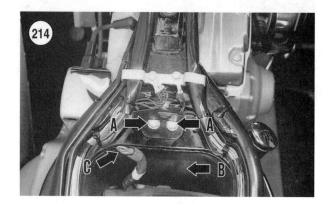

b. Push the oil vent and return lines *straight* into the fittings on the oil tank and crankcase until they lock into place. After the lines have locked into place into the fittings, pull straight out on the lines to make sure they are secure within the fittings.

c. Be sure to correctly route the battery positive cable behind the oil tank and the frame.

d. Refill the engine with oil as described in Chapter Three.

e. Start the engine and check for oil leaks.

f. Turn off the engine and check the oil level; readjust if necessary.

Oil Line Retainers and Fittings Replacement

The Oil Line Remover and Replacement tool (part No. HD-4445) is required to remove and install the oil line retainers at the oil tank and engine. Do not remove the retainers from the engine fittings or oil tank fittings unless the retainers, O-rings and/or spacers are damaged.

There are two sizes of oil line retainers and fittings and the correct size tool for all service procedures. The large tool is used on the crankcase fittings for the oil feed and return lines, the remaining fittings on the crankcase and oil tank use the small tool.

NOTE
This procedure is shown with the crankcase disassembled to better illustrate the steps.

1. Remove the oil line from the fitting on the oil tank and crankcase as previously described in this chapter.

2. Insert the correct size tool into the retainer on the fitting.

3. Squeeze the tabs on the oil line retainer and withdraw the tool, the retainer, both O-rings and the spacer from the fitting (**Figure 217**).

4. Discard the old retainer assembly.

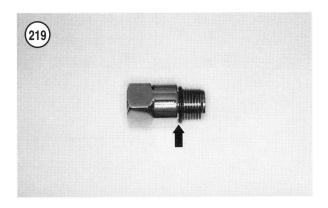

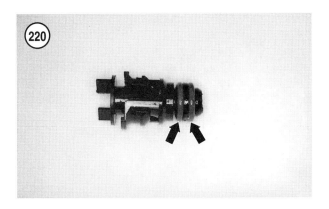

5. Unscrew and remove the fittings from the crankcase (**Figure 218,** typical).

6. Install a *new* O-ring (**Figure 219**) onto the fittings and apply a light coat of clean engine oil to the O-ring. Install the fittings into the crankcase and tighten securely.

7. Insert the correct size O-ring tool into the *new* retainer assembly.

CAUTION
Do not damage the O-rings (Figure 220)
during retainer installation.

8. Insert the new retainer assembly and special tool into the fitting until the tabs on the retainer lock into place.

9. Carefully withdraw the O-ring tool from the retainer assembly leaving the retainer assembly in place.

10. Apply Loctite pipe sealant to the crankcase fittings and tighten securely.

CAMSHAFT SUPPORT PLATE

A camshaft and crankshaft sprocket lock (JIMS part No. 1285), and a camshaft chain tensioner tool (JIMS part No. 1283) are required to remove and install the camshaft support plate. Refer to **Figure 221**.

Removal

1. Remove the exhaust system as described in Chapter Seven.

2. Drain the engine oil as described in Chapter Three.

3. Remove the pushrods, lifters and lifter covers as described in this chapter.

CAUTION
On 2000 models only, the cam position sensor wiring is routed through the camshaft cover. Move the cover out of the way and secure it to the frame with a piece of wire. Do not hang the cover by the wiring.

4. Using a crisscross pattern, loosen then remove the bolts securing the camshaft cover (**Figure 222**), and remove the cover and gasket.

5. To ensure the camshaft primary drive chain is reinstalled in the same direction of travel, mark one of the link plates with a permanent marking pen or a scribe.

6. Relieve the tension on the camshaft primary drive chain as follows:

   a. Install the camshaft chain tensioner tool (A, **Figure 223**) onto the primary chain tensioner (A, **Figure 224**).

CAMSHAFTS AND COVER

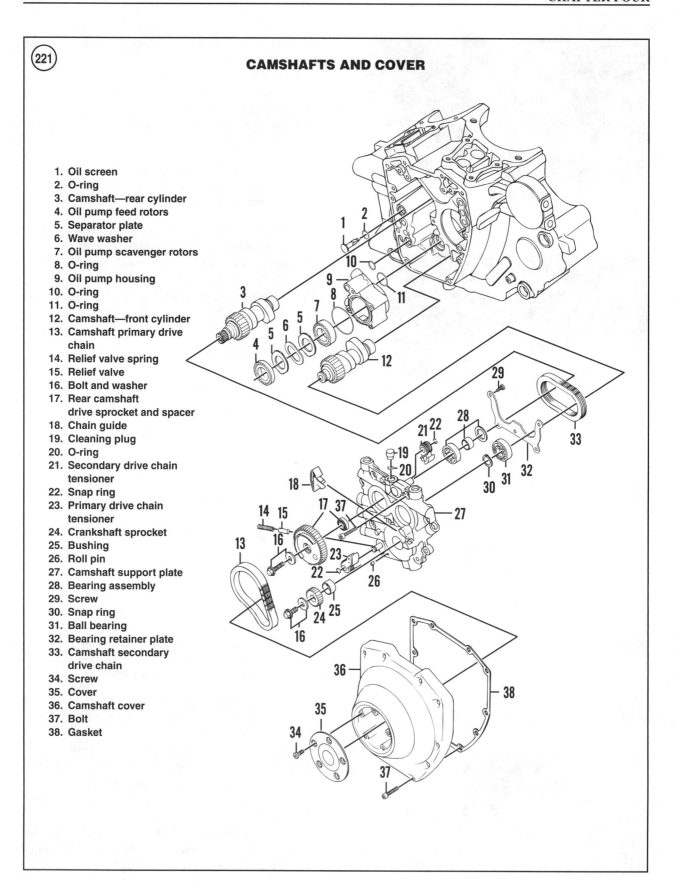

1. Oil screen
2. O-ring
3. Camshaft—rear cylinder
4. Oil pump feed rotors
5. Separator plate
6. Wave washer
7. Oil pump scavenger rotors
8. O-ring
9. Oil pump housing
10. O-ring
11. O-ring
12. Camshaft—front cylinder
13. Camshaft primary drive chain
14. Relief valve spring
15. Relief valve
16. Bolt and washer
17. Rear camshaft drive sprocket and spacer
18. Chain guide
19. Cleaning plug
20. O-ring
21. Secondary drive chain tensioner
22. Snap ring
23. Primary drive chain tensioner
24. Crankshaft sprocket
25. Bushing
26. Roll pin
27. Camshaft support plate
28. Bearing assembly
29. Screw
30. Snap ring
31. Ball bearing
32. Bearing retainer plate
33. Camshaft secondary drive chain
34. Screw
35. Cover
36. Camshaft cover
37. Bolt
38. Gasket

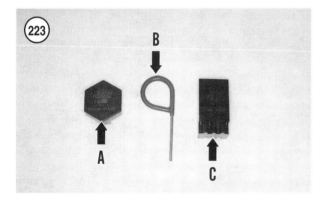

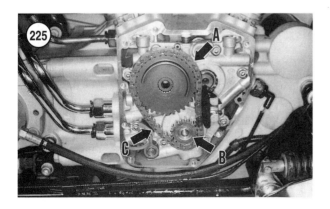

b. Using a wrench, rotate the tool *counterclockwise* and insert the hold pin (B, **Figure 223**) through the hole in the tensioner and into the hole in the support plate. Push the hold pin in until it bottoms (B, **Figure 224**).

c. Remove the wrench and tensioner tool from the tensioner.

7. Install and mesh the camshaft and crankshaft sprocket lock (C, **Figure 223**) between the camshaft and crankshaft sprockets (C, **Figure 224**).

8. Loosen the bolt securing the crankshaft sprocket (D, **Figure 224**).

CAUTION
*The rear camshaft sprocket bolt is secured with a threadlocking compound. Attempt to loosen the bolt with an impact driver or air impact wrench. If this is not successful, evenly heat the bolt head with a propane torch. Use caution, as excessive heat may damage tensioner assembly. Do **not** use excessive force to remove the bolt. If necessary, have a Harley-Davidson dealership remove the bolt.*

9. Loosen the bolt (E, **Figure 224**) securing the rear camshaft sprocket .

10. Remove the special tool installed in Step 6.

11. Remove camshaft sprocket bolt and the crankshaft sprocket bolt and washer.

NOTE
If it is difficult to loosen either sprocket from its respective shaft, use a small pry bar and gently loosen the sprocket(s) from the shaft(s).

12. Remove the rear camshaft drive sprocket (A, **Figure 225**), the crankshaft sprocket (B) and the primary camshaft drive chain (C) as an assembly. Pull the assembly straight off the shafts.

13. Remove the sprocket spacer (**Figure 226**) from the rear camshaft.

14. Squeeze the tabs and remove the camshaft chain guide (**Figure 227**).

15. Loosen the camshaft support plate Allen bolts in the following sequence:

a. Using a crisscross pattern, loosen and remove the four Allen bolts (A, **Figure 228**) securing the support plate to the oil pump assembly.

b. Using a crisscross pattern, loosen and remove the remaining six Allen bolts securing the support plate (B, **Figure 228**) to the crankcase.

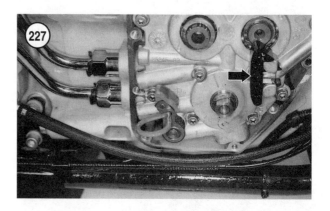

16. Withdraw the camshaft support plate assembly from the crankcase. If necessary, carefully pry the plate loose from the crankcase in the areas where the locating dowels are located (**Figure 229**).

17. Remove the O-ring (A, **Figure 230**) from the oil pump assembly and the lower O-ring (B).

18. Remove the upper O-ring (C, **Figure 230**) and the oil screen (**Figure 231**). Account for the two dowels (D, **Figure 230**).

19. If necessary, disassemble and remove the camshafts as described in this chapter.

Installation

NOTE
*Release the secondary chain tension to install the camshaft inner ends into the crankcase bearings (E, **Figure 230**). If the tension is not released, the inner ends of the camshafts will be pulled together and out of alignment with the bearings, making installation difficult if not impossible.*

1. Release the tension on the camshaft secondary chain tension as follows:

   a. Install the camshaft chain tensioner tool (A, **Figure 223**) onto the camshaft secondary chain tensioner.

   b. Using a wrench, rotate the tool *counterclockwise* (**Figure 232**) and insert the hold pin (A, **Figure 233**) through the hole in the outer surface of the support plate and into the hole in the tensioner. Push the hold pin in until it bottoms.

   c. Remove the wrench and tensioner tool from the tensioner.

2. Push in on the oil pump assembly to make sure it is correctly seated against the crankcase.

3. Install a *new* O-ring (A, **Figure 230**) onto the oil pump assembly and a *new* O-ring (B) onto the lower location. Apply a light coat of clean engine oil to the O-rings.

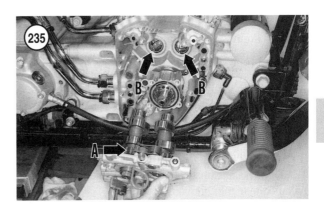

4. Install the oil screen (**Figure 231**) and a *new* upper O-ring (C, **Figure 230**). Apply a light coat of clean engine oil to the O-ring.

5. Lubricate the camshaft needle bearings (E, **Figure 230**) in the crankcase and the camshaft bearing surfaces (B, **Figure 233**) with clean engine oil.

6. If the camshafts were removed from the support plate, make sure the timing marks (**Figure 234**) on each camshaft are aligned with each other. If the marks are not aligned, reposition the camshafts prior to installing the assembly into the crankcase.

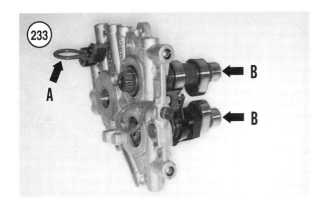

CAUTION
Do not force the camshaft support plate assembly into the crankcase. During installation, the camshaft ends may not be correctly aligned with the needle bearings. If force is applied, the needle bearing(s) will be damaged.

7. If removed, install the two locating dowels (D, **Figure 230**) onto the crankcase.

8. Slowly install the camshaft support plate assembly (A, **Figure 235**) into the crankcase. Guide the camshaft ends into the crankcase needle bearings (B, **Figure 235**). If necessary, slightly rotate and/or wiggle the end of the rear cylinder camshaft to assist in the alignment.

CAUTION
When properly aligned, the camshaft support plate assembly fits snugly against the crankcase mating surface. If they do not meet correctly, do not attempt to pull the parts together with the mounting bolts. Separate the camshaft support plate assembly and determine the cause of the interference.

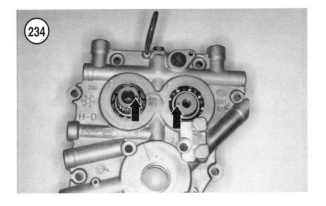

9. Push the camshaft support plate assembly onto the crankcase until it bottoms on the two locating dowels and the crankcase mating surface.

10. Make sure the timing marks on each camshaft are still aligned (**Figure 236**). If they are not aligned, correct the problem at this time.

11. Tighten the six camshaft support plate-to-crankcase Allen bolts in the following sequence:

    a. Install and loosely tighten the six Allen bolts (B, **Figure 228**).

    b. Tighten the Allen bolts in a crisscross pattern to 90-120 in.-lb. (10-14 N•m).

12. Tighten the camshaft four support plate-to-oil pump Allen bolts in the following sequence:

    a. Install the Allen bolts (A, **Figure 228**). Tighten the bolts until they just contact the support plate, then back them out 1/4 turn.

    b. Rotate the engine until the oil pump is in neutral center with no load on it.

    c. Tighten the bolts until they are snug against the support plate. Then tighten the Allen bolts in a crisscross pattern to 10-14 ft.-lb. (14-19 N•m).

13. After all ten Allen bolts are tightened, check the perimeter of the support plate to make sure it is seated against the crankcase mating surface.

14. Install an angled pick into the crankcase opening and against the secondary camshaft chain tensioner shoe (A, **Figure 237**). *Slowly* release the hold pin (B) and allow the tensioner shoe to gradually contact the chain surface. If it is released too fast, the shoe surface will slam against the chain and be damaged.

15. Squeeze the camshaft chain guide tabs and install it (**Figure 227**) onto the two posts.

NOTE
Step 16 is not necessary if the original camshaft support plate, both camshafts, rear camshaft sprocket, crankshaft drive sprocket and the crankshaft assembly are reused. If any of these components have been replaced, Step 16 is necessary to ensure correct alignment between the rear camshaft sprocket and the crankshaft drive sprocket. If the alignment is incorrect, the primary drive chain and both sprockets will bind and cause premature wear.

16. If new parts have been installed, perform the alignment procedure described under *Rear Camshaft Sprocket and Crankshaft Drive Sprocket Alignment*. If all original parts have been installed, proceed to Step 17.

17. Relieve the tension on the camshaft primary drive chain as follows:

    a. Install the camshaft chain tensioner tool (A, **Figure 238**) onto the camshaft primary chain tensioner.

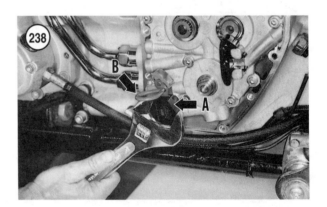

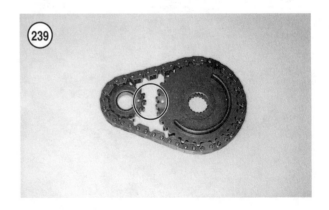

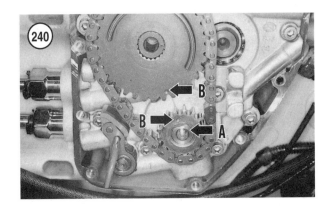

240

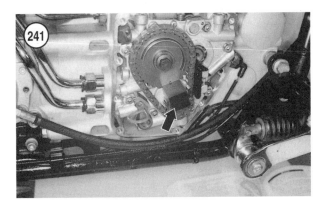

241

242

243

b. Using a wrench, rotate the tool counterclockwise and insert the hold pin (B, **Figure 238**) through the hole in the tensioner and into the hole in the support plate. Push the hold pin in until it bottoms.

c. Remove the wrench and tensioner tool from the tensioner.

18. Install the sprocket spacer (**Figure 226**) onto the rear camshaft with the manufacturer's marks facing the crankcase.

NOTE
Refer to the mark made prior to removal and position the camshaft primary drive chain so it will travel in the same direction. If it is installed incorrectly, the drive chain will wear prematurely.

19. Assemble the rear camshaft sprocket, the crankshaft drive sprocket and the primary drive chain as an assembly. Align the index mark on both sprockets so they face each other as shown in **Figure 239**.

20. On models so equipped, install the Woodruff key onto the rear camshaft.

21. Install the rear camshaft drive sprocket (A, **Figure 225**), the crankshaft sprocket (B), and the primary camshaft drive chain (C) as an assembly onto the crankshaft and rear camshaft. Align the flat on the crankshaft sprocket with the flat on the crankshaft (A, **Figure 240**). Check the alignment of the index mark on both sprockets, and make sure they face each other as shown in B, **Figure 240**. Realign the sprocket index marks if necessary.

22. Apply clean engine oil to the underside of both *new* sprocket bolts prior to installation.

23. Apply a small amount of ThreeBond TB1360 (red), or an equivalent, threadlocking compound to the threads of the *new* rear camshaft sprocket bolt. Do not apply the locking agent to the crankshaft bolt.

24. Install a *new* camshaft sprocket bolt and *new* crankshaft sprocket bolt and washer. Tighten the bolts finger-tight at this time.

25. Install and mesh the camshaft and crankshaft sprocket lock (**Figure 241**) between the camshaft and crankshaft sprockets.

26. Place a flat blade screwdriver (A, **Figure 242**) between the primary camshaft drive chain and the tensioner. Slowly release the hold pin (B, **Figure 242**), then slowly withdraw the screwdriver (**Figure 243**) and allow the tensioner to gradually contact the chain surface. If it is released too fast, the shoe surface will slam against the chain and be damaged.

27. Tighten both bolts as follows:

a. Tighten both bolts to 15 ft.-lb. (20 N•m).

b. Loosen both bolts one complete revolution (360°).

c. Tighten the rear camshaft bolt (**Figure 244**) to 34 ft.-lb. (46 N•m).

d. Tighten the crankshaft bolt to (**Figure 245**) 24 ft.-lb. (33 N•m).

28. Remove the tool (**Figure 241**) installed in Step 25.

29. Install a *new* camshaft cover gasket (**Figure 246**) onto the crankcase.

30. On 2000 models only, install the camshaft cover (**Figure 222**) onto the crankcase. Make sure the cam position sensor wiring is correctly positioned. Install the bolts and tighten them securely in a crisscross pattern.

31. Install the lifter covers, lifters and pushrods as described in this chapter.

32. Install the exhaust system as described in Chapter Seven.

Rear Camshaft Sprocket and Crankshaft Drive Sprocket Alignment

This procedure is required if the camshaft support plate, either or both camshafts, the rear camshaft sprocket, the crankshaft drive sprocket and/or the crankshaft assembly have been replaced.

If alignment between the rear camshaft sprocket and the crankshaft drive sprocket is incorrect, the primary drive chain and both sprockets will bind and cause premature wear.

1. Install the sprocket spacer (**Figure 247**) onto the rear camshaft with the manufacturer's marks facing the crankcase.

2. On models so equipped, install the Woodruff key onto the rear camshaft.

3. Apply clean engine oil to the camshaft splines and to the rear camshaft sprocket splines.

4. Install the rear camshaft sprocket onto the camshaft. Install the *used* mounting bolt and flat washer (A, **Figure 248**). Tighten the bolt finger-tight at this time.

> *NOTE*
> *Use a smaller outer diameter washer in Step 5 to allow room for the straightedge to be placed against the flat surface of the crankshaft sprocket face.*

5. Install the crankshaft sprocket (B, **Figure 248**) onto the crankshaft. Install the *used* mounting bolt and a *washer with a smaller outer diameter*. Tighten the bolt finger-tight at this time.

6. Install and mesh the camshaft and crankshaft sprocket lock (**Figure 241**) between the camshaft and crankshaft sprockets.

7. Tighten both bolts as follows:

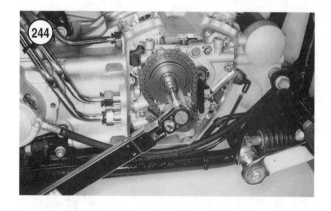

4

10. Try to insert a 0.005 in. (0.127 mm) feeler gauge (B, **Figure 249**) between the straightedge and the camshaft sprocket face.

11A. If the 0.005 in. (0.127 mm) feeler gauge can be inserted, the sprockets are correctly aligned. Remove both sprockets and proceed with Step 17 of *Camshaft Support Plate Installation* in the previous procedure.

11B. If a different thickness feeler gauge can be inserted, indicating a height difference other than 0.005 in. (0.127 mm), the rear camshaft spacer must be changed. Continue to insert feeler gauges of different thickness' until the dimension is determined. Record this dimension as it will be used to choose a new spacer.

12. Remove the rear camshaft sprocket bolt, washer and sprocket.

13. Remove the existing sprocket spacer (**Figure 247**) from the rear camshaft. Compare the part number stamped on the spacer with the part numbers in **Table 5** to determine the thickness.

14A. If the crankshaft sprocket is more than 0.005 in. (0.127 mm) above the camshaft sprocket, install the next *thicker* size spacer under the camshaft sprocket.

14B. If the crankshaft sprocket is less than 0.005 in. (0.127 mm) above the camshaft sprocket, install the next *thinner* size spacer under the camshaft sprocket.

15. Install a new spacer and repeat this procedure until the height difference is 0.005 in. (0.127 mm).

16. After the correct spacer thickness is established, remove the sprockets from the rear camshaft and crankshaft, then proceed with Step 17 of *Camshaft Support Plate Installation* in the previous procedure.

Camshaft Support Plate and Camshafts

A hydraulic press, camshaft chain tensioner tool (JIMS part No. 1283) and camshaft remover and installer (JIMS part No. 1277) are required to perform the following procedure.

Disassembly

1. Remove the camshaft support plate as described in this chapter.

2. Remove the snap ring (**Figure 250**) from the front cylinder camshaft.

3. Release the tension on the camshaft secondary chain tension as follows:

   a. Install the camshaft chain tensioner tool onto the camshaft secondary chain tensioner.

   b. Using a wrench, rotate the tool counterclockwise and insert the hold pin (**Figure 251**) through the

a. Tighten both bolts to 15 ft.-lb. (20 N•m).

b. Loosen both bolts one complete revolution (360°).

c. Tighten the rear camshaft bolt (**Figure 244**) to 34 ft.-lb. (46 N•m).

d. Tighten the crankshaft bolt to (**Figure 245**) 24 ft.-lb. (33 N•m).

8. Remove the special tool from the sprockets.

9. Place a straightedge (A, **Figure 249**) against the face of both sprockets. Push the straightedge against the *crankshaft sprocket* and hold it there.

hole in the outer surface of the support plate and into the hole in the tensioner. Push the hold pin in until it bottoms.

c. Remove the wrench and tensioner tool from the tensioner.

4. Loosen and remove the four T20 Torx screws (**Figure 252**) securing the bearing retainer plate. Remove the bearing retainer plate (**Figure 253**).

5. Press the camshafts and secondary drive chain out of the camshaft support plate as follows:

a. Turn the camshaft support cover face up on two support blocks in a press bed. Make sure the support blocks are tall enough to allow the complete removal of the camshafts from the cover.

b. Install the cups of the camshaft remover and installer onto the top of the camshafts (**Figure 254**) following the manufacturer's instructions.

c. Center the press ram over the center of the tool (**Figure 255**).

d. Slowly press the assembly out of the support cover.

e. Remove the assembly, cover and special tool from the press bed.

6. To ensure the camshaft secondary drive chain is reinstalled in the same direction of travel, mark one of the link plates on the bearing side with a permanent marking pen (**Figure 256**) or scribe.

7. Separate the camshafts from the secondary drive chain.

Inspection

There are no manufacturer's specifications available for the camshaft. The following procedure is a visual inspection to determine if the camshafts require replacement.

1. Check the camshaft lobes (**Figure 257**) for wear. The lobes should not be scored and the edges should be square.

4

2. Inspect the drive chain sprocket (**Figure 258**) for broken or chipped teeth. Also check the teeth for cracking or rounding. If the sprocket is damaged or severely worn, replace the camshaft.

3. If the camshaft sprockets are worn, check the camshaft secondary drive chain (**Figure 259**) for damage.

4. Inspect the external splines (A, **Figure 260**) on the rear cylinder's camshaft and the internal splines (B) on the sprocket. Check for worn or damaged splines and replace either or both parts if necessary. The sprocket must be a tight fit on the camshaft.

5. Check the snap ring groove (**Figure 261**) on the front cylinder's camshaft for wear or damage.

6. Inspect and rotate the ball bearing (**Figure 262**) on each camshaft. They should rotate smoothly with no roughness. If they are damaged, replace the ball bearings as described in this section.

7. Inspect the crankshaft bushing (**Figure 263**) for wear or damage.

Assembly

NOTE
This procedure is shown with the ball bearings in place on the camshafts.

1. Prior to installing the camshaft assembly, relieve the tension on the secondary cam chain tensioner as follows:

   a. Install the camshaft chain tensioner tool (**Figure 264**) onto the camshaft secondary chain tensioner.

   b. Using a wrench, rotate the tool *counterclockwise* (**Figure 265**) and insert the hold pin through the hole in the tensioner and into the hole in the support plate. Push the hold pin in until it bottoms (**Figure 266**).

   c. Remove the wrench and tensioner tool from the tensioner.

2. Assemble the camshafts and the secondary drive chain as follows:

   a. Locate the index marks on the front of the camshafts (**Figure 267**). Transfer these marks to the backside of the sprockets, in the same location with a permanent marking pen or scribe (**Figure 268**). These marks will be used for proper alignment of the camshaft as it is pressed into the camshaft support plate.

> *NOTE*
> *Refer to the mark made on one of the link plates in **Disassembly** Step 6 and position the camshaft secondary drive chain so it travels in the same direction as noted prior to removal. If it is installed incorrectly, the drive chain will wear prematurely.*

   b. Position the camshafts with the index marks facing directly opposite each other (**Figure 269**).

   c. Position the secondary chain with the marked link plate facing up (**Figure 256**) and install the secondary chain onto both camshafts.

   d. Rotate the camshafts in either direction several times and recheck the alignment of the index marks. If necessary, readjust one of the camshafts to achieve correct alignment (**Figure 269**).

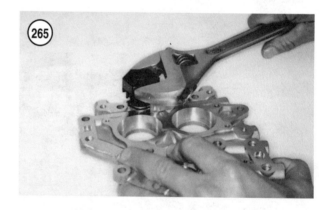

3. Apply a light coat of clean engine oil, or press lube, to the camshaft ends and to the bearing receptacles in the camshaft support plate.

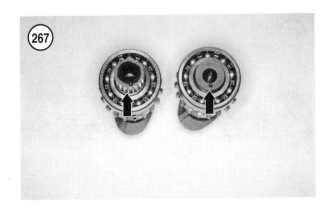

4

4. Place the camshaft support plate on the press bed with the bearing receptacles facing up (**Figure 270**).

5. Position the camshaft assembly on the camshaft support plate with the rear cylinder camshaft (**Figure 271**) located toward the back of the support plate. Align the bearings with the support plate receptacles and hold the assembly in place.

NOTE
*Prior to pressing the camshaft assembly into place, check the alignment of the camshaft index marks on the backside of the sprockets (**Figure 272**). If they are out of alignment, remove the assembly and correct this alignment.*

6. Install the cups of the camshaft remover and installer onto the top of the camshafts (**Figure 273**) following the manufacturer's instructions.

7. Center the press ram over the center of the tool (**Figure 274**).

8. Slowly press the assembly into the support cover until it bottoms.

9. Remove the assembly and special tool from the press bed.

10. Turn the assembly over and make sure the camshaft index marks are still correctly aligned as shown in **Figure 275**.

11. Rotate the camshafts several complete revolutions and check for binding.

12. Install the retainer plate (**Figure 253**).

13. Apply a small amount of ThreeBond TB1342 or an equivalent threadlocking compound to the Torx screw threads. Install the four T20 Torx screws (**Figure 252**) and tighten them securely.

14. Place a flat blade screwdriver between the secondary camshaft drive chain and the tensioner. Slowly release the hold pin (**Figure 251**), then slowly withdraw the screwdriver and allow the tensioner to gradually contact the chain surface. If it is released too fast, the shoe surface will slam against the chain and be damaged.

15. Install the snap ring (**Figure 276**) onto the front cylinder camshaft. Make sure the snap ring is correctly seated in the camshaft groove.

16. Install the camshaft support plate as described in this chapter.

Crankshaft bushing replacement

A crankshaft bushing tool (JIMS part No. 1281) is required to remove and install the crankshaft bushing (**Figure 263**).

1. Place the bushing support tool on the press bed.

NOTE
The crankshaft bushing edge is knurled on the side that faces the primary chain side.

2. Position the camshaft support plate with the primary chain side facing up. Place the camshaft support plate onto the bushing support tool and center the bushing over the tool (**Figure 277**).

3. Install the *remove side* of the driver (**Figure 278**) through the bushing and into the support tool until the shoulder of the driver contacts the edge of the bushing.

4. Press the bushing out of the support plate until the driver collar contacts the support plate.

5. If the bushing support tool was removed, place it on the press bed.

6. Position the camshaft support plate with the secondary chain side facing up. Place the camshaft support plate onto the bushing support tool.

7. Apply a light coat of clean engine oil, or press lube, to the outer surface of the bushing and to the support plate bushing receptacle.

8. Position the bushing into the receptacle with the knurled side facing up.

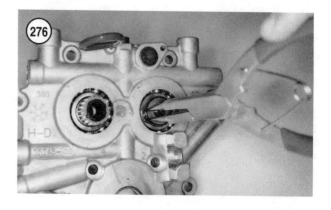

9. Install the *install side* of the driver (**Figure 279**) through the bushing and into the support tool until the driver contacts the edge of the bushing.

10. Press the bushing into the support plate until the driver collar contacts the support plate.

11. Remove the special tools and the support plate from the press bed.

Camshaft Bearing Replacement

Ball bearings

A hydraulic press, camshaft bearing puller (JIMS part No 1280), and camshaft remover and installer (JIMS part No. 1277) are required to remove and install the camshaft ball bearings.

1. Install the camshaft bearing puller tool onto the camshaft ball bearing (**Figure 280**) and remove the camshaft ball bearing following the manufacturer's instructions.

2. Repeat Step 1 for the other camshaft bearing.

NOTE
The ball bearing is installed in the camshaft support plate, not on the camshaft(s).

3. Install the ball bearing(s) into the camshaft support plate using the camshaft remover and installer as follows:

    a. Place the support block on the press bed.

    b. Place the camshaft support plate onto the support block (A, **Figure 281**). Make sure the support plate is indexed correctly into the support block.

    c. Apply a light coat of clean engine oil, or press lube, to the outer surface of the ball bearing and to the support plate bearing receptacle.

    d. Place the ball bearing onto the support plate (B, **Figure 281**).

    e. Install the bearing pilot (**Figure 282**) into the ball bearing.

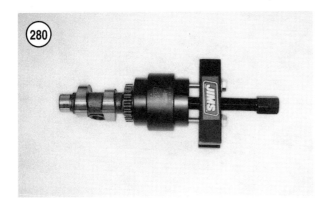

f. Press the bearing straight into the support plate until it bottoms.

g. Remove the pilot from the bearing and remove the support plate from the press bed.

Needle bearings

The inner cam bearing installer (JIMS part No. 1278) is used in the following procedure:

NOTE
*The camshaft needle bearings (**Figure 283**) can be removed with the engine mounted in the frame after the camshaft support plate is removed.*

NOTE
Replace both needle bearings as a set even if only one requires replacement.

1. Remove the camshaft support plate assembly from the engine as described in this chapter.

2. Install the puller portion of the tool set (A, **Figure 284**) part way into the needle bearing. Install a small hose clamp (B) onto the end that is closest to the needle bearing and tighten it. This closes the end of the tool so it can pass through the needle bearing. Push the puller all the way through the needle bearing and remove the hose clamp.

3. Assemble the remainder of the tool components onto the puller portion (**Figure 285**) following the manufacturer's instructions.

4. Place a 5/8 in. wrench on the flats of the puller (A, **Figure 286**).

5. Place a 1 1/8 in. wrench, or an adjustable wrench, on the large nut (B, **Figure 286**).

CAUTION
Do not turn the 5/8 in. wrench as this will damage the special tool and the crankcase receptacle.

6. Hold onto the 5/8 in. wrench (A, **Figure 286**) to keep the puller from rotating. Turn the 1 1/8 in. wrench B, **Figure 286**) *clockwise* on the large nut. Tighten the large nut and pull the needle bearing out of the crankcase receptacle.

7. Disassemble the special tool and remove the needle bearing from it.

8. Repeat Steps 2-7 for the other needle bearing.

9. Apply a light coat of clean engine oil, or press lube, to the outer surface of the *new* needle bearings and to the crankcase needle bearing receptacles (**Figure 287**).

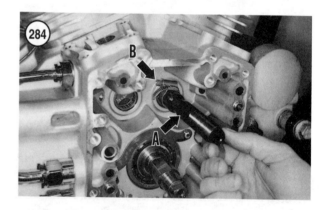

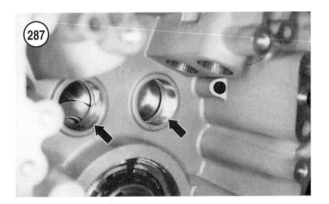

NOTE
The following photographs are shown with the crankcase disassembled to better illustrate the steps.

10. Apply a light coat of clean engine oil to the threads of the screw portion and to the installer plate.

11. Insert the screw portion of the special tool part way into the installer plate.

12. Push the installer onto the screw until it locks into place.

13. Position the new bearing with the manufacturer's marks facing out on the installer (**Figure 288**).

14. Install the installer plate onto the crankcase, aligning the tool to the bearing receptacle (A, **Figure 289**).

15. Install the thumb screws through the installer plate (B, **Figure 289**) and onto the crankcase threaded holes. Tighten the thumb screws securely.

16. Slowly tighten the screw until the bearing starts to enter the crankcase receptacle. Continue to tighten it until the installer contacts the crankcase surface. This will correctly position the needle bearing within the crankcase.

17. Remove the special tools.

18. Repeat Steps 10-17 for the other needle bearing.

Oil Pressure Relief Valve Removal/Installation

NOTE
This procedure is shown with the camshaft assembly removed to better illustrate the steps.

1. Remove the camshaft support plate assembly from the engine as described in this chapter.

2A. If the camshaft assembly is still in place, secure the camshaft support plate in a vise with soft jaws.

2B. If the camshaft assembly has been removed, place the camshaft support plate on a piece of soft wood.

3. Use a 1/8 in. punch to drive out the roll pin (**Figure 290**) securing the valve body and spring. Discard the roll pin (A, **Figure 291**).

4. Remove the valve body (B, **Figure 291**) and spring (C) from the bypass port of the camshaft support plate.

5. Inspect the valve body, spring and bypass port (**Figure 292**) for wear or damage. Replace as necessary.

6. Apply a light coat of clean engine oil to the bypass port and to the valve body.

7. Position the valve body (A, **Figure 293**) with the closed end going into the bypass port first.

8. Install the spring (B, **Figure 293**) into the valve body.

9. Push the valve body and spring into the bypass port, hold them in place and install a *new* roll pin (**Figure 294**). Tap the roll pin in until it bottoms (**Figure 290**).

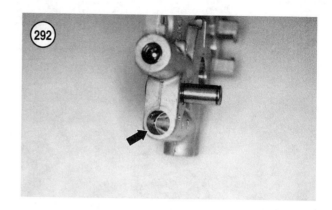

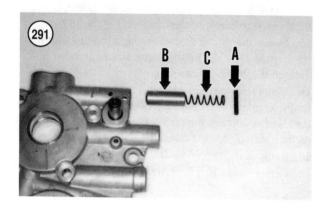

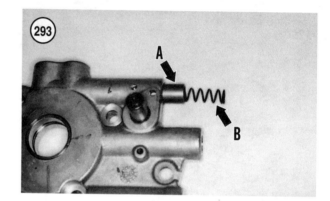

Cleaning Plug Removal/Installation

NOTE
This procedure is shown with the camshaft assembly removed to better illustrate the steps.

1. Remove the camshaft support plate assembly from the engine as described in this chapter.

2A. If the camshaft assembly is still in place, secure the camshaft support plate in a vise with soft jaws.

2B. If the camshaft assembly has been removed, place the camshaft support plate on piece of soft wood.

3. Use a pair of pliers to carefully remove the cleaning plug (**Figure 295**) from the camshaft support plate. Remove the O-ring.

4. Thoroughly clean the cleaning plug receptacle and support plate in solvent. Dry them with compressed air.

5. Apply low-pressure compressed air to the cleaning plug receptacle (**Figure 296**) to blow out any debris. Make sure the oil hole is clear.

6. Install a *new* O-ring onto the cleaning plug and install the cleaning plug. Press it in until it bottoms.

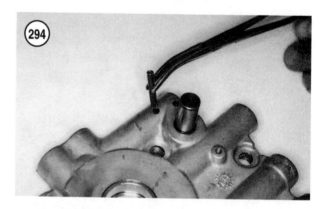

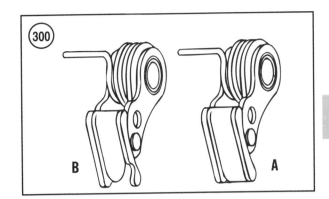

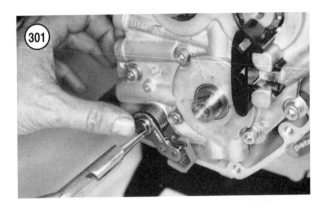

Camshaft Primary and Secondary Chain Tensioner Removal/Inspection/Installation

NOTE
The following illustrations show the primary chain tensioner. They also apply to the secondary chain tensioner.

1. Remove the camshaft primary and/or secondary chain as described in this chapter.

2. Remove the snap ring (**Figure 297**) securing the chain tensioner to the mounting post.

3. Slide the chain tensioner (A, **Figure 298**) off the mounting post.

4. Inspect the chain tensioner pad (A, **Figure 299**) for wear. If the pad surface is worn halfway through (A, **Figure** 300) or chipped (B), replace the assembly.

5. Check the spring (B, **Figure 299**) for sagging or damage. Replace the assembly if necessary.

6. Install the chain tensioner onto the mounting post and insert the spring end into the receptacle in the cover (B, **Figure 298**). Push the chain tension on until it bottoms.

7. Install a *new* snap ring (**Figure 301**). Make sure it is correctly seated in the mounting post groove.

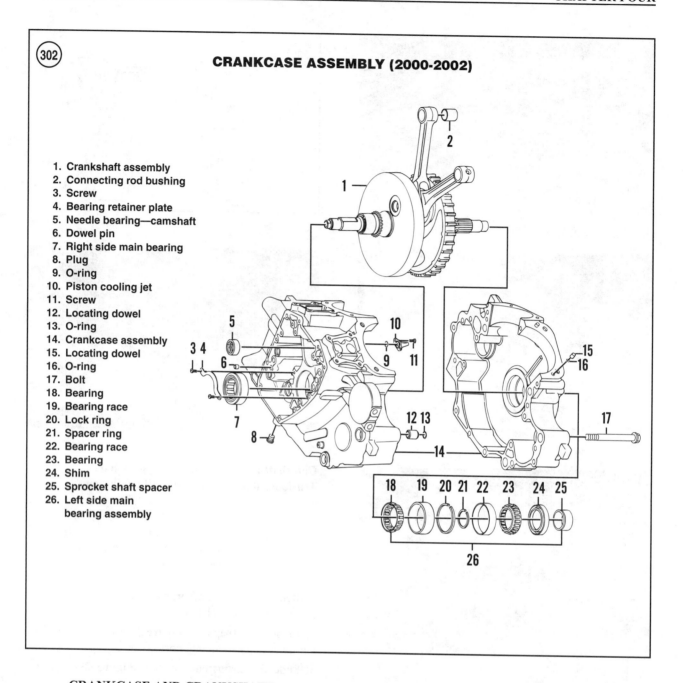

CRANKCASE ASSEMBLY (2000-2002)

302

1. Crankshaft assembly
2. Connecting rod bushing
3. Screw
4. Bearing retainer plate
5. Needle bearing—camshaft
6. Dowel pin
7. Right side main bearing
8. Plug
9. O-ring
10. Piston cooling jet
11. Screw
12. Locating dowel
13. O-ring
14. Crankcase assembly
15. Locating dowel
16. O-ring
17. Bolt
18. Bearing
19. Bearing race
20. Lock ring
21. Spacer ring
22. Bearing race
23. Bearing
24. Shim
25. Sprocket shaft spacer
26. Left side main
    bearing assembly

CRANKCASE AND CRANKSHAFT

Disassembly

A twin cam 88B engine stand (JIMS part No. 1142), base stand (JIMS part No. 1138) and crankcase assembly removing tool (JIMS part No. 1047-TP) are used in some of the following procedures:

CAUTION
On 2000-2002 models, prior to disassembling the crankcase, measure the crankshaft

*end play as described in **Crankshaft End Play Inspection.***

Refer to **Figure 302** and **Figure 303**.

1. Remove the engine from the frame as described in this chapter.

CAUTION
Do not lift the crankcase assembly by the cylinder studs. Bent or damaged cylinder studs may cause the engine to leak oil.

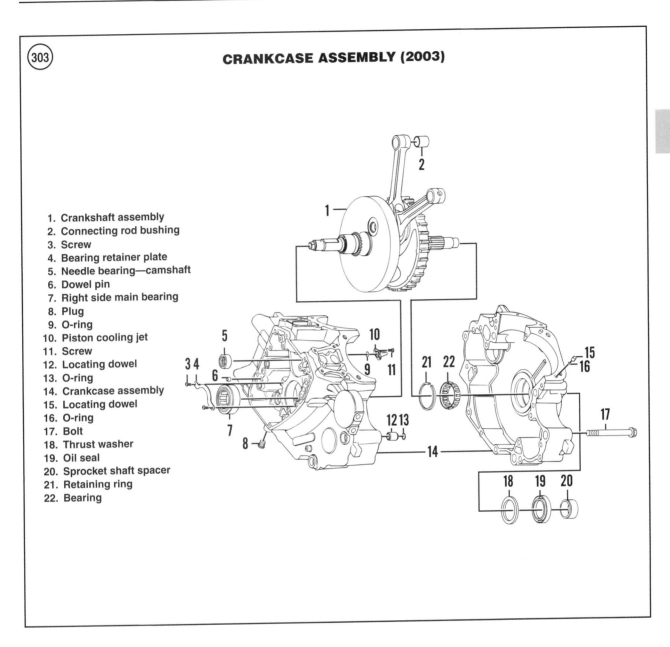

(303)

CRANKCASE ASSEMBLY (2003)

1. Crankshaft assembly
2. Connecting rod bushing
3. Screw
4. Bearing retainer plate
5. Needle bearing—camshaft
6. Dowel pin
7. Right side main bearing
8. Plug
9. O-ring
10. Piston cooling jet
11. Screw
12. Locating dowel
13. O-ring
14. Crankcase assembly
15. Locating dowel
16. O-ring
17. Bolt
18. Thrust washer
19. Oil seal
20. Sprocket shaft spacer
21. Retaining ring
22. Bearing

2. Remove the following components as described in this chapter:

   a. Cylinder heads and cylinders.

   b. Pistons.

   c. Pushrods and valve lifters.

   d. Camshaft assembly.

   e. Oil pump.

   f. Alternator rotor and stator assembly (Chapter Eight).

NOTE
Leave the bolts for the left side off so the case halves can be separated in the following steps.

3. If the special tool is available, attach the crankcase assembly to an engine stand (**Figure 304**) following the manufacturer's instructions.

4. Secure the engine base stand to the workbench.

5. Using the torque pattern shown in **Figure 305**, loosen the bolts in two to three stages and remove them from the left side of the crankcase (**Figure 306**).

6. Place the crankcase assembly on wooden blocks with the camshaft cover (left side) facing up. Use wooden blocks thick enough so the right side of the crankshaft clears the workbench surface.

7. Tap around the perimeter of the crankcase with a plastic mallet and remove the left crankcase half (**Figure 307**).

8. If the crankcase halves will not separate easily, perform the following:

   a. Install a crankcase assembly removing tool (A, **Figure 308**) onto the left side of the crankcase following the manufacturer's instructions.

   b. Apply clean engine oil, or press lube, to the end of the center screw and install it into the tool.

> *CAUTION*
> *Do not use a hand impact driver or air impact wrench on the center screw. They will damage the crankcase halves and the tool.*

   c. Slowly turn the center screw (B, **Figure 308**) with a wrench 1/2 turn at a time. After each turn, tap on the end of the center screw with a brass mallet to relieve the stress on the center screw and the tool.

   d. Repeat substep c until the center screw turns freely and the crankcase halves begin to separate (C, **Figure 308**).

   e. If used, remove the crankcase from the engine stand.

   f. Separate the crankcase halves (**Figure 309**).

   g. Remove the special tool from the left side crankcase unless the crankshaft is going to be removed in Step 10.

9. Remove the locating dowels and O-rings (**Figure 310**) from the right side crankcase.

> *CAUTION*
> *On 2003 models, after the counterbalancer assembly is removed, the crankshaft assembly is no longer secure in the left side crankcase. Be aware of this to avoid dropping the crankshaft assembly.*

10. Remove the counterbalancer assembly as described under *Counterbalancer Assembly* in this chapter.

> *WARNING*
> *Wear safety glasses to press out the crankshaft.*

> *CAUTION*
> *Do not drive the crankshaft out of the crankcase with a hammer.*

11A. On 2000-2002 models, if a hydraulic press is available, press the crankshaft out of the right crankcase half as follows:

   a. Support the right crankcase half on wooden blocks in a press with the outer surface facing up.

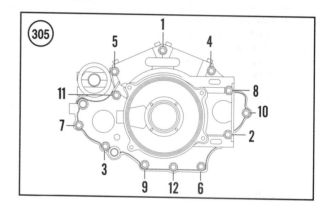

b. Center the press ram on the end of the crankshaft, then press the crankshaft out of the right crankcase half. Have an assistant support the crankshaft as it is being pressed out.

c. Remove the crankshaft.

d. Remove the right crankcase half from the press bed and place it on a workbench for further service.

11B. On 2000-2002 models, if a hydraulic press is not available, perform the following:

a. Install a crankcase assembly removing tool onto the left side of the crankcase following the manufacturer's instructions (**Figure 311**).

b. Apply clean engine oil, or press lube, to the end of the center screw and install it into the tool.

CAUTION
Do not use a hand impact driver or air impact wrench on the center screw, as they will damage the crankcase and the tool.

c. Secure the right side of the crankshaft with a wrench (A, **Figure 312**) to prevent it from rotating in the following step.

d. Slowly turn the center screw with a wrench (B, **Figure 312**) 1/2 turn at a time. After each turn, tap on the end of the center screw with a brass mallet to relieve the stress on the center screw and the tool.

e. Repeat substep d until the center screw pushes the crankshaft out of the left side crankcase half.

f. Remove the special tool from the left side crankcase half.

11C. On 2003 models, lift up and remove the crankshaft assembly from the left side crankcase half.

12A. On 2000-2002 models, to remove the left side crankshaft outer roller bearing and oil seal assembly, perform the following:

a. Place the left side crankcase on the workbench with the outer surface facing up.

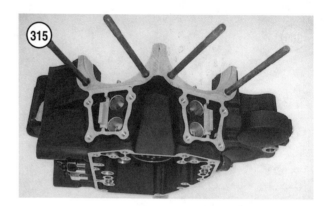

b. Carefully pry the sprocket shaft spacer out of the oil seal.

c. Carefully pry the oil seal out of the crankcase using a wide-blade screwdriver. Support the screwdriver with a rag to prevent damage to the crankcase.

d. Lift the outer roller bearing from the crankcase.

12B. On 2003 models, to remove the left side crankshaft bearing refer to *Left Side Main Bearing Assembly Replacement (2003 Models)* in this section.

Crankcase Cleaning and Inspection

1. Clean both case halves in solvent and dry them with compressed air.

2. Remove all gasket sealer residue from all mating surfaces.

3. Apply a light coat of oil to the races to prevent rust.

4. Inspect the right side (**Figure 313**) and left side (**Figure 314**) case halves for cracks or other damage. Especially in the lower areas.

5. Inspect all machined surfaces (**Figure 315**) for burrs, cracks or other damage.

6. Inspect the case studs (**Figure 316**) for bending, cracks or other damage. If necessary, replace studs as described under *Cylinder Stud Replacement* in this section.

7A. On 2000-2002 models, inspect the left side main bearing races. Refer to **Figure 317** for the outer bearing race and **Figure 318** for the inner bearing race. Also, check the roller bearings for wear or damage. The bearings should turn smoothly with no roughness. If any of these parts are worn, replace the bearing assembly as described under *Left Side Main Bearing Assembly Replacement (2000-2002 Models)* in this section.

7B. On 2003 models, inspect the left side assembled roller bearing for wear or damage. The bearing should turn smoothly with no roughness. If worn, replace the assembled bearing as described under *Left Side Main Bearing Assembly Replacement (2003 Model)* in this section.

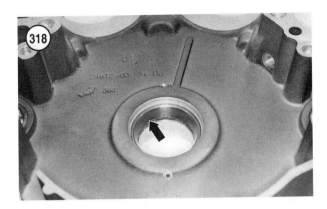

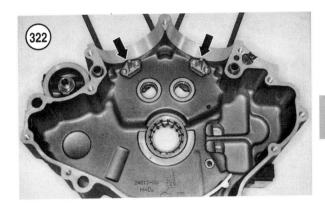

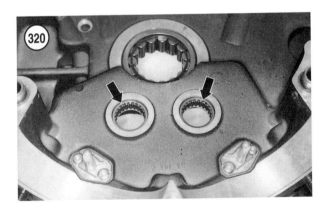

8. Inspect the right side main bearing (**Figure 319**) for wear or damage. The bearing should turn smoothly with no roughness. If it is damaged, replace the bearing assembly as described under *Right Side Main Bearing Replacement* in this section.

9. Inspect the camshaft needle bearings (**Figure 320**) in the right side crankcase for damage. To replace this bearing, refer to *Camshaft Support Plate* in this chapter.

10. Inspect the balance shaft bearings as described under *Balance Shaft Bearing Inspection/Replacement* in this chapter.

11. Inspect the valve lifter bore receptacles (**Figure 321**) for wear or damage. Refer to *Valve Lifters* in this chapter.

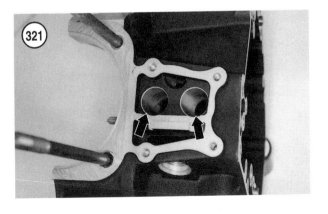

NOTE
If the original piston cooling jets are being reinstalled, apply Loctite No. 222 (purple) or an equivalent threadlocking compound to the screw threads prior to installation.

12. Make sure the piston cooling jets (**Figure 322**) are clear. If necessary, remove the T20 Torx mounting screws (**Figure 323**), cooling jets and O-rings. Clean the oil jets with compressed air. Install *new* O-rings and tighten the screws securely.

13. Check the oil filter fitting threads (**Figure 324**) for damage. Repair or replace if necessary.

14. If necessary, remove the oil gallery plugs and clean the oil paths with solvent. Refer to **Figure 325** and **Figure 326**. After cleaning the oil paths, apply compressed air to clear out any solvent residue. Apply Loctite pipe sealant to the plug threads and tighten securely.

15. Inspect the threaded holes for the transmission mounting bolts. Refer to **Figure 327** and **Figure 328**. Clean out with thread tap if necessary.

Crankshaft and Connecting Rods
Cleaning and Inspection

If any portion of the crankshaft and/or connecting rods are worn or damaged, replace them as one assembly. If necessary, have the crankshaft overhauled by a Harley-Davidson dealership.

1. Clean the crankshaft assembly in solvent and dry it thoroughly with compressed air.

2. Hold the shank portion of each connecting rod where it attaches to the crankshaft (**Figure 329**). Pull up and down on each connecting rod. Any amount of up and down movement indicates excessive lower bearing wear. If there is movement, have the crankshaft overhauled.

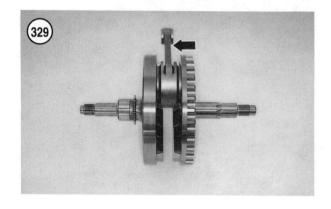

4

3. Measure connecting rod sideplay with a feeler gauge (**Figure 330**) and compare it to the service limit in **Table 2**.

4. Inspect the right side (pinion shaft) (**Figure 331**) and the left side (sprocket shaft) (**Figure 332**) for excessive wear or damage.

5. Inspect the balancer drive chain sprocket teeth (**Figure 333**). Check for chipped or missing teeth.

6. Support the crankshaft on a truing stand or in a lathe and check the runout at the flywheel outer rim (A, **Figure 334**) and the shaft adjacent to the flywheel (B) with a dial indicator. If the runout exceeds the service limit in **Table 2**, have the crankshaft trued or overhauled.

7. Inspect the crankshaft position sensor timing teeth on the left side flywheel for damaged or missing teeth.

8. On models so equipped, make sure the retaining ring (**Figure 335**) is secure on the right side of the crankshaft.

9. Inspect the connecting rod bushings (**Figure 336**) for wear. If necessary, replace as described under *Piston Pin Bushing Replacement* in this chapter.

Right Side Main Bearing Replacement (All Models)

A hydraulic press and a crankshaft bearing remover and installer (JIMS part No. 1146) are required for the follow-

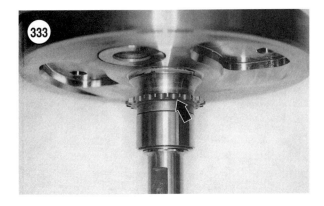

ing procedure. Refer to the manufacturer's instructions with the special tool.

Removal

1. Remove the two Torx screws (A, **Figure 337**) securing the bearing retainer plate (B) and remove the plate.

NOTE
The JIMS support tube is marked with either REMOVER or INSTALLER on the side.

2. Position the right side crankcase with the outer surface facing up.
3. Position the support tube with the REMOVER side facing down (**Figure 338**) and center the support tube onto the outer surface of the right side bearing (**Figure 339**).
4. Hold the support tube in place and turn the crankcase over (**Figure 340**) onto it.
5. Make sure the O-rings (**Figure 341**) are in place on the support tube.
6. Insert the driver/pilot (**Figure 342**) through the bearing and into the support tube below. Push the driver/pilot down until it bottoms on the bearing (**Figure 343**).
7. Place the crankcase and tools onto the press bed.
8. During removal, make sure that the curved edge on the pilot/driver matches the raised edge of the crankcase (**Figure 343**).
9. Center the press driver over the pilot/driver shaft.
10. Hold the crankcase half parallel to the press bed and have an assistant slowly apply pressure on the pilot/driver shaft until the bearing is free from the case half.
11. Remove the case half and special tools from the press bed.

Installation

1. Apply a light coat of clean engine oil to the outer surface of the bearing and to the crankcase receptacle.
2. Position the support tube with the INSTALLER side facing up and place it on the press bed.
3. Position the crankcase with the outer surface facing up and center it over the support tube. Align the leg of the support tube with the offset of the crankcase surface to allow the crankcase to set flat on the support tube.
4. Align the crankcase bearing receptacle with the support tube.
5. Position the new bearing over the crankcase receptacle and start it in by hand.
6. Insert the driver/pilot through the bearing and into the support tube below. Push the driver/pilot down until it bottoms on the bearing.

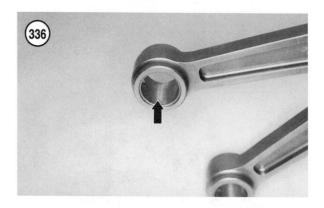

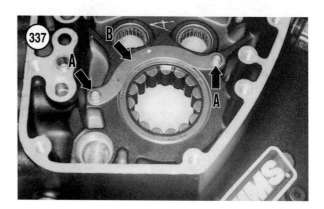

7. Center the press driver over the driver/pilot.

8. Slowly apply press pressure to the driver/pilot and press the bearing into the crankcase. Apply pressure until resistance if felt. Remove the driver/pilot.

9. Remove the crankcase and the support from the press bed.

10. Check each side of the crankcase to make sure the bearing is centered within the receptacle.

11. Install the bearing retainer plate (B, **Figure 337**). Apply medium strength threadlocking compound to the Torx screws (A, **Figure 337**) and install them. Tighten the screws securely.

12. Make sure the bearing rotates smoothly.

Left Side Main Bearing Assembly Replacement (2000-2002 Models)

Replace the left main bearing assembly as a complete set even if one bearing or race is damaged.

Tools

The following tools or their equivalents are required to remove and install the left side main bearing:

1. Hydraulic press.

2. Sprocket shaft bearing race tool (JIMS part No. 94547-80A).

3. Race and bearing installation tool handle (JIMS part No. 33416-80).

4. Snap ring removal and installation tool (JIMS part No. 1710).

5. Sprocket bearing race installation tool (JIMS part No. 2246).

Inner and outer bearing race replacement

> *CAUTION*
> *When replacing the bearing races in the following steps, do not remove the lock ring installed between the inner and outer bearing races. This ring is under heavy tension and will damage the bearing bore as it passes through it.*

1. Place the crankcase on the workbench with the inboard surface facing up.

2. If still in place, remove the crankshaft spacer and oil seal from the bearing bore.

3. Install half of the bearing race remover tool into the crankcase and push it against the inner bearing race (A, **Figure 344**).

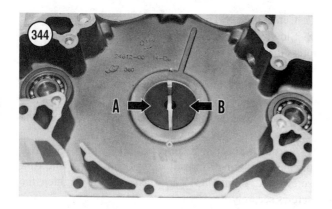

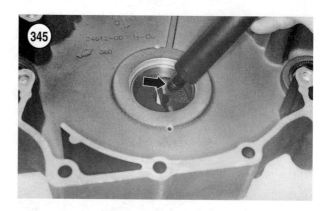

4. Install the other half of the bearing race remover tool into the crankcase and push it against the inner bearing race (B, **Figure 344**).

5. Hold the bearing race remover tools in place.

6. Insert the tool handle into the center of both race remover tools. Press it in until the ring (**Figure 345**) is locked into both bearing race remover tools (**Figure 346**).

7. Support the left crankcase half on the press bed with wooden blocks and with the tool handle facing up.

8. Center the press ram directly over the tool handle and slowly press the inner bearing race out of the crankcase.

9. Remove the crankcase and special tools from the press bed.

10. Place the crankcase on the workbench with the outboard surface facing up.

11. Install half of the bearing race remover tool into the crankcase and push it against the outer bearing race (A, **Figure 347**).

12. Install the other half of the bearing race remover tool into the crankcase and push it against the outer bearing race (B, **Figure 347**).

13. Hold the bearing race remover tools in place.

14. Insert the tool handle into the race remover tools. Press it in until the ring (**Figure 348**) is locked into both bearing race remover tools (**Figure 349**).

15. Support the left crankcase half on the press bed with wooden blocks and with the tool handle facing up.

16. Center the press ram directly over the tool handle and slowly press the outer bearing race out of the crankcase.

17. Remove the crankcase and special tools from the press bed.

18. Clean the crankcase half in solvent and dry it with compressed air.

19. Check the lock ring (**Figure 350**) for looseness or damage. If the lock ring is loose or damaged, perform the following:

4

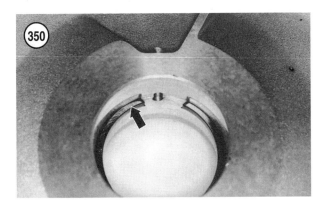

a. Place the crankcase on a workbench with the outboard side facing up.
b. With the gap of the lock ring at the 12 o'clock position, install the special tool clamps onto each side of the lock ring at the 10 o'clock and 2 o'clock positions.
c. Securely tighten the 9/16 in. Allen screws securing the clamps to the lock ring.
d. Use snap ring pliers to compress the lock ring and withdraw it from the crankcase groove.
e. Remove the clamps from the old lock ring and install them onto the new lock ring.
f. Squeeze the pliers (**Figure 351**) and insert the lock ring into the crankcase groove.
g. Make sure the lock ring gap is centered with the crankcase oil hole.

NOTE
Install both races with their larger diameter sides facing out. Install the bearing races with the same tool used to remove the old ones.

20. Apply clean engine oil, or press lube, to the bearing receptacles in the crankcase and to the outer surface of the inner bearing races.

NOTE
The large end of the installer base must contact the crankcase outer surface as shown in **Figure 352**.

21. Place the installer base on the press bed with the large end facing up.
22. Install the inboard outer race onto the crankcase receptacle (**Figure 353**).
23. Position the crankcase with the inboard surface facing up.
24. Install the crankcase onto the installer base so the crankcase retaining ring rests on top of the installer base.

25. Apply clean engine oil, or press lube, to the shaft of the pressing plug and install the pressing plug into the installer base (**Figure 354**). Push it down onto the bearing outer race (**Figure 355**).

26. Center the press ram directly over the pressing plug and slowly press the outer bearing race into the outboard surface of the crankcase until it touches the retaining ring (**Figure 356**).

27. Remove the crankcase and special tools from the press.

28. Turn the crankcase over and repeat Steps 23-26 for the outboard outer bearing race.

Crankshaft inner sprocket shaft bearing replacement

A sprocket shaft bearing cone installer (part No. HD-997225-55B) is required to install the sprocket shaft bearing (**Figure 357**).

1. Support the crankshaft with the bearing side facing up.

2. Install the bearing splitter under the bearing (**Figure 358**) and tighten it securely.

3. Attach a bearing puller to the splitter (**Figure 359**).

4. Slowly tighten the center screw and withdraw the bearing from the crankshaft shoulder.

5. Remove the bearing remover, splitter and bearing from the crankshaft.

6. Clean the sprocket shaft with contact cleaner. Check the sprocket shaft for cracks or other damage. If it is damaged, refer service to a Harley-Davidson dealership.

7. Slide the new bearing over the sprocket shaft.

8. Refer to **Figure 360** and install the new bearing as follows:

   a. Apply clean graphite lubricant to the threads of the pilot shaft, the flat washer and the bearing.

   b. Thread the pilot shaft (A) onto the crankshaft until it contacts the crankshaft shoulder.

   c. Slide the sleeve (B) over the pilot shaft until it contacts the bearing inner race.

   d. Install the bearing (C) and washer (D) over the pilot shaft and onto the top of the sleeve.

   e. Thread the handle (E) onto the pilot shaft (A).

   f. Slowly tighten the handle *clockwise* until the bearing bottoms on the crankshaft shoulder.

   g. Unscrew and remove all parts of the special tool.

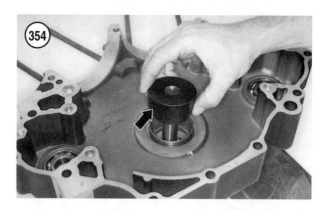

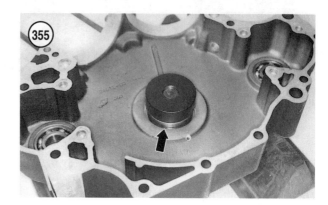

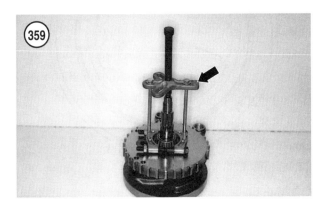

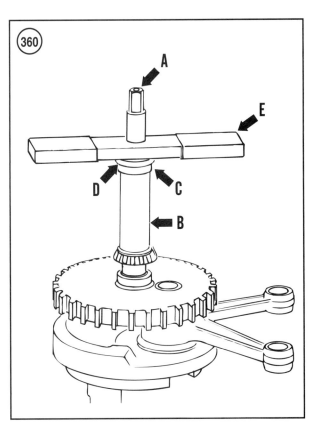

Left Side Main Bearing Assembly Replacement (2003 Model)

Tools

The following tools or their equivalents are required to remove and install the left side main bearing (**Figure 303**):

1. Hydraulic press.
2. Crankshaft roller bearing pilot/driver (HD-997225-55B).
3. Crankshaft roller bearing support tube (HD-42720-5).

> *NOTE*
> *The support tube ends are marked with an A and B. The A and B are referred to in the following procedure to indicate which side of the support tube must face.*

Bearing removal

1. Place the crankcase on the workbench with the inboard surface facing up.
2. If still in place, remove the crankshaft spacer from the bearing bore.
3. Carefully pull the thrust washer from the outer surface of the crankcase past the oil seal.
4. Place the support tube on the workbench with the *A* side facing up.
5. Position the crankcase with the inner surface facing up and place the bearing bore over the support tube.
6. Use a suitable size drift and tap the oil seal out of the bearing bore. Discard the oil seal.
7. Turn the crankcase over with the inner surface facing up.

> *CAUTION*
> *Do not damage the crankcase retaining ring groove with the screwdriver. The groove must remain sharp to correctly seat the retaining ring.*

8. The roller bearing (A, **Figure 361**) is secured in the crankcase with a retaining ring (B) on the inner surface of the bearing bore. Remove the retaining ring (C, **Figure 361**) as follows:
   a. Use a flat tip screwdriver and place it under the retaining ring. Carefully lift the edge of the retaining ring up and out of the crankcase groove.
   b. Slide the tip of the screwdriver around the edge of the bearing and continue to lift the retaining ring out of the crankcase groove.
   c. Remove the retaining ring.

9. Position the support tube (A, **Figure 362**) on the press bed with the *A* side facing up.

10. Position the crankcase half with the outer side facing up and position the crankshaft's bearing bore over the support tube. Correctly align the two parts.

11. Slide the pilot/driver (B, **Figure 362**) through the crankcase bearing and into the support.

12. Center the press ram (C, **Figure 362**) directly over the pilot/driver (B) and slowly press the bearing out of the crankcase.

13. Remove the crankcase and special tools from the press bed.

14. Clean the crankcase half in solvent and dry it with compressed air.

Bearing installation

1. Apply clean engine oil, or press lube, to the bearing receptacle in the crankcase and to the outer race of the *new* bearing.

2. Position the support tube (A, **Figure 363**) on the press bed with the *A* side facing up.

3. Position the crankcase half with the inner side facing up and position the crankshaft's bearing bore over the support tube. Correctly align the two parts.

4. Correctly position the *new* bearing (B, **Figure 363**) over the crankcase bore.

5. Slide the pilot/driver (C, **Figure 363**) through the new bearing and the crankcase and into the support.

6. Center the press ram (D, **Figure 363**) directly over the pilot/driver (C) and slowly press the bearing into the crankcase until it *lightly* bottoms in the crankshaft bearing bore.

7. Remove the crankcase and special tools from the press.

8. Make sure the bearing is has been pressed in past the retaining ring groove. If the groove is not visible above the bearing, repeat Steps 2-6 until the groove is visible.

9. Position the crankcase on the workbench with the inner surface facing up.

CAUTION
Do not damage the crankcase retaining ring groove with the screwdriver. The groove must remain sharp to correctly seat the retaining ring.

NOTE
If the retaining ring will not correctly seat in the crankcase groove, the bearing is not correctly seated in the crankcase bore. Repeat Steps 2-6

10. Install the bearing's *new* retainer ring as follows:

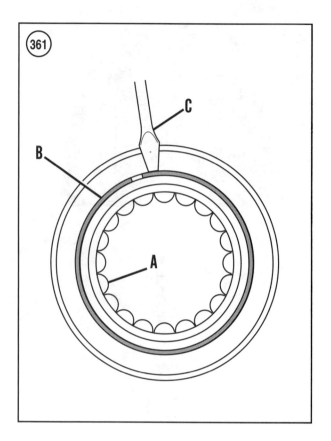

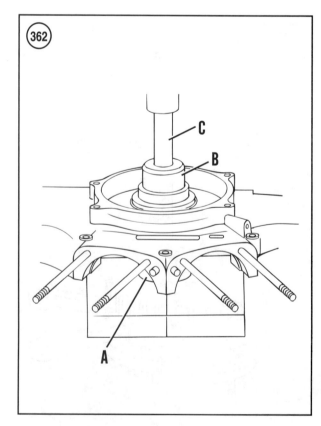

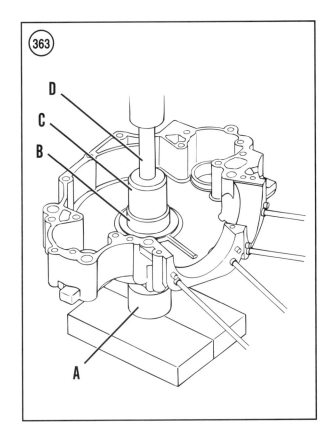

a. Work the retaining ring into the crankcase groove being careful not to damage the crankcase groove.

b. Use a flat tip screwdriver and push the retaining ring. Continue to push the retaining ring into the crankcase groove.

Crankshaft End Play Inspection (2000-2002 Models)

NOTE
The 2003 models are equipped with an assembled roller bearing and this procedure is not necessary.

The crankshaft end play *must* be between 0.001-0.005 in. (0.025-0.127 mm). End play is determined by the thickness of the shim between the inner and outer bearings on the left side. **Table 6** lists the shim part numbers and thickness.

If the end play was measured before disassembly and was within specification, and if the same components are reinstalled, then the same size shim can be reinstalled as a starting point.

Carefully measure the end play as described in Step 11. If there is *any* doubt about your abilities to properly set up the crankshaft end play, refer this procedure to a Harley-Davidson dealership.

Tools

The following tools or their equivalents are required to assemble the crankcase halves:

1. Sprocket shaft bearing installation tool (JIMS part No. 97225-55).

2. Crankshaft guide (JIMS part No. 1288).

3. Engine base stand (JIMS part No. 1138) and engine stand (JIMS part No. 1142).

Procedure

1. Position the crankshaft (**Figure 364**) with the left side facing up.

2. Apply clean engine oil or assembly lube to the inner bearing and to the left side crankcase inner bearing race.

3. Install the shim of the specified thickness onto the inner bearing inner race.

4. Place the left crankcase half over the crankshaft sprocket and onto the inner bearing.

5. Make sure the connecting rods are positioned within the crankcase openings (**Figure 365**).

6. Make sure the crankcase is located correctly on the crankshaft inner bearing.

7. Install the outer roller bearing onto the crankshaft (**Figure 366**) and push it into the outer bearing race.

8. Install the sprocket shaft bearing installation tool (**Figure 367**) onto the crankshaft following the manufacturer's instructions.

9. Hold onto the handle of the installation tool (A, **Figure 368**) and tighten the large nut with a wrench (B). Tighten the large nut until the outer bearing is seated correctly and makes firm contact with the shim installed in Step 3.

10. Remove the special tools and make sure the outer bearing is seated correctly.

11. Check crankshaft end play as follows:
   a. Securely attach a dial indicator to the left crankcase half (A, **Figure 369**).
   b. Position the dial indicator contact pointer on the end of the crankshaft (B, **Figure 369**).
   c. Push down hard on the crankcase (C, **Figure 369**) while turning it back and forth.
   d. Hold the crankcase down and zero the dial gauge.
   e. Pull up on the crankcase as far as it will go while turning it back and forth. Note the dial indicator reading.
   f. Repeat this step several times and note the readings. They should all be the same.
   g. The end play should be within 0.001-0.005 in. (0.025-0.127 mm). If the end play is incorrect, replace the shim with a shim of a different thickness. **Table 6** lists the various thickness shims and their part numbers.
   h. Remove the dial indicator.

Crankcase Assembly

One special tool, crankshaft guide (JIMS part No. 1288), is required to assemble the crankcase halves.

1. Perform Steps 1-9 of *Crankshaft End Play Inspection* (2000-2002 Models) in the proceeding procedure and install the crankshaft into the left side crankcase.

2. Turn the crankcase assembly over and place it on wooden blocks thick enough so the left side of the crankshaft clears the workbench surface.

3. Install the *new* O-rings (**Figure 370**) onto both locating dowels in both locations (**Figure 371**) in the right crankcase half. Apply clean engine oil to the O-rings.

4. Install the crankshaft guide (**Figure 372**) over the crankshaft.

5. Thoroughly clean and dry both crankcase gasket surfaces before applying gasket sealer in Step 6.

6. Apply a thin coat of a non-hardening gasket sealant to the crankcase mating surfaces. Use one of the following gasket sealants:
   a. Harley-Davidson crankcase sealant (part No. HD-99650-81).

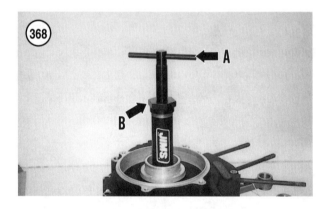

b. 3M #800 sealant.

c. ThreeBond Liquid Gasket 1104.

7. Align the crankcase halves and carefully lower the right crankcase half onto the crankshaft and left crankcase half. Press it down until it is seated correctly on the locating dowels. If necessary, carefully tap the perimeter of the right crankcase half until it is seated around the entire perimeter.

CAUTION
When properly aligned, the crankcase halves will fit snugly against each other around the entire perimeter. If they do not meet correctly, do not attempt to pull the case halves together with the mounting bolts. Separate the crankcase assembly and investigate the cause of the interference.

8. Remove the crankshaft guide (**Figure 373**) from the crankshaft.

9. If available, place the crankcase assembly in an engine stand. Secure the engine stand to the workbench.

10. Install the nine crankcase bolts into the left crankcase half (**Figure 374**) and tighten them as follows:

a. Alternately tighten the nine bolts finger-tight.

b. Using the torque pattern shown in **Figure 375**, tighten the bolts to 10 ft.-lb. (14 N•m).

c. Using the same sequence, tighten the bolts to 15-19 ft.-lb. (20-26 N•m).

11. Install the left crankcase oil seal as described in the following procedure.

12. Apply clean engine oil to the outer surface of the sprocket shaft spacer and install it onto the crankshaft and into the oil seal (**Figure 376**).

13. Install the following components as described in this chapter:

a. Alternator rotor and stator assembly (Chapter Eight).

b. Oil pump.

c. Camshaft assembly.

d. Pushrods and valve lifters.

e. Pistons.

f. Cylinder heads and cylinders.

14. Install the engine into the frame as described in this chapter.

Crankcase Left Side Oil Seal Replacement

Special Tools

The following tools or their equivalents are required to install the oil seal:

1. Sprocket shaft seal installer tool (JIMS part No. 39361-69).

2. Sprocket shaft bearing installation tool (JIMS part No. 97225-55).

Procedure

1. Remove the sprocket shaft spacer (**Figure 376**) from the crankshaft and the oil seal.

2. Carefully pry the old oil seal out of the bearing bore and discard it.

3. Position the *new* oil seal with the open side facing out.

4. Install the oil seal onto the crankshaft (**Figure 377**) and center it within the bearing bore.

5. Apply clean engine oil or press lube to the installer tool threads, both washers and the radial bearing.

6. Install the main body onto the crankshaft and screw it on until it stops (**Figure 378**).

7. Install the shaft seal installer tool following the manufacturer's instructions.

8. Hold onto the handle (A, **Figure 379**) of the main body and tighten the large nut (B) with a wrench. Tighten the large nut slowly and make sure the oil seal (C, **Figure 379**) is entering straight into the bearing bore.

9. Tighten the large nut until the shaft seal installer tool contacts the crankcase surface (**Figure 380**).

10. Remove the special tools.

11. Apply clean engine oil to the outer surface of the sprocket shaft spacer and install it onto the crankshaft and into the oil seal (**Figure 376**).

Cylinder Stud Replacement

Replace bent or damaged cylinder studs (A, **Figure 381**) to prevent cylinder block and cylinder head leaks.

1. If the engine lower end is assembled, block off the lower crankcase opening with clean shop cloths.

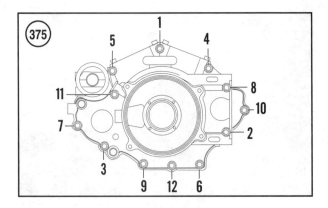

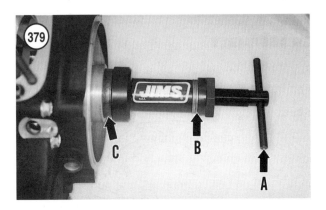

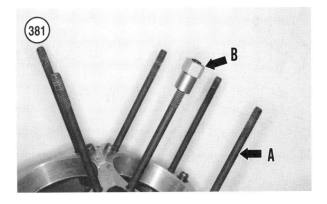

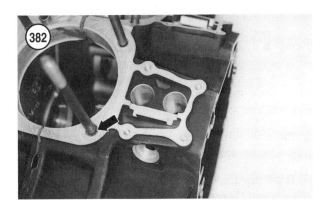

2A. If the stud has broken off with the top surface of the crankcase, remove it with a stud remover. Refer to Chapter One.

2B. If the stud is still in place, perform the following:

   a. Thread a 3/8 in.-16 nut onto the top of the stud.

   b. Thread an additional nut onto the stud and tighten it against the first nut so they are locked.

   c. Turn the bottom nut *counterclockwise* and unscrew the stud.

3. Clean the stud threads in the crankcase with a spiral brush, then clean them with an aerosol parts cleaner. If necessary, clean the threads with an appropriate size tap.

NOTE
If the new studs have a threadlocking compound patch already applied to the lower stud threads, do not apply any additional locking compound.

4. If the new stud does not have the threadlocking compound patch, apply ThreeBond TB1360 (red) or an equivalent to the studs lower threads.

NOTE
The cylinder studs have a shoulder on one end. This end must be installed next to the crankcase surface.

5A. Install the Motion Pro stud installation tool (part No. 08-0148) (B, **Figure 381**) onto the stud.

5B. Place a 0.313 in. diameter steel ball (H-D part No. 8860) into a cylinder head bolt, then thread the bolt onto the end of the new stud without the collar.

6. Position the stud with the shoulder end going in first and hand-thread the new stud into the crankcase.

CAUTION
Do not use a breaker bar, ratchet or similar tool to install the studs. These tools may bend the stud and cause the engine to leak oil.

7. Hold the air impact wrench directly in-line with the stud. *Slowly* tighten the new stud with an air impact wrench until the stud shoulder just contacts the top surface of the crankcase (**Figure 382**).

8. Tighten the stud to 10 ft.-lb. (14 N•m).

9. Remove the cylinder head bolt and steel ball or installation tool from the cylinder stud.

10. Repeat Steps 2-9 for any additional studs.

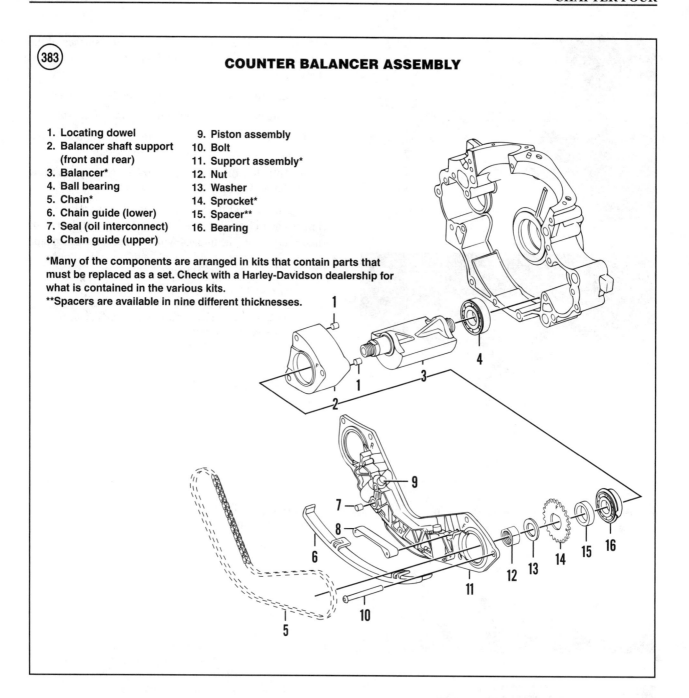

383

COUNTER BALANCER ASSEMBLY

1. Locating dowel
2. Balancer shaft support (front and rear)
3. Balancer*
4. Ball bearing
5. Chain*
6. Chain guide (lower)
7. Seal (oil interconnect)
8. Chain guide (upper)
9. Piston assembly
10. Bolt
11. Support assembly*
12. Nut
13. Washer
14. Sprocket*
15. Spacer**
16. Bearing

*Many of the components are arranged in kits that contain parts that must be replaced as a set. Check with a Harley-Davidson dealership for what is contained in the various kits.
**Spacers are available in nine different thicknesses.

COUNTER BALANCER ASSEMBLY

Special Tools

The following special tools are required to service the counter balancer assembly (**Figure 383**):

1. Balancer shaft retention pins (JIMS part No. 1163 or part No. HD-44062).

2. Hydraulic tensioner compressor (part No. HD-44063).

3. Hydraulic tensioner retainers (part No. HD-44408).

Removal

1. Separate the crankcase halves as described in this chapter.

2. Place the left side crankcase on the workbench supported by wooden blocks with the inner surface facing up.

3. If still in place, remove and discard the rubber oil interconnect seal (**Figure 384**).

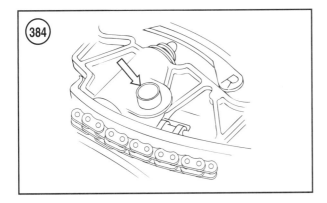

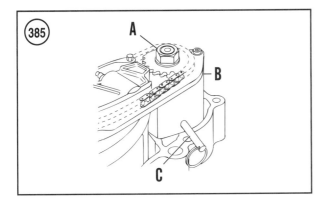

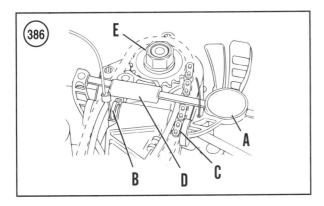

7. Pump the tensioner compressor handle and compress the hydraulic tensioner (A, **Figure 386**).

8. Move the retainer (D, **Figure 386**) over the tip of the tensioner (B).

9. Release the pressure on the tensioner compressor and remove it.

10. Repeat Steps 6-9 for the remaining tensioner assembly.

11. Loosen the self-locking hex nuts (E, **Figure 386**) on the balancer shafts. If the nuts are difficult to loosen an incorrect amount or type of threadlocking compound may have been applied during prior installation of the nuts. If necessary, heat the hex nuts to loosen the threadlocking compound. Do not remove the hex nuts at this time.

CAUTION
Do not apply heat to the hex nuts with any type of open flame (propane or welding torch).

NOTE
If necessary, an industrial type heat gun, capable of 248° F (120° C) may be required to loosen the hex nut on the balancer shafts.

12. Carefully pry on the tensioner guide to clear it from the locking post.

13. Use a small screwdriver and pry the front chain tensioner guide (1, **Figure 387**) upward from the locking post.

14. Repeat Step 13 for the rear chain tensioner guide (2, **Figure 387**).

15. Carefully pry the chain tensioner guide (3, **Figure 387**) away from the chain guide bracket assembly while freeing the two tensioner tabs (4) on the lower chain run.

16. Remove both self-locking hex nuts and washers (5, 6 **Figure 387**), loosened in Step 11, from the front and rear balance shafts.

17. Carefully pry the rear (7, **Figure 387**) and front (8) sprockets away from the chain guide bracket assembly and release the balancer chain (9). Remove the balancer chain and both sprockets.

18. Remove the spacer from the front balance shaft.

19. Remove the six T40 Torx screws (10, **Figure 387**) securing the chain guide support assembly to the balancer shaft supports and crankcase.

CAUTION
After removing the balancer shaft retaining pins, inspect the tip of each pin. If the small ball at the end is missing, locate it within the crankcase half and remove it. If the ball worked loose and stays within the

4. Rotate the crankshaft until the holes in the balance shafts (A, **Figure 385**) align with the holes in the shaft supports (B).

5. Insert a balancer shaft retaining pin (C, **Figure 385**) into the front and the rear supports to lock the balancer shafts (A) in place.

6. Install and clamp the tensioner compressor (A, **Figure 386**) over the balancer chain adjacent to the hydraulic tensioner (B) and the bottom of the chain guide bracket (C).

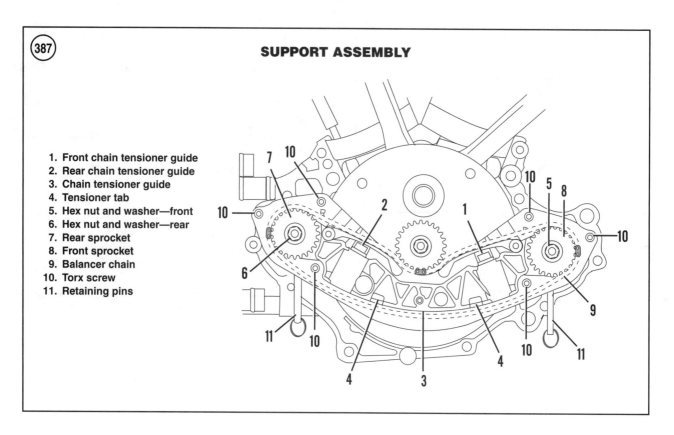

SUPPORT ASSEMBLY

1. Front chain tensioner guide
2. Rear chain tensioner guide
3. Chain tensioner guide
4. Tensioner tab
5. Hex nut and washer—front
6. Hex nut and washer—rear
7. Rear sprocket
8. Front sprocket
9. Balancer chain
10. Torx screw
11. Retaining pins

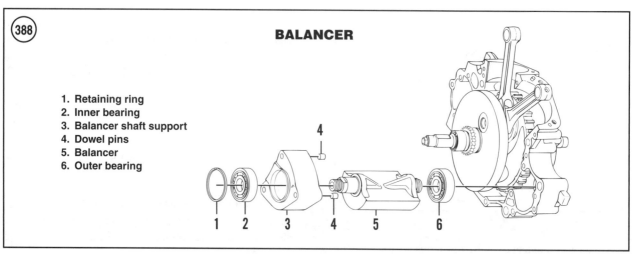

BALANCER

1. Retaining ring
2. Inner bearing
3. Balancer shaft support
4. Dowel pins
5. Balancer
6. Outer bearing

crankcase, severe engine damage could occur.

20. Remove both balancer shaft retaining pins (11, **Figure 387**), installed in Step 5, from the front and rear supports.

NOTE
The balancer shaft supports are marked with a F (front) and R (rear) and they must

be installed in the correct location during assembly. The balancer shafts are identical with the same part number.

21. Withdraw the front and rear balancer shaft supports and balancer shafts from the left side crankcase bearings (**Figure 388**). Do not lose the two dowel pins at each support location.

22. Inspect all components as described in this chapter.

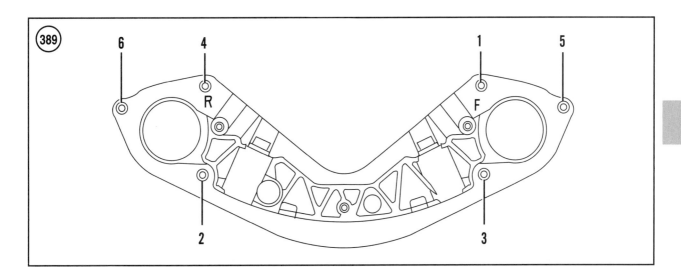

4

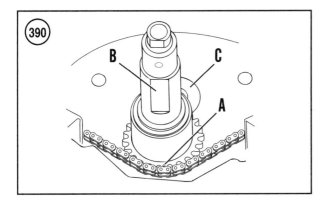

Installation

1. Place the left side crankcase on the workbench supported by wooden blocks with the inner surface facing up.

2. Apply clean engine oil to the balancer shaft bearings in the crankcase. Also apply oil to the balancer shafts where they engage the bearings.

3. Position the balancer shaft with the smooth end facing down and insert it into the crankcase bearing. Push the balancer shaft down until it bottoms.

4. Repeat Step 3 for the other balancer shaft.

5. Make sure both locating dowels are in place in the crankcase.

6. Install the front balancer shaft support marked with a *F* over the front balancer shaft into the crankcase front receptacle. Push the support down until it bottoms against the crankcase mating surface.

7. Install the rear balancer shaft support marked with a *R* over the rear balancer shaft into the crankcase rear receptacle. Push the support down until it bottoms against the crankcase mating surface.

8. Compress both hydraulic tensioners and install the chain guide support assembly over the front and rear balance shafts. Push the assembly down until it seats flush with the crankcase mating surface.

9. Apply a high strength threadlocking compound to the T40 Torx screws through the chain guide support assembly, the balancer shaft housings and into the crankcase. Tighten all six screws (10, **Figure 387**) finger tight and make sure the assembly is seated flush with the crankcase mating surface. Do not try to pull the assembly down with the Torx screws.

10. Tighten the six Torx screws to 18-22 ft.-lb. (24-30 N•m) in the sequence shown in **Figure 389**.

11. Rotate the crankshaft until the sprocket timing mark is at the 6 o'clock position (A, **Figure 390**) and the flat portion (B) is directly below the crankshaft crankpin hole (C).

12. Rotate the balance shafts until the holes in the balance shafts (A, **Figure 385**) align with the shaft supports (B).

13. Insert balance shaft retaining pins (C, **Figure 385**) into the front and rear supports and balancer shafts to lock the balancer shafts (A) in place. This will lock the balance shafts into correct timing with the crankshaft.

14. Install the spacer onto the *front* balance shaft.

15. Correctly position the chain sprockets with their marks facing UP. Install the front (8, **Figure 387**) and rear (7) sprockets onto the balance shafts.

16. Install the washer and an *old* hex nut onto each balance shaft and tighten the nuts sufficiently to hold the sprockets in place.

17. Perform *Front Sprocket Alignment* procedure as described in this section. This procedure must be done to ensure correct alignment between the sprockets and balance

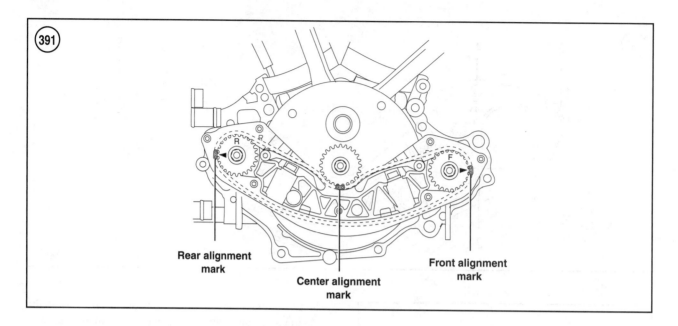

Rear alignment
mark

Center alignment
mark

Front alignment
mark

chain. If this alignment is incorrect, there will be premature wear on the sprockets and balancer chain.

18. Apply a thin coat of clean engine oil to the balancer chain.

19. Locate the balancer chain timing marks as shown in **Figure 391**. Loosely place the balancer chain next to the front and rear sprockets and crankshaft timing mark. Align the colored chain links next to the sprockets.

20. Slide the balancer chain over the sprockets starting with the rear sprocket. Align the colored chain link with the alignment arrow on the rear sprocket and mesh the chain onto the sprocket.

21. Pull the balancer chain taut and align the center colored chain link with the alignment mark on the crankshaft sprocket.

22. Pull the balancer chain taut, align the colored chain link with the alignment arrow on the front sprocket, then mesh the balancer chain onto the front sprocket.

CAUTION
All three balancer chain link alignment marks must be correctly aligned with the three sprockets. If alignment is incorrect, the balancer system will not function correctly, resulting in excessive vibration.

23. Verify that all three colored chain links are aligned with the marks on both front and rear sprockets and the crankshaft sprocket (**Figure 391**). Readjust if necessary.

NOTE
If new self-locking hex nuts are not available, apply a high-strength threadlocking

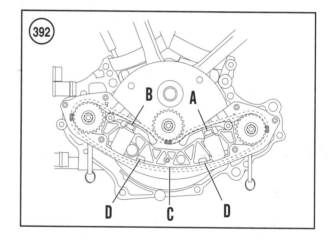

compound to the old nuts prior to installation.

24. Remove the old nuts installed in Step 16. Install *new* self-locking hex nuts (5, 6 **Figure 387**) and tighten to 78-82 ft.-lb. (106-111 N•m).

25. After the nuts have been tightened, once again verify that all three colored chain links are aligned with the marks on both front and rear sprockets and the crankshaft sprocket (**Figure 391**). Readjust if necessary.

26. Correctly position the front upper chain guide (A, **Figure 392**) with the *F* facing out. Install the front guide onto the post and push it down until it snaps into place.

27. Correctly position the rear upper chain guide (B, **Figure 392**) with the *R* facing out. Install the rear guide onto the post and push it down until it snaps into place.

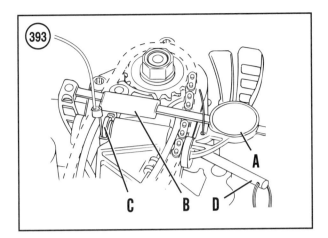

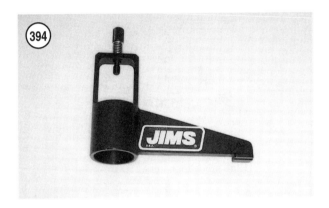

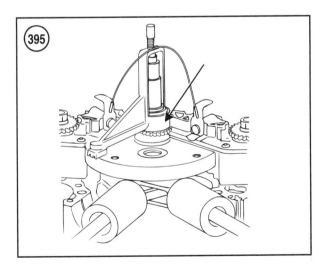

30. Pump the tensioner compressor handle and compress the hydraulic tensioner (C, **Figure 393**).

31. Slide the hydraulic tensioner retainer (B, **Figure 393**) away from the tip of the tensioner (C).

32. Slowly release pressure on the tensioner compressor and remove it.

CAUTION
After removing the balancer shaft retaining pins, inspect the tip of each pin. If the small ball at the end is missing, locate it within the crankcase half and remove it. If the ball worked loose and stays within the crankcase, severe engine damage could occur.

33. Repeat Steps 29-32 for the remaining tensioner.

34. Slowly remove the balancer shaft retaining pin (D, **Figure 393**), installed in Step 13, from the balancer shaft support and the balancer.

35. Install a *new* rubber interconnect (**Figure 384**).

Front Sprocket Alignment

The balancer sprocket alignment tool (JIMS part No. 1166 or part No. HD-44064) is required for this procedure (**Figure 394**).

This procedure if for the front sprocket only. The rear sprocket is not equipped with a spacer.

1. Slide the special tool (**Figure 395**) over the crankshaft and the timing sprocket shoulder.

2. Hold down the special tool in place on the crankshaft and move the tool over onto the *front* sprocket face.

3. Alignment is correct if the tool's *outside step* clears the top surface of the sprocket (**Figure 396**). Alignment clearance between the tool and the sprocket surface is 0.014 in. (0.356 mm). The tool's inside step *must not* pass over the sprocket face.

4. If alignment is incorrect, replace the spacer with a new one that will bring the front sprocket alignment into specification. Refer to **Table 7**.

Inspection

1. Clean all parts in solvent and dry with compressed air.

2. Check the flatness of each sprocket with a straightedge and flat feeler gauge. The sprocket must be flat within the service limit specification in **Table 2**.

3. Inspect the crankshaft and balancer sprockets for undercut or sharp teeth (**Figure 397**) or missing teeth.

NOTE
The balancer chain sprocket on the crankshaft is pressed into place. If severely dam-

28. Install the lower chain guide (C, **Figure 392**) into place and snap the two retention tabs (D) into place locking the guide in place.

29. Install and clamp the tensioner compressor (A, **Figure 393**) over the balancer chain adjacent to the hydraulic tensioner and the bottom of the chain guide bracket.

aged, have the sprocket replaced by a Harley-Davidson dealership.

4. If excessive wear or damage is evident, replace the balancer sprockets and balancer chain as a set. Rapid balancer chain wear occurs if the new chain is installed with worn sprockets.

5. Check the sprocket surface where it mates with the balancer surface. Make sure the surface is clean without any burrs or surface irregularities. Replace as necessary.

6. The balancer chain will darken to a brown color as the result of wear and the exposure of engine oil. If the chain has turned blue, it has overheated and should be replaced.

7. Inspect the inner plate chain links. They must be slightly polished on both sides. If the chain shows considerable uneven wear on one side, the sprockets are correctly aligned. Excessive wear requires the balancer chain and sprockets to be replaced.

8. Inspect the upper and lower chain guides for wear or damage. Replace any guide if a groove is worn to the wear limit in **Table 2**.

9. Inspect the chain guide support assembly for wear or distortion. Replace if necessary.

Balance Shaft Bearing Inspection/Replacement

Inspection

Refer to **Figure 388**.

Inspect the balancer bearing in the balance shaft support and in the left side crankcase (**Figure 398**). Turn each inner race by hand (**Figure 399**). The bearing must turn smoothly. Some axial play is normal, but radial play must be negligible. See **Figure 400**.

If the bearing(s) is damaged, replace it as described in the following.

Inner crankcase bearing replacement

A balancer shaft bearing remover and installer (JIMS part No. 1167) and a hydraulic press are required to service the counterbalancer shaft bearing.

1. Separate the crankcase and remove the balancer system as described in this chapter.

2. Thoroughly clean the crankcase half with solvent and dry with compressed air.

3. Place the left side crankcase half on towels or shop cloths to protect the exterior finish. Place the crankcase on the workbench.

4. Apply a light coat of graphite lubricant to the threads of the bearing puller and large nut.

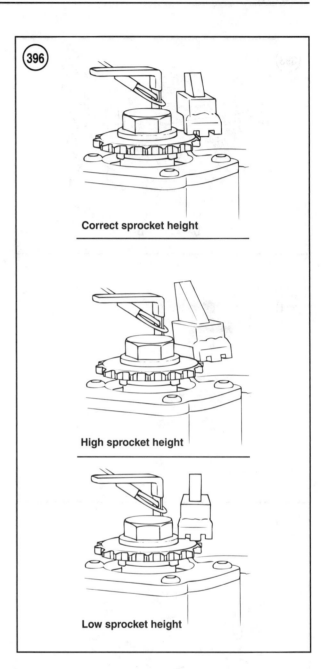

Correct sprocket height

High sprocket height

Low sprocket height

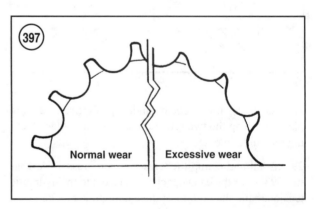

Normal wear   Excessive wear

4

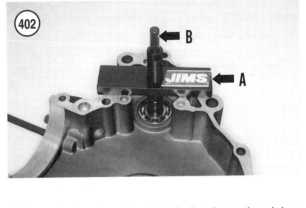

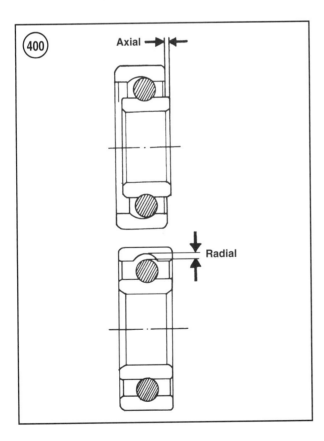

5. Insert the bearing puller onto the bearing and tap it into place (**Figure 401**) with a plastic mallet. Make sure the puller is seated correctly under the bearing inner race.

6. Install the plate (A, **Figure 402**) onto the puller and rest it flush with the crankcase sealing surface.

7. Insert the rod (B, **Figure 402**) into the puller and push it in until it bottoms.

8. Install the brass washer (A, **Figure 403**) and large nut (B) onto the puller and plate.

9. Secure the puller with a 5/8 in. open end wrench to keep it from rotating.

CAUTION
Do not turn the puller with the 5/8 in. wrench, just keep it from rotating.

10. Using a 1 1/8 in. wrench on the large nut (B, **Figure 403**), tighten the large nut until the bearing is pulled free from the crankcase receptacle.

11. Place the left side crankcase half on towels or shop cloths to protect the exterior finish. Place the crankcase on wooden blocks on the press bed.

12. Apply a light coat of clean engine oil to the crankcase bearing receptacle and to the bearing outer race surface.

13. Place the bearing onto the bearing receptacle.

14. Place the installer collar (**Figure 404**) onto the bearing.

15. Center the press ram directly over the installer collar and slowly press the bearing into the crankcase until it is seated.

16. Remove the crankcase and special tools from the press.

17. Rotate the bearing to make sure it rotates freely.

18. Repeat Steps 3-17 for the other bearing if necessary.

Outer support bearing replacement

A crankcase bearing remover (part No. HD-44065) and hydraulic press are required to replace the outer support bearing.

1. Remove the balancer shaft support as described in this chapter.

2. Thoroughly clean the support in solvent and dry with compressed air.

3. Place the bearing remover (A, **Figure 405**) on the press bed.

4. Place the bearing shaft support (B, **Figure 405**) upside down on the bearing remover.

5. Place a pilot (C, **Figure 405**) or suitable size socket onto the bearing outer race.

6. Center the press ram (D, **Figure 405**) over the pilot or socket.

7. Slowly apply pressure and remove the bearing and retaining ring from the support.

8. Release press pressure and remove the pilot or socket.

9. Discard the bearing and retaining ring.

10. Thoroughly clean the bore of the support and dry with compressed air.

11. Apply clean engine oil to the support bore surface and to the outer surface of the bearing.

12. Place the balancer shaft support (A, **Figure 406**) on a piece of wood on the press bed.

13. Install a *new* retaining ring onto the *new* bearing and make sure it seats correctly in the bearing groove.

14. Position the *new* bearing (B, **Figure 406**) and retaining ring (C) with the bearing letters facing up.

15. Place the bearing onto the support.

16. Place a pilot (D, **Figure 406**) or suitable size socket onto the bearing outer race.

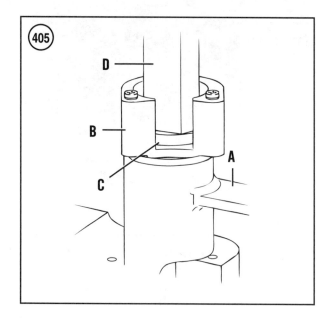

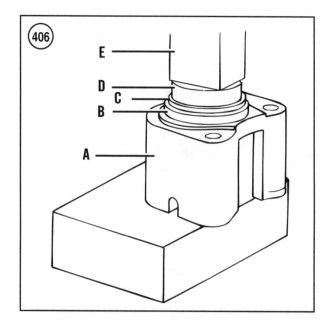

17. Center the press ram (E, **Figure 406**) over the pilot or socket.

18. Slowly apply pressure and press the bearing and retaining ring into the support until the retaining (C, **Figure 406**) fits flush against the housing surface.

19. Release press pressure and remove the pilot or socket.

20. Rotate the new bearing and make sure it rotates freely.

ENGINE BREAK-IN

Following cylinder service such as boring, honing and installing new rings, or major lower end work, break-in the engine as though it were new. The service and performance life of the engine depends on the break-in.

1. For the first 50 mi. (80 km), maintain engine speed below 2500 rpm in any gear. However, do not lug the engine. Do not exceed 50 mph during this period.

2. From 50-500 mi. (80-804 km), vary the engine speed. Avoid prolonged steady running at one engine speed. During this period, increase engine speed to 3000 rpm. Do not exceed 55 mph.

3. After the first 500 mi. (804 km), the engine break-in is complete.

4

Table 1 GENERAL ENGINE SPECIFICATIONS

Item	Specifications
Engine type	Four- stroke, 45 ° OHV V twin, Twin Cam 88B (balanced)
Bore and stroke	3.75 × 4.00 in. (95.25 × 101.6 mm)
Displacement	88 cubic inch (1450 cc)
Compression ratio	9.0 to 1
Torque	82 ft. lb. (111 N•m) @ 3000 rpm
Maximum sustained engine speed	5600 rpm
Engine and transmission weight	204 lbs. (92.5 kg)
Cooling system	Air-cooled

Table 2 ENGINE SERVICE SPECIFICATIONS

Item	New in. (mm)	Service limit in. (mm)
Cylinder head		
Warp	–	0.006 (0.15)
Valve guide fit in head	0.0020-0.0033 (0.051-0.084)	0.002 (0.051)
Valve seat fit in head	0.003-0.0045 (0.076-0.114)	0.002 (0.051)
Rocker arm		
Shaft-to-rocker arm bushing	0.0005-0.0020 (0.013-0.051)	0.0035 (0.089)
Shaft-to-rocker arm support	0.0007-0.0022 (0.018-0.056)	0.0035 (0.089)
End clearance	0.003-0.0013 (0.076-0.033)	0.025 (0.635)
Valves		
Valve stem-to-guide clearance		
Intake	0.0008-0.0026 (0.020-0.066)	–
Exhaust	0.0015-0.0033 (0.038-0.084)	–
Seat width	0.040-0.062 (1.02-1.58)	–
(continued)		

Table 2 ENGINE SERVICE SPECIFICATIONS (continued)

Item	New in. (mm)	Service limit in. (mm)
Valve stem protrusion	–	2.064 (52.43)
Valve springs		
Free length		
Outer	2.105-2.177 (53.47-55.3)	–
Inner	1.926-1.996 (48.9-50.7)	–
Piston-to-cylinder clearance	0.0006-0.0016 (0.015-0.041)	0.0053 (0.135)
Piston pin clearance in piston	0.0001-0.0004 (0.003-0.010)	0.001 (0.25)
Piston rings		
Compression ring end gap		
Top ring	0.007-0.020 (0.178-0.508)	0.020 (0.51)
Second ring	0.007-0.020 (0.178-0.508)	0.020 (0.51)
Oil control ring end gap	0.009-0.052 (0.23-1.32)	0.050 (1.27)
Compression ring side clearance		
Top ring	0.002-0.0045 (0.051-0.114)	0.0037 (0.09)
Second ring	0.0016-0.0041 (0.041-0.104)	0.0037 (0.09)
Oil control ring side clearance	0.0016-0.0076 (0.041-0.193)	0.0072 (0.18)
Cylinder		
Taper	–	0.002 (0.05)
Out of round	–	0.003 (0.08)
Warp		
At top (cylinder head)	–	0.006 (0.15)
At base (crankcase)	–	0.008 (0.20)
Cylinder bore		
Standard	–	3.753 (95.326)
Oversize 0.005 in	–	3.758 (95.453)
Oversize 0.010 in.	–	3.763 (95.580)
Oversize 0.020 in.	–	3.773 (95.834)
Oversize 0.030 in.	–	3.783 (96.088)
Connecting rod		
Connecting rod-to-crankpin clearance	0.0004-0.0012 (0.0102-0.0305)	0.002 (0.05)
Piston pin clearance in connecting rod	0.0003-0.0007 (0.008-0.018)	0.002 (0.05)
Side play	0.005-0.015 (0.13-0.38)	0.020 (0.51)
Valve lifters		
Lifter-to-guide clearance	0.0008-0.0020 (0.02-0.05)	0.003 (0.076)
Roller fit	–	0.0015 (0.038)
Roller end clearance	–	0.026 (0.660)
Camshaft support plate		
Camshaft chain tensioner shoe	–	0.080-0.090 (2.03-2.29)*
Camshaft support plate warpage	–	0.010 (0.25)
Camshaft bushing fit	–	0.0008-0.001 (0.0203-0.0254)
Oil pump rotor tip clearance	–	0.004 (0.10)
Sprocket shaft Timken bearing		
Cup fit in crankcase	0.003-0.005 (0.8-0.13)	–
Cone fit on shaft	0.005-0.0015 (0.013-0.038)	–
Crankshaft		
Runout (flywheel at rim)	0.000-0.010 (0.0-0.25)	0.015 (0.38)
Runout (shaft at flywheel)	0.000-0.002 (0.0-0.05)	0.003 (0.08)
End play	0.001-0.005 (0.03-0.13)	0.006 (0.015)
Balancer sprocket		
Flatness limit	–	0.008 (0.20)
Balancer chain		
Upper and lower chain guide groove limit	–	0.080-0.090 (2.03-2.29)*

*1/2 the thickness of the shoe.

Table 3 PUSH ROD AND LIFTER LOCATION

Cylinder	Lifter bore	Cylinder head/rocker housing bore
Front		
Intake	Inside	Rear
Exhaust	Outside	Front
Rear		
Intake	Inside	Front
Exhaust	Outside	Rear

Table 4 ENGINE TORQUE SPECIFICATIONS

Item	ft.-lb.	in.-lb.	N•m
Balancer shaft chain guide assembly			
Torx screws	18-22	–	24-30
Balancer shaft sprocket nuts	78-82	–	106-111
Bearing retainer plate screws	–	20-30	2-3
Breather cover bolts	–	90-120	10-14
Camshaft cover screws	–	125-155	14-17.5
Camshaft support plate Allen bolts	–	90-120	10-14
Camshaft support plate-to-			
oil pump Allen bolts	–	90-120	10-14
Camshaft position sensor cover screw	–	20-30	2-3
Camshaft position sensor screw	–	50-80	6-9
Crankshaft position sensor screw	–	90-120	10-14
Crankshaft sprocket bolt	Refer to text		
Crankcase bolts	15-19	–	20-26
Cylinder head bolts	Refer to text		
Cylinder head bracket bolts	28-35	–	38-47
Cylinder studs	10	–	14
Engine oil drain plug	–	120-144	14-16
Engine-to-transmission bolts			
Preliminary	15	–	20
Final	30-35	–	41-48
Engine upper mounting bracket			
Cylinder head-to-bracket bolts	25-30	–	34-41
Bracket-to-frame bolt	45-50	–	61–68
Engine front mount bolts	70-80	–	95-108
Engine upper mounting bracket			
Lower bracket-to-cylinder head bolts	25-30	–	34-41
Upper bracket-to-frame bolt	45-50	–	61-68
Lifter cover bolts	–	90-120	10-14
Oil fitting	–	120-144	14-16
Oil line cover bolts	–	90-108	10-12
Oil pump screws	–	90-120	10-14
Oil pressure sending unit	–	92-120	11-14
Pipe plug	–	120-144	14-16
Piston oil jet screw	–	25-35	3-4
Rear camshaft sprocket bolt	Refer to text		
Rocker arm			
Housing bolts	–	120-168	14-19
Support plate bolts	18-22	–	25-30
Cover bolt	15-18	–	20-24
Shift lever pinch bolt	18-22	–	24-30
Sprocket shaft nut	150-165	–	203-224
Drain plug	14-21	–	19-29
Voltage regulator bolts	–	70-100	8-11

Table 5 REAR CAMSHAFT SPROCKET SPACERS

Part No.	in.	mm
25717-00	0.327	8.31
25719-00	0.317	8.05
25721-00	0.307	7.79
25722-00	0.287	7.29
25723-00	0.297	7.54

Table 6 CRANKSHAFT LEFT SIDE BEARING SPACER SHIM (2000-2002)

Shim part No.	in.	mm
9110	0.0905-0.0895	2.299-2.273
9120	0.0925-0.0915	2.350-2.324
9121	0.0945-0.0935	2.400-2.375
9122	0.0965-0.0955	2.451-2.426
9123	0.0985-0.0975	2.502-2.476
9124	0.1005-0.0995	2.553-2.527
9125	0.1025-0.1015	2.602-2.578
9126	0.1045-0.1035	2.654-2.629
9127	0.1065-0.1055	2.705-2.680
9128	0.1085-0.1075	2.756-2.731
9129	0.1105-0.1095	2.807-2.781
9130	0.1125-0.1115	2.858-2.932
9131	0.1145-0.1135	2.908-2.883
9132	0.1165-0.1155	2.959-2.934
9133	0.1185-0.1175	3.010-2.985
9134	0.1205-0.1195	3.061-3.035

Table 7 BALANCER SPROCKET SPACERS

Part No.	in.	mm
14780-00	0.130	3.302
14781-00	0.140	3.356
14782-00	0.150	3.810
14783-00	0.160	4.064
14784-00	0.170	4.318
14785-00	0.180	4.572
14786-00	0.190	4.826
14787-00	0.200	5.080
14788-00	0.210	5.334

CHAPTER FIVE

CLUTCH AND PRIMARY DRIVE

This chapter describes service procedures for the clutch and primary drive assemblies.

Specifications are in **Tables 1-3** at the end of this chapter.

PRIMARY CHAINCASE COVER

Removal

Refer to **Figure 1**.

> *WARNING*
> *Disconnect the negative battery cable before working on the clutch or any primary drive component to avoid accidentally activating the starter.*

> *NOTE*
> *On models so equipped, always disarm the optional TSSM security system prior to disconnecting the battery or the siren will sound.*

1. Disconnect the negative battery cable as described in Chapter Eight.
2. On models so equipped, remove the left side floorboard as described in Chapter Fourteen.
3. On FLST models, remove the front portion of the shift lever assembly as described in Chapter Six.

4. Drain the primary chain oil as described in Chapter Three.

> *NOTE*
> *Note the location of the inspection cover screws. There are two different length screws and they must be reinstalled in the correct location.*

5. Remove the primary chain inspection cover and gasket (A, **Figure 2**).

> *NOTE*
> *Note the location of the outer cover bolts. There are two different length bolts and they must be reinstalled in the correct location.*

6. Remove the bolts and captive washers securing the chaincase cover (B, **Figure 2**) and remove the chaincase cover.
7. Remove the chaincase cover gasket.
8. Remove the dowel pins, if necessary.

Inspection

1. Remove all gasket residue from the chaincase cover (**Figure 3**) and chaincase housing gasket surfaces.
2. Clean the cover in solvent and dry it with compressed air.

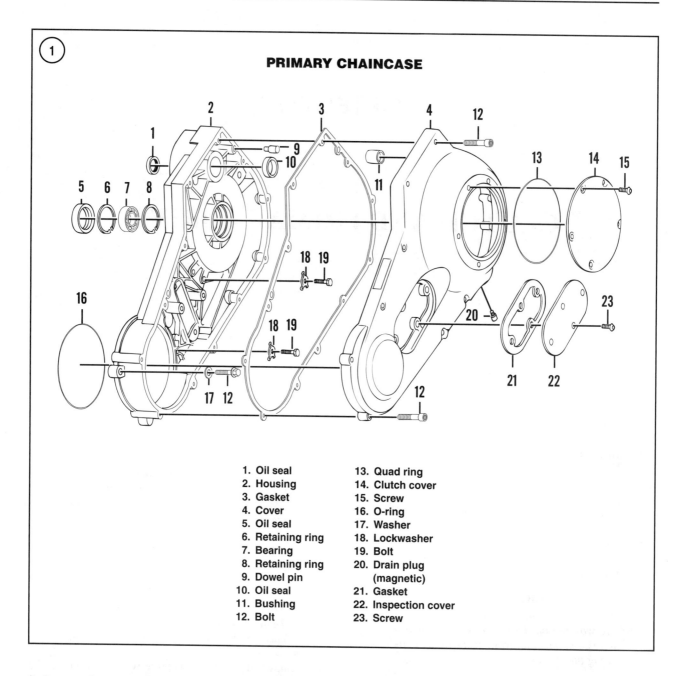

PRIMARY CHAINCASE

1. Oil seal
2. Housing
3. Gasket
4. Cover
5. Oil seal
6. Retaining ring
7. Bearing
8. Retaining ring
9. Dowel pin
10. Oil seal
11. Bushing
12. Bolt
13. Quad ring
14. Clutch cover
15. Screw
16. O-ring
17. Washer
18. Lockwasher
19. Bolt
20. Drain plug (magnetic)
21. Gasket
22. Inspection cover
23. Screw

3. Inspect the cover for cracks or damage. Check the lower portion (**Figure 4**) for any damage from road debris.

4. Inspect the starter jackshaft bushing (**Figure 5**) for excessive wear or damage. Replace the bushing as follows:

    a. Remove the bushing with a blind bearing removal tool.

    b. Clean the bushing bore in the housing.

    c. Press the new bushing in until its outer surface is flush with the edge of the bushing bore.

Installation

1. If removed, install the dowel pins (A, **Figure 6**) onto the chaincase housing.

> *CAUTION*
> *Harley-Davidson specifies that a **new** Print-O-Seal gasket must be installed every time the chaincase outer cover is removed.*

2. Install a *new* gasket (B, **Figure 6**) over the locating pins and seat it against the gasket surface of the chaincase housing.

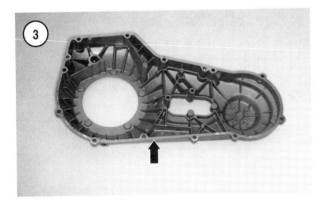

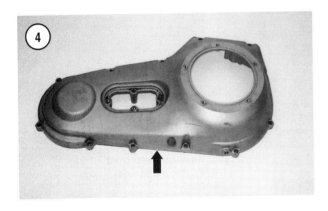

3. Install two *new* round gaskets (C, **Figure 6**) on the crankcase cover studs.

4. Slide the primary cover (B, **Figure 2**) over the locating dowels and seat it flush against the gasket.

NOTE
The gasket sealing surface is very thin and the overall size of the gasket is very large. The gasket may shift prior to the installation of the cover bolts. Make sure the gasket is positioned correctly during installation of the cover bolts in Step 5.

5. Install the primary cover bolts and captive washers into the locations noted during removal. Tighten the primary cover bolts to 108-120 in.-lb. (12-14 N•m). Make sure the gasket seats flush around the cover.

6. Install the primary chain inspection cover and gasket (A, **Figure 2**). Tighten the primary chain inspection cover screws to 84-108 in.-lb. (9-12 N•m).

7. On FLST models, install the front portion of the shift lever assembly as described in Chapter Six.

8. On models so equipped, install the left side floorboard as described in Chapter Fourteen.

9. Refill the primary chaincase with the type and quantity of oil specified under *Primary Chaincase Lubrication* in Chapter Three.

10. Connect the negative battery cable as described in Chapter Eight.

CLUTCH ASSEMBLY

This section describes removal, inspection and installation of the clutch plates. If the clutch requires additional service, refer to the clutch shell procedures in this chapter.

Refer to **Figure 7**.

⑦ **CLUTCH ASSEMBLY**

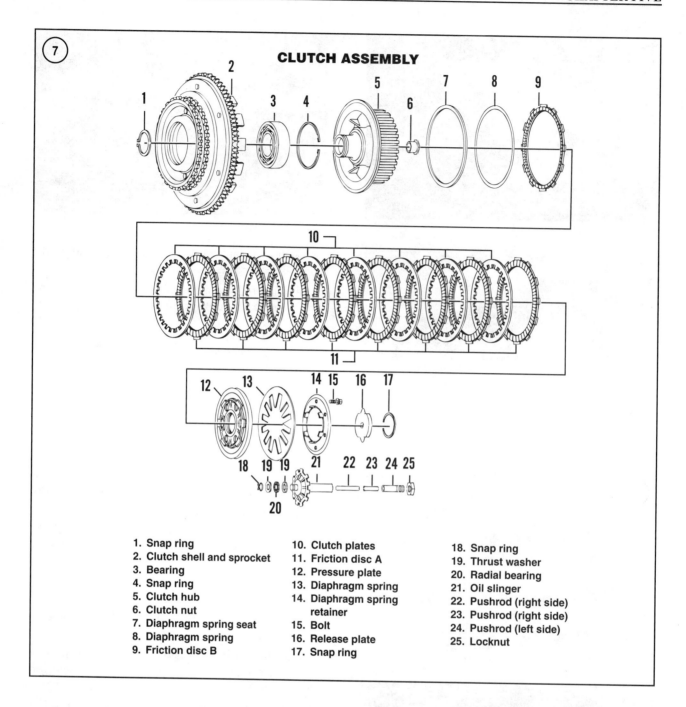

1. Snap ring
2. Clutch shell and sprocket
3. Bearing
4. Snap ring
5. Clutch hub
6. Clutch nut
7. Diaphragm spring seat
8. Diaphragm spring
9. Friction disc B

10. Clutch plates
11. Friction disc A
12. Pressure plate
13. Diaphragm spring
14. Diaphragm spring retainer
15. Bolt
16. Release plate
17. Snap ring

18. Snap ring
19. Thrust washer
20. Radial bearing
21. Oil slinger
22. Pushrod (right side)
23. Pushrod (right side)
24. Pushrod (left side)
25. Locknut

Removal

NOTE
On models so equipped, always disarm the optional TSSM security system prior to disconnecting the battery or the siren will sound.

1. Disconnect the negative battery cable as described in Chapter Eight.

2. Remove the clutch mechanism inspection cover and quad ring (C, **Figure 2**).

3. At the clutch mechanism, loosen the clutch adjusting screw locknut (A, **Figure 8**) and turn the adjusting screw (B) *counterclockwise* to allow slack against the diaphragm spring.

4. Remove the primary chaincase outer cover as described in this chapter.

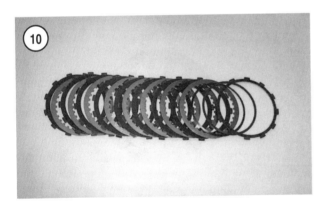

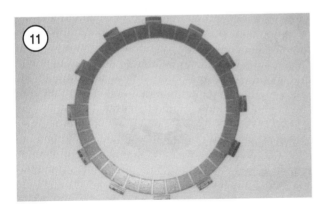

5. Loosen the bolts securing the diaphragm spring retainer (A, **Figure 9**) in a crisscross pattern. Remove the bolts and the retainer and diaphragm spring (B, **Figure 9**).

6. Remove the pressure plate.

7. Remove the clutch plates and friction discs from the clutch shell.

8. Remove the damper spring and damper spring seat from the clutch shell. Keep all parts in order as shown in **Figure 10**.

Inspection

When measuring the clutch components, compare the actual measurements to the specifications in **Table 1**. Replace parts that are out of specification or show damage as described in this section.

1. Clean all parts in solvent and thoroughly dry them with compressed air.

2. Inspect the friction discs as follows:

NOTE
*If any friction disc is damaged or out of specification as described in the following steps, replace **all** of the friction discs as a set. Never replace only one or two discs.*

a. Inspect the friction material (**Figure 11**) for excessive or uneven wear, cracks and other damage. Check the disc tangs for surface damage. The sides of the disc tangs must be smooth where they contact the clutch shell finger; otherwise, the discs cannot engage and disengage correctly.

NOTE
If the disc tangs are damaged, inspect the clutch shell fingers carefully as described later in this section.

b. Measure the thickness of each friction disc with a vernier caliper (**Figure 12**). Measure at several places around the disc.

3. Inspect the clutch plates (**Figure 13**) as follows:

a. Inspect the clutch plates for cracks, damage or color change. Overheated clutch plates will have a blue discoloration.

b. Check the clutch plates for oil glaze buildup. Remove buildup by lightly sanding both sides of each plate with 400 grit sandpaper placed on a surface plate or piece of glass. Clean off all sandpaper residue after cleaning the clutch plate(s).

c. Place each clutch plate on a flat surface and check for warp with a feeler gauge (**Figure 14**).

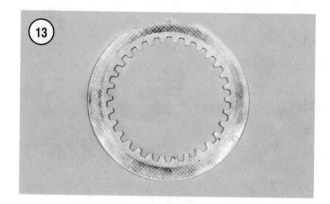

d. The clutch plate inner teeth mesh with the clutch hub splines. Check the clutch plate teeth for roughness or damage. The teeth contact surfaces must be smooth; otherwise, the plates cannot engage and disengage correctly.

NOTE
If the clutch plate teeth are damaged, inspect the clutch hub splines carefully as described later in this section.

4. Inspect the diaphragm spring (**Figure 15**) for cracks or damage.

5. Inspect the diaphragm spring retainer for cracks or damage. Also check for bent or damaged tabs (**Figure 16**).

6. Inspect the pressure plate inner contact surface (**Figure 17**) for cracks or other damage.

7. Inspect the pressure plate outer surface (**Figure 18**) where the diaphragm spring makes contact for wear marks (**Figure 19**).

8. If necessary, disassemble the pressure plate as follows:

a. Remove the snap ring and remove the release plate, left side pushrod and locknut (**Figure 20**) from the pressure plate.

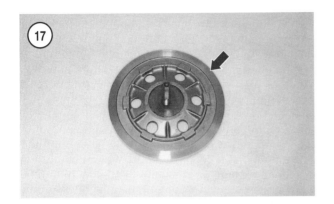

5

b. Inspect the release plate, left side pushrod and locknut for wear or damage.

c. Inspect the snap ring groove for damage (**Figure 21**).

d. Position the release plate with the OUT mark facing out (**Figure 22**) and install the assembly into the pressure plate.

e. Install the snap ring and make sure it is correctly seated in the pressure plate groove.

Installation

NOTE
*The original equipment clutch (**Figure 10**) has nine friction plates, eight steel plates, one damper spring and one damper spring seat. Make sure each part is installed. When installing an aftermarket clutch plate assembly, follow the manufacturer's instructions.*

1. Soak the clutch friction disc and clutch plates in new primary drive oil for approximately five minutes before installing them.

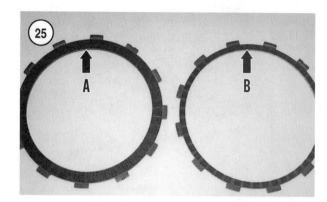

2. Install the damper spring seat (**Figure 23**) into the clutch hub and push it in until it seats within the clutch hub.

3. Position the damper spring with the dished side facing out and install it onto the clutch hub against the damper spring seat (**Figure 24**).

NOTE
*There are two different types of clutch friction discs (**Figure 25**). The wider friction disc A is the normal width disc. The narrow width friction disc B is installed first, as it works in conjunction with the damper spring and damper spring seat.*

4. Install the clutch friction disc *B* (**Figure 26**) onto the clutch shell and clutch hub. Push it on until it bottoms within the clutch hub and the damper spring and damper spring seat.

5. Install a clutch plate (**Figure 27**), then a friction disc *A* (**Figure 28**). Continue to alternately install the clutch plates and friction discs. The last part installed is a friction disc *A* (**Figure 29**). Make sure it is locked into place in the clutch shell (**Figure 30**).

6. Install the pressure plate onto the clutch hub (**Figure 31**).

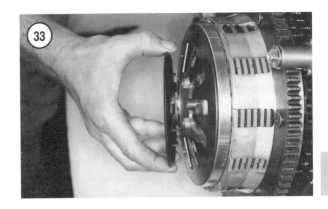

5

7. Position the diaphragm spring with the dished side facing out and install it onto the pressure plate (**Figure 32**). Hold the pressure plate in place.

8. Position the diaphragm spring retainer with the finger side (**Figure 33**) facing in toward the diaphragm spring and install the diaphragm spring retainer (**Figure 34**) and bolts.

9. Tighten the bolts (**Figure 35**) in a crisscross pattern to 90-110 in.-lb. (10-12 N•m).

10. Make sure the left side pushrod and nut (A, **Figure 36**) are in place, then install the release plate (B).

11. Secure the release plate with the snap ring (**Figure 37**). Make sure the snap ring is seated correctly in the pressure plate groove (**Figure 38**).

12. Install the primary chaincase cover as described in this chapter.

13. Install the clutch mechanism inspection cover and quad ring.

14. Connect the negative battery cable as described in Chapter Eight.

CLUTCH SHELL, COMPENSATING SPROCKET AND PRIMARY DRIVE CHAIN

Removal

This procedure describes clutch shell (**Figure 39**), primary chain and compensating sprocket removal (**Figure 40**). These components must be removed from the engine and transmission as an assembly.

> *NOTE*
> *On models so equipped, always disarm the optional TSSM security system prior to disconnecting the battery or the siren will sound.*

1. Disconnect the negative battery cable as described in Chapter Eight.

2. Remove the primary chaincase cover as described in this chapter.

3. If necessary, remove the diaphragm spring, pressure plate, clutch plates and friction discs as described in this chapter. This procedure is shown with these components removed.

4A. If a special tool is available, such as a primary drive locking tool (JIMS part No. 2234), place it onto the primary chain next to the clutch housing (**Figure 41**).

4B. If the special tool is not available, shift the transmission into fifth gear. Have an assistant apply the rear brake.

> *CAUTION*
> *The clutch nut has **left-hand threads**. Turn the clutch nut **clockwise** to loosen it.*

5. Loosen the clutch nut with an impact wrench. Remove the clutch nut (**Figure 42**).

6. Loosen the compensating sprocket nut with an impact wrench.

7. Remove the compensating sprocket nut, cover assembly (**Figure 44**) and sliding cam (A, **Figure 45**).

8. Loosen the primary chain shoe adjuster locknut (B, **Figure 45**) and push the tensioner assembly down (C) to relieve tension on the primary chain. Remove the locknut.

9. Remove the compensating sprocket (A, **Figure 46**), primary chain (B) and clutch assembly (C) at the same time.

10. Remove the shaft extension (**Figure 47**) and the spacer (**Figure 48**).

11. Inspect the various components as described in this chapter.

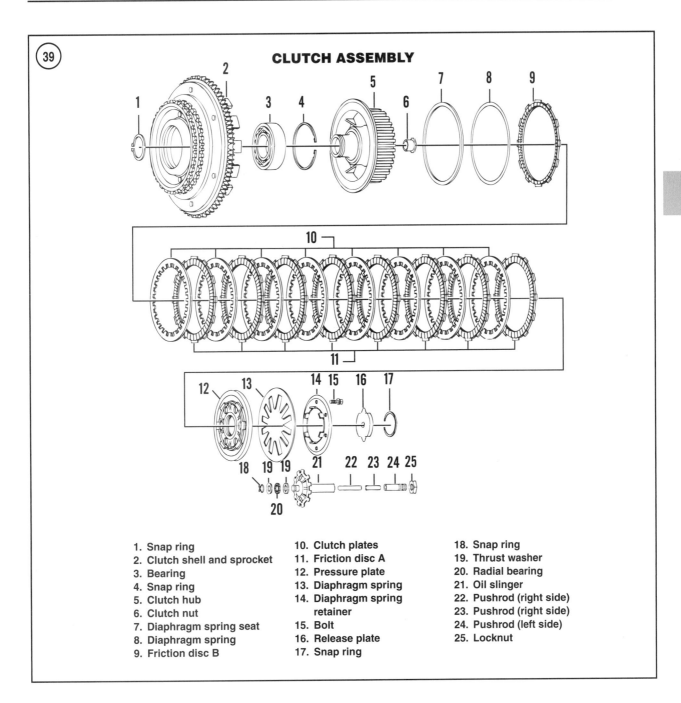

CLUTCH ASSEMBLY

1. Snap ring
2. Clutch shell and sprocket
3. Bearing
4. Snap ring
5. Clutch hub
6. Clutch nut
7. Diaphragm spring seat
8. Diaphragm spring
9. Friction disc B
10. Clutch plates
11. Friction disc A
12. Pressure plate
13. Diaphragm spring
14. Diaphragm spring retainer
15. Bolt
16. Release plate
17. Snap ring
18. Snap ring
19. Thrust washer
20. Radial bearing
21. Oil slinger
22. Pushrod (right side)
23. Pushrod (right side)
24. Pushrod (left side)
25. Locknut

Installation

1. Remove all threadlocking compound residue from the crankshaft and mainshaft threads, and from the compensating sprocket nut and the clutch nut.

2. Remove all gasket residue from the inner primary housing gasket surfaces.

3. Install the spacer (**Figure 48**) and the shaft extension (**Figure 47**) onto the crankshaft.

4. Assemble the compensating sprocket, primary chain and clutch.

5. Install the compensating sprocket (A, **Figure 46**), primary chain (B) and clutch assembly (C) at the same time.

6. Install the sliding cam (A, **Figure 45**) and the cover assembly (**Figure 44**).

7A. Install the same tool set-up (**Figure 41**) used during removal to prevent the compensating sprocket and clutch shell from rotating during the following steps.

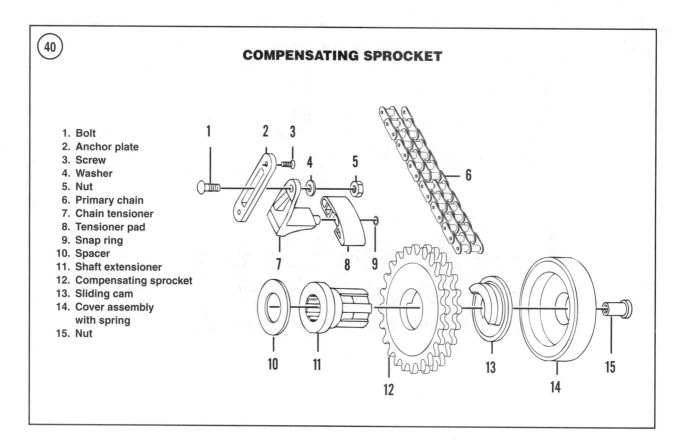

COMPENSATING SPROCKET

1. Bolt
2. Anchor plate
3. Screw
4. Washer
5. Nut
6. Primary chain
7. Chain tensioner
8. Tensioner pad
9. Snap ring
10. Spacer
11. Shaft extensioner
12. Compensating sprocket
13. Sliding cam
14. Cover assembly with spring
15. Nut

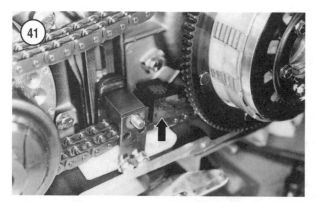

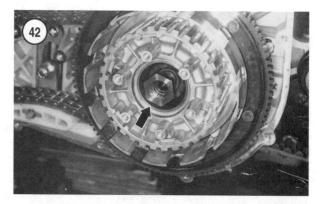

CAUTION
When using the clutch holder in Step 7B, make sure to secure it squarely onto the clutch shell. If the clutch holder starts to slip, stop tightening the clutch nut and reposition the clutch holder. If the clutch holder slips while tightening the clutch nut, it may damage the clutch shell splines.

7B. If the special tool is not available, hold the clutch shell with a clutch holder (A, **Figure 49**).

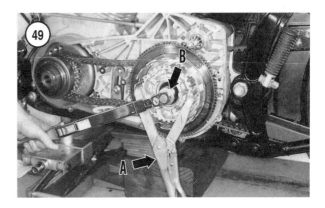

NOTE
*The clutch nut has **left-hand threads**. Turn the nut **counterclockwise** to tighten it.*

8. Apply two drops of ThreeBond TB1360 or an equivalent to the clutch nut threads. Install the nut (**Figure 42**) and tighten it (B, **Figure 49**) to 70-80 ft.-lb. (95-108 N•m).

9. Apply two drops of ThreeBond TB1360 or an equivalent to the compensating sprocket nut threads. Install the nut (**Figure 43**) and tighten it (**Figure 50**) to 150-165 ft.-lb. (203-204 N•m).

10. If used, remove the special tool from the clutch shell.

11. Adjust the primary chain as described in Chapter Three.

12. If removed, install the clutch plates and friction discs, pressure plate, and the diaphragm spring as described in this chapter.

13. Install the primary chaincase outer cover as described in this chapter.

14. Adjust the clutch as described in Chapter Three.

15. Connect the negative battery cable as described in Chapter Eight.

CLUTCH SHELL, CLUTCH HUB AND SPROCKET

Inspection

The clutch shell is a subassembly consisting of the clutch shell, the clutch hub, the bearing and two snap rings.

1. Remove the clutch shell as described in this chapter.

2. Hold the clutch shell and rotate the clutch hub by hand. The bearing is damaged if the clutch hub binds or turns roughly.

3. Check the sprocket (A, **Figure 51**) and the starter ring gear (B) on the clutch shell for cracks, deep scoring, excessive wear or heat discoloration.

4. If the sprocket or ring gear is worn or damaged, replace the clutch shell. If the primary chain sprocket is worn, also check the primary chain and the compensating sprocket as described in this chapter.

5. Inspect the clutch hub for the following conditions:

   a. The clutch plate teeth slide in the clutch hub splines (A, **Figure 52**). Inspect the splines for rough spots, grooves or other damage. Repair minor damage with a file or oil stone. If the damage is severe, replace the clutch hub.

   b. Inspect the clutch hub inner splines (**Figure 53**) for galling, severe wear or other damage. Repair minor damage with a fine cut file. If damage is severe, replace the clutch hub.

   c. Inspect the bolt towers and threads (B, **Figure 52**) for thread damage or cracks at the base of the tower. Repair thread damage with the correct size metric tap. If any of the towers are cracked or damaged, replace the clutch hub.

6. Check the clutch shell. The friction disc tangs slide in the clutch housing grooves (C, **Figure 52**). Inspect the grooves for cracks or galling. Repair minor damage with a file. If the damage is severe, replace the clutch housing.

7. If the clutch hub, clutch shell or bearing is damaged, replace them as described in the following procedure.

Disassembly/Assembly

Do not separate the clutch hub and shell unless either part or the bearing is going to be replaced. If the two parts are separated, the bearing will be damaged. Removal and installation of the bearing requires a hydraulic press.

1. Remove the clutch as described in this chapter. Remove the clutch shell assembly from the primary drive chain.

2. Remove the snap ring (**Figure 54**) from the clutch hub groove.

3. Support the clutch hub and clutch shell in a press with the primary chain sprocket side facing up (**Figure 55**).

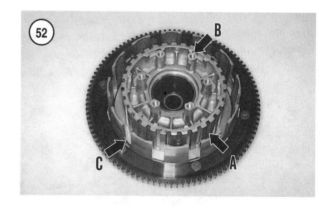

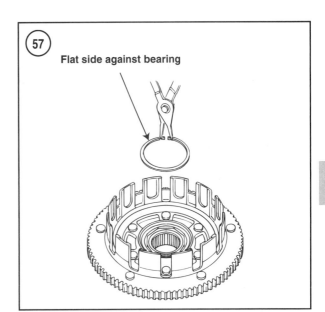

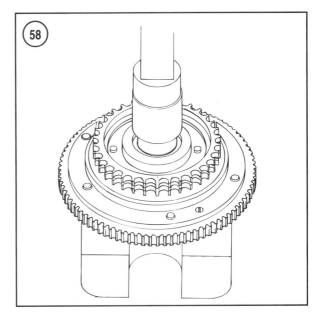

4. Place a suitable size arbor in the clutch hub surface and press the clutch hub (A, **Figure 56**) out of the bearing.

5. Remove the clutch shell from the press (B, **Figure 56**).

6. On the inner surface of the clutch shell, remove the bearing retaining snap ring (**Figure 57**) from the groove in the middle of the clutch shell.

CAUTION
Press the bearing out through the primary chain sprocket side of the clutch shell. The bearing bore has a shoulder on the primary chain side.

7. Support the clutch shell in the press with the primary chain sprocket side *facing up.*

8. Place a suitable size arbor on the bearing inner race and press the bearing out of the clutch shell (**Figure 58**).

9. Thoroughly clean the clutch hub and shell in solvent and dry them with compressed air.

10. Inspect the bearing bore in the clutch shell for damage or burrs. Clean off any burrs that would interfere with new bearing installation.

11. Support the clutch shell in the press with the primary chain sprocket side *facing down.*

12. Apply chaincase lubricant to the clutch shell bearing receptacle and to the outer surface of the bearing.

13. Align the bearing with the clutch shell receptacle.

14. Place a suitable size arbor on the bearing outer race and slowly press the bearing into the clutch shell until it bottoms on the lower shoulder. Press only on the outer bearing race. Applying force to the bearing's inner race will damage the bearing. Refer to *Basic Service Methods* in Chapter One for additional information.

15. Position the new snap ring with the flat side against the bearing and install the snap ring into the clutch shell groove (**Figure 57**). Make sure the snap ring is seated correctly in the clutch shell groove.

16. Press the clutch hub into the clutch shell as follows:

CAUTION
Failure to support the inner bearing race properly will cause bearing and clutch shell damage.

a. Place the clutch shell in a press. Support the inner bearing race with a sleeve as shown in **Figure 59**.

b. Align the clutch hub with the bearing and slowly press the clutch hub into the bearing until the clutch hub shoulder seats against the bearing inner race.

c. Install a *new* snap ring (**Figure 54**) into the clutch hub. Make sure the snap ring is seated correctly in the clutch hub groove.

17. After completing assembly, hold the clutch shell (A, **Figure 60**) and rotate the clutch hub (B) by hand. The shell should turn smoothly with no roughness or binding. If the clutch shell binds or turns roughly, the bearing was installed incorrectly. Repeat this procedure until this problem is corrected.

PRIMARY CHAIN AND GUIDE INSPECTION

1. Remove the primary chain as described under the *Clutch, Compensating Sprocket and Primary Drive Chain* procedure in this chapter.

2. Clean the primary chain in solvent and dry it thoroughly.

3. Inspect the primary chain (**Figure 61**) for excessive wear, cracks or other damage. If the chain is worn or damaged, check both sprockets for wear and damage.

NOTE
*If the primary chain is near the end of its adjustment level or if no more adjustment is available, and the adjusting guide (***Figure 62***) is not worn or damaged, the primary chain is excessively worn and must be re-*

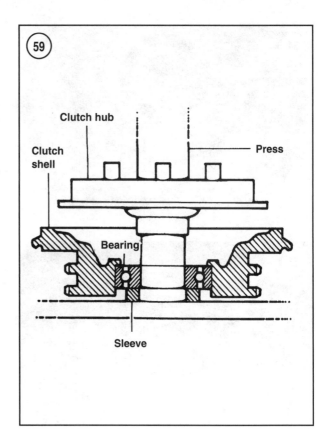

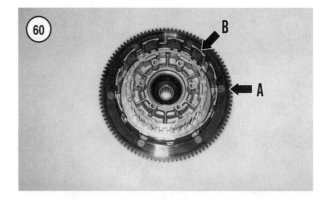

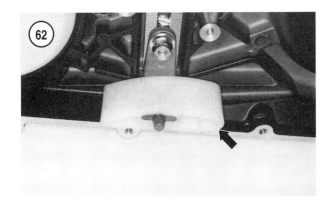

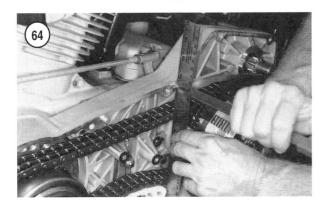

placed. Service specifications for chain wear are not available.

4. Inspect the adjusting guide (**Figure 62**) for cracks, severe wear or other damage. Replace the adjusting shoe if necessary.

PRIMARY CHAIN ALIGNMENT

A spacer, installed behind the compensating sprocket, aligns the compensating and clutch sprockets. Install the original spacer when reinstalling the compensating sprocket, primary chain and clutch assembly. However, if the primary chain is showing wear on one side, or if new components that could affect alignment have been installed, perform the following steps:

1. Remove the chaincase cover as described in this chapter.
2. Adjust the primary chain tension so the chain is snug against both the compensating sprocket and clutch shell sprocket.
3. Push the primary chain toward the engine and transmission (at both sprockets) as far as it will go.
4. Place a straightedge across the primary chain side plates as close to the compensating sprocket as possible.
5. Close to the compensating sprocket, measure the distance from the chain link side plates to the primary chaincase housing gasket surface (**Figure 63**). Record the measurement.
6. Repeat Steps 4 and 5 with the end of the straightedge as close to the clutch sprocket as possible (**Figure 64**). Record the measurement.
7. The difference between the two measurements should be within 0.030 in. (0.76 mm) of each other. If the difference exceeds this amount, replace the spacer (**Figure 65**) with a suitable size spacer. Refer to **Table 3** for spacer thickness and part numbers.
8. To replace the spacer, refer to *Clutch Shell, Compensating Sprocket and Primary Drive Chain* in this chapter.
9. Install the primary cover as described in this chapter.
10. Check and adjust the primary chain tension as described in Chapter Three.

COMPENSATING SPROCKET INSPECTION

Refer to **Figure 40**.
1. Remove the compensating sprocket assembly as described in this chapter.
2. Clean all parts in solvent and dry them with compressed air.
3. Check the cam surfaces (**Figure 66**) for cracks, deep scoring or wear.

4. Check the compensating sprocket gear teeth (**Figure 67**) for cracks or wear.

> *NOTE*
> *If the compensating sprocket teeth are worn, also check the primary chain and the clutch shell gear teeth (B, Figure 51) for wear.*

5. Check the compensating sprocket inner bushing (**Figure 68**) for wear.
6. Check the sliding cam inner splines (**Figure 69**) for wear.
7. Check the shaft extension splines for wear or galling.
8. Check the cover (**Figure 70**) for damage.
9. Inspect the inner threads (**Figure 71**) of the nut for damage.
10. If any of these components were replaced, check the primary chain alignment as described in this chapter.

PRIMARY CHAINCASE HOUSING

The primary chaincase housing (**Figure 72**) is bolted to the engine and transmission. It houses the primary drive assembly, flywheel, starter jackshaft, and the mainshaft oil seal and bearing assembly.

Removal

Refer to **Figure 73**.

> *NOTE*
> *On models so equipped, always disarm the optional TSSM security system prior to disconnecting the battery or the siren will sound.*

1. Disconnect the negative battery cable as described in Chapter Eight.
2. Remove the shift lever assembly as described under *External Shift Mechanism* in Chapter Six.
3. Remove the primary chaincase cover as described in this chapter.
4. Remove the compensating sprocket, primary chain and clutch assembly as described in this chapter.
5. Remove the starter motor as described in Chapter Eight.
6. Pry the lockwasher tabs away from the front two primary housing bolts. Loosen the four primary housing-to-engine mounting bolts (**Figure 74**).
7. Pry the lockwasher tabs away from the rear four primary housing bolts. Loosen the four primary housing-to-transmission mounting bolts (**Figure 75**).

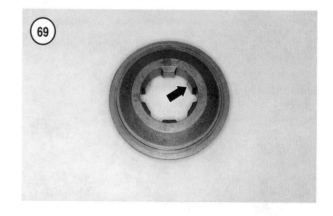

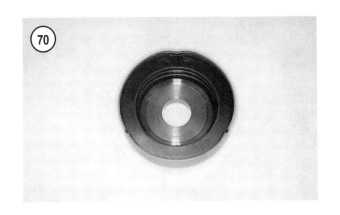

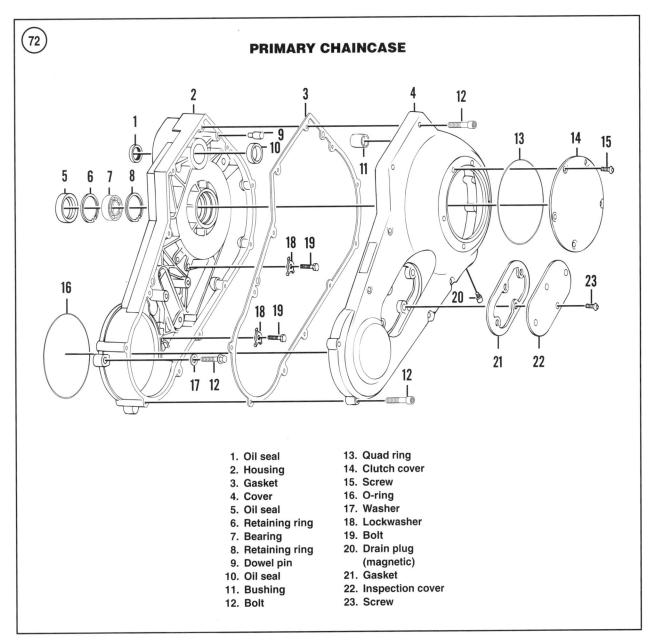

PRIMARY CHAINCASE

1. Oil seal
2. Housing
3. Gasket
4. Cover
5. Oil seal
6. Retaining ring
7. Bearing
8. Retaining ring
9. Dowel pin
10. Oil seal
11. Bushing
12. Bolt
13. Quad ring
14. Clutch cover
15. Screw
16. O-ring
17. Washer
18. Lockwasher
19. Bolt
20. Drain plug
    (magnetic)
21. Gasket
22. Inspection cover
23. Screw

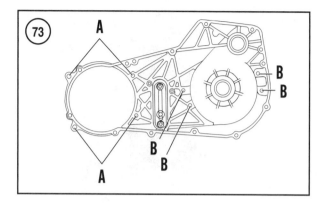

8. Remove all eight bolts securing the housing to the engine and the transmission. Discard all lockwashers as new ones must be installed.

9. Remove the starter jackshaft assembly from the housing as described in this chapter.

10. Tap the primary housing loose.

11. Remove the housing from the engine, transmission and gearshift shaft.

12. Remove the O-ring (**Figure 76**) from the engine crankcase shoulder.

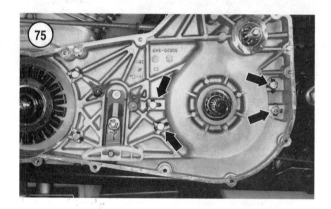

Inspection

1. Remove all gasket residue from the housing gasket surfaces (A, **Figure 77**).

2. Clean the housing in solvent and dry it thoroughly.

3. Check the housing (**Figure 78**) for cracks or other damage.

4. Check the starter jackshaft oil seal for excessive wear or damage. If necessary, replace the oil seal as follows:

    a. Note the direction the oil seal lip faces in the housing.

    b. Pack the new oil seal lips with grease.

    c. Pry the oil seal out of the inner primary housing.

    d. Carefully drive the *new* oil seal into the housing until it seats against the housing shoulder.

5. Inspect the starter jackshaft bushing (B, **Figure 77**) for wear, cracks or other damage. If necessary, replace the bushing as follows:

    a. Remove the bushing with a blind bearing removal tool.

    b. Clean the bushing bore in the housing.

    c. Press the new bushing in until its outer surface is flush with the edge of the bushing bore.

6. Turn the inner bearing race (**Figure 79**) by hand. Replace the bearing as follows:

    a. Remove the oil seal (**Figure 80**) as described in Step 7.

    b. Remove the inner and outer bearing snap rings.

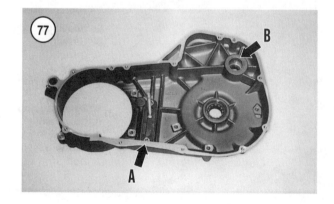

c. Support the housing and press the bearing out.

d. Install the outer snap ring (clutch side). Make sure the snap ring is correctly seated in the groove.

CAUTION
When pressing the bearing into the housing, support the outer snap ring. The force required to press the bearing into the inner primary housing may force the snap ring out of its groove, damaging the housing.

e. Support the inner housing and outer snap ring.

f. Press the bearing into the inner housing until it seats against the snap ring.

g. Install the inner snap ring. Make sure the snap ring is seated correctly in the groove.

h. Install a *new* oil seal as described in Step 7.

7. Inspect the primary housing oil seal (**Figure 80**) for excessive wear, tearing or other damage. If necessary, replace the oil seal as follows:

a. Remove the oil seal with a wide-blade screwdriver.

b. Clean the oil seal bore.

c. Pack the oil seal lip with a waterproof bearing grease.

d. Position the oil seal with its closed side facing out. Press the *new* oil seal in until its outer surface is flush with the edge of the bearing bore.

8. Check the primary chain adjuster rack screws (**Figure 81**) for looseness. Tighten the screws if necessary.

Installation

1. Thoroughly clean the *outer surface* of the eight bolt holes of the inner cover. Apply a light coat of black RTV sealant to the inner surfaces.

2. Install the *new* O-ring (**Figure 76**) onto the engine crankcase shoulder.

3. To prevent the transmission mainshaft splines from damaging the inner cover oil seal as it passes over, wrap the mainshaft splines with tape.

4. If removed, install the drive belt prior to installing the inner housing.

5. Align the inner housing with the engine and transmission, and install it. Push the inner housing on until it stops.

6. Install all eight bolts and *new* lockwashers securing the inner housing to the engine and the transmission.

7. Tighten the inner housing bolts in the following order.

a. Tighten the four primary housing-to-engine mounting bolts (**Figure 74**) to 17-21 ft.-lb. (23-29 N•m). Bend the lockwasher tabs against the four bolt heads.

b. Tighten the four primary housing-to-transmission mounting bolts (**Figure 75**) to 17-21 ft.-lb. (23-29

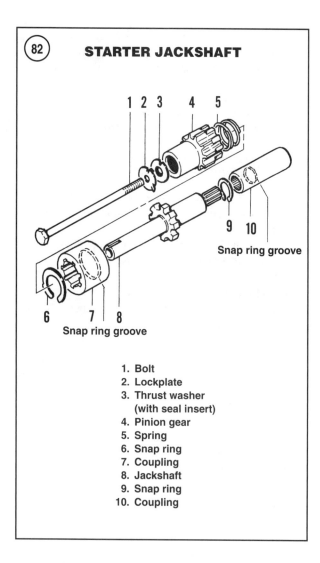

STARTER JACKSHAFT

Snap ring groove

Snap ring groove

1. Bolt
2. Lockplate
3. Thrust washer
   (with seal insert)
4. Pinion gear
5. Spring
6. Snap ring
7. Coupling
8. Jackshaft
9. Snap ring
10. Coupling

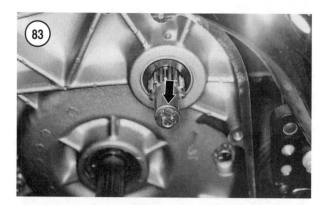

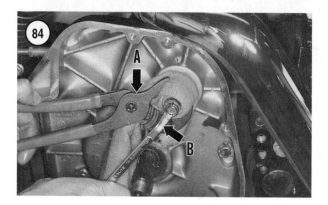

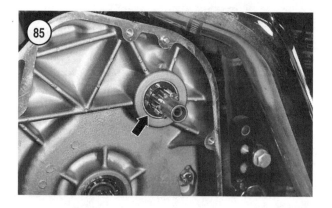

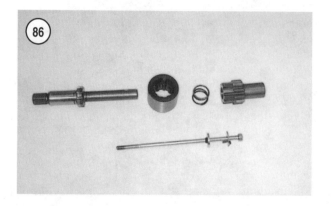

N•m). Bend the lockwasher tabs against the four bolt heads.

8. Install the starter jackshaft as described in this chapter.

9. Install the starter motor as described in Chapter Eight.

10. Install the compensating sprocket, primary chain and clutch assembly as described in this chapter.

11. Install the primary chaincase cover as described in this chapter.

12. Connect the negative battery cable as described in Chapter Eight.

STARTER JACKSHAFT

Removal

Refer to **Figure 82.**

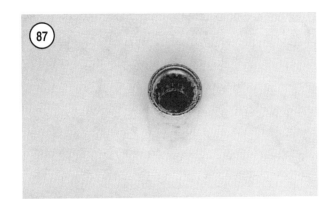

NOTE
On models so equipped, always disarm the optional TSSM security system prior to disconnecting the battery or the siren will sound.

1. Disconnect the negative battery cable as described in Chapter Eight.
2. Remove the primary chaincase cover as described in this chapter.

NOTE
*The pinion gear components (1-5, **Figure 82**) can be removed with the clutch/primary chain assembly in place. If only these parts require service, do not perform Step 3.*

3. Remove the compensating sprocket, primary chain and clutch assembly as described in this chapter.
4. Straighten the tab on the lockplate (**Figure 83**).
5. Wrap the pinion gear with a cloth to protect the finish, then secure it with pliers (A, **Figure 84**).
6. Loosen and remove the bolt (B, **Figure 84**), lockplate and thrust washer from the starter jackshaft assembly and the end of the starter motor.
7. Remove the pinion gear (**Figure 85**) and spring from the jackshaft.
8. Remove the jackshaft assembly and the coupling from the inner housing.

Inspection

1. Clean the jackshaft assembly (**Figure 86**) in solvent and dry it with compressed air.
2. Check the snap ring installed in each coupling (**Figure 87**) and (**Figure 88**). Replace any loose or damaged snap rings.
3. Replace all worn or damaged parts.

Installation

NOTE
*Before installing the coupling in Step 4, note the snap ring (**Figure 87**) installed inside the coupling. The coupling side with the snap ring closest to its end slides over the jackshaft.*

1. Install the jackshaft (**Figure 89**) into the housing. Push it in until it stops.
2. Position the coupling with its counterbore facing toward the jackshaft and install the coupling (**Figure 90**) into the housing bushing.
3. Install the spring (**Figure 91**) onto the jackshaft.

4. Install the pinion gear (**Figure 92**) onto the jackshaft.

5. Push in on the pinion gear (A, **Figure 93**) and install the bolt, lockplate and thrust washer (B) onto the jackshaft.

6. Push the assembly on until it bottoms.

7. Align the lockplate tab with the thrust washer, then insert the tab into the notch in the end of the jackshaft.

8. Screw the bolt into the starter motor shaft by hand.

9. Wrap the pinion gear with a cloth to protect the finish, then secure it with pliers (A, **Figure 84**).

10. Tighten the starter jackshaft bolt (B, **Figure 84**) to 84-108 in.-lb. (9-12 N•m). Bend the outer lockplate tab against the bolt head (**Figure 83**).

11. To ensure the components have been installed correctly, perform the following:

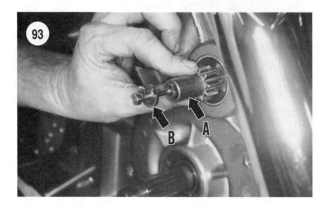

   a. Install the clutch shell onto the transmission mainshaft.

   b. With the starter motor not engaged, the pinion gear (A, **Figure 94**) must not engage the clutch shell gear (B).

   c. To check for proper engagement, pull out on the pinion gear and engage it with the clutch shell gear. Then rotate the clutch shell in either direction and make sure the pinion gear rotates with it.

   d. If engagement is incorrect, remove the clutch shell and correct the problem.

   e. Remove the clutch shell.

12. Install the compensating sprocket, primary chain and clutch assembly as described in this chapter.

13. Install the primary chaincase cover as described in this chapter.

14. Connect the negative battery cable as described in Chapter Eight.

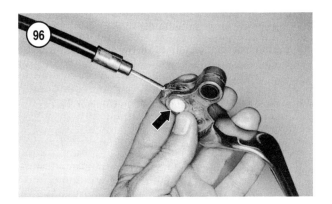

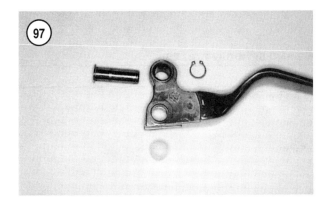

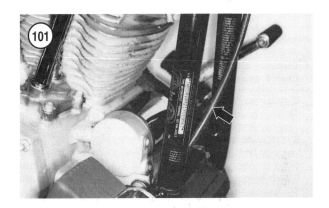

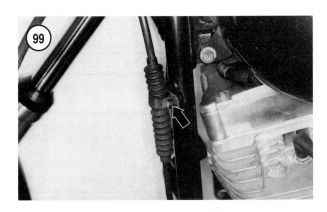

CLUTCH CABLE REPLACEMENT

1. Before removing the clutch cable, make a drawing of its routing path from the handlebar to the transmission side door.

2. Disconnect the clutch cable from the clutch release mechanism (**Figure 95**) as described under *Transmission Side Cover* in Chapter Six.

3. Remove the snap ring from the base of the clutch lever pivot pin.

4. Remove the pivot pin and slide the clutch lever out its perch.

5. Remove the plastic anchor pin (**Figure 96**) and disconnect the clutch cable from the lever.

6. Check the clutch lever components (**Figure 97**) for worn or damaged parts.

7. Make sure the anti-slack spring screw (**Figure 98**) on the bottom of the clutch lever is tight.

8. Remove the screw and bracket (**Figure 99**) securing the clutch cable to the frame front down tube cross member.

9. Carefully pull the clutch cable down through the steering stem upper and lower brackets (**Figure 100**, typical) and out from behind the voltage regulator/rectifier (**Figure 101**, typical).

5

10. Route the new clutch cable from the handlebar to the transmission side cover following the drawing made in Step 1.

11. Fit the clutch cable into its lever and secure it with the plastic anchor pin (**Figure 96**).

12. Slide the clutch lever into the perch and install the pivot pin.

13. Secure the pivot pin with the snap ring.

14. Reconnect the clutch cable to the clutch release mechanism as described under *Transmission Side Cover* in Chapter Six.

15. Adjust the clutch as described in Chapter Three.

Table 1 CLUTCH SPECIFICATIONS AND SPROCKET SIZES

Clutch type	Wet, multiplate disc
Clutch lever free play	1/16-1/8 in. (1.6-3.2 mm)
Clutch friction plate thickness	
service limit	0.143 in. (3.62 mm)
Clutch plate warp	
service limit	0.006 in. (0.15 mm)
Compensating sprocket	25 teeth
Clutch sprocket	36 teeth
Transmission sprocket	32 teeth

Table 2 CLUTCH AND PRIMARY CHAINCASE TORQUE SPECIFICATIONS

Item	ft.-lb.	in.-lb.	N•m
Diaphragm spring bolts	–	90-108	10-12
Clutch hub nut*	70-80	–	95-108
Compensating sprocket nut*	150-165	–	203-224
Primary chaincase cover bolts	–	108-120	12-14
Primary chaincase inspection cover			
long and short screws	–	84-108	9-12
Primary chaincase			
housing-to-engine and transmission bolts	17-21	–	23-29
Starter jackshaft bolt	–	84-108	9-12
*Apply threadlocking compound			

Table 3 COMPENSATING SPROCKET ALIGNMENT SPACERS

Spacer part No.	in.	mm
35850-84	0.010	0.25
35851-84	0.020	0.51
35852-84	0.030	0.76
24032-70	0.060	1.52
24033-70	0.090	2.29
24034-70	0.120	3.05
24035-70	0.150	3.81
24036-70	0.180	4.57
24037-70	0.210	5.33

CHAPTER SIX

TRANSMISSION

This chapter covers procedures for the transmission and shift linkage. Specifications are in **Tables 1-3** at the end of the chapter. Special tool requirements are described in the procedures. All of the special tools used in this manual and their part numbers are listed in **Table 12** of Chapter One.

All models are equipped with a five-speed transmission that is separate unit attached to the rear of the engine. The transmission shaft and shifter assemblies can be serviced with the transmission case mounted in the frame.

SHIFTER ASSEMBLY

The shifter assembly (**Figure 1**) consists of the external shift linkage and internal shift cam and shift arm components. The internal components can be serviced with the transmission case installed in the frame by removing the top cover.

If a shifting problem is encountered, refer to the troubleshooting procedures in Chapter Two and eliminate all clutch and shifter mechanism possibilities *before* considering transmission repairs. Improper clutch adjustment (Chapter Three) is often a cause of poor shifting.

Shift Linkage Adjustment

The shift linkage assembly connects the transmission shift rod lever to the foot-operated shift levers. The shift linkage does not require adjustment unless it is replaced or the transmission gears do not engage properly.

> *CAUTION*
> *On FLST models, the heal shift lever must never touch the footboard when shifting gears. To ensure proper gear engagement and avoid possible transmission damage, there must be a minimum clearance of 3/8 in. (9.5 mm) between the bottom of the heal shift lever and the top of the footboard. If the clearance is not correct, reposition the heal shift lever as described under **External Shift Mechanism** in this chapter.*

> *NOTE*
> *On models so equipped, always disarm the optional TSSM security system prior to disconnecting the battery or the siren will sound.*

1. Disconnect the negative battery cable as described in Chapter Eight.

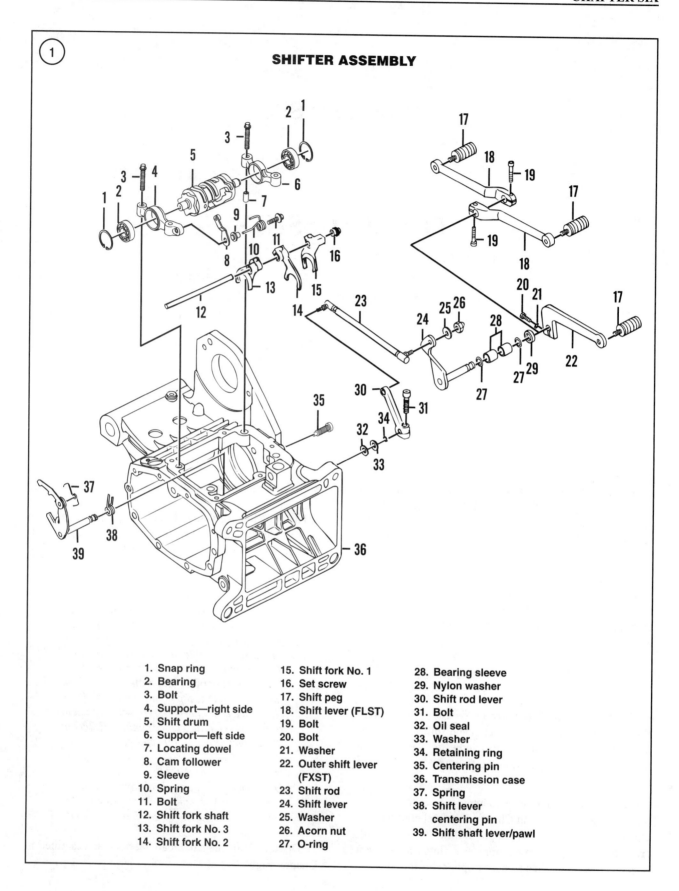

SHIFTER ASSEMBLY

1. Snap ring
2. Bearing
3. Bolt
4. Support—right side
5. Shift drum
6. Support—left side
7. Locating dowel
8. Cam follower
9. Sleeve
10. Spring
11. Bolt
12. Shift fork shaft
13. Shift fork No. 3
14. Shift fork No. 2
15. Shift fork No. 1
16. Set screw
17. Shift peg
18. Shift lever (FLST)
19. Bolt
20. Bolt
21. Washer
22. Outer shift lever (FXST)
23. Shift rod
24. Shift lever
25. Washer
26. Acorn nut
27. O-ring
28. Bearing sleeve
29. Nylon washer
30. Shift rod lever
31. Bolt
32. Oil seal
33. Washer
34. Retaining ring
35. Centering pin
36. Transmission case
37. Spring
38. Shift lever centering pin
39. Shift shaft lever/pawl

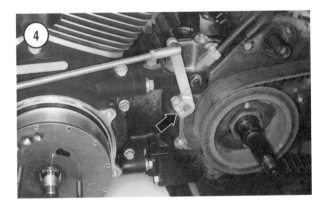

2. Loosen the two shift linkage rod locknuts (A, **Figure 2**).

3. Remove the acorn nut (**Figure 3**) and washers securing the shift linkage rod to the inner shift lever.

4. Turn the shift linkage rod (B, **Figure 2**) as necessary to change the linkage adjustment.

5. Reconnect the shift linkage rod to the front shift lever and tighten the locknuts to 20-24 ft.-lb. (27-32 N•m).

6. Recheck the shifting. Readjust if necessary.

7. If this adjustment does not correct the shifting, check the shift linkage for interference problems.

EXTERNAL SHIFT MECHANISM

Removal/Installation

Refer to **Figure 1**.

NOTE
On models so equipped, always disarm the optional TSSM security system prior to disconnecting the battery or the siren will sound.

1. Disconnect the battery negative lead as described in Chapter Eight.

2. Support the motorcycle with the front wheel off the ground. See *Motorcycle Stands* in Chapter Eight.

3. On models so equipped, remove the front left side footboard as described in Chapter Fourteen.

4A. On FXST models, perform the following:

    a. Make an alignment mark on the outer shift lever and the end of the shift shaft lever.

    b. Remove the clamp bolt and remove the outer shift lever.

4B. On FLST models, perform the following:

    a. Make an alignment mark on the heal shift lever and the end of the shift shaft lever.

    b. Remove the clamp bolt and remove the heal shift lever.

    c. Make an alignment mark on the toe shift lever that relates to the end of the shift lever shaft.

    d. Remove the clamp bolt and remove the toe shift lever.

5. Remove the nylon washer from the inner shift lever.

6. Remove the acorn nut (**Figure 3**) and washers securing the shift linkage rod to the inner shift lever.

7. Remove the jiffy stand and mounting bracket assembly as described in Chapter Fourteen.

8. Remove the primary chaincase assembly as described in Chapter Five.

9. Remove the clamp bolt securing the shift rod lever (**Figure 4**) to the transmission case.

10. Remove the shift rod lever, shift rod, inner and outer shift levers (**Figure 5**) and shift lever shaft as an assembly.

11. Install by reversing these removal steps. Tighten the clamp bolts securely.

TRANSMISSION TOP COVER

The transmission top cover assembly can be serviced with the transmission case installed in the frame.

6

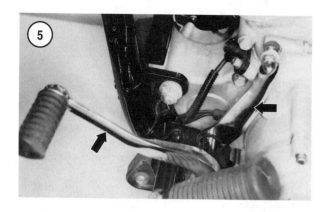

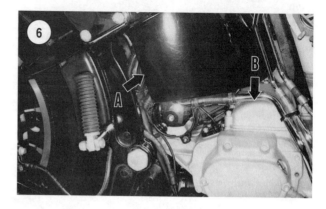

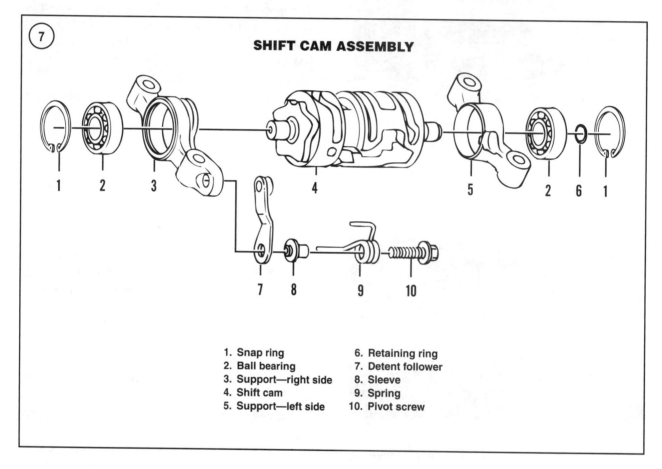

SHIFT CAM ASSEMBLY

1. Snap ring
2. Ball bearing
3. Support—right side
4. Shift cam
5. Support—left side
6. Retaining ring
7. Detent follower
8. Sleeve
9. Spring
10. Pivot screw

Removal/Installation

1. Remove the exhaust system as described in Chapter Seven.

2. Remove the battery as described in Chapter Eight.

3. Remove the oil tank (A, **Figure 6**) and oil lines as described in Chapter Four.

4. Disconnect the wire from the neutral indicator switch.

5. Disconnect the vent hose from the top cover or the fittings.

6. Remove the bolts and washers securing the transmission cover (B, **Figure 6**) to the transmission case. Remove the top cover and the gasket.

7. Remove the gasket residue from the transmission cover and transmission case gasket surfaces.

8. Install a *new* gasket onto the transmission case.

9. Install the transmission top cover, three bolts and washers. Tighten the bolts in a crisscross pattern to 84-108 in.-lb. (9-12 N•m).

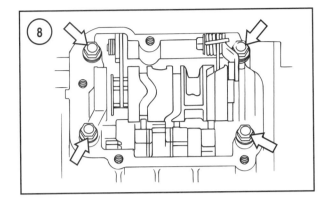

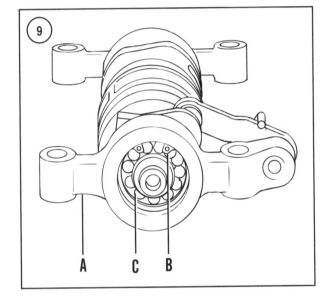

A C B

10. Reconnect the vent hose to the fitting and install a *new* hose clamp.

11. Connect the wire to the neutral indicator switch.

12. Install the oil tank as described in Chapter Four.

13. Install the battery as described in Chapter Eight.

14. Install the exhaust system as described in Chapter Seven.

SHIFT CAM

The shift cam assembly (**Figure 7**) can be serviced with the transmission case installed in the frame by removing the battery, oil tank and transmission top cover.

Removal

1. Remove the transmission top cover as described in this chapter.

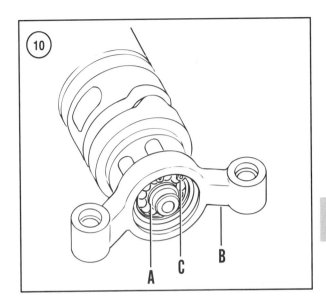

A C B

2. Remove the shift cam support block mounting bolts (**Figure 8**).

3. Lift the shift cam pawl off the cam pins to free the assembly.

4. Carefully lift the shifter cam assembly up and out of the transmission case.

5. Remove the four dowel pins from the transmission case.

Installation

1. Install the four dowel pins into the transmission case.

2. Lift the shift cam pawl up out of the way.

3. Carefully install the shift cam assembly into the transmission case. Align the shift fork pins with the shift cam slots.

4. Lower the shift cam pawl and engage it with the cam pins.

5. Install the shift cam support block mounting bolts. Tighten the bolts in a crisscross pattern to 84-108 in.-lb. (9-12 N•m).

6. Install the transmission top cover as described in this chapter.

Disassembly

1. On the right side, perform the following:
   a. Slide the right side support block (A, **Figure 9**) off the shift cam.
   b. Remove the snap ring (B, **Figure 9**) and withdraw the bearing (C) from the support block.

2. On the left side, perform the following:
   a. Remove the small retaining ring (A, **Figure 10**) from the shifter cam.

b. Slide the left side support block (B, **Figure 10**) off the shifter cam.

c. Remove the large retaining ring (C, **Figure 10**) and withdraw the bearing from the support block.

3. To remove the detent follower, unscrew the pivot bolt (A, **Figure 11**). Remove the spring (B), spring sleeve (C) and the detent follower (D).

Inspection

1. Clean all parts, except the support block bearings, in solvent and dry them thoroughly.

2. Check the shift cam grooves (**Figure 12**) for wear or roughness. Replace the shift cam if the groove profiles are excessively worn or damaged.

3. Check the shift cam ends where the cam contacts the bearings. If the ends are worn or damaged, replace the shift cam and both support block bearings.

4. Check the support block bearings for excessive wear, cracks or other damage. See **Figure 13**, typical. If necessary, refer to *Basic Service Methods* in Chapter One to replace the bearings.

5. Check the support blocks for wear, cracks or other damage. Replace the support blocks if necessary.

Assembly

1. Coat all bearing and sliding surfaces with assembly oil.

2. Install the detent follower as follows:

   a. Slide the spring sleeve (C, **Figure 11**) into the spring (B).

   b. Insert the pivot bolt (A, **Figure 11**) through the spring and sleeve.

   c. Correctly position the detent follower onto the bolt and place the spring end over the detent follower.

   d. Install the detent follower assembly onto the right side support and insert the spring's other end into the receptacle in the right side support. Screw the bolt into place and tighten it to 84-108 in.-lb. (9-12 N•m).

3. On the left side, perform the following:

   a. Position the bearing with the manufacturer's numbers facing out. Install the bearing into the support block.

   b. Position a *new* snap ring (C, **Figure 10**) so the larger tab will be on the right side when looking at the end of the support block. Install the snap ring.

   c. Make sure the snap ring is correctly seated in the groove.

   d. Slide the left side support block (B, **Figure 10**) onto the shifter cam.

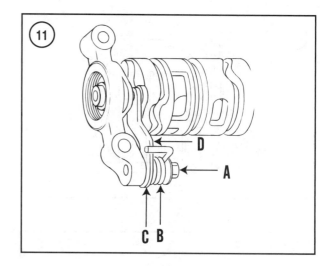

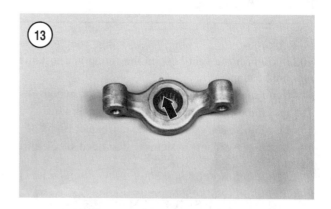

e. Install a *new* small retaining ring (A, **Figure 10**) onto the shifter cam.

f. Make sure the retaining ring is correctly seated in the groove.

4. On the right side, perform the following:

   a. Position the bearing with the manufacturer's numbers facing out. Install the bearing into the support block.

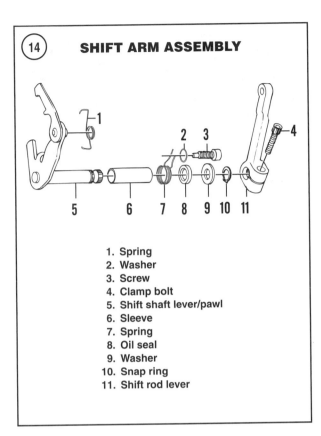

SHIFT ARM ASSEMBLY

14

1. Spring
2. Washer
3. Screw
4. Clamp bolt
5. Shift shaft lever/pawl
6. Sleeve
7. Spring
8. Oil seal
9. Washer
10. Snap ring
11. Shift rod lever

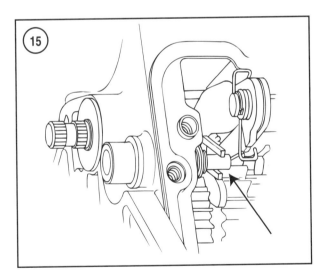

b. Position a *new* snap ring (B, **Figure 9**) with the beveled side facing out when looking at the end of the support block. Install the large retaining ring.

c. Make sure the snap ring is correctly seated in the groove.

d. Slide the right side support block (A, **Figure 9**) onto the shifter cam.

SHIFT ARM ASSEMBLY

Removal/Disassembly

Refer to **Figure 14**.

1. Remove the transmission side door assembly as described in this chapter.
2. Make an alignment mark on the shift rod lever and the end of the shift shaft lever/pawl.
3. Remove the clamp bolt and remove the shift rod lever from the shift shaft lever/pawl.
4. Remove the snap ring and washer from the shift lever shaft.
5. Withdraw the shift shaft lever/pawl, sleeve and spring from the inner surface of the transmission case.

Inspection

1. Check the shift pawl for wear. Replace the pawl if it is damaged.
2. Check the springs for wear or damage.
3. Check the shift shaft lever for wear or damage. Check the end splines for wear or damage.
4. Check the shift rod lever for wear or damage. Check the internal splines for wear or damage.

Assembly/Installation

1. Check that the sleeve is still in place in the transmission case.
2. Slide the shift shaft lever spring over the shift shaft lever. Align the opening on the spring with the tab on the lever.
3. Place the spring on the shift shaft lever/pawl.
4. Install the shift shaft lever assembly into the transmission case.
5. Align the spring with the screw in the case (**Figure 15**).
6. Install the washer and snap ring onto the shaft. Make sure the snap ring is correctly seated in the shaft.
7. Refer to the alignment marks made in Step 1 of *Removal/Disassembly* and instal the shift rod lever onto the end of the shift shaft lever/pawl. Push it on until the bolt hole aligns with the shaft lever/pawl groove.
8. Install the clamp bolt and tighten it to 18-24 ft.-lb. (24-30 N•m).
9. Install the transmission side door assembly as described in this chapter.

SHIFT FORKS

The shift forks can be serviced with the transmission case installed in the frame by removing the battery, oil tank and transmission top cover.

6

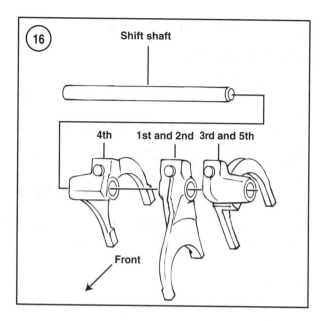

Shift shaft

4th   1st and 2nd   3rd and 5th

Front

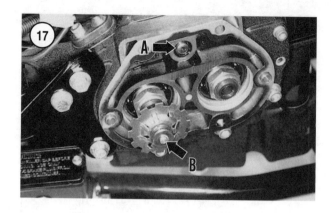

Removal

Refer to **Figure 1**.

1. Remove the transmission top cover as described in this chapter.

2. Remove the shift cam as described in this chapter.

3. Remove the transmission side cover as described in this chapter.

NOTE
*Use a waterproof felt-tip pen or scribe to mark the installed position of each shift fork in the transmission (**Figure 16**). All three shift forks are unique and must be reinstalled in the correct position.*

4. Slide the shift shaft (A, **Figure 17**, typical) out of the transmission case and remove the shift forks (**Figure 18**) from the transmission case.

Inspection

1. Inspect each shift fork (**Figure 19**) for excessive wear or damage. Replace worn or damaged shift forks as required.

2. Measure the thickness of each shift fork finger (A, **Figure 20**) where it contacts the sliding gear groove (**Figure 21**). Replace any shift fork with a finger thickness worn to the specification in **Table 2**.

3. Check the shift forks for arc-shaped wear or burn marks (B, **Figure 20**). Replace damaged shift forks.

4. Roll the shift fork shaft on a flat surface and check for bends. Replace the shaft if it is bent.

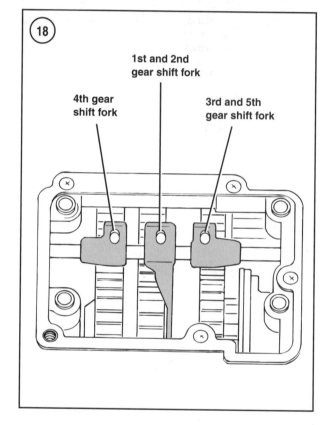

1st and 2nd
gear shift fork

4th gear
shift fork

3rd and 5th
gear shift fork

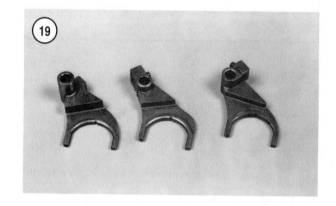

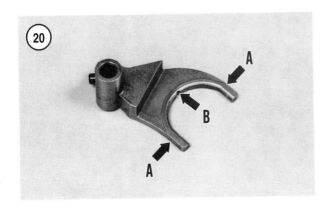

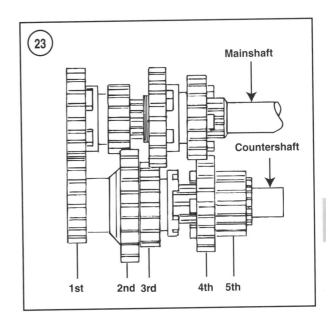

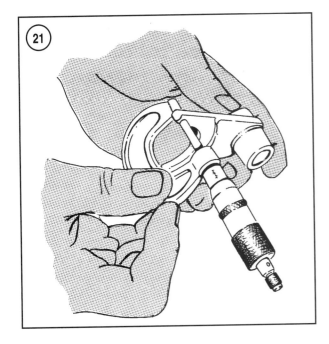

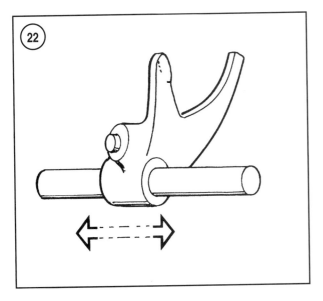

5. Install each shift fork on the shift shaft. The shift forks must slide smoothly with no binding or roughness (**Figure 22**).

Assembly

Refer to **Figure 23** to identify the transmission gears.

1. Coat all bearing and sliding surfaces with assembly oil.
2. To install the shift forks and shaft (**Figure 16**), perform the following:
   a. Insert the No. 1 shift fork into the mainshaft first gear groove.
   b. Install the No. 2 shift fork into the countershaft third gear groove.
   c. Install the No. 3 shift fork into the mainshaft second gear groove.
3. Insert the shift shaft (A, **Figure 17**) through each of the three shift forks and into the transmission case.
4. Install the transmission side door as described in this chapter.
5. Make sure the shift forks move smoothly when shifting the gears by hand.
6. Install the shift cam as described in this chapter.

TRANSMISSION SIDE DOOR AND TRANSMISSION SHAFT ASSEMBLIES

The transmission side door and transmission shaft assemblies can be serviced with the transmission case installed in the frame.

The following special tools are used during disassembly and assembly:

6

1. Mainshaft bearing race puller and installation tool (JIMS part No. 34902-84).
2. Five-speed door puller (JIMS part No. 2283).
3. Transmission door bearing remover and installer (JIMS part No. 1078).
4. Transmission shaft installers (JIMS part No. 2189).

Removal

Remove the transmission and side door assembly as follows:

1. Remove the exhaust system as described in Chapter Seven.
2. Drain the transmission oil as described in Chapter Three.
3. Remove the primary chaincase cover as described in Chapter Five.
4. Remove the clutch release cover and clutch assembly as described in Chapter Five.
5. Remove the primary chaincase housing as described in Chapter Five.
6. Remove the shift forks as described in this chapter.
7. Remove the bearing inner race (**Figure 24**) from the mainshaft as follows:
   a. Attach the mainshaft bearing race puller and installation tool (**Figure 25**) to the inner bearing race following the manufacturer's instructions.
   b. Tighten the puller bolt (A, **Figure 26**) and withdraw the inner race (B) from the mainshaft.
8. Remove the oil slinger assembly (B, **Figure 17**).
9. Turn the transmission by hand and shift the transmission into two different gears to keep the gears from turning.

> *NOTE*
> *The mainshaft and countershaft have left-hand threads. Turn the nuts **clockwise** to loosen them.*

10. If the transmission gear assemblies are going to be removed from the side door, loosen, but do not remove, the countershaft and mainshaft locknuts.
11. If the main drive gear is going to be removed, remove the drive sprocket as described under *Drive Sprocket* in Chapter Nine.
12. Remove the bolts securing the transmission side door to the transmission case.

> *CAUTION*
> *When removing the transmission side door in Step 13, do not tap the transmission shafts from the opposite side. This will damage the side door bearings.*

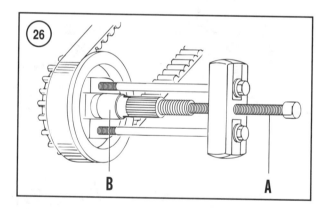

13. Tap the transmission side door to loosen its seal with the transmission case.

14. Install the five-speed door puller (**Figure 27**) onto the door following the manufacturer's instructions. Tighten the outside screws one-half turn at a time alternating from side-to-side until the door releases from the transmission case. Remove the special tool.

15. Slowly withdraw the transmission side door and the transmission gear assemblies from the transmission case.

16. Remove the transmission side door gasket. Do not lose the locating pins.

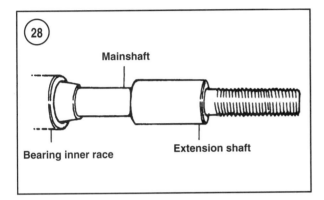

28

Mainshaft

Bearing inner race

Extension shaft

17. If necessary, service the side door and transmission assembly as described in this chapter.

Installation

1. If the main drive gear was removed, install it as described in this chapter.

2. Remove all gasket residue from the side door and transmission case mating surfaces.

3. Install a *new* gasket onto the transmission case. If the locating pins were removed, install them.

4. Install the side door and transmission assembly into the transmission case. Make sure the side door fits flush against the transmission case.

5. Install the transmission side door 5/16 in. and 1/4 in. bolts finger-tight. Tighten the 5/16 in. bolts to 13-16 ft.-lb. (18-22 N•m). Then tighten the 1/4 in. bolts to 84-108 in.-lb. (9-12 N•m).

6. Turn the transmission by hand and shift the transmission into two different gears to keep the gears from turning.

7. Install the bearing inner race (**Figure 24**) onto the mainshaft as follows:

    a. The bearing inner race is 0.950-1.000 in. (24.13-25.40 mm) long. When installing a *new* race,

measure it to confirm its length. Race length determines its installation position.

    b. Use the same special tool set-up used for bearing inner race removal.

    c. Apply clean oil to the transmission shaft bearing surface, shaft threads and inner surface of the inner race.

    d. Position the bearing inner race with the chamfered end going on first and slide it onto the mainshaft (**Figure 28**).

    e. Install the extension shaft onto the mainshaft.

    f. Place the pusher tube, the two flat washers and nut over the extension shaft.

NOTE
*The mainshaft and countershaft nut have left-hand threads. Turn each nut **counterclockwise** to tighten it in substep g.*

CAUTION
Install the inner bearing race to the dimension in substep g. This aligns the race with the bearing outer race installed in the primary chaincase. Installing the wrong race or installing it incorrectly will damage the bearing and race assembly.

    g. Hold the extension shaft and tighten the nut to press the bearing inner race onto the mainshaft. Install the race so its inside edge is 0.100-0.150 in. (2.540-3.810 mm.) away from the main drive gear.

    h. Remove the special tools.

8. Install the oil slinger assembly (B, **Figure 17**).

9. Install the shift forks as described in this chapter.

10. Install the primary chaincase housing as described in Chapter Five.

11. Install the clutch assembly and clutch release cover as described in Chapter Five.

12. Install the primary chaincase cover as described in Chapter Five.

13. Install the drain plug and refill the transmission oil as described in Chapter Three.

14. Install the exhaust system as described in Chapter Seven.

15. Test-ride the motorcycle slowly and check for proper transmission operation.

TRANSMISSION SHAFTS

This section describes service to the side door and both transmission shaft assemblies.

6

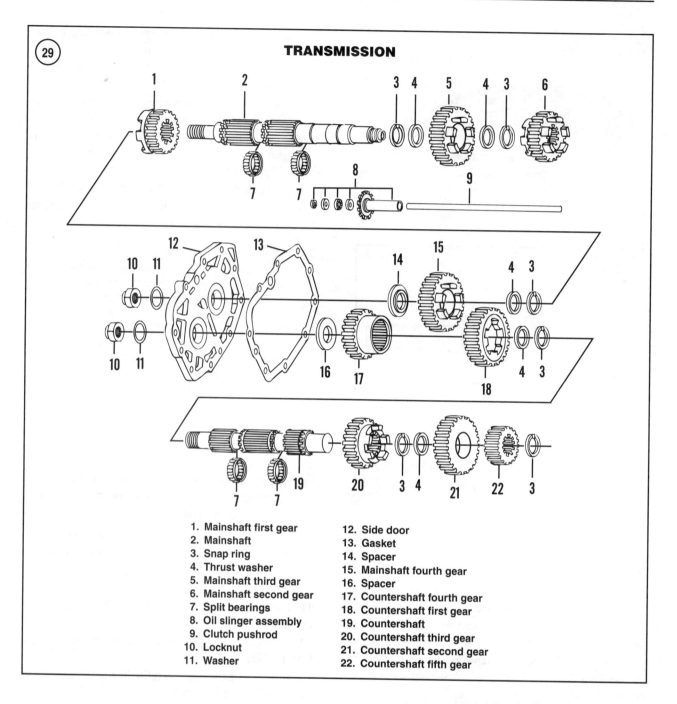

TRANSMISSION

1. Mainshaft first gear
2. Mainshaft
3. Snap ring
4. Thrust washer
5. Mainshaft third gear
6. Mainshaft second gear
7. Split bearings
8. Oil slinger assembly
9. Clutch pushrod
10. Locknut
11. Washer
12. Side door
13. Gasket
14. Spacer
15. Mainshaft fourth gear
16. Spacer
17. Countershaft fourth gear
18. Countershaft first gear
19. Countershaft
20. Countershaft third gear
21. Countershaft second gear
22. Countershaft fifth gear

Disassembly

The transmission shaft assemblies (**Figure 29**) must be partially disassembled prior to removing both shafts from the side door. Do not try to remove the shafts with all of the gears in place.

The snap rings are difficult to loosen and remove even with high-quality snap ring pliers. Heavy-duty retaining ring pliers (H-D part No. J-5586), or an equivalent, is recommended for this procedure.

Store all of the transmission gears, snap rings, washers and split bearings in the order of removal.

1. Remove the transmission side door and transmission shaft assemblies as described in this chapter.

2. Protect the splines and threads on the mainshaft with tape or a plastic sleeve (**Figure 30**).

3. Remove the mainshaft second gear (**Figure 31**).

4. Remove the snap ring (**Figure 32**) from the countershaft.

5. Remove the countershaft fifth gear (**Figure 33**).

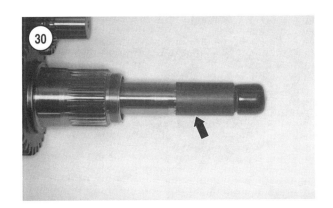

6

6. Remove the countershaft second gear (**Figure 34**).

CAUTION
Do not expand the split bearings any more
than necessary to slide them off the shaft.
The bearing carriers are plastic and will
fracture if expanded too far.

7. Remove the split bearing (**Figure 35**) from the countershaft.

8. Slide off the washer and remove the snap ring (**Figure 36**) from the countershaft.

9. Remove the countershaft third gear (**Figure 37**).

NOTE
The snap ring in Step 10 must be released and moved in order to gain access to the snap ring on the other side of the third gear.

10. Using snap ring pliers, release the snap ring (**Figure 38**) behind the mainshaft third gear. Slide the snap ring away from the third gear.

11. Slide the third gear toward the side door and remove the snap ring (**Figure 39**) and washer.

12. Remove the mainshaft third gear (**Figure 40**).

13. Remove the washer and snap ring (**Figure 41**).

14. Remove the split bearing (**Figure 42**) from the countershaft.

15. Place a brass or aluminum washer (**Figure 43**) between the countershaft fourth gear and the mainshaft fourth gear. This locks both transmission shafts from rotation.

16. If not loosened during *Removal*, loosen and remove the locknuts and washers (**Figure 44**) securing the shaft assemblies to the side door. Remove the brass or aluminum washer from between the shafts. New locknuts must be installed during assembly.

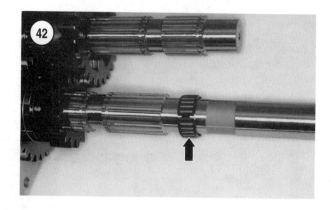

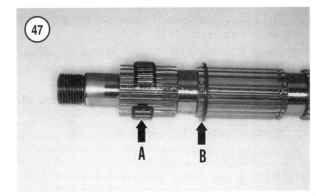

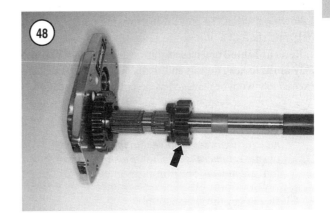

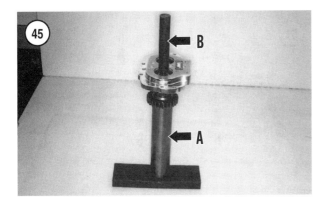

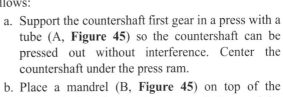

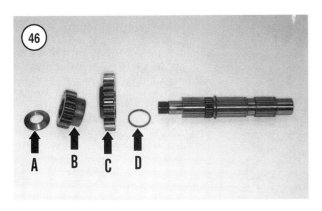

17. Press the countershaft out of its side door bearing as follows:

    a. Support the countershaft first gear in a press with a tube (A, **Figure 45**) so the countershaft can be pressed out without interference. Center the countershaft under the press ram.

    b. Place a mandrel (B, **Figure 45**) on top of the countershaft and press the countershaft out of the side door.

18. Remove the spacer (A, **Figure 46**), fourth gear (B), first gear (C) and washer (D) from the countershaft.

19. Remove the split bearing (A, **Figure 47**) from the countershaft.

20. If necessary, remove the snap ring (B, **Figure 47**) from the countershaft.

21. Remove the first gear (**Figure 48**) from the mainshaft.

22. Remove the ring snap and washer (A, **Figure 49**) from the mainshaft.

23. Press the mainshaft out of its side door bearing as follows:

    a. Support the mainshaft fourth gear on a tube (A, **Figure 50**) in a press so the mainshaft can be pressed out without interference. Center the mainshaft under the press ram.

   b. Place a mandrel (B, **Figure 50**) on top of the mainshaft and press the mainshaft out of the side door.

24. Remove the fourth gear and spacer (B, **Figure 49**) from the mainshaft.

25. Inspect all parts as described in this section.

Inspection

Maintain the alignment of the transmission components when cleaning and inspecting the individual parts in the following section. To prevent intermixing parts, work on only one shaft at a time.

Refer to **Table 2** and inspect the service clearance and end play of the indicated gears and shafts. Replace parts that are excessively worn or damaged as described in this section.

CAUTION
Do not clean the split bearings in solvent. Removing all traces of solvent from the bearing plastic retainers is difficult. Flush the bearings clean with new transmission oil.

1. Clean and dry the shaft assembly.

2. Inspect the mainshaft and countershaft for:
   a. Worn or damages splines (A, **Figure 51**).
   b. Excessively worn or damaged bearing surfaces.
   c. Cracked or rounded-off snap ring grooves (B, **Figure 51**).
   d. Worn or damaged threads (C, **Figure 51**).

3. Check each gear for excessive wear, burrs, pitting, or chipped or missing teeth. Check the inner splines (**Figure 52**) on sliding gears and the bore on stationary gears for excessive wear or damage.

4. Check the gear bushings (**Figure 53**) for wear, cracks or other damage.

5. To check stationary gears for wear, install them in their original operating positions. If necessary, use the old snap rings to secure them in place. Then spin the gear by hand. The gear should turn smoothly. A rough turning gear indicates heat damage. Check for a dark blue color or galling on the operating surfaces. Rocking indicates excessive wear to the gear and/or shaft.

6. To check the sliding gears, install them in their original operating positions. The gear should slide back and forth without any binding or excessive play.

7. Check the shift fork groove (**Figure 54**) for wear or damage.

8. Check the dogs on the gears for excessive wear, rounding, cracks or other damage. Refer to **Figure 55**. When

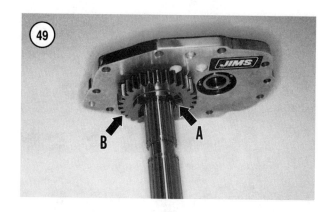

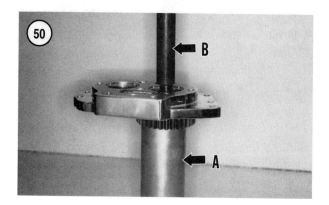

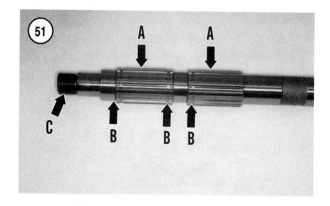

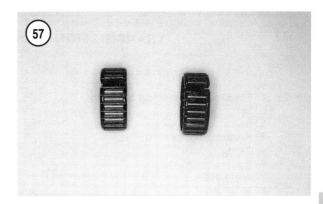

6

wear is noticeable, make sure it is consistent on each gear dog. If one dog is worn more than the others, the others will be overstressed during operation and will eventually crack and fail. Check engaging gears as described in Step 10.

9. Check each gear dog slot for cracks, rounding and other damage. Check engaging gears as described in Step 10.

10. Check engaging gears by installing the two gears on their respective shafts and in their original operating position. Mesh the gears together. Twist one gear against the other and check the dog engagement. Then reverse the thrust load to check the other operating position. Make sure the engagement in both directions is positive and there is no slippage. Make sure there is equal engagement across all of the engagement dogs.

> *NOTE*
> *If there is excessive or uneven wear to the gear engagement dogs, check the shift forks carefully for bends and other damage. Refer to **Shifter Assembly** in this chapter.*

> *NOTE*
> *Replace defective gears and their mating gears, though the mating gears may not show as much wear or damage.*

11. Check the spacers (**Figure 56**) for wear or damage.

12. Check the split bearings (**Figure 57**) for excessive wear or damage.

13. Replace all of the snap rings during reassembly. Check the washers for burn marks, scoring or cracks. Replace as necessary.

Side door bearings inspection and replacement

The side door bearings (**Figure 58**) are pressed into place and secured with a snap ring. They can be removed and installed with a transmission door bearing remover

58

TRANSMISSION CASE, BEARINGS AND COVERS

1. Speed sensor electrical connector
2. Secondary lock
3. Bolt
4. Neutral indicator switch
5. O-ring
6. Bolt
7. Vent hose
8. 90° fitting
9. Cover
10. Screw
11. Speed sensor
12. O-ring
13. Gasket
14. Dowel pin
15. Transmission case
16. Mainshaft bearing (left side)
17. Snap ring
18. Quad seal
19. Oil seal
20. Sprocket spacer
21. Bearing
22. Dowel pin
23. Bolt
24. Washer
25. Screw
26. Washer
27. Screw
28. Mounting bracket
29. O-ring
30. Drain plug
31. Transmission side door
32. Gasket
33. Locating pin
34. Locknut
35. Washer
36. Snap ring
37. Bearing
38. Bolt
39. Bolt
40. Clutch release cover
41. Screw
42. O-ring
43. O-ring
44. Filler plug/dipstick
45. Outer ramp
46. Coupling
47. Ball (3)
48. Inner ramp
49. Snap ring
50. Gasket

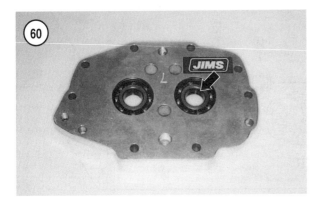

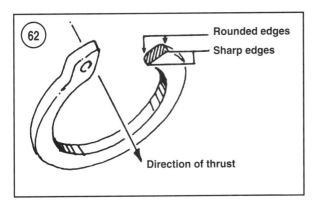

Rounded edges
Sharp edges
Direction of thrust

and installer (JIMS part No. 1078) (**Figure 59**). If this special tool set is not available, a press is required.

1. Clean the side door and bearings in solvent, and dry them with compressed air.

2. Turn each bearing inner race (**Figure 60**) by hand. The bearings must turn smoothly. If they need to be replaced, continue to Step 3.

3. Remove both snap rings (**Figure 61**) from the outer surface of the side door.

4A. To remove the bearings with the special tool set, follow the manufacturer's instructions.

4B. Remove the bearings with a press as follows:

    a. Support the side door on the press bed with the outer surface facing up.

    b. Use a driver or socket to press the bearing out of the backside of the side door.

    c. Repeat substep b for the opposite bearing.

5. Clean the side door in solvent and dry it thoroughly.

6. Inspect the bearing bores in the side cover for cracks or other damage. Replace the side door if it is damaged.

NOTE
Both side door bearings have the same part number.

7A. To install the bearing with the special tool set, follow the manufacturer's instructions.

7B. Install the bearing with a press as follows:

    a. Support the side door in a press with the backside facing up.

    b. Install bearings with their manufacturer's marks facing out.

    c. Use a driver that matches the bearing outer race. Press the bearing into the side door until it bottoms.

    d. Repeat substeps b and c for the opposite bearing.

8. Position the beveled snap ring with the sharp side (**Figure 62**) facing toward the bearing outer race and install the snap ring. Make sure the snap ring is correctly seated in the side door groove.

Assembly

Refer to **Figure 63**.

CAUTION
*Install **new** snap rings at every location to ensure proper gear alignment and engagement. Never reinstall a snap ring that has been removed since it is distorted and weakened, and may fail. Make sure each **new** snap ring is correctly seated in its respective shaft groove.*

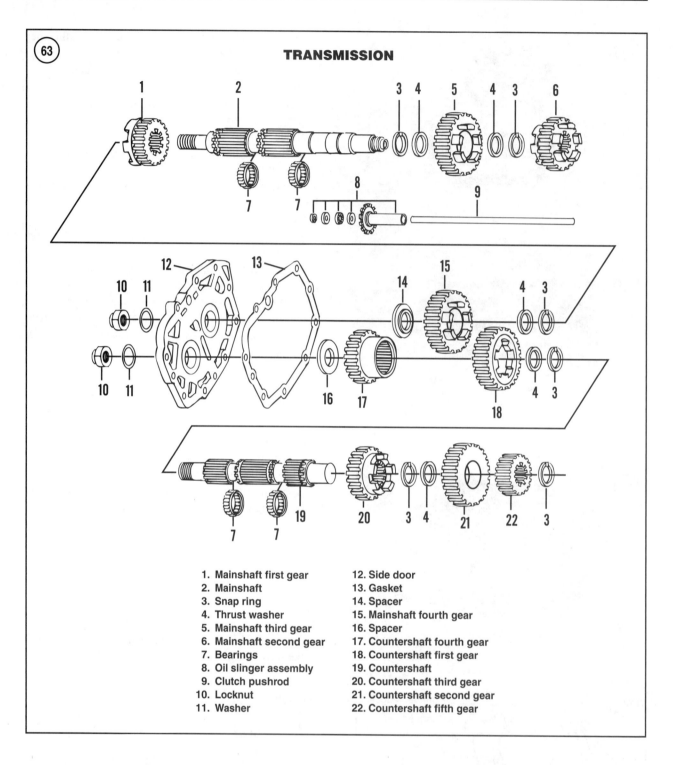

TRANSMISSION

1. Mainshaft first gear
2. Mainshaft
3. Snap ring
4. Thrust washer
5. Mainshaft third gear
6. Mainshaft second gear
7. Bearings
8. Oil slinger assembly
9. Clutch pushrod
10. Locknut
11. Washer
12. Side door
13. Gasket
14. Spacer
15. Mainshaft fourth gear
16. Spacer
17. Countershaft fourth gear
18. Countershaft first gear
19. Countershaft
20. Countershaft third gear
21. Countershaft second gear
22. Countershaft fifth gear

1. Apply a light coat of clean transmission oil to all mating gear surfaces and to all split bearing halves before assembly.

2. If removed, install the side door bearings as described in this chapter.

3. Install the following onto the mainshaft:

a. If the snap ring was removed, install a *new* snap ring (**Figure 64**).

b. Position the first gear with the shift dog side going on last and install the first gear (**Figure 65**).

c. Install the snap ring (A, **Figure 66**) and washer (B).

d. Install the split bearing (**Figure 67**).

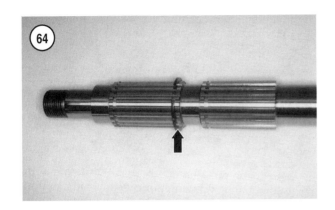

6

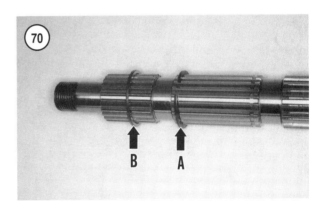

e. Position the fourth gear with the shift dog side going on first and install the fourth gear (**Figure 68**).

f. Position the spacer with the beveled side facing out (**Figure 69**) and install the spacer.

4. Install the following onto the countershaft:

a. If the snap ring was removed, install a *new* snap ring (A, **Figure 70**).

b. Install the washer (B, **Figure 70**) and push it against the snap ring.

c. Install the split bearing (**Figure 71**).

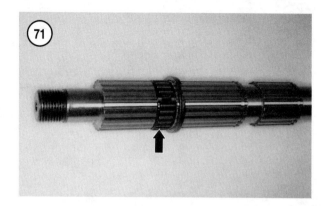

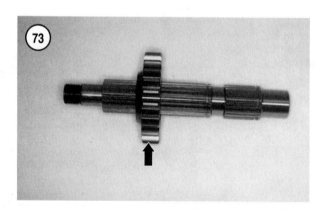

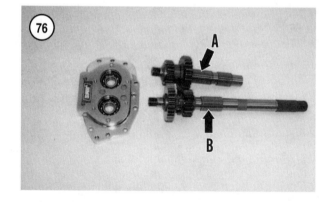

d. Position the first gear with the shoulder side (**Figure 72**) going on last and install the first gear onto the split bearing (**Figure 73**).

e. Position the fourth gear with the wide shoulder (**Figure 74**) going on first and install the fourth gear.

f. Position the spacer with the beveled side facing out (**Figure 75**) and install the spacer.

5. Apply transmission oil to the inner race of both bearings and to the shoulder of both shaft assemblies. Also ap-

ply transmission oil to the inner threads and ends of the special tools used in Step 8.

6. Position the countershaft (A, **Figure 76**) on the left side of the side door. Position the mainshaft (B, **Figure 76**) on the right side of the side door.

7. Mesh the two shaft assemblies together and start them into the side door bearings (**Figure 77**).

8. Attach the shaft installers (JIMS part No. 2189) onto the ends of both shafts.

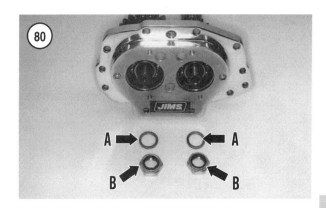

6

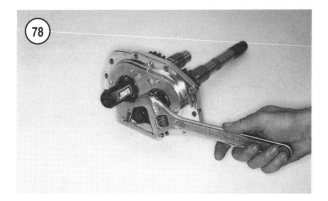

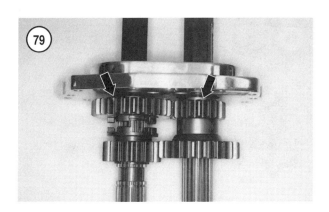

9. Tighten the shaft installers (**Figure 78**), alternating between both shafts, until both shaft shoulders bottom on the inner race of the side door bearings (**Figure 79**).

10. Unscrew and remove the special tools.

CAUTION
*Always install **new** locknuts. If an old locknut is reinstalled, it may work loose and cause transmission damage.*

11. Install the spacers (A, **Figure 80**) and *new* locknuts (B).

12. Start the *new* locknuts by hand until the locking portion of the nut touches the end of the transmission shaft.

13. Place a brass or aluminum washer between the countershaft fourth gear and the mainshaft fourth gear. This will lock both transmission shafts.

14. Tighten the locknuts (**Figure 81**) to 45-55 ft.-lb. (61-75 N•m).

15. Install the following onto the mainshaft:

   a. Install the split bearing (**Figure 82**).

   b. Move the snap ring (A, **Figure 83**) installed in Step 3 out of the groove and toward the first gear.

c. Install the washer (B, **Figure 83**) and slide it against the snap ring (A, **Figure 84**).

d. Position third gear with the shift dogs side (B, **Figure 84**) going on last. Install the third gear onto the split bearing (**Figure 85**).

e. Install the washer (A, **Figure 86**) and snap ring (B). Make sure the snap ring is correctly seated in the mainshaft groove.

f. Move third gear away from the first gear, and up against the washer and snap ring installed in substep e.

g. Reposition the washer and snap ring behind third gear. Make sure the snap ring is correctly seated in the mainshaft groove.

16. Install the following onto the countershaft:

a. Position the third gear with the shift fork groove (**Figure 87**) side going on last and install the third gear.

b. Install the snap ring (A, **Figure 88**) and washer (B).

c. Install the split bearing (**Figure 89**).

6

d. Position the second gear with the shift dog side (**Figure 90**) going on first. Install the second gear onto the split bearing (**Figure 91**).

17. On the mainshaft, position the second gear with the shift fork groove (**Figure 92**) side going on first and install the second gear (**Figure 93**).

18. On the countershaft, install the fifth gear (**Figure 94**), then install the snap ring (**Figure 95**). Make sure the snap ring is correctly seated in the countershaft groove.

19. Refer to **Figure 96** for correct placement of all gears. Also make sure the gears mesh properly to the adjoining

gear where applicable. Make sure the gears are correctly assembled before installing the shaft assemblies into the transmission case.

MAIN DRIVE GEAR

The main drive gear (**Figure 97**) and bearing assembly are pressed into the transmission case. If the transmission case is installed in the frame, a special transmission main drive gear tool set (JIMS part No. 35316-80) (**Figure 98**) is required to remove the main drive gear. If the transmission has been removed, use a press to remove and install the main drive gear.

Whenever the main drive gear is removed, the main drive gear bearing must be replaced at the same time.

Removal

1. Remove the transmission shaft assemblies from the transmission case as described in this chapter.
2. Remove the spacer from the main drive gear oil seal.
3. Remove the circlip behind the bearing.

> *NOTE*
> *If the main drive gear will not loosen from the bearing in Step 4 due to corrosion, remove the special tools and heat the bearing with a heat gun.*

4. Assemble the special tool set onto the main drive gear following the manufacturer's instructions. Then tighten the puller nut slowly to pull the main drive gear from the bearing in the transmission case.
5. Remove the main drive gear bearing from the transmission case as described in this section.

Inspection

1. Clean the main drive gear in solvent and dry it with compressed air, if available.
2. Check each gear tooth (A, **Figure 99**) for excessive wear, burrs, galling and pitting. Check for missing teeth.
3. Check the gear splines (B, **Figure 99**) for excessive wear, galling or other damage.
4. Inspect the two main drive gear needle bearings for excessive wear or damage. Refer to **Figure 100** and **Figure 101**. Insert the mainshaft into the main drive gear to check bearing wear. If necessary, replace the bearings as described in this section.

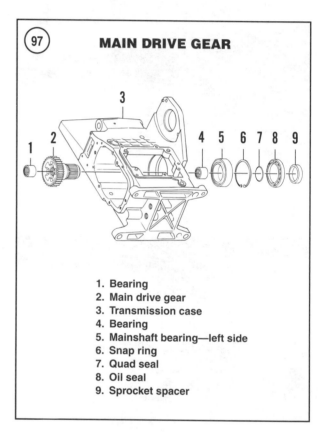

MAIN DRIVE GEAR

1. Bearing
2. Main drive gear
3. Transmission case
4. Bearing
5. Mainshaft bearing—left side
6. Snap ring
7. Quad seal
8. Oil seal
9. Sprocket spacer

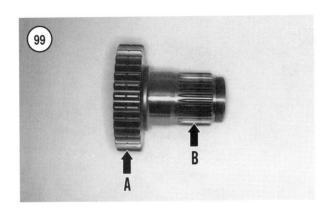

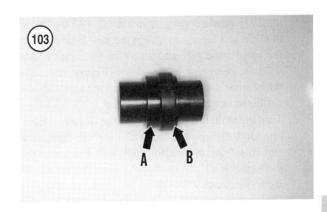

6

Bearing Replacement

Main drive gear needle bearings

Both main drive gear needle bearings must be installed to a correct depth within the main drive gear. The correct depth is obtained with a main drive gear bearing tool (JIMS part No. 37842-91). This tool also installs the oil seal. If this tool is not available, a press is required.

If the special tool is not available, measure the depth of both bearings before removing them.

Replace both main drive gear needle bearings as a set.

CAUTION
Never reinstall a main drive gear needle bearing, as it is distorted during removal.

1. Remove the oil seal (**Figure 102**) from the clutch side of the main drive gear.

2. If the special tool is not used, measure and record the depth of both bearings.

3. Support the main drive gear in a press and press out one needle bearing. Then turn the gear over and press out the opposite bearing.

4. Clean the gear and its bearing bore in solvent and dry them thoroughly.

5. Apply transmission oil to the bearing bore in the main drive gear and to the outer surface of both bearings.

NOTE
Install both needle bearings with their man-ufacturer's name and size code facing out.

6A. Install the bearings with the special tool as follows:

   a. The special tool has two different length ends. The tool's long side (A, **Figure 103**) is for the clutch side of the main drive gear (**Figure 101**). The tool's short side (B, **Figure 103**) is for the transmission side of the main drive gear (**Figure 100**).

b. Install the main drive gear in a press with the transmission end facing up. Align the new bearing with the main drive gear and insert the installation tool with the *short side facing down* (**Figure 104**) into the bearing. Operate the press until the tool's shoulder bottoms against the gear.

c. Turn the main drive gear over so the inner end faces up. Align the *new* bearing with the main drive gear and insert the installation tool with the *long side facing down* into the bearing. Operate the press until the tool's shoulder bottoms against the gear.

6B. If the bearings are being installed without the installation tool, use a suitable mandrel to press in the bearing to the depth recorded in Step 2.

7. Install a *new* oil seal (**Figure 102**) into the clutch side of the main drive gear.

Mainshaft bearing

The left side mainshaft bearing (5, **Figure 97**) is pressed into the transmission case. If the transmission case is installed in the frame, a transmission main bearing remover set (JIMS part No. 1720) (**Figure 105**), or equivalent, is required to remove the main drive gear bearing. If the transmission has been removed, use a press to remove the main drive gear bearing.

Whenever the main drive gear is removed, the mainshaft drive gear bearing is damaged and must be replaced at the same time.

> *CAUTION*
> *Failure to use the correct tools to install the bearing will cause premature failure of the bearing and related parts.*

1. Remove the main drive gear from the transmission case as described in this chapter.

2. Assemble the special tool set onto the mainshaft bearing following the manufacturer's instructions. Then tighten the bolt and nut slowly to pull the mainshaft bearing from the transmission case.

3. Clean the bearing bore and dry it with compressed air. Check the bore for nicks or burrs. Check the snap ring groove for damage.

> *NOTE*
> *Install the bearing into the transmission case with the bearing manufacturer's name and size code facing out.*

4. Apply transmission oil to the bearing bore in the transmission case and to the outer surface of the bearing. Also apply oil to the nut and threaded shaft of the installer tool.

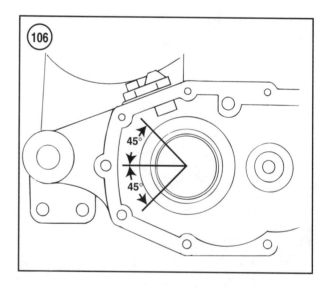

5. Install the bearing onto the installation tool and assemble the installation tool following the manufacturer's instructions.

6. Slowly tighten the puller nut to pull the bearing into the transmission case. Continue until the bearing bottoms in the case.

7. Disassemble and remove the installation tool.

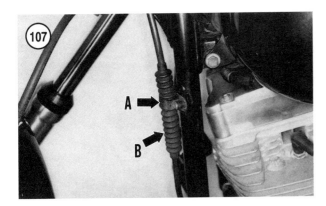

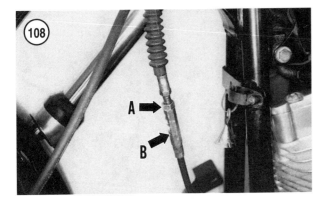

Installation

1. Replace the mainshaft bearing and oil seal as described in the previous procedure.

2. Install a *new* snap ring with the flat side facing the bearing.

3. Position the snap ring with the open end facing the rear of the transmission and within a 45° angle to horizontal (**Figure 106**). Make sure it is fully seated in the snap ring groove.

4. Install the *new* oil seal into the case so its closed side faces out.

5. Apply transmission oil to the bearing bore and to the outer surface of the main drive gear. Also apply oil to the nut and threaded shaft of the installer tool.

6. Insert the mainshaft into the mainshaft bearing as far as it will go. Hold it in place and assemble the special tool onto the main drive gear and transmission case following the manufacturer's instructions.

7. Slowly tighten the puller nut to pull the main drive gear into the bearing in the transmission case. Continue until the gear bottoms in the bearings inner race.

8. Disassemble and remove the installation tool.

9. Install the spacer into the main drive gear oil seal.

10. Install the transmission shaft assemblies from the transmission case as described in this chapter.

TRANSMISSION CLUTCH RELEASE MECHANISM COVER

Removal

1. Remove the exhaust system as described in Chapter Seven.

2. Drain the transmission oil as described in Chapter Three.

NOTE
If the cover is difficult to remove, apply the clutch lever after the mounting bolts have been removed. This will usually break the cover loose.

3. Remove the release cover mounting bolts, the side cover and the gasket. Do not lose the locating dowels.

4. At the clutch cable in-line adjuster, perform the following:

    a. Remove the clamp (A, **Figure 107**) and slide the rubber boot (B) off the clutch in-line cable adjuster.

    b. Loosen the adjuster locknut (A, **Figure 108**) and turn the adjuster (B) to provide maximum cable slack.

Disassembly

Refer to **Figure 109**.

NOTE
Before removing the snap ring in Step 1, note the position of the snap ring opening. The snap ring must be reinstalled with its opening in the same position.

1. Remove the snap ring (A, **Figure 110**) from the groove in the side cover.

2. Lift the inner ramp (A, **Figure 111**) out of the cover and disconnect it from the clutch cable coupling (B).

3. Remove the clutch cable coupling (A, **Figure 112**).

4. Remove the inner ramp and balls (B, **Figure 112**).

5. If necessary, remove the clutch cable (B, **Figure 110**) from the side cover.

Inspection

1. Clean the side cover and all components thoroughly in solvent and dry them with compressed air.

6

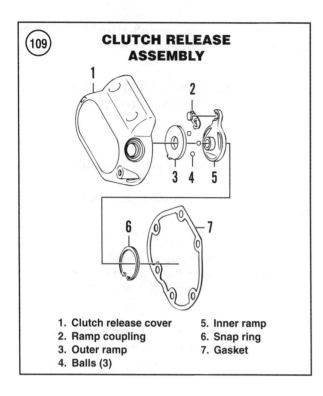

CLUTCH RELEASE ASSEMBLY

1. Clutch release cover
2. Ramp coupling
3. Outer ramp
4. Balls (3)
5. Inner ramp
6. Snap ring
7. Gasket

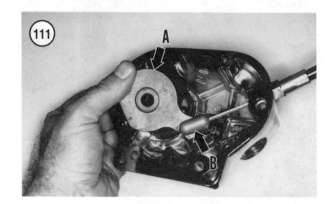

2. Check the release mechanism balls and ramp ball sockets for cracks, deep scoring or excessive wear (**Figure 113**).

3. Check the side cover (**Figure 114**) for cracks or damage. Check the clutch cable threads and the coupling snap ring groove for damage. Check the ramp bore in the side cover for excessive wear, or lips or grooves that could catch the ramps and bind them sideways, causing improper clutch adjustment.

4. Replace the clutch cable O-ring if it is damaged.

5. Replace all worn or damaged parts.

Assembly

1. If removed, screw the clutch cable into the side cover. Do not tighten the cable fitting at this time.

2. Install the inner ramp and balls (B, **Figure 112**). Center a ball into each socket.

3. Install the clutch cable coupling onto the clutch cable as shown in A, **Figure 112**.

4. Connect the inner ramp onto the clutch cable coupling (B, **Figure 111**).

5. Align the inner ramp socket with the balls and install the inner ramp as shown in **Figure 115**.

6. Install the snap ring into the side cover groove. Position the snap ring so its opening faces to the right of the outer ramp tang slot as shown in A, **Figure 110**. Make sure the snap ring is seated correctly in the groove.

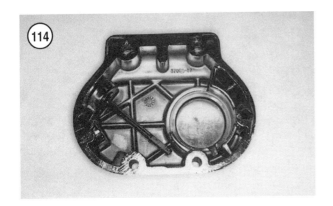

6

Installation

1. If removed, install the locating dowels.

2. Install a *new* gasket.

3. Install the release cover and bolts. Tighten the bolts in a crisscross pattern to 84-108 in.-lb. (9-12 N•m).

4. Refill the transmission with oil as described in Chapter Three.

5. Install the exhaust system as described in Chapter Seven.

6. Adjust the clutch as described in Chapter Three.

TRANSMISSION DRIVE SPROCKET

Removal/Installation

> *NOTE*
> *The mainshaft bearing race does not need to be removed for the transmission drive sprocket to be removed.*

1. Remove the primary chain case assembly as described in Chapter Five.

2. If necessary, install a sprocket locker tool (JIMS part No. 2260) (**Figure 116**) onto the transmission drive sprocket following the manufacturer's instructions.

3. Remove the two Allen bolts and the lock plate (**Figure 117**).

4A. Shift the transmission into gear.

4B. If the drive belt is still in place, have an assistant apply the rear brake.

5. Use a countershaft sprocket nut wrench (JIMS part No. 946600-37A) to install the inner collar (**Figure 118**) onto the mainshaft.

> *CAUTION*
> *The sprocket nut has left-hand threads. Turn the tool **clockwise** to loosen it in Step 6.*

6. Install the wrench onto the nut (**Figure 119**) and turn it *clockwise* to loosen the nut.

7. Remove the special tools and the nut from the mainshaft.

8. Carefully remove the transmission drive sprocket from the mainshaft. Do not damage the bearing race.

9. Install by reversing these removal steps. Note the following:

    a. Use the same tool set up used during removal.

    b. Apply Loctite TB1360 or an equivalent to the nut and Allen bolts prior to installation.

    c. Position the nut with the flanged side facing the drive sprocket.

> *CAUTION*
> *In substep d, do not tighten the nut past an additional 45° to align the lock plate bolt holes or the nut will be damaged.*

    d. Tighten the nut *counterclockwise* to 50 ft.-lb. (68 N•m). Then tighten it an additional 30° until the lock plate holes are aligned.

TRANSMISSION CASE

Only remove the transmission case (**Figure 58**) if it requires replacement or to perform extensive frame repair or replace the frame. All internal transmission components can be removed with the case in the frame.

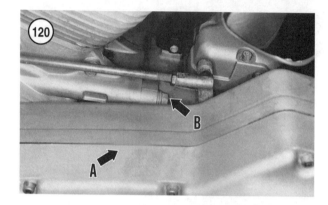

Removal/Installation

1. Drain the transmission oil and primary chain case lubricant as described in Chapter Three.

2. Remove the exhaust system as described in Chapter Seven.

3. Remove the primary chaincase cover (A, **Figure 120**) as described in Chapter Five.

4. Remove the clutch assembly as described in Chapter Five.

5. Remove the transmission side cover and clutch release mechanism as described in this chapter.

6. Remove the primary chaincase housing as described in Chapter Five.

7. Remove the oil tank and oil lines (A, **Figure 121**) as described in Chapter Four.

8. Remove the transmission drive sprocket as described in this chapter.

9. Remove the transmission shaft assemblies as described in this chapter.

10. Remove the external shift linkage as described in this chapter.

11. Make an alignment mark on the shift rod lever and the end of the shift shaft.

12. Remove the clamp bolt (A, **Figure 122**) securing the shift rod lever (B).

13. Use a T50 Torx wrench to back the centering screw (A, **Figure 123**) out until it clears the centering slot in the shift pawl assembly.

14. Remove the snap ring (B, **Figure 123**) and flat washer (C) from the shift shaft (D).

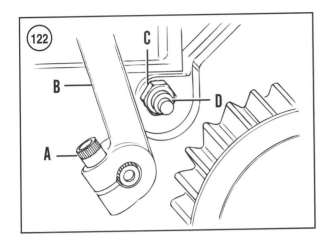

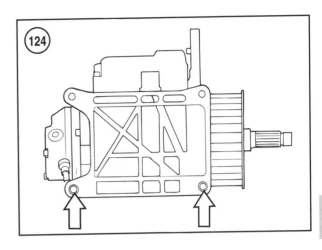

6

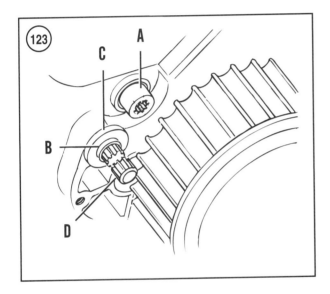

15. Remove the swing arm as described in Chapter Twelve.

16. On California models, remove the charcoal canister as described in Chapter Seven.

17. Remove the starter as described in Chapter Eight.

18. Support the transmission case with a jack or wooden blocks. Apply sufficient jack pressure on the transmission prior to removing the engine-to-transmission mounting bolts.

NOTE
Figure 120 *shows only the upper mounting bolt, remove the lower bolt also.*

19. Remove the two bolts and washers on each side securing the transmission to the engine. Refer to B, **Figure 121** and B, **Figure 120**.

20. Move the transmission case to the rear to clear the two lower locating dowels.

21. Move the transmission toward the right side and remove the transmission case from the frame.

22. Install the transmission case by reversing these removal steps. Note the following:
   a. Make sure the two locating dowels are in place on the engine or transmission case (**Figure 124**).
   b. Tighten the transmission mounting bolts in a crisscross pattern to a preliminary torque of 15 ft.-lb. (20 N•m).
   c. Continue to tighten the mounting bolts in a crisscross pattern to 30-35 ft.-lb. (41-48 N•m).

Tables 1-3 are on the following pages.

Table 1 TRANSMISSION GENERAL SPECIFICATIONS

Transmission type	Five-speed, constant mesh
Gear ratios	
First	3.21
Second	2.21
Third	1.57
Fourth	1.23
Fifth	1.00
Transmission fluid capacity	
Oil change	20-24 U.S. oz. (591-709 ml)
Rebuild (dry)	24 U.S. oz. (709 ml)

Table 2 TRANSMISSION SERVICE SPECIFICATIONS

Item	in.	mm
Countershaft		
Runout	0.000-0.003	0.00-0.08
Endplay	None	
First gear		
Clearance	0.003-0.0019	0.080-0.048
End play	0.005-0.0039	0.127-0.099
Second gear		
Clearance	0.003-0.0019	0.008-0.048
End play	0.005-0.0440	0.127-1.118
Third gear		
Clearance	0.000-0.0080	0.000-0.0203
Fourth gear		
Clearance	0.000-0.0080	0.000-0.0203
End play	0.005-0.0390	0.127-0.991
Fifth gear		
Clearance	0.000-0.0080	0.000-0.0203
End play	0.005-0.0400	0.127-0.102
Mainshaft		
Runout	0.00-0.003	0.00-0.08
Endplay	None	
First gear		
Clearance	0.000-0.0080	0.000-0.203
Second gear		
Clearance	0.000-0.0800	0.000-2.032
Third gear		
Clearance	0.003-0.0019	0.008-0.048
End play	0.005-0.0420	0.127-1.067
Fourth gear		
Clearance	0.0003-0.0019	0.008-0.048
End play	0.005-0.0310	0.127-0.787
Main drive gear (fifth)		
Bearing fit in transmission case	0.0003-0.0017	0.0076-0.043
Fit in bearing		
Tight fit	0.0009	0.023
Loose fit	0.0001	0.0025
Fit on mainshaft	0.0001-0.0009	0.0025-0.023
End play	None	
Shifter cam assembly		
Right edge of middle cam groove to right support block distance	1.992-2.002	50.60-50.85
Shifter cam end play	0.001-0.004	0.025-0.10

(continued)

Table 2 TRANSMISSION SERVICE SPECIFICATIONS (continued)

Item	in.	mm
Shifter forks		
Shifter fork-to-cam groove end play	0.0017-0.0019	0.043-0.048
Shifter fork-to-gear groove end play	0.0010-0.0011	0.025-0.0279
Shift fork finger thickness	0.165	4.19
Side door bearing		
Fit in side door	0.0014-0.0001	0.036-0.0025
Fit on countershaft		
Tight fit	0.0007	0.018
Loose fit	0.0001	0.0025
Fit on mainshaft		
Tight fit	0.0007	0.018
Loose fit	0.001	0.025

6

Table 3 TRANSMISSION TORQUE SPECIFICATIONS

Item	ft.-lb.	in.-lb.	N•m
Clutch cable fitting	–	30-60	3-7
Clutch release cover bolts	–	84-108	9-12
Shift rod lever clamp bolt	18-22	–	24-30
Shift rod locknuts	20-24	–	27-32
Shift cam support block bolts	–	84-108	9-12
Transmission top cover bolts	–	84-108	9-12
Transmission main and countershaft			
locknuts at side door	45-55	–	61-75
Transmission case door			
1/4 in. fasteners	–	84-108	9-12
5/16 in. fasteners	13-16	–	18-22
Transmission drain plug	14-21	–	19-28
Engine-to-transmission bolts			
Preliminary	15	–	20
Final	30-35	–	41-48
Detent follower bolt	–	84-108	9-12
Transmission drive sprocket			
Mounting nut*	50	–	68
Lockplate bolts	–	84-108	9-12

*Tighten an additional 30°–not to exceed 45°.

CHAPTER SEVEN

FUEL, EXHAUST AND EMISSION CONTROL SYSTEMS

This chapter includes procedures for the fuel, exhaust and emission control systems (California models). Electronic fuel injection (EFI) models are also covered. Routine air filter maintenance is described in Chapter Three. Specifications and carburetor jet sizes are in **Tables 1-3** at the end of the chapter.

> *WARNING*
> *Gasoline is carcinogenic and extremely flammable, and must be handled carefully. Wear latex gloves to avoid skin contact. If gasoline does contact skin, immediately and thoroughly wash the area with soap and warm water.*

AIR FILTER BACKPLATE

Removal

Refer to **Figure 1** and **Figure 2**.

1. Remove the air filter cover screw (A, **Figure 3**) and remove the cover (B).

2. Remove the Torx screws and bracket (**Figure 4**, typical) from the air filter element.

3. Gently pull the air filter element away from the backplate and disconnect the two breather hoses (A, **Figure 5**) from the hollow bolts on the backplate. Remove the air filter element (B, **Figure 5**).

4. Unscrew and remove the breather hollow bolts (A, **Figure 6**) securing the backplate to the cylinder heads.

5A. On California carbureted models, pull the backplate (B, **Figure 6**) partially away from the cylinder heads and the carburetor, then disconnect the evaporation emission control clean air inlet hose (**Figure 7**).

5B. On all other models, pull the backplate (B, **Figure 6**) away from the cylinder heads and remove it.

6. Remove the carburetor or fuel injection module gasket from the air filter, the backing plate or the fuel injection module (**Figure 8**).

Inspection

1. Inspect the backplate for damage.

2. On California models, make sure the trap door swings freely (**Figure 9**).

3. Make sure the breather hollow bolts and breather hoses (**Figure 10**) are clear. Clean them out if necessary.

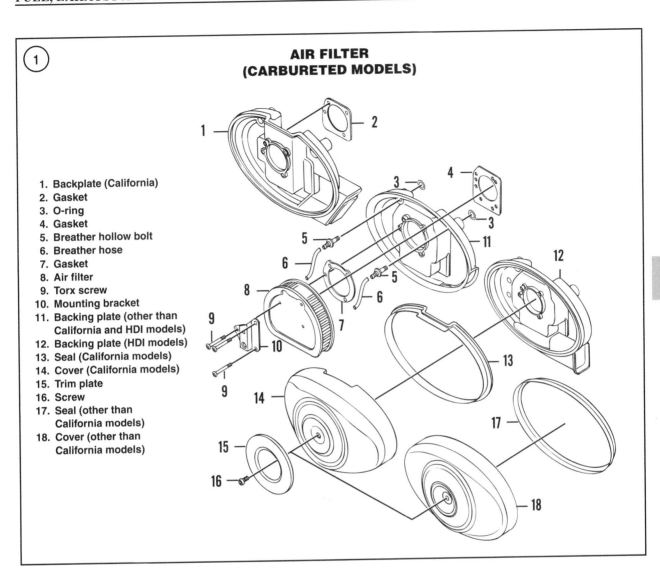

AIR FILTER (CARBURETED MODELS)

1. Backplate (California)
2. Gasket
3. O-ring
4. Gasket
5. Breather hollow bolt
6. Breather hose
7. Gasket
8. Air filter
9. Torx screw
10. Mounting bracket
11. Backing plate (other than California and HDI models)
12. Backing plate (HDI models)
13. Seal (California models)
14. Cover (California models)
15. Trim plate
16. Screw
17. Seal (other than California models)
18. Cover (other than California models)

Installation

1. Apply a couple dabs of gasket sealer to the *new* gasket and install it onto the air filter, the backing plate or the fuel injection module (**Figure 8**).

2. Move the backplate into position.

3. On California carbureted models, move the backplate part way into position. Connect the evaporation emission control clean air inlet hose (**Figure 7**) to the fitting on the backside of the backplate.

4. Position the backplate (B, **Figure 6**) against the carburetor, or fuel injection module, and cylinder heads. Make sure the Torx bolt holes of the gasket and backplate are aligned with the carburetor or fuel injection module. Reposition the gasket if necessary.

5. Install the breather hollow bolts (A, **Figure 6**) securing the backplate to the cylinder heads. Tighten them to 120-144 in.-lb. (14-16 N•m).

6. Position the element (B, **Figure 5**) with the flat side facing down and attach the breather hoses (A) to the backside of the element.

NOTE
If an aftermarket air filter element is being installed, position it onto the backplate following the manufacturer's instructions.

7. Move the element into position and install the mounting bracket (**Figure 4**) and the Torx screws. Tighten the Torx screws to 20-40 in.-lb. (2-4 N•m).

8. Apply a drop of ThreeBond TB1342 (blue) or an equivalent threadlocking compound to the cover screw prior to installation.

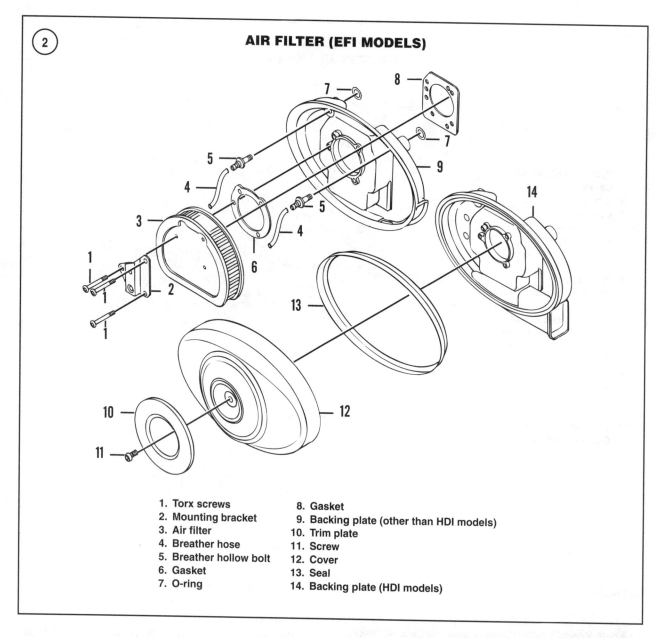

AIR FILTER (EFI MODELS)

1. Torx screws
2. Mounting bracket
3. Air filter
4. Breather hose
5. Breather hollow bolt
6. Gasket
7. O-ring
8. Gasket
9. Backing plate (other than HDI models)
10. Trim plate
11. Screw
12. Cover
13. Seal
14. Backing plate (HDI models)

9. Inspect the seal ring (**Figure 11**) on the air filter cover for hardness or deterioration. Replace it if necessary.

10. Install the air filter cover (B, **Figure 3**) and the screw (A). Tighten the screw to 36-60 in.-lb. (4-7 N•m).

CARBURETOR

Operation

An understanding of the function of each of the carburetor components and their relation to one another is a valuable aid for pinpointing the source of carburetor trouble.

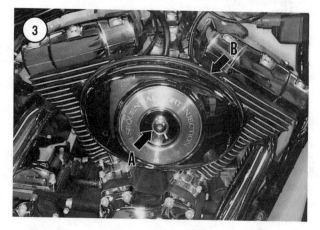

7

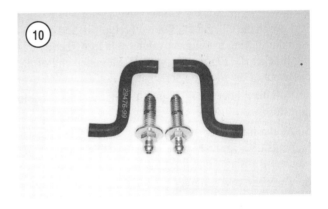

The carburetor's purpose is to supply and atomize fuel, and mix it in correct proportions with the air drawn in through the air intake. At the primary throttle opening (idle), a small amount of fuel is siphoned through the pilot jet by the incoming air. As the throttle is opened further, the air stream begins to siphon fuel through the main jet and needle jet. The tapered needle increases the effective flow capacity of the needle jet as it is lifted, and occupies progressively less of the area of the jet. At full throttle, the carburetor venturi is fully open and the needle is lifted far enough to permit the main jet to flow at full capacity.

The choke circuit is a starting enrichment valve system. The choke knob under the fuel tank on the left side of the engine opens an enrichment valve; rather than closing a butterfly in the venturi area as on some carburetors. In the open position, the slow jet discharges a stream of fuel into the carburetor venturi to enrich the mixture when the engine is cold.

The accelerator pump circuit reduces engine hesitation by injecting a fine spray of fuel into the carburetor intake passage during sudden acceleration.

Removal

1. Remove the air filter and backplate as described in this chapter.

2. Remove the fuel tank as described in this chapter.

3. Loosen the locknut (A, **Figure 12**, typical) and disconnect the starting enrichment valve cable from the mounting bracket (B, **Figure 12**, typical). Move the end of the cable out of the mounting bracket.

4. Roll the rubber boots (**Figure 13**) off the throttle cable adjusters.

5. At the handlebar, loosen both control cable adjuster locknuts (A, **Figure 14**), then turn the cable adjusters (B) *clockwise* as far as possible to increase cable slack.

6. There are two different throttle cables. Label the two cables at the carburetor before disconnecting them. One is the throttle control cable (A, **Figure 15**) and the other is the idle control cable (B).

7. Disconnect the fuel supply hose (**Figure 16**) from the carburetor fitting.

8. Twist and pull the carburetor off the seal ring and intake manifold.

9. Disconnect the vacuum hose from the carburetor fitting.

10. Disconnect the throttle control cable (A, **Figure 17**) and the idle control cable (B) from the carburetor cable guide and the throttle wheel.

11. Drain the gasoline from the carburetor assembly.

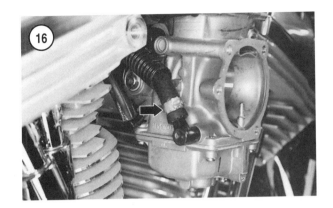

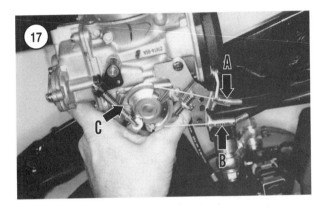

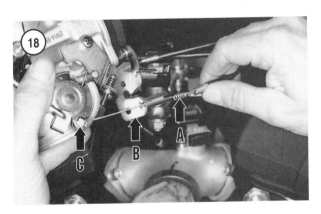

12. Inspect the carburetor seal ring on the intake manifold for wear, hardness, cracks or other damage. Replace it if necessary.

13. If necessary, service the intake manifold as described under *Intake Manifold* in this chapter.

14. Cover the intake manifold opening.

Installation

1. If removed, seat the seal ring onto the intake manifold. Make sure it is correctly seated to avoid a vacuum leak.

2. Route the starting enrichment valve cable between the cylinders and toward its mounting bracket on the left side.

3. Connect the idle cable to the carburetor as follows:
   a. The idle cable has the small spring (A, **Figure 18**) on the end of the cable.
   b. Insert the idle cable sheath into the rear cable bracket guide on the carburetor (B, **Figure 18**).
   c. Attach the end of the idle cable to the throttle wheel (C, **Figure 18**).

4. Connect the throttle cable to the carburetor as follows:
   a. Insert the throttle cable sheath into the front cable bracket guide on the carburetor.
   b. Attach the end of the throttle cable to the throttle wheel.

5. Operate the hand throttle a few times. Make sure the throttle wheel operates smoothly with no binding. Also make sure both cable ends are seated squarely in their cable bracket guides and in the throttle wheel.

> *CAUTION*
> *The carburetor must fit squarely onto the intake manifold. If it is misaligned, it may damage the intake manifold seal ring, resulting in a vacuum leak.*

6. Align the carburetor squarely with the intake manifold (**Figure 19**), then push it into the manifold until it bottoms. Position the carburetor so it sits square and vertical with the manifold.

7. Connect the vacuum hose to the carburetor fitting. Make sure it is seated correctly.

8. Slide a *new* hose clamp over the fuel supply hose, then connect the fuel hose to the hose fitting on the carburetor (**Figure 16**).

9. Insert the starting enrichment valve cable into the mounting bracket (B, **Figure 12**), then tighten the locknut (A) securely.

10. Before installing the fuel tank, recheck the idle and throttle cable operation. Open and release the hand throttle. Make sure the carburetor throttle valve opens and closes smoothly. Make sure both cables are routed prop-

7

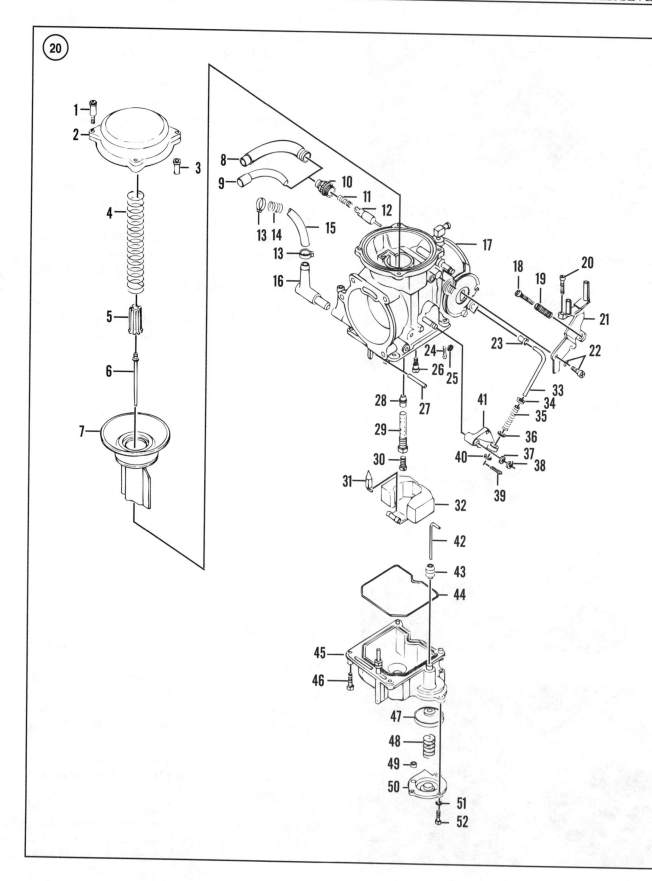

CARBURETOR

1. Screw
2. Cover
3. Collar
4. Spring
5. Spring seat
6. Jet needle
7. Vacuum piston
8. Cable sealing cap
9. Cable guide
10. Starting enrichment cap
11. Spring
12. Starting enrichment valve
13. Hose clamp
14. Spring
15. Hose
16. Fuel inlet fitting
17. Body
18. Screw
19. Spring
20. Screw
21. Throttle cable bracket
22. Screw and washer
23. Collar
24. Pin
25. Washer
26. Pilot jet
27. Float pivot pin
28. Needle jet
29. Main jet holder
30. Main jet
31. Valve
32. Float
33. Rod
34. Washer
35. Spring
36. Collar
37. Washer
38. E-clip
39. Pin
40. Washer
41. Lever
42. Rod
43. Boot
44. O-ring gasket
45. Float bowl
46. Screw
47. Diaphragm
48. Spring
49. O-ring
50. Cover
51. Washer
52. Screw

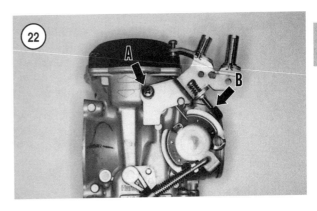

7

erly. If necessary, adjust the throttle cables as described in Chapter Three.

11. Install the air filter backplate and air filter as described in this chapter.

12. Install the fuel tank as described in this chapter.

13. Start the engine and allow it to idle. Check for fuel leaks.

14. Turn the handlebar from side to side. The idle speed should remain the same. If the idle speed increases while the handlebars are turned, the cables are installed incorrectly or are damaged. Remove the fuel tank and inspect the cables.

Disassembly

Refer to **Figure 20**.

1. Unscrew and remove the starting enrichment valve and cable (**Figure 21**).

2. Remove the screw and washer (A, **Figure 22**) on the side and the top screw (A, **Figure 23**) securing the throttle cable bracket to the carburetor. Remove the bracket (B, **Figure 23**).

3. Remove the collar (**Figure 24**) from the cover.

4. Remove the remaining cover screws (**Figure 25**). Remove the cover and spring (A, **Figure 26**).

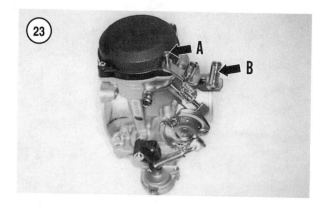

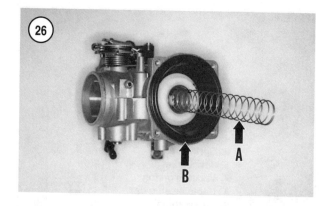

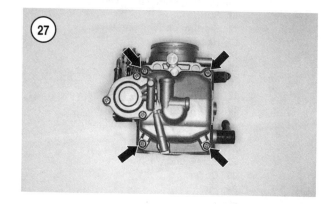

5. Remove the vacuum piston (B, **Figure 26**) from the carburetor housing. Do not damage the jet needle extending out of the bottom of the vacuum piston.

6. Remove the float bowl as follows:

   a. Remove the screws (**Figure 27**) securing the float bowl to the carburetor.

   b. Slowly remove the float bowl body and withdraw the pump rod (**Figure 28**) from the boot on the bowl.

   c. Disconnect the pump rod from the lever assembly on the carburetor (**Figure 29**).

7

CAUTION
One of the float pin pedestals has an inter-
ference fit that holds the float pin in place.
*An arrow, (**Figure 30**) cast into the carbure-*
tor, points to this pedestal. To remove the
float pin, tap it out from the interference side
in the direction of the arrow. If the float pin
is removed opposite of the arrow, the oppo-
site pedestal may crack or break off. If this
occurs, the carburetor must be replaced.

7. Carefully tap the float pin (**Figure 31**) out of the pedestals and remove it.

8. Remove the float and needle valve assembly (**Figure 32**).

9. Unscrew and remove the pilot jet (**Figure 33**).

10. Unscrew and remove the main jet (**Figure 34**).

11. Unscrew and remove the needle jet holder (**Figure 35**).

12. Remove the needle jet (A, **Figure 36**) from the needle jet bore in the carburetor.

Cleaning and Inspection

Replace worn or damaged parts as described in this section.

CAUTION
The carburetor body is equipped with plas-
tic parts that cannot be removed. Do not dip

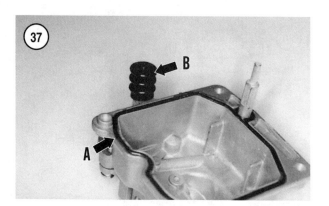

the carburetor body, O-rings, float assembly, needle valve or vacuum piston in a carburetor cleaner or another harsh solution that can damage these parts. The use of a caustic carburetor cleaning solvent is not recommended. Instead, clean the carburetor and related parts in a petroleum based solvent, or Simple Green. Then rinse them in clean water.

1. Initially clean all parts in a mild petroleum based cleaning solution. Then clean them in hot, soapy water and rinse with cold water. Blow them dry with compressed air.

> *CAUTION*
> *If compressed air is not available, allow the parts to air dry or use a clean, lint-free cloth. Do **not** use a paper towel to dry carburetor parts, as small paper particles may plug openings in the carburetor housing or jets.*

2. Allow the carburetors to dry thoroughly before assembly. Blow out the jets and the needle jet holder with compressed air.

> *CAUTION*
> *Do **not** use wire or drill bits to clean jets as minor gouges in the jet can alter the air/fuel mixture.*

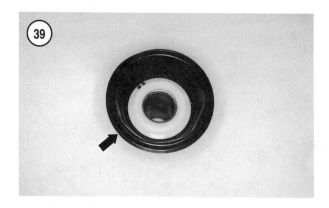

3. Inspect the float bowl O-ring gasket (A, **Figure 37**) for hardness or deterioration.

4. Inspect the accelerator pump boot (B, **Figure 37**) for hardness or deterioration.

5. Make sure the accelerator pump cover (**Figure 38**) screws are tight.

6. Inspect the vacuum piston diaphragm (**Figure 39**) for cracks or deterioration. Check the vacuum piston sides (**Figure 40**) for excessive wear. Install the vacuum piston into the carburetor body and move it up and down in the bore. The vacuum piston should move smoothly with no

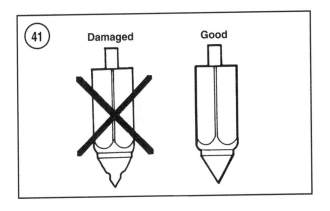

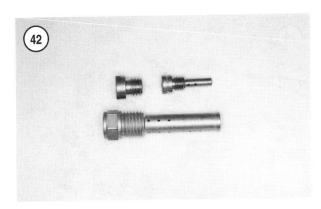

7

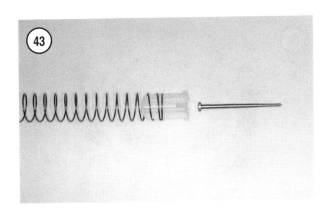

binding or excessive play. If there is excessive play, the vacuum piston slide and/or carburetor body must be replaced.

7. Inspect the needle valve tapered end for steps, uneven wear or other damage (**Figure 41**).

8. Inspect the needle valve seat (B, **Figure 36**) for steps, uneven wear or other damage. Insert the needle valve and slowly move it back and forth to check for smooth operation. If either part is worn or damaged, replace both parts as a pair for maximum performance.

9. Inspect the needle jet holder, pilot jet and main jet (**Figure 42**). Make sure all holes are open and none of the parts are either worn or damaged.

10. Inspect the jet needle, spring and spring seat (**Figure 43**) for deterioration or damage.

11. Inspect the jet needle tapered end for steps, uneven wear or other damage.

12. Inspect the float (**Figure 44**) for deterioration or damage. If the float is suspected of leakage, place it in a container of water and push it down. If the float sinks or if bubbles appear, there is a leak and the float must be replaced.

13. Make sure the throttle plate (**Figure 45**) screws are tight. Tighten them if necessary.

14. Move the throttle wheel (**Figure 46**) back and forth from stop to stop and check for free movement. The throt-

tle lever should move smoothly and return under spring tension.

15. Check the throttle wheel return spring (**Figure 47**) for free movement. Make sure it rotates the throttle wheel back to the stop position with no hesitation.

16. Make sure all openings in the carburetor housing are clear. Clean them out if they are plugged, then apply compressed air to all openings.

17. Inspect the carburetor body for internal or external damage. If there is damage, replace the carburetor assembly, as the body cannot be replaced separately.

18. Check the top cover for cracks or damage.

19. Check the starting enrichment valve and cable as follows:

    a. Check the end of the valve (**Figure 48**) for damage.

    b. Check the entire length of the cable for bends, chaffing or other damage.

    c. Check the knob, nut and lockwasher for damage. Move the knob and check for ease of movement.

Assembly

NOTE
The needle jet has two different sides and must be installed as described in Step 1.

1. Position the needle jet with the long end going in first (**Figure 49**) and install it (A, **Figure 36**).

2. Install the needle jet holder (**Figure 35**) into the main jet passage. Make sure it passes through the opening in the venturi (**Figure 50**), then tighten it securely.

3. Install the main jet and tighten it securely (**Figure 34**).

4. Install the pilot jet and tighten it securely (**Figure 33**).

5. Install the fuel valve onto the float (**Figure 51**) and position the float onto the carburetor so the valve drops into its seat.

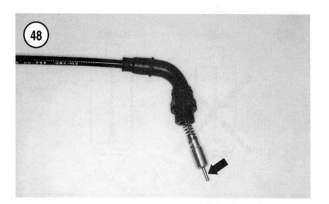

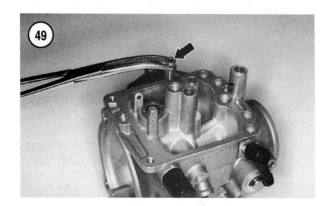

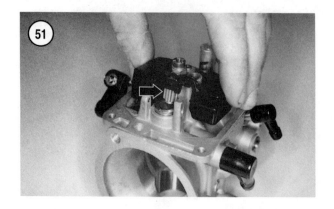

CAUTION
The pedestals that support the float pin are
fragile. In the next step, support the pedestal
on the arrow side while tapping the float pin
into place.

6. Align the float pin with the two pedestals.

7. Install the float pin (A, **Figure 52**) from the side opposite the arrow (B). Support the pedestal and tap the float pin into place in the pedestal.

8. Check the float level as described in this chapter.

9. Install the float bowl as follows:

a. Make sure the float bowl O-ring seal (A, **Figure 37**) and accelerator rod boot (B) are in place.

b. Connect the pump rod to the lever assembly on the carburetor (**Figure 53**).

c. Slowly install the float bowl body and insert the accelerator pump rod through the boot (**Figure 28**) on the float bowl. Engage the rod with the diaphragm while installing the float bowl.

d. Install the float bowl and screws (**Figure 27**). Tighten the screws securely in a crisscross pattern.

10. Insert the jet needle (**Figure 54**) through the center hole in the vacuum piston.

11. Install the spring seat (A, **Figure 55**) and spring (B) over the top of the needle to secure it in place.

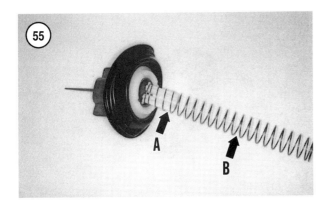

12. Align the slides (A, **Figure 56**) on the vacuum piston with the grooves (B) in the carburetor bore and install the vacuum piston (B, **Figure 26**). The slides on the piston are offset, so the piston can only be installed one way. When installing the vacuum piston, make sure the jet needle drops through the needle jet.

13. Seat the outer edge of the vacuum piston diaphragm into the piston chamber groove (**Figure 57**).

14. Align the free end of the spring with the carburetor top and install the top onto the carburetor.

15. Hold the carburetor top in place and lift the vacuum piston with a finger (**Figure 58**). The piston should move smoothly. If the piston movement is rough or sluggish, the

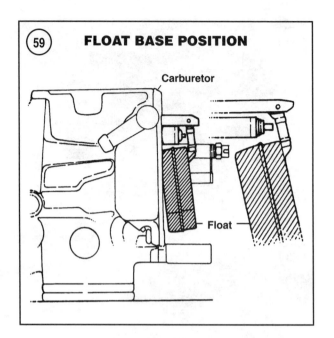

FLOAT BASE POSITION

Carburetor

Float

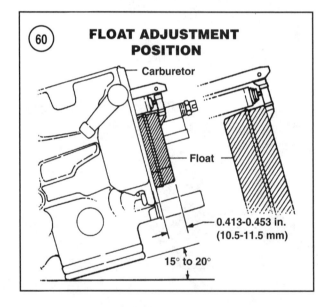

FLOAT ADJUSTMENT POSITION

Carburetor

Float

0.413-0.453 in.
(10.5-11.5 mm)

15° to 20°

spring is installed incorrectly. Remove the carburetor top and reinstall the spring.

16. Install the carburetor top screws (**Figure 25**) finger-tight.

17. Install the collar (**Figure 24**) into the cover.

18. Install the throttle cable bracket (B, **Figure 23**) onto the carburetor so the end of the idle speed screw engages the top of the throttle cam stop (B, **Figure 22**). Hold the bracket in place and install the bracket's side mounting screw and washer (A, **Figure 22**). Tighten the screw securely.

19. Install the top screw (A, **Figure 23**) and tighten it securely.

20. Install the starting enrichment cable and valve into the carburetor body. Tighten the nut securely (**Figure 21**).

Float Adjustment

The carburetor must be removed and partially disassembled for this adjustment.

1. Remove the carburetor as described in this chapter.

2. Remove the float bowl as described in this chapter.

3. Place the engine manifold side of the carburetor on a clean, flat surface as shown in **Figure 59**. This is the base position.

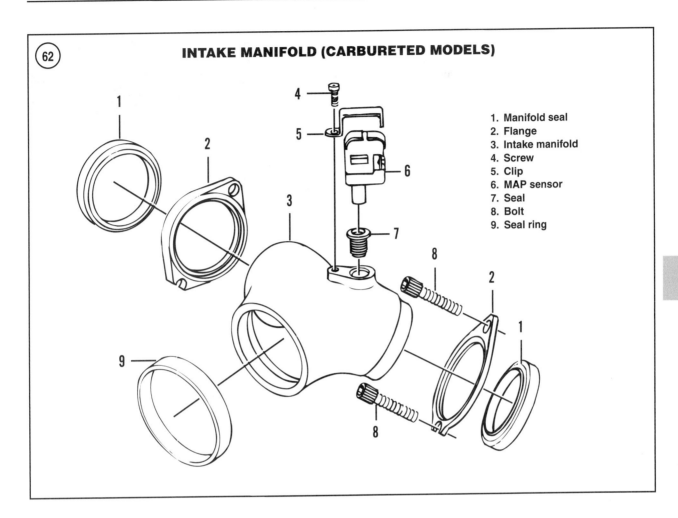

INTAKE MANIFOLD (CARBURETED MODELS)

62

1. Manifold seal
2. Flange
3. Intake manifold
4. Screw
5. Clip
6. MAP sensor
7. Seal
8. Bolt
9. Seal ring

7

4. Tilt the carburetor upward 15-20° as shown in **Figure 60**. In this position, the float will come to rest without compressing the pin return spring.

NOTE
If the carburetor is tilted less than 15° or more than 20°, the float measurement will be incorrect.

5. Measure from the carburetor flange surface to the top of the float as shown in **Figure 60**. When measuring float level, do not compress the float. The correct float level measurement is 0.413-0.453 in. (10.5-11.5 mm).
6. If the float level is incorrect, remove the float pin and float as described under *Carburetor Disassembly* in this chapter.
7. Slowly bend the float tang (**Figure 61**) with a screwdriver and adjust it to the correct position.
8. Reinstall the float and the float pin as described under *Carburetor Assembly* in this chapter. Recheck the float level.
9. Repeat Steps 4-8 until the float level is correct.

10. Install the float bowl and carburetor as described in this chapter.

INTAKE MANIFOLD (CARBURETED MODELS)

Removal/Installation

Refer to **Figure 62**.
1. Remove the carburetor as described in this chapter.

NOTE
The front and rear intake manifold flanges are different. If the flanges are not marked, label them with an F and R so they will be reinstalled in the correct location.

2. Disconnect the electrical connector from the MAP sensor (A, **Figure 63**) on top of the intake manifold.

NOTE
***Figure 63** shows only two of the Allen bolts. Remove all four bolts.*

3. Remove the four Allen bolts (B, **Figure 63**) securing the intake manifold to the cylinder heads.

4. Remove the intake manifold, flanges and manifold seals.

5. Inspect the intake manifold as described in this section.

6. Install the flanges (A, **Figure 64**) and manifold seals (B) onto the intake manifold.

7. Install the intake manifold onto the cylinder head intake ports.

8. Make sure the front and rear seals seat squarely against the cylinder head mating surfaces.

9. Install all four Allen bolts finger-tight at this time.

10. Temporarily install the carburetor (**Figure 65**) into the intake manifold.

CAUTION
Do not attempt to align the intake manifold after tightening the bolts. This will damage the manifold seals. If necessary, loosen the bolts, then align the manifold.

11. Make sure the intake manifold seats squarely against the cylinder heads. Then make sure the carburetor seats squarely in the intake manifold. Remove the carburetor.

NOTE
It is very difficult to get an Allen wrench and torque wrench onto the two inboard Allen bolts to tighten them to a specific torque value. Tighten the outboard Allen bolts to the specified torque value, then tighten the inboard Allen bolts to the same approximate tightness.

12. Tighten the intake manifold Allen bolts to 97-141 in.-lb. (11-16 N•m).

13. If the MAP sensor was removed, install a *new* seal in the manifold receptacle, then install the MAP sensor.

14. Connect the electrical connector onto the MAP sensor (A, **Figure 63**).

15. Install the carburetor as described in this chapter.

Inspection

1. Check the intake manifold seals (B, **Figure 64**) for wear, deterioration or other damage. Replace the seals as a set if necessary.

2. Check the intake manifold seal ring (C, **Figure 64**) for cracks, flat spots or other damage. Replace it if necessary.

3. If necessary, remove the self-tapping screw and clamp, and remove the MAP sensor.

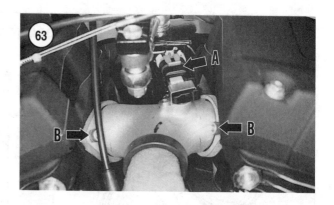

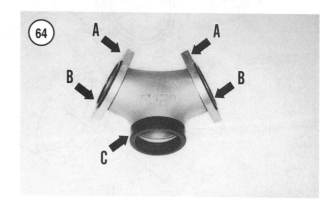

ELECTRONIC FUEL INJECTION (EFI)

This section describes the components and operation of the sequential port electronic fuel injection (EFI) system. The advantages of a map controlled fuel and ignition system working together are tremendous. It allows for the elimination of an inefficient cold start enrichment devise and allows for accurate control of the idle speed. Without a carburetor there is no need for periodic adjustments and altitude compensation is automatic. Improved torque characteristics are achieved, while at the same time allowing for greater fuel economy and low exhaust emissions due to the matching of the air/fuel ratio and ignition point, dependent upon load conditions. Engine performance modification is possible by simply installing an electronic control module (ECM) with different map characteristics.

Complete service of the system requires a Harley-Davidson Scanalyzer and a number of other specialty tools. However, basic troubleshooting diagnosis is no different on a fuel-injected machine than on a carbureted one. If the check engine light comes on or there is a driveability problem, make sure all electrical connections are clean and secure. A high or erratic idle speed may indicate a vacuum leak. Make sure there is an adequate supply of fresh gasoline. If basic tests fail to reveal the

cause of a problem, refer service to a Harley-Davidson dealership. Incorrectly performed diagnostic procedures can result in damage to the fuel injection system.

Electronic Control Module (ECM) and Sensors

The electronic control module (ECM) (**Figure 66**), mounted under the seat, determines the optimum fuel injection and ignition timing based on input from six or seven sensors. The sensors (**Figure 67** and **Figure 68**) and their locations and functions are as follows:

1. The throttle position sensor (TP), located on the front of the induction module and attached directly to the throttle shaft, indicates throttle angle. The ECM determines the air volume entering the engine based on the throttle angle.

2. The crankshaft position sensor (CKP), located on the forward position of the left crankcase, is an inductive type sensor. The ECM determines the engine speed by how fast the machined teeth on the flywheel pass by the sensor.

NOTE
The 2001-on models are not equipped with the camshaft position sensor.

3. The camshaft position (CMP), on 2000 models only, located in the camshaft cover, is also an inductive sensor. The ECM determines the camshaft position when the semicircular ridge on the rear cylinder's primary camshaft chain sprocket passes the sensor.

4. The engine temperature sensor (ET) on 2001-on models, is located on the front cylinder head. The ECM adjusts the injector opening time based on input from this sensor.

5. The intake air temperature sensor (IAT) is located inside the induction module (rear cylinder's intake runner). The ECM determines the air density and adjusts the injector opening time based on input from this sensor.

6. The manifold absolute pressure sensor (MAP) is located on top of the intake module. The MAP monitors intake manifold pressure (vacuum) and sends this information to the ECM.

7. The idle air control (IAC) valve is located on top of the induction module. The ECM control the engine speed by moving the IAC to open or close the passage around the throttle plate.

8. The bank angle sensor (BAS), located within the turn signal module (TSM) or the turn signal security module (TSSM), interrupts the ignition and shuts off the engine if the motorcycle's lean angle is greater than 45 ° from vertical for more than one second.

Make sure the ECM is securely mounted on the rubber isolators to prevent damage from vibration. Do not tamper with the ECM; it is sealed to prevent moisture contamination.

Fuel Supply System

Fuel pump and filters

The fuel pump and filter assembly is located inside the fuel tank. This assembly is part of the removable canopy attached to the top of the fuel tank. The canopy provides easy removal and installation of the attached components without having to work within the fuel tank cavity. An inlet screen on the fuel pump and the secondary fuel filter canister are located downstream from the fuel pump to provide maximum filtration before the fuel reaches the fuel injectors.

Fuel line

The fuel line is attached to the base of the fuel tank with quick-disconnect fittings.

The fuel supply line pressure is 58 psi (400 kPa). A check valve is located on the fuel line where it attaches to the fuel tank.

7

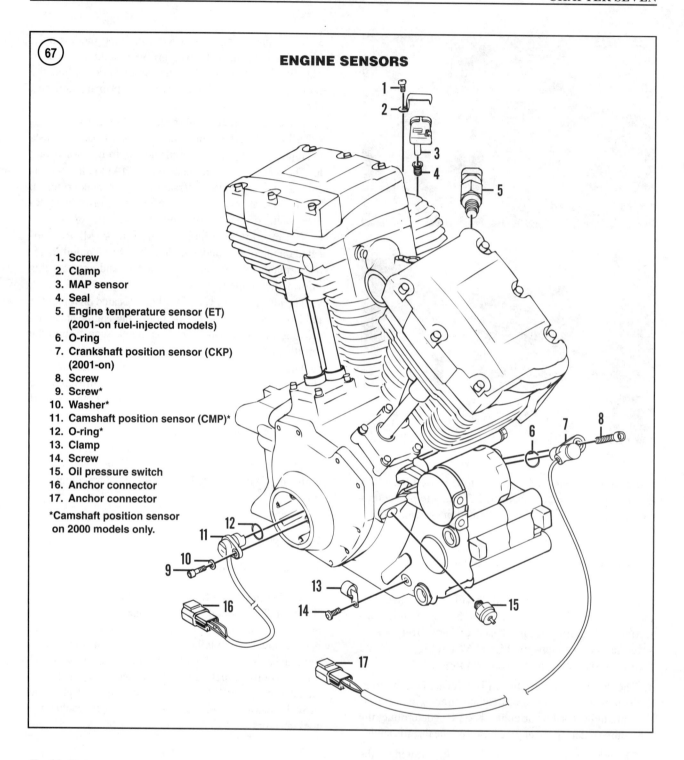

67

ENGINE SENSORS

1. Screw
2. Clamp
3. MAP sensor
4. Seal
5. Engine temperature sensor (ET)
   (2001-on fuel-injected models)
6. O-ring
7. Crankshaft position sensor (CKP)
   (2001-on)
8. Screw
9. Screw*
10. Washer*
11. Camshaft position sensor (CMP)*
12. O-ring*
13. Clamp
14. Screw
15. Oil pressure switch
16. Anchor connector
17. Anchor connector

*Camshaft position sensor
 on 2000 models only.

Fuel injectors

The solenoid-actuated constant-stroke pintle-type fuel injectors consist of a solenoid plunger, needle valve and housing. The fuel injector's opening is fixed and fuel pressure is constant.

The ECM controls the time the injectors open and close.

Induction Module

The induction module (**Figure 68**) consists of the two fuel injectors, fuel pressure regulator, throttle position sensor, intake air temperature sensor, idle speed lever, fuel supply line fitting and the idle speed control actuator.

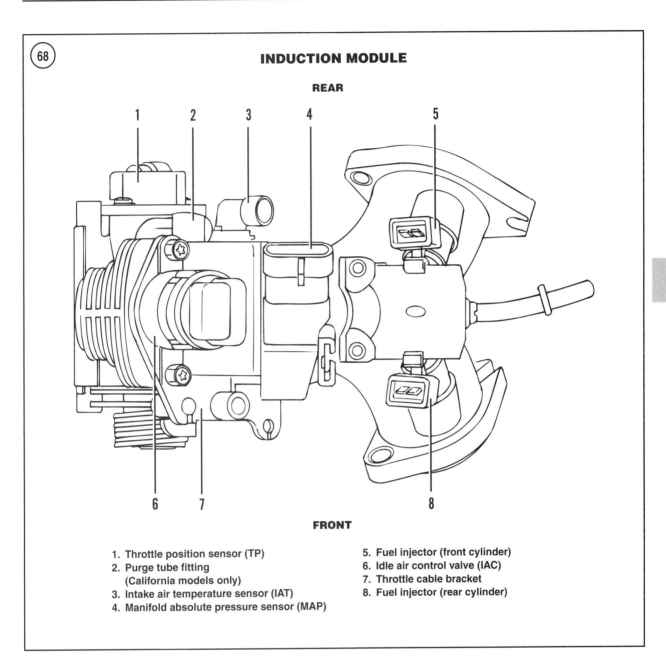

INDUCTION MODULE

REAR

FRONT

1. Throttle position sensor (TP)
2. Purge tube fitting
   (California models only)
3. Intake air temperature sensor (IAT)
4. Manifold absolute pressure sensor (MAP)

5. Fuel injector (front cylinder)
6. Idle air control valve (IAC)
7. Throttle cable bracket
8. Fuel injector (rear cylinder)

DEPRESSURIZING THE FUEL SYSTEM (EFI MODELS)

The fuel system is under pressure at all times, even when the engine is not operating. The system must be depressurized prior to loosening fittings or disconnecting fuel lines within the fuel injection system. Gasoline will spurt out unless the system is depressurized.

1. Remove the seat as described in Chapter Fourteen.

2. At the rear of fuel tank, disconnect the fuel pump single-pin black electrical connector (**Figure 69**).

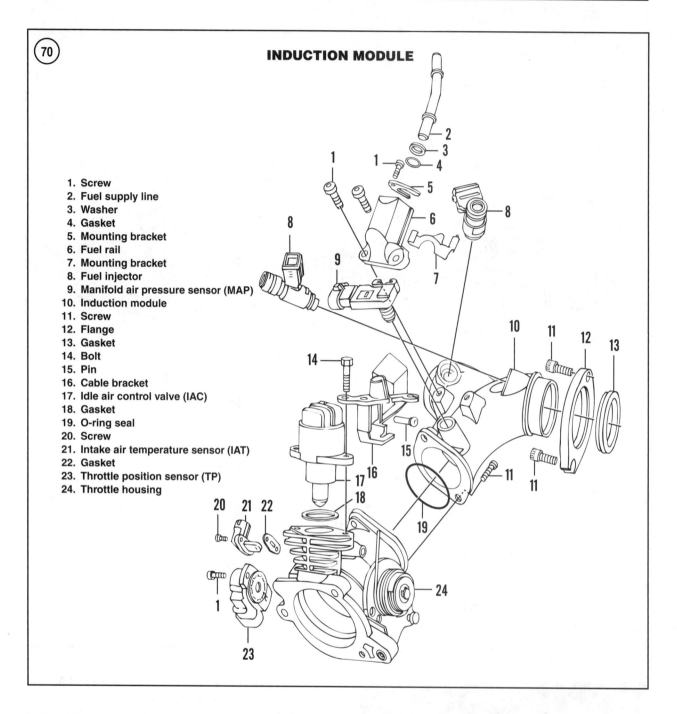

70 **INDUCTION MODULE**

1. Screw
2. Fuel supply line
3. Washer
4. Gasket
5. Mounting bracket
6. Fuel rail
7. Mounting bracket
8. Fuel injector
9. Manifold air pressure sensor (MAP)
10. Induction module
11. Screw
12. Flange
13. Gasket
14. Bolt
15. Pin
16. Cable bracket
17. Idle air control valve (IAC)
18. Gasket
19. O-ring seal
20. Screw
21. Intake air temperature sensor (IAT)
22. Gasket
23. Throttle position sensor (TP)
24. Throttle housing

3. Start the engine and allow it to idle until it runs out of gasoline.

4. After the engine has stopped, operate the starter for three seconds to eliminate any residual gasoline in the fuel lines.

5. After all service procedures have been completed, connect the fuel pump single-pin black electrical connector (**Figure 69**).

6. Install the seat.

**INDUCTION MODULE
(EFI MODELS)**

Removal

Refer to **Figure 70**.

1. Remove the fuel tank as described in this chapter.

2. Remove the air filter assembly as described in this chapter.

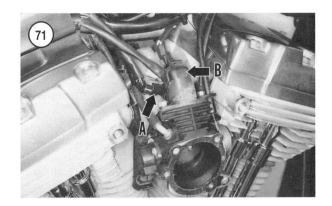

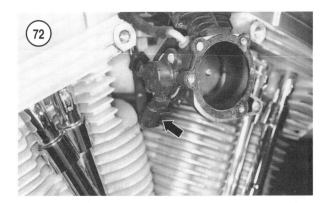

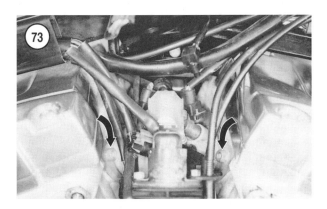

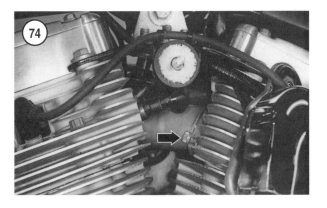

3. On California models, disconnect the EVAP hose from the port on the induction module. Plug the end of the hose to keep out debris.

4. *Carefully* disconnect the electrical connector from each fuel injector by rocking the connector back and forth.

5. Disconnect the following electrical connectors from the induction module:

    a. Intake air temperature sensor (IAT) (A, **Figure 71**).

    b. Idle air control valve (IAC) (B, **Figure 71**).

    c. Manifold pressure sensor (MAP).

    d. Throttle position sensor (TP) (**Figure 72**).

    e. Fuel injectors.

6. Disconnect the throttle cables from the induction module as described in this chapter.

7

> *NOTE*
> *The front and rear intake manifold flanges are different. If the flanges are not marked, label them with an F and R so they will be reinstalled in the correct locations.*

> *NOTE*
> *The type of bolts securing the induction module differs with the various years. Some models are equipped with hex-head bolts while others are fitted with Allen bolts. On models equipped with Allen bolts, use a 1/4 inch ball Allen bit with a 4 in. extension.*

7. Working on the right side of the motorcycle, loosen and remove the lower two bolts (**Figure 73**) securing the cylinder head mounting flanges to the cylinder heads. Loosen, but do not remove, the upper two Allen bolts securing the cylinder head mounting flanges to the cylinder heads.

8. Working on the left side of the motorcycle, loosen and remove the lower two bolts (**Figure 74**) securing the cylinder head mounting flanges to the cylinder heads. Loosen, but do not remove, the upper two Allen bolts securing the cylinder head mounting flanges to the cylinder heads.

9. Slide the induction module part way out of the cylinder head ports past the upper bolts.

10. Depress the button (A, **Figure 75**) on the fuel line fitting. Disconnect the fuel line and fitting (B, **Figure 75**) from the induction module fitting (C) and remove the induction module.

11. Remove the mounting flanges and discard the seals.

12. Inspect the induction module and fuel hoses as described in this section.

Installation

1. Install the flanges onto the correct side of the induction module with the slotted hole at the top. Refer to the marks made during *Removal*. Install *new* seals onto the induction module.

2. Partially install the induction module and fuel line assembly. Slide the fuel line connector (B, **Figure 75**) onto the induction module fitting (C) until it clicks. Gently pull on the fuel line to ensure the fitting is locked in place. Slide the induction module on the upper two bolts.

3. Connect both throttle cables to the induction module as described in this chapter.

4. Align the mounting flanges and install the two lower bolts by hand. Use the same tool set up used to loosen the bolts. Do not tighten the bolts at this time.

5. Working on the right side of the motorcycle, tighten the lower two bolts until snug, do not tighten to the final torque specification at this time. Use the same tool set up used to loosen the bolts.

6. Working on the left side of the motorcycle, tighten the upper two bolts to 71-124 in.-lb. (8-14 N•m).

7. Working on the right side of the motorcycle, tighten the lower two bolts to 71-124 in.-lb. (8-14 N•m).

8. Carefully attach the electrical connector to each fuel injector. Align the grooves in the female connector with the tabs in the male space housing. Push the connector halves together until both latches click.

NOTE
In Step 9, push the electrical connector halves together until the female latches slot connector is fully engaged with the tabs on the male space housing.

9. Connect the following electrical connectors from the induction module:
   a. Fuel injectors.
   b. Throttle position sensor (TP) (**Figure 72**).
   c. Manifold pressure sensor (MAP).
   d. Idle air control valve (IAC) (B, **Figure 71**).
   e. Intake air temperature sensor (IAT) (A, **Figure 71**).

10. On California models, connect the EVAP hose to the port on top of the induction module.

11. Install the air filter assembly as described in this chapter.

12. Install the fuel tank as described in this chapter.

Inspection

Check the induction module assembly for wear, deterioration or other damage. Replace the seals as a set if nec-

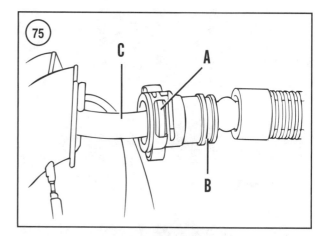

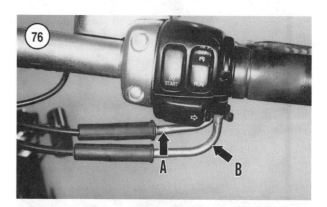

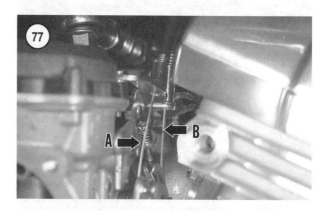

essary. The throttle housing is not serviceable and must be replace if damaged.

THROTTLE AND IDLE CABLES (CARBURETED MODELS)

There are two different throttle cables. At the throttle grip, the front cable is the throttle control cable (A, **Figure 76**) and the rear cable is the idle control cable (B). At the

carburetor, the outboard cable is the throttle control cable (A, **Figure 77**) and the inboard cable is the idle control cable (B).

Removal

1. Remove the fuel tank as described in this chapter.

2. Remove the air filter and backing plate as described in this chapter.

3. Make a drawing or take a picture of the cable routing from the carburetor through the frame to the right side handlebar.

4. At the right side handlebar, loosen both control cable adjuster locknuts (A, **Figure 78**), then turn the cable adjusters (B) *clockwise* as far as possible to increase cable slack.

> *CAUTION*
> *Failure to install the spacer in Step 5 will result in damage to the rubber boot and plunger on the front brake switch.*

5. Insert a 5/32 in. (4 mm) thick spacer between the brake lever and lever bracket. Make sure the spacer stays in place during the following steps.

6. Remove the screws securing the right side switch assembly together (A, **Figure 79**).

7. Remove the front master cylinder (B, **Figure 79**) as described in Chapter Thirteen.

8. Remove the brass ferrules from the notches on the inboard side of the throttle grip (**Figure 80**). Remove the ferrules from the cable end fittings.

9. Remove the friction shoe from the end of the tension adjust screw.

10. Remove the throttle grip from the handlebar.

> *NOTE*
> *Use a rocking motion while pulling on the control cable housings in Step 11. If necessary, place a drop of engine oil on the housings retaining rings to ease removal.*

11. Pull the crimped inserts at the end of the throttle and idle control cable housings from the switch lower housing.

12. Remove all clips and tie-wraps securing the throttle and idle control cables to the frame.

13. Remove the cables from the right side of the steering head and rubber trim (**Figure 81**).

14. Clean the throttle grip assembly and dry it thoroughly. Check the throttle slots for cracks or other damage. Replace the throttle if necessary.

7

15. The friction adjust screw is secured to the lower switch housing with a circlip. If necessary, remove the friction spring, circlip, spring and friction adjust screw. Check these parts for wear or damage. Replace damaged parts and reinstall. Make sure the circlip seats in the friction screw groove completely.

16. Clean the throttle area on the handlebar with solvent.

Installation

1. Apply a light coat of graphite to the housing inside surfaces and to the handlebar.

2. On the lower switch housing, push the larger diameter silver throttle cable insert into the larger hole in front of the tension adjust screw. Push it in until it snaps into place.

3. Push the smaller diameter gold throttle cable insert into the smaller hole in the rear of the tension adjust screw. Push it in until it snaps into place.

4. Position the friction shoe with the concave side facing up and install it so the pin hole is over the point of the adjuster screw.

5. Install the throttle grip onto the handlebar. Push it on until it stops, then pull it back about 1/8 in. (3.2 mm). Rotate it until the ferrule notches are at the top.

6. Place the lower switch housing below the throttle grip. Install the brass ferrules onto the cables so the end fittings seat in the ferrule recess. Seat ferrules in their respective notches on the throttle control grip. Make sure the cables are captured in the molded grooves in the grip.

7. Assemble the upper and lower switch housings (A, **Figure 79**) and the throttle grip. Install the lower switch housing screws and tighten them finger-tight.

8. If it is not in place, insert the 5/32 in. (4 mm) thick spacer between the brake lever and lever bracket. Make sure the spacer stays in place during the following steps.

9. Install the front master cylinder (B, **Figure 79**) onto the handlebar as described in Chapter Thirteen.

10. Securely tighten the switch housing screws.

11. Remove the cardboard insert from the front master cylinder.

12. Operate the throttle and make sure both cables move in and out properly.

13. Correctly route the cables (**Figure 81**) from the handlebar, through the frame and to the carburetor.

14. Connect the idle cable to the carburetor as follows:

   a. The idle cable has the small spring (A, **Figure 82**) on the end of the cable.

   b. Insert the idle cable sheath into the rear cable bracket guide on the carburetor (B, **Figure 82**).

   c. Attach the end of the idle cable into the throttle wheel (C, **Figure 82**).

15. Connect the throttle cable to the carburetor as follows:

   a. Insert the throttle cable sheath into the front cable bracket guide on the carburetor.

   b. Attach the end of the throttle cable to the throttle wheel.

16. At the throttle grip, tighten the cables to keep the cable ends from being disconnected from throttle wheel.

17. Operate the hand throttle a few times. Make sure the throttle barrel operates smoothly with no binding. Also

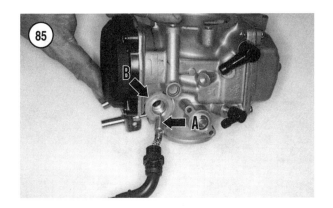

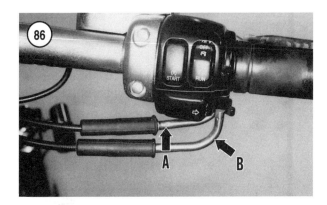

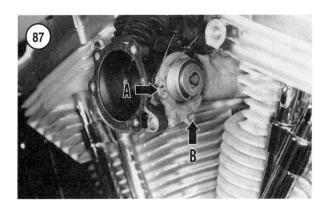

make sure both cable ends are seated squarely in their cable bracket guides and in the throttle barrel.

18. Adjust the throttle and idle cables as described in Chapter Three.

19. Reinstall the carburetor as described in this chapter.

20. Install the air filter backplate and air filter as described in this chapter.

21. Install the fuel tank as described in this chapter.

22. Start the engine and check for fuel leaks with the engine idling. Then turn the handlebar from side to side. Do not operate the throttle. If the engine speed increases

when turning the handlebar assembly, the throttle cables are routed incorrectly or are damaged. Recheck cable routing and adjustment.

> *WARNING*
> *Do not ride the motorcycle until the throttle cables are properly adjusted. Improper cable routing and adjustment can cause the throttle to stick open. This could cause loss of control.*

STARTING ENRICHMENT VALVE (CHOKE) CABLE REPLACEMENT (CARBURETED MODELS)

1. Remove the air filter and backplate as described in Chapter Three.
2. Note the routing of the enrichment cable from its mounting bracket to the carburetor.
3. Loosen the locknut (A, **Figure 83**) and disconnect the starting enrichment valve cable from the mounting bracket (B). Move the end of the cable out of the mounting bracket.
4. Partially remove the carburetor, as described in this chapter, until the starting enrichment valve cable can be disconnected from the backside of the carburetor.
5. Unscrew and remove the starting enrichment valve and cable (**Figure 84**) from the carburetor and remove the cable from the frame.
6. Install by reversing these removal steps. Note the following:
   a. Align the starting enrichment valve needle (A, **Figure 85**) with the needle passage in the carburetor (B) and install the starting enrichment valve. Tighten the valve nut securely.
   b. Position the starting enrichment valve cable into the mounting bracket (B, **Figure 83**), then tighten the locknut (A) securely.

THROTTLE AND IDLE CABLES (EFI MODELS)

There are two different throttle cables. At the throttle grip, the front cable is the throttle control cable (A, **Figure 86**) and the rear cable is the idle control cable (B).

At the induction control module, the idle control cable is located at the top of the throttle wheel (A, **Figure 87**) and the throttle control cable (B) is located at the bottom.

Removal

1. Remove the fuel tank as described in this chapter.

7

2. Remove the air filter and backing plate as described in this chapter.

3. Make a drawing or take a picture of the cable routing from the induction module through the frame to the right side handlebar.

4. At the right side handlebar, loosen both control cable adjuster locknuts (A, **Figure 88**), then turn the cable adjusters (B) *clockwise* as far as possible to increase cable slack.

5. At the induction module, use needlenose pliers to disconnect the throttle cable (A, **Figure 89**) and the idle cable (B) from the throttle barrel (C).

6. Release the cables from the integral cable guides in the induction module.

CAUTION
Failure to install the spacer in Step 7 will result in damage to the rubber boot and plunger on the front brake switch.

7. Insert a 5/32 in. (4 mm) thick spacer between the brake lever and lever bracket. Make sure the spacer stays in place during the following steps.

8. Remove the screws securing the right side switch assembly together (A, **Figure 90**).

9. Remove the front master cylinder (B, **Figure 90**) as described in Chapter Thirteen.

10. Remove the brass ferrules from the notches on the inboard side of the throttle grip (**Figure 91**). Remove the ferrules from the cable end fittings.

11. Remove the friction shoe from the end of the tension adjust screw.

12. Remove the throttle grip from the handlebar.

NOTE
Use a rocking motion while pulling on the control cable housings in Step 13. If necessary, place a drop of engine oil on the housings retaining rings to ease removal.

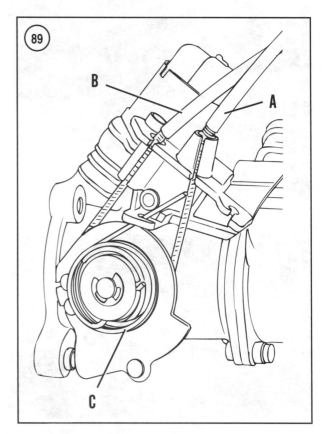

13. Pull the crimped inserts at the end of the throttle and idle control cable housings from the switch lower housing.

14. Remove the cables from the right side of the steering head and rubber trim (**Figure 92**).

15. At the induction module, perform the following:

   a. Carefully pull the throttle and idle control cables from the integral cable guides in the induction module.

   b. Disconnect the throttle and idle control cables from the throttle barrel.

16. Remove the cables from the frame.

17. Clean the throttle grip assembly and dry it thoroughly. Check the throttle slots for cracks or other damage. Replace the throttle if necessary.

18. The friction adjust screw is secured to the lower switch housing with a circlip. If necessary, remove the friction spring, circlip, spring and friction adjust screw. Check these parts for wear or damage. Replace damaged parts and reinstall. Make sure the circlip seats in the friction screw groove completely.

19. Clean the throttle area on the handlebar with solvent.

Installation

1. Apply a light coat of graphite to the housing inside surfaces and to the handlebar.

2. On the lower switch housing, push the larger diameter silver throttle cable insert into the larger hole in front of the tension adjust screw. Push it in until it snaps into place.

3. Push the smaller diameter gold throttle cable insert into the smaller hole in the rear of the tension adjust screw. Push it in until it snaps into place.

4. Position the friction shoe with the concave side facing up and install it so the pin hole is over the point of the adjuster screw.

5. Install the throttle grip onto the handlebar. Push it on until it stops, then pull it back about 1/8 in. (3.2 mm). Rotate it until the ferrule notches are at the top.

6. Place the lower switch housing below the throttle grip. Install the brass ferrules onto the cables so the end fittings seat in the ferrule recess. Seat ferrules in their respective notches on the throttle control grip. Make sure the cables are captured in the molded grooves in the grip.

7. Assemble the upper and lower switch housings (A, **Figure 90**) and the throttle grip. Install the lower switch housing screws and tighten them finger-tight.

8. If it is not in place, insert the 5/32 in. (4 mm) thick spacer between the brake lever and lever bracket. Make sure the spacer stays in place during the following steps.

9. Install the front master cylinder (B, **Figure 90**) as described in Chapter Thirteen.

10. Securely tighten the switch housing screws.

11. Remove the cardboard insert from the front master cylinder.

12. Operate the throttle and make sure both cables move in and out properly.

13. Correctly route the cables from the handlebar to the induction module.

14. At the induction module, perform the following:

    a. Install the idle cable (B, **Figure 89**) ball end over the top of the throttle barrel (C) and install the cable ball end into the upper hole in the throttle barrel. Make sure it is properly seated.

    b. Install the throttle cable (A, **Figure 89**) ball end under the bottom of the throttle barrel (C) and install the cable ball ends into the lower hole in the throttle barrel. Make sure they are properly seated.

    c. Install the cables into the integral cable guides in the induction module.

15. At the throttle grip, tighten the cables to keep the ball ends from being disconnected from throttle barrel.

16. Operate the hand throttle a few times. Make sure the throttle barrel operates smoothly with no binding. Also make sure both cable ends are seated squarely in their cable bracket guides and in the throttle barrel.

17. Adjust the throttle and idle cables as described in Chapter Three.

18. Install the backing plate and air filter as described in this chapter.

19. Install the fuel tank as described in this chapter.

20. Start the engine and check for fuel leaks with the engine idling. Then turn the handlebar from side to side. Do not operate the throttle. If the engine speed increases when turning the handlebar assembly, the throttle cables

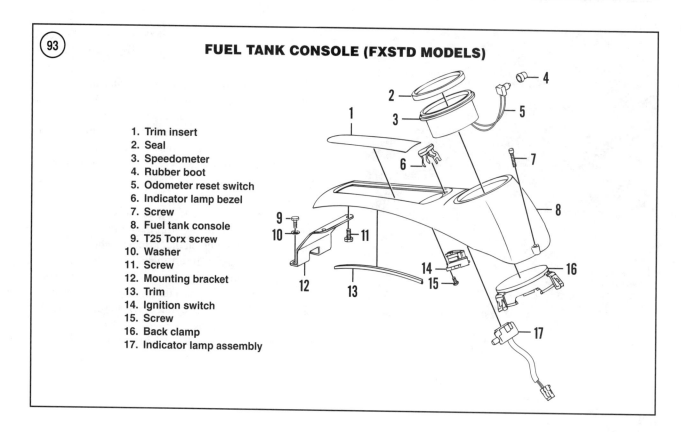

FUEL TANK CONSOLE (FXSTD MODELS)

93

1. Trim insert
2. Seal
3. Speedometer
4. Rubber boot
5. Odometer reset switch
6. Indicator lamp bezel
7. Screw
8. Fuel tank console
9. T25 Torx screw
10. Washer
11. Screw
12. Mounting bracket
13. Trim
14. Ignition switch
15. Screw
16. Back clamp
17. Indicator lamp assembly

are routed incorrectly or are damaged. Recheck cable routing and adjustment.

> *WARNING*
> *Do not ride the motorcycle until the throttle cables are properly adjusted. Improper cable routing and adjustment can cause the throttle to stick open. This could cause loss of control.*

FUEL TANK CONSOLE

Removal/Installation

Refer to **Figure 93** and **Figure 94**.

> *NOTE*
> *On models so equipped, always disarm the optional TSSM security system prior to disconnecting the battery or the siren will sound.*

1. Disconnect the negative battery cable as described in Chapter Eight.
2. Remove the seat as described in Chapter Fourteen.
3A. On FXSTD models, perform the following:
   a. Remove the T27 Torx screw securing the front of the console to the fuel tank.

b. Remove the two T25 Torx screws and washers securing the rear of the console mounting bracket to the frame.
c. Lift the console partially up off the fuel tank, and disconnect the electrical connector from the ignition switch, the indicator lamp and speedometer.
d. Remove the reset switch from the console.
e. Carefully remove the console and lay it upside down on shop cloths or towels.
3B. On all models except FXSTD, perform the following:
   a. Remove the rubber boot (**Figure 95**) from the odometer reset switch on the left side.
   b. Remove the acorn nut and washer (**Figure 96**) securing the console to the fuel tank.
   c. On fuel injected models, disconnect the fuel pump electrical connector.
   d. Lift the console partially up off the fuel tank and lay it upside down on shop cloths or towels.
   e. Unhook the ignition switch harness from the clip (**Figure 97**) on the side of the console.
   f. Disconnect the electrical connector from the ignition switch (A, **Figure 98**), the speedometer (B) and the indicator lamp assembly (C).
   g. Remove the odometer reset switch from the left side of the console.

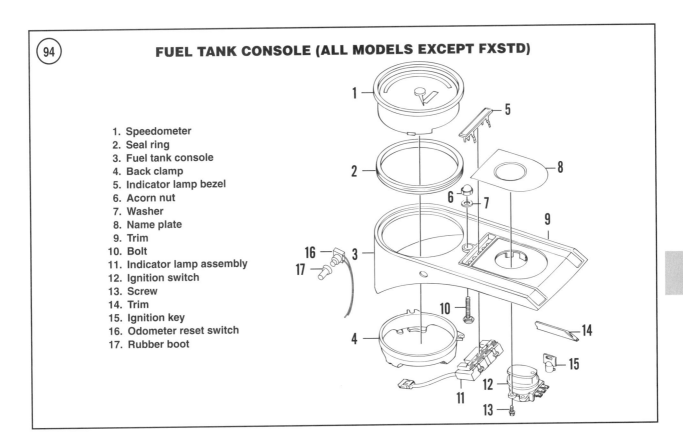

94 **FUEL TANK CONSOLE (ALL MODELS EXCEPT FXSTD)**

1. Speedometer
2. Seal ring
3. Fuel tank console
4. Back clamp
5. Indicator lamp bezel
6. Acorn nut
7. Washer
8. Name plate
9. Trim
10. Bolt
11. Indicator lamp assembly
12. Ignition switch
13. Screw
14. Trim
15. Ignition key
16. Odometer reset switch
17. Rubber boot

7

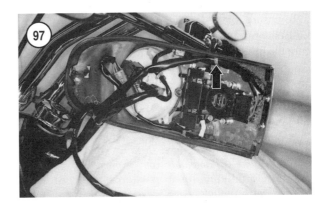

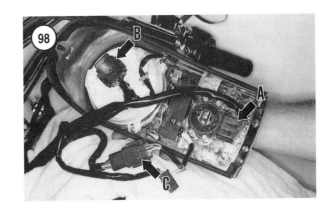

4. Install by reversing these removal steps. Note the following:

   a. Make sure the perimeter trim (**Figure 99**) is in place on the console.

   b. Carefully position the console in place and carefully route the electrical cables between the console and fuel tank (**Figure 100**) so they will not get pinched.

   c. Turn the ignition switch to the ON position and make sure the indicator lamps are illuminated.

   d. Start the engine to make sure the ignition switch is working. Turn off the engine.

FUEL HOSE AND CLAMPS

The fuel tank crossover fuel hose is connected to the tank fittings with non-reusable hose clamps. The hose clamps must be removed with cutting pliers and discarded. Do *not* re-use a hose clamp that has been removed.

When installing the original equipment (OE) type hose clamps, the new hose clamps must be installed with hose clamp pliers (H-D part No. 97087-65B). A screw-type hose clamp may be substituted in place of the OE hose clamp.

If OE hose clamps are going to be installed, disconnect the left side of the crossover hose from the fuel tank. There is insufficient room on the right side for the hose clamp pliers and the clamp during installation.

To ensure a leak-free connection when using the OE hose clamps, squeeze hard on the hose clamp pliers to secure the hose clamp and hose onto the fitting .

FUEL TANK (CARBURETED MODELS)

WARNING
Some fuel may spill from the fuel tank hose during this procedure. Because gasoline is extremely flammable and explosive, perform this procedure away from all open flames, including appliance pilot lights, and sparks. Do not smoke or allow anyone to smoke in the work area, as an explosion and fire may occur. Always work in a well-ventilated area. Wipe up any spills immediately.

WARNING
Route the fuel tank vapor hoses so they cannot contact hot engine or exhaust components. These hoses contain flammable vapors.

Removal/Installation

Refer to **Figure 101** or **Figure 102**.

1. Remove the fuel tank console as described in this chapter.

2. Turn the fuel valve (A, **Figure 103**) to the OFF position .

3. Remove the hose clamp and disconnect the fuel hose (B, **Figure 103**) from the valve.

NOTE
A crossover hose connects the two fuel tank compartments. Drain both sides of the tank before removing the tank in the following steps.

4. Drain the fuel tank as follows:

NOTE
A vacuum-operated fuel valve is installed on all carburetted models. A hand-operated vacuum pump is required to drain the fuel tank.

   a. Connect the drain hose to the fuel valve and secure it with a hose clamp. Insert the end of the drain hose into a gas can.

   b. Disconnect the vacuum hose from the fuel valve.

   c. Connect a hand-operated vacuum pump (**Figure 104**) to the fuel valve vacuum hose fitting.

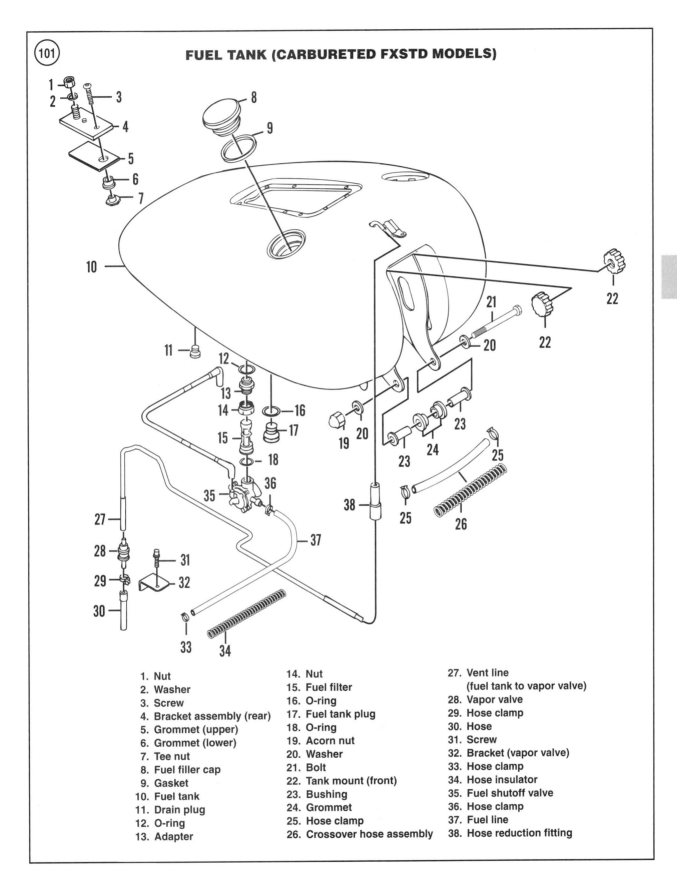

FUEL TANK (CARBURETED FXSTD MODELS)

1. Nut	14. Nut	27. Vent line
2. Washer	15. Fuel filter	(fuel tank to vapor valve)
3. Screw	16. O-ring	28. Vapor valve
4. Bracket assembly (rear)	17. Fuel tank plug	29. Hose clamp
5. Grommet (upper)	18. O-ring	30. Hose
6. Grommet (lower)	19. Acorn nut	31. Screw
7. Tee nut	20. Washer	32. Bracket (vapor valve)
8. Fuel filler cap	21. Bolt	33. Hose clamp
9. Gasket	22. Tank mount (front)	34. Hose insulator
10. Fuel tank	23. Bushing	35. Fuel shutoff valve
11. Drain plug	24. Grommet	36. Hose clamp
12. O-ring	25. Hose clamp	37. Fuel line
13. Adapter	26. Crossover hose assembly	38. Hose reduction fitting

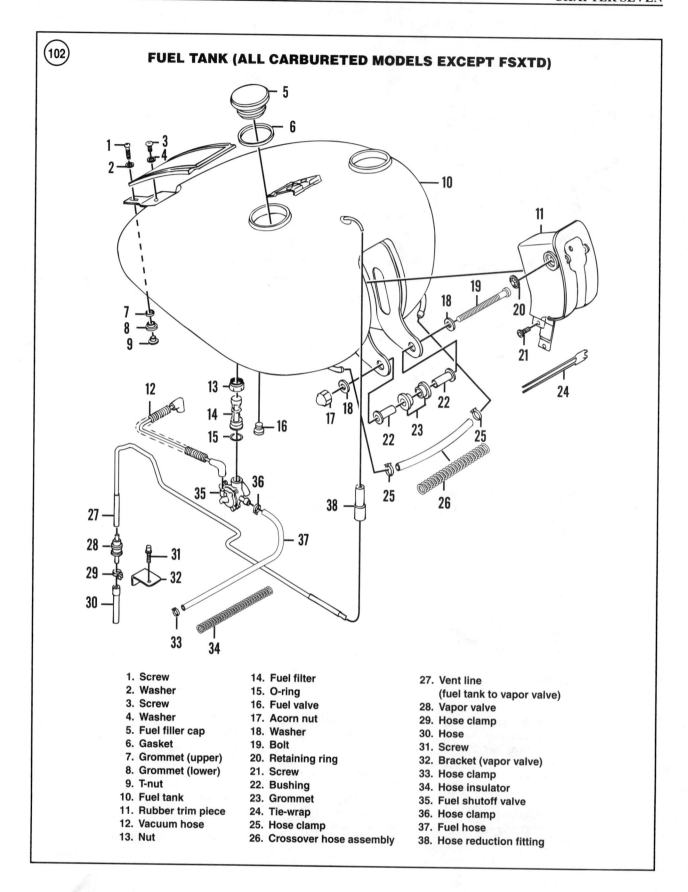

FUEL TANK (ALL CARBURETED MODELS EXCEPT FSXTD)

1. Screw
2. Washer
3. Screw
4. Washer
5. Fuel filler cap
6. Gasket
7. Grommet (upper)
8. Grommet (lower)
9. T-nut
10. Fuel tank
11. Rubber trim piece
12. Vacuum hose
13. Nut
14. Fuel filter
15. O-ring
16. Fuel valve
17. Acorn nut
18. Washer
19. Bolt
20. Retaining ring
21. Screw
22. Bushing
23. Grommet
24. Tie-wrap
25. Hose clamp
26. Crossover hose assembly
27. Vent line
   (fuel tank to vapor valve)
28. Vapor valve
29. Hose clamp
30. Hose
31. Screw
32. Bracket (vapor valve)
33. Hose clamp
34. Hose insulator
35. Fuel shutoff valve
36. Hose clamp
37. Fuel hose
38. Hose reduction fitting

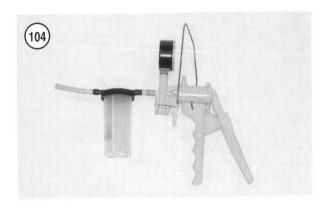

d. Turn the fuel valve to the RES position.

CAUTION
In the following step, do not apply more vacuum than 25 in. (635 mm) Hg or the fuel valve diaphragm will be damaged.

e. Gently operate the vacuum pump handle and apply a *maximum* of 25 in. (635 mm) Hg of vacuum. Once the vacuum is applied, the fuel will start to flow into the gas can.

f. When fuel stops flowing through the hose, turn the fuel valve OFF and release the vacuum. Disconnect the vacuum pump and drain hose.

5. Disconnect the vent hose from the fuel tank.

6. Disconnect the crossover hose from the left side of the fuel tank. Plug the tank opening and apply a hemostat to the crossover hose.

7A. On FXSTD models, remove the nut and washer securing the rear of the fuel tank to the frame.

7B. On all models except FXSTD, remove the T40 Torx bolt and washer securing the rear of the fuel tank to the frame.

8. At the front of the fuel tank, remove the acorn nut and washers from the through bolt. Withdraw the through bolt from the left side securing the fuel tank to the frame.

9. Lift and remove the fuel tank.

NOTE
Store the fuel tank in a safe place away from open flames or where it could be damaged.

10. Drain any remaining fuel into a gas can.

11. Inspect the fuel tank as described in this chapter.

12. Installation is the reverse of these steps while noting the following:

   a. Tighten the front and rear bolts and nuts to the specification in **Table 2**.

   b. Reconnect the fuel hose to the fuel valve and secure it with a *new* hose clamp.

   c. Refill the tank and check for leaks.

FUEL TANK (EFI MODELS)

WARNING
Some fuel may spill from the fuel tank hose during this procedure. Because gasoline is extremely flammable and explosive, perform this procedure away from all open flames, including appliance pilot lights, and sparks. Do not smoke or allow anyone to smoke in the work area, as an explosion and fire may occur. Always work in a well-ventilated area. Wipe up any spills immediately.

WARNING
Route the fuel tank vapor hoses so they cannot contact hot engine or exhaust components. These hoses contain flammable vapors.

Draining

1. Depressurize the fuel system as described in this chapter.

2. Make a drain hose from a 5/16 in. inner diameter hose and securely plug one end. Make it long enough to go from the fuel tank crossover hose fitting to a gas can.

3. Disconnect the crossover hose from the fittings on the left side of the fuel tank. Immediately connect the drain hose to the fuel tank fitting.

4. Place the plugged end of the drain hose into the gas can and remove the plug. Drain the fuel from that side of the fuel tank.

5. Disconnect the drain hose and reinstall the plug into the end.

6. Repeat Steps 3-5 for the other side of the fuel tank.

7. Plug the fuel tank crossover fittings to prevent the fuel from draining.

7

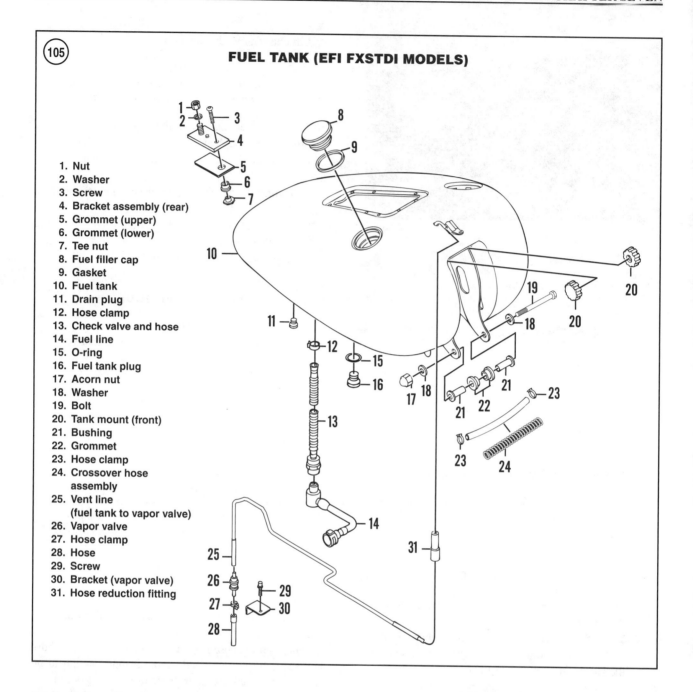

FUEL TANK (EFI FXSTDI MODELS)

1. Nut
2. Washer
3. Screw
4. Bracket assembly (rear)
5. Grommet (upper)
6. Grommet (lower)
7. Tee nut
8. Fuel filler cap
9. Gasket
10. Fuel tank
11. Drain plug
12. Hose clamp
13. Check valve and hose
14. Fuel line
15. O-ring
16. Fuel tank plug
17. Acorn nut
18. Washer
19. Bolt
20. Tank mount (front)
21. Bushing
22. Grommet
23. Hose clamp
24. Crossover hose assembly
25. Vent line (fuel tank to vapor valve)
26. Vapor valve
27. Hose clamp
28. Hose
29. Screw
30. Bracket (vapor valve)
31. Hose reduction fitting

Removal/Installation

Refer to **Figure 105** or **Figure 106**.

1. Depressurize the fuel system as described in this chapter.

2. Drain the fuel tank as described in this chapter.

3. Remove the seat as described in Chapter Fifteen.

4. Remove the fuel tank console as described in this chapter.

5. On the left side, disconnect the fuel pump electrical connector (**Figure 107**).

WARNING
A small amount of fuel will drain out of the fuel tank when the fuel lines are disconnected from the base of the tank. Place several shop cloths under the fuel line fittings to catch spilled fuel prior to disconnecting them. Discard the shop cloths in a safe manner.

6. Pull up on the chrome sleeve on the quick disconnect fitting and disconnect the fuel line (**Figure 108**) from the fuel tank.

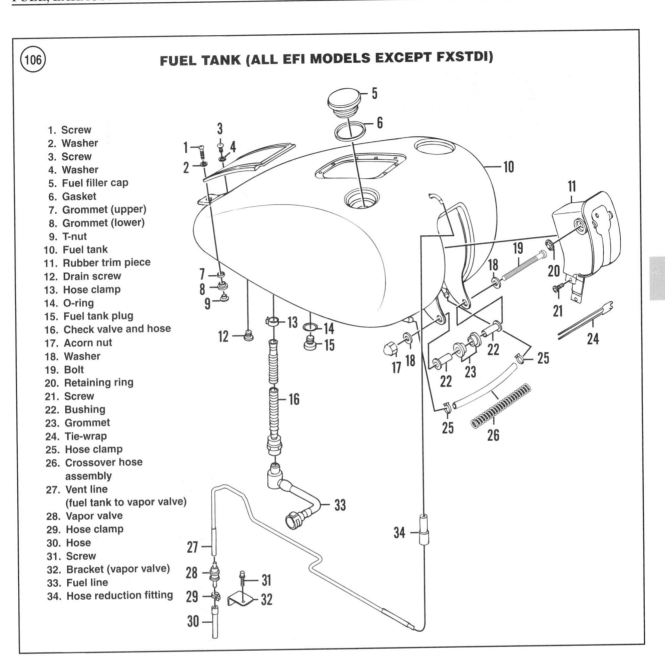

(106) FUEL TANK (ALL EFI MODELS EXCEPT FXSTDI)

1. Screw
2. Washer
3. Screw
4. Washer
5. Fuel filler cap
6. Gasket
7. Grommet (upper)
8. Grommet (lower)
9. T-nut
10. Fuel tank
11. Rubber trim piece
12. Drain screw
13. Hose clamp
14. O-ring
15. Fuel tank plug
16. Check valve and hose
17. Acorn nut
18. Washer
19. Bolt
20. Retaining ring
21. Screw
22. Bushing
23. Grommet
24. Tie-wrap
25. Hose clamp
26. Crossover hose
    assembly
27. Vent line
    (fuel tank to vapor valve)
28. Vapor valve
29. Hose clamp
30. Hose
31. Screw
32. Bracket (vapor valve)
33. Fuel line
34. Hose reduction fitting

7

7. Disconnect the vent line (**Figure 109**) from the fitting on the front of the fuel tank.

8A. On FXSTDI models, remove the nut and washer securing the rear of the fuel tank to the frame.

8B. On all models except FXSTDI, remove the Torx bolt and washer (**Figure 110**) securing the rear of the fuel tank to the frame.

9. At the front of the fuel tank, remove the acorn nut and washers from the through bolt (**Figure 111**). Withdraw the through bolt from the left side securing the fuel tank to the frame.

10. Lift and remove the fuel tank (**Figure 112**).

11. Inspect the fuel line quick-disconnect fitting for signs of leaks. Replace as necessary.

12. Drain any remaining fuel left in the tank into a gas can.

13. Inspect the fuel tank as described in this chapter.

WARNING
Store the fuel tank in a safe place away from open flames or where it could be damaged.

14. Installation is the reverse of these steps while noting the following:

    a. Tighten the front and rear bolts and nuts to the specification in **Table 2**.

    b. Reconnect the fuel line quick–disconnect fitting (**Figure 113**) onto the fuel tank until it clicks into the locked position. Pull down on the fuel line to make sure it is secured.

    c. On all models except FXSTDI, make sure the vent line runs along the right side of the frame backbone under the rubber trim.

    d. Refill the tank and check for leaks.

FUEL TANK INSPECTION (ALL MODELS)

1. Inspect the fuel hoses (A, **Figure 114**) and vent hoses for cracks, deterioration or damage. Replace damaged hoses with the same type and size materials. The fuel lines must be flexible and strong enough to withstand engine heat and vibration.

2. Check the fuel line insulator(s) for damage.

3. Check for damaged fuel tank mounting brackets. Refer to **Figure 115** and B, **Figure 114**.

4. Make sure the fuel level gauge wiring harness clamp is tight (**Figure 116**).

5. On fuel injected models, check the quick disconnect fitting (A, **Figure 117**) for tightness and fuel leakage.

6. On all models, check the fuel tank plug (B, **Figure 117**) for tightness and fuel leakage.

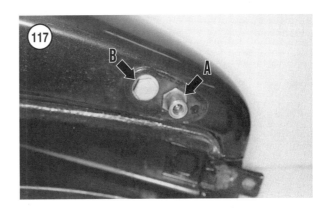

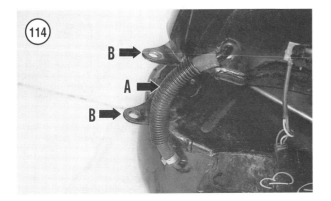

7. Remove the filler cap and inspect the tank for rust or contamination. If there is a rust buildup inside the tank, clean and flush the tank as described in this chapter.

8. Inspect the fuel tank for leaks.

FUEL PUMP AND FUEL FILTER (EFI MODELS)

Refer to **Figure 118**.

Top Plate Assembly Removal/Installation

1. Depressurize the fuel system as described in this chapter.

2. Remove the seat as described in Chapter Fourteen.

3. Remove the fuel tank console as described in this chapter.

4. Drain the fuel tank as described in this chapter.

5. Remove the ten screws securing the top plate (**Figure 119**) to the top of the fuel tank. Discard the screws.

6. Partially lift the top plate up away from the fuel tank.

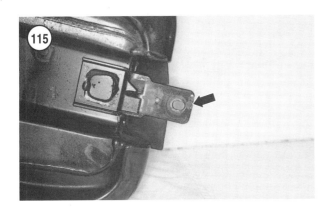

> *CAUTION*
> *Do not cut the fuel supply hose while cutting the hose clamp in the following step.*

7. On the right side of the fuel tank, carefully cut the hose clamp securing the outlet hose to the fuel filter fitting.

8. Carefully pull the top plate assembly straight up and out of the fuel tank. Do not damage the fuel gauge sending unit float during removal.

9. Remove the top plate gasket.

10. Installation is the reverse of these removal steps while noting the following:

    a. Raise the float to the up (FULL) position and install the assembly until the rubber spacer rests on the bottom of the fuel tank.

    b. Slip a *new* hose clamp onto the outlet hose prior to installing the assembly into the fuel filter fitting.

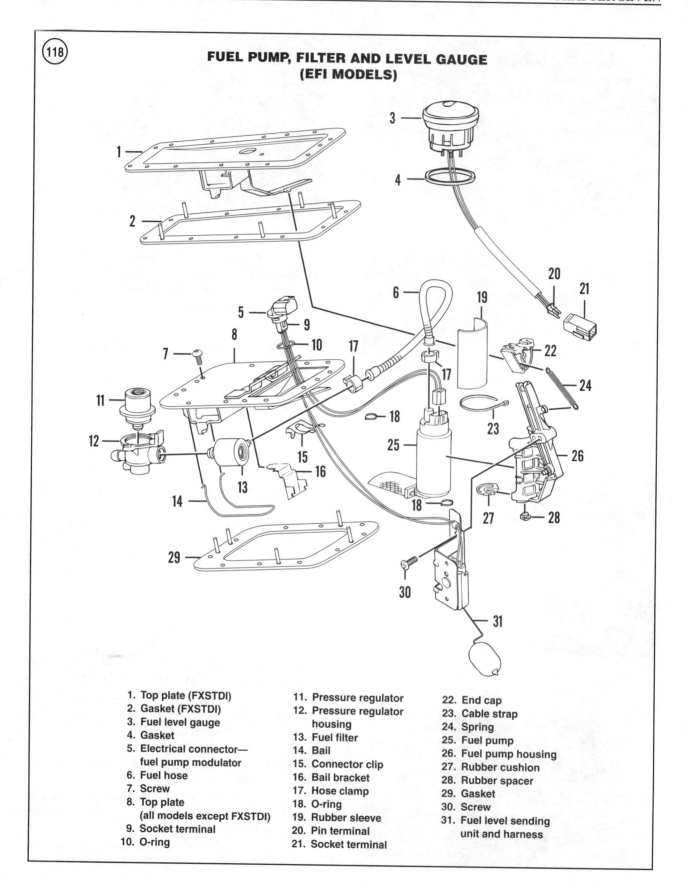

**FUEL PUMP, FILTER AND LEVEL GAUGE
(EFI MODELS)**

1. Top plate (FXSTDI)
2. Gasket (FXSTDI)
3. Fuel level gauge
4. Gasket
5. Electrical connector—
   fuel pump modulator
6. Fuel hose
7. Screw
8. Top plate
   (all models except FXSTDI)
9. Socket terminal
10. O-ring

11. Pressure regulator
12. Pressure regulator
    housing
13. Fuel filter
14. Bail
15. Connector clip
16. Bail bracket
17. Hose clamp
18. O-ring
19. Rubber sleeve
20. Pin terminal
21. Socket terminal

22. End cap
23. Cable strap
24. Spring
25. Fuel pump
26. Fuel pump housing
27. Rubber cushion
28. Rubber spacer
29. Gasket
30. Screw
31. Fuel level sending
    unit and harness

c. Install the outlet onto the fuel filter fitting and crimp the hose clamp.

d. Pivot the top plate and push down so the end cap engages the fuel pump housing.

e. Install a *new* top plate gasket.

f. Install *new* screws securing the top plate and tighten securely.

Fuel Filter Removal/Installation

1. Remove the top plate assembly as previously described in this chapter.

2. Carefully pull the wire bail from the slots on the fuel filter canister bracket. Move the wire bail out of the way.

3. Carefully pull the fuel filter out of the pressure regulator housing.

4. Use side cutting pliers to cut the hose clamp and remove it from the fuel filter hose.

5. Disconnect the fuel filter from the fuel pump hose.

6. Discard the fuel pump.

7. Installation is the reverse of removal while noting the following:

   a. Use a *new* hose clamp.

   b. Use a *new* O-ring on the fuel filter.

Fuel Pressure Regulator
Removal/Installation

1. Remove the fuel filter from the fuel pressure regulator.

2. Slide the fuel pressure regulator assembly forward to free its arms from the top plate.

3. Use a rocking motion and remove the fuel pressure regulator from the housing.

4. Installation is the reverse of removal. Apply clean engine oil to the new fuel pressure regulator O-rings.

Fuel Pump
Removal/Installation

NOTE
During the removal procedure, the fuel pump mounting bracket will be damaged and must be replaced along with the fuel pump. Make sure the fuel pump is defective prior to removing it from the bracket.

1. Remove the top plate assembly as previously described in this chapter.

2. Depress the external latch and disconnect the electrical connector from the fuel pump.

3. Use side cutting pliers to cut the hose clamp, and remove it from the fuel pump hose.

4. Remove the screw and remove the fuel level sending unit from the post on the fuel pump mounting bracket.

5. Disconnect the spring from the hook on the fuel pump mounting bracket.

6. Insert a flat screwdriver tip and crack the webbing at top of the fuel pump mounting bracket hinge. Remove the hinge from the mounting bracket.

7. Remove and discard the fuel pump and bracket assembly.

8. Installation is the reverse of removal while noting the following:

   a. Use a *new* hose clamp.

   b. Install a new fuel pump and fuel pump mounting bracket.

FUEL SHUTOFF VALVE
(CARBURETED MODELS)

A three-way vacuum-operated fuel shutoff valve is mounted to the left side of the fuel tank. A replaceable fuel filter is mounted to the top of the fuel shutoff valve.

To troubleshoot this valve, refer to *Vacuum Operated Fuel Shutoff Valve Testing* in Chapter Two.

Removal

WARNING
Gasoline is very volatile and flammable. Work in a well-ventilated area away from any open flames, including pilot lights on household appliances. Do not allow anyone to smoke in the area and have a fire extinguisher rated for gasoline fires on hand.

1. Disconnect the negative battery cable as described in Chapter Eight.

2. Turn the fuel shutoff valve to the OFF position.

7

3. Drain the fuel tank as described under *Fuel Tank Removal/Installation* in this chapter.

NOTE
*The fuel shutoff valve can be removed with the fuel tank in place. **Figure 120** is shown with the fuel tank removed to better illustrate the step.*

4. Loosen the fuel valve fitting (A, **Figure 120**) and remove the fuel shutoff valve (B) from the fuel tank. Drain residual gasoline still in the tank after the valve is removed.

Cleaning and Inspection

1. Inspect the filter mounted on top of the fuel valve. Remove contamination from the filter. Replace the filter if it is damaged.
2. Install a *new* filter gasket before installing the filter onto the fuel valve.
3. Remove all sealant residue from the fuel tank and fuel valve threads.

Installation

1. Install a *new* filter gasket onto the fuel shutoff valve, then install the filter.
2. Coat the fuel valve threads with Loctite Teflon pipe sealant.
3. Insert the fuel valve into the tank, then start the hex fitting onto the fuel tank threads two turns.
4. Hold the hex fitting and start the fuel valve into the fitting by turning it *counterclockwise* two turns.
5. Hold the fuel valve and tighten the hex fitting to 15-20 ft. lb. (20-27 N•m).

WARNING
If the hex fitting is turned more than two turns on the valve, it may bottom out on the valve and cause a fuel leak.

6. Install the insulator tube over the fuel hose.
7. Reconnect the fuel hose to the fuel shutoff valve and secure it with a hose clamp.
8. Refill the fuel tank and check for leaks.

FUEL TANK GAUGE

WARNING
Gasoline is extremely flammable and explosive, perform this procedure away from all open flames, including appliance pilot

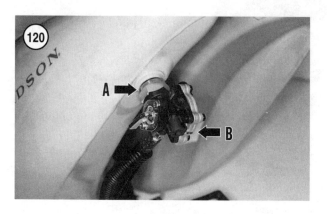

lights, and sparks. Do not smoke or allow someone to smoke in the work area, as an explosion and fire may occur. Always work in a well-ventilated area. Wipe up any spills immediately.

2000 Models (Except FXSTD)
Removal/Installation

Refer to **Figure 121**.
1. Remove the seat as described in Chapter Fourteen.
2. Disconnect the negative battery cable as described in Chapter Eight.
3. Remove the fuel tank as described in this chapter.

NOTE
*The fuel gauge sending unit electrical wires are routed through a tube in the fuel tank and are secured with a clamp at the bottom of the fuel tank. Loosen the clamp (**Figure 116**) and make sure there is enough slack in the wires to allow the gauge to be pulled up and out of the fuel tank.*

4. To remove the fuel gauge only, perform the following:

CAUTION
Do not twist the fuel gauge in Step 4 as the fuel gauge will be damaged.

  a. Carefully pull straight up and partially withdraw the fuel gauge from the fuel tank.
  b. Mark the wire connectors and the terminal on the fuel gauge to ensure correct installation.
  c. Disconnect the electrical connectors from the back of the fuel gauge. Do not disconnect the wires from the sending unit.
  d. Remove the fuel gauge and gasket.
5. To remove the fuel gauge sending unit, perform the following:

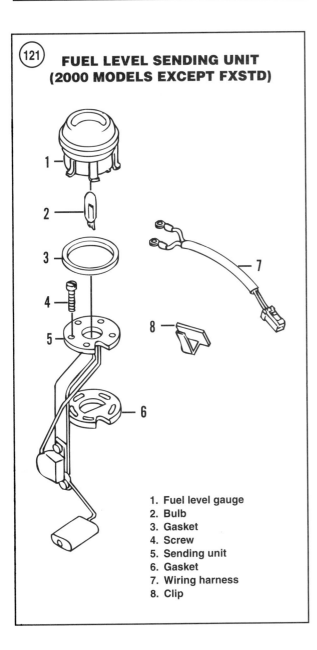

FUEL LEVEL SENDING UNIT (2000 MODELS EXCEPT FXSTD)

1. Fuel level gauge
2. Bulb
3. Gasket
4. Screw
5. Sending unit
6. Gasket
7. Wiring harness
8. Clip

a. Remove the fuel gauge as described in Step 4.
b. Remove the screws securing the sending unit to the fuel tank.
c. Disconnect the sending unit electrical connector from the wires in the fuel tank.

CAUTION
Do not bend the float arm during removal of the sending unit. If bent, the gauge will give inaccurate readings.

d. Carefully withdraw the sending unit while moving it back and forth, and while lifting and turning it in either direction.

e. Remove the gasket from the fuel tank.
6. Install by reversing these removal steps while noting the following:
a. Install *new* gaskets between the fuel gauge and fuel tank.
b. Install the sending unit *carefully* to avoid damage to the float arm.
c. Tighten all screws securely.

2000-on FXSTD Models
Removal/Installation

Refer to **Figure 122**.
1. Remove the seat as described in Chapter Fourteen.
2. Disconnect the negative battery cable as described in Chapter Eight.
3. Remove the fuel tank as described in this chapter.

NOTE
*The fuel gauge sending unit electrical wires are routed through a tube in the fuel tank and are secured with a clamp at the bottom of the fuel tank. Loosen the clamp (**Figure 116**) and make sure there is enough slack in the wires to allow the gauge to be pulled up and out of the fuel tank.*

4. To remove the fuel gauge only, perform the following:

CAUTION
Do not twist the fuel gauge in Step 4 as the fuel gauge will be damaged.

a. Carefully pull straight up and partially withdraw the fuel gauge from the fuel tank.
b. Mark the wire connectors and the terminal on the fuel gauge to ensure correct installation.
c. Disconnect the electrical connectors from the back of the fuel gauge. Do not disconnect the wires from the sending unit.
d. Remove the fuel gauge and gasket.
5. To remove the fuel gauge sending unit, perform the following:
a. Remove the fuel gauge as described in Step 4.
b. Disconnect the electrical harness from the connector (A, **Figure 123**) on the top plate.
c. Remove the T20 Torx screws (B, **Figure 123**) securing the top plate.

CAUTION
Do not bend the float arm during removal of the sending unit. If bent, the gauge will give inaccurate readings.

7

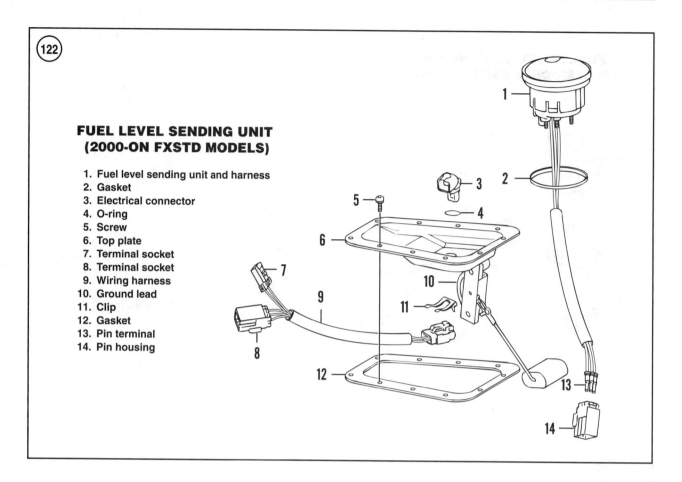

**FUEL LEVEL SENDING UNIT
(2000-ON FXSTD MODELS)**

1. Fuel level sending unit and harness
2. Gasket
3. Electrical connector
4. O-ring
5. Screw
6. Top plate
7. Terminal socket
8. Terminal socket
9. Wiring harness
10. Ground lead
11. Clip
12. Gasket
13. Pin terminal
14. Pin housing

d. Carefully withdraw the top plate (C, **Figure 123**) and sending unit while moving it back and forth, and while lifting and turning it in either direction.

e. Remove the gasket from the fuel tank and discard it.

6. Install by reversing these removal steps while noting the following:

NOTE
*Do **not** apply any type of gasket sealer to the top plate gasket.*

a. Install *new* gaskets between the fuel gauge and fuel tank.

b. Install the sending unit *carefully* to avoid damage to the float arm.

c. Tighten all screws securely.

**2001-On Models (Except FXSTD)
Removal/Installation**

Refer to **Figure 124**.

1. Remove the seat as described in Chapter Fourteen.

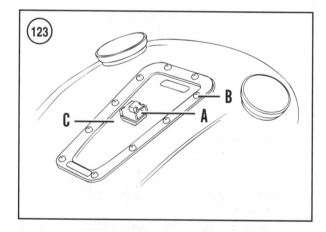

2. Disconnect the negative battery cable as described in Chapter Eight.

3. Remove the fuel tank as described in this chapter.

NOTE
The fuel gauge sending unit electrical wires are routed through a tube in the fuel tank and are secured with a clamp at the bottom

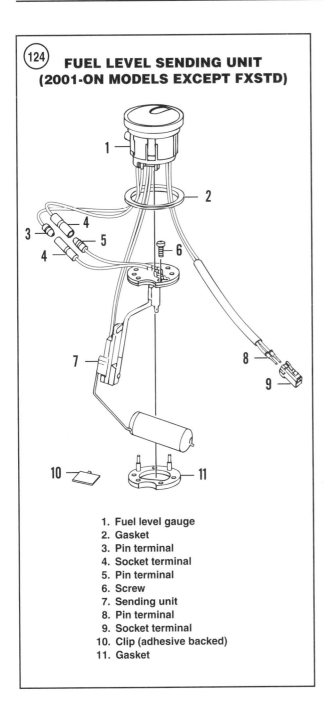

124 **FUEL LEVEL SENDING UNIT (2001-ON MODELS EXCEPT FXSTD)**

1. Fuel level gauge
2. Gasket
3. Pin terminal
4. Socket terminal
5. Pin terminal
6. Screw
7. Sending unit
8. Pin terminal
9. Socket terminal
10. Clip (adhesive backed)
11. Gasket

of the fuel tank. Loosen the clamp (**Figure 116**) and make sure there is enough slack in the wires to allow the gauge to be pulled up and out of the fuel tank.

4. To remove the fuel gauge only, perform the following:

CAUTION
Do not twist the fuel gauge in Step 3 as the fuel gauge will be damaged.

a. Carefully pull straight up and partially withdraw the fuel gauge from the fuel tank.
b. Disconnect the sending unit and fuel gauge wiring electrical connectors.
c. Remove the fuel gauge and gasket.

5. To remove the fuel gauge sending unit, perform the following:
a. Remove the fuel gauge as described in Step 3.
b. Remove the screws securing the fuel gauge sending unit plate.

CAUTION
Do not bend the float arm during removal of the sending unit. If bent, the gauge will give inaccurate readings.

c. Carefully withdraw the sending unit while moving it back and forth, and while lifting and turning it in either direction.
d. Remove the gasket from the fuel tank and discard it.

6. Install by reversing these removal steps while noting the following:

NOTE
*Do **not** apply any type of gasket sealer to the top plate gasket.*

a. Install *new* gaskets between the fuel gauge and fuel tank.
b. Install the sending unit *carefully* to avoid damage to the float arm.
c. Tighten all screws securely.

EXHAUST SYSTEM (FLSTF AND FXSTD MODELS)

Removal

Refer to **Figure 125**.

NOTE
If the system joints are corroded or rusty, spray all connections with WD-40, or an equivalent, and allow the penetrating oil to soak in sufficiently to free the rusted joints.

1. Support the motorcycle on a work stand. See *Motorcycle Stands* in Chapter Nine.
2. On models so equipped, remove the footboards as described in Chapter Fourteen.
3. Label the heat shields prior to removal for aid during installation. They look very similar but all have slight differences. Use the numbers assigned to these parts in **Figure 125**.

7

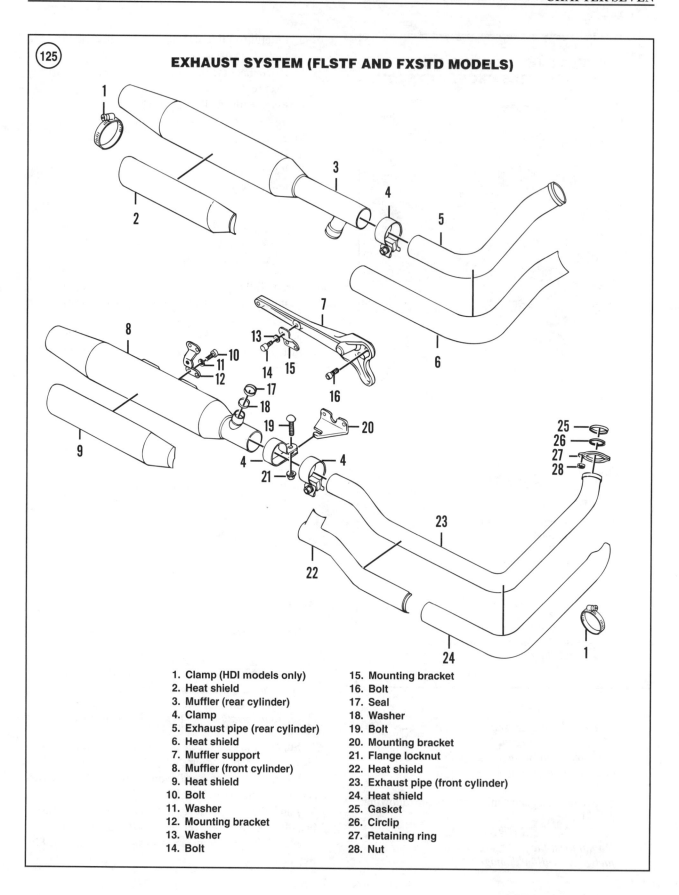

125

EXHAUST SYSTEM (FLSTF AND FXSTD MODELS)

1. Clamp (HDI models only)
2. Heat shield
3. Muffler (rear cylinder)
4. Clamp
5. Exhaust pipe (rear cylinder)
6. Heat shield
7. Muffler support
8. Muffler (front cylinder)
9. Heat shield
10. Bolt
11. Washer
12. Mounting bracket
13. Washer
14. Bolt
15. Mounting bracket
16. Bolt
17. Seal
18. Washer
19. Bolt
20. Mounting bracket
21. Flange locknut
22. Heat shield
23. Exhaust pipe (front cylinder)
24. Heat shield
25. Gasket
26. Circlip
27. Retaining ring
28. Nut

4. To remove the muffler assembly, perform the following:
   a. Remove the carriage bolt and nut securing the Torca clamp to the lower muffler-to-exhaust pipe mounting bracket.
   b. Remove the screws and washers on both muffler brackets.
   c. Pull the muffler assembly toward the rear and disconnect both mufflers from the front and rear exhaust pipes. Leave the mufflers attached to the interconnect fittings on both mufflers.

5. To remove the exhaust pipes, perform the following:
   a. Remove the mufflers as described in Step 4.
   b. Loosen the clamps and remove both heat shields.
   c. At each cylinder head, loosen and remove the two flange nuts securing both the front and rear exhaust pipes to the cylinder heads.
   d. Slide the exhaust flange and retaining ring off the cylinder head studs.
   e. Remove the exhaust pipes from the cylinder heads.
   f. Remove the circlip, then remove the exhaust port gaskets.

6. Inspect the exhaust system as described in this chapter.

7. Store the exhaust system components in a safe place until they are reinstalled.

Installation

NOTE
New Torca clamps must be installed to ensure correct sealing integrity. The new Torca clamps eliminate the need for graphite or silicone tape during installation of the mufflers.

NOTE
To prevent exhaust leaks, do not tighten any of the mounting bolts and nuts or the Torca clamps until all exhaust components are in place.

1. Scrape the exhaust port surfaces to remove all carbon residue. Then wipe the port with a rag.

2. Install a *new* exhaust port gasket into each exhaust port with the tapered side facing out. Install the circlips to secure the gaskets.

3. To install the exhaust pipes, perform the following:
   a. Install the front header pipe onto the front cylinder head exhaust port. Install the flange nuts and tighten them finger-tight.
   b. Install the rear header pipe onto the rear cylinder head exhaust port. Install the flange nuts and tighten them finger-tight.
   c. Move the open end of the exhaust pipes into position to accept the muffler assembly.

   d. Install the *new* Torca clamps onto the end of the exhaust pipes.

4. To install the muffler assembly, perform the following:
   a. Move the muffler assembly into position and attach them to the exhaust pipes.
   b. Install the screws and washers securing the mufflers to the mounting brackets. Tighten the screws finger-tight.
   c. Move the Torca clamps into position and tighten finger-tight.

5. Check the entire exhaust system to make sure none of the exhaust components are touching the frame. If necessary, make slight adjustments to avoid any contact that would transmit vibrations to the rider through the frame.

6. Check the exhaust assembly alignment, then tighten the mounting bolts and nuts as follows:
   a. Front cylinder head flange nuts. Tighten the upper nut to 60-80 in.-lbs. (7-9 N•m), then tighten the lower nut to 60-80 in.-lbs. (7-9 N•m).
   b. Rear cylinder head flange nuts. Tighten the upper nut to 60-80 in.-lbs. (7-9 N•m), then tighten the lower nut to 60-80 in.-lbs. (7-9 N•m).
   c. Tighten the carriage bolt and nut securing the Torca clamp to the lower muffler-to-exhaust pipe mounting bracket to 45-60 ft.-lbs. (61-81 N•m).
   d. Tighten the screws and washers on both muffler brackets to 15-19 ft.-lbs. (20-25 N•m).

7. Open the heat shield clamps completely. Position the clamp so the screw is on the outboard side in the most accessible position. Install the heat shields in the locations marked during removal. Tighten the clamps securely.

8. Check all heat shields to make sure none are touching the frame. If necessary, make slight adjustments to avoid any contact that would transmit vibrations to the rider through the frame.

9. Start the engine and check for leaks.

10. On models so equipped, install the footboards as described in Chapter Fourteen.

EXHAUST SYSTEM (FLSTS MODELS)

Removal

Refer to **Figure 126**.

NOTE
If the system joints are corroded or rusty, spray all connections with WD-40, or an equivalent, and allow the penetrating oil to soak in sufficiently to free the rusted joints.

1. Support the motorcycle on a work stand. See *Motorcycle Stands* in Chapter Nine.

7

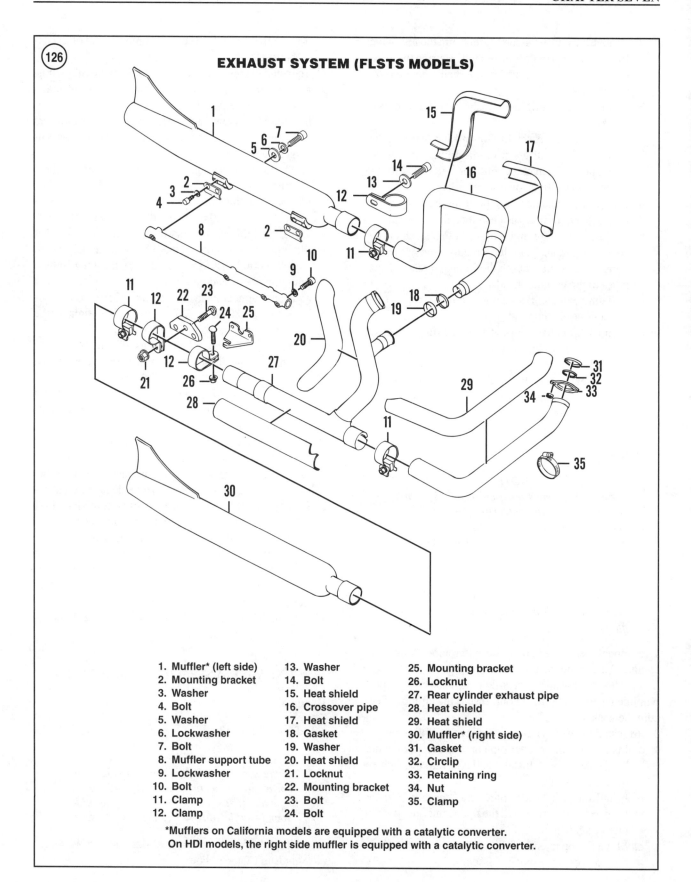

EXHAUST SYSTEM (FLSTS MODELS)

1. Muffler* (left side)
2. Mounting bracket
3. Washer
4. Bolt
5. Washer
6. Lockwasher
7. Bolt
8. Muffler support tube
9. Lockwasher
10. Bolt
11. Clamp
12. Clamp
13. Washer
14. Bolt
15. Heat shield
16. Crossover pipe
17. Heat shield
18. Gasket
19. Washer
20. Heat shield
21. Locknut
22. Mounting bracket
23. Bolt
24. Bolt
25. Mounting bracket
26. Locknut
27. Rear cylinder exhaust pipe
28. Heat shield
29. Heat shield
30. Muffler* (right side)
31. Gasket
32. Circlip
33. Retaining ring
34. Nut
35. Clamp

*Mufflers on California models are equipped with a catalytic converter.
On HDI models, the right side muffler is equipped with a catalytic converter.

2. Remove both saddlebags as described in Chapter Fourteen.

3. Remove the footboards as described in Chapter Fourteen.

4. Label the heat shields prior to removal for aid during installation. They look very similar but all have slight differences. Use the numbers assigned to these parts in **Figure 126**.

5. Loosen the clamps and remove the heat shields.

6. To remove the mufflers, perform the following:
   a. Loosen the Torca clamp securing the muffler to the exhaust pipe.
   b. Remove the bolts, lockwashers and washers securing the muffler to the muffler support tube.
   c. Pull the muffler toward the rear and disconnect the muffler from the exhaust pipe.
   d. Repeat for the other muffler.

7. To remove the exhaust pipes, perform the following:
   a. On the right side, loosen the clamp securing the front cylinder exhaust pipe to the rear cylinder exhaust pipe.
   b. Remove the bolt and locknut securing the rear portion of the rear cylinder exhaust pipe to the mounting bracket on the frame.
   c. Remove the screw and washer securing the cross over clamp to the passenger footboard.
   d. Remove the cross over pipe from the rear exhaust pipe.
   e. At each cylinder head, loosen and remove the two flange nuts securing both the front and rear exhaust pipes to the cylinder heads.
   f. Slide the exhaust flange and retaining ring off the cylinder head studs.
   g. Remove the exhaust pipes from the cylinder heads.
   h. Remove the circlip, then remove the exhaust port gaskets.

8. Inspect the exhaust system as described in this chapter.

9. Store the exhaust system components in a safe place until they are reinstalled.

Installation

NOTE
New Torca clamps must be installed to ensure correct sealing integrity. The new Torca clamps eliminate the need for graphite or silicone tape during installation of the mufflers.

NOTE
To prevent exhaust leaks, do not tighten any of the mounting bolts and nuts or the Torca clamps until all exhaust components are in place.

1. Scrape the exhaust port surfaces to remove all carbon residue, then wipe the port with a rag.

2. Install a *new* exhaust port gasket into each exhaust port with the tapered side facing out. Install the circlips to secure the gaskets.

3. To install the exhaust pipes, perform the following:
   a. Install the front header pipe onto the front cylinder head exhaust port. Install the flange nuts and tighten them finger-tight.
   b. Install the rear header pipe onto the rear cylinder head exhaust port. Install the flange nuts and tighten them finger-tight.
   c. Install the *new* Torca clamps onto the end of the exhaust pipes.
   d. Connect the front cylinder head exhaust pipe to the rear cylinder head exhaust pipe. Push them together until they bottom.
   e. Install the bolt and locknut securing the rear portion of the rear cylinder exhaust pipe to the mounting bracket on the frame.
   f. Install a *new* washer and gasket onto the cross over pipe.
   g. Install the cross over pipe to the rear cylinder exhaust pipe and push it on until it bottoms.
   h. Install the screw and washer securing the cross over clamp to the passenger footboard.
   i. Move the open end of the exhaust pipes into position to accept the mufflers.

4. To install the mufflers, perform the following:
   a. Install the *new* Torca clamp onto the end of the exhaust pipe.
   b. Move the muffler into position and attach it to the exhaust pipe.
   c. Install the bolts, lockwashers and washers securing the muffler to the muffler support tube. Tighten the bolts finger-tight.
   d. Move the Torca clamps into position and tighten finger-tight.
   e. Repeat for the other muffler.

5. Check the entire exhaust system to make sure none of the exhaust components are touching the frame. If necessary, make slight adjustments to avoid any contact that would transmit vibrations to the rider through the frame.

6. Check the exhaust assembly alignment, then tighten the mounting bolts and nuts as follows:
   a. Front cylinder head flange nuts. Tighten the upper nut to 9-18 in.-lbs. (1-2 N•m). Tighten the lower nut to 120 in.-lbs. (14 N•m) then tighten the upper nut to 120 in.-lbs. (14 N•m).

7

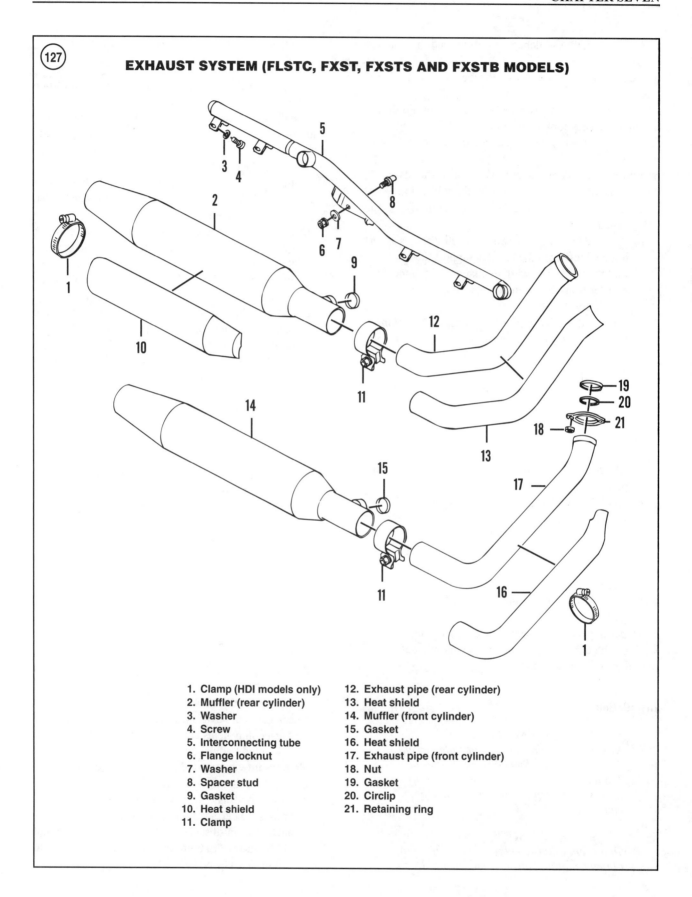

127

EXHAUST SYSTEM (FLSTC, FXST, FXSTS AND FXSTB MODELS)

1. Clamp (HDI models only)
2. Muffler (rear cylinder)
3. Washer
4. Screw
5. Interconnecting tube
6. Flange locknut
7. Washer
8. Spacer stud
9. Gasket
10. Heat shield
11. Clamp
12. Exhaust pipe (rear cylinder)
13. Heat shield
14. Muffler (front cylinder)
15. Gasket
16. Heat shield
17. Exhaust pipe (front cylinder)
18. Nut
19. Gasket
20. Circlip
21. Retaining ring

b. Rear cylinder head flange nuts. Tighten the upper nut to 9-18 in.-lbs. (1-2 N•m). Tighten the lower nut to 120 in.-lbs. (14 N•m) then tighten the upper nut to 120 in.-lbs. (14 N•m).

c. Tighten the bolts securing the mufflers to the support tube securely.

d. Tighten the screw securing the cross over pipe clamp to the passenger footboard securely.

e. Tighten the bolts and locknut securing the rear portion of the rear cylinder exhaust pipe to the mounting brackets securely.

f. Tighten the Torca clamp securing the front cylinder exhaust pipe to the rear cylinder exhaust pipe to 45-60 ft.-lbs. (61-81 N•m).

7. Open the heat shield clamps completely. Position the clamp so the screw is on the outboard side in the most accessible position. Install the heat shields in the locations marked during removal. Tighten the clamps securely.

8. Check all heat shields to make sure none are touching the frame. If necessary, make slight adjustments to avoid any contact that would transmit vibrations to the rider through the frame.

9. Start the engine and check for leaks.

10. Install the footboards as described in Chapter Fourteen.

11. Install both saddlebags as described in Chapter Fourteen.

EXHAUST SYSTEM
(FXST, FLSTC, FXSTS AND FXSTB MODELS)

Removal

Refer to **Figure 127**.

NOTE
If the system joints are corroded or rusty, spray all connections with WD-40, or an equivalent, and allow the penetrating oil to soak in sufficiently to free the rusted joints.

1. Support the motorcycle on a work stand. See *Motorcycle Stands* in Chapter Nine.

2. On models so equipped, remove the footboards as described in Chapter Fourteen.

3. On models so equipped, remove the saddlebags as described in Chapter Fourteen.

4. Label the heat shields prior to removal for aid during installation. They look very similar but all have slight differences. Use the numbers assigned to these parts in **Figure 127**.

5. Loosen the clamps and remove the heat shields.

6. To remove the muffler assembly, perform the following:

a. Remove the flange locknuts securing the interconnecting tube to the frame.

b. Loosen the clamps securing the mufflers to the exhaust pipes.

c. Pull the muffler assembly toward the rear and disconnect both mufflers from the front and rear exhaust pipes. Leave the mufflers attached to the interconnect tube on both mufflers.

7. To remove the exhaust pipes, perform the following:

a. Remove the mufflers as described in Step 6.

b. Loosen the clamps and remove both heat shields.

c. At each cylinder head, loosen and remove the two flange nuts securing both the front and rear exhaust pipes to the cylinder heads.

d. Slide the exhaust flange and retaining ring off the cylinder head studs.

e. Remove the exhaust pipes from the cylinder heads.

f. Remove the circlip, then remove the exhaust port gaskets.

8. Inspect the exhaust system as described in this chapter.

9. Store the exhaust system components in a safe place until they are reinstalled.

Installation

NOTE
To prevent exhaust leaks, do not tighten any of the mounting bolts and nuts or the Torca clamps until all exhaust components are in place.

1. Scrape the exhaust port surfaces to remove all carbon residue. Then wipe the port with a rag.

2. Install a *new* exhaust port gasket into each exhaust port with the tapered side facing out. Install the circlips to secure the gaskets.

3. To install the exhaust pipes, perform the following:

a. Install the front header pipe onto the front cylinder head exhaust port. Install the flange nuts and tighten them finger-tight.

b. Install the rear header pipe onto the rear cylinder head exhaust port. Install the flange nuts and tighten them finger-tight.

c. Move the open end of the exhaust pipes into position to accept the muffler assembly.

d. Install the *new* clamps onto the end of the exhaust pipes.

4. To install the muffler assembly, perform the following:

a. Move the muffler assembly into position and attach them to the exhaust pipes.

7

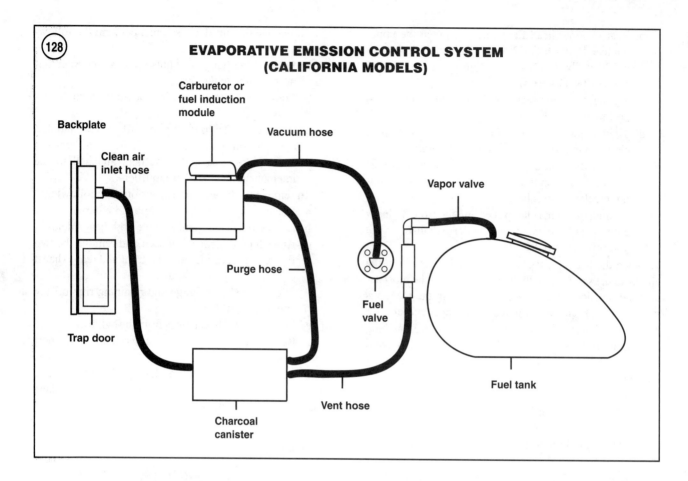

EVAPORATIVE EMISSION CONTROL SYSTEM (CALIFORNIA MODELS)

b. Install the flange locknuts securing the interconnecting tube to the frame and tighten them finger-tight.

c. Move the clamps into position and tighten finger-tight

5. Check the entire exhaust system to make sure none of the exhaust components are touching the frame. If necessary, make slight adjustments to avoid any contact that would transmit vibrations to the rider through the frame.

6. Check the exhaust assembly alignment, then tighten the mounting bolts and nuts as follows:

a. Front cylinder head flange nuts. Tighten the lower nut to 10 in.-lbs. (1 N•m). Tighten the upper nut to 60-80 in.-lbs. (7-9 N•m), then tighten the lower nut to 60-80 in.-lbs. (7-9 N•m).

b. Rear cylinder head flange nuts. Tighten the lower nut to 10 in.-lbs. (1 N•m). Tighten the upper nut to 60-80 in.-lbs. (7-9 N•m), then tighten the lower nut to 60-80 in.-lbs. (7-9 N•m).

c. Tighten the flange locknuts securing the interconnecting tube to the frame to 30-33 ft.-lbs. (41-45 N•m).

7. Open the heat shield clamps completely. Position the clamp so the screw is on the outboard side in the most accessible position. Install the heat shields in the locations marked during removal. Tighten the clamps securely.

8. Check all heat shields to make sure none are touching the frame. If necessary, make slight adjustments to avoid any contact that would transmit vibrations to the rider through the frame.

9. Start the engine and check for leaks.

10. On models so equipped, install the footboards as described in Chapter Fourteen.

11. On models so equipped, install the saddlebags as described in Chapter Fourteen.

EXHAUST SYSTEM

Inspection (All Models)

1. Replace rusted or damaged exhaust system components.

2. Inspect all pipes for rust or corrosion.

3. Remove all rust from exhaust pipes and muffler mating surfaces.

4. The Torca clamps are not reusable.

5. Replace damaged exhaust pipe retaining rings.

6. Replace worn or damaged heat shield clamps as required.

7. Check the mounting bracket bolts and nuts for tightness.

EVAPORATIVE EMISSION CONTROL SYSTEM (CALIFORNIA MODELS)

The evaporative emission control system prevents gasoline vapor from escaping into the atmosphere.

When the engine is not running, the system directs the fuel vapor from the fuel tank through the vapor valve and into the charcoal canister. Also, when the engine is not running, the gravity-operated trap door in the air filter backplate blocks the inlet port of the air filter. This prevents hydrocarbon vapors from the carburetor venturi, or fuel injection induction module, from escaping into the atmosphere.

When the engine is running, these vapors are drawn through a purge hose and into the carburetor, or fuel injection induction module, where they burn in the combustion chambers. The vapor valve also prevents gasoline vapor from escaping from the carbon canister if the motorcycle falls onto its side.

Also, when the engine is running, the engine vacuum pulls the air filter backplate trap door open, allowing air to enter.

Charcoal Canister

Inspection

Refer to **Figure 128** for component placement and hose routing. Before removing the hoses from any of the parts, mark the hose and fitting with a piece of masking tape to identify them.

1. Check all emission control lines and hoses to make sure they are correctly routed and connected.

WARNING
Make sure the fuel tank vapor hoses are routed so they cannot contact hot engine or exhaust components. These hoses contain flammable vapor. If a hose melts from contact with a hot part, leaking vapor may ignite, causing severe motorcycle damage and rider injury.

2. Make sure there are no kinks in the lines or hoses. Also inspect the hoses and lines routed near engine hot spots for excessive wear or burning.

3. Check the physical condition of all lines and hoses in the system. Check for cuts, tears or loose connections. These lines and hoses are subjected to various temperatures and operating conditions, and eventually become brittle and crack. Replace damaged lines and hoses.

4. Check all components in the emission control system for damage, such as broken fittings.

Replacement

1. Support the motorcycle on a work stand with the rear wheel off the ground. See *Motorcycle Stands* in Chapter Nine.

2. Remove the rear wheel as described in Chapter Nine.

3. Remove the bolts securing the rear fender panel and remove the panel.

4. On the left side of the canister, use a screwdriver and lift up on the tang of the canister bracket on the frame.

5. On the left side of the canister, mark the two hoses (A, **Figure 129**) and the canister fittings prior to disconnecting the hoses from the fittings.

6. Slide the canister (B, **Figure 129**) to the left until it is free from the bracket, then lower it from the frame.

7. On carbureted models, disconnect the breather hose from the fitting on the right side of the canister.

8. Disconnect the hoses from the canister fittings and remove the canister.

9. Installation is the reverse of removal. Ensure that all hoses are connected to the correct fittings and are secure.

Vapor Valve Replacement

The vapor valve is an integral part of the fuel pressure relief system. The fuel tank vapor expands as the fuel tank temperature rises. This pressure must be relived to avoid excessive vapor buildup within the fuel tank.

7

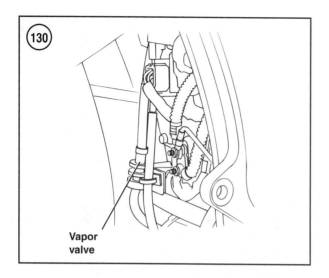

Vapor
valve

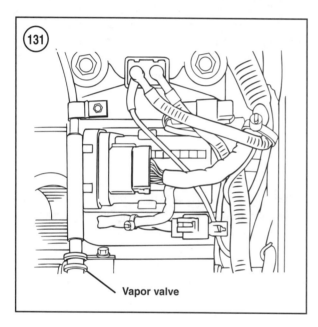

Vapor valve

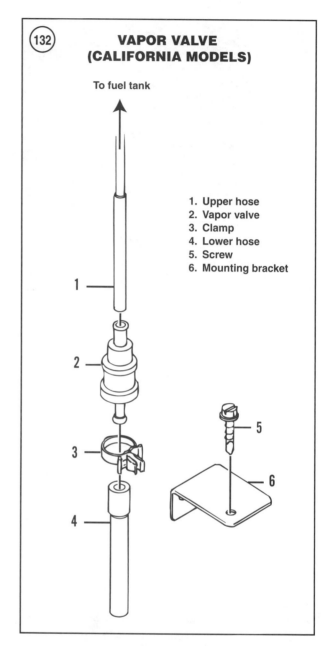

**VAPOR VALVE
(CALIFORNIA MODELS)**

To fuel tank

1. Upper hose
2. Vapor valve
3. Clamp
4. Lower hose
5. Screw
6. Mounting bracket

1
2
3
4
5
6

The lower hose is vented to the atmosphere or on California models it is connected to the evaporation canister.

Refer to **Figures 130-132**.

1. Remove the rear wheel as described in Chapter Nine.

2. Label the upper hose and lower hose where they are connected to the vapor valve fittings.

3. Disconnect the hoses from the vapor valve (**Figure 133**).

4. Remove the vapor valve from the clip on the mounting bracket.

WARNING
*The vapor valve must be mounted in the clip in a **vertical position** in order to operate*

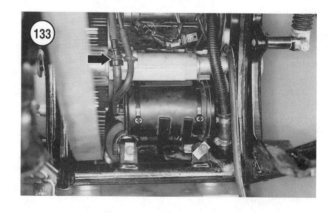

correctly. If installed incorrectly, excessive pressure can build up in the fuel tank that could result in a fire or an explosion resulting in serious injury.

5. Correctly position the vapor valve with the long neck fitting at the top and install the vapor valve into the clip on the mounting bracket.

6. Connect the upper and lower hoses to the vapor valve.

Table 1 CARBURETOR SPECIFICATIONS

Item	Specification
Main jet	190
Pilot jet	45
Float level	0.413-0.453 in. (10.5-11.5 mm)

Table 2 FUEL SYSTEM TORQUE SPECIFICATIONS

Item	ft.-lb.	in.-lb.	N•m
Air filter			
Backplate screws	–	20-40	2-4
Cover screw	–	36-60	4-7
Breather hollow bolts	–	120-144	14-16
Fuel valve adapter (FXSTD)		22-26	30-35
Fuel shutoff valve hex fitting	15-20	–	20-27
Fuel tank mounting bolts (FXSTD)			
Front	28-32	–	38-43
Rear	14-18	–	19-24
Fuel tank mounting bolts (all models except FXSTD)			
Front	28-32	–	38-43
Rear	18-22	–	24-30
Intake manifold bolts	–	97-141	11-16
Induction module bolts (EFI)	–	71-124	8-14

Table 3 EXHAUST SYSTEM TORQUE SPECIFICATIONS

Item	ft.-lb.	in.-lb.	N•m
Exhaust flange nuts	Refer to procedure in text.		
Torca clamp nuts	45-60	–	61-81

7

CHAPTER EIGHT

ELECTRICAL SYSTEM

This chapter contains service and test procedures for the electrical and ignition system components. Spark plug maintenance is in Chapter Three.

The electrical system includes the following systems:
1. Charging system.
2. Ignition system.
3. Starting system.
4. Lighting system.
5. Switches and other electrical components.

Refer to **Tables 1-7** at the end of the chapter for specifications. Wiring diagrams are located at the end of this manual.

ELECTRICAL COMPONENT REPLACEMENT

Most motorcycle dealerships and parts suppliers will not accept the return of any electrical part. If you cannot determine the *exact* cause of any electrical system malfunction, have a Harley-Davidson dealership retest that specific system to verify your test results. If you purchase a new electrical component(s), install it, and then find that the system still does not work properly, you will probably be unable to return the unit for a refund.

Consider any test results carefully before replacing a component that tests only *slightly* out of specification, especially resistance. A number of variables can affect test results dramatically. These include: the testing meter's internal circuitry, ambient temperature and conditions under which the machine has been operated. All instructions and specifications have been checked for accuracy; however, successful test results depend to a great degree upon individual accuracy.

ELECTRICAL CONNECTORS

Many electrical problems can be traced to damaged wiring, or contaminated or loose connectors.

The locations of the connectors vary by model. Also, if the motorcycle has been serviced previously, the connector may be in a different location.

The electrical system uses three types of connectors. If individual wires or terminals of a particular connector require repair or replacement, refer to *Electrical Connector Service* at the end of this chapter.

Always check the wire colors listed in the procedure or wiring diagrams to verify the location of the components.

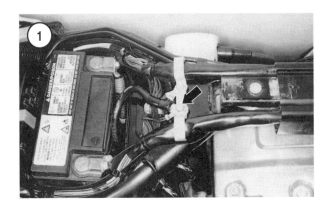

Perform the following steps first if an electrical system fault is encountered:

1. Inspect all wiring for fraying, burning and other visual damage.

2. Check the main fuse and make sure it is not blown. Replace it if necessary.

3. Check the individual fuse(s) for each circuit. Make sure it is not blown. Replace it if necessary.

4. Inspect the battery as described in this chapter. Make sure it is fully charged and the battery cables are clean and securely attached to the battery terminals.

5. Clean connectors with an aerosol electrical contact cleaner. After a thorough cleaning, pack multi-pin electrical connectors with dialectic grease to seal out moisture.

6. Disconnect electrical connectors in the suspect circuits and check for bent or damaged terminals. The male and female terminals must connect or an open circuit will result.

7. Make sure the terminals are pushed all the way into the plastic connector. If they are not, carefully push them in with a narrow-blade screwdriver.

8. After everything is checked, push the connectors together and make sure they are fully engaged and locked together.

9. Never pull on the electrical wires when disconnecting an electrical connector. Only pull on the connector plastic housing.

BATTERY

The battery is important to the motorcycle's electrical system, yet most electrical system problems can be traced to battery neglect. Clean and inspect the battery at periodic intervals. The original equipment battery is a maintenance-free sealed battery and the electrolyte level cannot be checked.

On all models in this manual, the negative side is the ground. When removing the battery, disconnect the negative cable first, then the positive cable. This minimizes the chance of a tool shorting to ground when disconnecting the battery positive cable.

Negative Cable

Some of the component replacement procedures and test procedures in this chapter require disconnecting the negative battery cable as a safety precaution.

NOTE
Always disarm the optional TSSM security system prior to disconnecting the battery or the siren will sound.

1. Remove the seat as described in Chapter Fourteen.

2. Remove the bolt or nut (**Figure 1**) securing the negative cable to the frame. Move the cable away from the battery to avoid making accidental contact with the battery post.

3. Connect the negative cable to the frame post. Reinstall the nut and tighten it securely.

4. Install the seat.

Cable Service

To ensure good electrical contact between the battery and the electrical cables, the cables must be clean and free of corrosion.

1. If the electrical cable terminals are badly corroded, disconnect them from the motorcycle's electrical system.

2. Thoroughly clean each connector with a wire brush and a baking soda solution. Rinse thoroughly with clean water and wipe dry with a clean cloth.

3. After cleaning, apply a thin layer of dielectric grease to the battery terminals before reattaching the cables.

4. Reconnect the electrical cables to the motorcycle's electrical system if they were disconnected.

5. After connecting the electrical cables, apply a light coat of dielectric grease to the terminals to retard corrosion and decomposition of the terminals.

Removal/Installation

NOTE
Always disarm the optional TSSM security system prior to disconnecting the battery or the siren will sound.

1. Remove the seat as described in Chapter Fourteen.

2. Remove the bolt or nut and disconnect the negative battery cable (**Figure 1**).

8

3. Remove the bolt and disconnect the positive battery cable (A, **Figure 2**).

4. Carefully lift the battery (B, **Figure 2**) up and out of the frame.

5. Inspect the battery tray and compartment (**Figure 3**) for corrosion or damage. Replace it if necessary.

6. Position the battery with the negative cable terminal on the right side of the frame.

7. Reinstall the battery onto the battery tray in the frame.

8. Install the battery, hold down and tighten the Torx bolt securely.

9. Connect the positive battery cable (A, **Figure 2**). Tighten the bolt securely.

10. Connect the negative battery cable (**Figure 1**). Tighten the bolt securely.

11. After connecting the electrical cables, apply a light coat of dielectric grease to the electrical terminals of the battery to retard corrosion and decomposition of the terminals.

12. Install the seat.

Inspection and Testing

The battery electrolyte level cannot be serviced in a maintenance-free battery. *Never* attempt to remove the sealing bar cap from the top of the battery. The battery does not require periodic electrolyte inspection or water refilling. Refer to the label (A, **Figure 4**) on top of the battery.

Even though the battery is sealed, protect eyes, skin and clothing. The corrosive electrolyte may have spilled out and can cause severe chemical skin burns and permanent injury. The battery case may be cracked and leaking electrolyte. If electrolyte is spilled or splashed on clothing or skin, immediately neutralize it with a baking soda and water solution, then flush with an abundance of clean water.

> *WARNING*
> *Electrolyte is extremely harmful to the eyes. Always wear safety glasses while working with a battery. If electrolyte gets into the eyes, call a physician immediately and force the eyes open and flood them with cool, clean water for approximately 15 minutes.*

1. Remove the battery as described in this chapter. Do not clean the battery while it is mounted in the frame.

2. Set the battery on a stack of newspapers or shop cloths to protect the surface of the workbench.

3. Check the entire battery case (**Figure 5**) for cracks or other damage. If the battery case is warped, discolored or has a raised top, the battery has been overcharged and overheated.

4. Check the battery terminal bolts, spacers and nuts (B, **Figure 4**) for corrosion or damage. Clean parts thoroughly with a baking soda and water solution. Replace corroded or damaged parts.

5. If the top of the battery is corroded, clean it with a stiff bristle brush using the baking soda and water solution.

6. Check the battery cable ends for corrosion and damage. If corrosion is minor, clean the battery cable ends with a stiff wire brush. Replace worn or damaged cables.

7. Connect a digital voltmeter between the battery negative and positive leads. Note the following:

   a. If the battery voltage is 13.0-13.2 volts (at 20° C [68° F]) the battery is fully charged.

   b. If the battery voltage is 12.0 to 12.5 volts (at 20° C [68° F]), or lower, the battery is undercharged and requires charging.

8. If the battery is undercharged, recharge it as described in this chapter. Then test the charging system as described in Chapter Two.

9. Inspect the battery case for contamination or damage. Clean it with a baking soda and water solution.

10. Install the battery as described in this chapter.

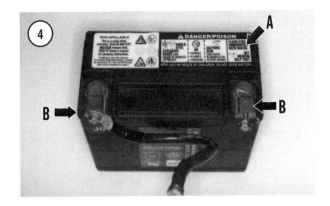

Charging

Refer to *Battery Initialization* in this chapter if the battery is new.

To recharge a maintenance-free battery, a digital voltmeter and a charger with an adjustable amperage output are required. If this equipment is not available, have the battery charged by a shop with the proper equipment. Excessive voltage and amperage from an unregulated charger can damage the battery and shorten service life.

The battery should only self-discharge approximately one percent of its given capacity each day. If a battery not in use, without any loads connected, loses its charge within a week after charging, the battery is defective.

If the motorcycle is not used for long periods of time, an automatic battery charger with variable voltage and amperage outputs is recommended for optimum battery service life.

WARNING
During charging, highly explosive hydrogen gas is released from the battery. Only charge the battery in a well-ventilated area away from open flames, including pilot lights on appliances. Do not allow smoking in the area. Never check the charge of the

battery by arcing across the terminals; the resulting spark can ignite the hydrogen gas.

CAUTION
Always disconnect the battery cables from the battery. If the cables are left connected during the charging procedure, the charger may damage the diodes within the voltage regulator/rectifier.

1. Remove the battery from the motorcycle as described in this chapter.
2. Set the battery on a stack of newspapers or shop cloths to protect the surface of the workbench.
3. Make sure the battery charger is turned off prior to attaching the charger leads to the battery.
4. Connect the positive charger lead to the positive battery terminal and the negative charger lead to the negative battery terminal.
5. Set the charger at 12 volts. If the output of the charger is variable, select the low setting.
6. The charging time depends on the discharged condition of the battery. Refer to **Table 2** for the suggested charging time. Normally, a battery should be charged at 1/10 its given capacity.

CAUTION
If the battery emits an excessive amount of gas during the charging cycle, decrease the charge rate. If the battery becomes hotter than 110° F (43° C) during the charging cycle, turn the charger off and allow the battery to cool. Then continue with a reduced charging rate and continue to monitor the battery temperature.

7. Turn the charger to the ON position.
8. After the battery has been charged for the predetermined time, turn the charger off, disconnect the leads and measure the battery voltage. Refer to the following:
   a. If the battery voltage is 13.0-13.2 volts (at 20° C [68° F]), the battery is fully charged.
   b. If the battery voltage is 12.5 volts (at 20° C [68° F]), or lower, the battery is undercharged and requires additional charging time.
9. If the battery remains stable for one hour, the battery is charged.
10. Install the battery into the motorcycle as described in this chapter.

Battery Initialization

A new battery must be *fully* charged before installation. To bring the battery to a full charge, give it an initial charge. Using a new battery without an initial charge will cause permanent battery damage. The battery will never be able to hold more than an 80% charge. Charging a new battery after it has been used will not bring its charge to 100%. When purchasing a new battery, verify its charge status.

> *NOTE*
> ***Recycle the old battery***. *When a new battery is purchased, turn in the old one for recycling. Most motorcycle dealerships will accept the old battery in trade for a new one. Never place an old battery in the household trash since it is illegal, in most states, to place any acid or lead (heavy metal) contents in landfills.*

Load Testing

A load test checks the battery's performance under full current load and is the best indication of battery condition.

A battery load tester is required for this procedure. When using a load tester, follow the manufacturer's instructions. **Figure 6** shows a typical load tester and battery arrangement.

1. Remove the battery from the motorcycle as described in this chapter.

> *NOTE*
> *Let the battery stand for at least one hour after charging prior to performing this test.*

2. The battery must be fully charged before beginning this test. If necessary, charge the battery as described in this section.

> *WARNING*
> *The battery load tester must be turned OFF prior to connecting or disconnecting the test cables to the battery. Otherwise, a spark could cause the battery to explode.*

> *CAUTION*
> *To prevent battery damage during load testing, do not load test a discharged battery and do not load test the battery for more than 20 seconds. Performing a load test on a discharged battery can cause permanent battery damage.*

3. Load test the battery as follows:
  a. Connect the load tester cables to the battery following its manufacturer's instructions.
  b. Load the battery at 50% of the cold cranking amperage (CCA) or 135 amperes.

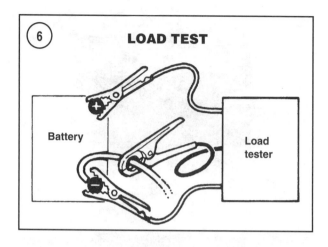

c. After 15 seconds, the voltage reading with the load still applied must be 9.6 volts or higher at 70° F (21° C). Now quickly remove the load and turn the tester OFF.

4. If the voltage reading was 9.6 volts or higher, the battery output capacity is good. If the reading was below 9.6 volts, the battery is defective.

5. With the tester OFF, disconnect the cables from the battery.

6. Install the battery as described in this chapter.

CHARGING SYSTEM

Refer to **Figures 7-10**. The charging system consists of the battery, alternator and a voltage regulator/rectifier. Alternating current generated by the alternator is rectified to direct current. The voltage regulator maintains the voltage to the battery and additional electrical loads, such as the lights and ignition system, at a constant voltage regardless of variations in engine speed and load.

A malfunction in the charging system generally causes the battery to remain undercharged. To prevent damage to the alternator and the regulator/rectifier when testing and repairing the charging system, note the following precautions:

> *NOTE*
> *Always disarm the optional TSSM security system prior to disconnecting the battery or the siren will sound.*

1. Always disconnect the negative battery cable, as described in this chapter, before removing a component from the charging system.

2. To charge the battery, remove the battery from the motorcycle and recharge it as described in this chapter.

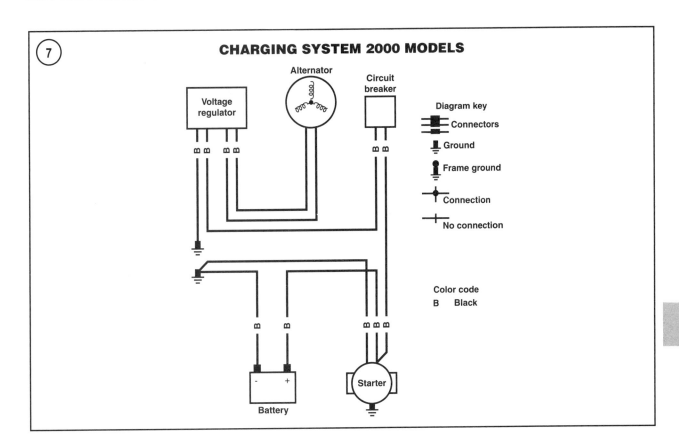

CHARGING SYSTEM 2000 MODELS

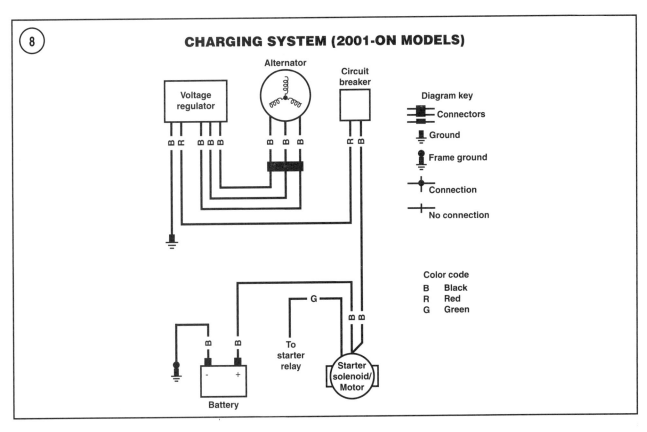

CHARGING SYSTEM (2001-ON MODELS)

8

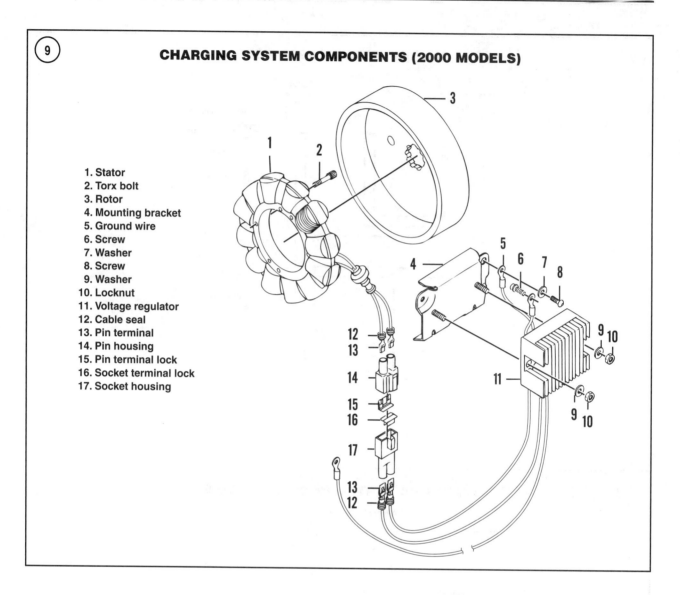

CHARGING SYSTEM COMPONENTS (2000 MODELS)

1. Stator
2. Torx bolt
3. Rotor
4. Mounting bracket
5. Ground wire
6. Screw
7. Washer
8. Screw
9. Washer
10. Locknut
11. Voltage regulator
12. Cable seal
13. Pin terminal
14. Pin housing
15. Pin terminal lock
16. Socket terminal lock
17. Socket housing

3. Inspect the battery case (**Figure 5**). Look for bulges or cracks in the case, leaking electrolyte or corrosion build-up.

4. Check the charging system wiring for signs of chafing, deterioration or other damage.

5. Check the wiring for corroded or loose connections. Clean, tighten or reconnect wiring as required.

Battery Current Draw Test

This test measures the current draw or drain on the battery when all electrical systems and accessories are off. Perform this test if the battery will not hold a charge when the motorcycle is not being used. A current draw that exceeds 5.5 mA will discharge the battery. The ECM (1 mA), voltage regulator (0.5 mA), TSM (0.5 mA), TSSM

disarmed (0.5 mA) and TSSM armed (3.0 mA) account for a 5.0 mA current draw. The battery must be fully charged to perform this test.

1. Disconnect the negative battery cable as described in Chapter Eight.

2. Connect an ammeter between the negative battery terminal and the battery ground cable as shown in **Figure 11**.

3. With the ignition switch, lights and all accessories turned off, read the ammeter. If the current drain exceeds 5.5 mA, continue with Step 4.

4. Refer to the wiring diagrams at the end of the manual for the necessary model. Check the charging system wires and connectors for shorts or other damage.

5. Unplug each electrical connector separately and check for a reduction in the current draw. If the meter reading changes after a connector is disconnected, the source of the

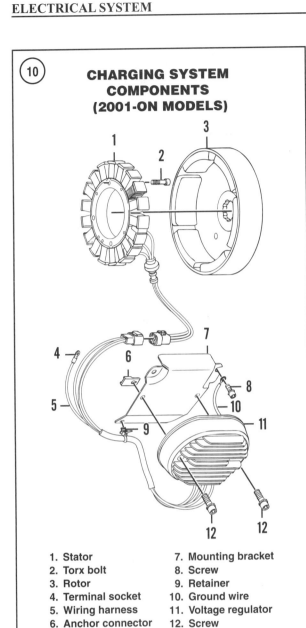

CHARGING SYSTEM COMPONENTS (2001-ON MODELS)

1. Stator
2. Torx bolt
3. Rotor
4. Terminal socket
5. Wiring harness
6. Anchor connector
7. Mounting bracket
8. Screw
9. Retainer
10. Ground wire
11. Voltage regulator
12. Screw

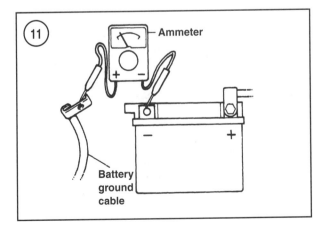

Ammeter

Battery ground cable

8

current draw has been found. Check the electrical connectors carefully before testing the individual component.

6. After completing the test, disconnect the ammeter and reconnect the negative battery cable.

Testing

A malfunction in the charging system generally causes the battery to remain undercharged. Perform the following visual inspection to determine the cause of the problem. If the visual inspection proves satisfactory, test the charging system as described under *Charging System* in Chapter Two.

1. Make sure the battery cables are connected properly (**Figure 12**). If polarity is reversed, check for a damaged voltage regulator/rectifier.

2. Inspect the terminals for loose or corroded connections. Tighten or clean them as required.

3. Inspect the battery case. Look for bulges or cracks in the case, leaking electrolyte or corrosion buildup.

4. Carefully check all connections at the alternator to make sure they are clean and tight.

5. Check the circuit wiring for corroded or loose connections. Clean, tighten or connect wiring as required.

ALTERNATOR

Rotor Removal/Installation

> *NOTE*
> *Always disarm the optional TSSM security system prior to disconnecting the battery or the siren will sound.*

1. Disconnect the negative battery cable as described in this chapter.

2. Remove the primary chain case cover and housing as described in Chapter Five.

3. Remove the primary chain, clutch assembly, chain tensioner assembly and compensating sprocket components as an assembly. Refer to Chapter Five.

4. If still in place, remove the shaft extension and washer from the crankshaft.

CAUTION
The holes in the rotor face are not threaded. Push the bolts in just enough to grasp the sides of the rotor holes. Do not push the bolts in too far as they will contact the stator coils and damage them.

5. Insert two bolts into the rotor face (**Figure 13**), then push outward to press the threads against the holes. Slide the rotor off the crankshaft.

6. Inspect the rotor magnets (**Figure 14**) for small bolts, washers or other metal debris that may be attached the magnets. Any debris will cause severe damage to the alternator stator assembly.

7. Check the inner splines (**Figure 15**) for wear or damage. Replace the rotor if necessary.

8. Install by reversing these removal steps. Align the rotor splines with the crankshaft splines and push the rotor on until it bottoms.

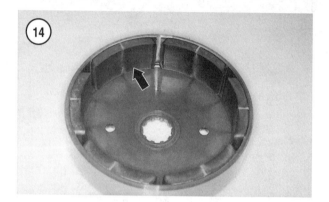

Stator Removal

1. Remove the rotor as described in this chapter.

2. Unplug the alternator rotor electrical connector (**Figure 16**) from the voltage regulator.

3. Insert a small screwdriver between the socket housing side of connector going to the alternator stator and the locking wedge on the socket housing. Gently pivot the screwdriver tip and pop the wedge loose.

4. Lift the terminal latches inside the socket housing and back the sockets through the wire end of connector.

5. Remove the three Torx screws (A, **Figure 17**) securing the stator assembly to the crankcase. New Torx screws must be used on installation.

NOTE
If necessary, spray electrical contact cleaner or glass cleaner around the wiring harness grommet to help ease it out of the crankcase boss receptacle.

6. Use an awl to carefully lift the capped lip on the grommet (**Figure 18**) from the crankcase and push it into the bore.

7. Carefully push the stator wires and grommet (B, **Figure 17**) through the crankcase bore and remove the stator assembly.

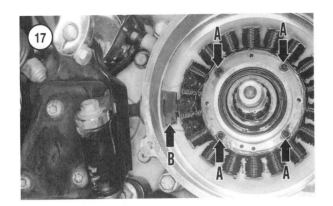

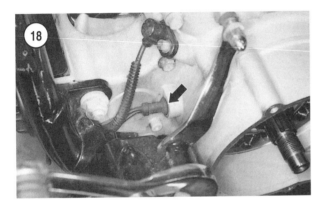

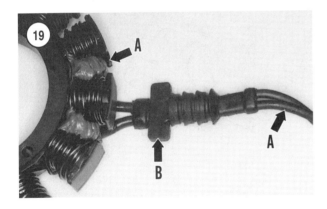

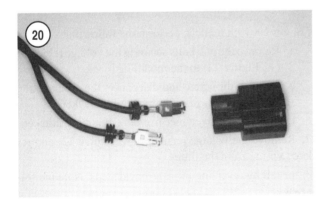

8. Inspect the stator mounting surface on the crankcase for oil residue from a damaged oil seal. Clean it off if necessary.
9. Inspect the stator wires (A, **Figure 19**, typical) for fraying or damage.
10. Inspect the rubber grommet (B, **Figure 19**) for deterioration or hardness.
11. Check the stator connector pins (**Figure 20**, typical) for looseness or damage.

Stator Installation

1. Apply a light coat of electrical contact cleaner or glass cleaner to the wiring harness grommet to help ease it into the crankcase boss receptacle.
2. Insert the electrical harness and grommet into the crankcase boss receptacle and carefully pull it through until the grommet is correctly seated.

CAUTION
New Torx screws must be installed. The threadlocking compound originally applied to the Torx screws is for one time use only. If a used Torx screw is installed, it can work loose and cause engine damage.

3. Move the stator into position on the crankcase and install four *new* Torx screws (A, **Figure 17**). Tighten the screws to the specification in **Table 5**.
4. Move the wires to the right side of the motorcycle.
5. Apply a light coat of dielectric compound to the electrical connector prior to assembling it. Reassemble the electrical connector socket by reversing Steps 4 and 5 of *Stator Removal*. Make sure it has locked together securely.
6. Install the rotor as described in this chapter.

VOLTAGE REGULATOR

Removal/Installation

Refer to **Figure 9** and **Figure 10**.
1. Disconnect the negative battery cable as described in this chapter.
2. Remove the rear fender inner panel as described in Chapter Fourteen.
3. Disconnect the voltage regulator lead (**Figure 21**) from the silver post on the main circuit breaker.

NOTE
Prior to removing the voltage regulator wires, note the routing of the wires through the frame. Note the location of cable straps and tie wraps. The wires must be rerouted in the same path.

8

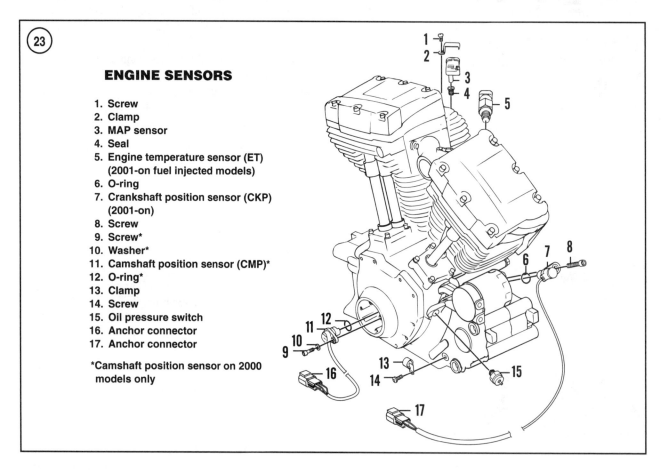

ENGINE SENSORS

1. Screw
2. Clamp
3. MAP sensor
4. Seal
5. Engine temperature sensor (ET)
   (2001-on fuel injected models)
6. O-ring
7. Crankshaft position sensor (CKP)
   (2001-on)
8. Screw
9. Screw*
10. Washer*
11. Camshaft position sensor (CMP)*
12. O-ring*
13. Clamp
14. Screw
15. Oil pressure switch
16. Anchor connector
17. Anchor connector

*Camshaft position sensor on 2000
models only

After disconnecting any straps, leave them in place on the frame as a reference for installation of the wiring.

4. Disconnect the voltage regulator electrical connector from the alternator stator (**Figure 16**).

5A. On 2000 models, perform the following:

   a. Remove the two nuts and washers securing the voltage regulator to the mounting bracket.

   b. Remove the screw and disconnect the ground strap from the backside of the voltage regulator. Do *not* disconnect it from the mounting bracket.

5B. On 2001-on models, perform the following:

   a. Remove the two bolts securing the voltage regulator (A, **Figure 22**) to the mounting bracket.

   b. Remove the screw and disconnect the ground strap (B, **Figure 22**) from the mounting bracket.

6. Unhook the wire retainer from the mounting bracket.

7. Remove the voltage regulator (A, **Figure 22**) and related wiring from the frame.

8. Install by reversing these removal steps. Note the following:

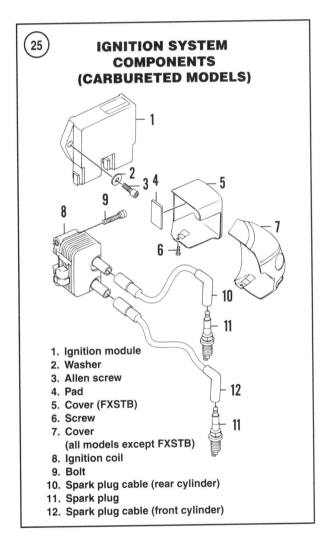

IGNITION SYSTEM COMPONENTS (CARBURETED MODELS)

1. Ignition module
2. Washer
3. Allen screw
4. Pad
5. Cover (FXSTB)
6. Screw
7. Cover
   (all models except FXSTB)
8. Ignition coil
9. Bolt
10. Spark plug cable (rear cylinder)
11. Spark plug
12. Spark plug cable (front cylinder)

a. Secure the ground strap to the voltage regulator (2000 models) or mounting bracket (2001-on models).

b. Tighten the mounting nut or bolts securely.

c. Apply a light coat of dielectric compound to the electrical connectors prior to installing them.

d. Install new cable straps and tie wraps securing electrical wires to the frame.

IGNITION SYSTEM

The ignition system consists of an ignition coil, two spark plugs, the ignition module (carburetted models), electronic control module (EFI models), crankshaft position sensor (CKP) (2001-on models), manifold absolute pressure sensor (MAP), camshaft position sensor (CMP) (2000 models only) and the bank angle sensor (BAS). Refer to **Figure 23** for the locations of the majority of the sensors.

The ignition module (carbureted models) or electronic control module (EFI models) is located behind the frame right side panel. It determines the spark advance for correct ignition timing based on signals from the CKP, MAP, BAS and CMP. The ignition system fires the spark plugs near top dead center for starting, then varies the spark advance from 0° to 50° depending on engine speed, crankshaft position and intake manifold pressure. It also regulates the low-voltage circuits between the battery and the ignition coil. The ignition module is not repairable and must be replaced if defective.

The MAP sensor is located on top of the intake manifold or throttle housing (**Figure 24**). This sensor monitors the intake manifold vacuum and sends this information to the ignition module (carbureted models) or electronic control module (EFI models). The module adjusts the ignition timing advance curve for maximum performance.

The rotor and camshaft position sensor (CMP) is located in the camshaft cover on the right side of the crankcase. The raised ridge on the rotor operates at one-half crankshaft speed and it breaks the magnetic field of the Hall-effect device on the camshaft position sensor. The logic-type signal of the Hall-effect device gives accurate timing information to the ignition module.

The bank angle sensor mounts on a frame-mounted panel behind the rear fender inner fender on 2000 models. On 2001-on models, the bank angle sensor is an integral part of the turn signal/turn signal security module (TSM/TSSM) and is also mounted on a frame-mounted panel behind the rear fender inner fender. The sensor consists of a small magnetic disc that rides within a V-shaped channel. If the motorcycle is tilted at a 45° angle, for more than one second, the ignition system is shut off. Once the sensor is activated, the motorcycle must be up-righted and the ignition turned OFF then ON. Then, the ignition system is operational and the engine can be restarted.

The basic components of a typical ignition system are shown in **Figure 25** for carbureted models or **Figure 26**

8

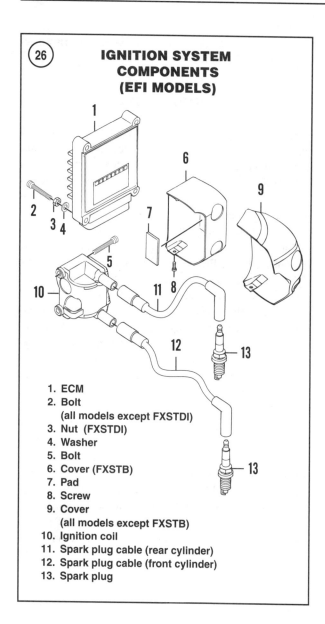

IGNITION SYSTEM COMPONENTS (EFI MODELS)

1. ECM
2. Bolt
   (all models except FXSTDI)
3. Nut (FXSTDI)
4. Washer
5. Bolt
6. Cover (FXSTB)
7. Pad
8. Screw
9. Cover
   (all models except FXSTB)
10. Ignition coil
11. Spark plug cable (rear cylinder)
12. Spark plug cable (front cylinder)
13. Spark plug

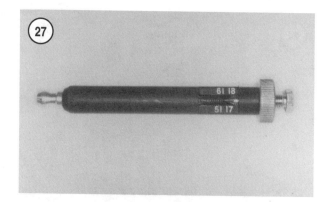

for EFI models. When servicing the ignition system, refer to the wiring diagrams located at the end of the manual.

Ignition Coil

Performance test

1. Disconnect the plug wire and remove one of the spark plugs as described in Chapter Three.

NOTE
*A spark tester is useful for testing the ignition system spark output. **Figure 27** shows the Motion Pro Ignition System Tester (part No. 08-0122). This tool is inserted in the spark*

plug cap and its base is grounded against the cylinder head. The tool's air gap is adjustable and it allows the visual inspection of the spark while testing the intensity of the spark.

2. Insert a clean shop cloth into the spark plug hole in the cylinder head to reduce gasoline vapors emitting from the hole.

3. Insert the spark plug (**Figure 28**), or spark tester (**Figure 29**), into its cap and touch the spark plug base against the cylinder head to ground it. Position the spark plug so the electrode is visible.

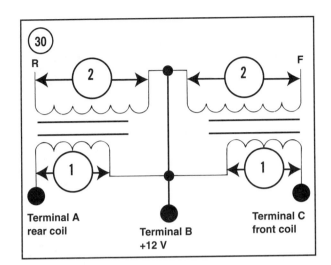

Terminal A
rear coil

Terminal B
+12 V

Terminal C
front coil

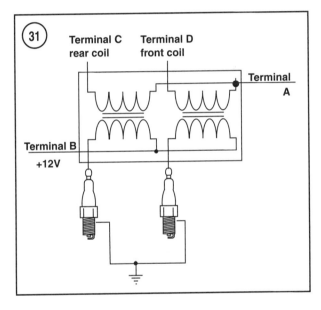

Terminal C
rear coil

Terminal D
front coil

Terminal
A

Terminal B
+12V

WARNING
Mount the spark plug, or tester, away from the spark plug hole in the cylinder so the spark or tester cannot ignite the gasoline vapors in the cylinder. If the engine is flooded, do not perform this test. The firing of the spark plug can ignite fuel ejected through the spark plug hole.

NOTE
When not using a spark tester, always use a new spark plug for this test procedure.

4. Crank the engine over with the starter. A fat blue spark should be evident across the spark plug electrode or spark tester. If there is strong sunlight on the plug, or tester,

shade it so the spark is more visible. Repeat for the other cylinder.

WARNING
*If necessary, hold onto the spark plug wire with a pair of insulated pliers. Do **not** hold the spark plug, wire or connector or a serious electrical shock could occur.*

5. If there is a fat blue spark, the ignition coil is good. If there is not, perform the following resistance test.

Resistance test (carbureted models)

NOTE
*Refer to **Electrical System Fundamentals** in Chapter One.*

1. Remove the ignition coil as previously described.
2. Disconnect the secondary wires from the ignition coil.
3. Use an ohmmeter set at R × 1 to measure the primary coil resistance between terminals A and B, then terminals B and C (**Figure 30**) at the backside of the ignition coil. The specified resistance is in **Table 1**.
4. Use an ohmmeter set at R × 1000 to measure the secondary coil resistance between terminals B and R, then terminals B and F (**Figure 30**) at the backside of the ignition coil. The specified resistance is in **Table 1**.
5. If the resistance is less than specified, there is probably a short in the coil windings. Replace the coil.
6. If the resistance is more than specified, this may indicate corrosion or oxidation of the coil's terminals. Thoroughly clean the terminals, then spray them with an aerosol electrical contact cleaner. Repeat Steps 3 and 4. If the resistance is still high, replace the coil.
7. If the coil resistance does not meet (or come close to) either of these specifications, replace the coil. If the coil is visibly damaged, replace it as described in this chapter.
8. Install the ignition coil as described in this chapter.

Resistance test (EFI models)

NOTE
*Refer to **Electrical System Fundamentals** in Chapter One.*

1. Remove the ignition coil as previously described.
2. Disconnect the secondary wires from the ignition coil.
3. Use an ohmmeter set at R × 1 to measure the primary coil resistance between terminals A and D, then terminals A and C (**Figure 31**) at the backside of the ignition coil. The specified resistance is in **Table 1**.

8

4. Use an ohmmeter set at R × 1000 to measure the secondary coil resistance between terminals B and C, then terminals B and D (**Figure 31**) at the backside of the ignition coil. The specified resistance is in **Table 1**.

5. If the resistance is less than specified, there is probably a short in the coil windings. Replace the coil.

6. If the resistance is more than specified, this may indicate corrosion or oxidation of the coil's terminals. Thoroughly clean the terminals, then spray them with an aerosol electrical contact cleaner. Repeat Steps 3 and 4. If the resistance is still high, replace the coil.

7. If the coil resistance does not meet (or come close to) either of these specifications, replace the coil. If the coil is visibly damaged, replace it as described in this chapter.

8. Install the ignition coil as described in this chapter.

Removal/installation

> *NOTE*
> *Always disarm the optional TSSM security system prior to disconnecting the battery or the siren will sound.*

1. Disconnect the negative battery cable as described in this chapter.

> *NOTE*
> *Label all wiring connectors prior to disconnecting them in the following steps.*

2. If necessary, disconnect the secondary lead from each spark plug.

3. Remove the small screw securing the cover and remove the cover.

4. Disconnect the secondary leads (**Figure 32**) from the coil towers.

> *NOTE*
> *On FLSTS models, to avoid removing the rear exhaust pipe, use a swivel socket and ball ended Allen wrenches to remove the coil fasteners.*

5. Remove the bolts and lockwashers (**Figure 33**) securing the ignition coil to the seat post.

6. Move the ignition coil away from the seat post and disconnect the primary wire connector (**Figure 34**) from the ignition coil.

7. Remove the ignition coil.

8. Install the ignition coil by reversing these steps.

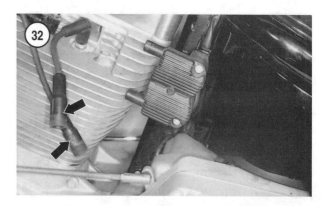

Ignition Module (Carbureted Models) Removal/Installation

The ignition module is located under the seat.

> *NOTE*
> *Always disarm the optional TSSM security system prior to disconnecting the battery or the siren will sound.*

1. Disconnect the negative battery cable as described in this chapter.

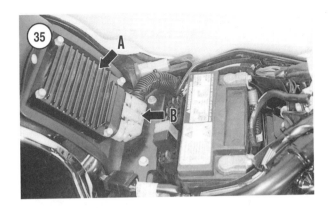

2. Remove the seat as described in Chapter Fourteen.

3. Remove the screws securing the ignition module to the mounting bracket.

4. Depress the external latches on the two multi-pin electrical connectors. Gently pull and disconnect the black and gray electrical connectors from the ignition module.

5. Remove the ignition module from the frame.

6. Install the ignition module by reversing these steps. Note the following:

    a. Apply a light coat of dielectric compound to the electrical connectors prior to installing them.

    b. Make sure the electrical connectors are pushed tightly onto the ignition module.

Electronic Control Module (ECM) (EFI Models) Removal/Installation

The ECM is located under the seat.

NOTE
Always disarm the optional TSSM security system prior to disconnecting the battery or the siren will sound.

1. Disconnect the negative battery cable as described in this chapter.

2. Remove the seat as described in Chapter Fourteen.

3. Remove the nuts and washers (FXSTDI models), or screws (all models except FXSTDI) securing the ECM (A, **Figure 35**) to the mounting bracket.

4. Depress the external latch and use a rocking motion to disconnect the 36-pin electrical connector (B, **Figure 35**) from the ECM.

5. Install the ECM by reversing these removal steps while noting the following:

    a. Apply a light coat of dielectric compound to the electrical connector prior to installing them.

    b. Make sure the electrical connector is pushed tightly onto the ECM.

Manifold Absolute Pressure (MAP) Sensor (Carbureted Models) Removal/Installation

The MAP sensor (**Figure 23**) is located on top of the intake manifold.

NOTE
Always disarm the optional TSSM security system prior to disconnecting the battery or the siren will sound.

1. Disconnect the negative battery cable as described in this chapter.

2. Remove the fuel tank as described in Chapter Seven.

3. Remove the carburetor as described in Chapter Seven. Place a lint-free shop cloth into the intake manifold opening (A, **Figure 36**) to prevent the entry of debris.

4. Remove the screw and clip (B, **Figure 36**) securing the MAP sensor to the top of the intake manifold.

5. Pull the MAP sensor (C, **Figure 36**) straight up out of the seal in the intake manifold.

6. Disconnect the electrical connector from the MAP sensor and remove the sensor.

7. Install the MAP sensor by reversing these steps. Note the following:

    a. Apply a light coat of dielectric compound to the electrical connector prior to installing it.

    b. Make sure the electrical connector is pushed tightly onto the MAP sensor.

    c. If necessary, replace the seal in the intake manifold.

8

Manifold Absolute Pressure (MAP) Sensor (EFI Models)
Removal/Installation

The MAP sensor (**Figure 23**) is located on top of the induction module.

> *CAUTION*
> *Do not try to remove the MAP sensor with the induction module installed on the engine as the sensor will be damage.*

1. Remove the induction module as described in Chapter Seven.

> *CAUTION*
> *Do not apply excessive heat to the idle air control unit as it will be damaged.*

2. Use a heat gun and apply sufficient heat to the front screw securing both the idle air control valve and the throttle housing stop to the throttle body. Heat the front screw to break loose the thread locking compound. Remove the front screw and discard it.

3. Remove the throttle housing screw.

4. Carefully pry the MAP sensor up and out of the intake manifold. The grommet may come out with the sensor or may stay in the intake manifold. Remove the grommet and discard it.

5. Install a *new* grommet onto the sensor and press it into the intake manifold until it bottoms.

> *NOTE*
> *The new screw is coated with a threadlocking compound. Do **not** add additional compound.*

6. Install a *new* screw securing the idle air control valve and the throttle housing stop to the throttle body. Tighten the screw finger-tight at this time.

7. Install the throttle housing screw and tighten to 18 in.-lbs. (2 N•m).

8. Tighten the throttle housing stop screw to 25 in.-lbs. (3 N•m).

9. Install the induction module as described in Chapter Seven.

Idle Air Control (IAC) Valve (EFI Models)
Removal/Installation

The IAC valve (**Figure 37**) is located on top of the induction module.

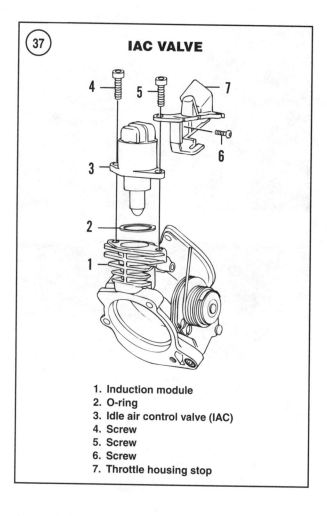

(37) IAC VALVE

4 5 7

3

2

1

6

1. Induction module
2. O-ring
3. Idle air control valve (IAC)
4. Screw
5. Screw
6. Screw
7. Throttle housing stop

> *CAUTION*
> *Do not try to remove the IAC valve with the induction module installed on the engine as the sensor will be damage.*

1. Remove the induction module as described in Chapter Seven.

> *CAUTION*
> *Do not apply excessive heat to the idle air control unit as it will be damaged.*

2. Use a heat gun and apply sufficient heat to the front screw securing both the idle air control valve and the throttle housing stop to the throttle body. Heat the front screw to break loose the thread locking compound. Remove the front screw and discard it.

3. Remove the throttle housing screw.

4. Remove the IAC valve and O-ring out of the intake manifold.

5. Install a *new* O-ring onto the sensor and press it into the intake manifold until it bottoms.

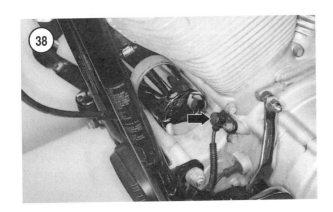

NOTE
*The new screw is coated with a threadlocking compound. Do **not** add additional compound.*

6. Install a *new* screw securing the idle air control valve and the throttle housing stop to the throttle body. Tighten the screw finger-tight at this time.

7. Install the throttle housing screw and tighten to 18 in.-lbs. (2 N•m).

8. Tighten the throttle housing stop screw to 25 in.-lbs. (3 N•m).

9. Install the induction module as described in Chapter Seven.

Crankshaft Position Sensor (CKP) (2001-on Models) Removal/Installation

The CKP sensor (**Figure 38**) is mounted on the front left side of the crankcase next to the oil filter.

1. Remove the seat as described in Chapter Fourteen.

NOTE
Always disarm the optional TSSM security system prior to disconnecting the battery or the siren will sound.

2. Disconnect the negative battery cable from the battery as described in this chapter.

3. Remove the voltage regulator (A, **Figure 39**) as described in this chapter.

4. Remove the voltage regulator mounting bracket (B, **Figure 39**).

5. Disconnect the sensor's two-pin electrical connector (one red, one black wire) from the harness.

6. On the left side of the motorcycle, remove the Allen screw (**Figure 38**) and withdraw the CKP sensor and O-ring from the crankcase.

7. Install by reversing these removal steps. Note the following:

   a. Apply a light coat of dielectric compound to the electrical connector prior to installing them.

   b. Apply clean engine oil to the *new* O-ring on the CKP sensor prior to installation. Install the sensor and tighten the Allen screw to 20-30 in.-lb. (2-3 N•m).

Camshaft Position Sensor (CMP) (2000 Models) Removal/Installation

The CMP sensor is located in the camshaft cover on the right side of the crankcase.

1. Remove the seat as described in Chapter Fourteen.

NOTE
Always disarm the optional TSSM security system prior to disconnecting the battery or the siren will sound.

2. Disconnect the negative battery cable as described in this chapter.

3. Remove the exhaust system as described in Chapter Seven.

4. Locate the CMP sensor harness three-pin Mini-Deutsch electrical connector at the right side of the frame adjacent to the rear brake line.

5. Remove the cable straps on the protective sheath to uncover the three-pin CMP and three-pin CKP electrical connectors. Detach the electrical connectors from the support bracket on the rear brake line.

6. Disconnect the three-pin CMP Mini-Deutsch connector (one red/white, one green/white, one black/white) from the wiring harness.

7. Use needle nose pliers to remove the secondary locking wedge from the pin side of the electrical connector.

8. Gently depress the terminal latches inside the pin housing and back the pins out through the holes in the wire seal. Remove the red/white, green/white and black/white wires.

8

9. Remove the T20 Torx screws securing the inspection cover and remove the cover.

10. Tie a piece of string to the end of the wiring harness.

11. Remove the screw and washer securing the CMP sensor to the camshaft cover. Remove the sensor and O-ring from the cover.

12. Tape a piece of string to the three individual electrical connectors in the CMP harness. Tie the other end of the string to the frame cross-member.

NOTE
Figure 40 is shown with the camshaft cover removed to better illustrate the step.

13. Carefully pull the electrical harness, with the piece of string, out through both openings in the camshaft cover (**Figure 40**).

14. Install by reversing these removal steps. Note the following:

   a. Attach the string to the new CMP electrical connectors.

   b. Slowly pull the wires and connectors back through both openings in the camshaft cover. Remove the string.

   c. Apply a light coat of dielectric compound to the electrical connector(s) prior to installing them.

   d. Apply clean engine oil to the *new* O-ring on the CMP sensor prior to installation. Install the sensor and tighten the Allen screw to 20-30 in.-lb. (2-3 N•m).

Engine Temperature Sensor (2001-on EFI Models) Removal/Installation

The engine temperature sensor (**Figure 41**) is located in the rear left side of the front cylinder head.

NOTE
All carbureted engines are not equipped with the engine temperature sensor circuit.

1. Remove the seat as described in Chapter Fourteen.

NOTE
Always disarm the optional TSSM security system prior to disconnecting the battery or the siren will sound.

2. Disconnect the negative battery cable as described in this chapter.

3. Remove the fuel tank as described in Chapter Seven.

4. On the left side of the front cylinder head, pull the rubber boot back off the sensor (**Figure 41**).

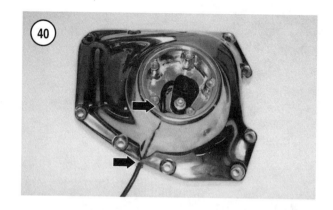

5. Pull on the external latch and disconnect the electrical connector from the sensor.

6. Use a 3/4 in. deep socket and loosen the sensor. When the socket turns easily, remove the socket and completely unscrew the sensor by hand.

7. Install a new sensor and start it by hand. Use the socket to tighten the sensor to 10-14 ft.-lb. (14-20 N•m).

8. Apply a light coat of dielectric compound to the electrical connector prior to installing it.

9. Install the electrical connector and push it on until it locks into place.

10. Pull the rubber boot back over the electrical connector.

11. Attach the negative battery cable.

12. Install the seat as described in Chapter Fourteen.

Bank Angle Sensor (BAS) (2000) Removal/Installation

The bank angle sensor mounts on a frame-mounted panel behind the rear fender inner fender on 2000 models. On 2001-on models, the BAS is an integral part of the turn signal/turn signal security module (TSM/TSSM) and is also mounted on a frame-mounted panel behind the rear fender inner fender.

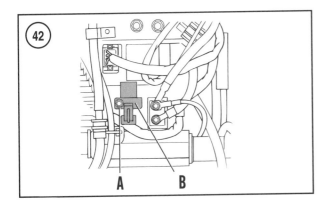

NOTE
*On 2001-on models, the bank angle sensor is an integral part of the turn signal module/turn signal security module (TSSM). Refer to **Turn Signal Security Module** in this chapter.*

1. Remove the seat as described in Chapter Fourteen.

NOTE
Always disarm the optional TSSM security system prior to disconnecting the battery or the siren will sound.

2. Disconnect the negative battery cable from the battery as described in this chapter.

3. Refer to *Electrical Panel* in this chapter to gain access to the BAS.

4. Remove the mounting screw (A, **Figure 42**) and partially remove the sensor (B) from the electrical panel.

5. Pull the external latch outward and disconnect the electrical connector from the bank angle sensor.

6. Install by reversing these removal steps. Note the following:

    a. Apply a light coat of dielectric compound to the electrical connector prior to installing it.

    b. Tighten the screw securely.

STARTING SYSTEM

When servicing the starting system, refer to the wiring diagrams located at the end of the manual.

CAUTION
Do not operate the starter for more than five seconds at a time. Let it cool approximately ten seconds before operating it again.

Troubleshooting

Refer to Chapter Two.

Starter Removal

1. Remove the seat as described in Chapter Fourteen.

NOTE
Always disarm the optional TSSM security system prior to disconnecting the battery or the siren will sound.

2. Disconnect the negative battery cable as described in this chapter.

3. Remove the primary drive outer cover as described in Chapter Five.

4. Remove the oil tank (A, **Figure 43**) as described in Chapter Four.

5. Remove the bolt and cover (B, **Figure 43**) from the end of the starter.

6. Straighten the tab on the lockplate (**Figure 44**).

7. Wrap the pinion gear with a cloth to protect the finish, then secure it with pliers (A, **Figure 45**).

8. Loosen and remove the bolt (B, **Figure 45**), lockplate and thrust washer from the starter jackshaft assembly at the end of the starter.

8

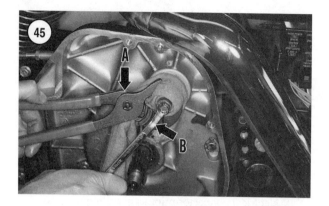

9. Remove the pinion gear (**Figure 46**) and spring from the jackshaft.

10. Remove the jackshaft assembly and the coupling from the inner housing.

11. Remove the starter mounting bolts and washers (**Figure 47**).

12. Slide back the rubber boot, remove the nut (A, **Figure 48**) and disconnect the positive cable from the starter terminal. Note the location of the circuit breaker cable terminal ring (B, **Figure 48**) under the front bolt and washer.

13. Disconnect the solenoid electrical connector (C, **Figure 48**) from the starter.

14. Pull the starter straight out of the crankcase and remove it.

15. If necessary, service the starter as described in this chapter.

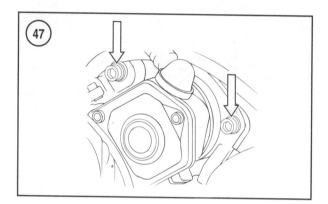

Starter Installation

1. Install the starter into the crankcase. Push it in until it bottoms.

2. Install the starter mounting bolts and washers (**Figure 47**). Tighten the bolts to 13-20 ft.-lb. (18-27 N•m).

3. Connect the solenoid electrical connector (C, **Figure 48**) onto the starter motor.

4. Install the circuit breaker cable terminal ring (B, **Figure 48**) under the front bolt and washer.

5. Connect the positive cable onto the starter terminal and install the nut (A, **Figure 48**). Tighten the nut securely, then slide the rubber boot into position.

6. Install the cover onto the end of the starter and secure with the bolt. Tighten the bolt securely.

7. Install the jackshaft (**Figure 49**) into the inner housing if it was removed. Push it in until it stops.

8. Position the coupling with its counterbore facing toward the jackshaft and install the coupling (**Figure 50**) into the inner housing bushing.

9. Install the spring (**Figure 51**) onto the jackshaft.

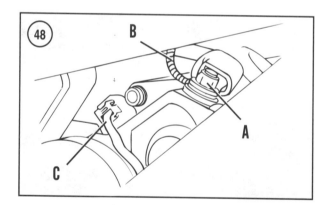

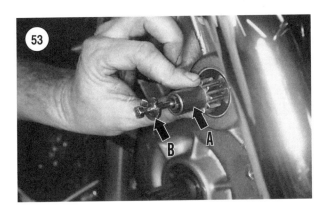

10. Install the pinion gear (**Figure 52**) onto the jackshaft.

11. Push in on the pinion gear (A, **Figure 53**) and install the bolt, lockplate and thrust washer (B) onto the jackshaft.

12. Push the assembly on until it bottoms.

13. Align the lockplate tab with the thrust washer, then insert the tab into the notch in the end of the jackshaft.

14. Screw the bolt into the starter shaft by hand.

15. Wrap the pinion gear with a cloth to protect the finish, then secure it with pliers (A, **Figure 45**).

16. Tighten the starter jackshaft bolt (B, **Figure 45**) to 84-108 in.-lb. (9-12 N•m). Bend the outer lockplate tab against the bolt head (**Figure 44**).

17. Ensure the components have been installed correctly as follows:

    a. Install the clutch shell onto the transmission mainshaft.

    b. With the starter not engaged, the pinion gear (A, **Figure 54**) must not engage the clutch shell gear (B).

    c. To check for proper engagement, pull out on the pinion gear and engage it with the clutch shell gear. Then rotate the clutch shell in either direction and make sure the pinion gear rotates with it.

    d. If the engagement is incorrect, remove the clutch shell and correct the problem.

    e. Remove the clutch shell.

18. Install the oil tank as described in Chapter Four.

19. Install the cover and the bolt (B, **Figure 43**) onto the end of the starter.

20. Install the oil tank (A, **Figure 43**) as described in Chapter Four.

21. Install the primary drive outer cover as described in Chapter Five.

22. Connect the negative battery cable.

23. Install the seat.

8

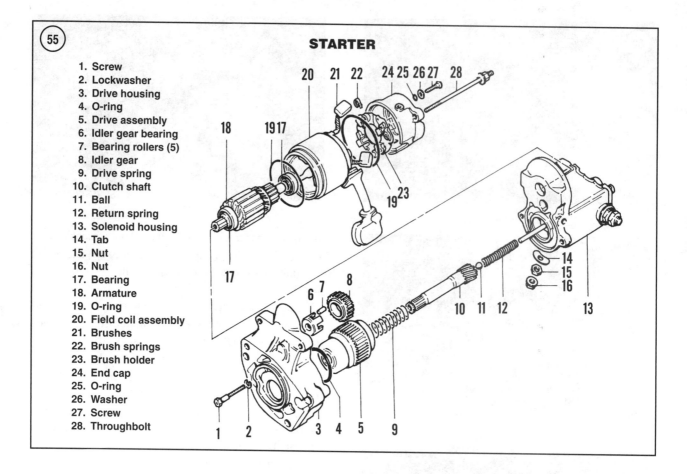

STARTER

1. Screw
2. Lockwasher
3. Drive housing
4. O-ring
5. Drive assembly
6. Idler gear bearing
7. Bearing rollers (5)
8. Idler gear
9. Drive spring
10. Clutch shaft
11. Ball
12. Return spring
13. Solenoid housing
14. Tab
15. Nut
16. Nut
17. Bearing
18. Armature
19. O-ring
20. Field coil assembly
21. Brushes
22. Brush springs
23. Brush holder
24. End cap
25. O-ring
26. Washer
27. Screw
28. Throughbolt

Starter Disassembly

NOTE
*If only the solenoid assembly requires service, refer to **Starter Solenoid** in this chapter.*

1. Clean all grease, dirt and carbon from the exterior of the starter assembly (**Figure 55**).

2. Remove the two through bolts (**Figure 56**).

3. Remove the two drive housing Phillips screws (**Figure 57**) and lockwashers.

4. Tap the drive housing and remove it from the starter assembly (**Figure 58**).

5. Disconnect the C terminal field wire (A, **Figure 59**) from the solenoid housing.

6. Separate the field coil (B, **Figure 59**) from the solenoid housing (C).

7. Remove the end cap screws, washers and O-rings (A, **Figure 60**). Then remove the end cap (B).

8. Pull the brush holder (A, **Figure 61**) away from the commutator and remove the armature (B) from the field coil assembly.

9. Remove the two field coil brushes from the brush holder (**Figure 62**).

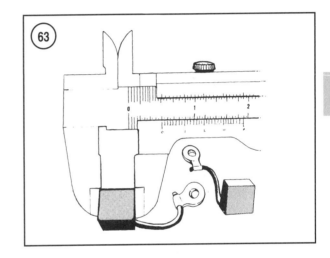

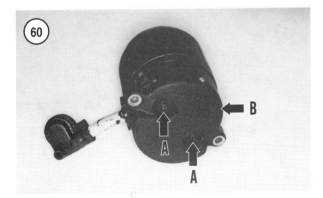

8

10. Clean all grease, dirt and carbon from the armature, field coil assembly and end covers.

> *CAUTION*
> *Be extremely careful when selecting a solvent to clean the electrical components. Do not immerse any of the wire windings in solvent, because the insulation may be damaged. Wipe the windings with a cloth lightly moistened with solvent, then allow the solution to dry thoroughly.*

11. To service the drive housing assembly, refer to *Drive Housing Disassembly/Inspection/Assembly* in this section.

12. To service the solenoid housing, refer to *Solenoid Housing Disassembly/Inspection/Assembly* in this section.

Starter Inspection

1. Measure the length of each brush with a vernier caliper (**Figure 63**). If the length is less than the minimum speci-

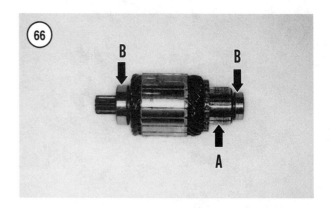

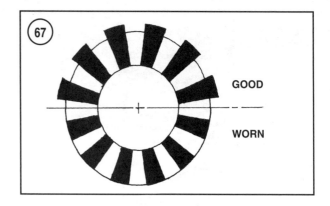

fied in **Table 3**, replace all of the brushes as a set. See **Figure 64** for the field coil and **Figure 65** for the brush holder.

> *NOTE*
> *The field coil brushes (**Figure 64**) are soldered into position. To replace them, unsolder the brushes by heating their joints with a soldering gun, then pull them out with a pair of pliers. Position the new brushes and solder them in place with rosin core solder. Do not use acid core solder.*

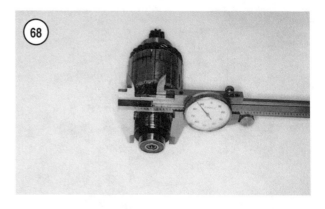

2. Inspect the commutator (A, **Figure 66**). The mica should be below the surface of the copper commutator segments (**Figure 67**). If the commutator bars are worn to the same level as the mica insulation, have the commutator serviced by a dealership or electrical repair shop.

3. Inspect the commutator copper segments for discoloration. If the commutator segments are rough, discolored or worn, have the commutator serviced by a dealership or electrical repair shop.

4. Measure the outer diameter of the commutator with a vernier caliper (**Figure 68**). Replace the armature if it is worn to the service limit in **Table 3**.

5. Use an ohmmeter to perform the following tests:

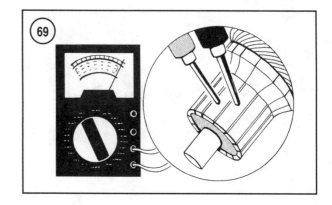

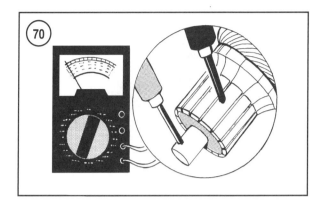

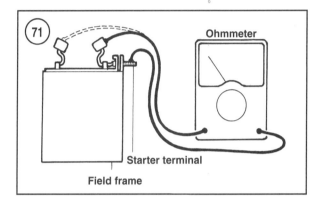

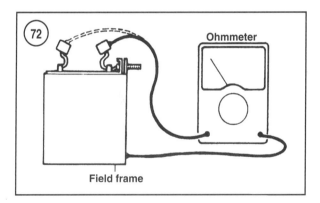

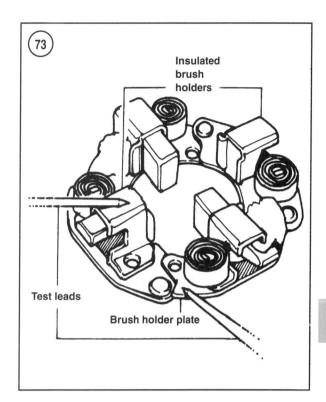

a. Check for continuity between the commutator bars (**Figure 69**); there should be continuity between pairs of bars.

b. Check for continuity between any commutator bar and the shaft (**Figure 70**). There should be no continuity.

c. If the unit fails either test, replace the armature.

6. Use an ohmmeter to perform the following tests:

a. Check for continuity between the starter cable terminal and each field frame brush (**Figure 71**); there should be continuity.

b. Check for continuity between the field frame housing and each field frame brush (**Figure 72**); there should be no continuity.

c. If the unit fails either test, replace the field frame assembly.

7. Use an ohmmeter to check for continuity between the brush holder plate and each brush holder (**Figure 73**); there should be no continuity. If the unit fails this test, replace the brush holder plate.

8. Service the armature bearings as follows:

a. Check the bearings (B, **Figure 66**) on the armature shaft. Replace worn or damaged bearings.

b. Check the bearing bores in the end cover and solenoid housing. Replace the cover or housing if the area is worn or cracked.

Starter Assembly

1. Assemble the drive housing as described in this chapter if it was serviced.

2. Assemble the solenoid housing as described in this chapter if it was serviced.

3. Lubricate the armature bearings (B, **Figure 66**) with high-temperature grease.

4. Install two *new* O-rings onto the field coil shoulders (**Figure 74**).

5. Install the two field coil brushes into the brush plate holders (**Figure 75**).

6. Install the armature partway through the field coil as shown in **Figure 61**. Then pull the brushes back and push the armature forward, so when released, all of the brushes contact the commutator as shown in **Figure 76** and **Figure 77**.

7. Install the end cap (**Figure 78**) and the two screws, washers and O-rings. Tighten the screws securely.

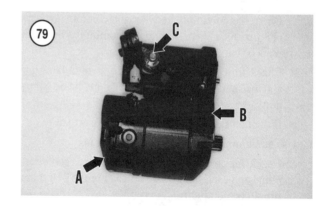

8. Align the field coil (A, **Figure 79**) with the solenoid housing (B) and assemble both housings. Hold the assembly together while installing the drive housing in Step 9.

9. Align the drive housing (**Figure 80**) with the field coil and solenoid housing assembly, and install it. Install the two drive housing screws and lockwashers (**Figure 57**). Tighten them securely.

10. Install the two through bolts, washers and O-rings (**Figure 56**). Tighten them securely.

11. Reconnect the C terminal field wire (C, **Figure 79**) at the solenoid housing.

Drive Housing Disassembly/Inspection/Assembly

The drive housing was removed during starter disassembly.

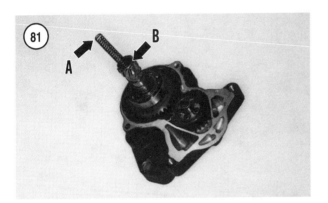

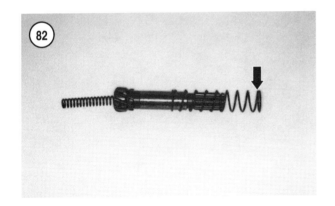

8

1. Remove the return spring (A, **Figure 81**), ball, clutch shaft (B) and drive spring (**Figure 82**) from the drive assembly.

2. Remove the idler gear (**Figure 83**) from the drive housing.

3. Remove the idler gear bearing and cage assembly (A, **Figure 84**). There are five individual bearing rollers (**Figure 85**).

4. Remove the drive assembly (B, **Figure 84**).

5. Replace the drive housing O-ring (**Figure 86**) if it is worn or damaged. Lubricate the O-ring with high temperature grease.

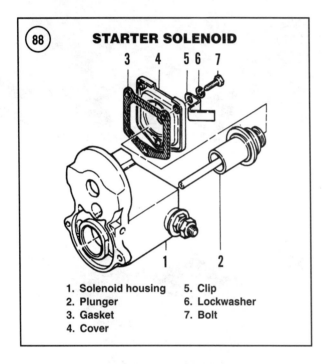

STARTER SOLENOID

1. Solenoid housing
2. Plunger
3. Gasket
4. Cover
5. Clip
6. Lockwasher
7. Bolt

6. Inspect the idler gear bearing and cage assembly (**Figure 85**) for worn or damaged parts.

> *CAUTION*
> *The drive assembly (**Figure 87**) is a sealed unit. Do not clean or soak it in any type of solvent.*

7. Inspect the drive assembly and its bearings (**Figure 87**) for worn or damaged parts. If the bearings are worn or damaged, replace the drive assembly and bearings as a set.
8. Assemble the drive housing by reversing these steps. Note the following:
9. Lubricate the following components with high temperature grease.
   a. Idler gear bearing and cage assembly (**Figure 85**).
   b. Drive housing O-ring and shaft (**Figure 86**).

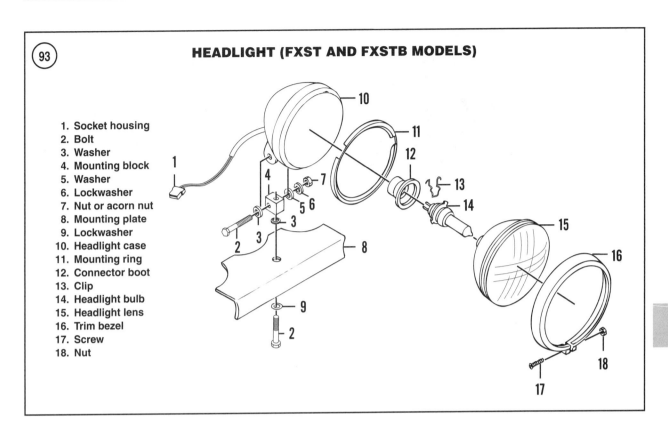

HEADLIGHT (FXST AND FXSTB MODELS)

93

1. Socket housing
2. Bolt
3. Washer
4. Mounting block
5. Washer
6. Lockwasher
7. Nut or acorn nut
8. Mounting plate
9. Lockwasher
10. Headlight case
11. Mounting ring
12. Connector boot
13. Clip
14. Headlight bulb
15. Headlight lens
16. Trim bezel
17. Screw
18. Nut

c. Drive assembly (**Figure 87**).

d. Clutch shaft, drive spring, return spring and ball.

10. Install the idler gear bearing and cage assembly so the open side of the cage (A, **Figure 84**) faces toward the solenoid housing.

Solenoid Housing Disassembly/Inspection/Assembly

1. Remove the solenoid housing (**Figure 88**) as described during starter disassembly.

2. Remove the screws, washers and clip securing the end cover to the solenoid housing. Then remove the end cover (**Figure 89**) and the gasket.

3. Remove the plunger assembly (**Figure 90**).

4. Inspect the plunger (**Figure 91**) for scoring, deep wear marks or other damage.

5. Inspect the solenoid housing (**Figure 92**) for wear, cracks or other damage.

6. The solenoid housing is a separate assembly and cannot be serviced. If any part is defective, the solenoid housing must be replaced as an assembly.

7. Assemble the solenoid housing by reversing these steps. Lubricate the solenoid plunger with high temperature grease.

LIGHTING SYSTEM

The lighting system consists of a headlight, passing lamps, taillight/brake light combination and turn signals.

Always use the correct wattage bulb. The use of a larger wattage bulb will give a dim light and a smaller wattage bulb will burn out prematurely. **Table 4** lists replacement bulb specifications.

CAUTION
All models are equipped with a quartz-halogen bulb. Do not touch the bulb glass. Traces of oil on the bulb will drastically reduce the life of the bulb. Clean all traces of oil from the bulb glass with a cloth moistened in alcohol or lacquer thinner.

Headlight Bulb Replacement (FXST and FXSTB Models)

Refer to **Figure 93**.

WARNING
If the headlight has just burned out or just turned off, it will be hot. To avoid burned fingers, allow the bulb to cool prior to removal.

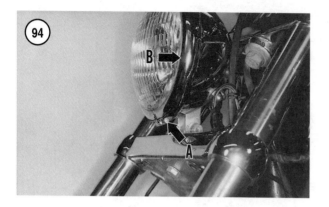

1. Loosen the screw (A, **Figure 94**) at the base of the trim bezel (B) and remove the trim bezel from the headlamp lens assembly.

2. Pull the lens assembly part way out of the headlight case.

3. Pull *straight out* on the electrical connector and disconnect it from the bulb (**Figure 95**). Remove the headlight assembly.

4. Remove the connector cover (**Figure 96**) from the back of the headlight lens. Check the rubber cover for tears or deterioration; replace it if necessary.

5. Unhook the light bulb retaining clip (**Figure 97**) and pivot it out of the way.

6. Remove and discard the blown bulb (**Figure 98**).

7. Align the tangs on the new bulb with the notches in the headlight lens and install the bulb.

8. Securely hook the retaining clip onto the bulb (**Figure 97**).

9. Install the connector cover (**Figure 96**) and make sure it is correctly seated against the bulb and the retainer.

10. Correctly align the electrical plug terminals with the bulb and connect the plug. Push it *straight on* until it bottoms on the bulb and the connector cover (**Figure 95**).

11. Check headlight operation.

12. Insert the lens into the headlight housing and seat it correctly.

13. Install the trim bezel (B, **Figure 94**) into place and tighten the screw (A) securely.

14. Check headlight adjustment as described in this chapter.

**Headlight Bulb Replacement
(FLSTS, FXSTD and FXSTS Models)**

Refer to **Figure 99**.

*WARNING
If the headlight has just burned out or just
turned off, it will be hot. To avoid burned*

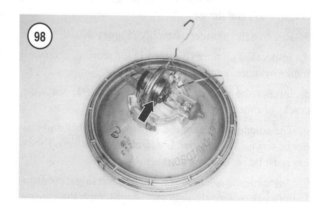

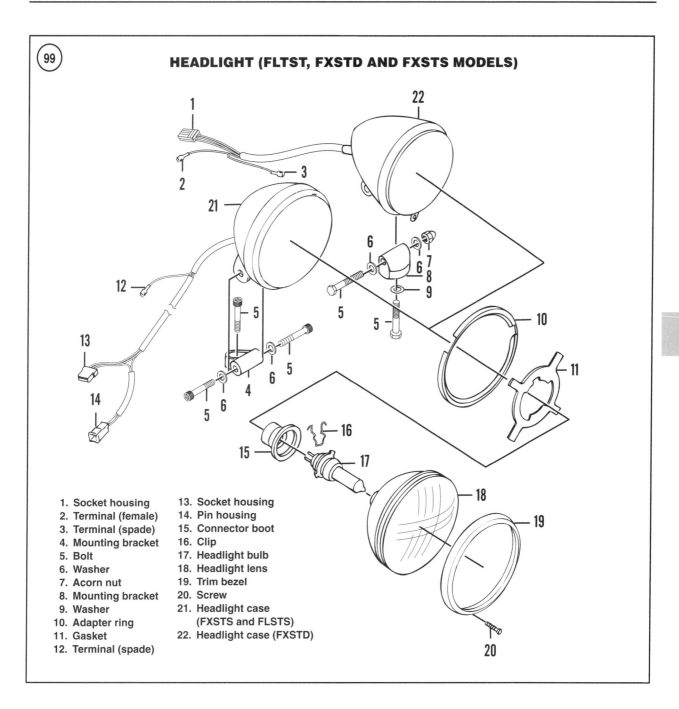

HEADLIGHT (FLTST, FXSTD AND FXSTS MODELS) ⑨⑨

1. Socket housing
2. Terminal (female)
3. Terminal (spade)
4. Mounting bracket
5. Bolt
6. Washer
7. Acorn nut
8. Mounting bracket
9. Washer
10. Adapter ring
11. Gasket
12. Terminal (spade)
13. Socket housing
14. Pin housing
15. Connector boot
16. Clip
17. Headlight bulb
18. Headlight lens
19. Trim bezel
20. Screw
21. Headlight case
    (FXSTS and FLSTS)
22. Headlight case (FXSTD)

fingers, allow the bulb to cool prior to removal.

1. Remove the screw at the base of the trim bezel and remove the trim bezel from the headlight lens assembly.

2. Pull the lens assembly part way out of the headlight case.

3. Pull *straight out* on the electrical connector and disconnect it from the bulb. Remove the headlight assembly.

4. Remove the connector boot (**Figure 96**) from the back of the headlight lens. Check the rubber boot for tears or deterioration; replace it if necessary.

5. Squeeze the light bulb retaining clip (**Figure 97**) and pivot it out of the way.

6. Remove and discard the blown bulb (**Figure 98**).

7. Align the tangs on the new bulb with the notches in the headlight lens and install the bulb.

8. Securely hook the retaining clip onto the bulb.

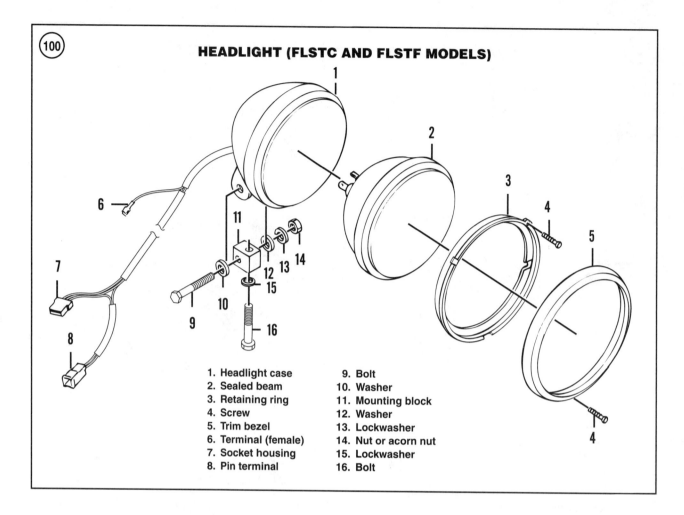

HEADLIGHT (FLSTC AND FLSTF MODELS)

1. Headlight case
2. Sealed beam
3. Retaining ring
4. Screw
5. Trim bezel
6. Terminal (female)
7. Socket housing
8. Pin terminal
9. Bolt
10. Washer
11. Mounting block
12. Washer
13. Lockwasher
14. Nut or acorn nut
15. Lockwasher
16. Bolt

9. Install the connector boot and make sure it is correctly seated against the bulb and the retainer.

10. Correctly align the electrical plug terminals with the bulb and connect the plug. Push it *straight on* until it bottoms on the bulb and the connector boot.

11. Check headlight operation.

12. Insert the lens into the headlight housing and seat it correctly.

13. Install the trim bezel and screw. Tighten the screw securely.

14. Check headlight adjustment as described in this chapter.

**Headlight Bulb Replacement
(FLSTC and FLSTF Models)**

Refer to **Figure 100**.

WARNING
If the headlight has just burned out or just turned off, it will be hot. To avoid burned

fingers, allow the headlight assembly to cool prior to removal.

NOTE
*On FLSTC and FLSTF HDI models, refer to **Headlight Bulb Replacement (FXST and FXSTB Models)** in this chapter. These models are not equipped with a sealed beam headlight assembly.*

1. Remove the screw at the base of the trim bezel.

2. Carefully remove the trim bezel. Do not bend the two top locating tabs at the top of the trim bezel.

3. Remove the three screws securing the retaining ring and remove it while holding the headlight assembly in place.

4. Pull the headlight assembly out of the headlight case.

5. Pull *straight out* on the electrical connector and disconnect it from the headlight assembly. Remove the headlight assembly.

6. Remove and discard the blown headlight assembly.

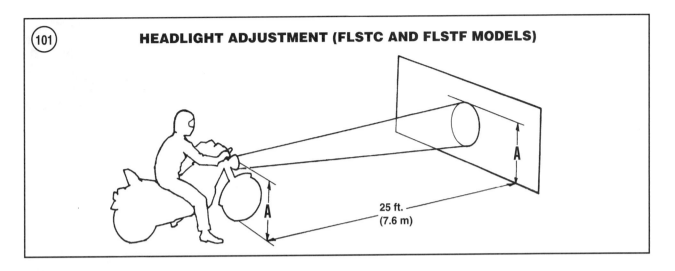

HEADLIGHT ADJUSTMENT (FLSTC AND FLSTF MODELS)

25 ft.
(7.6 m)

A

A

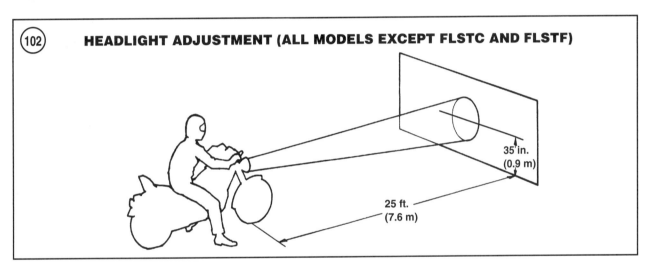

HEADLIGHT ADJUSTMENT (ALL MODELS EXCEPT FLSTC AND FLSTF)

8

35 in.
(0.9 m)

25 ft.
(7.6 m)

7. Correctly align the electrical plug terminals with the bulb and connect the plug. Push it *straight on* until it bottoms on the headlight assembly.

8. Check headlight operation.

9. Insert the headlight assembly into the headlight case and seat it correctly.

10. Install the retaining ring and three screws. Tighten them securely.

11. Install the two top locating tabs on the trim bezel and snap the trim bezel into place. Install the screw and tighten it securely.

12. Check headlight adjustment as described in this chapter.

Headlight Adjustment

1. Park the motorcycle on a level surface approximately 25 ft. (7.6 m) from the wall.

2. Check tire inflation pressure. Readjust it if necessary, as described in Chapter Three.

3A. On FLSTC and FLSTF models, draw a horizontal line on the wall the same height as the center of the headlight (**Figure 101**).

3B. On all models except FLSTC and FLSTF, draw a horizontal line on the wall 35 in. (0.9 m) above the floor **Figure 102**.

4. Have an assistant (with the same approximate weight as the primary rider) sit on the seat.

5. Aim the headlight at the wall. Switch the headlight to the HIGH beam. Point the front wheel straight ahead.

6. Turn the key switch to the IGNITION position.

7. Check the headlight beam alignment. The broad, flat pattern of light (main beam of light) must be centered on the horizontal line with an equal area of light above and below line.

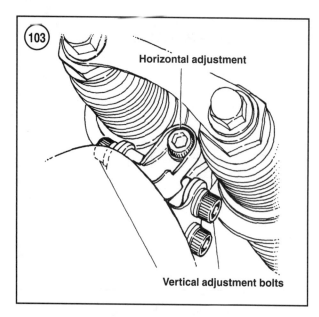

Horizontal adjustment

Vertical adjustment bolts

8. Check the headlight beam lateral alignment. With the headlight beam pointed straight ahead, there should be an equal area of light to the left and right of center.

9. If the beam is incorrect, adjust it as follows:

10A. On FXSTS and FLSTS models, perform the following:

    a. Loosen the two vertical adjust bolts (**Figure 103**) to move the headlight up and down. Tighten the bolts to the specification in **Table 5**.

    b. Loosen the horizontal adjust bolt (**Figure 103**) to move the headlight beam from side-to-side. Then move the headlight adjustment mechanism forward to the end of the bracket slot. Tighten the bolt to the specification in **Table 5**.

CAUTION
Move the headlight assembly as far forward as possible (see substep b) to prevent the headlight from making contact with the front springs. Compress the front fork to ensure this adjustment is correct prior to riding the motorcycle.

10B. On all models except FXSTS and FLSTS, perform the following:

    a. Loosen the upper adjust bolt (**Figure 104**) to move the headlight up and down. Tighten the bolts to the specification in **Table 5**.

    b. Loosen the lower horizontal adjust bolt (**Figure 105**) to move the headlight beam from side-to-side. Then move the headlight adjustment mechanism forward to the end of the bracket slot. Tighten the bolt to the specification in **Table 5**.

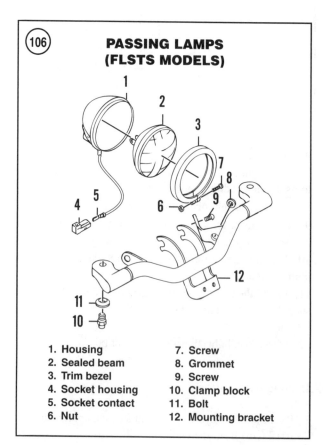

PASSING LAMPS (FLSTS MODELS)

1. Housing	7. Screw
2. Sealed beam	8. Grommet
3. Trim bezel	9. Screw
4. Socket housing	10. Clamp block
5. Socket contact	11. Bolt
6. Nut	12. Mounting bracket

11. Recheck headlight aim.

Passing Light and Front Turn Signal Bulb Replacement (FLSTS and FLSTC Models)

Refer to **Figure 106**.

1. Remove the passing light bulb as follows:
    a. Remove the screw (**Figure 107**) at the base of the trim bezel and remove the trim bezel from the passing light housing.
    b. Carefully pull the bulb/lens assembly partially out of the housing.
    c. Loosen the two screws securing the wiring harness (**Figure 108**) to the bulb/lens assembly and remove it.
    d. Connect the wiring harness to the *new* bulb/lens assembly and tighten the screws securely.
    e. Push the bulb/lens assembly into the housing and install the trim bezel.
    f. Tighten the screw securely.

2. On FLSTC models, remove the front turn signal bulb as follows:
    a. Remove the screws securing the lens (**Figure 109**).
    b. Push in on the bulb, rotate it and remove it (**Figure 110**).
    c. Install a new bulb and lens.
    d. Tighten the screws securely. Do not overtighten the screws as the lens may crack.

Front Turn Signal Bulb Replacement (All Models Except FLSTS)

1. Remove the screws securing the lens and remove the lens (**Figure 111**).
2. Push in on the bulb, rotate it and remove it.
3. Install a new bulb and lens.
4. Install the screws and tighten them securely. Do not overtighten the screws as the lens may crack.

8

Rear Turn Signal Bulb Replacement

1. Remove the screws securing the lens and remove the lens.
2. Push in on the bulb, rotate it and remove it.
3. Install a new bulb and lens.
4. Install the screws and tighten them securely. Do not overtighten the screws as the lens may crack.

Taillight/Brake and License Plate Light Replacement (FXSTD Models)

Refer to **Figure 112**.
1. Insert a small diameter screwdriver into the middle hole in the license plate cover. Push in on the screwdriver and release the internal clip.
2. Carefully pull the taillight/brake light assembly out and away from the housing.
3A. To replace the taillight/brake light bulb, perform the following:
   a. Rotate the bulb housing and socket *counterclockwise* and pull straight out.
   b. Rotate the bulb *counterclockwise* and pull straight out of the socket.
   c. Install a new bulb and rotate it *clockwise* into the socket.
   d. Rotate the bulb housing and socket *clockwise* and push it straight in until it bottoms.
3B. To replace the license plate bulb, perform the following:
   a. Rotate the bulb housing and socket *counterclockwise*. Pull it straight out and make sure the tabs clear of the notches in the housing.
   b. Pull the bulb straight out of the socket.
   c. Install a new bulb and push it into the socket.
   d. Align the socket tabs, push the socket into the housing and rotate it *clockwise*.
4. Correctly position the taillight/brake light assembly routing the electrical wires to either side of the assembly.
5. Insert the top clip under the edge of the fender to lock it into place.
6. Push the assembly toward the front of the motorcycle and engage the lower clip with the lower edge of the bottom opening in the fender.
7. Push down on the assembly until an audible click is heard. Pull out on the assembly to make sure it is locked into place in the housing.

Taillight/Brake Light Replacement (FLSTS Models)

Refer to **Figure 113**.
1. Remove the three screws securing the lens.

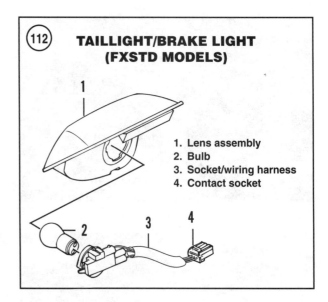

(112) **TAILLIGHT/BRAKE LIGHT (FXSTD MODELS)**

1. Lens assembly
2. Bulb
3. Socket/wiring harness
4. Contact socket

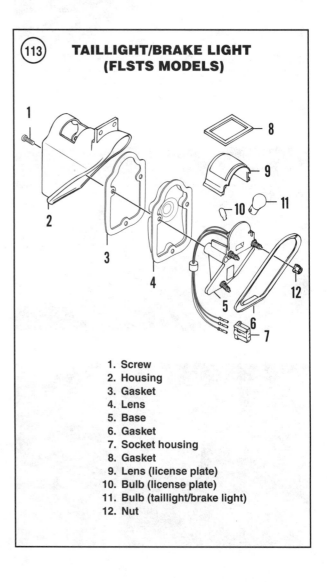

(113) **TAILLIGHT/BRAKE LIGHT (FLSTS MODELS)**

1. Screw
2. Housing
3. Gasket
4. Lens
5. Base
6. Gasket
7. Socket housing
8. Gasket
9. Lens (license plate)
10. Bulb (license plate)
11. Bulb (taillight/brake light)
12. Nut

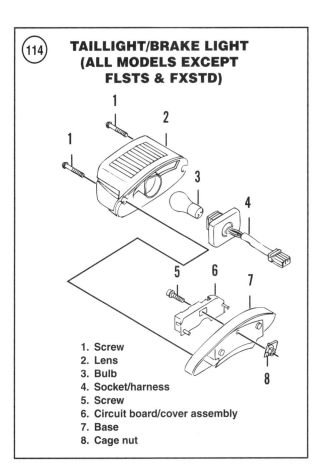

TAILLIGHT/BRAKE LIGHT (ALL MODELS EXCEPT FLSTS & FXSTD)

1. Screw
2. Lens
3. Bulb
4. Socket/harness
5. Screw
6. Circuit board/cover assembly
7. Base
8. Cage nut

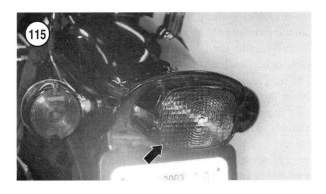

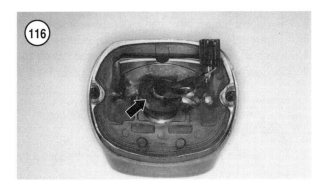

2. Pull the housing and lens off the base.

3. Rotate the bulb and remove it from the socket assembly.

4. Install a new bulb, then install the housing and lens onto the base.

5. Install the screws and tighten them securely.

6. Replace the light base as follows:

   a. Remove both seats as described in Chapter Fourteen.

   b. Disconnect the negative battery cable as described in this chapter.

   c. Remove the right side saddlebag as described in Chapter Fourteen.

   d. Disconnect the light base three-pin Amp multi-lock connector. Refer to *Electrical Connector Service* at the end of this chapter.

   e. From underneath the rear fender, disconnect the wiring harness from the backside of the fender. Note the harness routing prior to disconnect it from the fender clips.

   f. Remove the three nuts securing the base to the underside of the rear fender.

   g. Carefully pull the light base and rubber grommets from the rear fender. Pull the wiring harness out of the rear fender and remove the light base assembly.

   h. Install by reversing these steps.

**Taillight/Brake Light Replacement
(All Models Except FLSTS and FXSTD)**

Refer to **Figure 114**.

1. Remove the screws securing the lens (**Figure 115**).

2. Pull the lens off the base and disconnect the four-pin electrical connector.

3. Pull the bulb/socket assembly (**Figure 116**) out from the backside of the lens.

4. Rotate the bulb and remove it from the socket assembly (**Figure 117**).

5. Install a new bulb, then install the socket assembly into the lens.

6. Connect the electrical connector, and install the lens onto the base.

7. Install the screws and tighten them securely. Do not overtighten the screws as the lens may crack.

8. Replace the base as follows:

    a. From underneath the rear fender, disconnect the wiring harness from the backside of the base.

    b. Remove the screw securing the printed circuit board and base to the rear fender.

    c. Remove the base.

    d. Install by reversing these steps.

Front Fender Tip Light Replacement (FLSTS Models)

Refer to **Figure 118**.

1. Remove the rear screw securing the light cover.

2. From underneath the front fender, secure the crimp nut and loosen remove the front screw securing the light cover.

3. Remove the light cover.

4. Carefully pull the bulb straight back out of the socket.

5. Install a new bulb, then install the light cover. Make sure it is seated correctly on the mounting pad.

6. Install the screws and tighten them securely.

7. Replace the light lens/socket assembly as follows:

    a. Remove the light cover as previously described.

    b. Remove both seats as described in Chapter Fourteen.

    c. Disconnect the negative battery cable as described in this chapter.

    d. Remove the fuel tank as described in Chapter Seven.

    e. Disconnect the light lens/socket assembly two-pin Amp multi-lock connector. Refer to *Electrical Connector Service* at the end of this chapter.

    f. Disconnect or cut all straps securing the wiring harness to the frame and front fender.

    g. From underneath the front fender, disconnect the wiring harness from the backside of the fender. Note the harness routing prior to disconnect it from the fender clips.

    h. Use a long screwdriver and carefully pry the metal clips away from the fender.

    i. Carefully pull the lens/socket and rubber grommet from the front fender. Pull the wiring harness out of the front fender and remove the light base assembly.

    j. Install by reversing these steps.

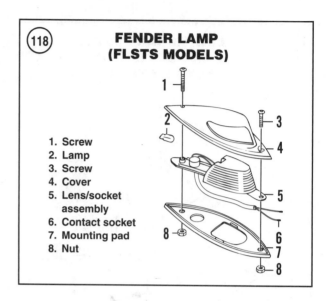

FENDER LAMP (FLSTS MODELS)

1. Screw
2. Lamp
3. Screw
4. Cover
5. Lens/socket assembly
6. Contact socket
7. Mounting pad
8. Nut

SWITCHES

Testing

Test switches for continuity by using an ohmmeter (see Chapter One) or a self-powered test light at the switch connector plug and operating the switch in each of its operating positions. Compare the results with the switch operating diagrams included in the wiring diagrams located at the end of the manual.

For example, **Figure 119** shows the continuity diagram for a typical ignition switch. It shows which terminals should show continuity when the switch is in a given position. When the ignition switch is in the IGNITION position, there should be continuity between the red/black, red and red/gray terminals. Note the line on the continuity diagram. An ohmmeter connected between these three terminals should indicate little or no resistance, or a test light should light. When the starter switch is OFF, there should be no continuity between the same terminals. Replace the switch or button if it does not perform properly.

When testing the switches, note the following:

1. Check the battery as described under *Battery* in this chapter. Charge or replace the battery if necessary.

2. Disconnect the negative battery cable as described in this chapter before checking the continuity of any switch.

3. Detach all connectors located between the switch and the electrical circuit.

CAUTION
Do not attempt to start the engine with the battery disconnected.

4. When separating two connectors, pull on the connector housings and not the wires.

IGNITION SWITCH (TYPICAL)

Switch / Position	Red/black	Red	Red/gray
Off		●	
Accessory		●———————————●	
Ignition	●————————————●	●	

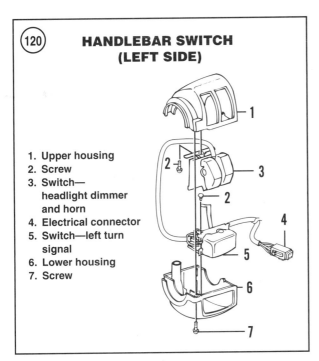

HANDLEBAR SWITCH (LEFT SIDE)

1. Upper housing
2. Screw
3. Switch—headlight dimmer and horn
4. Electrical connector
5. Switch—left turn signal
6. Lower housing
7. Screw

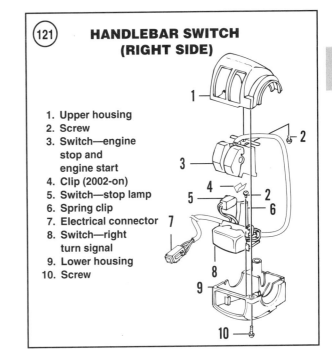

HANDLEBAR SWITCH (RIGHT SIDE)

1. Upper housing
2. Screw
3. Switch—engine stop and engine start
4. Clip (2002-on)
5. Switch—stop lamp
6. Spring clip
7. Electrical connector
8. Switch—right turn signal
9. Lower housing
10. Screw

5. After locating a defective circuit, check the connectors to make sure they are clean and properly connected. Check all wires going into a connector housing to make sure each wire is positioned properly and the wire end is not loose.

6. To reconnect connectors properly, push them together until they click or snap into place.

Handlebar Switches

Left handlebar switch description

The left side handlebar switch housing (**Figure 120**) is equipped with the following switches:

1. Headlight dimmer.
2. Horn.
3. Left side turn signal.

Right handlebar switch description

The right side handlebar switch housing (**Figure 121**) is equipped with the following switches:

1. Engine stop/run.
2. Start.
3. Right side turn signal.
4. Front brake light.

Handlebar switch replacement

1. Remove the screws securing the left side switch housing (**Figure 122**) to the handlebar. Then carefully separate the switch housing to access the defective switch (**Figure 123**).

2. Remove the screws securing the right side switch housing (**Figure 124**) to the handlebar. Then carefully separate the switch housing to access the defective switch (**Figure 125**).

NOTE
*To service the front brake light switch, refer to **Front Brake Light Switch Replacement** in this chapter.*

3A. On models without splices, remove the screw and bracket.

3B. On models with splices, remove the cable strap.

4. Pull the switch(es) out of the housing.

5. Cut the switch wire(s) from the defective switch(es).

6. Slip a piece of heat shrink tubing over each wire cut in Step 2.

7. Solder the wire end(s) to the new switch. Then shrink the tubing over the wire(s).

8. Install the switch by reversing these steps. Note the following:

   a. When clamping the switch housing onto the handlebar, check the wiring harness routing position to make sure it is not pinched between the housing and handlebar.

   b. To install the right side switch housing, refer to *Throttle and Idle Cable Replacement* in Chapter Seven.

WARNING
Do not ride the motorcycle until the throttle cables are properly adjusted. Also, the cables must not catch or pull when the handlebars are turned. Improper cable routing and

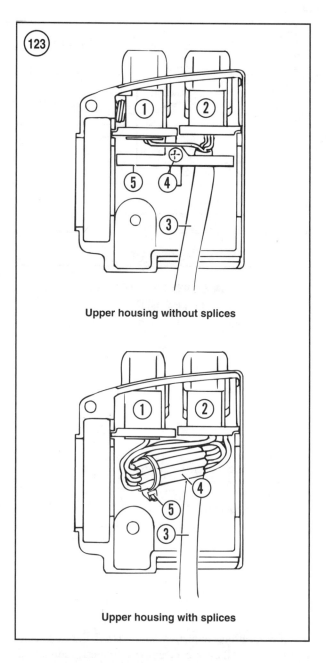

Upper housing without splices

Upper housing with splices

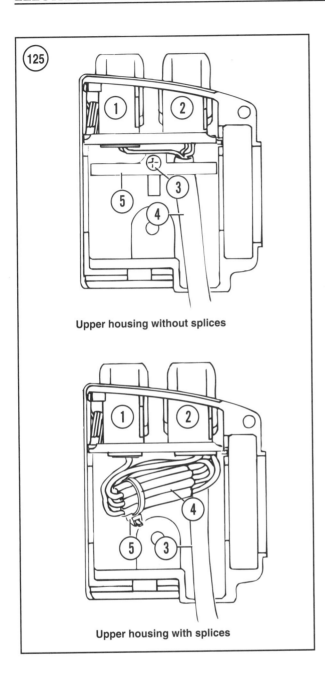

Upper housing without splices

Upper housing with splices

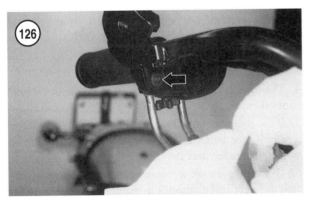

adjustment can cause the throttle to stick open. This could cause loss of control.

Front Brake Light Switch Replacement

The front brake light switch (**Figure 126**) is mounted in the right side switch lower housing.

1. Separate the right side switch housing as described under *Handlebar Switch Replacement* in this chapter.

2. If the wedge between the switch and the switch housing is still in place, remove it.

3. Cut the switch wires 1.0 in. (25.4 mm) from the defective switch.

4. While depressing the switch plunger, slowly rotate the switch upward, rocking it slightly, and remove it from the switch housing.

5. Check that the plunger is square in the bore and that the boot is not compressed, collapsed or torn. Work the plunger in and out until the boot is fully extended.

6. Slip a piece of heat shrink tubing over each wire cut in Step 3.

7. Solder the wire ends to the new switch. Then shrink the tubing over the wires.

8. Install the switch by reversing these steps. Note the following:

   a. When clamping the switch housing onto the handlebar, check the wiring harness routing position to make sure it is not pinched between the housing and handlebar.

   b. To install the right side switch housing, refer to *Throttle and Idle Cable Replacement* in Chapter Seven.

> *WARNING*
> *Do not ride the motorcycle until the throttle cables are properly adjusted. The cables must not catch or pull when the handlebars are turned. Improper cable routing and adjustment can cause the throttle to stick open. This could cause a loss of control. Recheck the work before riding the motorcycle.*

Ignition/Light Switch Removal/Installation

Refer to **Figure 127** and **Figure 128**.

1. Remove the fuel tank console as described under *Fuel Tank Console* in Chapter Seven.

2. Turn the fuel tank console over onto towels on the workbench.

3. Remove the four screws securing the ignition switch (**Figure 129**) to the bottom surface of the fuel tank console.

4. Remove the ignition switch.

8

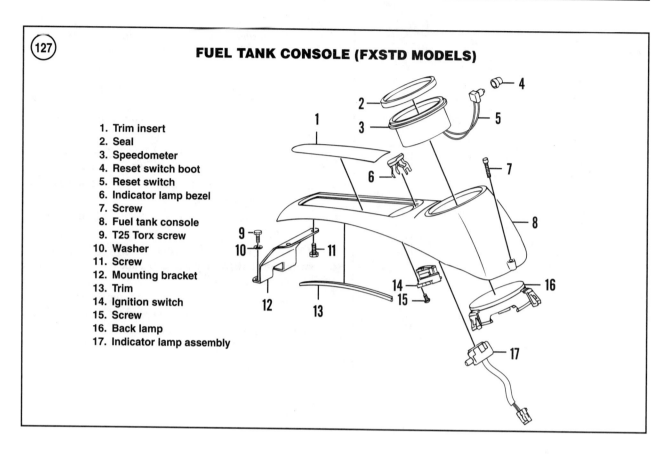

FUEL TANK CONSOLE (FXSTD MODELS)

1. Trim insert
2. Seal
3. Speedometer
4. Reset switch boot
5. Reset switch
6. Indicator lamp bezel
7. Screw
8. Fuel tank console
9. T25 Torx screw
10. Washer
11. Screw
12. Mounting bracket
13. Trim
14. Ignition switch
15. Screw
16. Back lamp
17. Indicator lamp assembly

5. Install the new ignition switch with the electrical connector terminal facing toward the rear of the fuel console. Tighten the screws securely.

6. Install the fuel tank console as described under *Fuel Tank Console* in Chapter Seven.

Oil Pressure Switch

Operation

The oil pressure switch is located on the front right side of the crankcase.

A pressure-actuated diaphragm-type oil pressure switch is used. When the oil pressure is low or when oil is not circulating through a running engine, spring tension inside the switch, holds the switch contacts closed. This completes the signal light circuit and causes the low oil pressure indicator lamp to light.

The oil pressure signal light should turn on when any of the following occurs:

1. The ignition switch is turned on prior to starting the engine.

2. The engine speed idle is below of 950-1050 rpm.

3. The engine is operating with low oil pressure.

4. Oil is not circulating through the running engine.

NOTE
The oil pressure indicator light may not come on when the ignition switch is turned off then back on immediately. This is due to the oil pressure retained in the oil filter housing. Test the electrical part of the oil pressure switch in the following steps. If the oil pressure switch, indicator lamp and related wiring are in good condition, inspect the lubrication system as described in Chapter Two.

Testing/replacement

1. Remove the rubber boot (A, **Figure 130**) and disconnect the electrical connector from the switch.

2. Turn the ignition switch ON.

3. Ground the switch wire to the engine.

4. The low oil pressure indicator lamp on the instrument panel should light.

5. If the indicator lamp does not light, check for a defective indicator lamp, and inspect all wiring between the switch, or sender, and the indicator lamp.

6A. If the oil pressure warning light operates properly, attach the electrical connector to the pressure switch. Make

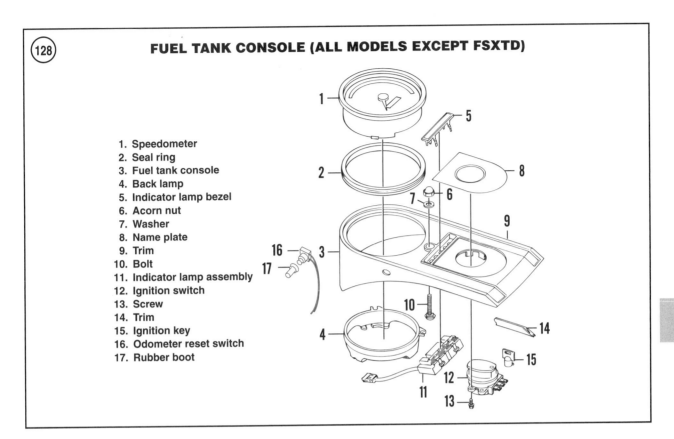

FUEL TANK CONSOLE (ALL MODELS EXCEPT FSXTD)

1. Speedometer
2. Seal ring
3. Fuel tank console
4. Back lamp
5. Indicator lamp bezel
6. Acorn nut
7. Washer
8. Name plate
9. Trim
10. Bolt
11. Indicator lamp assembly
12. Ignition switch
13. Screw
14. Trim
15. Ignition key
16. Odometer reset switch
17. Rubber boot

8

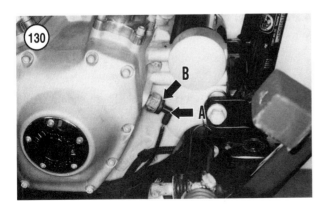

sure the connection is tight and free of oil. On models with a switch, slide the rubber boot back into position.

6B. If the warning light remains on when the engine is running, shut the engine off. Check the engine lubrication system as described in Chapter Two.

7. To replace the switch, perform the following:

a. Use a 1-1/16 in. open-end wrench and unscrew the switch (B, **Figure 130**) from the engine.

NOTE
If the original switch is going to be reinstalled, perform sub step b. A new switch already has a sealant contact path on the threads. Do not add any additional sealant to a new switch.

b. If reinstalling the original switch, apply Teflon Loctite pipe sealant to the switch threads prior to installation.

c. Install the switch and tighten it to 96-144 in.-lb. (11-16 N•m).

d. Test the new switch as described in Steps 1-4.

Neutral Indicator Switch Replacement

The neutral indicator switch is located on the transmission top cover. The neutral indicator light on the instrument panel should light when the ignition is turned ON and the transmission is in NEUTRAL.

1. Disconnect the electrical connector from the neutral indicator switch.

2. Turn the ignition switch ON.

3. Ground the neutral indicator switch wire to the transmission case.

4. If the neutral indicator lamp lights, the neutral switch is defective. Replace the neutral indicator switch and retest.

5. If the neutral indicator lamp does not light, check for a defective indicator lamp, faulty wiring or a loose or corroded connection.

NOTE
The electrical connector can be attached to either stud on the switch.

6A. If the neutral switch operates correctly, attach the electrical connector to the neutral switch. Make sure the connection is tight and free of oil.

6B. If the neutral switch is defective, replace the neutral indicator switch.

7. To replace the old switch, perform the following:

   a. Shift the transmission into NEUTRAL.

   b. Disconnect the oil tank feed line (A, **Figure 131**) as described in Chapter Four.

   c. Unscrew and remove the old switch and O-ring (B, **Figure 131**) from the transmission top cover.

   d. Apply clean transmission oil to the *new* O-ring seal.

   e. Install the new switch and tighten it to 120-180 in.-lb. (14-20 N•m).

Rear Brake Light Switch Testing/Replacement

A hydraulic, normally-open rear brake light switch is used on all models. The rear brake light is attached to the rear brake caliper brake hose assembly. When the rear brake pedal is applied, hydraulic pressure closes the switch contacts, providing a ground path so the rear brake lamp comes on. If the rear brake lamp does not come on, perform the following:

NOTE
Removal of the exhaust system is not necessary, but it provides additional work room if necessary for this procedure.

1. If necessary, remove the exhaust system from the right side as described in Chapter Seven.

2. Turn the ignition switch OFF.

3. Disconnect the electrical connector (A, **Figure 132**) from the switch.

4. Connect an ohmmeter between the switch terminals. Check the following:

   a. Apply the rear brake pedal. There should be continuity.

   b. Release the rear brake pedal. There should be no continuity.

   c. If the switch fails either of these tests, replace the switch.

5. Place a drip pan under the switch, as some brake fluid will drain out when the switch is removed.

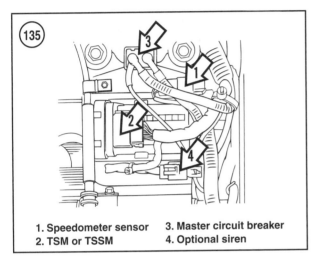

1. Speedometer sensor   3. Master circuit breaker
2. TSM or TSSM   4. Optional siren

6. Loosen and remove the switch (B, **Figure 132**) from the fitting on the rear brake line.

7. Thread the new switch into the fitting and tighten it to 96-120 in.-lb. (11-14 N•m).

8. Reconnect the switch electrical connectors.

9. Bleed the rear brake as described in Chapter Thirteen.

10. Check the rear brake light with the ignition switch turned ON and the rear brake applied.

HORN

Testing

1. Remove the seat.

2. Refer to the following procedure and partially remove the horn to gain access to the electrical connector.

3. Disconnect the electrical connector (**Figure 133**) from the backside of the horn.

4. Connect a positive voltmeter test lead to the yellow/black electrical connector and the negative test lead to ground.

5. Turn the ignition switch to the ON position.

6. Press the horn button. If battery voltage is present, the horn is faulty or is not grounded properly. If there is no battery voltage, either the horn switch or the horn wiring is faulty.

7. Replace the horn or horn switch as necessary.

Replacement

1. Remove the seat as described in Chapter Fourteen.

2. Disconnect the negative battery cable as described in this chapter.

3A. On FLSTS models, remove the screws securing the horn assembly to the passing lamp mounting bracket.

3B. On all models except FLSTS, remove the acorn nut and washer (A, **Figure 134**) securing the horn assembly bracket (B) to the engine mounting bracket.

4. Move the horn assembly to the frame and engine, and disconnect the electrical connector (**Figure 133**) from the horn spade terminals.

5. Remove the large nut securing the horn to the mounting bracket, and remove the horn.

6. Install the horn by reversing these removal steps. Note the following:

    a. Make sure the electrical connectors and horn spade terminals are free of corrosion.

    b. Connect the wires to the horn's top spade terminals.

    c. Make sure the horn operates correctly.

ELECTRICAL PANEL

The electrical panel is located in front of the rear wheel behind the rear fender inner panel. The panel assembly houses the main circuit breaker, the vehicle speed sensor, turn signal module (2000 models) or turn signal security module (2001-on models) and security siren connector (models so equipped). Refer to **Figure 135**.

To gain access to the electrical panel, perform the following:

1. Remove the seat.

NOTE
Always disarm the optional TSSM security system prior to disconnecting the battery or the siren will sound.

2. Disconnect the negative battery cable as described in this chapter.

NOTE
The rear wheel can remain in place, but removal allows easier access to the components.

8

3. Remove the rear wheel as described in Chapter Nine.

4. Remove the two bolts (A, **Figure 136**) securing the rear fender inner panel.

5. Move the inner panel up, unhook it from the upper mounting tab (B, **Figure 136**) and remove the inner panel.

6. Install the inner panel and hook it onto the upper mounting tab. Pull down and make sure it is attached correctly.

7. Install the two lower bolts and tighten securely.

8. Install the rear wheel as described in Chapter Nine.

9. Connect the negative battery cable.

10. Install the seat.

TURN SIGNAL MODULE (2000 MODELS)

The turn signal module (TSM) is an electronic microprocessor that controls the turn signals and the four-way hazard flasher. The turn signal module receives its information from the speedometer and turn signal switches.

The turn signal module is located on the electrical panel located in front of the rear wheel.

If the following tests do not solve or confirm the problem, refer TSM testing to a Harley-Davidson dealership.

Operation

Refer to **Figure 137**.

1. When the left turn signal switch is pressed, a momentary 12 VDC pulse sent to Pin No. 8 (input) on the TSM module. The module responds to this signal by sending a series of 12 VDC pulses to Pin No. 4 (output) to flash the left front and rear turn signal lamps.

2. The TSM module then monitors the number of motorcycle sensor pulses sent from the speedometer sending unit to Pin No. 5. These pulses indicate the distance the motorcycle has traveled. When the number of speedometer pulses is equal to the quantity preset in the module program, the turn signal is cancelled.

NOTE
If the turn signal switch is pressed and held in, the turn signal will flash indefinitely until the switch is released.

3. When the right turn signal switch is pressed, a momentary 12 VDC pulse sent to Pin No. 7 (input) on the TSM module and an output signal at Pin No. 3 (output). The remaining signal process is identical to the left turn signal operation.

Preliminary Troubleshooting

If one of the turn signals does not flash perform the following:

1. Remove the lens and check for a defective bulb(s). Replace the bulb(s) if necessary.

2. If the bulb(s) is good, check for one of the following problems:

   a. Check the bulb socket contacts for corrosion. Clean the contacts and recheck. If there is a problem with corrosion building on the contacts, wipe the contacts with a dielectric grease before reinstalling the bulb.

   b. Check for a broken wire within the circuit. Repair the wire(s) or connector(s).

   c. Check for a loose bulb socket where it is staked to the housing. If the bulb socket is loose, replace the light assembly.

   d. Check for a poor ground connection. If the ground is poor, clean the ground mounting area or replace damaged ground wire(s), as required.

   e. Stuck turn signal button.

3. Remove the TSM as described in this chapter.

4. Disconnect the electrical connector from the TSM.

5. Check the electrical connectors in the TSM and in the wiring harness for corrosion. Clean off if necessary.

Distance Test

The turn signal module (TSM) recognizes four different speed ranges and uses these distances to activate the cancellation action. Refer to the speed ranges listed in **Table 6**.

1. Ride the motorcycle at the mid-point of speed range No. 1.

2. Press and release the right turn button and closely check the motorcycle speed and the odometer at the time

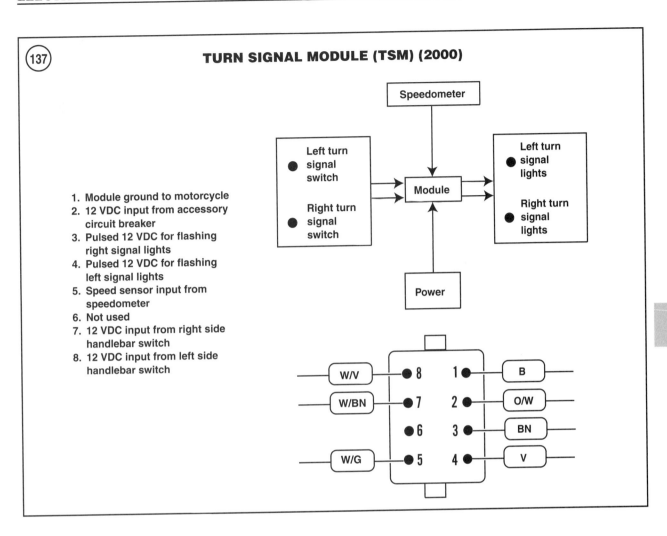

TURN SIGNAL MODULE (TSM) (2000)

1. Module ground to motorcycle
2. 12 VDC input from accessory circuit breaker
3. Pulsed 12 VDC for flashing right signal lights
4. Pulsed 12 VDC for flashing left signal lights
5. Speed sensor input from speedometer
6. Not used
7. 12 VDC input from right side handlebar switch
8. 12 VDC input from left side handlebar switch

the button is released and the time the turn signal is cancelled.

3. Repeat Step 1 and Step 2 for right and left turns at the midpoint of speed ranges No. 2 through No. 4.

4. If the distances observed in Steps 1-3 are not correct, check the following steps:

a. Check the TSM ground connection and module pin connections for corrosion.

b. Check all lamps and lamp connections.

c. Check the motorcycle speed sensor connections and ground for corrosion.

Time Test

This is an alternate test to the speed/distance test, to check if the TSM module is operating correctly. Measure the turn signal ON time at the four indicated constant speeds listed in **Table 7**.

If the TSM fails this test, replace the TSM and repeat with a good module.

Rider Preference Setting

If the rider desires the turn signals to flash for a longer or shorter distance that the pre-set time, perform the following:

1. Longer distance cycle—hold the turn signal longer and release it closer to the turning point.

2. Shorter distance cycle—press the button a second time to cancel the turn signals.

Turn Signal Module (TSM) Removal/Installation

Refer to **Figure 135**.

1. Remove the seat as described in Chapter Fourteen.

2. Disconnect the negative battery cable as described in this chapter.

3. Turn the ignition switch OFF.

4. Refer to *Electrical Panel* in this chapter to gain access to the TSM.

5. Disconnect thc eight-pin Deutsch connector from the module.

6. Remove the bolt securing the module to the electrical panel.

7. Install the module by reversing these removal steps while noting the following:

    a. Make sure the electrical connectors are free of corrosion.

    b. Tighten the bolt securely. Be sure to install the rubber washer.

    c. Make sure the turn signal and flasher systems work properly.

TURN SIGNAL MODULE AND TURN SIGNAL/SECURITY MODULE (2001-ON MODELS)

The turn signal module (TSM) is an electronic microprocessor that controls the turn signals and four-way hazard flasher. The turn signal module receives its information from the speedometer and turn signal switches. On models equipped with a security system (TSSM), it is incorporated into the TSM module. The bank angle sensor (BAS) provides motorcycle movement signals to the module. TSM and TSSM modules are not interchangeable.

The turn signal module, TSM or TSSM, is located on the electrical panel located in front of the rear wheel.

When there is a problem with either system, a diagnostic fault code(s) is set. The TSM or TSSM can only be tested with Harley-Davidson diagnostic equipment. The following information describes how the systems are designed to operate. If any portion of the module is inoperative, refer the testing to a Harley-Davidson dealership.

Turn Signal Operation

Automatic cancellation

NOTE
The TSM/TSSM will not cancel the signal before the turn is actually completed.

1. When the turn signal button is pressed and released, the system begins a 20 count. As long as the motorcycle is moving above 7 MPH (11 KPH) and the ISM does not receive any additional input, the turn signals will cancel after 20 bulb flashes.

2. If the motorcycle's speed drops to 7 MPH (11 KPH) or less, the turn signals will continue to flash. The count resumes when the motorcycle reaches 8 MPH (13 KPH) and

the turn signal will cancel when the total count equals 20 bulb flashes.

3. The turn signals will cancel two seconds after a turn of 45° or more is completed.

Manual cancellation

1. After the turn signal button is pressed and released, the system begins a 20 count. To cancel the turn signal, press the turn signal button a second time.

2. If the turn direction is changed, press the opposite turn signal button. The primary signal is cancelled and the opposite turn signal will flash.

Four-way flashing

1. Turn the ignition key to the ON position. On models so equipped, disarm the security system. Press the right and left turn signal buttons at the same time. All four turn signals will flash at the same time.

2. On models with the security system, the system can be armed so all four signals flash for up to two hours. Turn the ignition key to the OFF position and arm the security system. Press both the right and left turn signal buttons at the same time.

3. To cancel the four-way flashing, disarm the security system, on models so equipped, and press both the right and left turn signal buttons at the same time.

Bank angle sensor (BAS)

The bank angle sensor automatically shuts off the engine if the motorcycle tilts more than 45° for longer than one second. The shutoff will occur even at a very slow speed.

To restart the motorcycle, return the motorcycle to vertical. Turn the ignition key from OFF to ON, then restart the engine.

Security System (TSSM) Operation

If a theft attempt is detected and the TSSM is in operation, it immobilizes the starting and ignition systems. It also flashes the right and left turn signals alternately and sounds the siren, if so equipped. The following conditions activate the armed security system:

1. Small motorcycle movement—the turn signals flash three times and the optional siren chirps once. If the motorcycle is not returned to its original position, the warnings will reactivate after four seconds. This cycle will repeat a maximum of 255 times.

2. Large motorcycle movement—the system will activate for 30 seconds, then turn off. If the motorcycle is not returned to its original position, the warnings will reactivate after ten seconds. This cycle may repeat a maximum of ten times.

3. Tampering of the security lamp circuit—system activates for 30 seconds. The cycle will repeat for each tampering incident.

4. A battery ground or ground disconnect has occurred while the system is armed—the siren will sound, if so equipped, but the turn signals will not flash.

NOTE
Always disarm the optional TSSM prior to disconnecting the battery or the siren will sound. If the TSSM is in auto-alarming mode, disarm the system with two clicks of the key fob, and disconnect the battery or remove the TSSM fuse before the 30 second arming period expires.

Turn Signal Security Module (TSSM) Removal/Installation

1. Remove the seat as described in Chapter Fourteen.

2. Turn the ignition switch OFF.

3. Disconnect the negative battery cable as described in this chapter.

4. Refer to *Electrical Panel* in this chapter to gain access to the TSSM.

5. Carefully pull the TSSM (**Figure 138**) from the bracket on the electrical panel.

6. Disconnect the twelve-pin electrical Deutsch connector from the module and remove the module.

7. Install the module by reversing these removal steps. Note the following:

    a. Make sure the electrical connector is free of moisture.

    b. Make sure the protrusion on the module is secure in the hole in the electrical panel bracket.

    c. Make sure the turn signal and flasher systems work properly.

SPEEDOMETER SPEED SENSOR

8

All models are equipped with an electronic speedometer assembly that consists of the speedometer, speed sensor and function switch.

The speed sensor mounts on top of the transmission housing, directly over fourth gear.

Performance Check

The Harley-Davidson Speedometer Tester is required to check the performance of the speedometer.

NOTE
This test cannot be used to verify the calibration of the speedometer and will not verify the speedometer's function for legal proceedings. The test will verifies speedometer function for service diagnosis or repair, and verifies if the speedometer requires replacement.

Speedometer Speed Sensor Removal/Installation

The speedometer speed sensor mounts on top of the transmission case.

1. Remove the seat as described in Chapter Fourteen.

2. Disconnect the negative battery cable as described in this chapter.

3. Remove the Allen screw and remove the speed sensor (**Figure 139**) from the transmission case.

4. Disconnect the three-pin Mini-Deutsch connector containing one red, one black and one white wire.

5. Carefully pull the electrical connector out from under the frame crossmember. Disconnect the secondary locks on the Mini-Deutsch connector and disconnect the connector.

6. Tie a piece of string to the electrical connector. Tie the other end of the string to the frame crossmember.

7. Carefully pull the wiring harness and connector out of the frame on the right side. If the wire is tight or stuck, do not force it. If necessary, make a drawing of the wire routing through the frame. It is easy to forget the routing path after removing the wire.

8. Untie the string from the wiring harness.

9. Installation is the reverse of removal. Note the following:

    a. Tie the string to the wiring harness and connector.

    b. Carefully pull the string and the wiring harness and connector through the right side of the frame into position under the seat. Untie and remove the string.

    c. Apply a light coat of dielectric compound to the electrical connector(s) prior to installing them.

    d. Apply clean engine oil to the *new* O-ring on the speedometer sensor prior to installation. Install the sensor and tighten the Allen screw to 84-108 in.-lb (10-12 N•m).

STARTER RELAY SWITCH REPLACEMENT

The starter relay switch is mounted under the fuse cover on the left side of the frame.

1. Remove the seat as described in Chapter Fourteen.

2. Disconnect the negative battery cable as described in this chapter.

3. Pull straight up and remove the fuse block cover (**Figure 140**).

4. Unplug and remove the starter relay switch (A, **Figure 141**) from the rear fuse block.

5. Install by reversing these steps.

SPEEDOMETER AND INDICATOR LIGHTS

Removal/Installation

Refer to **Figure 127** and **Figure 128**.

1. Remove the seat.

> *NOTE*
> *Always disarm the optional TSSM security system prior to disconnecting the battery or the siren will sound.*

2. Disconnect the negative battery cable as described in this chapter.

3. Remove the fuel tank console as described under *Fuel Tank Console* in Chapter Seven.

4. Turn the fuel tank console over onto towels on the workbench.

5. If still in place, remove the rubber boot from the reset switch, then remove the nut securing the reset switch from the side of the fuel tank console.

6A. On FSXST models, perform the following:

    a. Unhook the retaining clip securing the indicator lamp wire to the backside of the speedometer.

    b. Disengage the clips securing the speedometer back clamp to the fuel tank console.

    c. Remove the speedometer and back clamp from the fuel tank console.

    d. If necessary, disengage the clips securing the back clamp to the speedometer and remove the back clamp.

6B. On all models except FXSTD, perform the following:

    a. Use a flat blade screwdriver and carefully pry between the three locking tabs on the back clamp (A, **Figure 142**) and the speedometer. Raise the back clamp, release it from the speedometer and remove the back clamp.

    b. Remove the speedometer (**Figure 143**) from the fuel tank console.

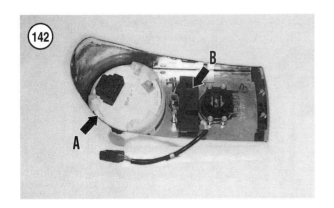

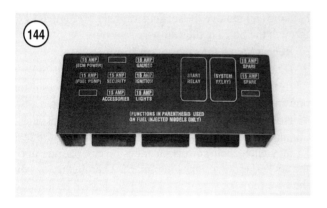

c. Remove the gasket from the speedometer.

7. To remove the indictor light assembly (B, **Figure 142**), depress the locking tabs and remove the light assembly from the fuel tank console.

8. Installation is the reverse of removal.

FUSES

All models are equipped with a series of 15 amp fuses to protect the electrical system. The number of fuses varies depending on the model. Refer to the wiring diagrams at the end of the manual.

The fuse panel is located under the seat, behind the battery. If there is an electrical failure, first check for a blown fuse. A blown fuse has a break in the element.

Whenever a fuse blows, find the reason for the failure before replacing the fuse. Usually, the trouble is a short circuit in the wiring. This may be caused by worn-through insulation or a disconnected wire shorted to ground. Check the circuit that the fuse protects.

Replacement

1. Remove the seat as described in Chapter Fourteen.

NOTE
Always disarm the optional TSSM security system prior to disconnecting the battery or the siren will sound.

2. Disconnect the negative battery cable as described in this chapter.
3. Pull straight up and remove the fuse block cover (**Figure 140**).

NOTE
Fuse description and location is printed on the fuse block cover (Figure 144).

4. Locate the blown fuse (B, **Figure 141**) and install a new fuse with the *same* amperage.

NOTE
Always carry spare fuses.

CIRCUIT BREAKER

All models use a single 30 amp circuit breaker to protect the electrical circuits.

Whenever a failure occurs in any part of the electrical system, the circuit breaker is self-resetting and will automatically return power to the circuit when the electrical fault is found and corrected.

CAUTION
If the electrical fault is not found and corrected, the circuit breaker will cycle on and off continuously. This will cause the motorcycle to run erratically.

Usually the problem causing a short circuit is in the wiring connected to the circuit breaker.

Determine the circuits protected by the circuit breaker by following the wiring diagrams at the end of the manual.

8

Do not consider a tripped circuit breaker a minor annoyance; it indicates something is wrong in the electrical system and must be corrected immediately.

Replacement

The circuit breaker is located on the electrical pan forward of the rear wheel.

1. Remove the seat as described in Chapter Fourteen.
2. Turn the ignition switch OFF.
3. Disconnect the negative battery cable as described in this chapter.
4. Refer to *Electrical Panel* in this chapter to gain access to the circuit breaker.

NOTE
Record the wire's colors and the terminal to which they are connected. The wires must be reinstalled onto the correct terminal.

5. Remove the nuts and wire connections at the circuit breaker (**Figure 145**).
6. Remove the circuit breaker from the mounting bracket on the electrical panel.
7. Install the circuit breaker by reversing these steps.

ELECTRICAL CONNECTOR SERVICE

A variety of electrical connectors are used throughout the electrical system. The following procedures are for disassembly of the connector in order to replace an individual electrical wire in the connector.

These connectors are designed for a superior seal to prevent dirt and moisture from entering the connector and damaging a pin connector.

Deutsch Electrical Connectors Socket Terminal Removal/Installation

This procedure shows how to remove and install the socket terminals from the socket housing connector half. This procedure is shown on a 12-pin Duetsch connector and is the same for two-, three-, four- and six-pin Duetsch connectors.

Refer to **Figure 146** and **Figure 147**.

1. Remove the seat as described in Chapter Fourteen.

NOTE
Always disarm the optional TSSM security system prior to disconnecting the battery or the siren will sound.

2. Disconnect the negative battery cable as described in this chapter.
3. Disconnect the connector housing.
4. Remove the secondary locking wedge (7, **Figure 147**) as follows:
   a. Locate the secondary locking wedge in **Figure 146** or **Figure 147**.
   b. Insert a wide-blade screwdriver between the socket housing and the locking wedge. Turn the screwdriver 90° to force the wedge up (**Figure 148**).
   c. Remove the secondary locking wedge (7, **Figure 147**).
5. Lightly press the terminal latches inside the socket housing and remove the socket terminal (14, **Figure 147**) through the holes in the rear wire seal.
6. Repeat Step 5 for each socket terminal.
7. If necessary, remove the wire seal (12, **Figure 147**).
8. Install the wire seal (12, **Figure 147**) into the socket housing if it was removed.
9. Hold onto the socket housing and insert the socket terminals (14, **Figure 147**) through the holes in the wire seal so they enter their correct chamber hole. Continue until the socket terminal locks into place. Then lightly tug on the wire to make sure it is locked into place.
10. Set the internal seal (8, **Figure 147**) onto the socket housing if it was removed.

NOTE
*With the exception of the three-pin Duetsch connector, all of the secondary locking wedges are symmetrical. When assembling the three-pin connector, install the connector so the arrow on the secondary locking wedge is pointing toward the external latch as shown in **Figure 149**.*

NOTE
If the secondary locking wedge does not slide into position easily, one or more of the

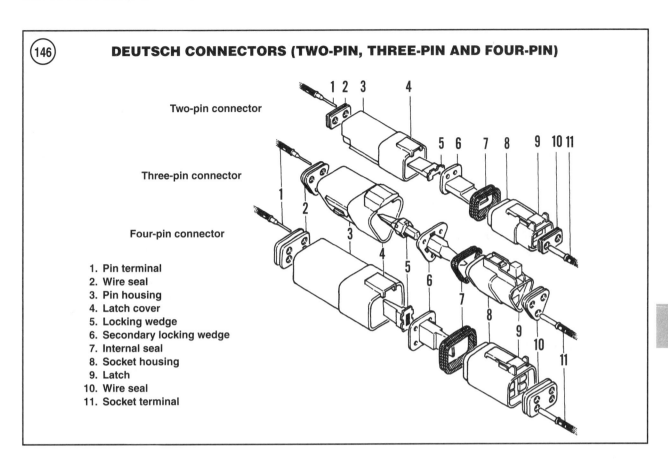

⑴⁴⁶ **DEUTSCH CONNECTORS (TWO-PIN, THREE-PIN AND FOUR-PIN)**

Two-pin connector

Three-pin connector

Four-pin connector

1. Pin terminal
2. Wire seal
3. Pin housing
4. Latch cover
5. Locking wedge
6. Secondary locking wedge
7. Internal seal
8. Socket housing
9. Latch
10. Wire seal
11. Socket terminal

8

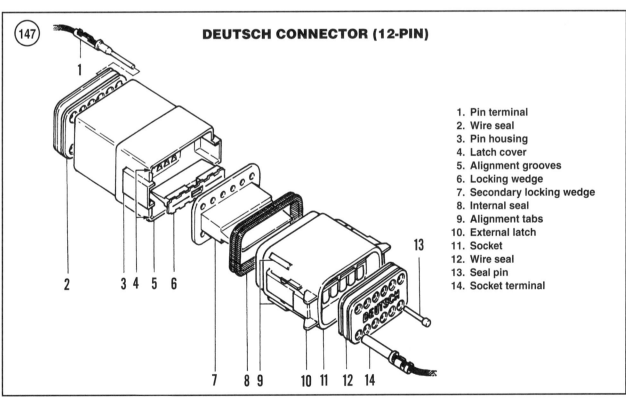

⑴⁴⁷ **DEUTSCH CONNECTOR (12-PIN)**

1. Pin terminal
2. Wire seal
3. Pin housing
4. Latch cover
5. Alignment grooves
6. Locking wedge
7. Secondary locking wedge
8. Internal seal
9. Alignment tabs
10. External latch
11. Socket
12. Wire seal
13. Seal pin
14. Socket terminal

*socket terminals are not installed correctly.
Correct the problem at this time.*

11. Install the secondary locking wedge into the socket housing as shown in **Figure 146** or **Figure 147**. Press the secondary locking wedge down until it locks into place.

Deutsch Electrical Connectors Pin Terminal Removal/Installation

This procedure shows how to remove and install the pin terminals from the pin housing connector half. This procedure is shown on a 12-pin Duetsch connector and relates to all of the Duetsch connectors (two-, three-, four- and six-pin).

Refer to **Figure 146** and **Figure 147**.

1. Remove the seat as described in Chapter Fourteen.

> *NOTE*
> *Always disarm the optional TSSM security system prior to disconnecting the battery or the siren will sound.*

2. Disconnect the negative battery cable as described in this chapter.

3. Disconnect the connector housing.

4. Use needlenose pliers to remove the locking wedge (6, **Figure 147**).

5. Lightly press the terminal latches inside the pin housing and remove the pin terminal(s) (1, **Figure 147**) through the holes in the rear wire seal.

6. Repeat Step 5 for each socket terminal.

7. If necessary, remove the wire seal (2, **Figure 147**).

8. Install the wire seal (2, **Figure 147**) into the socket housing if it was removed.

9. Hold onto the pin housing and insert the pin terminals (1, **Figure 147**) through the holes in the wire seal so they enter their correct chamber hole. Continue until the pin terminal locks into place. Then lightly tug on the wire to make sure it is locked into place.

> *NOTE*
> *With the exception of the three-pin Duetsch connector, all of the secondary locking wedges are symmetrical. When assembling the three-pin connector, install the connector so the arrow on the secondary locking wedge is pointing toward the external latch as shown in Figure 149.*

> *NOTE*
> *If the locking wedge does not slide into position easily, one or more of the pin termi-*

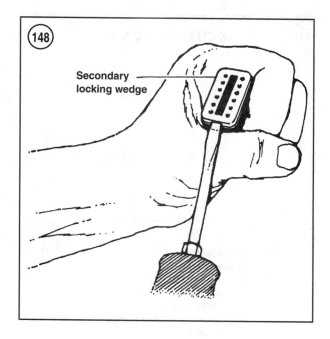

Secondary locking wedge

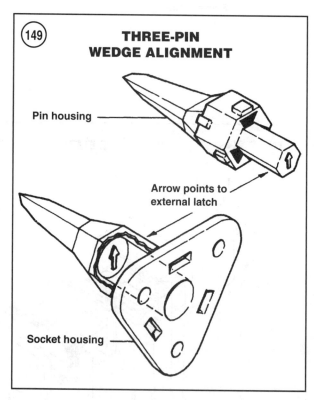

THREE-PIN
WEDGE ALIGNMENT

Pin housing

Arrow points to external latch

Socket housing

nals are not installed correctly. Correct the problem at this time.

10. Install the locking wedge into the pin housing as shown in **Figure 146** or **Figure 147**. Press the secondary locking wedge down until it locks into place. When prop-

(150) PACKARD CONNECTORS EXTERNAL LATCH TYPE

IAT sensor connector

Two-place

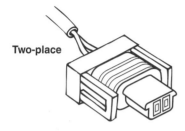

ET sensor connector

Two-place

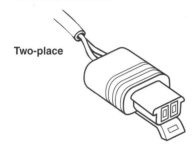

TP sensor connector

Three-place

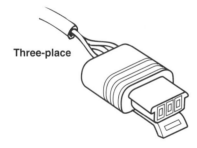

IAC valve connector

Four-place

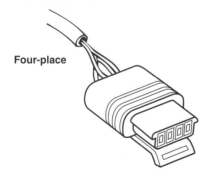

(151) PACKARD TERMINALS

1. Locate tang on latch side of chamber

2. Pivot end of pin to depress tang

3. Push on wire end of lead to remove terminal

4. Raise tang and reinstall terminal

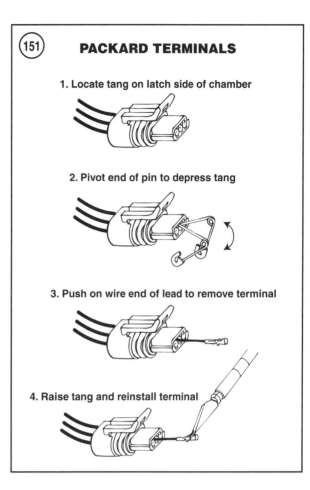

8

erly installed, the wedge will fit into the pin housing center groove.

Packard Electrical Connectors External Latch Type Removal/Installation

This procedure shows how to remove and install the electrical terminals from the external latch type connectors with pull-to-seat terminals (**Figure 150**).

1. Remove the seat as described in Chapter Fourteen.

NOTE
Always disarm the optional TSSM security system prior to disconnecting the battery or the siren will sound.

2. Disconnect the negative battery cable as described in this chapter.

3. Bend back the external latch(es) slightly and separate the connector.

4. Look into the mating end of the connector and locate the locking tang (1, **Figure 151**) in the middle chamber

and on the external latch side of connector. On locking ear connectors, the tang is on the side opposite the ear.

5. Insert the point of a one-inch safety pin about 1/8 in. into the middle chamber (2, **Figure 151**). Pivot the end of the safety pin up toward the terminal body until a click is heard. Repeat this step several times. The click is the tang returning to the locked position as it slips from the point of the safety pin. Continue to pick at the tang until the clicking stops and the safety pin seems to slide in at a slightly greater depth indicating the tang has been depressed.

6. Remove the safety pin, push the wire end of the lead and remove the lead from the connector (3, **Figure 151**). If additional slack is necessary, pull back on the harness conduit and remove the wire seal at the back of the connector.

7. To install the terminal and wire back into the connector, use a thin flat blade of an X-Acto knife to carefully bend the tang away from the terminal (4, **Figure 151**).

8. Carefully pull the lead and terminal into the connector until a click is heard indicating the terminal is seated correctly within the connector. Gently push on the lead to ensure the terminal is correctly seated.

9. If necessary, install the wire seal and push the harness conduit back into position on the backside of the connector.

10. Push the socket halves together until the latch(es) are locked together.

Packard Electrical Connectors Wire Form Type Removal/Installation

This procedure shows how to remove and install the electrical terminals from the wire form type latch connectors with pull-to-seat terminals (**Figure 152**).

1. Remove the seat as described in Chapter Fourteen.

> *NOTE*
> *Always disarm the optional TSSM security system prior to disconnecting the battery or the siren will sound.*

2. Disconnect the negative battery cable as described in this chapter.

3. Depress the wire form and separate the connector.

4. Hold the connector so the wire form is facing down.

5. Look into the mating end of the connector and locate the plastic rib that separates the wire terminals. The terminal is on each side of the rib with the tang at the rear.

6. Use the thin flat blade of an X-Acto knife to depress the tang. Tilt the blade at an angle and place the tip at the inboard edge of the terminal. Push down slightly until the spring tension is relieved and a click is heard. Repeat this

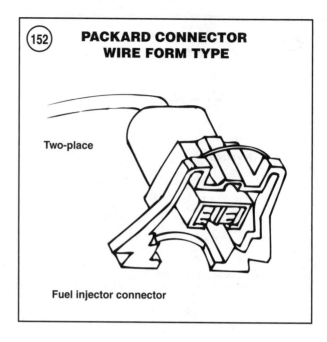

PACKARD CONNECTOR WIRE FORM TYPE

Two-place

Fuel injector connector

step several times. The click represents the tang returning to the locked position as it slips from the point of the knife blade. Continue to push down until the clicking stops indicating the tang has been depressed.

7. Remove the knife blade, push the wire end of the lead and remove the lead from the connector. If additional slack is necessary, pull back on the harness conduit and remove the wire seal at the back of the connector.

8. To install the terminal and wire back into the connector, use a thin flat blade of an X-Acto knife to carefully bend the tang away from the terminal.

9. Carefully pull the lead and terminal into the connector until a click is heard indicating the terminal is seated correctly within the connector. Gently pull on the lead to ensure the terminal is correctly seated.

10. If necessary, install the wire seal and push the harness conduit back into position on the backside of the connector.

11. Push the socket halves together until the latch(es) are locked together.

Amp Electrical Connectors Socket and Pin Terminals Removal/Installation

This procedure shows how to remove and install the socket and pin terminals from the pin and socket housing connector. This procedure relates to all of the Amp connectors (three-, six- and ten-pin).

Refer to **Figure 153**.

1. Remove the seat as described in Chapter Fourteen.

AMP MULTILOCK CONNECTORS

Three-place connector

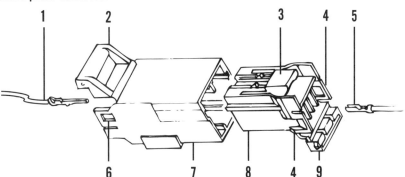

Six-place connector

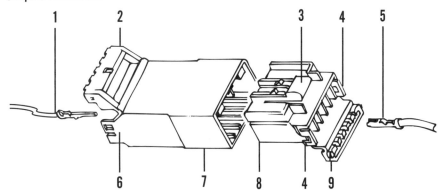

Ten-place connector

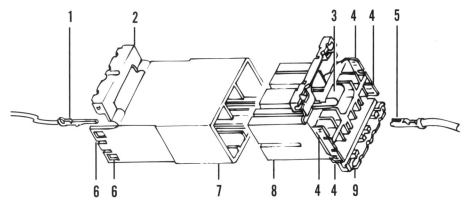

1. Pin terminal
2. Secondary lock
3. Button
4. Latch
5. Socket terminal
6. Latch
7. Pin housing
8. Socket housing
9. Secondary lock

153

8

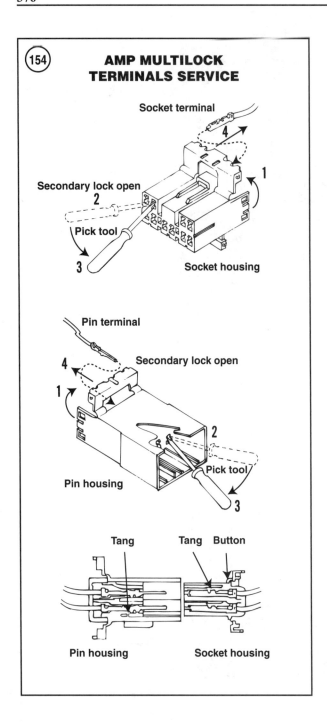

AMP MULTILOCK TERMINALS SERVICE

Socket terminal

Secondary lock open

Pick tool

Socket housing

Pin terminal

Secondary lock open

Pin housing

Pick tool

Tang   Tang   Button

Pin housing   Socket housing

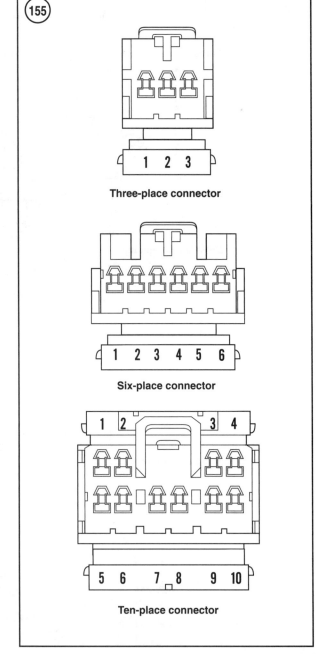

1 2 3

Three-place connector

1 2 3 4 5 6

Six-place connector

1 2   3 4

5 6   7 8   9 10

Ten-place connector

NOTE
Always disarm the optional TSSM security system prior to disconnecting the battery or the siren will sound.

2. Disconnect the negative battery cable as described in this chapter.

3. Press the button on the socket on the terminal side and pull the connector apart.

4. Slightly bend the latch back and free one side of the secondary lock. Repeat this step for the other side.

5. Rotate the secondary lock (**Figure 154**) out on the hinge to access the terminals within the connector.

NOTE
Do not pull too hard on the wire until the tang is released or the terminal will be difficult to remove.

6. Insert a pick tool (2, **Figure 154**) into the flat edge of the terminal cavity until it stops. Pivot the pick tool away (3) from the terminal and gently pull on the wire to pull the terminal (4) from the terminal cavity. Note the wire location number on the connector (**Figure 155**).

NOTE
The release button used to separate the connectors is at the top of the connector.

7. The tang in the chamber engages the pin terminal slot to lock the terminal into position. The tangs (**Figure 154**) are located as follows:

a. Pin housing side—the tangs are located at the bottom of each chamber. The pin terminal slot, on the side opposite the crimp tails, must face downward.

b. Socket housing side—the tangs are located at the top of each chamber. The pin terminal slot, on the same side as the crimp tails, must face upward.

8. On the secondary lock side of the connector, push the wire and terminal into the correct location until it snaps into place. Gently pull on the lead to ensure the terminal is correctly seated.

9. Rotate the hinged secondary lock down and inward until the tabs are fully engaged with the latches on both sides of the connector. Pull upward to make sure the tabs are locked in place.

10. Insert the socket housing into the pin housing and push it in until it locks into place.

WIRING DIAGRAMS

Wiring diagrams are located at the end of this manual.

8

Table 1 ELECTRICAL SPECIFICATIONS

Item	Specification
Battery capacity	12 volts, 19 amp hour/270 CCA*
Maximum current draw	5.5 mA
Alternator	
AC voltage output	
Carbureted	16-20 volts per 1000 rpm
EFI	19-26 VAC per 1000 rpm
Stator coil resistance	0.1-0.3 ohm
Voltage regulator	
Voltage output @ 3600 rpm	14.3-14.7 @ 75° F (24° C)
Amps @ 3000 rpm	
Carbureted	34-40 amps
EFI	41-48 amps
Ignition coil	
Primary resistance	0.5-0.7 ohm
Secondary resistance	5500-7500 ohms
Spark plug cable resistance	
Short cable (7.25 in./184 mm)	1812-4375 ohms
Long cable (19.0 in./483 mm)	4750-11,230 ohms
Circuit breaker	30 amp
Fuses	
Ignition	15 amp
Lighting	15 amp
Accessory	15 amp
Instrument	15 amp
Security	15 amp
Fuel pump (EFI)	15 amp
Electronic control module (EFI)	15 amp
* CCA. Cold cranking amperage	

Table 2 BATTERY CHARGING RATES/TIMES (APPROXIMATE)

Voltage	% of charge	3 amp charger	6 amp charger	10 amp charger	20 amp charger
12.8	100%	–	–	–	–
12.6	75%	1.75 hours	50 minutes	30 minutes	15 minutes
12.3	50%	3.5 hours	1.75 hours	1 hour	30 minutes
12.0	25%	5 hours	2.5 hours	1.5 hours	45 minutes
11.8	0%	6 hours and 40 minutes	3 hours and 20 minutes	2 hours	1 hour

Table 3 STARTER MOTOR SPECIFICATIONS

Minimum no-load speed @ 11.5 volts	3000 rpm
Maximum no-load current @ 11.5 volts	90 amp
Current draw	
normal	160-180 amps
maximum	200 amps
Brush length (minimum)	0.433 in. (11.0 mm)
Commutator diameter (minimum)	1.141 in. (28.981)

Table 4 REPLACEMENT BULBS

Item	wattage × quantity
Headlamp	
FLS models	40/60
FXS models	60/55
Position lamp[1]	4
Passing lamps	30
Fog lamps[1]	35
Tail lamp	7
Tail lamp[1]	5
Stop lamp	27
Stop lamp[1]	21
License plate lamp	
FLST/I	4.2
All models except FLST[1]	5
Front turn signal/running light	27/7 × 2
Front turn signal[1]	21 × 2
Rear turn signal	27 × 2
Rear turn signal[1]	21 × 2
Fender tip lamps	
FLSTC	1
FLSTS	4.2
1. Indicates bulb specification for HD International models.	

Table 5 ELECTRICAL SYSTEM TORQUE SPECIFICATIONS

Item	ft.-lb.	in.-lb.	N•m
Alternator stator Torx screws			
2000	–	30-40	3-5
2001-on	–	55-75	6-9
Camshaft position sensor (2000 only)			
Inspection cover screws	–	20-30	2-3
Sensor mounting screw	–	20-30	2-3
Crankshaft position sensor (CKP)			
Allen screw	–	90-120	10-14
Engine temperature sensor (EFI)	10-15	–	14-20
Fuel gauge sending unit			
Plate screws	–	16-22	2-3
Fuel tank console nut	–	80-100	9-11
Handlebar switch housing screws	–	35-45	4-5
Headlight adjust bolts			
FXSTS, FLSTS	25-35	–	34-48
FLSTC, FXSTB, FXST			
Horizontal bolt	30-35	–	41-48
Vertical bolt	35-45	–	48-61
FXSTD	25-30	–	34-41
Horn			
Mounting nut	–	110-120	12-14
Screws	–	23-28	2.6-3
Ignition coil bolts	10-15	–	14-20
Ignition module			
Mounting screws	–	15-21	1.7-2.4
Mounting nuts	–	30-35	3.4-4.0
Mounting plate nuts	–	70-80	8-9
Ignition switch Allen bolts			
(all FLHT models)	–	40-50	5-6
MAP sensor screw	–	25-35	3-4
Jackshaft lockplate bolt	–	84-108	9-12
Speed sensor screw	–	84-108	10-12
Starter			
Mounting bolts	13-20	–	18-27
Positive terminal nut	–	65-80	7-9
Switches			
Neutral	–	120-180	14-20
Oil pressure	–	96-144	11-16
Rear brake light	–	96-120	11-14
Tail/brake light			
Base screws	–	40-48	5-6
Lens screws	–	20-24	2-3
Voltage regulator			
Mounting bracket bolt	–	70-100	8-11
Mounting bolt	–	50-80	6-9

8

Table 6 TURN SIGNAL DISTANCE TEST (2000 ONLY)

Range	1	2	3	4
MPH	0-34	35-44	45-60	61+
KMH	0-56	56-71	72-97	98+
Feet	221	339	680	1051
Miles	0.04	0.06	0.13	0.20
Meters	67	103	207	320

Table 7 TURN SIGNAL TIME TEST (2000 ONLY)

Constant speed		
MPH	KMH	Turn signal ON time in seconds
25	40	5-7
38	61	5-7
52	84	8-10
65	105	10-12

CHAPTER NINE

WHEELS, HUBS AND TIRES

This chapter includes procedures for disassembly and repair of the front and rear wheels, and hubs and tire service. For routine maintenance, see Chapter Three.

Tables 1-3 are at the end of the chapter.

MOTORCYCLE STANDS

Many procedures in this chapter require the front or rear wheel to be lifted off the ground. A quality motorcycle front end stand (**Figure 1**), swing arm stand or suitable size jack is required. Before purchasing or using a stand, check the manufacturer's instructions to make sure the stand will work with the specific model being worked on. If any adjustments or accessories are required, perform the necessary adjustments and install the correct parts before lifting the motorcycle. When using the stand, have an assistant standing by to help. Some means to tie down one end of the motorcycle may also be required. Make sure the motorcycle is properly supported on the stand.

If a motorcycle stand is not available, use a scissor jack (**Figure 2**) with adapters that securely fit onto the frame tubes (**Figure 3**).

FRONT WHEEL

Removal (Non-Springer Fork Models)

1. Support the motorcycle with the front wheel off the ground. See *Motorcycle Stands* in this chapter.

2. Remove the caliper mounting bolts and remove the caliper (A, **Figure 4**) as described in Chapter Thirteen.

> *NOTE*
> *Place a plastic or wooden spacer between the brake pads in place of the disc. Then, if the brake lever is inadvertently applied, the pistons will not be forced out of the caliper. If the pistons are forced out, disassemble the caliper to reseat the pistons.*

3. On all models except FXSTD, insert a drift or screwdriver through the front axle hole on the right side to prevent it from rotating in the next step.

> *NOTE*
> *On FXSTD models, the front axle is equipped with two axle nuts. Loosen and remove only the left side axle nut.*

4A. On FXSTD models, loosen and remove the *left side* axle nut, lockwasher and flat washer.

4B. On all other models, loosen and remove the axle nut (B, **Figure 4**), lockwasher and flat washer.

5. On the right side, loosen the fork slider axle clamp nuts (**Figure 5**, typical).

6. Prior to removing the front axle, note the location of the right side spacer and left side spacer. The spacers must be reinstalled on the correct sides during installation.

7. Withdraw the front axle (**Figure 6**) from the fork sliders and front wheel.

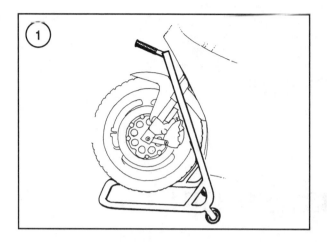

8. Pull the wheel away from the fork sliders and remove it.

9. On FLSTC models, the hub cap and spacer will come off with the wheel.

NOTE
The wheel spacers are different. Label the spacers before removing them.

10. On 2002-on FXSTD models, remove the outer right side spacer.

11. Remove the spacers from the right side (**Figure 7**) and the left side (**Figure 8**) of the wheel.

CAUTION
Do not set the wheel down on the brake disc surface, as it may be damaged.

12. Inspect the front wheel assembly as described in this chapter.

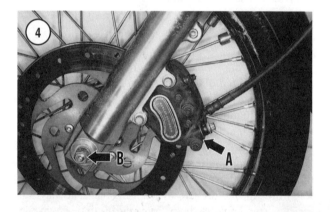

Installation
(Non-Springer Fork Models)

1. Clean the axle in solvent and dry it thoroughly. Make sure the axle bearing surfaces on both fork sliders and the axle are free of burrs and nicks.

2. Apply an antiseize lubricant to the axle shaft prior to installation.

3. If the oil seals or bearings were replaced, check front axle spacer alignment as described under *Front Hub* in this chapter.

4. Install the spacer onto the right side (**Figure 7**) and the left side (**Figure 8**) of the wheel.

5. On 2002-on FXSTD models, install the outer right side spacer.

6. On FLSTC models, install the hub cap and spacer on the right side of the wheel.

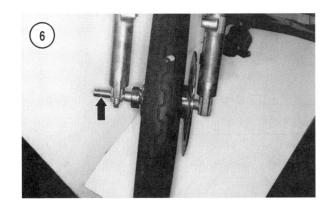

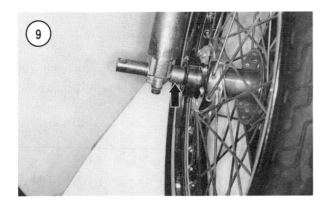

9

7. Install the wheel between the fork sliders and install the axle from the right side. Push the front axle through the right side fork, spacer (**Figure 9**), through the hub, the left side spacer (**Figure 10**) and left side fork.

8. Make sure axle spacers are installed correctly.

9A. On FXSTD models, install the flat washer, lockwasher and the *left side* axle nut finger-tight. Make sure axle spacers are installed correctly.

9B. On all other models, install the flat washer, lockwasher and axle nut (**Figure 11**) finger-tight.

10. On all models except FXSTD, insert a drift or screwdriver through the front axle hole on the right side to prevent it from rotating in the next step.

11. Tighten the front axle nut (B, **Figure 4**) to 50-55 ft.-lb. (68-75 N•m).

12. On the right side fork slider, tighten the nuts on the fork slider cap (**Figure 5**) to 11-15 ft.-lb. (15-20 N•m).

13. Make sure the front wheel is centered between the fork sliders. If it is not, check the position of the left and right axle spacers.

14. Install the front brake caliper (A, **Figure 4**) as described in Chapter Thirteen.

15. With the front wheel off the ground, rotate it several times and apply the front brake to seat the brake pads against the disc.

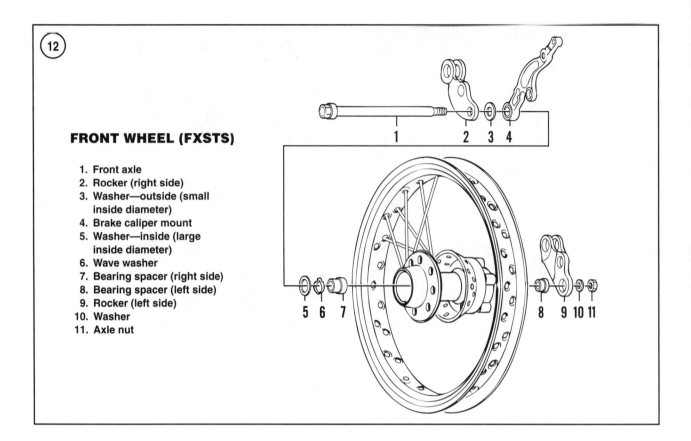

FRONT WHEEL (FXSTS)

1. Front axle
2. Rocker (right side)
3. Washer—outside (small inside diameter)
4. Brake caliper mount
5. Washer—inside (large inside diameter)
6. Wave washer
7. Bearing spacer (right side)
8. Bearing spacer (left side)
9. Rocker (left side)
10. Washer
11. Axle nut

16. Remove the stand and lower the front wheel to the ground.

Removal
(Springer Fork [FXSTS Models])

Refer to **Figure 12**.

1. Support the motorcycle with the front wheel off the ground. See *Motorcycle Stands* in this chapter.
2. Remove the front fender as described in Chapter Fourteen.
3. Remove the caliper as described in Chapter Thirteen.

NOTE
Place a plastic or wooden spacer between the brake pads in place of the disc. Then, if the brake lever is inadvertently applied, the pistons will not be forced out of the calipers. If the pistons are forced out, disassemble the caliper to reseat the pistons.

4. On the left side, loosen and remove the axle nut (**Figure 13**) and flat washer (**Figure 14**). Discard the axle nut.
5. Prior to removing the front axle, note the location of the right side spacer and left side spacer. The spacers must be reinstalled on the correct sides during installation.

NOTE
There are several small washers located between the wheel hub and the brake caliper mount and the fork rockers. Do not misplace them.

6. On the right side, *slowly* withdraw the front axle (A, **Figure 15**) from the left side fork rocker, front wheel, brake caliper mount (B) and right side fork rocker (C).

7. Roll the front wheel away from the fork rockers and remove the brake caliper mount (**Figure 16**).

NOTE
The right and left side wheel bearing spacers are different. Label the spacers before removing them.

8. On the right side of the wheel, perform the following:
   a. Remove the outside washer (small inner diameter) from between the rocker and the brake caliper mount.
   b. Remove the inside washer (large inner diameter) (**Figure 17**) and wave washer (**Figure 18**) from the bearing spacer.
   c. Remove the bearing spacer (**Figure 19**) from the hub.

CAUTION
Do not set the wheel down on the brake disc surface, as it may be damaged.

9. Inspect the front wheel assembly as described in this chapter.

Installation
(Springer Fork [FXSTS Models])

1. Clean the axle in solvent and dry it thoroughly. Make sure the axle bearing surfaces on both fork rockers, the

brake caliper mount bushing and the axle are free of burrs and nicks.

2. Apply an antiseize lubricant to the axle shaft prior to installation.

3. Move the wheel into position between the fork rockers.

4. Install the left side bearing spacer into the hub.

5. On the right side of the wheel, perform the following:

    a. Correctly position the bearing spacer (**Figure 20**) and install it into the hub.

    b. Install the wave washer (**Figure 18**) onto the bearing spacer.

    c. Install the inside washer (large inner diameter) (**Figure 17**) onto the bearing spacer.

    d. Correctly position the brake caliper mount (**Figure 21**) and install it onto the bearing spacer.

6. On the right side, *slowly* install the front axle (A, **Figure 15**) through the right side fork rocker (C), the outside washer (small inner diameter), brake caliper mount (B), front wheel and left side fork rocker.

7. Push the front axle all the way through until it bottoms.

8. On the left side, install the flat washer (**Figure 14**) and *new* axle nut (**Figure 13**).

9. Hold the front axle stationery and tighten the axle nut (**Figure 13**) to 60-65 ft.-lb. (81-88 N•m).

10. Make sure the front wheel is centered between the fork rockers. If it is not, check the position of the left and right bearing spacers.

11. Install the caliper as described in Chapter Thirteen.

12. Install the front fender as described in Chapter Fourteen.

13. With the front wheel off the ground, rotate it several times and apply the front brake to seat the brake pads against the disc.

14. Remove the stand and lower the front wheel to the ground.

Removal
(Springer Fork [FLSTS Models])

Refer to **Figure 22**.

1. Support the motorcycle with the front wheel off the ground. See *Motorcycle Stands* in this chapter.

2. Remove the caliper mounting bolts and remove the caliper as described in Chapter Thirteen.

NOTE
Place a plastic or wooden spacer between the brake pads in place of the disc. Then, if the brake lever is inadvertently applied, the pistons will not be forced out of the caliper. If the pistons are forced out, disassemble the caliper to reseat the pistons.

3. Remove the hub cap and seal from each side. Use the Harley-Davidson special tool, Hub Cap Remover/Installer (part No. HD-41494), or an equivalent.

4. On the left side, remove the retaining pin, then loosen and remove the front axle nut.

5. Remove the left side outer spacer, nylon insert and O-ring from the front axle.

NOTE
The front fender will remain attached to the fork assembly after the front axle is removed.

6. On the right side, *slowly* withdraw the front axle from the left side fork rocker, rubber spacer, Teflon-coated washer, brake caliper mount, left side bearing spacer, front hub, right side bearing spacer and right side fork rocker. As the front axle is withdrawn, catch the nylon insert and right side outer spacer. The right side O-ring may come off or stay with the front fender.

7. Pull the wheel away from the fork rockers and remove it.

NOTE
The wheel bearing spacers are different. Label the bearing spacers before removing them.

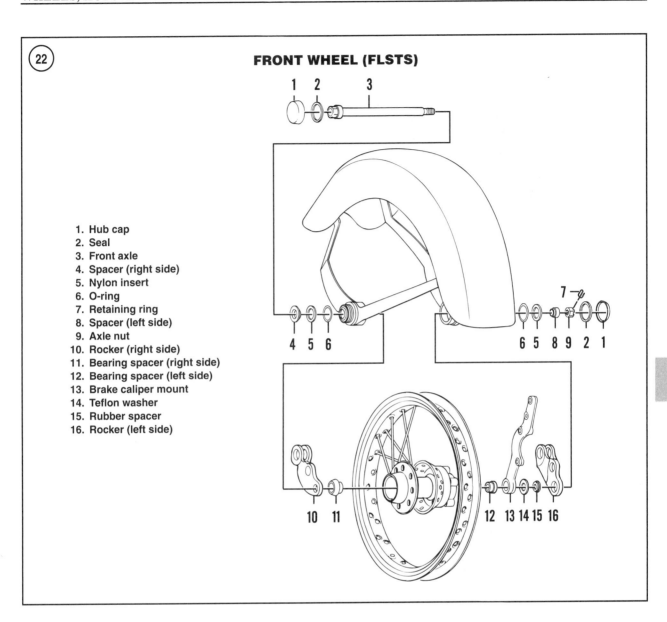

FRONT WHEEL (FLSTS)

1. Hub cap
2. Seal
3. Front axle
4. Spacer (right side)
5. Nylon insert
6. O-ring
7. Retaining ring
8. Spacer (left side)
9. Axle nut
10. Rocker (right side)
11. Bearing spacer (right side)
12. Bearing spacer (left side)
13. Brake caliper mount
14. Teflon washer
15. Rubber spacer
16. Rocker (left side)

9

8. Remove the bearing spacers from the right side and the left side of the wheel.

CAUTION
Do not set the wheel down on the brake disc surface, as it may be damaged.

9. Inspect the front wheel assembly as described in this chapter.

Installation
(Springer Fork [FLSTS Models])

1. Clean the axle in solvent and dry it thoroughly. Make sure the axle bearing surfaces on both fork rockers, the brake caliper mount bushing, the front fender mounts and the axle are free of burrs and nicks.

2. Apply an antiseize lubricant to the axle shaft prior to installation.

3. Install the spacer onto the right side and the left side of the wheel.

4. Insert the front axle in from the right side as follows:
   a. Right side spacer, nylon insert and O-ring.
   b. Right side fender brace.
   c. Right side rocker.
   d. Right side bearing spacer.
   e. Through the left side of the hub and the left side bearing spacer.
   f. Brake caliper mount and the Teflon-coated washer.

g. Rubber spacer and left side rocker.

h. Left side fender brace, O-ring, nylon washer.

5. Push the front axle all the way through until it bottoms.

6. Install a *new* axle nut.

7. Hold the front axle stationery and tighten the axle nut to 60-65 ft.-lb. (81-88 N•m). If necessary, tighten the rear axle nut to align the nut slot with the axle retaining pin hole.

8. Install the retaining pin and make sure it seats correctly.

9. Make sure the front wheel is centered between the fork sliders. If it is not, check the position of the left and right axle spacers.

10. Install the right and left side hub caps and seals. Use the same tool set-up and tighten the hub cap 1/4 turn after it make contact with the fender boss.

11. Install the front brake caliper as described in Chapter Fourteen.

12. With the front wheel off the ground, rotate it several times and apply the front brake to seat the brake pads against the disc.

13. Remove the stand and lower the front wheel to the ground.

Inspection (All Models)

Replace worn or damaged parts as described in this section.

1. Turn each bearing inner race by hand (**Figure 23**, typical). The bearing should turn smoothly. Some axial play is normal, but radial play should be negligible. See **Figure 24**. If one bearing is damaged, replace both bearings as a set. Refer to *Front and Rear Hubs* in this chapter.

2. Clean the axle and axle spacers in solvent to remove all grease and dirt. Make sure the axle contact surfaces are clean and free of dirt and old grease.

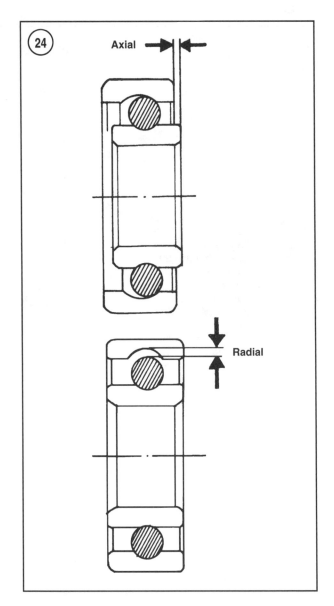

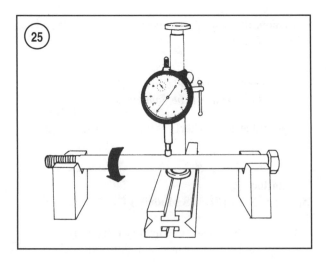

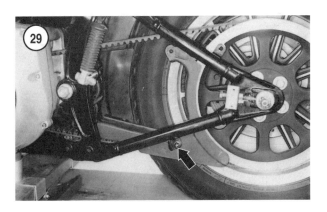

3. On Springer fork models, inspect the Teflon-coated washers. If the coating is worn through to expose the brass underneath; replace the washer.

4. Check the axle runout with a set of V-blocks and a dial indicator (**Figure 25**).

5. Check the spacers for wear, burrs and damage. Replace as necessary.

6. Check the brake disc bolts for tightness. To service the brake disc, refer to Chapter Twelve.

7. Check wheel runout and spoke tension (laced wheels) as described in this chapter.

REAR WHEEL

Removal

1. On models so equipped, remove saddlebags as described in Chapter Fourteen.

2. Remove both mufflers as described in Chapter Seven.

3. Support the motorcycle with an appropriate size jack with the rear wheel off the ground.

4. On models equipped with the optional chrome cover, perform the following:

    a. Remove the bolts and the rear axle chrome cover (**Figure 26**).

    b. If necessary, remove the mounting bracket (**Figure 27**) from the drive belt adjuster.

5. Remove the bolts securing the drive belt guard (**Figure 28**) and the debris deflector (**Figure 29**). Remove the belt guard and the deflector.

> *NOTE*
> *The rear wheel is heavy and can be difficult to remove. Check the tire-to-ground clearance before removing the rear axle. If necessary, have an assistant help in the removal or place wooden blocks under it.*

6. On HDI models, remove the axle nut cover.

7. Remove the spring clip (**Figure 30**) and loosen the rear axle nut.

> *NOTE*
> *Prior to removing the axle nut, mark the wheel bearing spacers and adjuster collars with a R (right side) and L (left side). The spacers and collars are unique and must be reinstalled onto the correct side of the wheel during installation.*

8. Loosen and remove the axle nut and washer (**Figure 31**).

9. Remove the rear brake pads as described in Chapter Thirteen.

9

10. Loosen the jam nut (A, **Figure 32**) and completely loosen the drive belt adjuster (B) on each side of the swing arm to allow maximum slack in the drive belt.

11. On the left side, remove the adjuster collar (**Figure 33**) from the rear axle.

12. On the left side, use a soft-faced mallet and gently tap the rear axle toward the right side. Remove the left side spacer.

13. From the right side, withdraw the rear axle (**Figure 34**) while holding onto the rear wheel. Remove the right side spacer. Lower the wheel to the wooden blocks or the ground.

14. Move the rear wheel forward and lift the drive belt off the driven sprocket.

15. Lift the rear caliper and move it toward the front of the motorcycle until the caliper notch clears the tab on the swing arm. Move the caliper out of the way and secure it with a bungee cord.

16. Raise the motorcycle sufficiently to allow the rear wheel to roll toward back and clear the rear fender.

17. Remove the rear wheel (**Figure 35**) and lower the motorcycle to a safe level.

18. If still in place, remove the wheel spacers from the right side and the left side of the wheel.

NOTE
Place a plastic or wooden spacer between the brake pads in place of the disc. Then, if the brake pedal is inadvertently depressed, the pistons will not be forced out of the caliper. If the pistons are forced out, disassemble the caliper to reseat the pistons.

CAUTION
Do not set the wheel down on the brake disc surface, as it may be damaged.

19. Install the wheel bearing spacers, adjuster collars and nut onto the axle in the same order of removal (**Figure 36**).

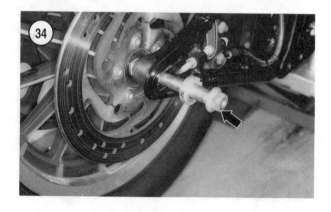

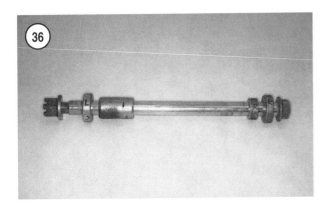

20. Inspect the rear wheel as described in this chapter.

Installation

> *CAUTION*
> *The rear wheel bearing spacer must be installed onto the correct side of the rear wheel. If installed incorrectly, the wheel will be off-set to the wrong side within the swing arm. This will result in the drive belt being out of alignment with the driven sprocket resulting in rapid drive belt wear.*

1. Remove the wheel bearing spacers, adjuster collars and nut from the rear axle and keep them in the same order (**Figure 36**).

2. Clean the axle in solvent and dry it thoroughly. Make sure the bearing surfaces on the axle are free of burrs and nicks.

3. Apply an antiseize lubricant to the axle shaft prior to installation.

4. Raise the motorcycle sufficiently to allow the rear wheel to roll forward and clear the rear fender.

5. Move the rear caliper into position and onto the locating tab on the swing arm (**Figure 37**).

6. Move the rear wheel forward (A, **Figure 38**) and install the drive belt onto the driven sprocket.

7. Lower the motorcycle to a level where the rear axle can be installed.

8. Make sure the right side axle adjuster (A, **Figure 39**) is in place on the rear axle.

9. Move the rear wheel into position and align it with the swing arm.

10. Move the rear caliper (B, **Figure 38**) up into position and align it with the rear axle receptacles in the swing arm.

11. Install the right side bearing spacer onto the wheel and hold it in place.

12. From the right side, carefully install the rear axle (**Figure 34**) through the right side of the swing arm, the

rear caliper (B, **Figure 38**), the right side bearing spacer (C) and rear hub.

13. Install the left side bearing spacer onto the wheel and hold it in place.

14. Continue to push the rear axle through the left side bearing spacer (A, **Figure 40**) and the swing arm.

15. Install the left side axle adjuster (B, **Figure 40**), washer and axle nut (C). Tighten the axle nut finger-tight at this time.

16. After the rear axle is installed, make sure both bearing spacers and axle adjusters are in the correct location and are still in place. The notch in the axle adjuster must align with the tip of the drive belt adjuster (**Figure 41**). Reposition at this time if incorrect.

17. Install the rear brake pads as described in Chapter Thirteen.

18. Check drive belt tension and adjustment as described in Chapter Three.

19. Tighten the rear axle nut to 60-65 ft.-lb. (81-88 N•m). If necessary, tighten the rear axle nut to align the nut slot with the axle spring pin hole. Install the spring pin (**Figure 42**) and snap it into place (**Figure 30**).

20. On HDI models, install the axle nut cover.

21. Install the drive belt debris deflector (**Figure 29**) and guard (**Figure 28**) and tighten the bolts securely.

22. On models equipped with the optional chrome cover, perform the following:

    a. If removed, install the mounting bracket (**Figure 27**) onto the drive belt adjuster.

    b. Install the rear axle chrome cover (**Figure 26**) and bolts and tighten securely.

23. Install both mufflers as described in Chapter Seven.

24. Rotate the wheel several times to make sure it rotates freely. Then apply the rear brake pedal several times to seat the pads against the disc.

25. Remove the stand and lower the rear wheel to the ground.

26. On models so equipped, install the saddlebags as described in Chapter Fourteen.

Inspection

Replace worn or damaged parts as described in this section.

1. Turn each bearing inner race by hand (**Figure 43**). The bearing should turn smoothly. Some axial play is normal, but radial play should be negligible. See **Figure 24**. If one bearing is damaged, replace both bearings as a set. Refer to *Front and Rear Hubs* in this chapter.

2. Clean the axle and axle spacers in solvent to remove all grease and dirt. Make sure the axle contact surfaces are free of dirt and old grease.

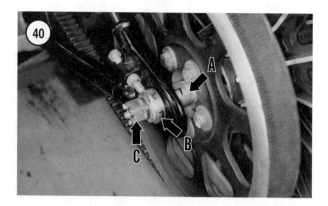

3. Check the axle runout with a set of V-blocks and a dial indicator (**Figure 25**).

4. Check the bearing spacers and axle adjusters (**Figure 36**) for wear, burrs and damage. Replace as necessary.

5. Check the brake disc bolts (**Figure 44**) for tightness. To service the brake disc, refer to Chapter Twelve.

6. Check the final drive sprocket bolts (**Figure 45**) for tightness. Service for the final drive sprocket is covered in this chapter.

7. Check wheel runout and spoke tension as described in this chapter.

FRONT AND REAR HUBS

Sealed ball bearings are installed on each side of the hub. Do not remove the bearing assemblies unless they require replacement.

Preliminary Inspection

Inspect each wheel bearing prior to removing it from the wheel hub.

> *CAUTION*
> *Do not remove the wheel bearings for inspection as they will be damaged during the removal process. Remove wheel bearings only if they are to be replaced.*

1. Perform Steps 1-3 of *Disassembly* in the following procedure.
2. Turn each bearing by hand (**Figure 46**). The bearings should turn smoothly with no roughness.
3. Inspect the play of the inner race of each wheel bearing. Check for excessive axial play and radial play (**Figure 24**). Replace the bearing if free play is excessive.

Disassembly

This procedure applies to both the front and rear wheel and hub assemblies. Differences between the different hubs are identified. Refer to **Figures 47** and **48**.

1A. Remove the front wheel as described in this chapter.
1B. Remove the rear wheel as described in this chapter.
2. Remove the axle spacers from each side of the hub if they are still in place.
3. If necessary, remove the bolts securing the brake disc (**Figure 44**) and remove the disc.
4. Before proceeding, inspect the wheel bearings as described in this chapter. If they must be replaced, proceed as follows.
5A. If the special tools are not used, perform the following:
   a. To remove the right and left bearings and spacer collar, insert a soft aluminum or brass drift into one side of the hub.
   b. Push the spacer collar over to one side and place the drift on the inner race of the lower bearing.
   c. Tap the bearing out of the hub with a hammer, working around the perimeter of the inner race (**Figure 49**). Remove the bearing and distance collar.

9

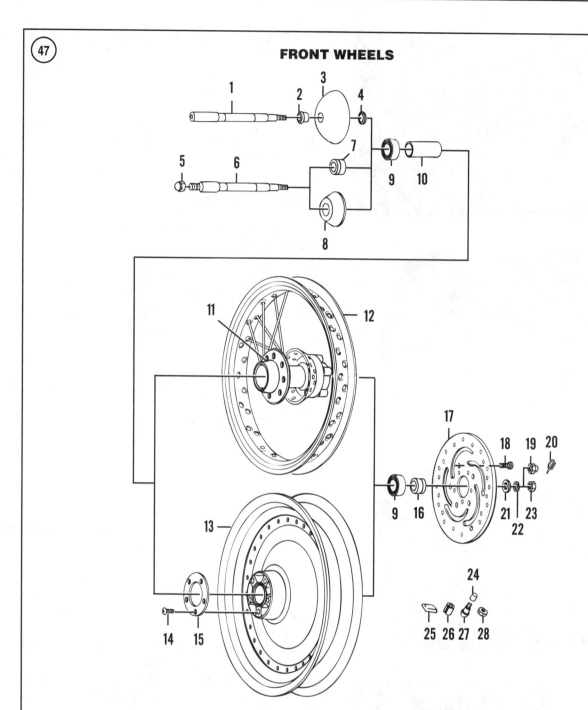

FRONT WHEELS

1. Front axle
   (all models except FXSTD)
2. Hub cap spacer (FLSTC)
3. Hub cap (FLSTC)
4. Snap ring (FLSTC)
5. Acorn nut (FXSTD)
6. Front axle (FXSTD)
7. Spacer—right side
   (all models except FXSTD 2002-on)
8. Spacer—right side (FXSTD 2002-on)
9. Wheel bearing
10. Spacer sleeve
11. Hub (laced wheel)
12. Laced wheel
13. Cast wheel
14. Screw
15. Cover
16. Spacer (left side)
17. Brake disc
18. Bolt
19. Acorn nut (FXSTD)
20. Retaining pin (FLSTS)
21. Washer
22. Lockwasher
23. Nut (all models except FXSTD)
24. Valve stem cap
25. Balance weight (cast wheel)
26. Balance weight (laced wheel)
27. Valve stem
28. Valve stem nut (laced wheel)

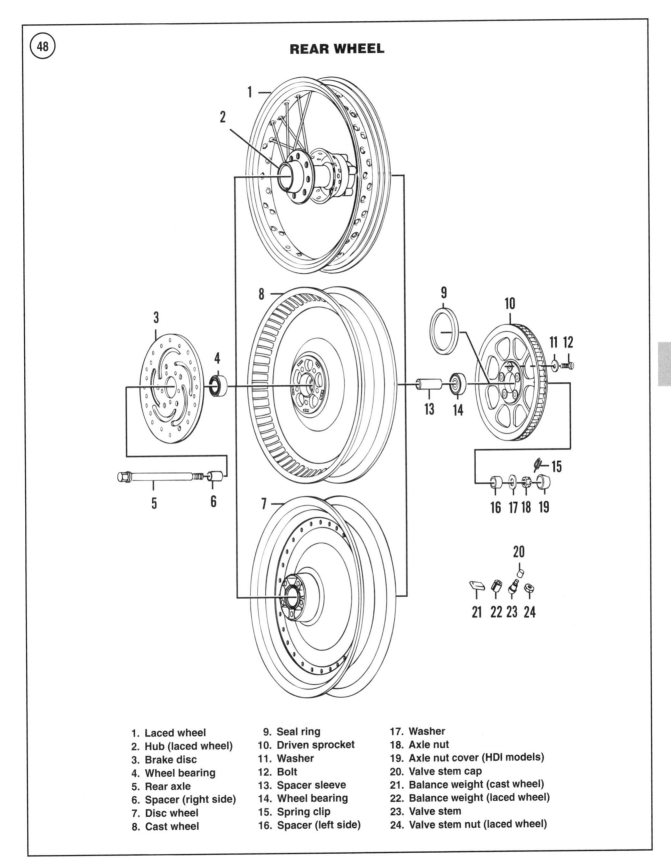

REED WHEEL

REAR WHEEL

1. Laced wheel
2. Hub (laced wheel)
3. Brake disc
4. Wheel bearing
5. Rear axle
6. Spacer (right side)
7. Disc wheel
8. Cast wheel
9. Seal ring
10. Driven sprocket
11. Washer
12. Bolt
13. Spacer sleeve
14. Wheel bearing
15. Spring clip
16. Spacer (left side)
17. Washer
18. Axle nut
19. Axle nut cover (HDI models)
20. Valve stem cap
21. Balance weight (cast wheel)
22. Balance weight (laced wheel)
23. Valve stem
24. Valve stem nut (laced wheel)

d. Repeat sub steps b and c for the bearing on the other side.

NOTE
The Kowa Seiki Wheel Bearing Remover set can be ordered through a K&L Supply Co. dealer.

WARNING
Be sure to wear safety glasses while using the wheel bearing remover set.

5B. To remove the bearings with the Kowa Seiki Wheel Bearing Remover set, perform the following:
a. Select the correct size remover head tool and insert it into the bearing.
b. Turn the wheel over and insert the remover shaft into the backside of the adapter. Tap the wedge and force it into the slit in the adapter (**Figure 50**). This will force the adapter against the bearing inner race.
c. Tap the end of the wedge bar with a hammer (**Figure 51**) to drive the bearing out of the hub. Remove the bearing and the distance collar.
d. Repeat substeps a-c for the bearing on the other side.

6. Clean the inside and the outside of the hub with solvent. Dry it with compressed air.

Assembly

CAUTION
*The removal process will generally damage the bearings. Replace the wheel bearings in pairs. **Never** reinstall bearings after they are removed. Always install **new** bearings.*

1. Blow any debris out of the hub prior to installing the new bearings.
2. Apply a light coat of wheel bearing grease to the bearing seating areas of the hub. This will make bearing installation easier.

CAUTION
Install non-sealed bearings with the single sealed side facing outward. Tap the bearings squarely into place and tap on the outer race only. Do not tap on the inner race or the bearing might be damaged. Make sure the bearings are completely seated.

3. Select a driver, or socket (**Figure 52**), with an outside diameter slightly smaller than the bearing's outside diameter.
4. Tap the right side bearing squarely into place and tap on the outer race only. Tap the bearing into the hub bore until it bottoms. Make sure the bearing is completely seated.

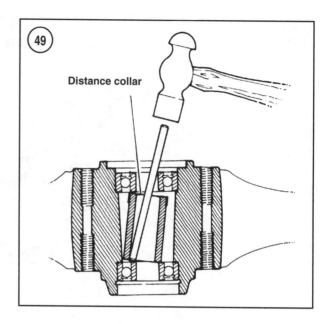

49

Distance collar

5. Turn the wheel over (right side up) on the workbench and install the spacer collar.
6. Use the same tool set-up to drive in the left side bearing.
7. If the brake disc was removed, install it as described in Chapter Thirteen.
8A. Install the front wheel as described in this chapter.
8B. Install the rear wheel as described in this chapter.

DRIVEN SPROCKET ASSEMBLY

Inspection

Inspect the sprocket teeth (**Figure 53**). If the teeth are visibly worn, replace the drive belt and both sprockets.

Removal/Installation

1. Remove the rear wheel as described in this chapter.
2. Remove the bolts and washers (**Figure 45**) securing the driven sprocket to the hub, and remove the sprocket.
3. Position the driven sprocket onto the rear hub.
4. Apply a light coat of ThreeBond TB1360, or an equivalent, to the bolts prior to installation.
5. Install the bolts and washers and tighten the bolts to 55-60 ft.-lb. (75-81 N•m).

DRIVE SPROCKET

The drive sprocket is covered in Chapter Six under *Transmission Drive Sprocket*.

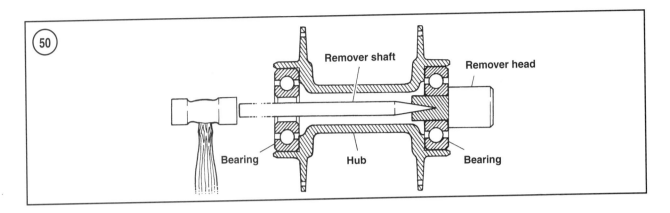

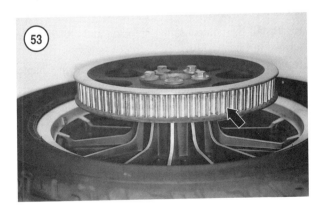

DRIVE BELT

CAUTION
When handling a new or used drive belt, never wrap the belt in a loop smaller than 5 in. (130 mm) or bend it sharply. This will weaken or break the belt fibers and cause premature belt failure.

Removal

NOTE
If the existing drive belt is being reinstalled, install it so it travels in the same direction. Before removing the belt, draw an arrow on the top surface of the belt facing forward.

1. Remove the exhaust system as described in Chapter Seven.
2. Remove the compensating sprocket and clutch as described in Chapter Five.
3. Remove the primary chain inner housing as described in Chapter Five.
4. Remove the rear wheel as described in this chapter.
5. Remove the two bolts (A, **Figure 54**) securing the inner fender panel. Move the inner fender up to release if from the frame hook and remove the inner fender panel (B).
6. Place wooden blocks or a floor jack under the transmission and engine assembly to support it after the swing arm pivot shaft is partially removed.
7. On the right side, secure the pivot shaft (**Figure 55**) to keep it from rotating in the following step.
8. On the left side, loosen and remove the pivot shaft flange nut and hardened washer (**Figure 56**).
9. Support the swing arm on a box and tap on the left side of the pivot shaft with a drift.
10. Drive the pivot shaft from the left side of the frame until the left side spacer collar (**Figure 57**) can be removed, then remove it from between the swing arm and

the transmission case. Do not drive the pivot shaft out any farther than necessary.

11. Remove the drive belt (**Figure 58**) from the drive sprocket and remove the drive belt from between the swing arm and transmission case.

12. If the drive belt is going to remain off for a period of time, install the left side spacer collar and tap the pivot shaft back into place through the collar and the frame. Install the nut and tighten securely.

Installation

> *NOTE*
> *If the existing drive belt is being reinstalled, install it so it travels in the same direction as noted prior to removal. If a new drive belt is being installed, it can be installed in either direction.*

1. Insert the drive belt through the space between the swing arm and the transmission case.

2. Install the drive belt onto the drive sprocket.

3. If reinstalled, remove the nut from the pivot shaft and drive the pivot shaft out until it is flush with the left side of the transmission case.

4. Position the left side spacer collar (**Figure 57**) with the flange side facing the transmission case and install it between the transmission case and the swing arm.

5. Push the pivot shaft through the left side spacer collar, the swing arm bushing and left side of the frame pivot area. Push the pivot shaft in until it bottoms.

> *NOTE*
> *Do not substitute another type of washers in place of the hardened washers.*

6. Install the *L* marked hardened washer onto the pivot shaft.

7. On the right side, secure the pivot shaft (**Figure 55**) to keep it from rotating in the following step.

8. Apply ThreeBond No. 1360 (red) threadlocking compound to the pivot shaft threads prior to installing the flange nut.

9. On the left side, install the flange nut (**Figure 56**) and tighten to 90-110 ft.-lb. (122-149 N•m).

10. Slowly raise and lower the swing arm to ensure ease of movement. If binding occurs, repeat Step 9 and correct the problem.

11. Install the inner fender and hook it onto the frame hook. Install the two bolts (A, **Figure 54**) securing the inner fender (B) and tighten securely.

12. Install the rear wheel as described in this chapter.

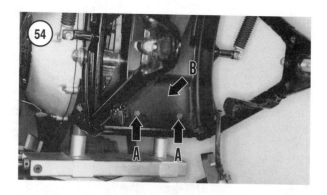

13. Remove the wooden blocks or floor jack from under the transmission and engine assembly.

14. Install the primary chain inner housing as described in Chapter Five.

15. Install the compensating sprocket and clutch as described in Chapter Five.

16. Install the exhaust system as described in Chapter Seven.

Inspection

Do not apply any type of lubricant to the drive belt. Inspect the drive belt and teeth (**Figure 59**) for severe wear, damage or oil contamination.

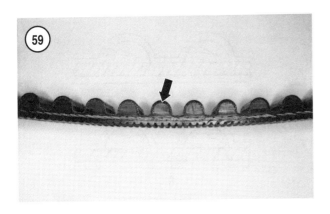

Refer to **Figure 60** for various types of drive belt wear or damage. Replace the drive belt if it is worn or damaged.

WHEEL RUNOUT

1. Remove the front or rear wheel as described in this chapter.

2. Install the wheel in a wheel truing stand and check the wheel for excessive wobble or runout.

3. If the wheel is not running true, remove the tire from the rim as described in this chapter. Then remount the wheel into the truing stand, and measure axial and lateral runout (**Figure 61**) with a pointer or dial indicator. Compare actual runout readings with the service limit specification in **Table 1**. Note the following:

   a. Disc or cast wheels—if the runout meets or exceeds the service limit in **Table 1**, check the wheel bearings as described under *Front and Rear Hub* in this chapter. If the wheel bearings are acceptable, replace the cast or disc wheel as it cannot be serviced. Inspect the wheel for cracks, fractures, dents or bends. Replace a damaged wheel.

> *WARNING*
> *Do not try to repair damage to a disc wheel as it will result in an unsafe riding condition.*

   b. Laced wheels—if the wheel bearings, spokes, hub and rim assembly are not damaged, the runout can be corrected by truing the wheel. Refer to *Spoke Adjustment* in this chapter. If the rim is dented or damaged, replace the rim and rebuild the wheel.

4. While the wheel is off, perform the following:

   a. Check the brake disc mounting bolts (**Figure 44**) for tightness as described in Chapter Thirteen.

   b. On the rear wheel, check the driven sprocket bolts for tightness as described in this chapter.

RIM AND LACED WHEEL SERVICE

The laced wheel assembly consists of a rim, spokes, nipples and hub containing the bearings, and spacer collar.

Component Condition

Wheels are subjected to a significant amount of punishment. Inspect the wheel regularly for lateral (side-to-side) and radial (up-and-down) runout, even spoke tension and visible rim damage. When a wheel has a noticeable wobble, it is out of true. This is usually cause by loose spokes, but it can be caused by an impact-damaged rim.

Truing a wheel corrects the lateral and radial runout to bring the wheel back into specification. The condition of the individual wheel components will effect the ability to successfully true the wheel. Note the following:

1. Spoke condition—Do not attempt to true a wheel with bent or damaged spokes. Doing so places an excessive amount of tension on the spoke and rim. The spoke may break and/or pull through the spoke nipple hole in the rim. Inspect the spokes carefully and replace any spokes that are damaged.

9

2. Nipple condition—When truing the wheels, the nipples should turn freely on the spoke. It is common for the spoke threads to become corroded and make turning the nipple difficult. Spray a penetrating liquid onto the nipple and allow sufficient time for it to penetrate before trying to force the nipple loose. Work the spoke wrench in both directions and continue to apply penetrating liquid. If the spoke wrench rounds off the nipple, remove the tire from the rim and cut the spoke(s) out of the wheel.

3. Rim condition—Minor rim damage can be corrected by truing the wheel; however, trying to correct excessive runout caused by impact damage causes hub and rim damage due to spoke overtightening. Inspect the rims for cracks, flat spots or dents. Check the spoke holes for cracks or enlargement. Replace rims with excessive damage.

Wheel Truing Preliminaries

Before checking runout and truing the wheel, note the following:

1. Make sure the wheel bearings are in good condition. Refer to *Front and Rear Hubs* in this chapter.

2. A small amount of wheel runout is acceptable, do not try to true the wheel to a perfect zero reading. Doing so causes excessive spoke tension and possible rim and hub damage. **Table 1** lists the lateral (side-to-side) and radial (up-and-down) runout limit specifications.

3. The runout can be checked on the motorcycle by mounting a pointer against the fork or swing arm and slowly rotating the wheel.

4. Perform major wheel truing with the tire removed and the wheel mounted in a truing stand (**Figure 61**). If a stand is not available, mount the wheel on the motorcycle with spacers on each side of the wheel to prevent it from sliding on the axle.

5. Use a spoke nipple wrench of the correct size. Using the wrong type of tool or one that is the incorrect size will round off the spoke nipples, making adjustment difficult. Quality spoke wrenches have openings that grip the nipple on four corners to prevent nipple damage.

6. Refer to the spoke nipple torque specification in **Table 2** when using a torque wrench.

Wheel Truing Procedure

1. Position a pointer facing toward the rim (**Figure 61**). Then spin the wheel slowly and check the lateral and radial runout. If the rim is out of adjustment, continue with Step 2.

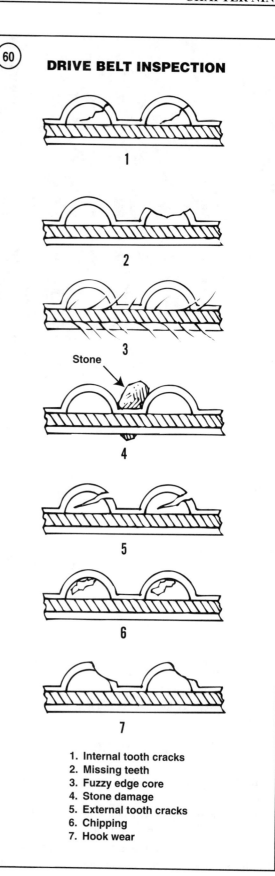

60

DRIVE BELT INSPECTION

1

2

3

Stone

4

5

6

7

1. Internal tooth cracks
2. Missing teeth
3. Fuzzy edge core
4. Stone damage
5. External tooth cracks
6. Chipping
7. Hook wear

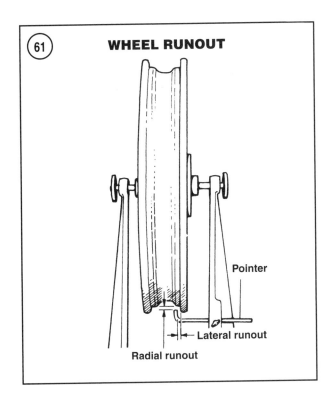

WHEEL RUNOUT

Pointer

Lateral runout

Radial runout

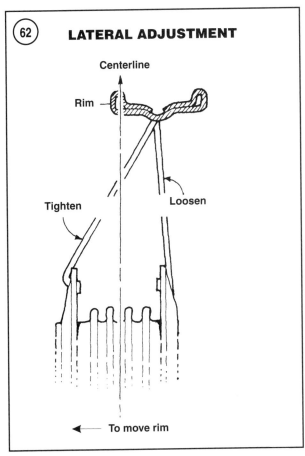

LATERAL ADJUSTMENT

Centerline

Rim

Tighten

Loosen

To move rim

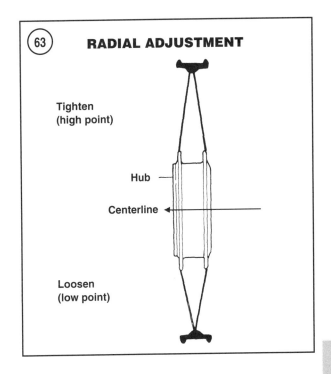

RADIAL ADJUSTMENT

Tighten
(high point)

Hub

Centerline

Loosen
(low point)

9

NOTE
If there is a large number of loose spokes, make sure the hub is centered in the rim. This must be done visually as there are no hub and rim centering specifications for these models.

NOTE
The number of spokes to loosen and tighten in Steps 2 and 3 depends on how far the runout is out of adjustment. As a minimum, always loosen two or three spokes, then tighten the opposite two or three spokes. If the runout is excessive and affects a greater area along the rim, a greater number of spokes will require adjustment.

2. If the lateral (side-to-side) runout is out of specification, adjust the wheel by using **Figure 62** as an example. To move the rim to the left, loosen and tighten the spokes as shown. Always loosen and tighten the spokes an equal number of turns.

3. If the radial (up and down) runout is out of specification, the hub is not centered in the rim. Draw the high point of the rim toward the centerline of the wheel by tightening the spokes in the area of the high point and on the same side as the high point, and loosening the spokes on the side opposite the high point (**Figure 63**). Tighten spokes in equal amounts to prevent distortion.

4. After truing the wheel, seat each spoke in the hub by tapping it with a flat nose punch and hammer. Then re-

check the spoke tension and wheel runout. Readjust if necessary.

5. Check the ends of the spokes where they are threaded in the nipples. Grind off ends that protrude through the nipples.

DISC AND CAST WHEELS

Disc and cast wheels consist of a single assembly equipped with bearings, and a spacer sleeve.

While these wheels are virtually maintenance free, they must be checked periodically for damage. Also, the disc wheel should be checked prior to installing a new tire. Wheel bearing service is described in this chapter.

Inspection

Before checking runout and truing the wheel, note the following:

1. Make sure the wheel bearings are in good condition. Refer to *Front and Rear Hubs* in this chapter.

2. Perform wheel runout with the tire removed and the wheel mounted in a truing stand (**Figure 64**). If a stand is not available, mount the wheel on the motorcycle with spacers on each side of the wheel to prevent it from sliding on the axle.

3. The maximum lateral (side-to-side) and radial (up-and-down) runout is listed in **Table 1**.

> *WARNING*
> *Do not try to repair any damage to a disc or cast wheels as it will result in an unsafe riding condition.*

WHEEL BALANCE

An unbalanced wheel is unsafe. Depending on the degree of unbalance and the speed of the motorcycle, the rider may experience anything from a mild vibration to a violent shimmy that may causes loss of control.

On cast or disc wheels, weights are attached to the flat surface on the rim (**Figure 65**). On laced wheels, the weights are attached to the spoke nipples (**Figure 66**).

Before attempting to balance the wheel, make sure the wheel bearings are in good condition and properly lubricated. The wheel must rotate freely.

1A. Remove the front wheel as described in this chapter.

1B. Remove the rear wheel as described in this chapter.

2. Mount the wheel on a fixture (**Figure 67**) so it can rotate freely.

3. Spin the wheel and let it coast to a stop. Mark the tire at the lowest point.

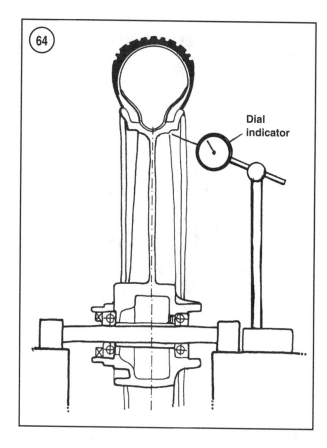

Dial indicator

4. Spin the wheel several more times. If the wheel keeps coming to rest at the same point, it is out of balance.

5A. On cast or disc wheels, tape a test weight to the upper or light side of the wheel (**Figure 65**).

5B. On laced wheels, attach a weight to the spoke (**Figure 66**) on the upper or light side of the wheel.

6. Experiment with different weights until the wheel comes to a stop at a different position each time it is spun.

7. On cast or cast wheels, remove the test weight and install the correct size weight.

   a. Attach the weights to the flat surface on the rim (**Figure 65**). Clean the rim of all road residue before installing the weights; otherwise, the weights may fall off.

   b. Add weights in 1/4 oz. (7g) increments. If 1 oz. (28 g) or more must be added to one location, apply half the amount to each side of the rim.

   c. To apply Harley-Davidson wheel weights, remove the paper backing from the weight and apply three drops of Loctite 420 Superbonder to the bottom of the weight. Position the weight on the rim, press it down and hold in position for 10 seconds. To allow the adhesive to cure properly, do not use the wheel for 8 hours.

8. When fitting weights on laced wheels for the final time, crimp the weights onto the spoke with slip-joint pliers.

TIRES

Tire Safety

Maintain the tire inflation pressure at the specification in **Table 3**. If a different brand of tire is used, follow the inflation recommendation provided by the tire manufacturer. Tire inflation specifications are cold inflation speci-fications. Do not check/adjust tire pressure after riding the motorcycle.

Always allow the tires to warm up by riding before subjecting them to high cornering loads. Warm tires provide more adhesion.

New tires provide significantly less adhesion until they are broken in. Do not subject new tires to high speed or high cornering forces for at least 60 mile (100 km). Be especially careful when encountering wet conditions with new tires.

TIRE CHANGING

The cast or disc wheels can easily be damaged during tire removal. Take special care with tire irons when changing a tire to avoid scratches and gouges to the outer rim surface. Insert scraps of leather between the tire iron and the rim to protect the rim from damage. All original equipment cast or disc wheels are designed for use with tubeless tires only. All laced wheels use a tube and tire combination.

When removing a tubeless tire, take care not to damage the tire beads, inner liner of the tire or the wheel rim flange. Use tire levers or flat handle tire irons with rounded heads.

Tire Removal

CAUTION
To avoid damage when removing the tire, support the wheel on two wooden blocks, so the brake disc or the driven sprocket does not contact the floor.

NOTE
To make tire removal easier, warm the tire to make it softer and more pliable. Place the wheel and tire assembly in the sun. If possible, place the wheel assembly and the new tire in a completely closed motorcycle.

1A. Remove the front wheel as described in this chapter.
1B. Remove the rear wheel as described in this chapter.
2. If not already marked by the tire manufacturer, mark the valve stem location on the tire, so the tire can be installed in the same location for easier balancing.
3. Remove the valve cap and unscrew the core from the valve stem and deflate the tire or tube.

NOTE
*Removal of tubeless tires from their rims can be difficult because of the exceptionally tight tire bead-to-rim seal. Breaking the bead seal may require a special tool (**Figure**)*

68). If unable to break the seal loose, take the wheel to a motorcycle dealership or tire repair shop, and have them break it loose on a tire changing machine.

> **CAUTION**
> *The inner rim and tire bead areas are the sealing surfaces on the tubeless tire. Do not scratch the inside of the rim or damage the tire bead.*

4. Press the entire bead on both sides of the tire away from the rim and into the center of the rim. If the bead it tight, use a bead breaker.

5. Lubricate both beads with soapy water.

> **CAUTION**
> *Use rim protectors (part No. HD-01289), or an equivalent (**Figure 69**) or insert scraps of leather between the tire iron and the rim to protect the rim from damage.*

> **NOTE**
> *Use only quality tire irons without sharp edges. If necessary, file the ends of the tire irons to remove rough edges.*

6. Insert a tire iron under the top bead next to the valve stem (**Figure 70**). Force the bead on the opposite side of the tire into the center of the rim and pry the bead over the rim with the tire iron.

7. Insert a second tire iron next to the first iron to hold the bead over the rim. Then work around the tire with the first tire iron, prying the bead over the rim (**Figure 71**). On tube-type tires, be careful not to pinch the inner tube with the tools.

8. On tube-type tires, use a thumb and push the valve stem from its hole in the rim to the inside of the tire. Carefully pull the tube out of the tire and lay it aside.

> **NOTE**
> *Step 9 is only necessary only if it is necessary to remove tire from the wheel completely, such as for tire replacement or tubeless tire repair.*

9. Stand the wheel upright. Insert a tire iron between the back bead and the side of the rim that the top bead was pried over (**Figure 72**). Force the bead on the opposite side from the tire iron into the center of the rim. Work around the tire and pry the back bead off the rim. On tube-type tires, remove the rim band.

10. Inspect the valve stem seal. Because rubber deteriorates with age, replace the valve stem when replacing the tire.

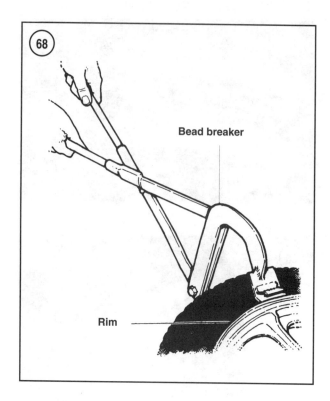

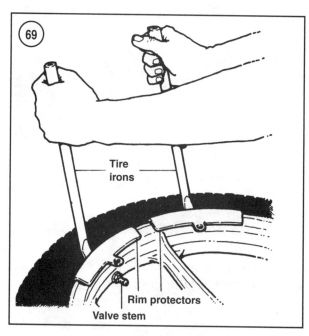

11. On tubeless tires, remove the old valve stem and discard it. Inspect the valve stem hole (**Figure 73**) in the rim. Remove any dirt or corrosion from the hole and wipe it dry with a clean cloth. Install a new valve stem and make sure it is properly seated in the rim.

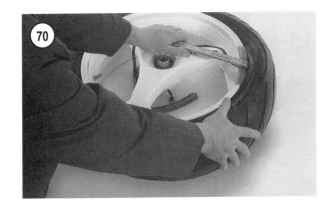

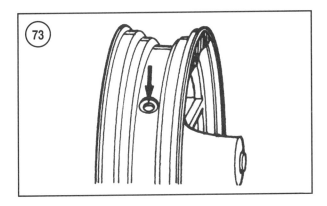

12. Carefully inspect the tire and wheel rim for damage as described in the following section.

Tire and Wheel Rim Inspection

1. Wipe off the inner surfaces of the wheel rim. Clean off any rubber residue or oxidation.

> *WARNING*
> *Carefully consider whether a tire should be replaced. If there is any doubt about the quality of the existing tire, replace it with a new one. Do not take a chance on a tire failure at any speed.*

2. On tubeless tires, inspect the valve stem rubber grommet for deterioration. If replacement is necessary, install only the OE valve stem assembly.

> *WARNING*
> *Install only OE tire valves and valve caps. A valve or valve/cap combination that is too long or heavier that OE parts may interfere with adjacent component when the motorcycle is under way. Damage to the valve will cause rapid tire deflation and loss of control.*

3. If any of the following conditions are observed, replace the tire:
   a. A puncture or split whose total length or diameter exceeds 0.24 in. (6 mm).
   b. A scratch or split on the side wall.
   c. Any type of ply separation.
   d. Tread separation or excessive abnormal wear pattern.
   e. Tread depth of less than 1/16 in. (1.6 mm) on original equipment tires. Tread depth minimum may vary on aftermarket tires.
   f. Scratches on either sealing bead.
   g. The cord is cut in any place.
   h. Flat spots in the tread from skidding.
   i. Any abnormality in the inner liner.

Tire Installation

1. A new tire may have balancing rubbers inside. These are not patches. Do not remove them. Most tires are marked with a colored spot near the bead (**Figure 74**) that indicates a lighter point on the tire. This should be placed next to the valve stem.

2. On tube-type tires, install the rim band over the wheel and align the hole in the rim band with the hole in the rim.

9

If installing a new rim band, make sure it is the correct diameter and width for the wheel.

3. Lubricate both beads of the tire with soapy water.

4. When installing the tire on the rim, make sure the correct tire (either front or rear) is installed on the correct wheel. Also make sure the direction arrow faces the direction of wheel rotation (**Figure 75**).

5. When remounting the old tire, align the mark made in Step 2 of *Removal* with the valve stem (**Figure 74**).

6. Place the backside of the tire onto the rim so the lower bead sits in the center of the rim while the upper bead remains outside the rim (**Figure 76**). Work around the tire in both directions and press the lower bead by hand into the center of the rim. Use a tire iron for the last few inches of bead.

7. On tube-type tires, perform the following:

   a. Dust the inner tube with talcum powder before installing it in the tire. The talcum powder will prevent the tube from sticking to the tire.

   b. Inflate the tube just enough to round it out. Too much air will make installation difficult.

   c. Place the tube on top of the tire, aligning the valve stem with the matching hole in the rim. Insert the tube into the tire.

   d. Lift the upper bead away from the rim with a hand and insert the tube's valve stem through the rim hole. Check to make sure the valve stem is straight up (90 degrees), not cocked to one side. If necessary, reposition the tube in the tire. If the valve stem wants to slide out of the hole and back into the tire, install the valve stem nut at the top of the valve; do not tighten the nut at this time.

8. Press the upper bead into the rim opposite the valve stem. Working on both sides of this initial point, pry the bead into the rim with the tire tool, and work around the rim to the valve stem (**Figure 77**). On tube-type tires, do not pinch the inner tube during the last few inches. If the tire wants to pull up on one side, either use another tire iron or one knee to hold the tire in place. The last few inches are usually the toughest to install. Continue to push the tire into the rim by hand. Re-lubricate the bead if necessary. If the tire bead pulls out from under the rim, use both knees to hold the tire in place. If necessary, use a tire iron for the last few inches (**Figure 78**).

9. On tube-type tires, check to make sure that the valve stem is straight up (90°), not cocked to one side (**Figure 79**). If necessary, slide the tire along the rim in either direction while holding the rim securely. When the valve stem is straight up, tighten the valve stem nut at the top of the valve; do not tighten it against the rim at this time. Check that the tube was not forced outward so that it rests

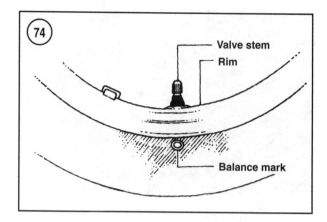

between the tire bead and the rim. If necessary, push the tube back into the tire.

10. Bounce the wheel several times, rotating it each time. This will force the tire bead against the rim flanges. After the tire beads are in contact with the rim, inflate the tire to seat the beads.

11A. On tube-type tires, perform the following:

   a. Inflate the tube to it maximum tire pressure to seat the tire beads in the rim.

   b. After inflating the tire, make sure the beads are fully seated and the rim lines are the same distance from the rim all the way around the tire (**Figure 80**).

   c. If the tire beads do not seat properly, release the air pressure and re-lubricate the tire beads.

   d. When the tire is seated correctly, remove the valve core and deflate the tire allowing the tube to straighten out within the tire.

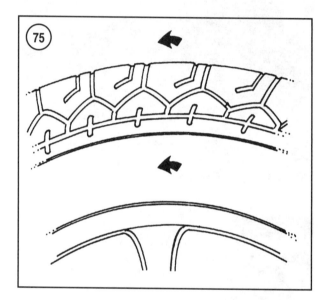

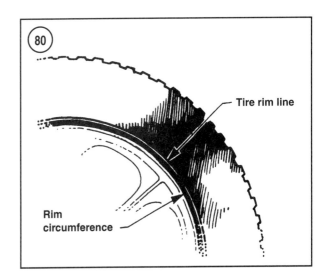

Tire rim line

Rim
circumference

e. Install the valve core and inflate the tire to the pressure in **Table 3**.

f. Tighten the valve stem nut securely and install the valve stem cap.

11B. On tubeless tires, perform the following:

a. Place an inflatable band around the circumference of the tire. Slowly inflate the band until the tire beads are pressed against the rim. Inflate the tire enough to make it seat, deflate the band and remove it.

WARNING
In the next step, never exceed 40 psi (276 kPa) inflation pressure as the tire could burst, causing severe injury. Never stand directly over a tire while inflating it.

b. After inflating the tire, make sure the beads are fully seated and the rim lines are the same distance from the rim all the way around the tire (**Figure 80**). If the beads will not seat, deflate the tire and lubricate the rim and beads with soapy water.

c. Re-inflate the tire to the pressure in **Table 3**. Install the valve stem cap.

12. Check tire runout as described in this chapter.

13. Balance the wheel as described in this chapter.

14A. Install the front wheel as described in this chapter.

14B. Install the rear wheel as described in this chapter.

TIRE REPAIRS
(TUBELESS)

NOTE
Changing or patching on the road is very difficult. A can of pressurized tire inflator

and sealer can inflate the tire and seal the hole, but this is only a temporary fix.

> *WARNING*
> *Do not install an inner tube inside a tubeless tire. The tube will cause an abnormal heat buildup in the tire.*

Tubeless tires have the TUBELESS molded into the sidewall and the rims have SUITABLE FOR TUBELESS TIRES or equivalent stamped or cast on them.

If the tire is punctured, remove it from the rim to inspect the inside of the tire and apply a combination plug/patch from inside the tire (**Figure 81**). Never attempt to repair a tubeless motorcycle tire using a plug or cord patch applied from outside the tire.

After repairing a tubeless tire, do not exceed 50 mph (80 km/h) for the first 24 hours.

As soon as possible, replace the patched tire with a new one.

Repair

Do not rely on a plug or cord patch applied from outside the tire. Use a combination plug/patch applied from inside the tire (**Figure 81**).

1. Remove the tire from the wheel rim as described in this chapter.
2. Inspect the rim inner flange. Smooth scratches on the sealing surface with emery cloth. If a scratch is deeper than 0.020 in. (0.5 mm), replace the wheel.
3. Inspect the inside and outside of the tire. Replace a tire if any of the following conditions are found.
   a. A puncture larger than 1/8 in. (3 mm) diameter.
   b. A punctured or damaged side wall.
   c. More than two punctures in the tire.
4. Apply the plug/patch following the manufacturer's instructions with the patch kit.
5. As soon as possible, replace the patched tire with a new one.

TIRE REPAIRS (TUBE-TYPE)

> *NOTE*
> *Changing or patching on the road is very difficult. A can of pressurized tire inflator and sealer can inflate the tire and seal the hole, but this is only a temporary fix.*

Patching a motorcycle tube is only a temporary fix. A motorcycle tire flexes too much and a patch can rub right off. As soon as possible, replace the tube with a new one.

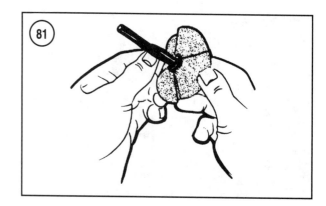

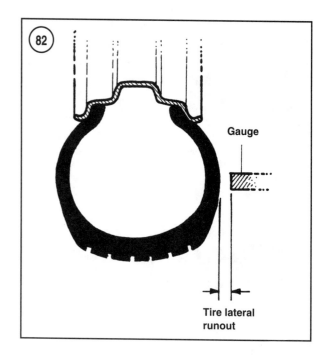

Gauge

Tire lateral runout

Tube Repair Kits

Tire repair kits are available from motorcycle dealerships and some auto supply retailers. When buying one, make sure the kit is for a motorcycle tire. Kits that vulcanize the patch to the tube with heat (hot patch) are strongest. Kits that attach the patch in place with adhesive are known as cold patch types. Purchase the repair kit and follow the manufacturer's instructions.

TIRE RUNOUT

Check the tires for excessive lateral and radial runout after a wheel has been mounted or if the motorcycle developed a wobble that cannot be traced to another compo-

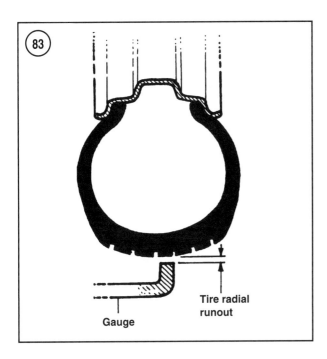

Tire radial runout

Gauge

not directly in line with the molded tire logo or any other raised surface.

b. Rotate the tire and measure lateral runout.

c. The lateral runout should not exceed 0.080 in. (2.03 mm). If runout is excessive, remove the tire from the wheel and recheck the wheel's lateral runout as described in this chapter. If the runout is excessive, the wheel must be trued (laced wheels) or replaced (alloy wheels). If wheel runout is correct, the tire runout is excessive and the tire must be replaced.

2. Check the tire for excessive up-and-down play radial runout as follows:

a. Position a fixed pointer at the center bottom of the tire tread as shown in **Figure 83**.

b. Rotate the tire and measure the amount of radial runout.

c. The radial runout should not exceed 0.090 in. (2.29 mm). If runout is excessive, remove the tire from the wheel and recheck the wheel's radial runout as described in this chapter. If the runout is excessive, true (laced wheel) or replace the wheel. If wheel runout is correct, the tire runout is excessive and the tire must be replaced.

nent. Mount the wheels on their axles when making the following checks:

1. Check the tire for excessive side-to-side play lateral runout as follows:

a. Position a fixed pointer next to the tire sidewall as shown in **Figure 82**. Position the pointer tip so it is

9

Table 1 WHEEL SPECIFICATIONS

	in.	mm
Wheel runout (maximum)		
Laced wheels		
Lateral and radial	0.031	0.79
Disc wheels		
Lateral	0.040	1.02
Radial	0.030	0.76
End play (service limit)		
Front and rear	0.002	0.051

Table 2 WHEEL TORQUE SPECIFICATIONS

Item	ft.-lb.	in.-lb.	N•m
Brake disc bolts			
Front wheel	16-24	–	22-32
Rear wheel	30-45	–	41-61
Driven sprocket bolts	55-60	–	75-81
Front axle nut			
FXST, FLSTC, FLSTF,			
FXSTB and FXSTD	50-55	–	68-75
FLSTS and FXSTS	60-65	–	81-88
Front fork			
Cap bolt	40-60	–	52-81
Drain screw			
FXSTD	–	12-18	1.4-2.0
All models except FXSTD	–	52-78	6-9
Fork slider cap	11-15	–	15-20
Front brake caliper (FLSTS and FXSTS)			
Upper mounting bolt	28-30	–	38-41
Lower mounting bolt	25-30	–	34-41
Front brake caliper			
(all models except FLSTS and FXSTS)			
Upper and lower mounting bolts	28-30	–	38-41
Rear axle nut	60-65	–	81-88
Springer fork (FLSTS and FXSTS)			
Rigid fork leg studs	60-65	–	81-88
Rocker pivot stud nut	45-50	–	61-68
Spring bridge acorn nut	30-35	–	41-48
Spring rod acorn nut	20-25	–	27-34
Spoke nipples	–	40-50	4-6
Swing arm pivot bolt locknut	90-110	–	122-149
Valve stem nut			
Tubeless tire	–	12-15	1-2
Tube type tire	–	25-35	3-4

Table 3 TIRE INFLATION PRESSURE (COLD)*

Model	kPa	PSI
Front wheels		
Rider only	207	30
Rider and passenger	207	30
Rear wheels		
Rider only	248	36
Rider and passenger	275	40
*Tire pressure for original equipment tires. Aftermarket tires may require different inflation pressure.		

CHAPTER TEN

FRONT SUSPENSION AND STEERING (TELESCOPIC FORK)

This chapter covers the handlebar, steering head and front fork assemblies for all models except the FXSTS and FLSTS. These two Springer front fork models are covered in Chapter Eleven.

Table 1 and **Table 2** are at the end of the chapter.

HANDLEBAR

Removal/Installation

Refer to **Figure 1**.

1. On models so equipped, remove the windshield as described in Chapter Fourteen.

2. Support the motorcycle with the front wheel off the ground. See *Motorcycle Stands* in Chapter Nine.

NOTE
Cover the fuel tank with a heavy cloth or plastic tarp to protect it from accidental scratches or dents when removing the handlebar.

NOTE
Before removing the handlebar, make a drawing of the clutch and throttle cable routing from the handlebar through the frame.

This information will help when reinstalling the handlebar and connecting the cables.

3. On the right side of the handlebar, perform the following:
   a. Unscrew and remove the mirror (A, **Figure 2**).
   b. Remove the screws securing the master cylinder (B, **Figure 2**). Do not disconnect the hydraulic brake line.
   c. Remove the screws securing the right side switch assembly (C, **Figure 2**) and separate the housing halves.
   d. Slide the throttle housing assembly (D, **Figure 2**) off the handlebar.

4. On the left side of the handlebar, perform the following:
   a. Unscrew and remove the mirror (A, **Figure 3**).
   b. Remove the screws securing the left side switch assembly (B, **Figure 3**) and separate the housing halves.
   c. Remove the clutch lever clamp (C, **Figure 3**) mounting screws and washers, and separate the clamp halves.

5. Disconnect or remove any wiring harness clamps at the handlebar.

6A. On FXSTD models, remove the two front handlebar clamp bolts, then the rear clamp bolts. Remove both clamps and the handlebar.

6B. On all models except FXSTD, remove the two front handlebar clamp bolts, then the rear clamp bolts (**Figure 4**). Remove the clamp and the handlebar.

6C. To remove the handlebar and the lower clamps as an assembly, remove the bolt, lockwasher and washer (**Figure 5**) on each side securing the assembly to the upper bracket. Remove the handlebar assembly.

7. Install the handlebar by reversing these steps. Note the following:

    a. Check the knurled rings on the handlebar for galling and bits of aluminum. Clean the knurled section with a wire brush.

    b. Check the handlebar for cracks, bends or other damage. Replace the handlebar if necessary. Do not attempt to repair it.

    c. Thoroughly clean the upper and lower clamp halves of all residue.

    d. After installing the handlebar, reposition the handlebar while sitting on the motorcycle.

    e. Tighten the handlebar clamp bolts securely.

    f. Adjust the mirrors.

FRONT FORK

Front Fork Service

Before assuming a fork is malfunctioning, drain the front fork oil and refill with the proper type and quantity fork oil as described in Chapter Three. If there is still a problem, such as poor damping, a tendency to bottom or top out, or leakage around the oil seals, follow the service procedures in this section.

To simplify fork service and to prevent the mixing of parts, remove, service and install the fork legs individually.

Removal (Fork Not To Be Serviced)

1. On FLSTC models, perform the following:

    a. Remove the windshield as described in Chapter Fourteen.

    b. Remove the headlight assembly as described in Chapter Eight.

    c. Remove the screws securing the front trim panel located behind the headlight assembly.

2. Support the motorcycle with the front wheel off the ground. See *Motorcycle Stands* in Chapter Nine.

3. Remove the front brake caliper as described in Chapter Thirteen.

4. Remove the front fender and front wheel as described in Chapter Nine.

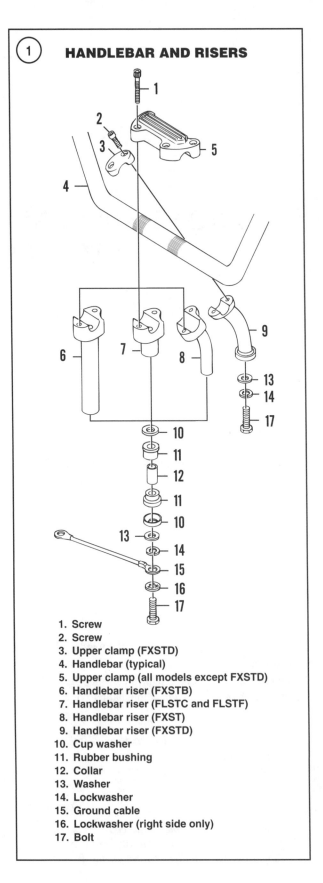

① HANDLEBAR AND RISERS

1. Screw
2. Screw
3. Upper clamp (FXSTD)
4. Handlebar (typical)
5. Upper clamp (all models except FXSTD)
6. Handlebar riser (FXSTB)
7. Handlebar riser (FLSTC and FLSTF)
8. Handlebar riser (FXST)
9. Handlebar riser (FXSTD)
10. Cup washer
11. Rubber bushing
12. Collar
13. Washer
14. Lockwasher
15. Ground cable
16. Lockwasher (right side only)
17. Bolt

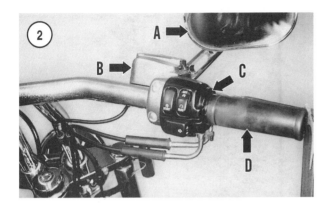

10

5. If removing both fork tube assemblies, mark them with an R (right side) and L (left side) so the assemblies will be reinstalled on the correct side.

NOTE
The fork cap bolt is not under spring pressure.

6. Loosen the fork cap bolt (**Figure 6**), then remove the bolt, spacer and oil seal (**Figure 7**) from the top of the fork tube.

7. Working at the side of the steering stem, loosen the lower bracket pinch bolt (**Figure 8**).

8. Carefully slide the fork tube out of the upper fork bracket.

9A. On FLSTC and FLSTF models, carefully slide the fork assembly out of the lower fork bracket and the chrome fork cover.

9B. On models other than FLSTC and FLSTF, slide the fork assembly out of the lower fork bracket.

10. Continue to slide the fork tube out of the lower fork bracket. It may be necessary to rotate the fork tube slightly while pulling it down and out. Remove the fork assembly and take it to the workbench for service. If the fork is not going to be serviced, wrap it in a bath towel or blanket to protect the surface from damage.

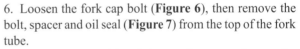

11. Repeat Steps 6-10 for the other fork assembly.

Installation (Fork Was Not Serviced)

1. Position the fork assembly so that one of the flats on the fork tube plug faces toward the inside of the motorcycle.

2A. On FLSTC and FLSTF models, carefully slide the fork assembly up through the lower fork bracket and the chrome fork cover.

2B. On models other than FLSTC and FLSTF, install a fork tube through the lower fork bracket.

3. Continue to push the fork tube up through the top fork bracket until it bottoms against the upper fork bracket.

4. Tighten the lower pinch bolt (**Figure 8**) finger tight at this time.

5. Install a *new* oil seal, spacer and fork cap bolt (**Figure 7**). Loosen the lower fork bracket bolt and tighten the fork cap bolt (**Figure 6**) to 40-60 ft.-lb. (52-81 N•m).

6. Tighten the lower bracket pinch bolt to 40 ft.-lb. (54 N•m).

7. Install the front fender and front wheel as described in Chapter Nine.

8. Install the front brake caliper as described in Chapter Thirteen.

9. On FLSTC and FLSTF models, perform the following:
    a. Install the front trim panel located behind the headlight assembly and tighten the screws securely.
    b. Install the headlight assembly as described in Chapter Eight.
    c. Install the windshield as described in Chapter Fourteen.

10. Apply the front brake and pump the front fork several times to seat the fork tubes and front wheel.

Removal (Fork To Be Serviced)

1. On FLSTC and FLSTF models, perform the following:
    a. Remove the windshield as described in Chapter Fourteen.
    b. Remove the headlight assembly as described in Chapter Eight.
    c. Remove the screws securing the front trim panel located behind the headlight assembly.

2. Support the motorcycle with the front wheel off the ground. See *Motorcycle Stands* in Chapter Nine.

3. Remove the front brake caliper as described in Chapter Thirteen.

4. Remove the front fender and front wheel as described in Chapter Nine.

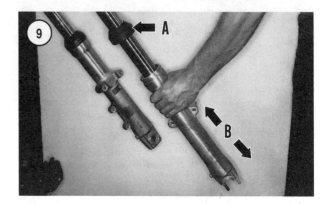

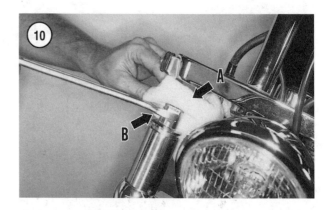

5. If removing both fork tube assemblies, mark them with an R (right side) and L (left side) so the assemblies will be reinstalled on the correct side.

NOTE
The fork cap bolt is not under spring pressure.

6. Loosen the fork cap bolt (**Figure 6**), then remove the bolt, spacer and oil seal (**Figure 7**) from the top of the fork tube.

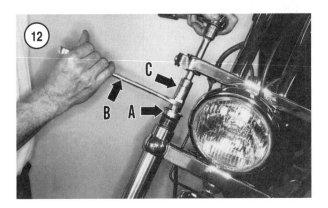

7. Working at the side of the steering stem, loosen the lower bracket pinch bolt (**Figure 8**).

8. Carefully slide the fork tube out of the upper fork bracket.

9. Slide the fork assembly part way down and retighten the lower bracket pinch bolt (**Figure 8**) securely.

10. Place a drain pan under the fork slider to catch the fork oil.

11. Use an 8 mm Allen wrench and impact driver and loosen the damper rod bolt at the base of the slider.

12. Remove the Allen bolt and washer and drain the fork oil. Pump the slider several times to expel most of the fork oil. Reinstall the Allen bolt to keep residual oil in the fork.

13. On models so equipped, slide the dust seal (A, **Figure 9**) up on the fork tube.

14. Remove the stopper ring from the fork slider.

15. Slide the fork slider down on the fork tube until it stops.

NOTE
It may be necessary to slightly heat the area on the slider around the oil seal prior to removal. Use a rag soaked in hot water; do not apply a flame directly to the fork slider.

16. There is a interference fit between the bushing in the fork slider and the bushing on the fork tube. Remove the fork tube from the slider, pull hard on the fork tube using quick up and down strokes (B, **Figure 9**). This will withdraw the bushing and the oil seal from the slider.

17. Remove the slider from the fork tube. Remove the oil lock piece from the damper rod if it is still in place.

WARNING
The fork tube plug is under spring pressure, protect yourself when removing the fork tube plug.

18. Place a shop cloth (A, **Figure 10**) between the upper fork bracket and the fork tube plug.

19. Slowly loosen the fork tube plug (B, **Figure 10**), then remove it and the O-ring seal.

20. Loosen the lower bracket pinch bolt.

21A. On FLSTC and FLSTF models, carefully slide the fork assembly out of the lower fork bracket and the chrome fork cover.

21B. On models other than FLSTC and FLSTF, slide the fork assembly out of the lower fork bracket (**Figure 11**).

22. It may be necessary to rotate the fork tube slightly while pulling it down and out. Remove the fork assembly and take it to the workbench for service.

23. Repeat Steps 6-22 for the other fork assembly.

10

Installation (Fork Was Serviced)

NOTE
Do not install the fork tube plug until the fork assembly is installed in the lower fork bracket. The fork spring must be compressed in order to install the fork tube plug and it is easier to accomplish this with the fork assembly partially installed in the frame.

1. Assemble the fork(s), only up to and including the fork spring, as described in this chapter.

2A. On FLSTC and FLSTF models, carefully slide the fork assembly up through the lower fork bracket and the chrome fork cover.

2B. On models other than FLSTC and FLSTF, install a fork tube through the lower fork.

3. Continue to push the fork tube up through the lower fork bracket until it is just above the top surface of the lower fork bracket (**Figure 11**).

4. Tighten the lower bracket pinch bolt securely.

5. Install the fork tube plug as follows:
    a. Install the fork tube plug on top of the fork spring (A, **Figure 12**).

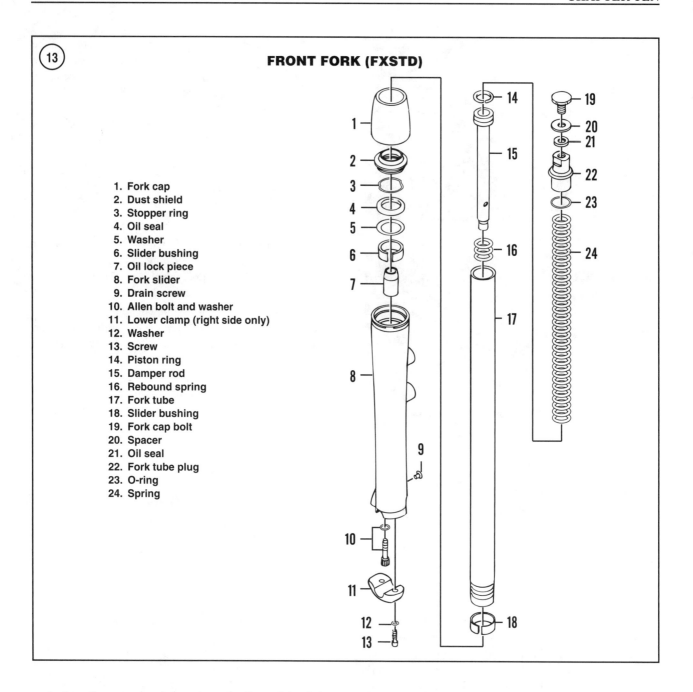

FRONT FORK (FXSTD)

1. Fork cap
2. Dust shield
3. Stopper ring
4. Oil seal
5. Washer
6. Slider bushing
7. Oil lock piece
8. Fork slider
9. Drain screw
10. Allen bolt and washer
11. Lower clamp (right side only)
12. Washer
13. Screw
14. Piston ring
15. Damper rod
16. Rebound spring
17. Fork tube
18. Slider bushing
19. Fork cap bolt
20. Spacer
21. Oil seal
22. Fork tube plug
23. O-ring
24. Spring

b. Install an open-end wrench on the flats of the fork tube plug (B, **Figure 12**).

c. Insert a socket that fits onto the top surface of the fork tube plug (C, **Figure 12**) and an extension down through the top fork bracket onto the top surface of the fork tube plug.

d. Press down on the socket and extension to compress the fork spring. Slowly thread the fork tube plug into the fork tube being careful to not cross-thread it. Tighten the fork tube plug securely. There is no torque specification for this plug.

6. Loosen the lower bracket pinch bolt.

7. Position the fork assembly so one of the flats on the fork tube plug faces toward the inside of the motorcycle.

8. Push the fork assembly up until it bottoms against the upper fork bracket.

9. Tighten the lower bracket pinch bolt (**Figure 8**) finger tight at this time.

10. Install a *new* oil seal, spacer and fork cap bolt (**Figure 7**). Loosen the lower fork bracket bolt and tighten the fork cap bolt (Figure 6) to 40-60 ft.-lb. (52-81 N•m).

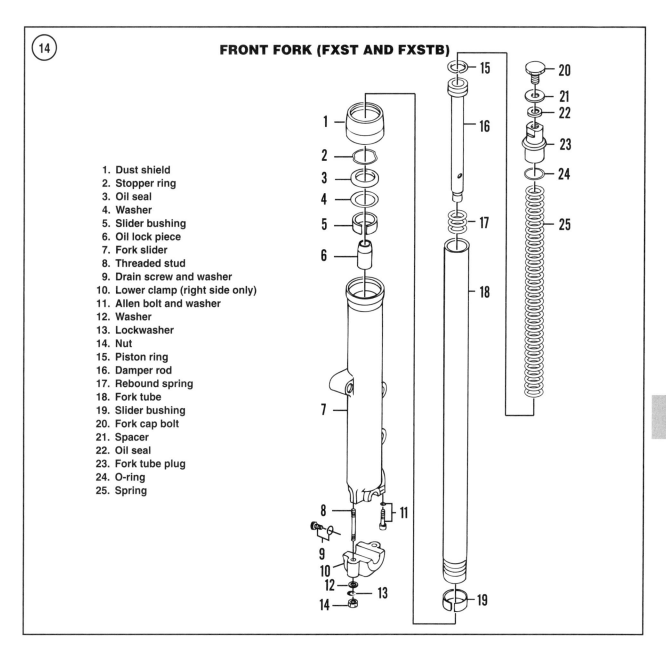

FRONT FORK (FXST AND FXSTB)

1. Dust shield
2. Stopper ring
3. Oil seal
4. Washer
5. Slider bushing
6. Oil lock piece
7. Fork slider
8. Threaded stud
9. Drain screw and washer
10. Lower clamp (right side only)
11. Allen bolt and washer
12. Washer
13. Lockwasher
14. Nut
15. Piston ring
16. Damper rod
17. Rebound spring
18. Fork tube
19. Slider bushing
20. Fork cap bolt
21. Spacer
22. Oil seal
23. Fork tube plug
24. O-ring
25. Spring

11. Tighten the lower bracket pinch bolt to 40 ft.-lb. (54 N•m).

12. Install the front fender and front wheel as described in Chapter Nine.

13. Install the front brake caliper as described in Chapter Thirteen.

14. On FLSTC and FLSTF models, perform the following:

   a. Install the front trim panel located behind the headlight assembly and tighten the screws securely.

   b. Install the headlight assembly as described in Chapter Eight.

   c. Install the windshield as described in Chapter Fourteen.

15. Apply the front brake and pump the front fork several times to seat the fork tubes and front wheel.

Disassembly (Without Special Tool)

   Refer to **Figures 13-15**.

1. Remove the fork tube plug as described under. *Removal (Fork To Be Serviced)* in this chapter.

2. Remove the fork spring, and drain any residual fork oil. Dispose of the fork oil properly.

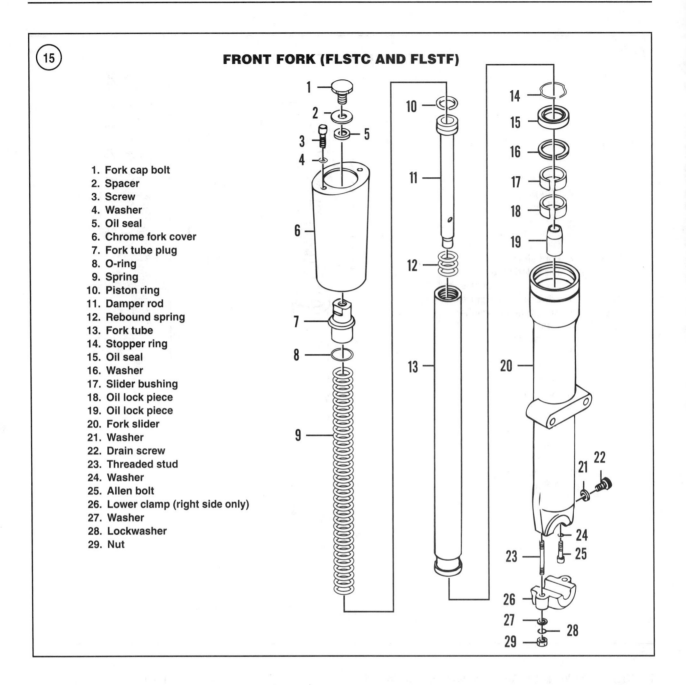

15

FRONT FORK (FLSTC AND FLSTF)

1. Fork cap bolt
2. Spacer
3. Screw
4. Washer
5. Oil seal
6. Chrome fork cover
7. Fork tube plug
8. O-ring
9. Spring
10. Piston ring
11. Damper rod
12. Rebound spring
13. Fork tube
14. Stopper ring
15. Oil seal
16. Washer
17. Slider bushing
18. Oil lock piece
19. Oil lock piece
20. Fork slider
21. Washer
22. Drain screw
23. Threaded stud
24. Washer
25. Allen bolt
26. Lower clamp (right side only)
27. Washer
28. Lockwasher
29. Nut

3. Turn the fork tube upside down, and remove the damper rod and rebound spring.

4. Slide the dust seal, oil seal, washer and fork slider bushing off the fork tube.

5. Inspect the fork assembly as described under *Inspection (All Models)* in this chapter.

Assembly (Without Special Tool)

1. Install a *new* O-ring (**Figure 16**) onto the fork top plug.

16

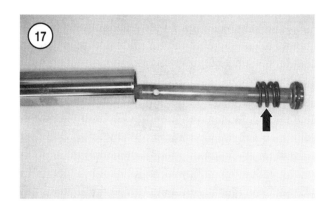

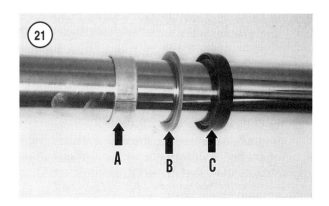

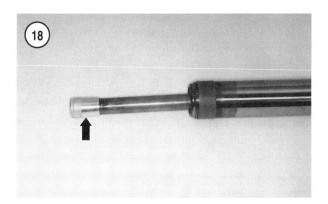

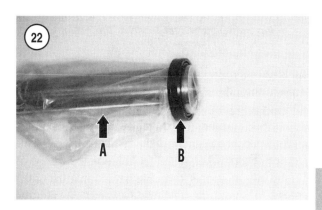

10

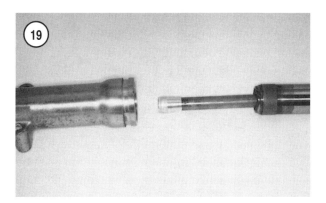

2. Coat all parts with Harley-Davidson Type E Fork Oil, or an equivalent, before assembly.

3. Install the rebound spring (**Figure 17**) onto the damper rod and slide the damper rod into the fork tube until it extends out the end of the fork tube.

4. Install the oil lock piece (**Figure 18**) onto the end of the damper rod.

5. Install the fork tube into the fork slider (**Figure 19**). Insert a Phillips screwdriver through the opening in the bottom of the fork tube and guide the damper rod end into the receptacle in the base of the slider. Remove the screwdriver.

6. Install a new washer onto the damper rod Allen bolt (**Figure 20**).

7. Apply a non-permanent threadlocking compound to the damper rod Allen bolt threads prior to installation. Insert the Allen bolt and washer through the lower end of the slider and thread it into the damper rod. Tighten the Allen bolt securely.

8. Slide the fork slider bushing (A, **Figure 21**) and washer (B) onto the fork tube.

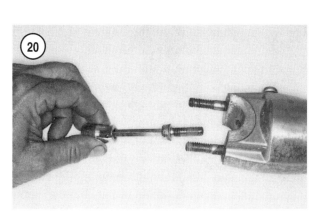

NOTE
*To protect the oil seal lips, place a thin plastic bag (A, **Figure 22**) on top of the fork tube. Before installing the seal in the follow-*

ing steps, lightly coat the bag and the seal lips with fork oil.

9. Position the *new* oil seal with the letters facing up (B, **Figure 22**) and slide it down the fork tube (C, **Figure 21**).

> *NOTE*
> *A fork seal driver is required to install the fork tube bushing and seal into the fork tube. A number of different aftermarket fork seal drivers (JIMS part No. 2046) are available. Another method is to use a piece of pipe or a metal collar with the correct dimensions to slide over the fork tube and seat against the seal. Select or fabricate a driver tool that has sufficient weight to drive the bushing and oil seal into the fork tube.*

10. Slide the fork seal driver down the fork tube and seat it against the oil seal (**Figure 23**).

11. Operate the driver and drive the fork slider bushing and new seal into the fork tube. Continue to operate the driver until the stopper ring groove in the tube is visible above the fork seal (**Figure 24**). Remove the fork seal driver tool.

12. Install the stopper ring (**Figure 25**) into the slider groove. Make sure the retaining ring seats in the groove.

13. On all models except FLSTC and FLSTF, install the dust seal (**Figure 26**) and seat it into the slider.

14. Fill the fork assemblies with the correct viscosity and quantity of fork as described under *Front Fork Oil Change* in this section.

15. Position the fork spring with the tighter wound coils going in first and install the fork spring into the fork tube (**Figure 27**).

16. Keep the fork assembly vertical and install it as described in this chapter.

17. After installation, make sure the Allen bolt is tight and that there is no fork oil leakage.

Disassembly (With Special Tool)

Refer to **Figures 13-15**.

> *NOTE*
> *If the fork tube cap was not loosened and removed during removal, a special fork holding tool is required to disassemble and assemble the fork assembly. The fork spring cannot be compressed enough by hand to loosen and remove the fork tube plug. This special tool is available from motorcycle dealerships or motorcycle parts supply houses.*

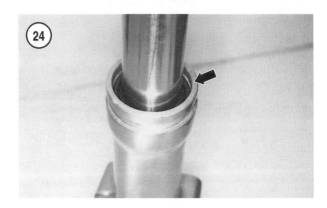

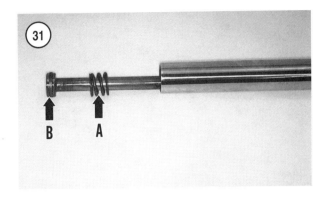

1. To protect the fork tube, place a steel washer (A, **Figure 28**) over the fork damper rod and up against the base of the fork tube.

2. Tighten the lower bolt (B, **Figure 28**) so it is seated below the steel washer. Do not over tighten the bolt as the damper rod will be damaged. Make sure the tool is indexed properly against the steel washer.

3. Install the special tool's upper bolt into the hole in the fork tube plug (A, **Figure 29**) following the manufacturer's instructions. Make sure the tool is indexed properly in the hole in the fork tube plug.

WARNING
Be careful when removing the fork top plug as the spring is under pressure. Protect eyes and face accordingly.

4. Hold onto the fork tube and loosen the fork tube plug (B, **Figure 29**). Slowly loosen the special tool while unscrewing the fork tube plug.

5. When the fork tube plug is completely unscrewed from the fork tube, loosen and remove the special tool from the fork assembly.

6. Remove the fork tube plug and fork spring, and drain any residual fork oil. Dispose of the fork oil properly.

7. Turn the fork tube upside down, and remove the damper rod and rebound spring.

8. Slide the dust seal, oil seal, washer and fork slider bushing off the fork tube.

9. Inspect the fork assembly as described under *Inspection (All Models)* in this section

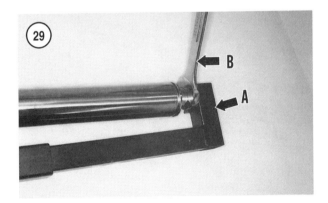

Assembly (With Special Tool)

1. Install a *new* O-ring onto the fork top plug (**Figure 30**).

2. Coat all parts with Harley-Davidson Type E Fork Oil, or an equivalent, before assembly.

3. Install the rebound spring (A, **Figure 31**) onto the damper rod and slide the damper rod (B) into the fork tube until it extends out the end of the fork tube.

10

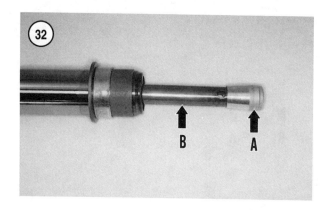

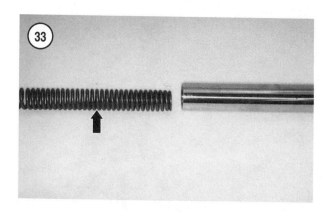

4. Install the oil lock piece (A, **Figure 32**) onto the end of the damper rod (B).

5. Position the fork spring with the tighter wound coils going in first (**Figure 33**) and install the fork spring into the fork tube.

6. To protect the fork tube, place a steel washer (A, **Figure 28**) over the fork damper rod and up against the base of the fork tube.

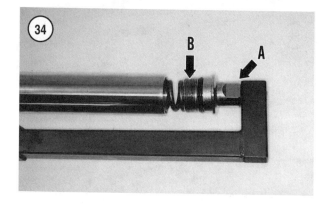

7. Tighten the lower bolt (B, **Figure 28**) so it is seated below the steel washer. Do not over tighten the bolt as the damper rod will be damaged. Make sure the tool is indexed properly against the steel washer.

8. Position the fork tube plug onto the top of the fork spring.

9. Install the special tool's upper bolt into the hole in the fork tube plug (A, **Figure 34**) following the manufacturer's instructions. Make sure the tool is indexed properly in the hole in the fork tube plug.

CAUTION
While tightening the special tool, do not jamb the fork tube plug into the threaded portion of the fork tube. This will damage the threads on both parts.

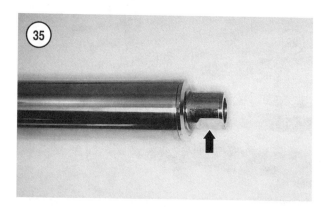

10. Hold onto the fork tube plug and slowly tighten the special tool while guiding the fork tube plug into the top of the fork tube (B, **Figure 34**).

11. Place a wrench on the fork tube plug (B, **Figure 29**) and screw the fork tube plug into the fork tube while tightening the special tool. Once the fork tube plug has started to thread into the fork tube, loosen the special tool and remove it from the fork assembly.

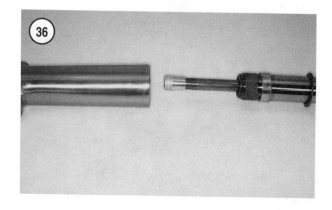

12. Place the slider in a vise with soft jaws and tighten the fork top plug (**Figure 35**) securely.

13. Push the fork slider and damper rod (**Figure 36**) into the fork slider. Insert a Phillips screwdriver through the opening in the bottom of the fork tube and guide the

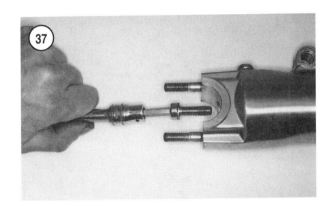

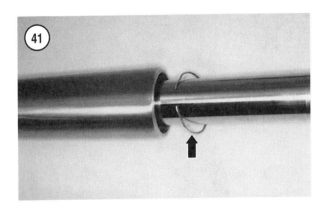

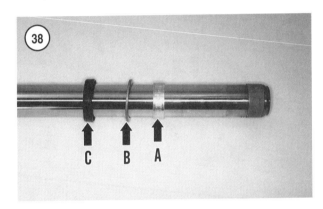

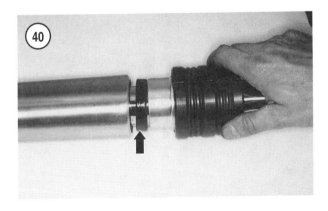

damper rod end into the receptacle in the base of the slider. Remove the screwdriver.

14. Install a new washer onto the damper rod Allen bolt.

15. Apply a non-permanent threadlocking compound to the damper rod Allen bolt threads prior to installation. Insert the Allen bolt (**Figure 37**) and washer through the lower end of the slider and thread it into the damper rod. Tighten the bolt securely.

NOTE
To protect the oil seal lips, place a thin plastic bag on top of the fork tube. Before installing the seal in the following steps, lightly coat the bag and the seal lips with fork oil.

16. Slide the fork slider bushing (A, **Figure 38**), washer (B) and oil seal (C) (with the letters facing up) down into the fork tube receptacle (**Figure 39**).

NOTE
A fork seal driver is required to install the fork tube bushing and seal into the fork tube. A number of different aftermarket fork seal drivers (JIMS part No. 2046) are available. Another method is to use a piece of pipe or a metal collar with the correct dimensions to slide over the fork tube and seat against the seal. Select or fabricate a driver tool that has sufficient weight to drive the bushing and oil seal into the fork tube.

17. Slide the fork seal driver down the fork tube and seat it against the oil seal (**Figure 40**).

18. Operate the driver and drive the fork slider bushing and new seal into the fork tube. Continue to operate the driver until the stopper ring groove in the tube is visible above the fork seal. Remove the fork seal driver tool.

19. Install the stopper ring (**Figure 41**) into the slider groove. Make sure the retaining ring seats in the groove (**Figure 42**).

10

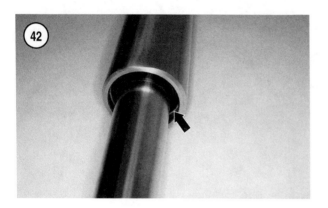

20. Fill the fork assemblies with the correct viscosity and quantity of fork as described under *Front Fork Oil Change* in this section

21. Install the fork tube as described in this chapter.

Inspection (All Models)

Replace worn or damaged parts.

1. Thoroughly clean all parts in solvent and dry them. Check the fork tube for signs of wear or scratches.

2. Check the fork tube for bending, nicks, rust or other damage. Place the fork tube on a set of V-blocks and check runout with a dial indicator. If the special tools are not available, roll the fork tube on a large plate glass or another flat surface. Harley-Davidson does not provide service specifications for runout.

3. Check the internal threads in the top of the fork tube (**Figure 43**) for stripping, cross-threading or sealer residue. Use a tap to true the threads and to remove sealer deposits.

4. Check the fork tube plug O-ring (A, **Figure 44**) for hardness or deterioration. Replace if necessary.

5. Check the external threads on the fork tube plug (B, **Figure 44**) for stripping, cross-threading or sealer residue. Use a die to true the threads and to remove sealer deposits.

6. Make sure the oil passage hole in the fork tube (**Figure 45**) is open. If it is clogged, flush it with solvent and dry it with compressed air.

7. Check the fork cap bolt O-ring (A, **Figure 46**) for hardness or deterioration. Replace if necessary.

8. Check the external threads on the fork cap (B, **Figure 46**) for stripping, cross-threading or sealer residue. Use a die to true the threads and to remove sealer deposits.

9. Check the slider (**Figure 47**) for dents or other exterior damage. Check the retaining ring groove (**Figure 48**) in the top of the slider for cracks or other damage.

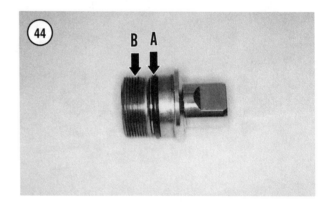

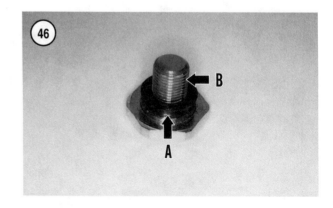

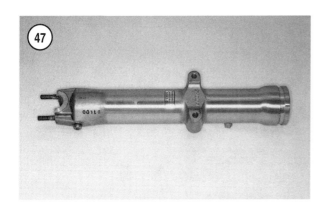

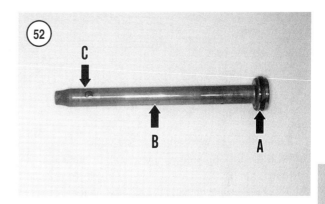

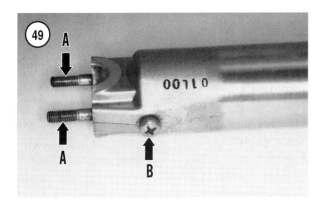

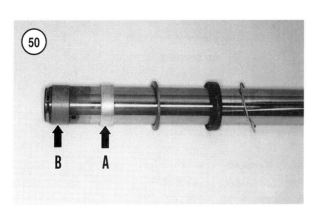

10

10. Check the front caliper mounting bosses for cracks or damage.

11. Check the threaded studs (A, **Figure 49**) on the base of the slider for thread damage. Repair if necessary.

12. Check the drain screw (B, **Figure 49**) and washer for damage.

13. Check the slider (A, **Figure 50**) and fork tube bushings (B) for excessive wear, cracks or damage.

14. Remove the fork tube bushing as follows:

    a. Expand the bushing slit (**Figure 51**) with a screwdriver and slide the bushing off the fork tube.

    b. Coat the new bushing with new fork oil.

    c. Install the new bushing by expanding the slit with a screwdriver.

    d. Seat the new bushing into the fork tube groove.

15. Check the damper rod piston ring (A, **Figure 52**) for excessive wear, cracks or other damage. If necessary, replace both rings as a set.

16. Check the damper rod (B, **Figure 52**) for straightness with a set of V-blocks and a dial indicator (**Figure 53**), or by rolling it on a piece of plate glass. Specifications for runout are not available. If the damper rod is not straight, replace it.

17. Make sure the oil passage hole in the damper rod (C, **Figure 52**) is open. If it is clogged, flush it with solvent and dry it with compressed air.

18. Check the internal threads in the bottom of the damper rod for stripping, cross-threading or sealer residue. Use a tap to true the threads and to remove sealer deposits.

19. Check the damper rod rebound spring and the fork spring for wear or damage. Service limit specifications for spring free length are not available. If necessary, replace both fork springs as a set.

20. Replace the oil seal whenever it is removed. Always replace both oil seals as a set.

Front Fork Oil Change

NOTE
Always adjust fork oil by measuring the fork oil level. Do not rely on the fork oil capacity. Inaccurate setting will result.

1. Secure the fork vertically in a vise with soft jaws.
2. Push the fork tube down into the slider until the tube bottoms.
3. Refer to **Table 2** and add the recommended amount of fork oil into the fork assembly.
4. Slowly raise and lower the fork tube several times to distribute the oil.
5. After the fork oil, settles fully compress the fork tube.
6. Use an accurate ruler or the Motion Pro oil gauge (part No. 08-0121) (**Figure 54**), or an equivalent, to achieve the correct oil level listed in **Table 2**.
7. Allow the oil to settle completely and recheck the oil level measurement. Adjust the oil level if necessary.
8. Remove the special tool.
9. Fully extend the fork tube and install the fork as described in this chapter.

STEERING HEAD AND STEM

Removal (FLSTC and FLSTF Models)

Refer to **Figure 55**.
1. On FLSTC models, remove the windshield as described in Chapter Fourteen.
2. Remove the fuel tank as described in Chapter Seven.
3. Remove the front fender and front wheel as described in Chapter Nine.
4. Remove both front fork legs as described in this chapter.
5. Remove the handlebar as described in this chapter.

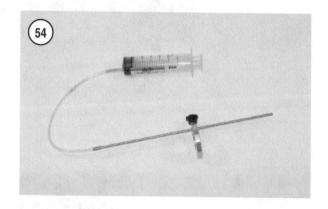

6. Remove the headlight and headlight bracket as described in Chapter Eight.

7. Remove the screws and nuts securing the front and back trim panels to the upper and lower brackets. Remove all three panels.

8. Remove the screws and lockwashers securing the fork tube covers and remove both covers.

9. Remove the bolt securing the front brake hose to the bottom of the lower fork bracket. Do not disconnect any brake hose connections.

10. Remove the steering stem cap.

11. Loosen the pinch bolt on the upper bracket.

CAUTION
Hold or secure the steering stem to keep it from falling after removal of the fork stem bolt and washer in Step 12.

12. Loosen and remove the fork stem bolt and washer.

13. Remove the upper fork bracket, then slide the steering stem/lower bracket out of the steering head.

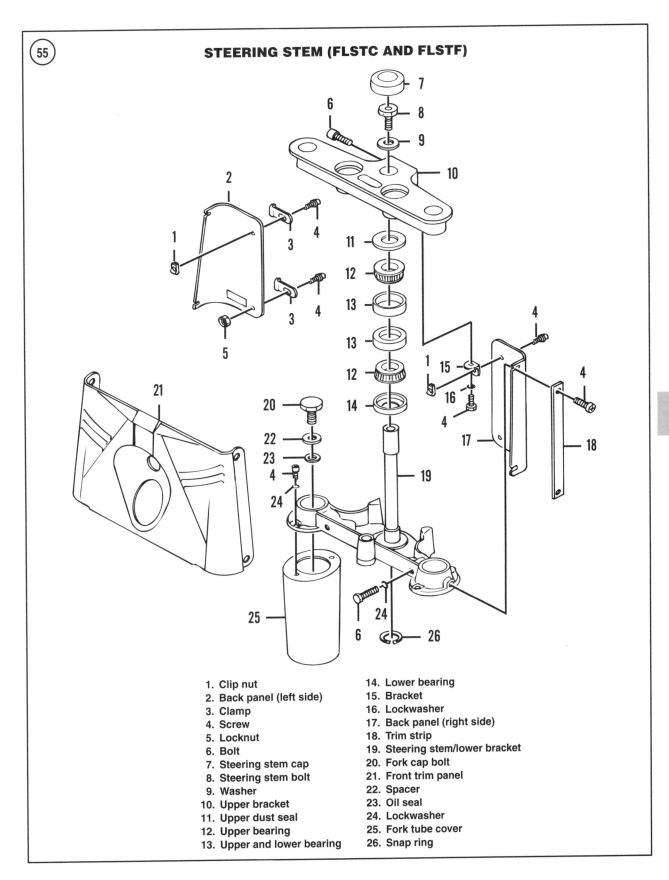

STEERING STEM (FLSTC AND FLSTF)

55

1. Clip nut
2. Back panel (left side)
3. Clamp
4. Screw
5. Locknut
6. Bolt
7. Steering stem cap
8. Steering stem bolt
9. Washer
10. Upper bracket
11. Upper dust seal
12. Upper bearing
13. Upper and lower bearing
14. Lower bearing
15. Bracket
16. Lockwasher
17. Back panel (right side)
18. Trim strip
19. Steering stem/lower bracket
20. Fork cap bolt
21. Front trim panel
22. Spacer
23. Oil seal
24. Lockwasher
25. Fork tube cover
26. Snap ring

10

14. Remove the upper dust shield and bearing from the steering head.

15. Inspect the steering stem and bearing assembly as described under *Inspection (All Models)* in this section.

Installation
(FLSTC and FLSTF Models)

1. If the steering head bearing races were replaced, make sure they are seated in the steering head.

2. Wipe the bearing races with a clean, lint-free cloth. Then lubricate each race with bearing grease.

3. Pack the upper and lower bearings with bearing grease.

4. If removed, install the lower dust shield and the lower bearing on the steering stem/lower bracket as described in this chapter.

5. Insert the steering stem/lower bracket into the frame steering head and hold it firmly in place.

6. Install the upper bearing over the steering stem and seat it into to the upper race. Install the upper dust shield.

7. Install the upper bracket, *new* washer and the steering stem bolt. Tighten the steering stem bolt finger-tight at this time.

8. Install the fork tube covers, lockwashers and screws. Tighten the screws securely.

9. Install the front fork legs as described in this chapter.

CAUTION
Do not overtighten the steering stem bolt in Step 9 or damage will occur to the bearings and races. Final adjustment of the fork stem will take place after the front wheel is installed.

10. Tighten the steering stem bolt until the steering stem/lower bracket can be turned from side to side with no axial or lateral play. When the play feels correct, tighten the steering stem bolt to 97-124 in.-lb. (11-14 N•m).

11. Install the steering stem cap.

12. Install the front brake hose to the bottom of the lower fork bracket and tighten the bolt securely.

13. Install the three front and back trim panels to the fork brackets. Tighten the screws and nuts securely.

14. Install the headlight bracket and headlight as described in Chapter Eight.

15. Install the handlebar as described in this chapter.

16. Install the front fender and front wheel as described in Chapter Nine.

17. Install the fuel tank as described in Chapter Seven.

18. On FLSTC models, install the windshield as described in Chapter Fourteen.

19. Adjust the steering play as described under *Steering Play Adjustment* in this chapter.

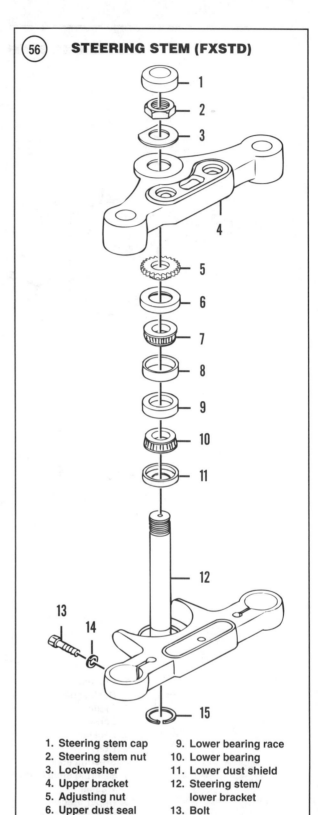

(56) STEERING STEM (FXSTD)

1. Steering stem cap	9. Lower bearing race
2. Steering stem nut	10. Lower bearing
3. Lockwasher	11. Lower dust shield
4. Upper bracket	12. Steering stem/
5. Adjusting nut	lower bracket
6. Upper dust seal	13. Bolt
7. Upper bearing	14. Lockwasher
8. Upper bearing race	15. Snap ring

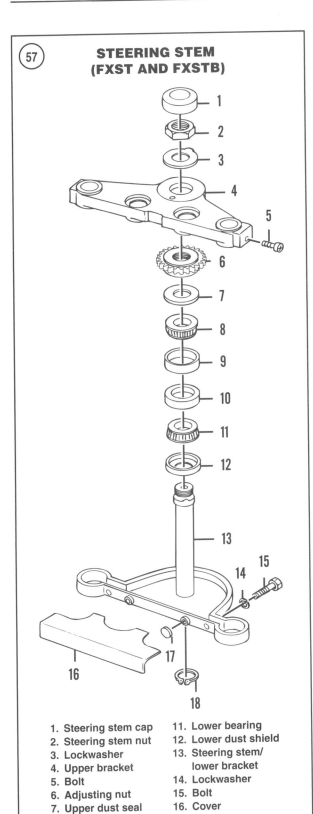

**STEERING STEM
(FXST AND FXSTB)**

1. Steering stem cap
2. Steering stem nut
3. Lockwasher
4. Upper bracket
5. Bolt
6. Adjusting nut
7. Upper dust seal
8. Upper bearing
9. Upper bearing race
10. Lower bearing race
11. Lower bearing
12. Lower dust shield
13. Steering stem/
    lower bracket
14. Lockwasher
15. Bolt
16. Cover
17. Pad
18. Snap ring

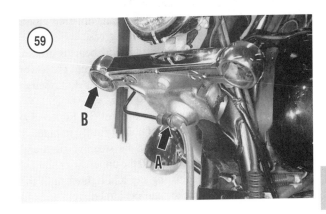

10

Removal
(FXSTD, FXST and FXSTB Models)

Refer to **Figure 56** and **Figure 57**.

1. Remove the fuel tank as described in Chapter Seven.

2. Remove the front fender and front wheel as described in Chapter Nine.

3. Remove both front fork legs as described in this chapter.

4. Unscrew and remove the steering stem cap (**Figure 58**).

5. Remove the bolt securing the front brake hose (A, **Figure 59**) assembly to the bottom of the lower fork bracket. Do not disconnect any brake hose connections.

6. Remove the handlebar (A, **Figure 60**) as described in this chapter.

7. Remove the headlight and headlight bracket (B, **Figure 60**) as described in Chapter Eight.

8. Pry the tab on the lockwasher away from the steering stem nut.

9. Remove the steering stem nut (C, **Figure 60**) and lockwasher. Discard the lockwasher.

10. Remove the upper fork bracket (D, **Figure 60**).

CAUTION
Hold or secure the steering stem to keep it from falling after removal of the bearing adjusting nut in Step 11.

11. Loosen and remove the bearing adjusting nut, then slide the steering stem/lower bracket (B, **Figure 59**) out of the steering head.

12. Remove the upper dust shield and bearing from the steering head.

13. Inspect the steering stem and bearing assembly as described under *Inspection (All Models)* in this section.

Installation
(FXSTD, FXST and FXSTB Models)

1. If the steering head bearing races were replaced, make sure they are seated in the steering head.

2. Wipe the bearing races with a clean, lint-free cloth. Then lubricate each race with bearing grease.

3. Pack the upper and lower bearings with bearing grease.

4. If removed, install the lower dust shield and the lower bearing on the steering stem/lower bracket as described in this chapter.

5. Insert the steering stem/lower bracket (B, **Figure 59**) into the frame steering head and hold it firmly in place.

6. Install the upper bearing over the steering stem and seat it into to the upper race. Install the upper dust shield.

7. Install the bearing adjusting nut and tighten until the steering stem/lower bracket can be turned from side to side with no axial or lateral play. When the play feels correct, tighten the bearing adjusting nut securely.

8. Install the upper bracket (D, **Figure 60**).

9. Install the *new* lockwasher and engage its pin with the hole in the upper bracket. This is necessary to keep the lockwasher from rotating.

10. Install the steering stem nut (C, **Figure 60**). Tighten the steering stem nut finger-tight at this time.

11. Install the front fork legs as described in this chapter.

> *CAUTION*
> *Do not overtighten the steering stem nut in Step 12 or damage will occur to the bearings and races. Final adjustment of the fork stem will take place after the front wheel is installed.*

12. Tighten the steering stem nut until the steering stem/lower bracket can be turned from side to side with no axial or lateral play. When the play feels correct, tighten the steering stem nut to 50-65 ft.-lb. (68-88 N•m).

13. Bend the tab on the lockwasher up against the flats on the steering stem nut.

14. Install the steering stem cap (**Figure 58**) and tighten securely.

15. Install the front brake hose assembly (A, **Figure 59**) onto the bottom of the lower fork bracket and tighten the bolt securely.

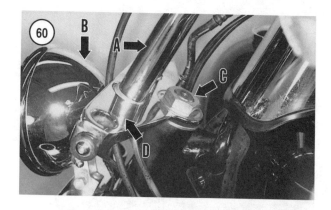

16. Install the headlight bracket and headlight (B, **Figure 60**) as described in Chapter Eight.

17. Install the handlebar (A, **Figure 60**) as described in this chapter.

18. Install the front fender and front wheel as described in Chapter Nine.

19. Install the fuel tank as described in Chapter Seven.

20. Adjust the steering play as described under *Steering Play Adjustment* in this chapter.

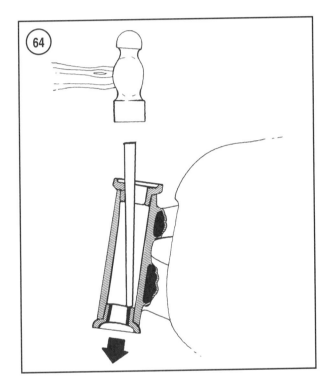

Inspection (All Models)

The bearing outer races are pressed into the steering head. Do not remove them unless they are going to be replaced.

1. Wipe the bearing races with a solvent-soaked rag and dry them with compressed air or a lint-free cloth. Check the races in the steering head (**Figure 61**) for pitting, scratches, galling or excessive wear. If any of these conditions exist, replace the races as described in this chapter. If the races are in good condition, wipe each race with grease.

2. Clean the bearings in solvent to remove all of the old grease. Blow the bearing dry with compressed air, making sure not to allow the air jet to spin the bearing. Do not re-

move the lower bearing from the fork stem unless it is to be replaced. Clean the bearing while it is installed in the steering stem.

3. After the bearings are dry, hold the inner race with one hand and turn the outer race with the other hand. Turn the bearing slowly. The bearing should turn smoothly with no roughness. Visually check the bearing (**Figure 62**) for pitting, scratches or visible damage. If the bearings are worn, check the dust covers for wear or damage, or for improper bearing lubrication. Replace the bearing if necessary. If a bearing is going to be reused, pack it with grease and wrap it with wax paper or another lint-free material until it is reinstalled. Do not store the bearings for any length of time without lubricating them to prevent rust.

4. Check the steering stem/lower bracket for cracks or damage. Check the threads at the top of the stem for damage. Check the steering stem bolt or nut for damage and thread it into the steering stem. Make sure the bolt or nut threads easily with no roughness.

5. Replace all worn or damaged parts. Replace bearing races as described in this chapter.

6. Replace the lower steering stem bearing (**Figure 63**) and the dust shield as described in this chapter.

7. Check for broken welds on the frame around the steering head. If any are found, have them repaired by a competent frame shop or welding service familiar with motorcycle frame repair.

STEERING HEAD BEARING RACE REPLACEMENT

The upper and lower bearing outer races are pressed into the frame. Do not remove the bearing races unless replacement is necessary. If they are removed, replace both the outer race and bearing at the same time. Never reinstall an outer race that has been removed as it is no longer true and will damage the bearing.

1. Remove the steering stem as described in this chapter.

2. To remove a race, insert an aluminum or brass rod into the steering head and carefully tap the race out from the inside (**Figure 64**). Tap all around the race so neither the race nor the steering head is bent.

3. Clean the steering head with solvent and dry it thoroughly.

4A. Install the bearing races with the steering head bearing race installer tool (JIMS part No. 1725) following the manufacturer's instructions.

4B. If the special tools are not available, install the bearing races as follows:

   a. Clean the race thoroughly before installing it.

   b. Align the upper race with the frame steering head and tap it slowly and squarely in place. Do not con-

10

tact the bearing race surfaces. See **Figure 65**. Drive the race into the steering head until it bottoms on the bore shoulder.

    c. Repeat substeps a-c to install the lower race into the steering head.

5. Apply bearing grease to the face of each race.

Fork Stem Lower Bearing Replacement

Do not remove the steering stem lower bearing and lower dust seal unless they are going to be replaced. The lower bearing can be difficult to remove. If the lower bearing cannot be removed as described in this procedure, take the steering stem to a Harley-Davidson dealership.

Never reinstall a lower bearing that has been removed; it is no longer true and will damage the bearing assembly.

1. Install the steering stem bolt or nut onto the top of the steering stem to protect the threads.

2. Loosen the lower bearing from the shoulder at the base of the steering stem with a chisel as shown in **Figure 66**. Slide the lower bearing and lower dust seal off the steering stem.

3. Clean the steering stem with solvent and dry it thoroughly.

4. Position the new lower dust seal with the flange side facing up.

5. Slide a *new* lower dust seal and the lower bearing onto the steering stem until the bearing stops on the raised shoulder.

6. Align the lower bearing with the machined shoulder on the steering stem. Press or drive the lower bearing onto the steering stem until it bottoms (**Figure 67**).

STEERING PLAY ADJUSTMENT

If aftermarket accessories have been installed on the steering assembly, they must be removed before attempting to adjust the steering play.

1. Use a floor jack centrally located under the frame. Support the motorcycle with both the front and rear wheels the same distance off the ground. If necessary, place a wooden block(s) under the rear wheel until the motorcycle is level on level ground.

2. On FLSTC models, remove the windshield as described in Chapter Fourteen.

3. If any control cable is routed so that it pulls the front end one way or the other, disconnect it.

4. Loosen the lower fork bracket pinch bolts.

5. Place a piece of masking tape transversely across the leading edge of the front fender.

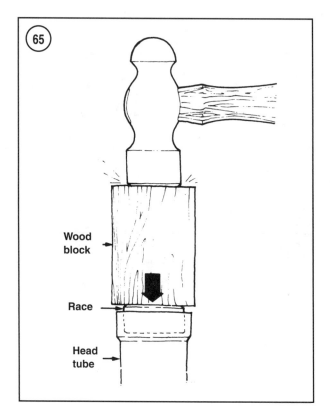

65

Wood block

Race

Head tube

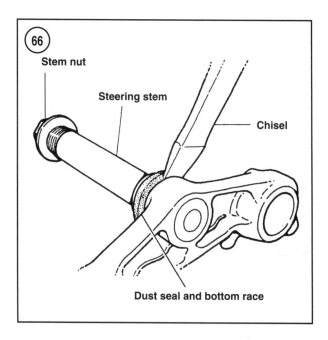

66

Stem nut

Steering stem

Chisel

Dust seal and bottom race

6. Swing the handlebar so that the front wheel faces straight ahead.

7. Place a pointer on a stand so that its tip points to the center of the fender when the wheel is facing straight ahead.

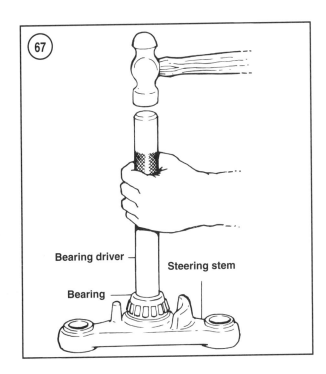

Bearing driver

Steering stem

Bearing

8. Lightly push the fender towards the right side until the front end starts to turn by itself. Mark this point on the piece of tape.

9. Repeat Step 8 for the left side.

10. Measure the distance between the two marks on the tape. For proper bearing adjustment, the distance should be 1-2 in. (25.4-50.8 mm). If the distance is incorrect, perform Step 11.

11. Adjust the steering head bearing as follows:

   a. If the distance is less than 1 in. (25.4 mm), tighten the adjusting nut, or steering stem bolt slightly.

   b. If the distance is greater than 2 in. (50.8 mm) loosen the adjusting nut, or steering stem bolt slightly.

   c. Repeat Steps 8-10 until adjustment is within 1-2 inches (25.4-50.8 mm).

   d. Tighten the lower fork bracket pinch bolts to 40 ft.-lb. (54 N•m).

12. Lower the motorcycle to the ground.

13. On FLSTC models, install the windshield as described in Chapter Fourteen.

14. Connect any control cable that was disconnected.

10

Table 1 FRONT SUSPENSION TORQUE SPECIFICATIONS

Item	ft.-lb.	in.-lb.	N•m
Brake hose bracket bolt	8-10	–	11-14
Front fork			
Cap bolt	40-60	–	52-81
Drain screw			
FXSTD	–	12-18	1.4-2.0
All models except FXSTD	–	52-78	6-9
Fork slider cap	11-15	–	15-20
Lower fork bracket pinch bolts	40	–	54
Steering stem nut			
FXSTD, FXST, FSXTB	50-65	–	68-88
Steering stem bolt			
FLSTC, FLSTF	–	97-124	11-14
Front fender bolts	14-18	–	19-24

Table 2 FRONT FORK OIL CAPACITY AND OIL LEVEL DIMENSION

Model	Capacity (each fork leg)	Oil level dimension
FLSTF, FLSTC	12.9 U.S. oz.	4.72 in. (119.9 mm)
FLSTC, FXST		
FXSTB	12.0 U.S. oz.	7.28 in. (184.9 mm)
FXSTD	11.6 U.S. oz.	7.48 in. (189.9 mm)

CHAPTER ELEVEN

FRONT SUSPENSION AND STEERING (SPRINGER FORK)

This chapter covers the handlebar, steering head and front fork assemblies for the FXSTS and FLSTS. All other models are covered in Chapter Ten.

Table 1 at the end of the chapter lists torque specifications.

> *WARNING*
> *All fasteners used on the Springer front suspension must be replaced with parts of the same type. Do not use a replacement part of lesser quality or substitute design. It may affect the performance of the front suspension or fail, leading to loss of control of the motorcycle. Use the torque specifications in **Table 1** during installation to ensure proper retention of these components.*

SPRINGER SERVICE PRECAUTIONS

1. Read the applicable service procedure prior to performing any service work. In some instances, it is necessary to have various special tools available. Acquire all necessary special tools prior to staring work.

2. The front wheel must be raised off the ground to perform some of the procedures. Make sure the motorcycle is secure in a safe manner. See *Motorcycle Stands* in Chapter Nine.

3. Make sure all front suspension parts and fasteners are replaced with the same type and grade. Do not assembly the Springer front fork with inferior parts or fasteners.

4. In most instances, there is a washer under the bolt head or nut to prevent galling of the part being installed. This also ensures the correct torque can be achieved when tightening the bolt or nut. If servicing the front suspension that had been previously been disassembled, refer to the illustrations in this chapter to ensure that all parts and washers are installed in the correct order.

5. The spring fork assembly is under spring pressure. If there is any uncertainty about being able to service the Springer fork assembly, refer this type of work to a Harley-Davidson dealership or competent motorcycle repair facility.

> *WARNING*
> *All of the components that make up the Springer front end (fork, tire and front fender) are designed to work together to offer optimum handling, steering and braking performance. Changing or modifying any of these components can alter the handling and steering characteristics of the Springer front end and may cause the loss of control. If any accessories are going to be added, consult with a Harley-Davidson dealership*

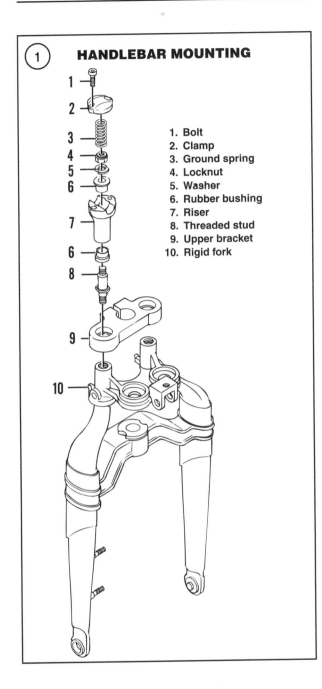

HANDLEBAR MOUNTING

1. Bolt
2. Clamp
3. Ground spring
4. Locknut
5. Washer
6. Rubber bushing
7. Riser
8. Threaded stud
9. Upper bracket
10. Rigid fork

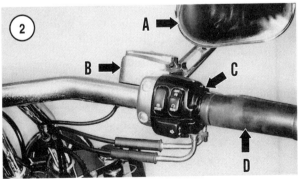

*first. Specifically, Harley-Davidson recommends that the following should **not** be added to or modified:*

a. Do not install a tire with a higher aspect ratio. During hard stops, the front tire could bind against the fender.

b. Do not lower the front fender from its stock position. During hard stops, or when hitting big road bumps or pot holes, the front tire could bind against the fender.

c. Do not install a tire/wheel combination other than that originally installed on the motorcycle. Doing so could adversely affect the handling characteristics of the motorcycle.

6. The rocker arm assemblies are subjected to road debris and water. Whenever the rocker arms are removed, thoroughly clean the spherical bearings, pivot studs and all pivoting parts. It may be necessary to clean the pivot studs with crocus cloth to remove any corrosion buildup. This type of cleaning is usually only necessary when the components have not been routinely serviced and lubricated. The front suspension will be stiff and will not operate correctly if these components have not been serviced correctly.

HANDLEBAR AND RISERS

Removal/Installation

Refer to **Figure 1**.

1. Support the motorcycle with the front wheel off the ground. See *Motorcycle Stands* in Chapter Nine.

> *CAUTION*
> *Cover the fuel tank with a heavy cloth or plastic tarp to protect it from accidental scratches or dents when removing the handlebar.*

> *NOTE*
> *Before removing the handlebar, make a drawing of the clutch and throttle cable routing from the handlebar through the frame. This information will help when reinstalling the handlebar and connecting the cables.*

2. On the right side of the handlebar, perform the following:
   a. Unscrew and remove the mirror (A, **Figure 2**).
   b. Remove the screws securing the master cylinder (B, **Figure 2**). Do not disconnect the hydraulic brake line.
   c. Remove the screws securing the right side switch assembly (C, **Figure 2**) and separate the housing halves.

11

d. Slide the throttle housing assembly (D, **Figure 2**) off the handlebar.

3. On the left side of the handlebar, perform the following:

    a. Unscrew and remove the mirror (A, **Figure 3**).

    b. Remove the screws securing the left side switch assembly (B, **Figure 3**) and separate the housing halves.

    c. Remove the clutch lever clamp (C, **Figure 3**) mounting screws and washers, and separate the clamp halves.

4. Disconnect or remove any wiring harness clamps at the handlebar.

5. Remove the two front handlebar clamp bolts, then the rear clamp bolts. Remove both clamps and the handlebar.

6. Remove the ground spring (A, **Figure 4**) from one of the risers.

7. To remove the riser, perform the following:

    a. Loosen and remove the locknut and washer securing the riser (B, **Figure 4**) to the threaded stud.

    b. Remove the riser from the threaded stud and if necessary, remove the rubber bushings from the each end of the riser.

8. If necessary, unscrew and remove the threaded stud from the top of the rigid fork.

9. Inspect the handlebar as follows:

    a. Check the knurled rings on the handlebar for galling and bits of aluminum. Clean the knurled section with a wire brush.

    b. Check the handlebar for cracks, bends or other damage. Replace the handlebar if necessary. Do not attempt to repair it.

    c. Thoroughly clean the upper clamps and risers of all residue.

10. Install the handlebar by reversing these steps. Note the following:

    a. If removed, tighten the riser threaded stud to 60-65 ft.-lb. (81-88 N•m).

    b. If removed, install new rubber bushings into the risers. Make sure the lip on the bottom bushing is fitted into the recess in the bottom surface of the riser.

    c. Position the risers (B, **Figure 4**) onto the threaded studs so the recess will be aligned correctly to accept the handlebar.

    d. Install *new* riser locknuts and tighten to 25-35 ft.-lb. (34-47 N•m).

    e. Install the ground spring (A, **Figure 4**) into the riser having a ground strap attached to it.

    f. After installing the handlebar, reposition the handlebar while sitting on the motorcycle.

    g. Tighten the handlebar clamp bolts to 144-180 in.-lb. (16-20 N•m).

    h. Adjust the mirrors.

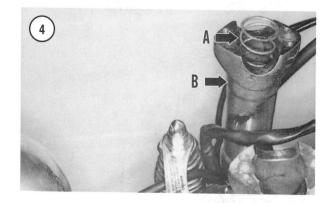

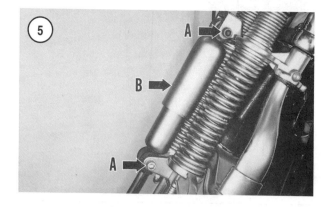

SHOCK ABSORBER

Removal/Installation

1. Support the motorcycle with the front wheel off the ground. See *Motorcycle Stands* in Chapter Nine.

> *NOTE*
> *Cover the front fender with a heavy cloth or towels to protect it from accidental scratches or dents when removing the shock absorber.*

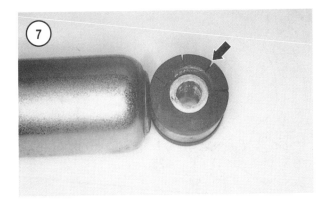

6. Clean all threadlocking residue from the mounting bolts and acorn nuts.

7. On FXSTS models, position the shock absorber with the H-D decal faced toward the front.

CAUTION
To protect the chrome finish, place a washer under each bolt head and between the mounting brackets and the acorn nuts when installing the shock mounting bolts and nuts in Steps 7 and 8.

8. Install the shock absorber into the upper mount and then the lower mount, then install the bolts and washers from the left side.

9. Apply ThreeBond TB1342 threadlocking compound to the bolt threads, then install the washers and acorn nuts onto the bolts.

10. Secure the bolts and tighten the acorn nuts to 45-50 ft.-lb. (61-68 N•m).

WARNING
After the mounting bolts and acorn nuts are tightened to the correct torque specification, there should be zero clearance between the shock absorber mounts and the shock mounting brackets on the fork. If there is measurable clearance between the shock absorber and mounting brackets, first check for loose or damaged bolts. If the bolts are tightened correctly, check the mounting brackets for cracks or other damage. Do not ride the motorcycle until the shock absorber is correctly installed and the bolts tightened to specification.

11. On FLSTS models, install the horn as described in Chapter Eight.

Inspection

There are no replacement parts for the shock absorber. If any part other than the mounting hardware is defective, replace the shock absorber.

1. Remove the shock absorber as described in this chapter.

2. Inspect the upper bushing (**Figure 6**) and lower bushing (**Figure 7**) for wear and deterioration.

3. Inspect the shock absorber mounting bolt holes for elongation.

4. Check the shock absorber (**Figure 8**) for fluid leakage .

2. On FLSTS models, remove the horn as described in Chapter Eight.

3. Remove the acorn nuts and washers (A, **Figure 5**) securing the shock absorber to the upper and lower mounts.

4. Carefully lower the shock absorber (B, **Figure 5**) from the upper mount and remove it. On FLSTS models, do not scratch the passing lamp mounting bar assembly.

5. The shock absorber cannot be serviced. Check the unit for oil leakage or loss of damping effect. Replace the shock absorber if necessary.

11

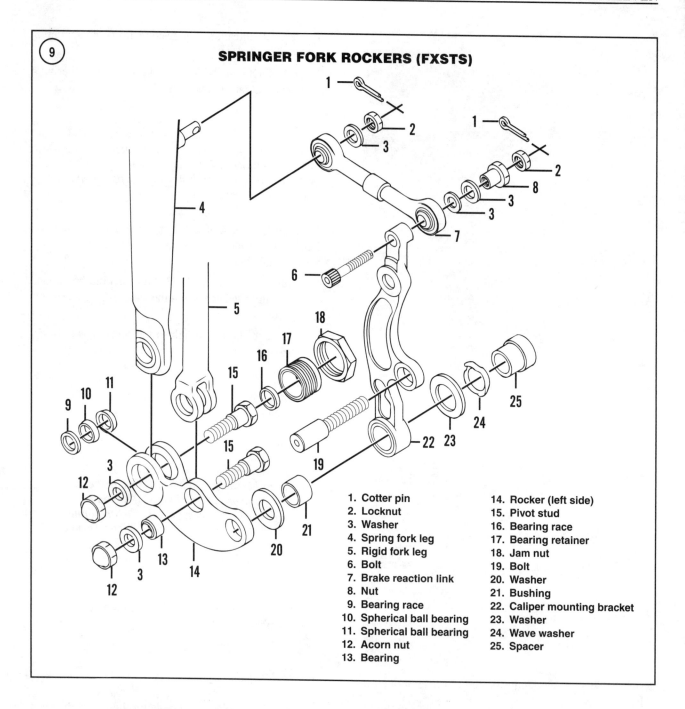

SPRINGER FORK ROCKERS (FXSTS)

1. Cotter pin
2. Locknut
3. Washer
4. Spring fork leg
5. Rigid fork leg
6. Bolt
7. Brake reaction link
8. Nut
9. Bearing race
10. Spherical ball bearing
11. Spherical ball bearing
12. Acorn nut
13. Bearing
14. Rocker (left side)
15. Pivot stud
16. Bearing race
17. Bearing retainer
18. Jam nut
19. Bolt
20. Washer
21. Bushing
22. Caliper mounting bracket
23. Washer
24. Wave washer
25. Spacer

FORK ROCKERS

Bearing Inspection and Adjustment

Refer to **Figure 9** and **Figure 10**.

The fork rockers pivot on the rigid fork leg via a split ball bearing assembly. Inspect the spherical bearings in each rocker assembly every 10,000 miles (16,000 km). At every 50,000 miles (80,000 km) inspect the Teflon coating of the outside surface of each bearing (**Figure 11**). Re-

place the bearings in each rocker if the coating is worn through to the metal at any point. If replacement is necessary, replace both bearings in both rockers at the same time.

This procedure is shown on a FXSTS model.

CAUTION
The spring fork legs must be secured to the rigid forks during this procedure. By doing this, the spring forks can be disconnected

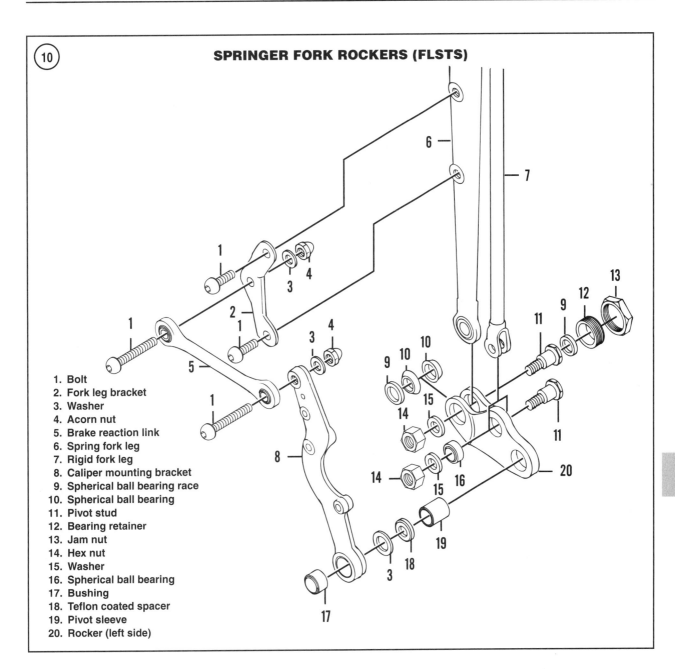

SPRINGER FORK ROCKERS (FLSTS)

1. Bolt
2. Fork leg bracket
3. Washer
4. Acorn nut
5. Brake reaction link
6. Spring fork leg
7. Rigid fork leg
8. Caliper mounting bracket
9. Spherical ball bearing race
10. Spherical ball bearing
11. Pivot stud
12. Bearing retainer
13. Jam nut
14. Hex nut
15. Washer
16. Spherical ball bearing
17. Bushing
18. Teflon coated spacer
19. Pivot sleeve
20. Rocker (left side)

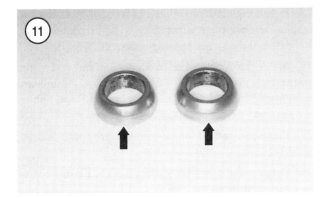

from the rockers without removing the fork assemblies from the motorcycle.

1. Support the motorcycle with the front wheel off the ground. See *Motorcycle Stands* in Chapter Nine.

2. Remove the front caliper as described in Chapter Thirteen. Do not disconnect the brake line from the caliper.

3. Remove the front wheel as described in Chapter Nine.

4. On FLSTS models, remove the front fender as described in Chapter Fourteen.

WARNING
If the spring fork legs are not secured to the rigid fork legs, the spring pressure will snap them forward with great force, which could cause personal injury. The spring fork legs must be secured with heavy duty cable ties or an equivalent.

5. Use a heavy-duty cable tie, or an equivalent, and secure each spring-fork to the adjacent rigid fork leg (A, **Figure 12**). Place the cable ties close to the boss at the lower end of the spring fork leg. Make sure the cable ties are secure.

NOTE
*The jam nut is located on different sides of the fork rocker depending on model. On FXSTS models, the jam nut (A, **Figure 13**) is on the inboard side of the rigid fork leg. On FLSTS models, the jam nut is on the outboard side of the rigid fork leg.*

NOTE
The jam nut requires a 1 1/2 in. open end wrench. Do not use a box wrench as it will not have enough contact surface on the jam nut that has been tightened to 95-105 ft.-lb. (129-142 N•m).

6. On the rigid fork leg, loosen but do not remove the bearing retainer jam nut (A, **Figure 13**) and bearing retainer (B) on the fork rocker.

7. On the spring fork, loosen the pivot studs and remove the acorn nut (FSXST) (B, **Figure 12**), or hex nut (FLSTS), and washer from each pivot stud (C, **Figure 13**). Leave the pivot stud in place at this time.

8. On the rigid fork, tighten the bearing retainer (**Figure 14**) to 25-35 in.-lbs. (3-4 N•m).

9. Secure the bearing retainer (A, **Figure 15**) to keep it from rotating and tighten the jam nut to (B) 95-105 ft.-lb. (129-142 N•m).

10. Remove the spring fork pivot stud (C, **Figure 13**) loosened in Step 7. Allow the fork rocker to pivot down away from the spring fork leg.

NOTE
While performing Step 11, check for abnormal noise or movement that may indicate damaged spherical bearing in the rigid fork leg.

11. Attach a torque wrench onto the rigid fork pivot stud (**Figure 16**) and rotate the fork rocker through its arc. The torque reading should be 25-35 in.-lbs. (3-4 N•m).

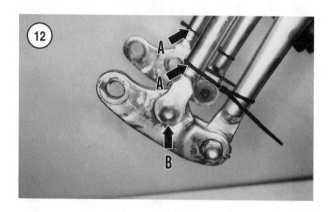

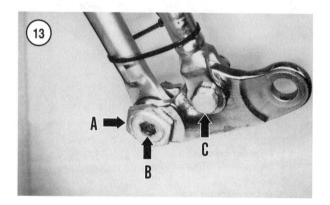

12. If the torque reading in Step 11 is out of specification, readjust the bearing retainer (Step 8) and repeat Step 11. Repeat until the torque reading is correct.

13. Move the fork rocker into position and install the spring fork pivot stud (C, **Figure 13**) from the inboard side. Install the washer and nut (B, **Figure 13**) and tighten the nut to 45-50 ft.-lb. (61-68 N•m).

14. Repeat Steps 6-13 for the bearing on the other fork assembly.

15. Remove the heavy-duty cable ties (A, **Figure 12**), or an equivalent, from the fork assemblies.

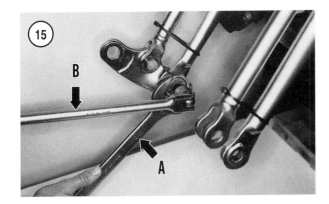

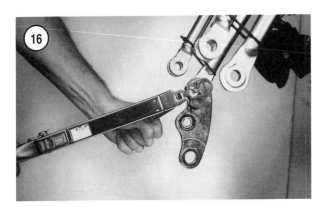

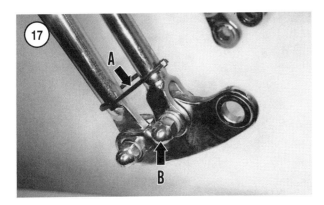

16. On FLSTS models, install the front fender as described in Chapter Fourteen.

17. Install the front wheel as described in Chapter Nine.

18. Install the front brake caliper as described in Chapter Thirteen.

Rocker Removal

CAUTION
The spring fork legs must be secured to the rigid forks during this procedure. By doing this, the spring forks can be disconnected from the rockers without removing the fork assemblies from the motorcycle.

1. Support the motorcycle with the front wheel off the ground. See *Motorcycle Stands* in Chapter Nine.

2. Remove the front caliper as described in Chapter Thirteen. Do not disconnect the brake line from the caliper.

3. Remove the front wheel as described in Chapter Nine.

4. On FLSTS models, remove the front fender as described in Chapter Fourteen.

WARNING
If the spring fork legs are not secured to the rigid fork legs, the spring pressure will snap them forward with great force, which could cause personal injury. The spring fork legs must be secured with heavy duty cable ties, or an equivalent.

5. Use a heavy-duty cable tie, or an equivalent, and secure each spring fork to the adjacent rigid fork leg. Place the cable ties (A, **Figure 17**) close to the boss at the lower end of the spring fork leg. Make sure the cable ties are secure.

6. On the spring fork, loosen the pivot stud (thick head) and remove the acorn nut (FXSTS) (B, **Figure 17**), or hex nut (FLSTS), and washer (**Figure 18**) from the pivot stud. Do not remove the pivot stud at this time.

NOTE
*The jam nut is located on different sides of the fork rocker depending on model. On FXSTS models, the jam nut (A, **Figure 13**) is on the inboard side of the rigid fork leg. On FLSTS models, the jam nut is on the outboard side of the rigid fork leg.*

NOTE
The jam nut requires a 1 1/2 in. open end wrench. Do not use a box wrench as it will not have enough contact surface on the jam nut and will round off the head of the nut. The nut has been tightened to 95-105 ft.-lb. (129-142 N•m).

11

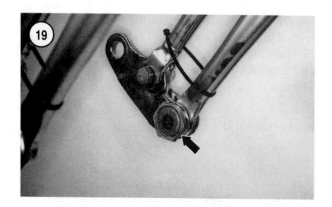

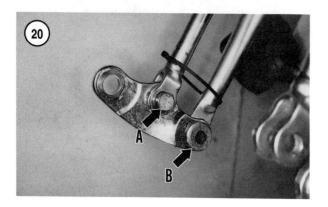

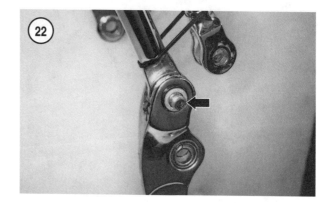

7. Loosen and remove the bearing retainer jam nut (**Figure 19**).

8. Remove the pivot stud (A, **Figure 20**) loosened in Step 6.

9. Loosen and remove the bearing retainer (B, **Figure 20**).

10. On the rigid fork, loosen the pivot stud (thick head) and remove the acorn nut (FSXST) (**Figure 21**), or hex nut (FLSTS), and washer (**Figure 22**) from the pivot stud.

11. Remove the pivot stud (**Figure 23**) from the rocker and the rigid fork leg.

12. Remove the fork rocker.

13. Remove the spherical bearings from fork rocker at the rigid fork pivot area. Reinstall the spherical bearings washer and nut onto the pivot stud (**Figure 24**) to avoid misplacing them.

14. Repeat Steps 6-13 for the other rocker assembly.

Rocker Inspection

1. Clean all parts in solvent and dry with compressed air (**Figure 25**).

2. Inspect the fork rockers (**Figure 26**) for cracks or damage.

3. Check the rocker arm pivot studs (A, **Figure 27**).

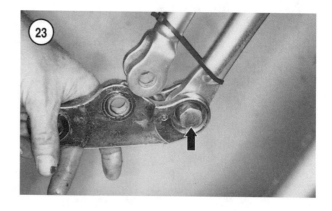

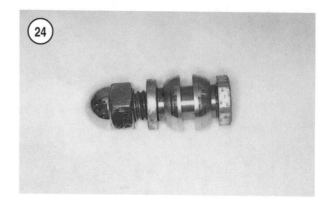

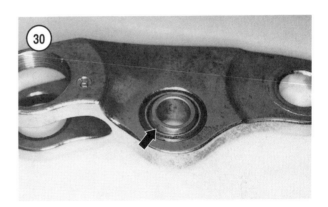

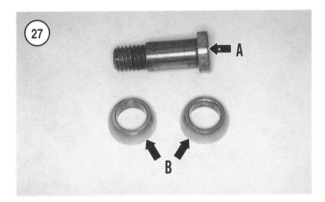

11

4. Check the spherical ball bearing surfaces (B, **Figure 27**) for cracks or excessive wear. If necessary, replace the bearings as a set.

5. Check the spherical bearing race in the rocker (**Figure 28**) and bearing retainer (**Figure 29**). If necessary, use a hydraulic press and replace the bearing races as a set. Refer to Chapter One.

6. Check the spherical bearing assembly in the rocker (**Figure 30**). If necessary, use a hydraulic press and replace the bearing. Refer to Chapter One.

7. Check the bearing retainer jam nut (A, **Figure 31**) and bearing retainer (B) for thread damage.

8. Check the spherical bearing in the rocker (**Figure 11**). If the Teflon coating is worn completely through at any point, with the metal surface visible, replace the bearing as a set as described in this chapter.

Rocker Installation

CAUTION
Be sure to install the fork rockers onto the correct side of the fork assemblies. The fork rockers are marked with a (R) right side (Figure 32) and (L) left side.

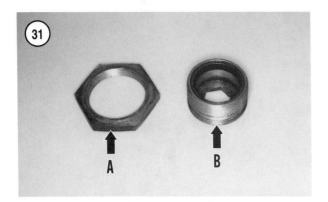

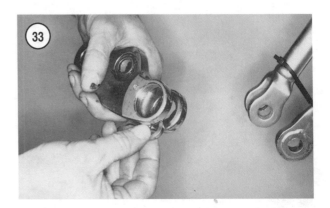

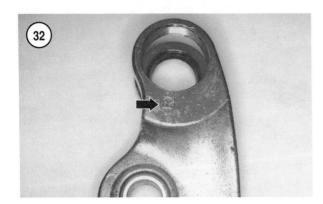

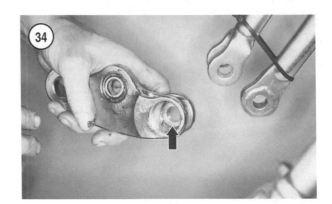

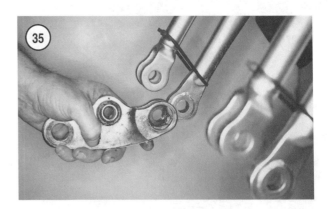

1. Thoroughly coat the bearing races with wheel bearing grease.

NOTE
The spherical surface on each bearing faces away from each other and toward their respective bearing race.

2. Install the *outer* spherical bearing half into the outer surface of the fork rocker race (**Figure 33**). Push it in until it bottoms (**Figure 34**).

3. Align the rocker with the rigid fork leg so that it faces in the normal operating direction (facing forward) (**Figure 35**). Make sure the spherical bearing does not fall out.

4. Install the *inner* spherical bearing half into the inner surface of the fork rocker race (A, **Figure 36**). Push it in until it bottoms.

5. Install the pivot stud (thin head) (B, **Figure 36**) through the rigid fork leg, spherical bearings and the other side of the rocker (**Figure 23**).

6. Apply ThreeBond TB1342 threadlocking compound to the pivot stud.

7. Install the washer (**Figure 37**), acorn nut (FXSTS) (**Figure 38**), or hex nut (FLSTS), and washer onto the pivot stud. Tighten the nut (**Figure 39**) to 45-50 ft.-lb. (61-68 N•m).

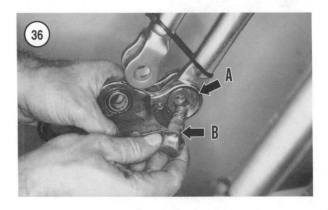

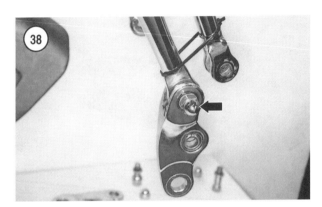

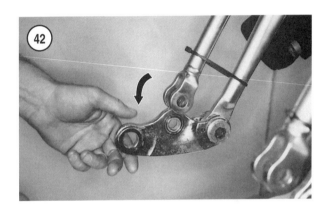

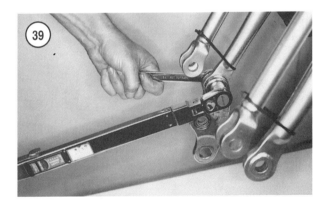

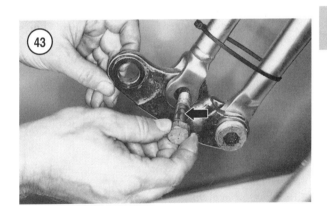

11

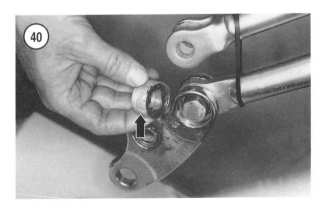

8. Apply and anti-seize lubricant to the threads of the bearing retainer (**Figure 40**). Also, apply a full amount to the bearing race, then install the bearing retainer (**Figure 41**). Tighten the bearing retainer securely at this time.

9. To ensure the spherical bearing are installed correctly, move the fork rocker up and down at this time (**Figure 42**). Check for easy of movement.

10. Install the bearing retainer jam nut.

11. Move the fork rocker up into position on the spring fork and temporarily install the pivot stud (**Figure 43**).

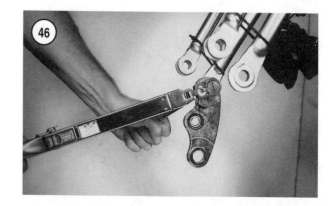

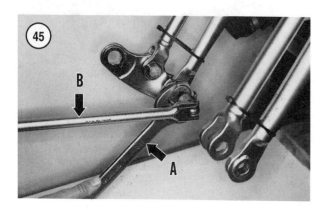

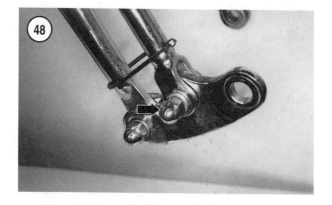

12. On the rigid fork, tighten the bearing retainer (**Figure 44**) to 25-35 in.-lbs. (3-4 N•m).

13. Secure the bearing retainer (A, **Figure 45**) to keep it from rotating and tighten the jam nut to (B) 95-105 ft.-lb. (129-142 N•m).

14. Remove the spring fork pivot stud (**Figure 43**), installed in Step 11. Allow the fork rocker to pivot down away from the spring fork leg.

NOTE
While performing Step 15, check for abnormal noise or movement that may indicate damaged spherical bearing in the rigid fork leg.

15. Attach a torque wrench onto the rigid fork pivot stud (**Figure 46**) and rotate the fork rocker through its arc. The torque reading should be 25-35 in.-lbs. (3-4 N•m).

16. If the torque reading in Step 11 is out of specification, readjust the bearing retainer (Step 8) and repeat Step 13. Repeat until the torque reading is correct.

17. Move the fork rocker into position and install the spring fork pivot stud (**Figure 43**) from the inboard side. Install the washer (**Figure 47**) and nut (**Figure 48**); tighten the nut (**Figure 49**) to 45-50 ft.-lb. (61-68 N•m).

18. Remove the heavy-duty cable ties from the fork assemblies.

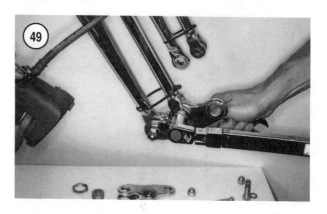

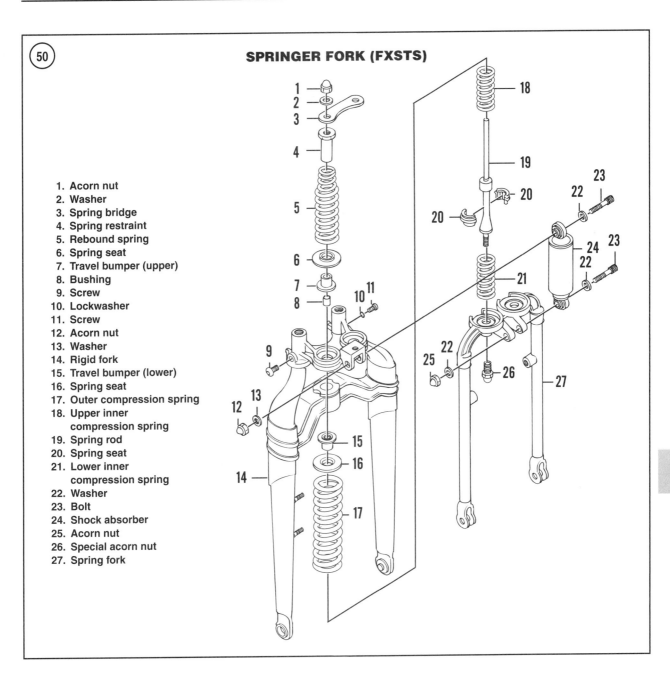

SPRINGER FORK (FXSTS)

50

1. Acorn nut
2. Washer
3. Spring bridge
4. Spring restraint
5. Rebound spring
6. Spring seat
7. Travel bumper (upper)
8. Bushing
9. Screw
10. Lockwasher
11. Screw
12. Acorn nut
13. Washer
14. Rigid fork
15. Travel bumper (lower)
16. Spring seat
17. Outer compression spring
18. Upper inner
    compression spring
19. Spring rod
20. Spring seat
21. Lower inner
    compression spring
22. Washer
23. Bolt
24. Shock absorber
25. Acorn nut
26. Special acorn nut
27. Spring fork

11

19. Repeat for the remaining rocker assembly.

20. On FLSTS models, install the front fender as described in Chapter Fourteen.

21. Install the front wheel as described in Chapter Nine.

22. Install the front caliper as described in Chapter Thirteen.

SPRINGER FORK

Removal

Refer to **Figure 50** and **Figure 51**.

The spring fork assembly can be removed from the rigid fork with the rigid fork installed in the frame. If necessary, the spring and rigid fork can be removed as an assembly as described under *Rigid Fork Removal* in this chapter.

There are no service specifications for the springs on this fork assembly. Label each spring as it is removed to ensure it will be installed on the correct side of the fork. After removing the springs, compare the two sets of springs for sag or distortion. If replacement is necessary, replace the springs as pairs. Take suspected distorted

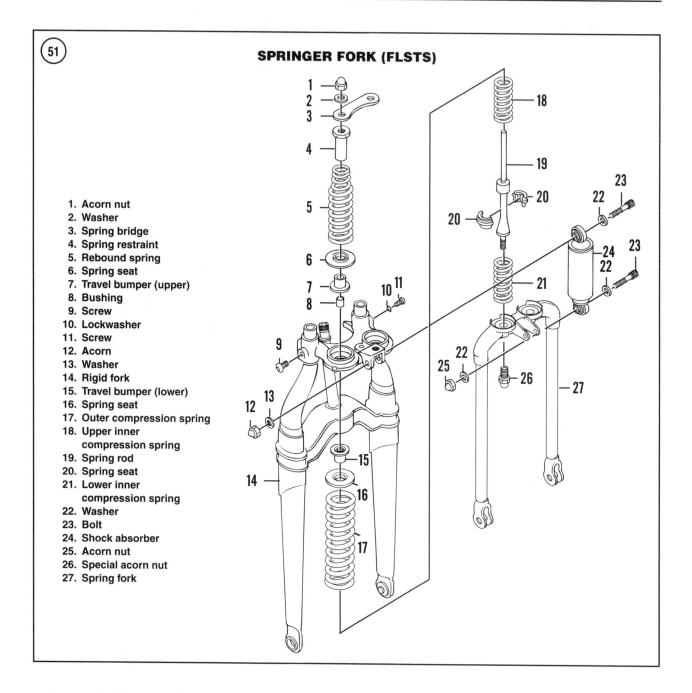

SPRINGER FORK (FLSTS)

1. Acorn nut
2. Washer
3. Spring bridge
4. Spring restraint
5. Rebound spring
6. Spring seat
7. Travel bumper (upper)
8. Bushing
9. Screw
10. Lockwasher
11. Screw
12. Acorn
13. Washer
14. Rigid fork
15. Travel bumper (lower)
16. Spring seat
17. Outer compression spring
18. Upper inner
    compression spring
19. Spring rod
20. Spring seat
21. Lower inner
    compression spring
22. Washer
23. Bolt
24. Shock absorber
25. Acorn nut
26. Special acorn nut
27. Spring fork

springs to a Harley-Davidson dealership and compare to new springs. The two upper rebound springs and the four inner and outer compression springs are located between the rigid and spring fork assemblies. During disassembly, keep the right and left side components in separate containers. Parts tend to create a wear pattern after prolonged use and it is advised to reinstall them in the same location during assembly.

One special tool is required to safely remove the fork springs. The Fork Spring Tool from Motion Pro (part No.

08-0144) (**Figure 52**) is available from a motorcycle dealership or motorcycle mail order houses. This tool can be fabricated from hardware store materials as shown in **Figure 53**. The block shown at the bottom should be made from cold-roll steel and the block should be cut so that it can fit between the shock absorber lower mounting eye on the spring fork. Then drill the hole through the block with a 3/8 in. drill.

CAUTION
After making the block, round off all corners with a file to avoid scratching any of the

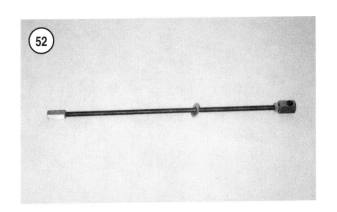

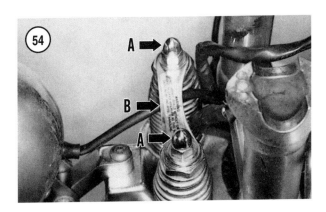

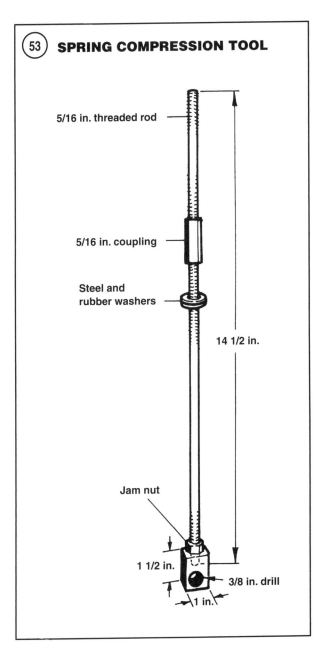

53 **SPRING COMPRESSION TOOL**

5/16 in. threaded rod

5/16 in. coupling

Steel and
rubber washers

14 1/2 in.

Jam nut

1 1/2 in.

3/8 in. drill

1 in.

*front fork components. Also, remove all
burrs from the drilled hole.*

1. Remove the handlebar as described in this chapter.

2. Remove the acorn nuts and washers (A, **Figure 54**) securing the spring bridge. Remove the spring bridge (B,
Figure 54).

3. Remove the shock absorber as described in this chapter.

4. Remove the headlight assembly as described in Chapter Eight.

5. On FLSTS models, remove the passing lamp assembly
as described in Chapter Eight.

6. Remove the front wheel as described in Chapter Nine.

7. Remove the front brake caliper as described in Chapter
Thirteen.

8. Remove the front fender as described in Chapter Fourteen.

9. Remove the front fender link as follows:
   a. Remove the fender link (**Figure 55**) from the pivot
      shaft on the spring fork.
   b. Remove the washer and rubber spacer (**Figure 56**)
      from the pivot shaft on the spring fork.

10. Install the special tool onto the fork as follows:
   a. Remove the coupling and washer from the threaded
      rod.

11

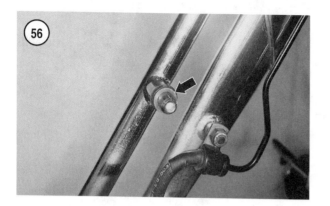

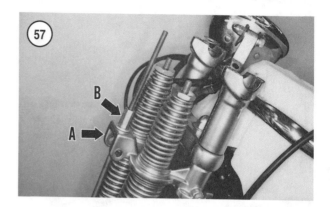

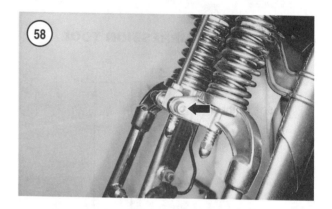

b. Insert the threaded rod up through the shock absorber upper mount (A, **Figure 57**).

c. Insert the block between the lower shock absorber mount on the spring fork.

d. Secure the block with the shock absorber bolt, washers and acorn nut (**Figure 58**).

e. Install the washers and long coupling onto the threaded rod (B, **Figure 57**).

11. Measure the distance from the top of the spring rod to the top of the spring restraint (**Figure 59**). Record this measurement since it will be used during assembly.

> *WARNING*
> *If the spring fork legs are not secured to the rigid fork legs, the spring pressure will snap them forward with great force, which could cause personal injury. The spring fork legs must be secured with heavy duty cable ties or an equivalent.*

12. Use heavy-duty cable ties, or an equivalent, and secure each spring fork to the adjacent rigid fork leg. Place the cable ties close to the boss at the lower end of the spring fork leg (A, **Figure 60**). Make sure the cable ties are secure.

13. Remove both rocker arm assemblies (B, **Figure 60**) as described in this chapter.

> *NOTE*
> *The spring seats and travel bumpers are installed between the rigid fork assembly and the spring cup at the top of the compression spring. The compression springs are the lower springs. The two upper springs are the rebound springs.*

14. Slowly tighten the long coupling with a wrench until the compression springs bottom out on their spring seats travel bumpers. This released the pressure on the upper rebound springs. Check to make sure the rebound springs (A, **Figure 61**) are no longer under pressure. If necessary, tighten the coupler an additional amount.

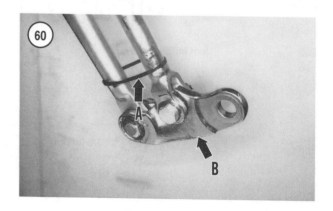

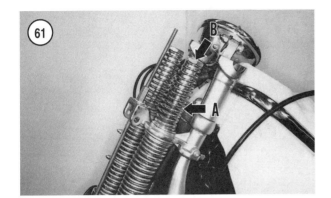

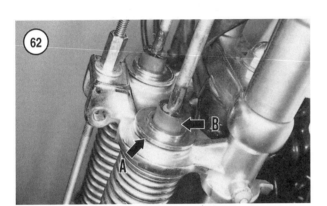

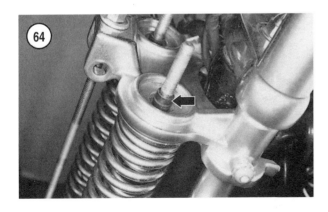

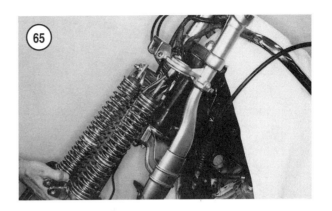

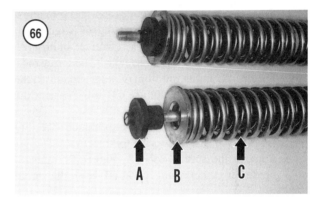

15. Unscrew and remove both spring restraints (B, **Figure 61**).

16. Pull straight up and remove both rebound springs (A, **Figure 61**) from the spring rods.

17. Remove the spring seat (A, **Figure 62**) and the travel bumper (B) from each spring rod.

18. Slowly loosen the long coupling (B, **Figure 57**) with a wrench releasing the tension on the compression springs (**Figure 63**).

19. Remove the bushing (**Figure 64**) from each spring rod.

20. Remove the plastic tie wraps.

21. Secure the spring fork assembly and remove the special tool from both fork assemblies.

22. Slide the spring fork assembly down and out of the rigid fork (**Figure 65**).

Disassembly

1. Remove the travel bumper (A, **Figure 66**), spring seat (B) and outer compression spring (C) from the spring rod. Remove the travel bumper, spring cup and outer compression spring from the other spring rod.

2. Remove the inner/upper compression spring (**Figure 67**) from the spring rod.

3. Remove the spring rod as follows:

11

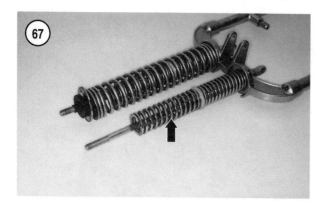

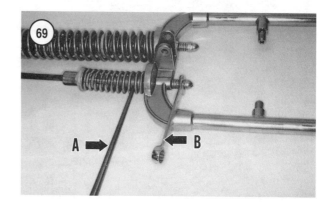

a. Rotate the inner/lower compression spring to allow access to the cross-hole in the spring rod (**Figure 68**).

b. Insert a No. 2 Phillips head screwdriver, or drift (A, **Figure 69**) through the cross-hole in the spring rod.

c. Secures the spring rod from rotating and loosen the special acorn nut (B, **Figure 69**) at the base of the spring rod.

d. Pull straight up and remove the spring rod assembly (**Figure 70**) from the spring fork.

e. Remove the spring seats (A, **Figure 71**) and inner/lower compression spring (B) from the spring rod.

f. Repeat for the other spring rod assembly.

CAUTION
*The spring rod (C, **Figure 71**) is comprised of an upper and lower rod assembly. Do not separate these two rods if either rod is damaged, replace the spring rod as an assembly.*

Inspection

Harley-Davidson does not provide any inspection specifications for the Springer fork assembly. Visually inspect the components for wear, damage or deterioration. If the front end was involved in an accident, have the motorcycle inspected by a Harley-Davidson dealership or competent motorcycle frame specialist.

As noted during removal/disassembly, do not intermix the right and left side components during the cleaning and inspection steps. Clean and inspect one set at a time.

1. Clean the travel bumpers in a non-chemical cleaner like Simple Green all-purpose cleaner. Do not use cleaning solvent as some types will cause permanent damage.

2. Clean all remaining components in solvent and dry with compressed air. Remove all anti-seize lubricant residue from the upper spring rod.

3. Inspect each fork assembly for cracks, bending or other damage. Check the rocker assembly mounting area

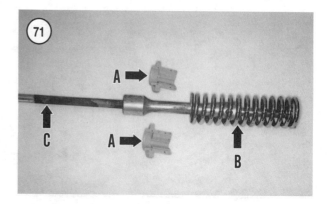

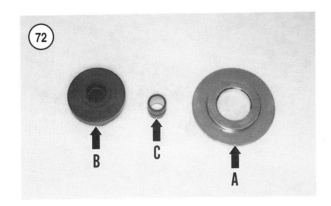

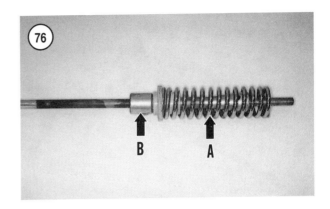

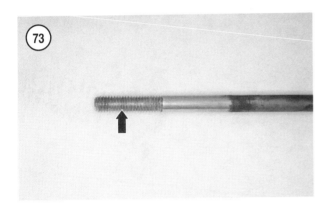

in both fork assemblies for damage. If either fork assembly is damaged, replace it.

4. Inspect the springs for wear or sag. Compare the right side spring(s) to the left side spring(s). If there is a difference in length, replace the springs as a set. Also inspect the springs for crack or other visual damage.

5. Inspect the spring rod for damage or bending (C, **Figure 71**). Check the threaded portion of each end for thread damage. Repair with a thread die if necessary. Replace the spring rod if bent or damaged.

6. Inspect the spring rod spring seats (A, **Figure 72**) for cracks or damage where the spring makes contact. Replace as a set.

7. Inspect the travel bumpers (B, **Figure 72**) for hardness or deterioration.

8. Check the bushing (C, **Figure 72**) for damage.

9. Inspect the threads in the spring restraints and special acorn nuts for damage. Repair with thread tap if necessary.

10. Inspect the threads in the spring rod (**Figure 73**) for damage. Repair with thread die if necessary.

11. Check the spring bridge for straightness and damage.

12. Inspect the front fender link (**Figure 74**) for damage. Check the shoulder bolt bearing surface (A, **Figure 75**) and front fender link (B) for damage.

Assembly/Installation

1. Assemble one spring rod at a time as follows:
   a. Install the inner/lower compression spring (A, **Figure 76**) over the spring rod.
   b. Install both spring seats (B, **Figure 76**) onto the spring rod to lock the spring in place. Make sure the spring seats are locked in place on the spring rod and inserted into the spring.
   c. Install the spring rod and inner/lower spring onto the receptacle on the spring fork (**Figure 77**).

11

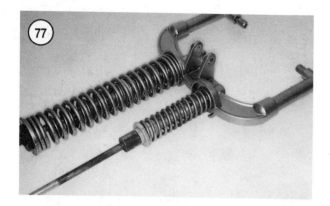

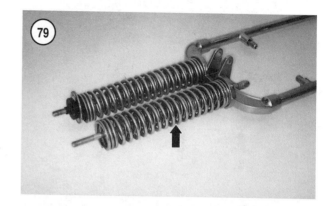

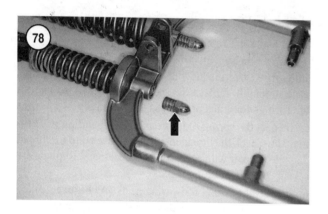

d. Install the special acorn nut (**Figure 78**) onto the spring rod and tighten finger tight at this time.

e. Rotate the inner/lower compression spring to allow access to the cross-hole in the spring rod (**Figure 68**).

f. Insert a No. 2 Phillips head screwdriver, or drift (A, **Figure 69**) through the cross-hole in the spring rod.

g. Secure the spring rod from rotating and tighten the special acorn nut (B, **Figure 69**) to 20-25 ft.-lb. (27-34 N•m).

2. Install the inner/upper compression spring (**Figure 67**) onto the spring rod.

3. Install the outer compression spring (**Figure 79**) over the inner/upper compression spring and onto the spring rod.

4. Correctly position the spring seat with the shoulder facing down (**Figure 80**) toward the outer compression spring and install it.

5. Correctly position the travel bumper with the smaller diameter portion (**Figure 81**) side going on first and install it onto the spring rod and into the spring seat (**Figure 82**).

6. Repeat Steps 1-5 for the other side.

7. Slide the spring fork assembly up and into the rigid fork (**Figure 83**). Make sure the lower travel bumpers, compression spring seats and compression springs properly engage the bottom of the rigid fork spring brace.

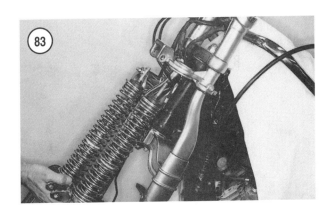

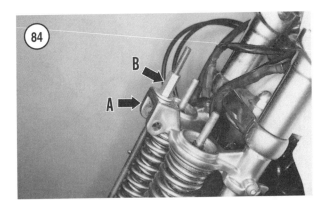

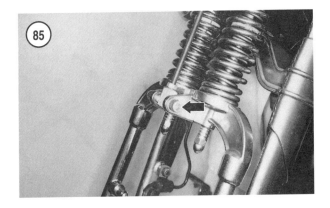

NOTE
Check that both sides of the spring fork are properly installed into the rigid fork.

8. Have an assistant hold the spring fork in place.
9. Install the special tool onto the fork as follows:
    a. Remove the coupling and washer from the threaded rod.
    b. Insert the threaded rod up through the shock absorber upper mount (A, **Figure 84**).
    c. Insert the block between the lower shock absorber mount on the spring fork.
    d. Secure the block with the shock absorber bolt, washers and acorn nut (**Figure 85**).
    e. Install the washers and long coupling onto the threaded rod.
10. Slowly tighten the long coupling (B, **Figure 84**) with a wrench until the two outer springs are compressed enough to secure the spring fork in place.

WARNING
If the spring fork legs are not secured to the rigid fork legs, the spring pressure will snap them forward with great force, which could cause personal injury. The spring fork legs must be secured with heavy duty cable ties or an equivalent.

11. Use heavy-duty cable ties, or an equivalent, and secure each spring fork to the adjacent rigid fork leg. Place the cable ties close to the boss at the lower end of the spring fork leg (**Figure 86**). Make sure the cable ties are secure.
12. Install the rebound springs as follows:
    a. Oil the spring rebound bushing and slide it onto the end of the spring rod. Push the bushing down on the rod until it bottoms (**Figure 64**).
    b. Install the travel bumper (A, **Figure 87**) over the spring rod and onto the bushing.
    c. Place the spring seat (B, **Figure 87**) over the travel bumper so that it shoulder faces up.

11

13. Repeat Step 12 for the other side.

14. Slowly tighten the long coupling (B, **Figure 84**) with a wrench until the compression springs bottom out on their spring seats travel bumpers.

15. Install both rocker arm assemblies (A, **Figure 88**) as described in this chapter.

16. Remove the heavy-duty cable ties from the boss at the lower end of the spring fork leg (B, **Figure 88**).

17. Make sure the travel bumpers and spring seats are still in the bottom of the receptacle in the rigid.

18. Position the rebound spring with the tapered spring end going on last (**Figure 89**). Install both rebound springs (A, **Figure 90**).

19. Apply a coat of anti-seize lubricant to the top 1/2 in. (12.7 mm) of both spring rod threads.

> *WARNING*
> *Tighten both spring restraints evenly. Not having the same amount of exposed spring rod on each side could adversely affect handling that could lead to loss of control of the motorcycle.*

20. Install the spring restraint (B, **Figure 90**) onto the spring rod and tighten it until spring rod protrudes 0.625-0.750 in. (16-19 mm) from the top of the spring restrainers (**Figure 91**).

21. Repeat Steps 19-21 for the other spring restraint maintaining the same distance of 0.625-0.750 in. (16-19 mm).

22. Remove the special tool.

23. Install the shock absorber as described in this chapter.

24. Correctly position the headlight electrical wire behind the rebound springs.

25. Install the acorn nuts (A, **Figure 92**) and spring bridge (B). Tighten the acorn nuts to 30-35 ft.-lb. (41-48 N•m).

26. Install the front fender link as follows:

    a. Install the rubber washer (**Figure 93**) and washer (**Figure 94**) onto the pivot shaft on the spring fork.

    b. Install the fender link (**Figure 95**) onto the pivot shaft on the spring fork. Push it on until it bottoms.

27. Install the handlebar as described in Chapter Ten.

28. Install the front fender as described in Chapter Fourteen.

29. Install the front brake caliper as described in Chapter Thirteen.

30. Install the front wheel as described in Chapter Nine.

31. On FLSTS models, install the passing lamp assembly as described in Chapter Eight.

32. Install the headlight assembly as described in Chapter Eight.

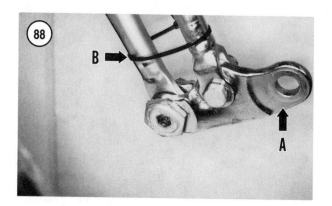

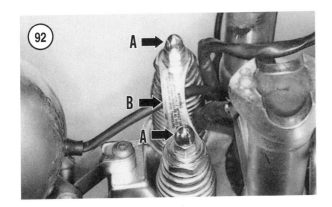

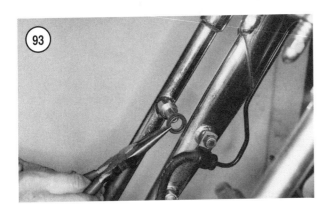

33. Lower the motorcycle to the ground and place it on the jiffy stand.

34. Apply the front brake and compress the front suspension several times and make sure there is no binding or abnormal noise.

35. Test ride the motorcycle slowly at first to make sure the front suspension is operating correctly.

WARNING
Do not ride the motorcycle until the front brake is operating correctly with full hydraulic advantage and that the front suspension is operating correctly.

RIGID FORK

Removal

Refer to **Figure 96** and **Figure 97**.

The rigid fork can be removed with the spring fork attached to it. This procedure outlines the removal of the rigid fork with the spring fork attached or removed.

1. Remove the shock absorber as described in this chapter.

2. Loosen the upper bracket clamp bolt (**Figure 98**).

3. Remove the headlight assembly (A, **Figure 99**) as described in Chapter Eight.

4. On FLSTS models, remove the passing lamp assembly as described in Chapter Eight.

5. Remove the front wheel as described in Chapter Nine.

6. Remove the front brake caliper as described in Chapter Thirteen.

7. Remove the front fender as described in Chapter Fourteen.

8. Remove the handlebar and risers (B, **Figure 99**) as described in this chapter.

9. If necessary, remove the spring fork as described in this chapter.

10. Remove the bolt and bracket (**Figure 100**) securing the front brake line to the side of the rigid fork.

11. Remove the bolt and bracket (**Figure 101**) securing the front brake line to the base of the rigid fork below the steering stem.

12. Loosen and remove the fork stem acorn nut and rubber washer (C, **Figure 99**).

13. Loosen and remove both rigid fork leg studs.

14. Remove the upper bracket.

NOTE
The rigid fork assembly can fall out of the steering head after the bearing retainer is

11

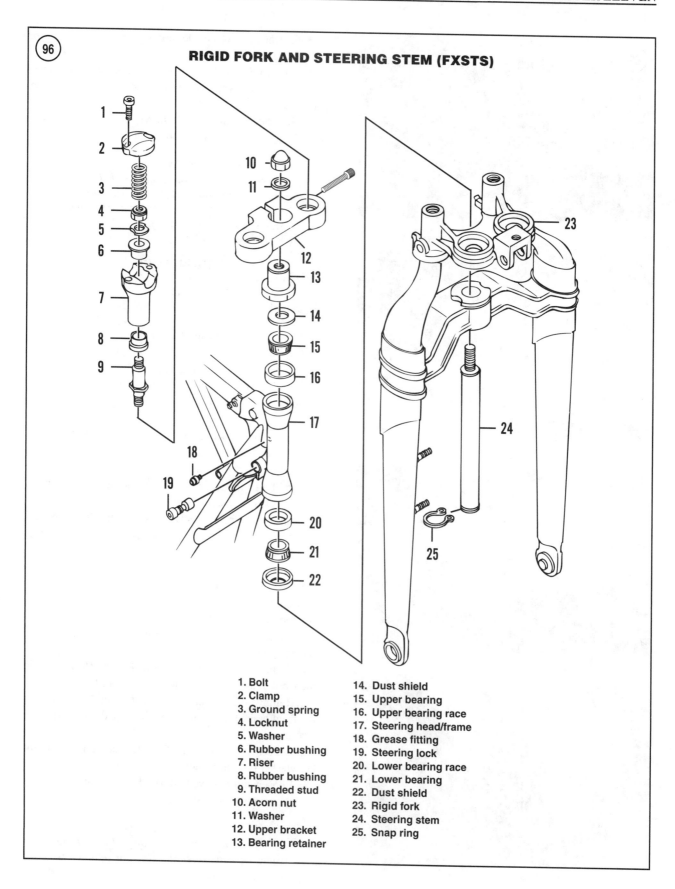

RIGID FORK AND STEERING STEM (FXSTS)

96

1. Bolt
2. Clamp
3. Ground spring
4. Locknut
5. Washer
6. Rubber bushing
7. Riser
8. Rubber bushing
9. Threaded stud
10. Acorn nut
11. Washer
12. Upper bracket
13. Bearing retainer
14. Dust shield
15. Upper bearing
16. Upper bearing race
17. Steering head/frame
18. Grease fitting
19. Steering lock
20. Lower bearing race
21. Lower bearing
22. Dust shield
23. Rigid fork
24. Steering stem
25. Snap ring

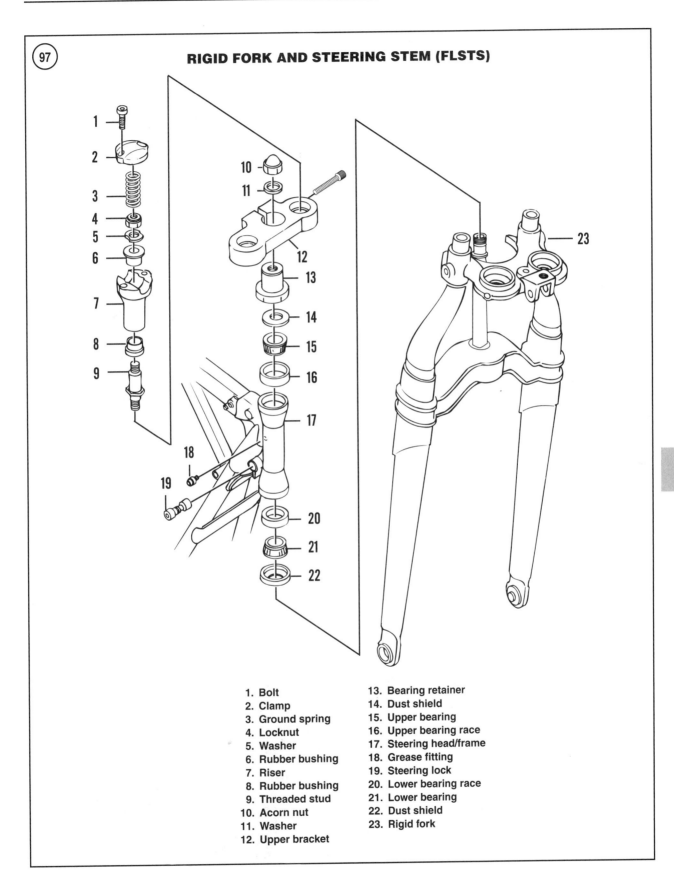

RIGID FORK AND STEERING STEM (FLSTS)

1. Bolt
2. Clamp
3. Ground spring
4. Locknut
5. Washer
6. Rubber bushing
7. Riser
8. Rubber bushing
9. Threaded stud
10. Acorn nut
11. Washer
12. Upper bracket
13. Bearing retainer
14. Dust shield
15. Upper bearing
16. Upper bearing race
17. Steering head/frame
18. Grease fitting
19. Steering lock
20. Lower bearing race
21. Lower bearing
22. Dust shield
23. Rigid fork

11

*removed in Step 15. Secure the rigid fork
prior to removing the bearing retainer.*

15. Loosen and remove the bearing retainer (**Figure 102**) and the dust shield (**Figure 103**).

16. Carefully slide the rigid fork assembly down and out of the steering head (A, **Figure 104**).

17. If necessary, remove the upper bearing (B, **Figure 104**) from the steering head.

Inspection

Harley-Davidson does not provide any inspection specifications for the rigid fork assembly. Visually inspect the components for wear, damage or deterioration. If the front end was involved in an accident, have the motorcycle inspected by a Harley-Davidson dealership or competent motorcycle frame specialist.

1. Clean all parts in solvent and dry with compressed air.

2. Inspect the rigid fork assembly for cracks, bending or other damage. If visual inspection indicated that the rigid fork is bent, have it inspected by a Harley-Davidson dealership or competent motorcycle frame specialist.

3. Check the rigid fork leg stud threads for being stripped or cross-threaded. Check the threaded portion on both ends of the stud for bending or other damage. Repair or replace the studs if necessary.

4. Check the rigid fork leg stud threaded holes in the rigid fork for being stripped or cross-threaded. Repair the threads if necessary.

5. Use compressed air and thoroughly clean out the threaded holes of all debris. Any buildup in the hole may hamper the threaded stud from being tightened to the correct torque.

6. Inspect the upper bracket for cranks or damage.

7. Inspect the bearing retainer for damage and thread damage. Repair the threads if necessary. If the hex portion of the bearing retainer is rounded off, replace it.

8. Inspect the steering stem portion and steering stem bearings as described under *Steering Stem* in this chapter.

Installation

1. Make sure the upper and lower bearing outer races are properly seated in the steering stem. Apply a light coat of bearing grease to each bearing race.

2. Pack the upper and lower bearings with grease before installation.

3. With the help of an assistant, carefully slide the rigid fork assembly up and into the steering head. Hold the fork assembly in place, then install the upper bearing onto the

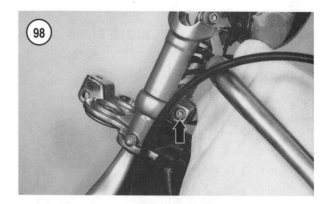

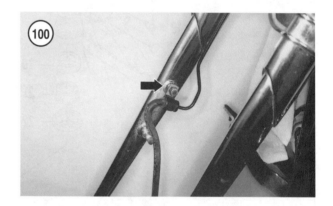

steering stem and push it down into the upper bearing race (B, **Figure 104**).

4. Install the dust shield (**Figure 103**) over the fork stem. Position the bearing retainer with the hex head facing down and install it onto the steering stem (**Figure 102**).

5. Tighten the bearing retainer as follows:

   a. Tighten the bearing retainer to 40 ft.-lb. (54 N•m).

   b. Loosen the bearing retainer and retighten to 72 in.-lb. (8 N•m).

6. Turn the rigid fork assembly from side-to-side; the fork should pivot smoothly with no sign of roughness or

tightness. If the fork does not pivot smoothly, remove the bearing retainer and recheck the bearings and fork stem.

7. Install the upper bracket onto the steering stem and rigid fork legs. Make sure it is seated correctly.

8. Install both rigid fork leg studs as follows:

   a. Thread both studs into the fork legs and tighten hand-tight.

   b. Tighten both studs to 60-65 ft.-lb. (81-88 N•m).

9. Install the upper bracket clamp bolt (**Figure 98**) and tighten to 25-30 ft.-lb. (34-41 N•m).

10. Install a *new* rubber washer and the acorn nut (C, **Figure 99**). Tighten the acorn nut to 30-35 ft.-lb. (41-48 N•m).

11. Adjust the steering as described under *Steering Adjustment* in this chapter.

12. Once again, turn the rigid fork assembly from side-to-side; the fork should pivot smoothly with no sign of roughness or tightness. If the fork does not pivot smoothly, readjust the steering as described in this chapter.

13. Move the brake line assembly into position on the base of the rigid fork below the steering stem. Install the bolt and bracket (**Figure 101**) and tighten securely.

14. Move the front brake line onto the side of the rigid fork and install the bolt and bracket (**Figure 100**). Tighten the bolt securely.

15. If removed, install the spring fork as described in this chapter.

16. Install the risers (B, **Figure 99**) and the handlebar as described in Chapter Ten.

17. Install the front fender as described in Chapter Fourteen.

18. Install the front brake caliper as described in Chapter Thirteen.

19. Install the front wheel as described in Chapter Nine.

20. On FLSTS models, install the passing lamp assembly as described in Chapter Eight.

21. Install the headlight assembly (A, **Figure 99**) as described in Chapter Eight.

22. Install the shock absorber as described in this chapter.

23. Remove the handlebar as described in this chapter.

24. Lower the motorcycle to the ground and place it on the jiffy stand.

25. Apply the front brake and compress the front suspension several times and make sure there is no binding or abnormal noise.

26. Test ride the motorcycle slowly at first to make sure the front suspension is operating correctly.

WARNING
Do not ride the motorcycle until the front brake is operating correctly with full hy-

11

*draulic advantage and that the front suspen-
sion is operating correctly.*

STEERING STEM

Steering Stem and Bearing Inspection

The upper and lower bearing outer races are pressed
into the frame. Do not remove the bearing races unless
they will be replaced.

1. Remove the entire fork assembly as described in this
chapter.

2. If still in place, remove the upper bearing from the
steering head.

3. Wipe the bearing races with a solvent soaked rag and
then dry with compressed air or a lint-free cloth. Check
the races in the steering head for pitting, scratches, galling
or excessive wear. Refer to **Figure 105** and **Figure 106**. If
any of these conditions exist, replace the races as described in this chapter. If the races are good, wipe each
race with grease.

4. Clean the bearings in solvent to remove all of the old
grease. Blow the bearing dry with compressed air, making
sure not to allow the air jet to spin the bearing. Do not remove the lower bearing from the fork stem unless it is to
be replaced. Clean the bearing while installed in the steering stem.

5. After the bearings are dry, hold the inner race with one
hand and turn the bearing with the other hand. Turn the
bearing slowly, the bearing must turn smoothly with no
roughness. Visually check the bearing (**Figure 107**) for
pitting, scratches or visible damage. If the bearings are
worn, check the dust covers for wear or damage or for improper bearing lubrication. Replace the bearing if necessary. If a bearing is going to be reused, pack it with grease
and wrap it with wax paper or another type of lint-free material until it is reinstalled. Do not store the bearings for
any length of time without lubricating them to prevent
rust.

6. Check the steering stem for cracks or damage. Check
the threads (**Figure 108**) at the top of the stem for damage.
Check the bearing retainer (**Figure 109**) for damage.
Thread it into the steering stem; make sure the nut threads
easily with no roughness.

7. Replace all worn or damaged parts. Replace bearing
races as described in this chapter.

8. Replace the lower steering stem bearing and the dust
shield as described in this chapter.

9. Check for broken welds on the frame around the steering head. If any are found, have them repaired by a competent frame shop or welding service familiar with
motorcycle frame repair.

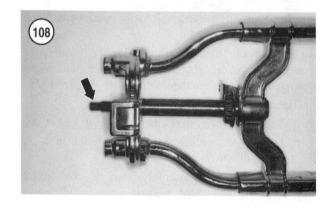

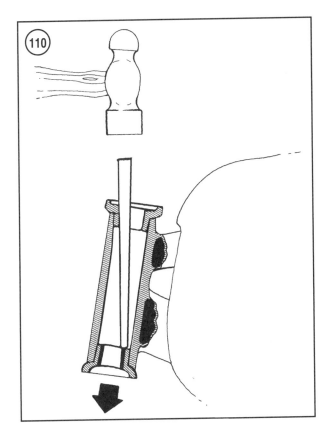

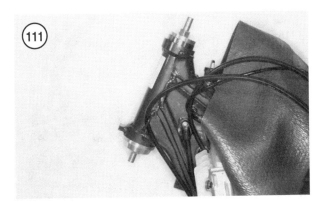

Steering Head Bearing Race Replacement

The upper and lower bearing outer races are pressed into the frame. Do not remove the bearing races unless replacement is necessary. If removed, replace both the outer race along with the bearing at the same time. Never reinstall an outer race that has been removed as it is no longer true and will damage the bearing.

1. Remove the entire fork assembly as described in this chapter.

2. If still in place, remove the upper bearing from the steering head.

3. To remove a race, insert an aluminum or brass rod into the steering head and carefully tap the race out from the inside (**Figure 110**). Tap all around the race so that neither the race nor the steering head is bent.

4. Clean the steering head with solvent and dry thoroughly.

5A. Install the bearing races with steering head bearing race installer tool (JIMS part No. 1725) (**Figure 111**) following the manufacturer's instructions.

5B. If the special tools are not available, install the bearing races as follows:

    a. Clean the race thoroughly before installing it.

    b. Align the upper race with the frame steering head (**Figure 112**) and tap it slowly and squarely in place. Do not contact the bearing race surfaces. See **Figure 113**. Drive the race into the steering head until it bottoms out on the bore shoulder.

    c. Repeat to install the lower race into the steering head.

6. Apply bearing grease to the face of each race.

Steering Stem Lower Bearing Replacement

Do not remove the steering stem lower bearing and lower seal unless it is going to be replaced. The lower bearing can be difficult to remove. If the lower bearing

11

cannot be removed as described in this procedure, take the steering stem to a Harley-Davidson dealership.

Never reinstall a lower bearing that has been removed since it is no longer true and will damage the rest of the bearing assembly.

1. Install the steering stem bearing retainer and acorn nut onto the top of the steering stem to protect the threads.

2. Remove the lower bearing (**Figure 114**) as follows:

   a. Place two large wide-blade screwdrivers into the fork stem bracket as shown in **Figure 115**.

   b. Slowly pry the lower bearing and dust shield up and off the steering stem raised shoulder.

   c. Slide the lower bearing and dust shield off the steering stem.

3. Clean the steering stem with solvent and dry thoroughly.

4. Position the new lower dust shield with the flange side facing up.

5. Slide a new the lower bearing onto the steering stem until it stops on the raised shoulder.

6. Align the lower bearing with the machined shoulder on the steering stem. Press or drive the lower bearing onto the steering stem until it bottoms (**Figure 114**).

7. If necessary, have the fork steering stem (**Figure 116**) replaced by a Harley-Davidson dealership.

STEERING PLAY ADJUSTMENT

Steering Tool Fabrication

By using this special tool, the steering head bearings can be adjusted with the handlebar, risers, rigid fork leg studs and upper bracket in place.

A steering adjustment tool must be fabricated to adjust the steering. Purchase the bearing retainer (part No. 48306-88) and three roll pins (part No. 614) from a Harley-Davidson dealership. See **Figure 117**.

Use a hacksaw and cut the pins so approximately 0.5 in. (12.7 mm) of the pin protrudes from the bottom surface of the retaining nut (**Figure 118**).

Coat the ends of the pins with Loctite Retaining Compound 620, or an equivalent, and insert them into the pre-drilled holes on the retaining nut. Allow the compound to set prior to using the tool.

> *CAUTION*
> *Do not use this tool to seat the upper bearing retainer nut. High torque will bend the pins in the tool.*

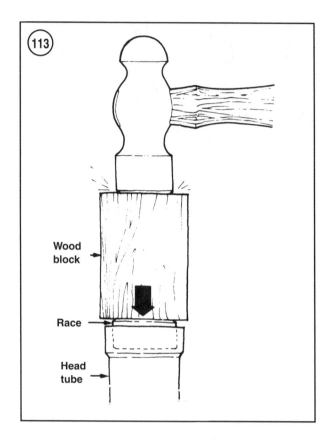

Wood block

Race

Head tube

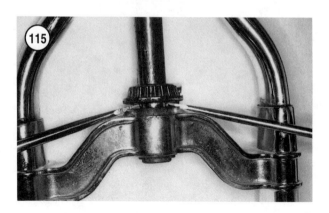

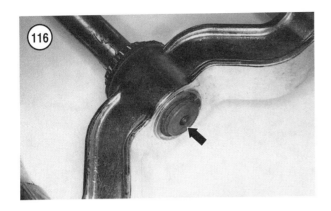

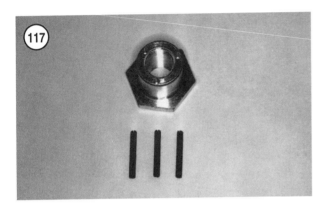

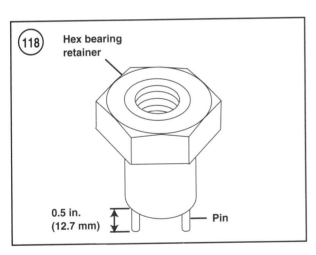

Hex bearing retainer

0.5 in. (12.7 mm)

Pin

Adjustment (FXSTS Models)

The motorcycle must be equipped with only the factory installed components. If any aftermarket components have been installed, they must be removed at this time as they could affect this adjustment.

1. Use a centrally located floor jack under the frame. Support the motorcycle with both the front and rear wheels off the ground the same distance. If necessary, place a wooden block(s) under the rear wheel until the motorcycle is level.

2. Disconnect the clutch cable from the handlebar. Refer to Chapter Five.

3. Disconnect the throttle cables from the handlebar. Refer to Chapter Seven.

4. Remove the acorn nut and rubber washer (C, **Figure 99**).

5. Loosen, but do not remove, the upper bracket pinch bolt (**Figure 98**).

6. Apply a strip of masking tape across the front end of the front fender. Draw a vertical line across the tape at the center of the fender.

7. Turn the handlebar so that the front wheel faces straight ahead.

8. Install pointer so the base is stationary on the floor and the pointer indicates the center of the fender tape mark when the wheel is facing straight ahead.

9. Lightly push the fender toward the right side until the front end starts to turn by itself. Mark this point on the tape.

10. Repeat Step 9 for the left side.

11. Measure the distance between the two marks on the tape. The correct distance is 1-2 in. (25-51 mm). If the distance is incorrect, perform Step 12.

12. If necessary, use the special tool and loosen or tighten the steering stem bearing retainer nut or bolt until the measurement is within the limits:

    a. If the distance is more than 2 in. (51 mm) loosen the bearing retainer nut.

    b. If the distance is less than 1 in. (25 mm) tighten the bearing retainer nut.

13. If used, remove the special tool from the bearing retainer.

14. Tighten the upper bracket pinch bolt (**Figure 98**) to 25-30 ft.-lb. (34-41 N•m).

15. Tighten the acorn nut and rubber washer (**Figure 99**) to 30-35 ft.-lb. (41-48 N•m).

16. Lower the motorcycle to the ground.

Adjustment (FLSTS Models)

The motorcycle must be equipped with only the factory installed components. If any aftermarket components have been installed, they must be removed at this time as they could affect this adjustment.

NOTE
The fork has more weight on the right side than on the left side. The balance point is just off the full left lock position.

11

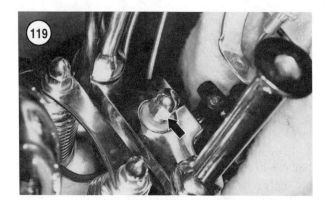

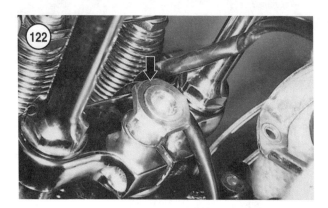

1. Use a centrally located floor jack under the frame. Support the motorcycle with both the front and rear wheels off the ground the same distance. If necessary, place a wooden block(s) under the rear wheel until the motorcycle is level.

2. Disconnect the clutch cable from the handlebar. Refer to Chapter Five.

3. Disconnect the throttle cables from the handlebar. Refer to Chapter Seven.

4. Remove the acorn nut and rubber washer (**Figure 119**).

5. Loosen, but do not remove the upper bracket pinch bolt (**Figure 120**).

6. Turn the fork to full left lock.

7. Hang a plumb bob from the hole in the rear of the fender.

8. Place a ruler on the floor directly under the plumb bob with the plumb bob pointing directly at zero.

9. Align the pins on the special tool with the holes in the bearing retainer (**Figure 121**). Push the tool in until it seats correctly (**Figure 122**).

10. Move the front wheel to the balance point and tap it until it begins to fall away *to the right*. Measure the distance from zero to the fall-away. Steering adjustment is correct when the zero to fall-away distance is 4-6 in. (101.6-152.4 mm). If necessary, use the special tool and adjust the bearing retainer until the adjustment is correct.

11. If used, remove the special tool from the bearing retainer.

12. Tighten the upper bracket pinch bolt (**Figure 120**) to 25-30 ft.-lb. (34-41 N•m).

13. Tighten the acorn nut and rubber washer (**Figure 119**) to 30-35 ft.-lb. (41-48 N•m).

14. Lower the motorcycle to the ground.

Table 1 FRONT SUSPENSION TORQUE SPECIFICATIONS (SPRINGER)

Item	ft.-lb.	in.-lb.	N•m
Bearing retainer	–	25-35	3-4
Bearing adjuster jam nut	95-105	–	129-143
Handlebar			
Clamp bolts	–	144-180	16-20
Riser lock nuts	25-35	–	34-47
Riser threaded stud	60-65	–	81-88
Rocker pivot stud			
Acorn or hex nut	45-50	–	61-68
Rigid fork leg studs	60-65	–	81-88
Rigid fork steering stem bearing retainer			
Preliminary	40	–	54
Final	–	72	8
Acorn nut	30-35	–	41-48
Shock absorber acorn nut	45-50	–	61-68
Spring bridge acorn nuts	30-35	–	41-48
Spring rod acorn nut	20-25	–	27-34
Upper bracket pinch bolt	25-30	–	34-41

11

CHAPTER TWELVE

REAR SUSPENSION

This chapter includes repair and replacement procedures for the rear suspension components. **Table 1** is located at the end of this chapter.

WARNING
*All fasteners used on the rear suspension must be replaced with parts of the same type. Do not use a replacement part of lesser quality or substitute design. It may affect the performance of the rear suspension or fail, leading to loss of control of the motorcycle. Use the torque specifications in **Table 1** during installation to ensure proper retention of these components.*

SPRING PRELOAD ADJUSTMENT

The shock absorber spring preload can be adjusted to compensate for the weight the motorcycle is to carry. A special tool is required for this procedure. The spanner wrench (HD-94455-89) is included in the motorcycle tool kit (**Figure 1**).

1. Thoroughly clean the threads on the shock absorber mount prior to loosening the locknut in Step 2. Remove all dirt and road debris to avoid damage to the threads.
2. Working under the motorcycle, loosen the locknut (**Figure 2**) on both shock absorber shafts. The locknut is located at the front of the shock absorber.

3. Mark alignment marks on the adjuster plate and the shock absorber case on each shock absorber.
4. Using the spanner wrench, rotate the adjuster plate in the following directions:
   a. To increase spring preload, rotate the adjuster plate out toward the locknut.
   b. To decrease spring preload, rotate the adjuster plate in toward the locknut.
5. Adjust both shock absorbers to the same setting.
6. Tighten the locknuts securely.

SHOCK ABSORBERS

All models are equipped with dual shock absorbers located horizontally under the transmission case.

Removal/Installation

Refer to **Figure 3**.
One special tool is required for shock absorber removal and installation. Use a Snap-on adapter (part No. SRES24), or an equivalent ratchet wrench, to access the bolt securing the shock absorber to the swing arm.

NOTE
This procedure is shown with the rear wheel removed to better illustrate the steps.

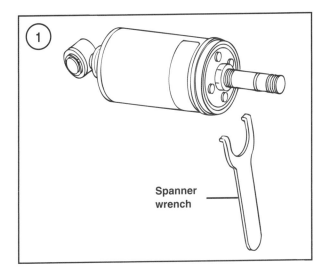

Spanner wrench

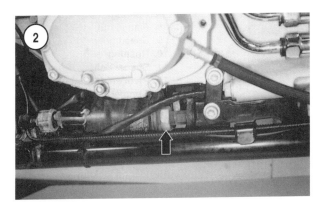

1. Support the motorcycle with the rear wheel *slightly* off the ground. See *Motorcycle Stands* in Chapter Nine.

2. On models so equipped, remove the saddlebags as described in Chapter Fourteen.

3. Using the special tool, remove the bolt and washer (**Figure 4**) securing the shock absorbers to the rear swing arm.

4. Remove the flange locknut and washer/grommet securing the shock absorber stud to the frame cross member (**Figure 5**).

5. Pull the shock absorber to the rear (**Figure 6**) and remove it from the motorcycle. Do not lose the bushing on the shock absorber stud.

6. Inspect the shock absorber as described in this chapter.

7. Install the bushing onto the end of the shock absorber stud.

8. Place the washer/grommet onto the inside surface of the frame and insert the shock absorber stud through the washer/grommet.

9. Install the flange locknut and tighten finger-tight.

10. Apply a few drops of ThreeBond TB1342, or an equivalent, to the shock mounting bolt threads.

11. Move the shock absorber into position on the rear swing arm and install the mounting bolt washer securing the shock absorber to the swing arm.

12. Tighten the mounting bolt and the flange locknut to the specifications in **Table 1**.

13. Repeat Steps 8-12 for the other shock absorber if necessary.

14. Adjust both shock absorbers equally as described in this chapter.

15. On models so equipped, install the saddlebag(s) as described in Chapter Fourteen.

16. Lower the motorcycle and test ride it to make sure the rear suspension is working properly.

Inspection

There are no shock replacement parts available for these models. If any part requires replacement, other than the mounting hardware, replace the shock assembly.

1. Remove the shock absorber as described in this chapter.

2. Inspect the shock bushing (**Figure 7**) for wear and deterioration.

3. Inspect the threaded stud (A, **Figure 8**) and nut (B) for thread damage and clean up if necessary.

4. Check the bushing (C, **Figure 8**) for wear.

5. Inspect the grommet/washer combination (**Figure 9**) for hardness or deterioration.

6. Check the adjuster locknut (**Figure 10**) for damage and for tightness.

7. Inspect the shock absorber body (**Figure 11**) for damage, replace the shock absorber if necessary.

8. Inspect the mounting bolt (**Figure 12**) for thread damage and clean up if necessary.

REAR SWING ARM

Rear Swing Arm Bearing Check

The swing arm bearings are sealed and lifetime lubricated. These bearings do not require any routing service and should last the life of the motorcycle unless they are damaged due to an accident or abuse. Worn or damaged bearings can produce erratic and dangerous handling. Common symptoms are wheel hop, pulling to one side during acceleration and pulling to the other side during braking.

1. On models so equipped, remove the saddlebags as described in Chapter Fourteen.

2. Remove the rear wheel as described in Chapter Nine.

12

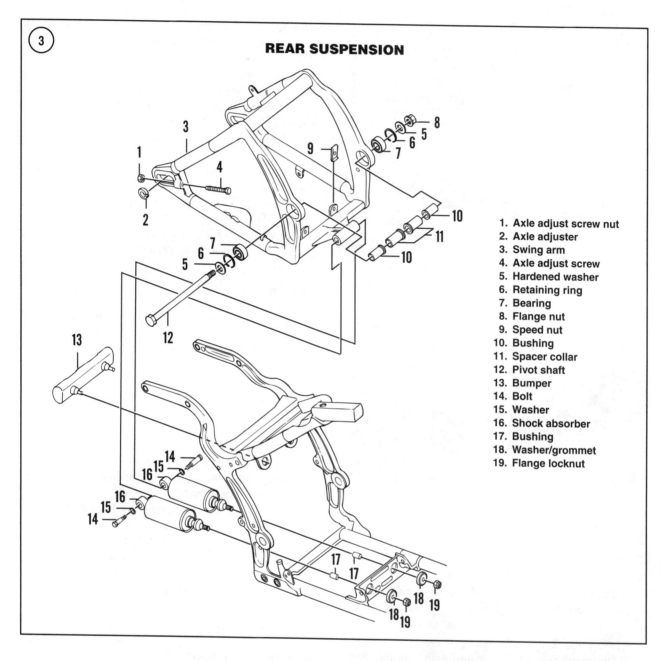

REAR SUSPENSION

1. Axle adjust screw nut
2. Axle adjuster
3. Swing arm
4. Axle adjust screw
5. Hardened washer
6. Retaining ring
7. Bearing
8. Flange nut
9. Speed nut
10. Bushing
11. Spacer collar
12. Pivot shaft
13. Bumper
14. Bolt
15. Washer
16. Shock absorber
17. Bushing
18. Washer/grommet
19. Flange locknut

3. Make sure the nut (**Figure 13**) securing the rear swing arm pivot shaft is tight.

4. Have an assistant hold the motorcycle securely.

5. Grasp the back of the rear swing arm and try to move it from side to side. Any play between the rear swing arm and the frame may indicate worn or damaged bearings. If there is any play, remove the swing arm and inspect the bearings.

6. Install the rear wheel as described in Chapter Nine.

7. On models so equipped, install the saddlebags as described in Chapter Fourteen.

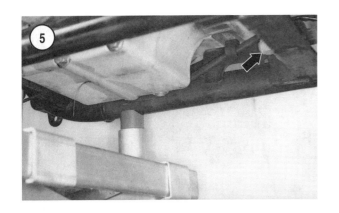

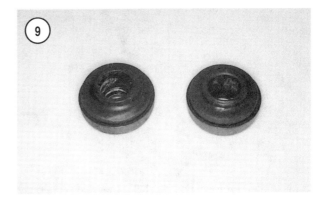

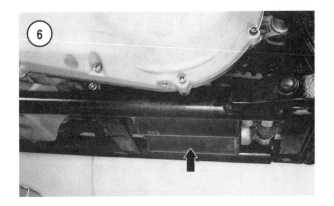

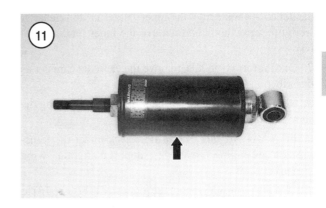

12

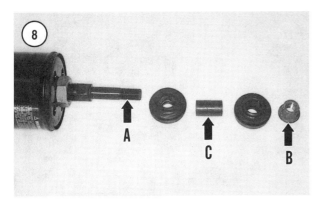

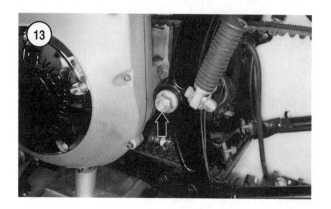

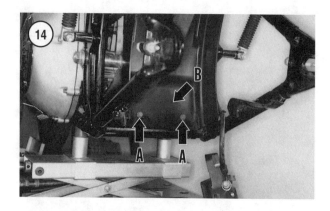

Removal

Refer to **Figure 3**.

1. Remove the exhaust system as described in Chapter Seven.

2. Remove the rear wheel as described in Chapter Nine.

3. On models so equipped, remove the saddlebags as described in Chapter Fourteen.

4. Remove the belt guard as described in Chapter Nine.

5. Remove the rear caliper as described in Chapter Thirteen.

6. Remove the two bolts (A, **Figure 14**) securing the inner fender panel. Move the inner fender up to release if from the frame hook and remove the inner fender panel (B).

7. On California models, remove the charcoal canister as described in Chapter Seven.

8. Remove the bolts and washers (**Figure 4**) securing the shock absorbers to the swing arm.

9. Place wooden blocks or a floor jack under the transmission and engine assembly to support it after the swing arm pivot shaft is removed.

10. On the right side, secure the pivot shaft (**Figure 15**) to keep it from rotating in the following step.

> *NOTE*
> *The pivot shaft hardened washers are unique (different part numbers) and must be installed on the correct side. After removal mark each washer with a **R** or **L** so ensure correct placement during installation.*

11. On the left side, loosen and remove the pivot shaft flange nut and hardened washer (**Figure 13**).

12. Support the swing arm on a box and tap on the left side of the pivot shaft with a drift. Drive the pivot shaft from the left side of the frame.

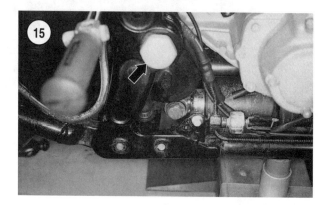

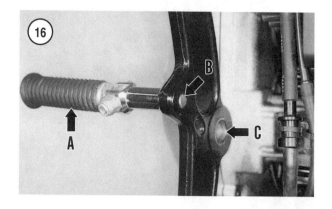

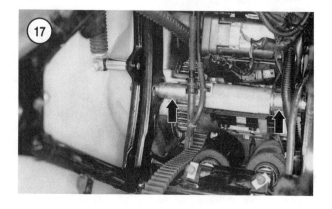

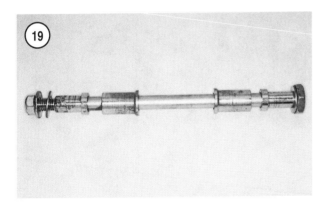

NOTE
In some cases, the rear footpeg mounting bolts protrude past the frame mounting area and will interfere with the removal of the swing arm.

13. If necessary, remove the rear footpeg assemblies (A, **Figure 16**) as described in Chapter Fourteen. An alternative is to grind off a small portion of the end of the mounting bolt (B) to gain necessary clearance.

14. Remove the pivot shaft and hardened washer from the frame. Remove the spacer collar (**Figure 17**) on each side of the pivot area on the transmission.

15. Pull the rear swing arm straight back and remove it from the frame and transmission case.

16. Remove the pivot bushing (**Figure 18**) from each side of the frame pivot locations.

17. Install the hardened washers, spacer collars, pivot bushings, washer and nut onto the pivot shaft in the correct order of removal (**Figure 19**).

18. Inspect the swing arm as described in this chapter.

Inspection

1. Wash the exterior of the swing arm in solvent and thoroughly dry it with compressed air.

2. Inspect the welded sections (**Figure 20**) on the rear swing arm for cracks or fractures.

3. Inspect the pivot shaft (**Figure 19**) for surface cracks, deep scoring, wear or heat distortion. Replace if necessary.

4. Clean the bearing bore with a clean shop cloth.

5. Turn the bearings (**Figure 21**) with a finger. The bearings should turn smoothly with no sign of roughness or damage. If necessary, replace the bearings as described in the following procedure. Replace the bearings as a pair if either is damaged.

12

6. Inspect the bushings and spacer collars for wear or damage.

7. Inspect the shock absorber mounting post threads (**Figure 22**) for thread damage and clean up if necessary.

8. Inspect the pivot shaft receptacles in the frame (C, **Figure 16**) for wear or elongation. Repair if necessary.

9. Check the rear axle adjuster bolt and jamb nut (**Figure 23**). Make sure the adjuster bolt turns freely within the treaded portion of the frame and clean up if necessary.

Bearing replacement

Remove and install the bearings only if the bearings must be replaced. Never install a bearing that has been removed. Both the bearings must be replaced as set.

1. Remove the retaining ring on the outer surface of the swing arm securing the bearing in place.

2. Place the rear swing arm on wooden blocks with the outside surface facing down.

3. Use a socket that matches the bearing outer race and will fit into the swing arm bearing receptacle.

4. Place the socket on the inner surface, tap squarely on the bearing squarely and drive the bearing out of the swing arm pivot bore.

5. Blow any debris out of the swing arm pivot bore prior to installing the new bearing.

6. Apply a light coat of bearing grease to the seating area of the pivot bore. This will make bearing installation easier.

7. Place the rear swing arm on wooden blocks with the outside surface facing up.

8. Select a driver with an outside diameter slightly smaller than the bearing's outside diameter.

9. Tap the *new* bearing squarely into place and tap on the outer race only. Tap the bearing into the pivot bore until it bottoms on the shoulder. Make sure the bearing is completely seated and that the retaining ring groove is visible.

10. Install a *new* retaining ring and make sure it is seated correctly in the groove.

11. Turn the bearing (**Figure 21**) with a finger and make sure the new bearing turns smoothly with no sign of roughness.

12. Turn the swing arm over and repeat for the bearing on the other side.

Installation

1. Install both bushings (**Figure 18**) into the pivot bearings in the swing arm. Push them in until the bottom.

2. Position the drive belt (A, **Figure 24**) on the inboard side of the swing arm and position the swing arm (B) onto

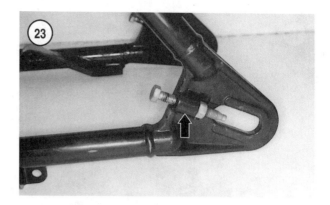

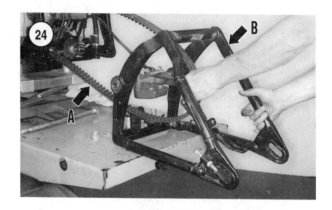

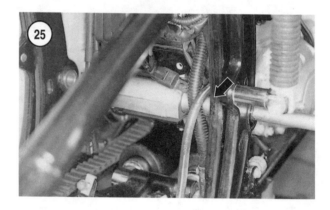

the pivot area of the transmission case and frame and support it in this position.

NOTE
Do not substitute another type of washer in place of the hardened washers.

3. Install the pivot shaft as follows:

 a. Coat the pivot shaft with Loctite antiseize, or an appropriate type of grease.

 b. Install the *R* marked hardened washer onto the pivot shaft.

c. Position the right side spacer collar (**Figure 25**) with the flange side facing the transmission case and install it between the transmission case and the swing arm.

d. Insert the pivot shaft (**Figure 26**) from the right side through the frame pivot area, the swing arm bushing, the right side spacer collar and the transmission case.

e. Position the left side spacer collar (**Figure 27**) with the flange side facing the transmission case and in-

stall it between the transmission case and the swing arm.

f. Continue to push the pivot shaft through the left side spacer collar, the swing arm bushing and left side of the frame pivot area. Push the pivot shaft in until it bottoms.

g. Make sure both spacer collars (**Figure 17**) are in place.

h. Install the *L* marked hardened washer onto the pivot shaft.

4. On the right side, secure the pivot shaft (**Figure 15**) to keep it from rotating in the following step.

5. Apply ThreeBond No. 1360 (red) threadlocking compound to the pivot shaft threads prior to installing the flange nut.

6. On the left side, install the flange nut (**Figure 13**) and tighten to 90-110 ft.-lb. (122-149 N•m).

7. Slowly raise and lower the swing arm to ensure ease of movement. If binding occurs, repeat Step 6 and correct the problem.

8. Install the shock absorbers as described in this chapter.

9. On California models, install the charcoal canister as described in Chapter Seven.

10. Install the inner fender and hook it onto the frame hook. Install the two bolts (A, **Figure 14**) securing the inner fender and tighten securely.

11. Install the rear caliper as described in Chapter Thirteen.

12. Install the rear wheel and the belt guard as described in Chapter Nine.

13. Remove the wooden blocks or floor jack from under the transmission and engine assembly.

14. Install the exhaust system as described in Chapter Seven.

15. On models so equipped, install both saddlebags as described in Chapter Fourteen.

12

Table 1 REAR SUSPENSION TORQUE SPECIFICATIONS

Item	ft.-lb.	in.-lb.	N•m
Rear axle nut	60-65	–	81-88
Shock absorber			
Mounting bolt	115-130	–	156-176
Flange locknut	32-39	–	43—53
Swing arm pivot bolt lock nut	90-110	–	122-149

CHAPTER THIRTEEN

BRAKES

This chapter includes repair and replacement procedures for all brake system components.

Refer to **Table 1** and **Table 2** located at the end of this chapter.

BRAKE SERVICE

WARNING
*Do not use brake fluid labeled **DOT 5.1**. This is a glycol-based fluid that is **not compatible** with silicone-based DOT 5. DOT 5 brake fluid is purple while DOT 5.1 is amber/clear. Do not intermix these two different types of brake fluid. It will lead to brake component damage and possible brake failure.*

WARNING
Do not intermix DOT 3, DOT 4, or DOT 5.1 brake fluids as they are not silicone-based. Using non-silicone brake fluid in these models can cause brake failure.

WARNING
*When working on the brake system, do **not** inhale brake dust. It may contain asbestos, which is a know carcinogen. Do **not** use compressed air to blow off brake dust. Use an aerosol brake cleaner. Wear a facemask and wash thoroughly after completing the work.*

The disc brake system transmits hydraulic pressure from the master cylinders to the brake calipers. This pressure is transmitted from the caliper(s) to the brake pads, which grip both sides of the brake disc(s) and slow the motorcycle. As the pads wear, the pistons move out of the caliper bores to automatically compensate for wear. As this occurs, the fluid level in the master cylinder reservoir goes down. Compensate for this by occasionally adding fluid.

The proper operation of this system depends on a supply of clean brake fluid (DOT 5) and a clean work environment when any service is being performed. Any particle of debris that enters the system can damage the components and cause poor brake performance.

Brake fluid is hygroscopic (easily absorbs moisture) and moisture in the system reduces brake performance. Purchase brake fluid in small containers and properly discard small quantities that remain. Small quantities of fluid will quickly absorb the moisture in the container. Only use fluid clearly marked DOT 5. If possible, use the same brand of fluid. Do not replace the fluid with a non-silicone fluid. It is not possible to remove all of the old fluid. Other types are not compatible with DOT 5. Do not reuse drained fluid. Discard old fluid properly. Do not combine brake fluid with fluids for recycling.

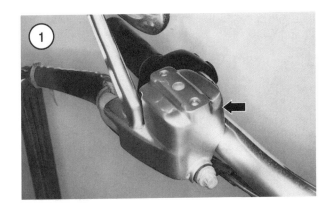

When adding fluid, punch a small hole into the edge of the fluid container's seal to help control the fluid flow. This is especially important to prevent spills while adding fluid to the small reservoirs.

Perform service procedures carefully. Do not use sharp tools inside the master cylinders or calipers or on the pistons. Damage to these components could cause a loss in the system's ability to maintain hydraulic pressure. If there is any doubt about the ability to correctly and safely service the brake system, have a professional technician perform the task.

Consider the following when servicing the brake system:

1. The hydraulic components rarely require disassembly. Make sure disassembly is necessary.

2. Keep the reservoir covers in place to prevent the entry of moisture and debris.

3. Clean parts with an aerosol brake part cleaner or isopropyl alcohol. Never use petroleum-based solvents on internal brake system components. They will cause seals to swell and distort.

4. Do not allow brake fluid to contact plastic, painted or plated parts. It will damage the surface.

5. Dispose of brake fluid properly.

6. If the hydraulic system, not including the reservoir cover has been opened, bleed the system to remove air from the system. Refer to *Bleeding the System* in this chapter.

7. The manufacturer does not provide wear limit specifications for the caliper and master cylinder assemblies. Use good judgment when inspecting these components or consult a professional technician for advice.

FRONT BRAKE PAD REPLACEMENT (FXSTS AND FLSTS MODELS)

There is no recommended mileage interval for changing the brake pads. Pad wear depends on riding habits and conditions. Frequently check the brake pads for wear. Increase the inspection interval when the wear indicator reaches the edge of the brake disc. After removal, measure the thickness of each brake pad with a vernier caliper or ruler, and compare measurements to the dimensions in **Table 1**.

Always replace both pads in the caliper at the same time to maintain even brake pressure on the disc. Do not disconnect the hydraulic brake hose from the brake caliper for brake pad replacement. Only disconnect the hose if the caliper assembly is going to be removed.

CAUTION
Check the pads more frequently when the lining approaches the pad metal backing plate. If pad wear is uneven for some reason, the backing plate may come in contact with the disc and cause damage.

NOTE
The brake disc and caliper are mounted on the right side of the front wheel on FXSTS models, on FLSTS models they are located on the left side.

1. Read the information under *Brake Service* in this chapter.

2. Park the motorcycle on a level surface.

3. To prevent the front brake lever from being applied, place a spacer between the brake lever and the throttle grip and secure it in place. Then if the brake lever is inadvertently squeezed, the piston will not be forced out of the cylinder.

4. To prevent the reservoir from overflowing while repositioning the piston in the caliper, perform the following:

    a. On models so equipped, remove the master cylinder chrome cover (**Figure 1**).

    b. Remove the screws securing the cover (A, **Figure 2**), and remove the cover (B) and diaphragm.

13

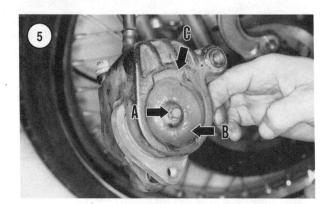

c. Use a shop syringe and remove about 50% of the brake fluid from the reservoir. Do *not* drain more than 50% of the brake fluid or air will enter the system. Discard the brake fluid properly.

5A. On FXSTS models, perform the following:

    a. Remove the cotter pin and washer (**Figure 3**) from the caliper upper mounting bolt.

    b. Gently push the caliper against the brake disc to push the piston back into the caliper to make room for the new brake pads.

    c. Remove the caliper upper mounting bolt and washers (A, **Figure 4**).

    d. Remove the caliper lower mounting bolt (B, **Figure 4**).

    e. Slide the brake caliper (C, **Figure 4**) off the brake disc.

5B. On FLSTS models, perform the following:

    a. Remove the spring pin from the caliper upper mounting bolt.

    b. Remove the lower and upper caliper mounting bolts. Do not lose the washer on the upper mounting bolt.

    c. Slide the brake caliper off the brake disc.

> *NOTE*
> *If the brake pads are going to be reused, mark them so they can be reinstalled into their original locations.*

6. Remove the outboard pad, pad holder and spring clip as an assembly (**Figure 6**).

7. Remove the bolt (A, **Figure 5**) and the pad retainer (B) securing the inner pad to the caliper.

8. Remove the inboard pad (**Figure 6**) and the outboard pad (**Figure 7**).

9. Push the outboard pad (A, **Figure 8**) free of the spring clip (B) and remove it.

10. Check the brake pads (**Figure 9**) for wear or damage. Measure the thickness of the brake pad friction material (**Figure 10**). Replace the brake pads if they are worn to the service limit in **Table 1**.

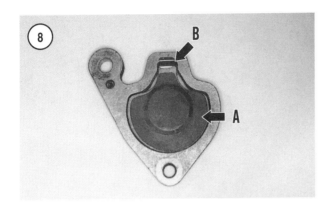

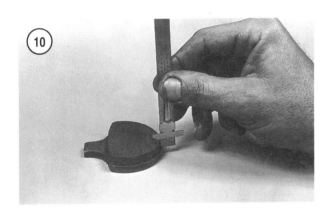

11. Check the friction surface of the new pads for any debris or manufacturing residue. If necessary, clean them off with an aerosol brake cleaner.

NOTE
When purchasing new pads, check with the dealership to make sure the friction compound of the new pad is compatible with the disc material. Remove roughness from the backs of the new pads with a fine-cut file, then thoroughly clean them off with brake cleaner.

12. Inspect the upper mounting bolt and the lower mounting pin. Replace them if they are damaged or badly corroded.

13. Replace the pad retainer (**Figure 11**) if it is damaged.

14. Check the piston dust boot (**Figure 12**) in the caliper. If the boot is swollen or damaged, or if brake fluid is leaking from the caliper, remove and overhaul the caliper. Refer to *Front Brake Caliper (FXSTS* and *FLSTS Models)* in this chapter.

15. Remove all corrosion from the pad holder.

16. Replace the spring clip if it is damaged or badly corroded.

17. Check the brake disc for wear as described under *Brake Disc* in this chapter. Service the brake disc if necessary.

18. Assemble the pad holder, spring clip and outboard brake pad as follows:

   a. Lay the pad holder on a workbench so the upper mounting screw hole is positioned at the upper right as shown in A, **Figure 13**.

   b. Install the spring clip (B, **Figure 13**) at the top of the pad holder so the spring loop faces in the direction shown in **Figure 14**.

   c. The outboard brake pad has an insulator pad mounted on its backside (A, **Figure 8**).

   d. Center the outboard brake pad into the pad holder so the lower end of the pad rests inside the pad holder.

13

Push the upper end of the brake pad past the spring clip and into the holder.

NOTE
Step 19 is not necessary if the piston was repositioned in Step 4.

19. After the installation of new brake pads, the caliper piston must be relocated into the caliper before the caliper is installed over the brake disc. This will force brake fluid back up into the reservoir. To prevent the reservoir from overflowing, perform the following:

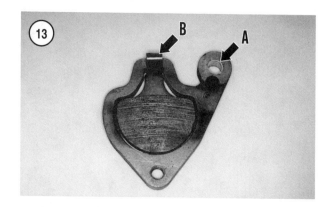

   a. Remove the screws (A, **Figure 2**) securing the cover (B) and remove the cover and diaphragm.

   b. Use a shop syringe and remove about 50% of the brake fluid from the reservoir. Do *not* drain more than 50% of the brake fluid or air will enter the system. Discard the brake fluid properly.

CAUTION
Do not allow the master cylinder to overflow during this step. Wash brake fluid off any painted, plated, or plastic surfaces immediately as it will damage most surfaces it contacts. Use soapy water and rinse completely.

   c. Install the old outer brake pad into the caliper and against the piston.

   d. Slowly push the outer brake pad and piston back into the caliper. Watch the brake fluid level in the master cylinder reservoir. If necessary, siphon off fluid before it overflows.

   e. Remove the old brake pad.

   f. Temporarily install the diaphragm and cover. Install the screws finger-tight at this time.

20. Install the inner brake pad (**Figure 15**) into the caliper from the inside surface. Push the pad into place.

21. Install the outer brake pad/pad holder assembly (**Figure 16**).

WARNING
*The spring clip loop and the brake pad friction material (**Figure 17**) must face away from the piston when the pad holder is installed in the caliper. Brake failure will occur if this assembly is installed incorrectly.*

22. Install the pad retainer (**Figure 18**) onto the backside of the caliper, indexing the tabs into the caliper recesses (C, **Figure 5**).

23. Install the bolt (A, **Figure 5**) through the pad retainer into the backside of the inner brake pad. Tighten the bolt to 40-50 in.-lb. (5-6 N•m).

24A. On FXSTS models, perform the following:

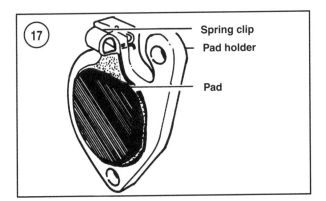

Spring clip

Pad holder

Pad

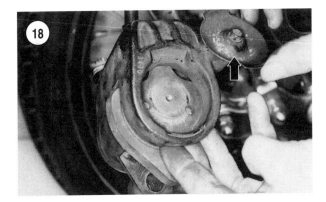

a. Carefully slide the brake caliper onto the brake disc. Align the bolt two mounting bolt holes with the mounting holes on the caliper mounting bracket.

b. Coat the outside surface of the lower mounting bolt with Dow Corning Moly 44 grease or an equivalent prior to installation.

c. Install the caliper lower mounting bolt (**Figure 19**) through the caliper mounting bracket and into the caliper. Tighten finger tight at this time.

d. Install the caliper upper mounting bolt and washers (**Figure 20**) and screw it into the threaded bushing. Tighten the bolt finger-tight at this time.

e. Tighten the upper and lower mounting bolts to the specifications in **Table 2**.

f. Install the washer (**Figure 21**) and *new* cotter pin onto the caliper upper mounting bolt. Bend the ends of the cotter pin over completely (**Figure 3**).

24B. On FLSTS models, perform the following:

a. Coat the outside surface of the lower mounting bolt with Dow Corning Moly 44 grease or an equivalent prior to installation.

b. Install the caliper mounting plate and brake pad onto the backside of the brake disc.

c. Install the brake caliper onto the brake disc.

d. Move the caliper mounting plate into position and align the hole in the caliper mounting plate with the raised boss on the brake caliper mounting bracket. Make sure the spring clip is positioned correctly in the brake caliper.

e. Install the upper bolt and washer through the brake caliper mounting bracket and into the brake caliper. Tighten finger-tight at this time.

f. Install the lower bolt through the caliper and into the brake caliper mounting bracket. Tighten finger-tight at this time.

g. Tighten the upper and lower mounting bolts to the specifications in **Table 2**.

h. Install the spring pin onto the upper mounting bolt.

13

25. Refill the master cylinder reservoir with DOT 5 brake fluid, if necessary, to maintain the correct fluid level. Install the diaphragm, top cover (B, **Figure 2**) and tighten the screws (A) to 6-8 in.-lb. (1 N•m).

26. Apply the front brake lever several times to seat the pads against the disc.

> *WARNING*
> *Do not ride the motorcycle until the front brake is operating correctly with full hydraulic advantage. If necessary, bleed the brakes as described in this chapter.*

27. On models so equipped, install the master cylinder chrome cover (**Figure 1**).

FRONT BRAKE PAD REPLACEMENT (ALL MODELS EXCEPT FXSTS AND FLSTS)

There is no recommended mileage interval for changing the brake pads. Pad wear depends on riding habits and conditions. Frequently check the brake pads for wear. Increase the inspection interval when the wear indicator reaches the edge of the brake disc. After removal, measure the thickness of each brake pad with a vernier caliper or ruler, and compare measurements to the dimensions in **Table 1**.

Always replace both pads in the caliper at the same time to maintain even brake pressure on the disc. Do not disconnect the hydraulic brake hose from the brake caliper for brake pad replacement. Only disconnect the hose if the caliper assembly is going to be removed.

> *CAUTION*
> *Check the pads more frequently when the lining approaches the pad metal backing plate. If pad wear is uneven for some reason, the backing plate may come in contact with the disc and cause damage.*

1. Read the information under *Brakes Service* in this chapter.

2. Park the motorcycle on level ground.

3. Place a spacer between the brake lever and the throttle grip, and secure it in place. If the brake lever is inadvertently squeezed, this will prevent the pistons from being forced out of the cylinders.

4. Clean the top of the master cylinder of all dirt and debris.

5. On models so equipped, remove the master cylinder chrome cover (**Figure 22**).

6. Remove the screws securing the cover (A, **Figure 23**), and remove the cover (B) and diaphragm.

7. Use a shop syringe and remove about 50% of the brake fluid from the reservoir. This will prevent the master cylinder from overflowing when the pistons are compressed for reinstallation. Do *not* drain more than 50% of the brake fluid or air will enter the system. Discard the brake fluid properly.

> *CAUTION*
> *Do not allow the master cylinder to overflow during Step 7. Wash brake fluid off any painted, plated, or plastic surfaces immediately as it will damage most surfaces it contacts. Use soapy water and rinse completely.*

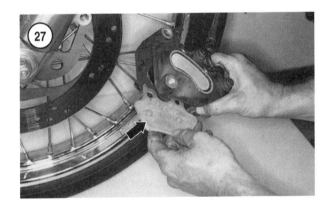

8. Loosen the pad pin bolts (**Figure 24**).

CAUTION
The brake disc is thin in order to dissipate heat and may bend easily. When pushing against the disc in the following step, support the disc adjacent to the caliper to prevent damage to the disc.

9. Hold the caliper body from the outside and push it toward the brake disc. This will push the outer pistons into the caliper bores to make room for the new brake pads.

Constantly check the reservoir to make sure brake fluid does not overflow. Remove fluid, if necessary, before it overflows. Install the diaphragm and cover. Tighten the screws finger-tight.

10. Remove the caliper mounting bolts (**Figure 25**) and remove the caliper from the front fork.

11. Remove the pad pin bolts (**Figure 24**).

12. Remove the inboard and outboard brake pads from the caliper.

13. Check the brake pads for wear or damage. Measure the thickness of the brake pad friction material. Replace the brake pads if they are worn to the service limit in **Table 1**.

14. Carefully remove rust or corrosion from the disc.

15. Thoroughly clean the pad pin bolts of corrosion or road dirt.

16. Check the friction surface of the new pads for debris or manufacturing residue. If necessary, clean them off with an aerosol brake cleaner.

NOTE
When purchasing new pads, check with the dealership to make sure the friction compound of the new pad is compatible with the disc material. Remove roughness from the backs of the new pads with a fine-cut file, then thoroughly clean them off.

NOTE
The pads are not symmetrical. The pad with one tab (A, Figure 26) must be installed on the inboard side of the left side caliper and on the outboard side of the right side caliper. The pad with two tabs (B, Figure 26) must be installed on the outboard side of the left side caliper and on the inboard side of the right side caliper.

NOTE
The front and rear caliper brake pads are identical with the exception of the FXSTD models. The FXSTD rear brake pads have a vertical slot cut into them. Do not interchange the rear brake pads with the front brake pads.

17. Install the outboard pad (**Figure 27**). Hold the pad in place against the anti-rattle spring and install both pad pin bolts (**Figure 28**) through the caliper and the outboard brake pad.

18. Install the inboard pad (**Figure 29**) into the caliper. Hold the pad in place against the anti-rattle spring and push both pad pin bolts through the inboard brake pad and into the caliper. Tighten the pad pin bolts finger-tight.

19. Separate the brake pads (**Figure 30**) to allow room for the brake disc.

13

20. Carefully install the caliper onto the brake disc and install the mounting bolts (**Figure 25**). Tighten the bolts to 28-38 ft.-lb. (38-52 N•m).

21. Tighten the pad pin bolts (**Figure 24**) to 180-200 in.-lb. (20-30 ft.-lb.).

22. Remove the spacer from the front brake lever.

23. Make sure there is sufficient brake fluid in the master cylinder reservoir. Top it off if necessary.

24. Pump the front brake lever several times to reposition the brake pads against the brake disc.

25. Refill the master cylinder reservoir, if necessary, to maintain the correct fluid level as indicated on the side of the reservoir. Install the diaphragm and the top cover. Tighten the screws to 6-8 in.-lb. (1 N•m).

NOTE
Do not ride the motorcycle until the front brake is operating correctly with full hydraulic advantage. If necessary, bleed the brakes as described in this chapter.

FRONT BRAKE CALIPER (FXSTS AND FLSTS MODELS)

NOTE
On FXSTS models, the brake disc and caliper are mounted on the right side of the front wheel, on FLSTS models they are located on the left side.

Removal (FXSTS Models)

Refer to **Figure 31**.

1. Remove the cotter pin and washer (**Figure 32**) from the caliper upper mounting bolt.

2. Remove the caliper upper mounting bolt and washers (A, **Figure 33**).

3. Remove the caliper lower mounting bolt (B, **Figure 33**).

4. Slide the brake caliper (C, **Figure 33**) off the brake disc.

NOTE
Step 5 is only necessary if the caliper is going to be serviced.

5. If the caliper assembly is going to be disassembled for service, perform the following:

NOTE
If the brake pads are going to be reused, mark them so they can be reinstalled into their original locations.

a. Remove the brake pads as described in this chapter.

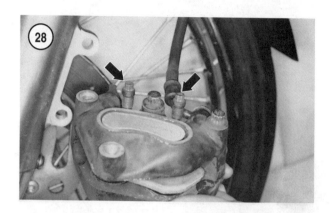

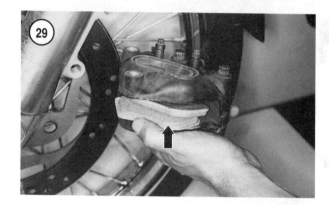

b. Slowly apply the front brake lever to push the piston part way out of the caliper assembly for ease of removal during caliper service.

6. Drain the brake fluid from the front brake hose as described under *Brake Hose and Line Replacement* in this chapter.

7. Loosen the banjo bolt at the caliper (D, **Figure 33**). Remove the banjo bolt and the two washers.

8. Move the brake hose out of the way and place it in a plastic bag.

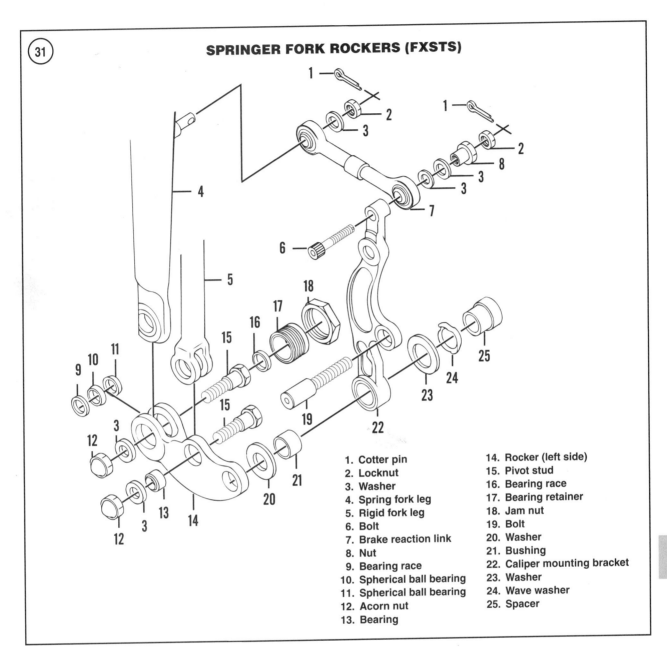

③ **SPRINGER FORK ROCKERS (FXSTS)**

1. Cotter pin
2. Locknut
3. Washer
4. Spring fork leg
5. Rigid fork leg
6. Bolt
7. Brake reaction link
8. Nut
9. Bearing race
10. Spherical ball bearing
11. Spherical ball bearing
12. Acorn nut
13. Bearing
14. Rocker (left side)
15. Pivot stud
16. Bearing race
17. Bearing retainer
18. Jam nut
19. Bolt
20. Washer
21. Bushing
22. Caliper mounting bracket
23. Washer
24. Wave washer
25. Spacer

13

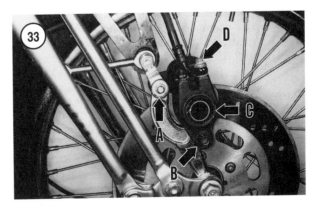

9. If the front caliper is not going to be serviced, place it in a reclosable plastic bag to keep it clean.

Installation (FXSTS Models)

Refer to **Figure 31**.

1. If the caliper was disassembled for service, install the brake pads as described in this chapter.
2. Carefully slide the brake caliper (C, **Figure 33**) onto the brake disc. Align the bolt two mounting bolt holes with the bolt holes on the caliper mounting bracket.
3. Coat the outside surface of the lower mounting bolt with Dow Corning Moly 44 grease or an equivalent prior to installation.
4. Install the caliper upper mounting bolt and washers (A, **Figure 33**) and screw it into the threaded bushing. Tighten the bolt finger-tight at this time.
5. Install the caliper lower mounting bolt (B, **Figure 33**) through the caliper mounting bracket and into the caliper. Tighten finger-tight at this time.
6. Tighten the upper and lower mounting bolts to the specifications in **Table 2**.
7. Install the washer (**Figure 34**) and *new* cotter pin onto the caliper upper mounting bolt. Bend the ends of the cotter pin over completely (**Figure 32**).
8. Install the brake line onto the caliper with a *new* washer on both sides of the brake line fitting, then secure the fitting to the caliper with the banjo bolt (D, **Figure 33**). Tighten the banjo bolt to 17-22 ft.-lb. (23-30 N•m). Make sure the fitting seats against the caliper locating tabs.
9. Refill the master cylinder reservoir with DOT 5 brake fluid, if necessary, to maintain the correct fluid level. Install the diaphragm, top cover and tighten the screws to 6-8 in.-lb. (1 N•m).
10. Apply the front brake lever several times to seat the pads against the disc.
11. Bleed the brakes as described under *Bleeding the System* in this chapter.

> *WARNING*
> *Do not ride the motorcycle until the front brakes operate correctly with full hydraulic advantage. If necessary, bleed the brakes as described in this chapter.*

Removal (FLSTS Models)

Refer to **Figure 35**.

1. Remove the spring pin from the caliper upper mounting bolt.
2. Remove the lower and upper caliper mounting bolts. Do not lose the washer on the upper mounting bolt.

3. Slide the brake caliper off the brake disc.

> *NOTE*
> *Step 4 is only necessary if the caliper is going to be serviced.*

4. If the caliper assembly is going to be disassembled for service, perform the following:

> *NOTE*
> *If the brake pads are going to be reused, mark them so they can be reinstalled into their original locations.*

5. Remove the brake pads as described in this chapter.
6. Drain the brake fluid from the front brake hose as described under *Brake Hose and Line Replacement* in this chapter.
7. Loosen the banjo bolt at the caliper. Remove the banjo bolt and the two washers.
8. Move the brake hose out of the way and place it in a plastic bag.
9. If the front caliper is not going to be serviced, place it in a reclosable plastic bag to keep it clean.

Installation (FLSTS Models)

Refer to **Figure 35**.

1. If the caliper was disassembled for service, install the brake pads as described in this chapter.
2. Coat the outside diameter of the lower mounting bolt with Dow Corning Moly 44 grease or an equivalent prior to installation.
3. Install the caliper mounting plate and brake pad onto the backside of the brake disc.
4. Install the brake caliper onto the brake disc.
5. Move the caliper mounting plate into position and align the hole in the caliper mounting plate with the raised boss on the brake caliper mounting bracket. Make sure the spring clip is positioned correctly in the brake caliper.

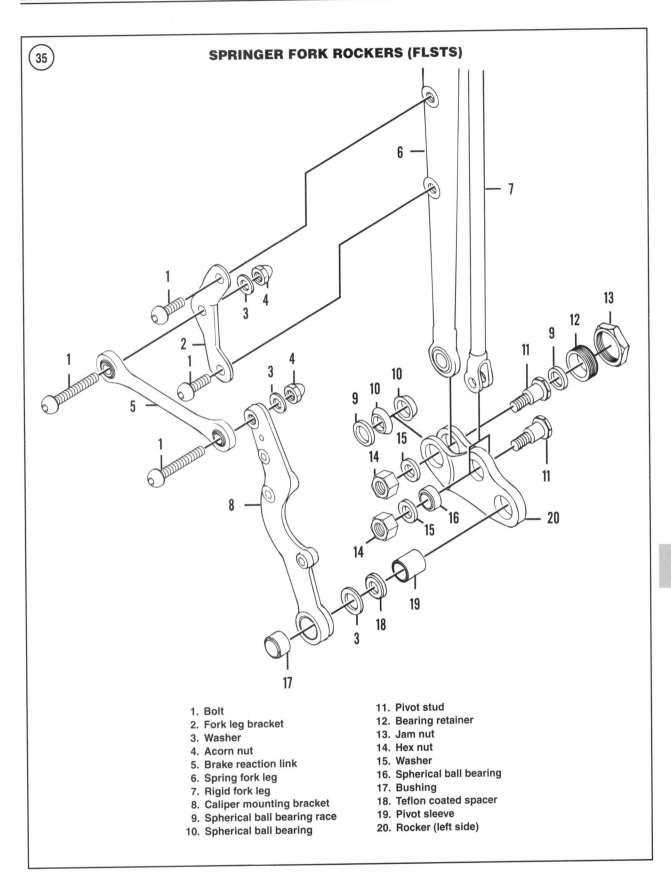

SPRINGER FORK ROCKERS (FLSTS)

1. Bolt
2. Fork leg bracket
3. Washer
4. Acorn nut
5. Brake reaction link
6. Spring fork leg
7. Rigid fork leg
8. Caliper mounting bracket
9. Spherical ball bearing race
10. Spherical ball bearing
11. Pivot stud
12. Bearing retainer
13. Jam nut
14. Hex nut
15. Washer
16. Spherical ball bearing
17. Bushing
18. Teflon coated spacer
19. Pivot sleeve
20. Rocker (left side)

13

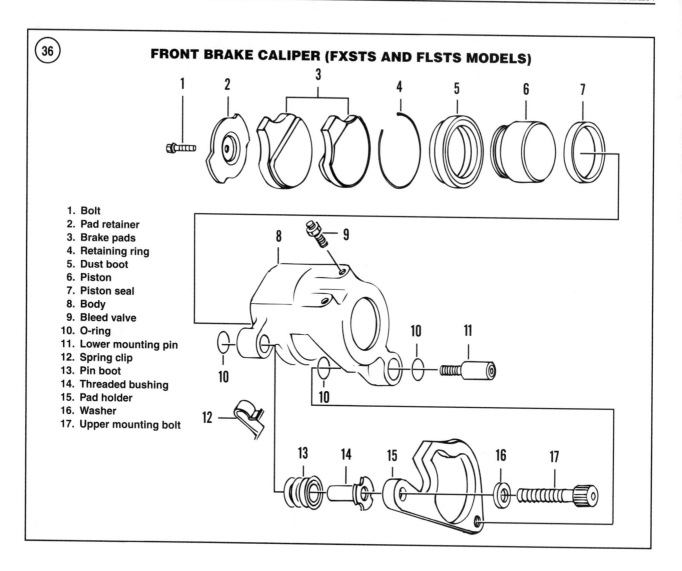

FRONT BRAKE CALIPER (FXSTS AND FLSTS MODELS)

1. Bolt
2. Pad retainer
3. Brake pads
4. Retaining ring
5. Dust boot
6. Piston
7. Piston seal
8. Body
9. Bleed valve
10. O-ring
11. Lower mounting pin
12. Spring clip
13. Pin boot
14. Threaded bushing
15. Pad holder
16. Washer
17. Upper mounting bolt

6. Install the upper bolt and washer through the brake caliper mounting bracket and into the brake caliper. Tighten finger-tight at this time.

7. Install the lower bolt through the caliper and into the brake caliper mounting bracket. Tighten finger-tight at this time.

8. Tighten the upper and lower mounting bolts to the specifications in **Table 2**.

9. Install the spring pin onto the upper mounting bolt.

NOTE
Install new steel banjo bolt washers in Step 10.

10. If the brake line was removed, install it onto the caliper with a *new* washer on both sides of the brake line fitting, then secure the fitting to the caliper with the banjo bolt. Tighten the banjo bolt to 17-22 ft.-lb. (23-30 N•m). Make sure the fitting seats against the caliper.

11. Refill the master cylinder reservoir with DOT 5 brake fluid, if necessary, to maintain the correct fluid level. Install

the diaphragm, top cover and tighten the screws to 6-8 in.-lb. (1 N•m).

12. Apply the front brake lever several times to seat the pads against the disc.

WARNING
Do not ride the motorcycle until the front brake operates correctly with full hydraulic advantage.

13. Bleed the brakes as described under *Bleeding the System* in this chapter.

Disassembly (FXSTS and FLSTS Models)

Refer to **Figure 36**.

1. Partially remove the piston from the caliper as described during caliper removal in this chapter.

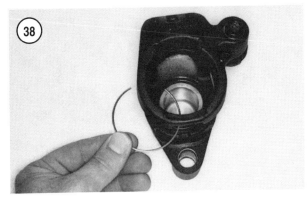

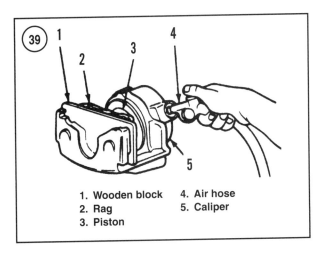

1. Wooden block   4. Air hose
2. Rag   5. Caliper
3. Piston

WARNING
Compressed air will force the piston out of
the caliper under considerable force. Do not
block the piston by hand as injury will occur.

2. Insert a small screwdriver into the notched groove machined in the bottom of the piston bore (**Figure 37**). Then pry the retaining ring (**Figure 38**) out of the caliper body.

3. If the piston did not come partially out of the caliper bore, perform the following:

a. Place a rag and a piece of wood in the caliper (**Figure 39**). Keep fingers out of the way of the piston.

b. Apply compressed air through the brake hose port and force the piston out of the caliper.

4. Remove the piston and dust boot assembly (**Figure 40**).

5. Remove the piston seal (**Figure 41**) from the groove in the caliper body.

6. Pull the threaded bushing (A, **Figure 42**) out of the caliper, then remove the pin boot (B).

7. Remove the O-rings from the caliper body (**Figure 43**).

Inspection

Service specifications for the front caliper components are not available. Replace worn, damaged or questionable parts.

1. Clean the caliper body and piston in clean DOT 5 brake fluid or isopropyl alcohol, and dry them with compressed air.

2. Make sure the fluid passageway in the base of the piston bore is clear. Apply compressed air to the opening to make sure it is clear. Clean it out, if necessary, with clean brake fluid.

3. Inspect the piston seal groove in the caliper body for damage. If it is damaged or corroded, replace the caliper assembly.

13

4. Inspect the banjo bolt threaded hole in the caliper body. If it is worn or damaged, clean it out with a metric thread tap or replace the caliper assembly.

5. Inspect the bleed valve threaded hole in the caliper body. If it is worn or damaged, clean it out with a metric thread tap or replace the caliper assembly.

6. Inspect the bleed screw. Apply compressed air to the opening and make sure it is clear. Clean it out, if necessary, with clean brake fluid. Install the bleed valve and tighten it to 80-100 in.-lb. (9-11 N•m).

7. Inspect the caliper body for damage.

8. Inspect the cylinder wall and piston (**Figure 44**) for scratches, scoring or other damage.

9. If the brake caliper mounting bracket was removed, inspect the bracket (**Figure 45**) for cracks or damage. Inspect the front axle bushing (**Figure 46**) for wear.

Assembly

1. A Harley-Davidson rebuild kit (part No. 44020-83) includes a piston seal (A, **Figure 47**), piston (B), dust boot (C) and retaining ring (D).

NOTE
Never reuse an old dust boot or piston seal. Very minor damage or age deterioration can make the boot and seal ineffective.

2. Soak the new dust and piston seal in clean DOT 5 brake fluid.

3. Carefully install the *new* piston seal into the groove. Make sure the seal is properly seated in its groove.

4. Install *new* O-rings into the caliper grooves.

5. Wipe the inside of the pin boot with Dow Corning MOLY 44 grease. Then insert the boot into the bushing bore with the flange end seating in the bore groove (**Figure 48**).

6. Insert the threaded bushing into the boot (**Figure 49**).

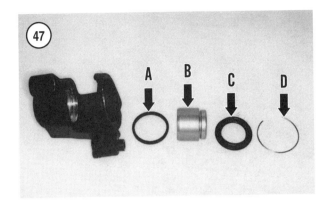

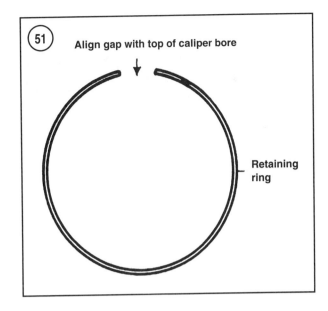

Align gap with top of caliper bore

Retaining ring

7. Install the piston dust boot on the piston before the piston is installed in the caliper bore. Perform the following:

    a. Place the piston on the workbench with its open side facing up.

    b. Align the piston dust boot with the piston so the shoulder on the dust boot faces up.

    c. Slide the piston dust boot onto the piston until the inner lip on the dust boot seats in the piston groove (**Figure 40**).

8. Coat the piston and the caliper bore with DOT 5 brake fluid.

9. Align the piston with the caliper bore so its open end faces out (**Figure 40**). Then push the piston in until it bottoms.

10. Seat the piston dust boot (**Figure 50**) into the caliper bore.

11. Locate the retaining ring groove in the top end of the caliper bore. Align the retaining ring so its gap (**Figure 51**) is at the top of the caliper bore and install the ring into the ring groove. Make sure the retaining ring is correctly seated in the groove.

12. Apply a light coat of Dow Corning MOLY 44 grease to the caliper mounting lug bores.

13. If the bleed valve assembly was removed, install it and tighten it to 80-100 in.-lb. (9-11 N•m).

14. Install the caliper and brake pads as described in this chapter.

15. Bleed the brakes as described under *Bleeding the System* in this chapter.

13

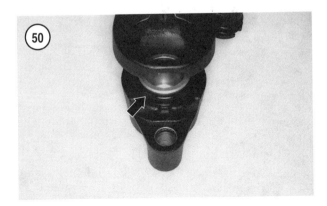

BRAKE REACTION LINK

Removal/Installation (FXSTS Models)

Refer to **Figure 31**.

1. Remove the cotter pin, locknut (**Figure 52**) and shaft nut (**Figure 53**) from the mounting bolt.

2. Remove the mounting bolt securing the reaction link to the caliper mounting bracket and front fender. Do not lose the washer (**Figure 54**) between the reaction link and the fender.

3. Remove the cotter pin, locknut and washer (**Figure 55**) securing the reaction link to the threaded post on the rigid fork. Discard the locknut.

4. Remove the reaction link (**Figure 56**) from the rigid fork post.

5. Install the reaction link (A, **Figure 57**) onto the threaded post (B) on the rigid fork. Push the reaction link on until it bottoms.

6. Install the washer and *new* locknut onto the threaded post, Tighten the locknut (**Figure 55**) securely and install a *new* cotter pin. Bend the ends over completely.

7. Correctly position the reaction link with the caliper mounting bracket and front fender.

8. Install a washer (A, **Figure 58**) between the reaction link and the front fender and hold it in place and partially install the mounting bolt (B).

9. Install the rubber spacer and washer (A, **Figure 59**) onto the shaft nut, then push the mounting bolt (B) all the way through all components. Tighten the shaft nut securely (**Figure 53**).

10. Install the washer (**Figure 60**), *new* locknut and shaft nut (**Figure 52**). Tighten the locknut securely then install a *new* cotter pin. Bend the ends over completely.

11. Repeat for the other side if necessary.

Removal/Installation (FLSTS Models)

Refer to **Figure 35**.

1. Remove the front brake caliper as described in this chapter.

2. Remove the front wheel as described in Chapter Nine.

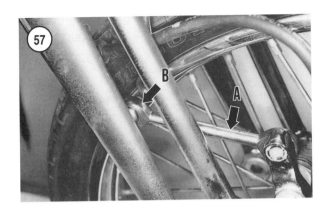

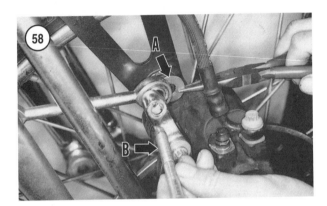

3. Remove the front fender as described in Chapter Fourteen.

4. Remove the bolt, acorn locknut and washer securing the brake reaction link to the caliper mounting bracket. Discard the acorn locknut.

5. Remove the caliper mounting bracket, Teflon-coated washer, rubber washer and left side pivot sleeve from the fork rocker.

6. Remove the bolt, acorn locknut and washer securing the brake reaction link to the fork leg bracket. Discard the acorn locknut. Remove the brake reaction link.

7. If necessary, remove the bolts securing the fork leg bracket to the rigid fork and remove the bracket.

8. Installation is the reverse of the removal steps. Note the following:

   a. Install *new* acorn locknuts.

   b. Tighten locknuts to 35-40 ft.-lb. (48-54 N•m).

Inspection (All Models)

1. Check the reaction link for bending or other damage (**Figure 61**).

2. Inspect the spherical bearing (**Figure 62**) at each end. If damaged, replace the reaction link.

3. On FXSTS models, inspect the mounting hardware (**Figure 63**) for damage.

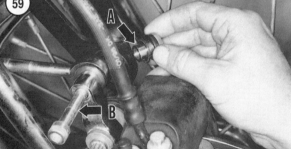

13

FRONT BRAKE CALIPER
(ALL MODELS EXCEPT FXSTS AND FLSTS)

Removal/Installation

> *CAUTION*
> *Do not spill brake fluid on the front fork or front wheel. Wash brake fluid off any painted, plated, or plastic surfaces immediately as it will destroy most surfaces it contacts. Use soapy water and rinse completely.*

1. If the caliper assembly is going to be disassembled for service, perform the following:

> *NOTE*
> *By performing Steps 1b and 1c, compressed air may not be necessary for piston removal during caliper disassembly.*

   a. Remove the brake pads as described in this chapter.

> *CAUTION*
> *Do not allow the pistons to travel out far enough to come in contact with the brake disc. If this happens, the pistons may scratch or gouge the disc during caliper removal.*

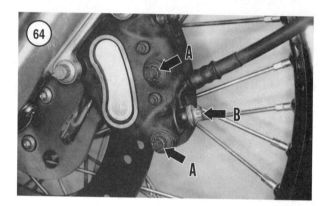

   b. Slowly apply the brake lever to push the pistons part way out of the caliper assembly for ease of removal during caliper service.

   c. Loosen the two caliper body mounting bolts (A, **Figure 64**).

   d. Loosen the brake hose banjo bolt (B, **Figure 64**).

2. Remove the banjo bolt and sealing washers (B, **Figure 64**) attaching the brake hose to the caliper assembly. Do not lose the sealing washer on each side of the hose fittings.

3. Place the loose end of the brake hose in a reclosable plastic bag to prevent the entry of debris and to prevent residual brake fluid from leaking out.

4. Remove the caliper mounting bolts (**Figure 65**) and remove the caliper from the front fork.

5. If necessary, disassemble and service the caliper assembly as described in this chapter. If the front caliper is not going to be serviced, place it in a reclosable plastic bag to keep it clean.

6. Install by reversing these removal steps. Note the following:

   a. Install the caliper assembly onto the disc, being careful not to damage the leading edge of the brake pads.

   b. Install the bolts (**Figure 65**) securing the brake caliper assembly to the front fork and tighten them to 28-38 ft.-lb. (38-52 N•m).

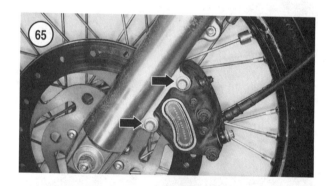

   c. Apply clean DOT 5 brake fluid to the rubber portions of the new sealing washers prior to installation.

   d. Install a *new* sealing washer on each side of the brake hose fitting and install the banjo bolt (B, **Figure 64**). Tighten the banjo bolt to 17-22 ft.-lb. (23-30 N•m).

   e. Bleed the brakes as described under *Bleeding the System* in this chapter.

> *WARNING*
> *Do not ride the motorcycle until the front brake operates correctly with full hydraulic advantage. If necessary, bleed the brakes as described in this chapter.*

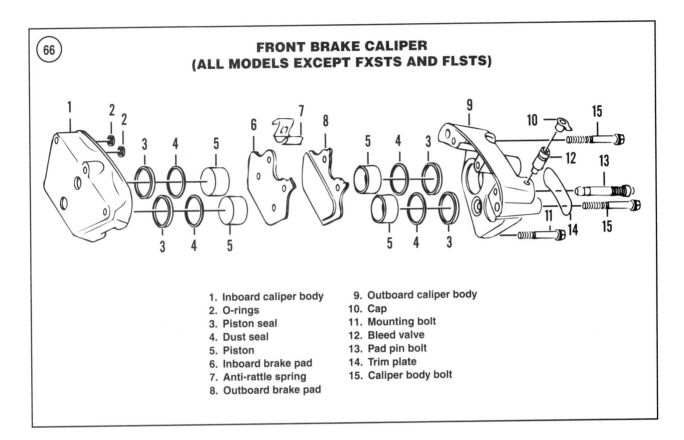

**FRONT BRAKE CALIPER
(ALL MODELS EXCEPT FXSTS AND FLSTS)**

1. Inboard caliper body
2. O-rings
3. Piston seal
4. Dust seal
5. Piston
6. Inboard brake pad
7. Anti-rattle spring
8. Outboard brake pad
9. Outboard caliper body
10. Cap
11. Mounting bolt
12. Bleed valve
13. Pad pin bolt
14. Trim plate
15. Caliper body bolt

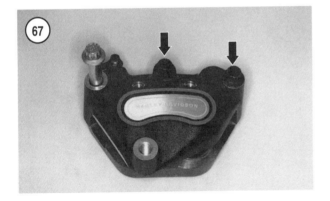

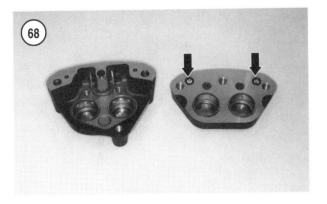

Disassembly

1. Remove the caliper and brake pads (**Figure 66**) as described in this chapter.

2. Remove the two caliper body bolts (**Figure 67**) loosened during the removal procedure.

3. Separate the caliper body halves. Remove the O-ring seals (**Figure 68**). *New* O-ring seals must be installed every time the caliper is disassembled.

NOTE
If the pistons were partially forced out of the caliper body during removal, Steps 4-6 may not be necessary. If the pistons or caliper bores are corroded or very dirty, a small amount of compressed air may be necessary to completely remove the pistons from the body bores.

4. Place a piece of soft wood or a folded shop cloth over the end of the pistons and the caliper body. Turn the assembly over and place it on the workbench with the pistons facing down.

WARNING
Compressed air will force the pistons out of the caliper bodies under considerable force.

13

Do no block the piston by hand as injury will occur.

5. Apply the air pressure in short spurts to the hydraulic fluid passageway to force out the pistons. Repeat this for the other caliper body half. Use a service station air hose if compressed air is not available.

CAUTION
In Step 6, do not use a sharp tool to remove the dust and piston seals from the caliper cylinders. Do not damage the cylinder surface.

6. Use a piece of wood or a plastic scraper to carefully push the dust seal and the piston seal (**Figure 69**) in toward the caliper cylinder and out of their grooves. Remove the dust and piston seals.

7. If necessary, unscrew and remove the bleed valve (A, **Figure 70**).

8. Inspect the caliper assembly as described in this section.

Inspection

1. Clean both caliper body halves and pistons in clean DOT 5 brake fluid or isopropyl alcohol, and dry them with compressed air.

2. Make sure the fluid passageways (**Figure 71**) in the piston bores are clear. Apply compressed air to the openings to make sure they are clear. Clean them out, if necessary, with clean brake fluid.

3. Make sure the fluid passageways (A, **Figure 72**) in both caliper body halves are clear. Apply compressed air to the openings to make sure they are clear. Clean them out, if necessary, with clean brake fluid.

4. Inspect the piston and dust seal grooves (**Figure 73**) in both caliper bodies for damage. If they are damaged or corroded, replace the caliper assembly.

5. Inspect the banjo bolt threaded hole (B, **Figure 70**) in the outboard caliper body. If it is worn or damaged, clean it out with a metric thread tap or replace the caliper assembly.

6. Inspect the bleed valve threaded hole in the caliper body. If it is worn or damaged, clean it out with a metric thread tap or replace the caliper assembly.

7. Inspect the bleed valve. Apply compressed air to the opening and make sure it is clear. Clean it out, if necessary, with clean brake fluid. Install the bleed valve and tighten it to 80-100 in.-lb. (9-11 N•m).

8. Inspect both caliper bodies for damage. Check the inboard caliper mounting bolt hole threads (B, **Figure 72**)

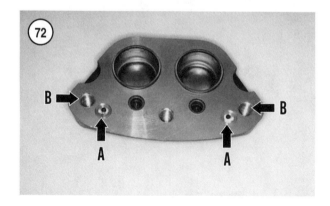

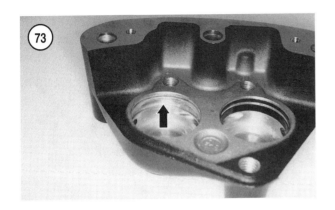

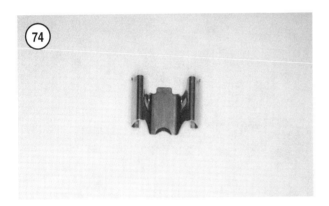

for wear or damage. Clean the threads with an appropriately sized metric tap or replace the caliper assembly.

9. Inspect the cylinder walls and pistons for scratches, scoring or other damage.

10. Check the anti-rattle spring (**Figure 74**) for wear or damage.

Assembly

> *WARNING*
> *Never reuse old dust seals or piston seals. Very minor damage or age deterioration can make the seals ineffective.*

1. Soak the new dust and piston seals in clean DOT 5 brake fluid.

2. Coat the piston bores and pistons with clean DOT 5 brake fluid.

3. Carefully install the new piston seals into the lower grooves. Make sure the seals are properly seated in their respective grooves.

4. Carefully install the new dust seals into the upper grooves. Make sure all seals are properly seated in their respective grooves (**Figure 75**).

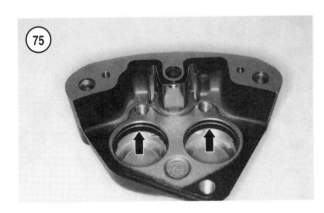

5. Repeat Step 3 and Step 4 for the other caliper body half.

6. Position the pistons with the open end facing out and install the pistons into the caliper cylinders (A, **Figure 76**). Push the pistons in until they bottom (B, **Figure 76**).

7. Repeat Step 6 for the other caliper body half. Make sure all pistons are installed correctly.

8. Coat the *new* O-ring seals in DOT 5 brake fluid and install the O-rings (**Figure 68**) into the inboard caliper half.

9. Install the anti-rattle spring (**Figure 77**) onto the boss on the outboard caliper half.

10. Make sure the O-rings are still in place and assemble the caliper body halves.

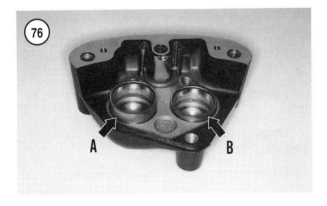

13

11. Install one of the caliper mounting bolts through the upper hole (A, **Figure 78**) to correctly align the caliper halves.

12. Install the two caliper body bolts (B, **Figure 78**) and tighten them securely. They will be tightened to the specification after the caliper is installed on the front fork.

13. If the bleed valve assembly was removed, install it and tighten it to 80-100 in.-lb. (9-11 N•m).

14. Install the caliper and brake pads as described in this chapter.

15. Tighten the two caliper body mounting bolts (A, **Figure 64**) to 28-38 ft.-lb. (38-52 N•m).

16. Bleed the brakes as described under *Bleeding the System* in this chapter.

FRONT MASTER CYLINDER

Removal

> *CAUTION*
> *Cover the fuel tank and front fender with a heavy cloth or plastic tarp to protect them from accidental brake fluid spills. Wash brake fluid off painted, plated, or plastic surfaces immediately as it will destroy most surfaces it contacts. Use soapy water and rinse completely.*

1. On models so equipped, remove the windshield as described in Chapter Fourteen.

2. Remove the mirror (A, **Figure 79**) from the master cylinder.

3. Clean the top of the master cylinder of all dirt and debris.

> *CAUTION*
> *Failure to install the spacer in Step 2 will result in damage to the rubber boot and plunger on the front brake switch.*

4. Insert a 5/32 in. (4 mm) thick spacer between the brake lever and lever bracket. Make sure the spacer stays in place during the following steps.

5. On models so equipped, remove the master cylinder chrome cover (B, **Figure 79**).

6. Remove the screws securing the cover (A, **Figure 80**), and remove the cover (B) and diaphragm.

7. Use a shop syringe to draw all of the brake fluid out of the master cylinder reservoir. Temporarily reinstall the diaphragm and the cover. Tighten the screws finger-tight.

8. Remove the banjo bolt and sealing washers (C, **Figure 79**) securing the brake hose to the master cylinder.

9. Place the loose end of the brake hose in a reclosable plastic bag to prevent the entry of moisture and debris. Tie the loose end of the hose to the handlebar.

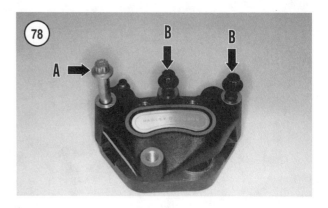

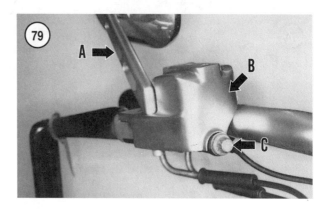

10. Remove the screw securing the right side switch together and separate the switch.

11. Remove the bolts and washers securing the clamp and master cylinder to the handlebar.

12. Remove the master cylinder assembly from the handlebar.

13. Drain any residual brake fluid from the master cylinder and dispose of it properly.

14. If the master cylinder assembly is not going to be serviced, reinstall the clamp and Torx bolts to the master cyl-

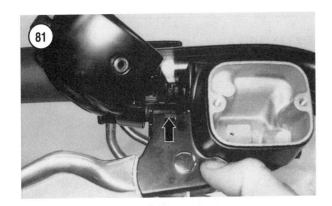

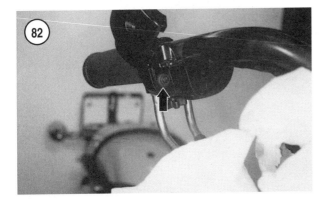

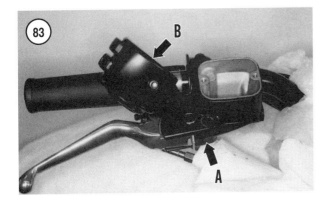

inder. Place the assembly in a reclosable plastic bag to protect it from debris.

Installation

1. Insert the 5/32 in. (4 mm) thick spacer between the brake lever and lever bracket if not in place. Make sure the spacer stays in place during the following steps.

2. Position the front master cylinder onto the handlebar. Align the master cylinder notch (**Figure 81**) with the locating tab on the lower portion of the right side switch.

CAUTION
*Do not damage the front brake light switch and rubber boot (**Figure 82**, typical) when installing the master cylinder in Step 3.*

3. Push the master cylinder all the way onto the handlebar (A, **Figure 83**). Hold it in this position and install the upper portion of the right side switch (B, **Figure 83**). Install the switch's clamping screw and tighten it securely.

4. Position the clamp and install the bolts and washers. Tighten the upper mounting bolt, then the lower bolt. Tighten the bolts to 70-80 in.-lb (8-9 N•m).

5. Apply clean DOT 5 brake fluid to the rubber portions of the new sealing washers prior to installation.

6. Install *new* sealing washers and the banjo bolt (C, **Figure 79**) securing the brake hose to the master cylinder. Tighten the banjo bolt to 17-22 ft.-lb. (23-30 N•m).

7. Remove the spacer from the brake lever.

8. Install the mirror (A, **Figure 79**) onto the master cylinder.

9. On models so equipped, install the windshield or front fairing.

10. Temporarily install the diaphragm and top cover (B, **Figure 80**) onto the reservoir. Tighten the screws finger-tight at this time.

11. On models so equipped, install the master cylinder chrome cover (B, **Figure 79**).

12. Refill the master cylinder reservoir and bleed the brake system as described under *Bleeding the System* in this chapter.

13. On models so equipped, install the windshield as described in Chapter Fourteen.

Disassembly

1. Store the master cylinder components (**Figure 84**) in a divided container, such as a restaurant-size egg carton, to help maintain their correct alignment positions.

2. Remove the screws securing the top cover if they are still in place. Remove the top cover and the diaphragm from the master cylinder.

3. Remove the master cylinder assembly as described in this chapter.

4. Remove the snap ring (A, **Figure 85**) and pivot pin securing the hand lever to the master cylinder. Remove the hand lever (B, **Figure 85**).

5. Remove the retainer (A, **Figure 86**) and the rubber boot (B) from the area where the hand lever actuates the piston assembly.

6. Remove the piston assembly (**Figure 87**) and the spring.

7. Inspect all parts as described in this section.

13

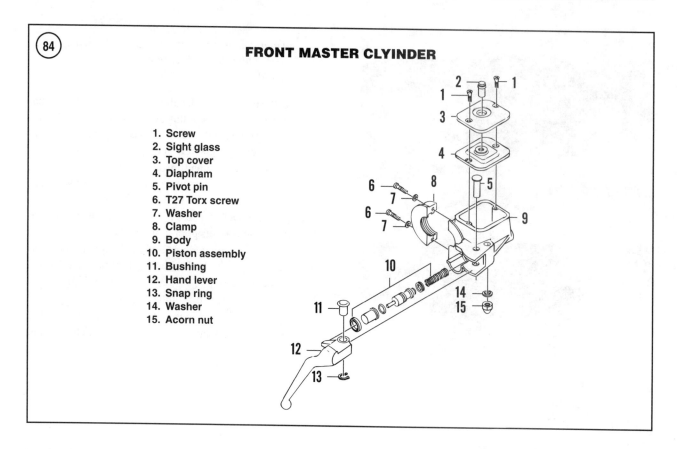

FRONT MASTER CLYINDER

1. Screw
2. Sight glass
3. Top cover
4. Diaphram
5. Pivot pin
6. T27 Torx screw
7. Washer
8. Clamp
9. Body
10. Piston assembly
11. Bushing
12. Hand lever
13. Snap ring
14. Washer
15. Acorn nut

Inspection

Replace worn or damage parts as described in this section. It is recommended that a new piston kit assembly be installed every time the master cylinder is disassembled.

1. Clean all parts in isopropyl alcohol or clean DOT 5 brake fluid. Inspect the body cylinder bore surface for signs of wear and damage. If it is less than perfect, replace the master cylinder assembly. The body cannot be replaced separately.

2. Inspect the piston cup (A, **Figure 88**) and O-ring (B) for signs of wear and damage.

3. Make sure the fluid passage (**Figure 89**) in the bottom of the master cylinder reservoir is clear. Clean it out if necessary.

4. Inspect the piston contact surface for signs of wear and damage.

5. Check the end of the piston (C, **Figure 88**) for wear caused by the hand lever.

6. Check the hand lever pivot lugs in the master cylinder body for cracks or elongation.

7. Inspect the hand lever pivot hole and bushing (A, **Figure 90**), and the pivot pin (B) for wear, cracks or elongation.

8. Inspect the piston cap and retainer (**Figure 91**) for wear or damage.

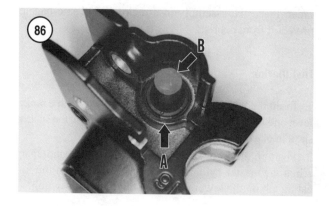

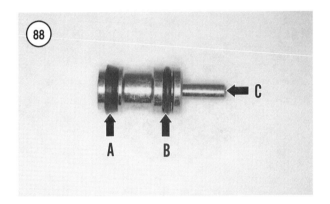

9. Inspect the threads in the bore for the banjo bolt. If they are worn or damaged, clean them out with a thread tap or replace the master cylinder assembly.

10. Check the top cover and diaphragm for damage or deterioration.

11. If necessary, separate the cover from the diaphragm as follows:

    a. Pull straight up on the sight glass (**Figure 92**) and remove it from the cover and diaphragm.

    b. Separate the diaphragm from the cover.

    c. The trim plate may separate from the cover.

13

Assembly

NOTE
When installing a new piston assembly, coat all parts with the lubricant provided with the Harley-Davidson parts kit. When installing existing parts, coat them with DOT 5 brake fluid.

NOTE
Make sure the new piston kit is for a single front disc motorcycle.

CAUTION
The cover and diaphragm must be assembled as described. If the sight glass is not in-

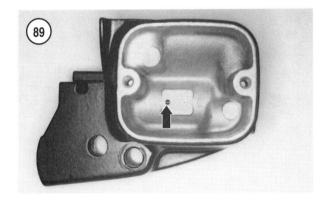

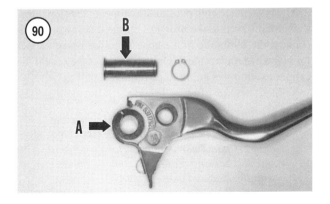

stalled correctly through the cover and diaphragm neck, brake fluid will leak past these components.

1. If the cover and the diaphragm were disassembled, assemble them as follows:
   a. Install the trim plate (**Figure 93**) onto the cover if it was removed.
   b. Insert the neck of the diaphragm into the cover. Press it in until it seats correctly and the outer edges are aligned with the cover.
   c. Push the sight glass (**Figure 92**) straight down through the cover and the neck of the diaphragm (**Figure 94**) until it snaps into place. The sight glass must lock these two parts together to avoid a brake fluid leak.

2. Soak the *new* cup, O-ring and piston assembly in clean DOT 5 brake fluid for 15 minutes to make them pliable. Coat the inside of the cylinder bore with clean brake fluid prior to the assembly of parts.

> *CAUTION*
> *When installing the piston assembly, do not allow the cup to turn inside out as it will be damaged and allow brake fluid leaks within the cylinder bore.*

3. Install the spring and piston assembly into the cylinder (**Figure 95**). Push them in until they bottom in the cylinder (**Figure 87**).

4. Position the retainer with the flat side going on first, and install the piston cap and retainer onto the piston end.

5. Push down on the piston cap (**Figure 96**). Hold it in place and press the retainer down until it correctly seats in the cylinder groove (A, **Figure 86**).

6. Make sure the bushing is in place in the hand lever pivot area.

7. Install the hand lever (B, **Figure 85**) into the master cylinder. Install the pivot pin and secure it with the snap ring. Make sure the snap ring is correctly seated in the pivot pin groove (A, **Figure 85**).

8. Slowly apply the lever to make sure it pivots freely.

9. Install the master cylinder as described in this chapter.

REAR BRAKE PAD REPLACEMENT

There is no recommended mileage interval for changing the brake pads. Pad wear depends on riding habits and conditions. Frequently check the pads for wear. Increase the inspection interval when the wear indicator reaches the edge of the brake disc. After removal, measure the thickness of each brake pad with a vernier caliper or ruler, and compare measurements to the dimensions in **Table 1**.

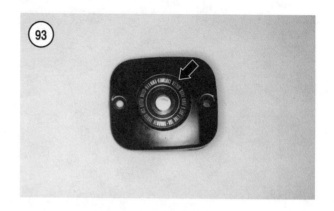

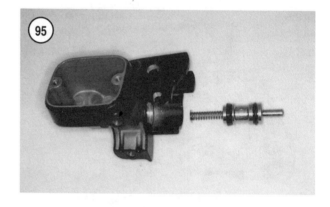

Always replace both pads in the caliper at the same time to maintain even brake pressure on the disc. Do not disconnect the hydraulic brake hose from the brake caliper for brake pad replacement. Only disconnect the hose if the caliper assembly is going to be removed.

> *CAUTION*
> *Check the pads more frequently when the lining approaches the pad metal backing plate. If pad wear is uneven for some reason, the backing plate may come in contact with the disc and cause damage.*

7. Use a shop syringe to remove about 50% of the brake fluid from the reservoir. This will prevent the master cylinder from overflowing when the pistons are compressed for reinstallation. Do *not* drain more than 50% of the brake fluid or air will enter the system. Discard the brake fluid.

8. Loosen the pad pin bolts.

CAUTION
Do not allow the master cylinder to overflow during Step 9. Wash brake fluid off painted, plated, or plastic surfaces immediately as it will destroy most surfaces it contacts. Use soapy water and rinse completely.

CAUTION
The brake disc is thin and easily damaged. When pushing against the disc in the following step, support the disc adjacent to the caliper to prevent damage.

9. Hold the caliper body from the outside and push it toward the brake disc. This will push the outer pistons into the caliper bores to make room for the new brake pads. Constantly check the reservoir to make sure brake fluid does not overflow. Remove fluid, if necessary, before it overflows. Install the diaphragm and cover. Tighten the screws finger-tight.

10. Remove the pad pin bolts (**Figure 98**).

11. Remove the inboard and outboard brake pads from the caliper.

12. Check the brake pads for wear or damage. Measure the thickness of the brake pad friction material. Replace the brake pads if they are worn to the service limit in **Table 1**.

13. Carefully remove any rust or corrosion from the disc.

14. Thoroughly clean the pad pins of any corrosion or debris.

15. Check the friction surface of the new pads for debris or manufacturing residue. If necessary, clean them off with an aerosol brake cleaner.

NOTE
When purchasing new pads, check with the dealership to make sure the friction compound of the new pad is compatible with the disc material. Remove roughness from the backs of the new pads with a fine-cut file then thoroughly clean them off.

NOTE
*The pads are not symmetrical. The pad with one tab (A, **Figure 99**) must be installed on the outboard side. The pad with two tabs (B,*

13

1. Read *Brake Service* in this chapter.

2. Park the motorcycle on level ground.

3. Tie the end of the brake pedal to the frame. If the brake pedal is inadvertently applied, this will prevent the piston from being forced out of the cylinder.

4. On models so equipped, remove the right side saddlebag as described in Chapter Fourteen.

5. Clean the top of the rear master cylinder of all dirt and debris.

6. Remove the screws securing the cover, and remove the cover (**Figure 97**) and diaphragm.

Figure 99) must be installed on the inboard side of the caliper.

NOTE
The rear and front caliper brake pads are identical with the exception of the FXSTD models. The FXSTD rear brake pads have a vertical slot cut into them. Do not interchange them with the front brake pads.

16. Install the outboard pad (**Figure 100**) into the caliper.
17. Hold the pad in place and install the pad pin bolts (**Figure 98**) part way in to hold the outboard pad in place.
18. Install the inboard pad (**Figure 101**) into the caliper.
19. Push the pad pin bolts (**Figure 98**) through the inboard pad and tighten them to 180-200 in.-lb. (20-23 N•m).
20. Make sure there is sufficient brake fluid in the master cylinder reservoir. Top it off if necessary.
21. Untie the brake pedal from the frame and pump the rear brake pedal to reposition the brake pads against the brake disc. Roll the motorcycle back and forth. Continue to pump the brake pedal as many times as it takes to refill the cylinders in the caliper and correctly position the brake pads against the disc.
22. Refill the master cylinder reservoir, if necessary, to maintain the correct fluid level as indicated on the side of the reservoir. Install the diaphragm and the top cover. Tighten the screws to 6-8 in.-lb. (1 N•m).

WARNING
Do not ride the motorcycle until the rear brake is operating correctly with full hydraulic advantage. If necessary, bleed the brakes as described in this chapter.

REAR BRAKE CALIPER

Removal/Installation

CAUTION
Do not spill brake fluid on the swing arm or rear wheel. Wash brake fluid off any painted, plated, or plastic surfaces immediately as it will damage most surfaces it contacts. Use soapy water and rinse completely.

1. If the caliper assembly is going to be disassembled for service, perform the following:

NOTE
By performing Steps 1b and 1c, compressed air may not be necessary for piston removal during caliper disassembly.

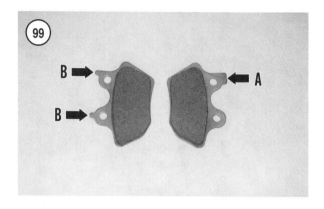

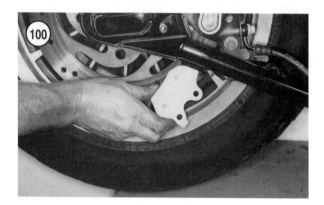

a. Remove the brake pads as described in this chapter.

CAUTION
Do not allow the pistons to travel out far enough to come in contact with the brake disc. If this happens, the pistons may scratch or gouge the disc during caliper removal.

b. Slowly apply the brake lever to push the pistons part way out of the caliper assembly for ease of removal during caliper service.

c. Loosen the brake hose banjo bolt (A, **Figure 102**).

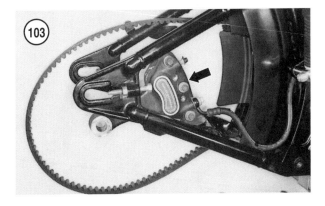

d. Loosen the three body mounting bolts (B, **Figure 102**).

2. Loosen the banjo bolt (A, **Figure 102**) attaching the brake hose to the caliper assembly.

3. Place the loose end of the brake hose in a reclosable plastic bag to prevent the entry of debris and to prevent residual brake fluid from leading out.

4. Remove the rear wheel as described in Chapter Nine.

5. Remove the banjo bolt and sealing washers (A, **Figure 102**) attaching the brake hose to the rear caliper assembly.

6. Remove the rear caliper assembly (**Figure 103**) from the swing arm.

7. If necessary, disassemble and service the caliper assembly as described in this chapter.

8. If the rear caliper is not going to be serviced, place it in a reclosable plastic bag to keep it clean.

9. Installation is the reverse of removal. Note the following:

    a. Install the caliper assembly onto the disc, being careful not to damage the leading edge of the brake pads.

    b. Refer to Chapter Nine to complete the installation of the rear axle.

    c. Apply clean DOT 5 brake fluid to the rubber portions of the *new* sealing washers prior to installation.

    d. Install a *new* sealing washer on each side of the brake hose fitting and install the banjo bolt (A, **Figure 102**). Tighten the banjo bolt to 17-22 ft.-lb (23-30 N•m).

    e. If disassembled, tighten the three body mounting bolts (B, **Figure 102**) to 28-38 ft.-lb. (38-52 N•m).

    f. Bleed the brakes as described under *Bleeding the System* in this chapter.

> *WARNING*
> *Do not ride the motorcycle until the rear brake is operating correctly with full hydraulic advantage. If necessary, bleed the brakes as described in this chapter.*

Disassembly

1. Remove the caliper and brake pads (**Figure 104**) as described in this chapter.

2. Remove the three caliper body bolts (**Figure 105**) loosened during the removal procedure.

3. Separate the caliper body halves. Remove the O-ring seals (**Figure 106**). New O-ring seals must be installed every time the caliper is disassembled.

> *NOTE*
> *If the pistons were partially forced out of the caliper body during removal, Steps 4-6 may not be necessary. If the pistons or caliper bores are corroded or very dirty, a small amount of compressed air may be necessary to completely remove the pistons from the body bores.*

4. Place a piece of soft wood or a folded shop cloth over the end of the pistons and the caliper body. Turn the assembly over and place it on the workbench with the pistons facing down.

> *WARNING*
> *Compressed air will force the pistons out of the caliper bodies under considerable force. Do not block the piston by hand as injury will occur.*

5. Apply the air pressure in short spurts to the hydraulic fluid passageway to force out the pistons. Repeat this for the other caliper body half. Use a service station air hose if compressed air is unavailable.

> *CAUTION*
> *In Step 7, do not use a sharp tool to remove the dust and piston seals from the caliper cylinders. Do not damage the cylinder surface.*

13

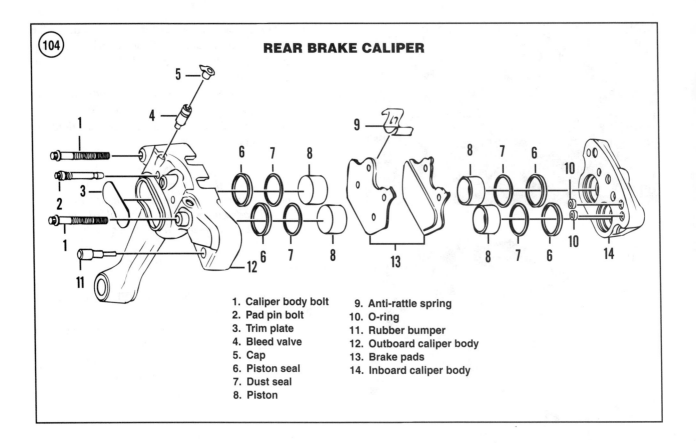

REAR BRAKE CALIPER

1. Caliper body bolt
2. Pad pin bolt
3. Trim plate
4. Bleed valve
5. Cap
6. Piston seal
7. Dust seal
8. Piston
9. Anti-rattle spring
10. O-ring
11. Rubber bumper
12. Outboard caliper body
13. Brake pads
14. Inboard caliper body

6. Use a piece of wood or a plastic scraper to carefully push the dust seal and the piston seal in toward the caliper cylinder and out of their grooves. Remove the dust and piston seals.

7. If necessary, unscrew and remove the bleed valve (**Figure 107**).

8. Inspect the caliper assembly as described in this section.

Inspection

1. Clean both caliper body halves and pistons in clean DOT 5 brake fluid or isopropyl alcohol and dry them with compressed air.

2. Make sure the fluid passageways (**Figure 108**) in the piston bores are clear by applying compressed air to the openings. Clean them out, if necessary, with clean brake fluid.

3. Make sure the fluid passageways (**Figure 109**) in both caliper body halves are clear by applying compressed air to the openings. Clean them out, if necessary, with clean brake fluid.

4. Inspect the piston and dust seal grooves in both caliper bodies for damage. If they are damaged or corroded, replace the caliper assembly.

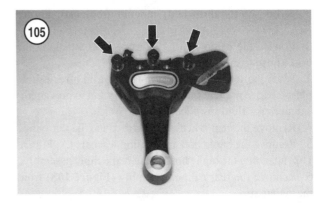

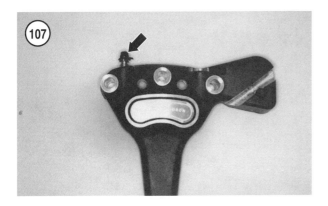

5. Inspect the banjo bolt threaded hole in the outboard caliper body. If it is worn or damaged, clean it out with a metric thread tap or replace the caliper assembly.

6. Inspect the bleed valve threaded hole in the caliper body. If it is worn or damaged, clean it out with a metric thread tap or replace the caliper assembly.

7. Inspect the bleed valve. Apply compressed air to the opening and make sure it is clear. Clean it out if necessary with clean brake fluid. Install the bleed valve and tighten it to 80-100 in.-lb. (9-11 N•m).

8. Inspect both caliper bodies for damage. Check the inboard caliper mounting bolt hole threads (**Figure 110**) for wear or damage. Clean them with an appropriate size metric tap or replace the caliper assembly.

9. Inspect the cylinder walls and pistons for scratches, scoring or other damage.

10. Check the anti-rattle spring for wear or damage.

Assembly

> *WARNING*
> *Never reuse old dust seals or piston seals. Very minor damage or age deterioration can make the seals ineffective.*

1. Soak the new dust and piston seals in clean DOT 5 brake fluid.

2. Coat the piston bores and pistons with clean DOT 5 brake fluid.

3. Carefully install the new piston seals into the lower grooves. Make sure the seals are properly seated in their respective grooves.

4. Carefully install the new dust seals into the upper grooves. Make sure all seals are properly seated in their respective grooves.

5. Repeat Step 3 and Step 4 for the other caliper body half.

6. Position the pistons with the open end facing out and install the pistons into the caliper cylinders. Push the pistons in until they bottom.

7. Repeat Step 6 for the other caliper body half. Make sure all pistons are installed correctly.

8. Coat the *new* O-ring seals in DOT 5 brake fluid and install the O-rings into the inboard caliper half.

9. Install the anti-rattle spring (**Figure 111**) onto the boss on the outboard caliper half.

10. Make sure the O-rings are still in place and assemble the caliper body halves.

11. Install the three caliper body bolts (**Figure 105**) and tighten them securely. They will be tightened to the specified torque after the caliper is installed on the rear disc.

13

12. Install a *new* rubber bumper (**Figure 112**) if it was removed.

13. Install the bleed valve assembly (**Figure 107**) if it was removed and tighten it to 80-100 in.-lb. (9-11 N•m).

14. Install the caliper and brake pads as described in this chapter.

15. Tighten the three caliper body mounting bolts to 28-38 ft.-lb. (38-52 N•m).

16. Bleed the brakes as described under *Bleeding the System* in this chapter.

REAR MASTER CYLINDER

Removal

1. Remove the exhaust system as described in Chapter Seven.

2. On models so equipped, refer to Chapter Fourteen and perform the following:

   a. Remove the right side saddlebag.

   b. Remove the right side footboard.

3. At the rear brake caliper, perform the following:

   a. Insert a hose onto the end of the bleed valve (**Figure 113**). Insert the open end of the hose into a container.

   b. Open the bleed valve and operate the rear brake pedal to drain the brake fluid. Remove the hose and close the bleed valve after draining the assembly. Discard the brake fluid properly.

4. Remove the screws securing the cover, and remove the cover (**Figure 97**) and diaphragm.

5. Remove the banjo bolt and sealing washers (A, **Figure 114**) securing the brake hose to the front of the master cylinder cartridge body.

6. Remove and/or release clips or tie-wraps securing the rear brake line to the chassis until there is only enough slack in the brake line to allow the removal of the brake line from the front of the master cylinder fitting.

7. Disconnect the rear brake line from the front of the master cylinder. Place the loose end of the brake hose in a

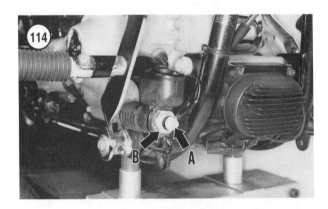

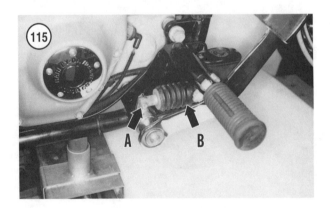

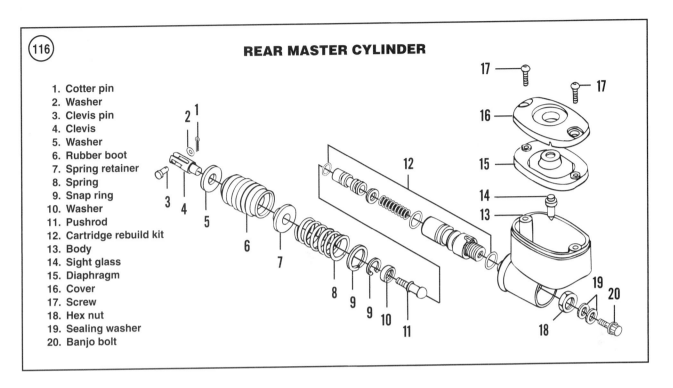

REAR MASTER CYLINDER

1. Cotter pin
2. Washer
3. Clevis pin
4. Clevis
5. Washer
6. Rubber boot
7. Spring retainer
8. Spring
9. Snap ring
10. Washer
11. Pushrod
12. Cartridge rebuild kit
13. Body
14. Sight glass
15. Diaphragm
16. Cover
17. Screw
18. Hex nut
19. Sealing washer
20. Banjo bolt

reclosable plastic bag to prevent the entry of debris and to prevent any residual brake fluid from leaking out.

8. Use a 1 1/8 in. open-end wench, remove the hex nut (B, **Figure 114**) securing the front of the master cylinder cartridge assembly to the frame boss. Pull the master cylinder free from the square hole in the frame boss.

9. Remove the cotter pin and washer from the clevis pin.

10. Withdraw the clevis pin (A, **Figure 115**) and disconnect the master cylinder (B) from the rear brake pedal assembly. Remove the master cylinder assembly from the frame.

11. If necessary, service the master cylinder as described in this chapter. If the master cylinder is not going to be serviced, place it in a reclosable plastic bag to keep it clean.

Installation

1. Install the master cylinder onto the rear brake pedal assembly.

2. Install the clevis pin through the two parts, then install the washer and *new* cotter pin. Bend the ends over completely.

3. Insert the front of the master cylinder through the hole in the mounting bracket.

4. Apply ThreeBond TB1342 or an equivalent threadlocking compound to the hex nut threads prior to installation. Install the hex nut (B, **Figure 114**) and tighten it to 50 ft.-lb. (68 N•m).

5. Connect the rear brake line to the front of the master cylinder cartridge body.

6. Lubricate the *new* steel/rubber washers on each side with fresh DOT5 brake fluid.

7. Install a *new* steel/rubber washer on each side of the brake hose banjo fitting. Insert the banjo bolt through the washers and banjo fitting and thread it into the cartridge body (A, **Figure 114**). Then tighten the banjo bolt to 17-22 ft.-lb. (23-30 N•m).

8. Secure the rear brake line to the chassis using tie-wraps or new clips.

9. Bleed the brakes as described under *Bleeding the System* in this chapter.

10. On models so equipped, refer to Chapter Fourteen and perform the following:

   a. Install the right side footboard.

   b. Install the right side saddlebag.

11. Install the exhaust system as described in Chapter Seven.

> *WARNING*
> *Do not ride the motorcycle until the rear brake is operating correctly with full hydraulic advantage. If necessary, bleed the brakes as described in this chapter.*

Disassembly

Refer to **Figure 116**.

1. Clean the exterior master cylinder housing with clean DOT 5 brake fluid or isopropyl alcohol and dry it.

13

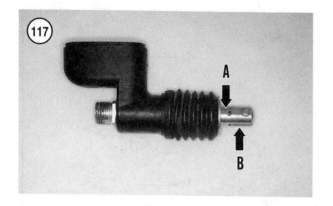

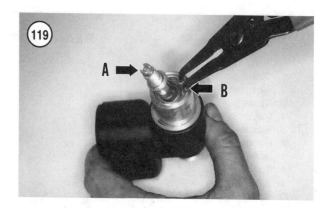

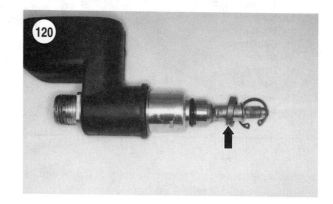

2. Store the master cylinder components in a divided container, such as a restaurant-size egg carton, to help maintain their correct alignment positions.

3. Remove the master cylinder cover and diaphragm if it is still installed.

4. Compress the spring, rubber boot and washer.

NOTE
On 2003 models, the pushrod, clevis pin and spacer washer are an integral component.

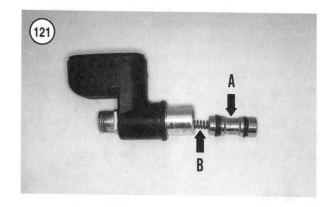

5. On 2000-2002 models, support the master cylinder in a vise. Use a brass drift to carefully tap out the pushrod pin (A, **Figure 117**) from the clevis. Separate the clevis (B) from the pushrod.

6. Remove the washer, rubber boot, spring retainer and spring (**Figure 118**).

7. Depress the pushrod (A, **Figure 119**) and remove the snap ring (B).

8. Remove the pushrod (**Figure 120**).

9. Remove the piston assembly (A, **Figure 121**) and spring (B) from the cartridge.

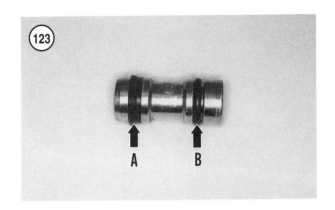

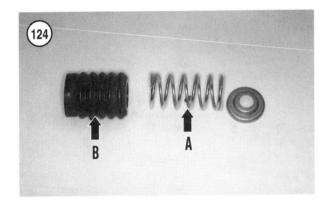

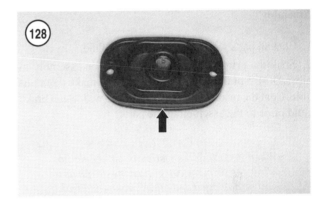

Inspection

1. Clean all parts in clean DOT 5 brake fluid or isopropyl alcohol and dry them with compressed air. Replace worn or damage parts as described in this section. It is recommended that a new cartridge rebuild kit assembly be installed every time the master cylinder is disassembled.

2. Inspect the cartridge body cylinder bore surface (**Figure 122**) for signs of wear and damage. Do not hone the cartridge bore to clean or repair it. If it is less than perfect, replace the cartridge and/or the master cylinder reservoir.

3. Check the piston primary cup (A, **Figure 123**) and the O-ring (B) for deterioration or damage.

4. Check the spring (A, **Figure 124**) for bending, unequally spaced coils or corrosion.

5. Inspect the boot (B, **Figure 124**) for tears or deterioration.

6. Check the pushrod, washer and snap ring (**Figure 125**) for bending, wear or damage.

7. Check the reservoir body (**Figure 126**) for corrosion or other damage. Make sure the opening (**Figure 127**) in the base is clear.

8. Check the reservoir cap and diaphragm (**Figure 128**) for damage.

13

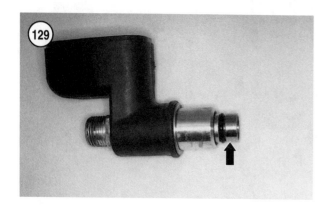

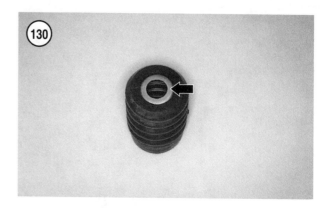

Assembly

1. Coat all parts with clean DOT 5 brake fluid.

2. Soak the primary cup, O-ring and piston assembly in clean DOT 5 brake fluid for 15 minutes to make them pliable. Coat the inside of the cartridge bore with clean brake fluid prior to the assembling the parts.

> *CAUTION*
> *When installing the piston assembly, do not allow the primary cup to turn inside out as it will be damaged and allow brake fluid leaks in the cartridge cylinder bore.*

3. Install the spring (B, **Figure 121**) into the cartridge.

4. Position the piston assembly with the primary cup (A, **Figure 121**) end going in first. Make sure the piston cup does not tear as it passes through the bore entrance (**Figure 129**).

5. Turn the reservoir on its end on a shop cloth. Carefully push the piston assembly into the cartridge with a Phillips screwdriver. Push the piston assembly in, then let it move out several times to check for ease of movement.

6. Position the pushrod onto the end of the piston (**Figure 120**) and push the piston into the cartridge. Hold the push rod in place (A, **Figure 119**) and install the snap ring (B). Make sure the snap ring is correctly seated in the cartridge groove.

7. Install the spring and spring seat (**Figure 118**) onto the pushrod and cartridge.

8. Install the washer into the boot and push it all the way to the end (**Figure 130**).

9. Install the boot (**Figure 131**) onto the pushrod and cartridge.

> *NOTE*
> *On 2003 models, the pushrod, clevis pin and spacer washer are all one part.*

10. On 2000-2002 models, perform the following:

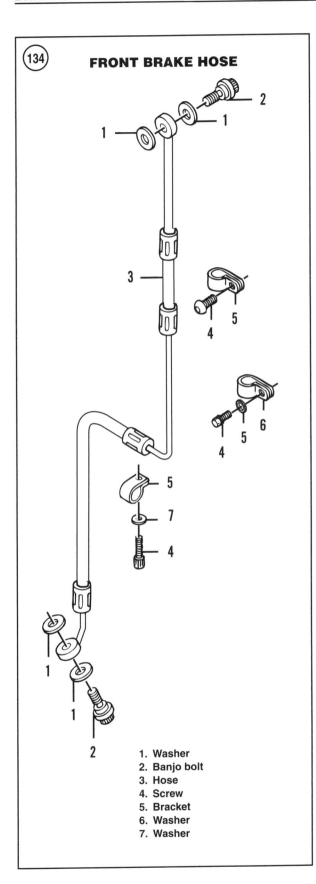

FRONT BRAKE HOSE

1. Washer
2. Banjo bolt
3. Hose
4. Screw
5. Bracket
6. Washer
7. Washer

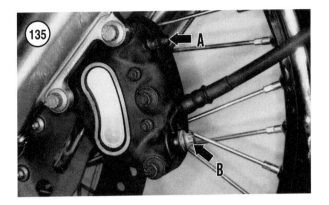

a. Install the clevis and tighten it against the pushrod until the roll pin holes are aligned.

b. Install a *new* roll pin (**Figure 132**) and tap it into place until it is flush.

11. Install the diaphragm and reservoir cover (**Figure 133**).

BRAKE HOSE AND LINE REPLACEMENT

A combination of steel and flexible brake lines connect the master cylinder to the brake calipers. Banjo fittings and bolts connect brake hoses to the master cylinder and brake calipers. Steel washers seal the banjo fittings.

Replace a hose if the flexible portion is swelling, cracking or damaged. Replace the brake hose if the metal portion leaks or if there are dents or cracks.

Front Brake Hose Removal/Installation

A single combination steel/flexible brake hose (**Figure 134**) connects the front master cylinder to the front brake caliper. When purchasing a new hose, compare it to the old hose to make sure the length and angle of the steel hose portion are correct. Install *new* banjo bolt washers at both ends.

> *CAUTION*
> *Do not spill brake fluid on the front fork or front wheel. Wash brake fluid off painted, plated, or plastic surfaces immediately as it will damage most surfaces it contacts. Use soapy water and rinse completely.*

1. On models so equipped, refer to Chapter Fourteen and remove the windshield assembly.

2. Drain the front brake system as follows:

a. Connect a hose over the bleed valve (A, **Figure 135**).

b. Insert the loose end of the hose into a container to catch the brake fluid.

13

c. Open the bleed valve and apply the front brake lever to pump the fluid out of the master cylinder and brake line. Continue until the fluid is removed.

d. Close the bleed valve and disconnect the hose.

e. Dispose of the brake fluid. Never reuse brake fluid. Contaminated brake fluid will cause brake failure.

3. Before removing the brake line assembly, note the brake line routing from the master cylinder to the caliper. Note the number and position of metal hose clamps and/or plastic ties used to hold the brake line in place.

4. Remove any metal clamp or cut any plastic ties.

5A. On FXSTS and FLSTS models, perform the following:

a. Remove the bolt securing the brake hose and mounting plate (**Figure 136**) to the lower portion of the rigid fork.

b. Remove the bolt and washer securing the brake hose and mounting plate (**Figure 137**) to the lower portion of the rigid fork leg below the steering stem.

5B. On models other than FXSTS and FLSTS, remove the bolt securing the brake hose and mounting plate (**Figure 138**) to the lower steering stem. On models so equipped, do not lose the guide plate between the hose mounting plate and the steering stem.

6. Remove the screw or nut securing the metal clamps around the brake line. Spread the clamp and remove it from the brake line.

7. Remove the banjo bolt and washers (B, **Figure 135**) securing the hose to the brake caliper.

8. Remove the banjo bolt and washers (A, **Figure 139**) securing the hose to the front master cylinder.

9. Cover the ends of the brake hose to prevent brake fluid from leaking out.

10. Remove the brake hose assembly (B, **Figure 139**) from the motorcycle.

11. If the existing brake hose assembly is going to be reinstalled, inspect it as follows:

a. Check the metal pipes where they enter and exit at the flexible hoses. Check the crimped clamp for looseness or damage.

b. Check the flexible hose portions for swelling, cracks or other damage.

c. If wear or damage is found, replace the brake hose assembly.

12. Install the brake hose, *new* sealing washers and banjo bolts (**Figure 134**) in the reverse order of removal. Note the following:

a. Install *new* sealing washers against the side of each hose fitting.

b. Carefully install the clips and guides to hold the brake hose in place.

c. Tighten the banjo bolts to 17-22 ft.-lb. (23-30 N•m).

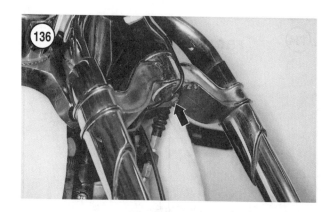

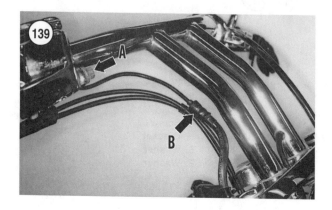

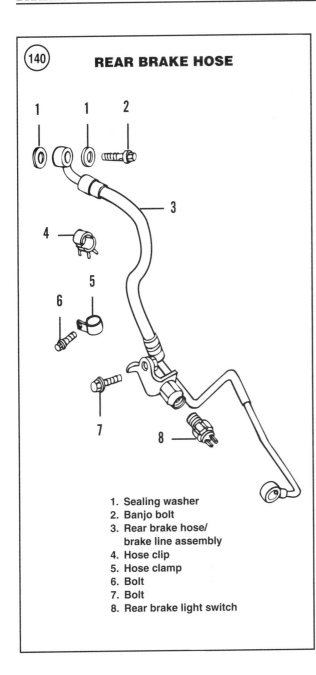

REAR BRAKE HOSE

1. Sealing washer
2. Banjo bolt
3. Rear brake hose/
   brake line assembly
4. Hose clip
5. Hose clamp
6. Bolt
7. Bolt
8. Rear brake light switch

d. Refill the front master cylinder with clean brake fluid clearly marked DOT 5. Bleed the front brake system as described in this chapter.

WARNING
Do not ride the motorcycle until the front brakes operate correctly with full hydraulic advantage.

Rear Brake Hose Removal/Installation

A single combination steel and rubber brake hose (**Figure 140**) connects the rear master cylinder to the rear brake caliper. The rear brake switch is installed in the rear brake hose. When buying a new hose, compare it to the old hose. Make sure the length and angle of the steel hose portion are correct. Install *new* banjo bolt washers at both hose ends.

CAUTION
Do not spill brake fluid on the swing arm, frame or rear wheel. Wash brake fluid off any painted, plated or plastic surfaces immediately as it will damage most surfaces it contacts. Use soapy water and rinse completely.

1. Remove the exhaust system as described in Chapter Seven.
2. On models so equipped, remove the right side saddlebag as described in Chapter Fourteen.
3. Drain the hydraulic brake fluid from the rear brake system as follows:
    a. Connect a hose to the rear caliper bleed valve (**Figure 141**).
    b. Insert the loose end of the hose in a container to catch the brake fluid.
    c. Open the caliper bleed valve and operate the rear brake pedal to pump the fluid out of the master cylinder and brake line. Continue until all of the fluid is removed.
    d. Close the bleed valve and disconnect the hose.
    e. Dispose of the brake fluid. Never reuse brake fluid. Contaminated brake fluid will cause brake failure.
4. Before removing the brake line, note the brake line routing from the master cylinder to the caliper. Note the number and position of the metal hose clamps, plastic clips and plastic ties used to hold the brake line in place. The metal clamp and plastic clips can be reused.

NOTE
To open the cable clips, insert a small screwdriver into the gap at the side of the clip and carefully rotate the screwdriver.

13

5. Open the cable clips on the lower frame tube. Refer to A, **Figure 142** and **Figure 143**.

6. At the rear brake light switch, cut the plastic tie securing the rear brake light switch wires, voltage regulator wires and the engine sensor harness to the frame lower tube.

7. Disconnect the electrical connector from the rear brake switch (A, **Figure 144**).

8. Remove the bolt (B, **Figure 144**) securing the brake light switch to the frame bracket.

9. Remove the banjo bolt and washers (B, **Figure 142**) securing the hose to the brake caliper.

10. Remove the banjo bolt and washers (**Figure 145**) securing the hose to the master cylinder.

11. Carefully move the rear brake line assembly forward and away from the rear swing arm bracket. Remove the brake hose assembly from the motorcycle.

12. If the existing brake hose assembly is going to be reinstalled, inspect it as follows:

    a. Check the metal pipe where it enters and exits the flexible hose. Check the crimped clamp for looseness or damage.

    b. Check the flexible hose portion for swelling, cracks or other damage.

    c. If wear or damage is found, replace the brake hose.

13. If replacement is necessary, remove the brake light switch from the rear brake hose fitting.

14. Installation is the reverse of removal. Note the following:

    a. Install and tighten the stoplight switch securely.

    b. Install *new* sealing washers against the side of each hose fitting.

    c. Carefully install the clips and guides to hold the brake hose in place.

    d. Tighten the banjo bolts to 17-22 ft.-lb. (23-30 N•m).

    e. Refill the master cylinder with clean brake fluid clearly marked DOT 5. Bleed the rear brake system as described in this chapter.

> *WARNING*
> *Do not ride the motorcycle until the rear brake is operating correctly with full hydraulic advantage.*

BRAKE DISC

The brake discs are separate from the wheel hubs and can be removed once the wheel is removed from the motorcycle.

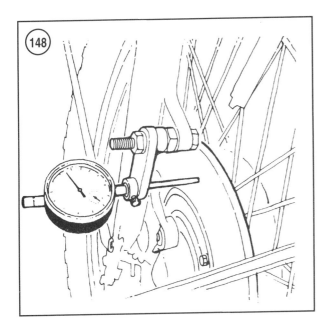

Inspection

It is not necessary to remove the disc from the wheel to inspect it. Small nicks and marks on the disc are not important, but radial scratches deep enough to snag a finger-

nail reduce braking effectiveness and increase brake pad wear. If these grooves are present, and the brake pads are wearing rapidly, replace the disc.

The specifications for the standard and wear limits are in **Table 1**. Each disc is also marked with the minimum (MIN) thickness. If the specification marked on the disc differs from the one in **Table 1**, use the specification on the disc.

When servicing the brake discs, do not have the discs surfaced to compensate for warp. The discs are thin, and grinding will only reduce their thickness, causing them to warp rapidly. A warped disc may be caused by the brake pads dragging on the disc, due to a faulty caliper, and overheating the disc. Overheating can also be caused by unequal pad pressure on the disc.

Three main causes of unequal brake pad pressure are:
1. The brake caliper piston seals are worn or damaged.
2. The master cylinder's small relief port is plugged.
3. The primary cup on the master cylinder piston is worn or damaged.

NOTE
It is not necessary to remove the wheel to measure the disc thickness. The measurement can be performed with the wheel installed or removed from the motorcycle.

4. Measure the thickness of the disc at several locations around the disc with a vernier caliper or a micrometer (**Figure 146**). Replace the disc if the thickness in any area is less than the MIN dimension on the disc (**Figure 147**).
5. Make sure the disc mounting bolts are tight prior to running this check. Check the disc runout with a dial indicator as shown in **Figure 148**.

NOTE
When checking the front disc, turn the handlebar all the way to one side, then to the other side.

6. Slowly rotate the wheel and watch the dial indicator. If the runout exceeds the specification in **Table 1**, replace the disc.
7. Clean the disc of any rust or corrosion and wipe it clean with brake cleaner. Never use an oil-based solvent that may leave an oil residue on the disc.

Removal/Installation

1. Remove the front or rear wheel as described in Chapter Nine.
2. Remove the Torx bolts (**Figure 149**) securing the brake disc to the hub and remove the disc.

13

3. Check the brake disc bolts for thread damage. Replace worn or damaged fasteners.

4. Check the threaded bolt holes for the brake disc in the wheel hub for thread damage. True them with a tap if necessary.

5. Clean the disc and the disc mounting surface thoroughly with brake cleaner. Allow the surfaces to dry before installation.

6. Install the disc onto the wheel hub.

7. Apply a drop of ThreeBond TB1342 or an equivalent to the threads of *new* Torx bolts prior to installation.

8. Install the bolts and tighten the specification in **Table 2**.

BLEEDING THE SYSTEM

If air enters the brake system, the brake will feel soft or spongy and braking pressure will be reduced. Bleed the system to remove the air. Air can enter the system if there is a leak in the system, the brake fluid level in a master cylinder runs low, a brake line is opened or the brake fluid is replaced.

The brakes can be bled with a brake bleeder or manually. This section includes procedures for both.

Before bleeding the brake system:

1. Check the brake lines to make sure all fittings are tight.

2. Make sure the caliper piston does not stick or bind in its bore.

3. Check piston movement in each master cylinder. Operate the lever or brake pedal, making sure there is no binding or other abnormal conditions.

Brake Bleeder Process

This procedure uses the Mityvac hydraulic brake bleeding kit (**Figure 150**) available from motorcycle or automotive supply stores and mail order outlets.

> *NOTE*
> *This procedure is shown on the rear wheel and relates to the front wheel as well.*

1. Remove the dust cap from the caliper bleed valve.

2. Place a clean shop cloth over the caliper to protect it from accidental brake fluid spills.

3. Open the bleed screw approximately a half turn.

4. Assemble the brake bleeder according to its manufacturer's instructions. Secure it to the caliper bleed valve.

5. Clean the top of the master cylinder of all dirt and debris.

6. Remove the screws securing the master cylinder top cover, and remove the cover and rubber diaphragm.

7. Fill the reservoir almost to the top with DOT 5 brake fluid, and reinstall the diaphragm and cover. Leave the cover in place during this procedure to prevent the entry of dirt.

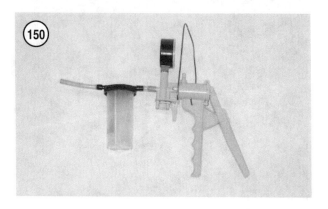

> *WARNING*
> *Do not intermix DOT 3, DOT 4, or DOT 5.1 brake fluids as they are not silicone-based. Non-silicone brake fluid used in these models can cause brake failure.*

8. Operate the pump several times to create a vacuum in the line (**Figure 151**, typical). Brake fluid will quickly flow from the caliper into the pump's reservoir. Tighten the caliper bleed valve before the fluid stops flowing through the hose. To prevent air from being drawn through the master cylinder, add fluid to maintain the level at the top of the reservoir.

> *NOTE*
> *Do not allow the master cylinder reservoir to empty during the bleeding operation or more air will enter the system. If this occurs, the procedure must be repeated.*

9. Continue the bleeding process until the fluid drawn from the caliper is bubble free. If bubbles are in the brake fluid, more air is trapped in the line. Repeat Step 8, making sure to refill the master cylinder to prevent air from being drawn into the system.

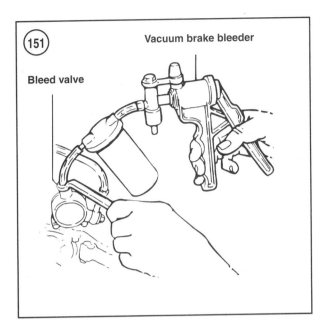

151

Vacuum brake bleeder

Bleed valve

der, turn the handlebar until the reservoir is level. Add fluid until it is level with the reservoir gasket surface. The fluid level in the rear master cylinder must be slightly below the upper gasket surface.

12. Reinstall the reservoir diaphragm and cover. Install the screws and tighten securely.

13. Test the feel of the brake lever or pedal. It should be firm and offer the same resistance each time it is operated. If it feels spongy, there is probably still air in the system. Bleed the system again. After bleeding the system, check for leaks and tighten all fittings and connections as necessary.

WARNING
Do not ride the motorcycle until the front and/or rear brakes are operating correctly with full hydraulic advantage.

14. Test ride the motorcycle slowly at first to make sure the brakes are operating properly.

Without a Brake Bleeder

NOTE
Before bleeding the brakes, make sure all brake hoses and lines are tight.

1. Connect a length of clear tubing to the bleed valve on the caliper. Place the other end of the tube into a clean container. Fill the container with enough clean DOT 5 brake fluid to keep the end of the tube submerged. The tube must be long enough so a loop can be made higher than the bleeder valve to prevent air from being drawn into the caliper during bleeding.

2. Clean the top of the master cylinder of all debris.

3. Remove the screws securing the master cylinder top cover, and remove the cover and diaphragm.

4. Fill the reservoir almost to the top with DOT 5 brake fluid, and reinstall the diaphragm and cover. Leave the cover in place during this procedure to prevent the entry of dirt.

WARNING
Do not intermix DOT 3, DOT 4, or DOT 5.1 brake fluids as they are not silicone-based. Non-silicone brake fluid used in these models can cause brake failure.

NOTE
During this procedure, check the fluid level in the master cylinder reservoir often. If the reservoir runs dry, air will enter the system.

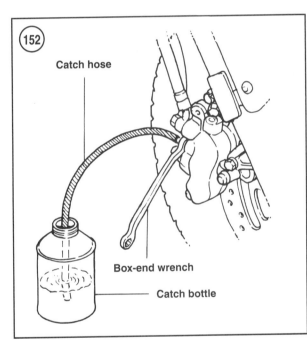

152

Catch hose

Box-end wrench

Catch bottle

10. When the brake fluid is free of bubbles, tighten the bleed valve and remove the brake bleeder assembly. Reinstall the bleed valve dust cap.

NOTE
Dispose of the brake fluid expelled during the bleeding process. Do not reuse the brake fluid.

11. If necessary, add fluid to correct the level in the master cylinder reservoir. When topping off the front master cylin-

13

5. Slowly apply the brake lever several times. Hold the lever in the applied position and open the bleed valve about a half turn (**Figure 152**, typical). Allow the lever to travel to its

limit. When the limit is reached, tighten the bleed valve, then release the brake lever. As the brake fluid enters the system, the level will drop in the master cylinder reservoir. Maintain the level at the top of the reservoir to prevent air from being drawn into the system.

6. Continue the bleeding process until the fluid emerging from the hose is completely free of air bubbles. If the fluid is being replaced, continue until the fluid emerging from the hose is clean.

NOTE
If bleeding is difficult, allow the fluid to stabilize for a few hours. Repeat the bleeding procedure when the bubbles in the system dissipate.

7. Hold the lever in the applied position and tighten the bleed valve. Remove the bleed tube and install the bleed valve dust cap.

NOTE
Dispose of the brake fluid expelled during the bleeding process. Do not reuse the brake fluid.

8. If necessary, add fluid to correct the level in the master cylinder reservoir. When topping off the front master cylinder, turn the handlebar until the reservoir is level. Add fluid until it is level with the reservoir gasket surface. The fluid level in the rear master cylinder must be slightly below the upper gasket surface.

9. Install the diaphragm and top cover, and tighten the screws securely.

10. Test the feel of the brake lever or pedal. It should be firm and offer the same resistance each time it is operated. If it feels spongy, there is probably still air in the system and it must be bled again. After bleeding the system, check for leaks and tighten all fittings and connections as necessary.

WARNING
Do not ride the motorcycle until the front and/or rear brakes are operating correctly with full hydraulic advantage.

11. Test ride the motorcycle slowly at first to make sure the brakes are operating properly.

REAR BRAKE PEDAL

Removal/Installation

1. Remove the exhaust system as described in Chapter Seven.

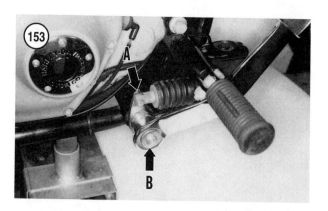

2. On models so equipped, remove the right side floorboard as described in Chapter Fourteen.

3. Remove the cotter pin and washer from the clevis pin (A, **Figure 153**).

4. Withdraw the clevis pin and disconnect the master cylinder from the rear brake pedal assembly.

5. Remove the bolt and washer (B, **Figure 153**) securing the rear brake pedal to the mounting post on the footrest.

6. Inspect the brake pedal bushings for fractures or damage, and replace it if necessary.

7. Check the O-ring seal on each side of the bushings for hardness or deterioration and replace if necessary.

8. Make sure the grease fitting is clear. Apply grease with a gun and make sure it is passing through the fitting and the brake pedal. Clean out if necessary.

9. Install the pedal by reversing these removal steps. Note the following:
   a. Apply waterproof grease to the bushings and O-rings prior to installation.
   b. Apply a medium strength threadlocking compound to the mounting bolt threads, then tighten the bolt to 15-18 ft.-lb. (20-24 N•m).
   c. Apply waterproof grease to the fitting (**Figure 154**).

Table 1 BRAKE SYSTEM SPECIFICATIONS

Brake fluid	DOT 5 silicone base
Brake pad minimum thickness	
FLSTS & FXSTS	1/16 in. (1.6 mm)
All other models	0.04 in. (1.02 mm)
Brake disc runout (max.)	0.008 in. (0.2 mm)

Table 2 BRAKE SYSTEM TORQUE SPECIFICATIONS

Item	ft.-lb.	in.-lb.	N•m
Bleed valves	–	80-100	9-11
Brake disc bolts			
Front wheel	16-24	–	22-32
Rear wheel	30-45	–	41-61
Brake pad pins (Non-Springer models)			
Front and rear calipers	–	180-200	20-23
Brake reaction link (FLSTS)			
Acorn locknut	35-40	–	48-54
Caliper body mounting bolts			
Front and rear (Non-Springer models)	28-38	–	38-52
Front brake caliper (Springer models)			
Inner brake pad retainer screw	–	40-50	5-6
Upper mounting bolt	28-30	–	38-41
Lower mounting bolt	25-30	–	34-41
Front brake caliper (Non-Springer models)			
Upper mounting bolt	28-38	–	38-52
Lower mounting bolt	28-38	–	38-52
Front master cylinder			
Clamp screw	–	70-80	8-9
Cover screws	–	6-8	1
Rear master cylinder			
Cartridge mounting hex nut	50	–	68
Cover screws	–	6-8	1
Rear brake pedal locknut	15-18	–	20-24
Brake line banjo bolts	17-22	–	23-30

13

CHAPTER FOURTEEN

BODY

SEAT

Removal/Installation

1. Place the motorcycle on level ground on the jiffy stand.

2A. On FXST, FXSTB and FXSTS models, remove the bolt and washer (**Figure 1**) securing the seat. Remove the seat from the slot in the frame backbone (**Figure 2**).

2B. On FLSTF and FLSTC models, remove the side thumbscrews securing the rider's seat and remove the seat. Remove the rear thumbscrew securing the passenger seat and remove the seat out from the seat strap.

2C. On FLSTS models, remove the rear thumbscrew securing the passenger seat and remove the seat from the rider's seat mount. Remove the nuts securing the rider's seat and remove the seat.

3. Inspect the seat front mounting tab and bracket(s). Replace if necessary.

4. Installation is the reverse of removal. Note the following:

   a. Push the rider's seat forward and engage the front bracket into the slot in the frame backbone.

   b. Tighten all thumb screws securely.

   c. Pull up on the front of the seat (**Figure 2**) to ensure the seat front hook is secured in the frame backbone slot.

FRONT FENDER

Removal/Installation
(FLSTC and FLSTF Models)

1. Remove the front wheel as described in Chapter Nine.

2. On FLSTC models, disconnect the electrical connector for the front fender lamp (under the fuel tank) as described in Chapter Eight. Pull the electrical cable free from the frame and secure it to the front fender.

3. Remove the screws, or nuts, securing the front fender to the fork sliders.

4. Carefully remove the front fender from between the fork sliders.

5. Installation is the reverse of removal. Tighten the screws and nuts securely.

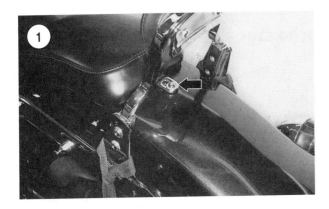

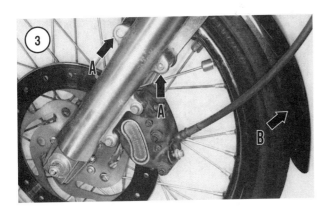

Removal/Installation
(FXSTD, FXST and FXSTB Models)

1. Place the motorcycle on the jiffy stand on level ground.

2A. On FXSTD models, remove the four screws and washers securing the front fender to the fork sliders.

2B. On FXST and FXSTB models, remove the acorn nut and washers and screws securing the front fender to the fork sliders (A, **Figure 3**).

3. Carefully remove the front fender (B, **Figure 3**) from between the fork sliders.

4. Installation is the reverse of removal. Tighten the screws and/or acorn nut securely.

Removal/Installation
(FXSTS Models)

Refer to **Figure 4**.

1. On the right side, remove cotter pin (**Figure 5**), locknut (A, **Figure 6**), shaft nut (**Figure 7**), washers (B, **Figure 6**) and screw securing the brake reaction link to the front fender.

2. On the left side, repeat Step 2.

NOTE
The rubber spacers and washers may come off with the shaft nuts or may stay with the fender bracket bushing.

3. The brake reaction links (A, **Figure 8**) are now free from the fender. Let them pivot down out of the way.

4A. On the right side, remove the locknut and shoulder bolts (B, **Figure 8**) securing the pivot link and caliper mounting bracket to the front fender. Remove the fender insert and place it on the shoulder bolt and nut to avoid misplacing them.

4B. On the left side, remove the locknut and shoulder bolts securing the pivot link to the front fender. Remove the fender insert and place it on the shoulder bolt and nut to avoid misplacing them.

5. Very carefully, lift the fender out from the forks and the pivot links.

6. Move the fender into place over the front wheel.

7. Install the fender insert and bearing (**Figure 9**) into the receptacle in the front fender on both sides.

8. Move the pivot link into place. Install the shoulder bolts (B, **Figure 8**) securing the pivot link to the front fender. Tighten the shoulder bolts securely.

9. Move the pivot link (A, **Figure 8**) and the caliper mounting bracket into position on the front fender.

10. Install the washer (**Figure 10**) in between the pivot link and the fender.

11. Install the bolt (A, **Figure 11**) through the caliper mounting bracket, washer and pivot link. Push the bolt in until it bottoms.

12. Install the shaft nut, rubber spacer and washer (B, **Figure 11**) onto the bolt.

13. Tighten the shaft nut onto the bolt (**Figure 12**) to 10-20 ft.-lbs. (14-27 N·m).

14. Install the washer (**Figure 13**) onto the bolt and the nut (A, **Figure 6**). Tighten the nut to 10-20 ft.-lbs. (14-27 N·m).

14

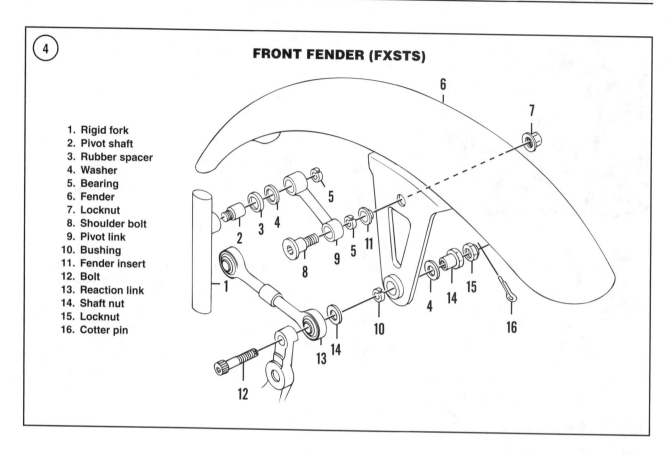

FRONT FENDER (FXSTS)

1. Rigid fork
2. Pivot shaft
3. Rubber spacer
4. Washer
5. Bearing
6. Fender
7. Locknut
8. Shoulder bolt
9. Pivot link
10. Bushing
11. Fender insert
12. Bolt
13. Reaction link
14. Shaft nut
15. Locknut
16. Cotter pin

15. Install a new cotter pin (**Figure 5**) and bend the ends over completely.

16. Repeat Steps 8-15 for the other side.

Removal/Installation
(FLSTS Models)

Refer to **Figure 14**.

Read this procedure thoroughly prior to starting to remove the front fender. Each step must be taken slowly and carefully and in the proper order to avoid damage to the finish of the front fender and the springer fork assembly.

CAUTION
Removal of the front fender is very difficult due its the close proximity of the spring fork legs.

To protect the finish, cover the front fender and left side fork assembly with a towel or large, heavy cloth. Tape the towel or cloth onto the front fender and to the fork with duct tape.

1. Remove the front wheel as described in Chapter Nine.

2. Remove the front brake caliper as described in Chapter Thirteen.

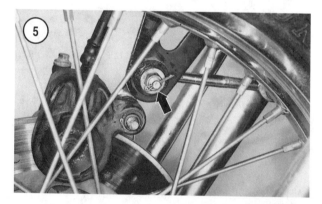

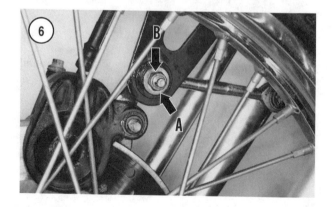

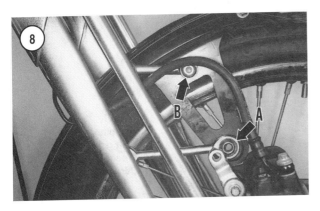

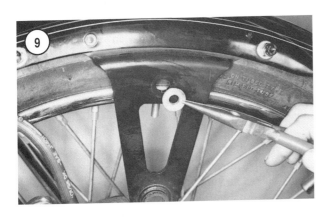

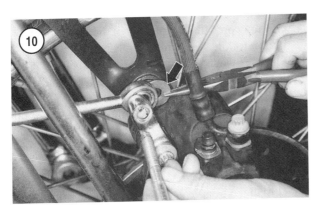

14

3. Disconnect the front fender lamp (under the fuel tank) as described in Chapter Eight. Pull the electrical cable free from the frame and secure it to the front fender.

4. On the left side, remove the spring clip and nut from the screw securing the front fender to the bracket.

5. Insert the front axle through the front fender pivot area to support the fender assembly.

6. Support the front fender and on the left side, remove the screw and washer.

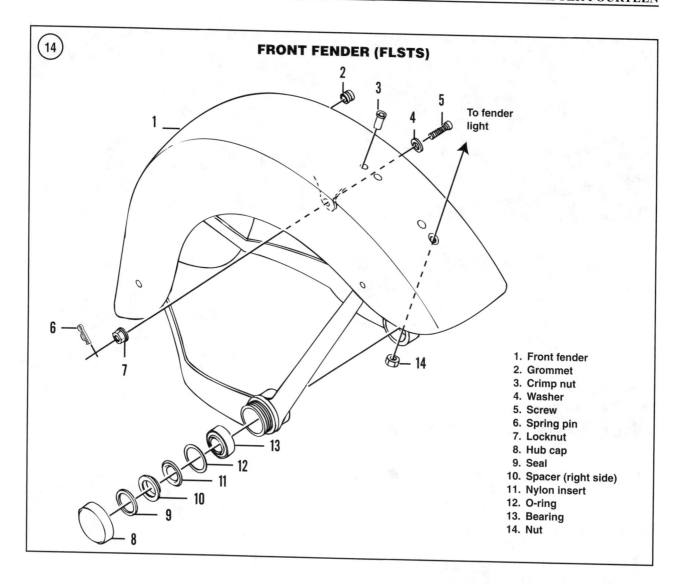

FRONT FENDER (FLSTS)

To fender light

1. Front fender
2. Grommet
3. Crimp nut
4. Washer
5. Screw
6. Spring pin
7. Locknut
8. Hub cap
9. Seal
10. Spacer (right side)
11. Nylon insert
12. O-ring
13. Bearing
14. Nut

7. Working on the right side of the fork assembly, slide the front fender down until the mounting bracket is just in front of the left side rigid fork leg.

8. While holding onto the right side fender braces, carefully rotate the front fender down between both fork legs and remove the fender.

9. Installation is the reverse of removal. Note the following:

   a. Install a *new* nut on the fender bracket.

   b. Tighten the nut to 18-22 ft.-lbs. (24-30 N·m).

Front Fender Bearing Replacement (FLSTS Models)

CAUTION
As previously noted during fender removal, protect the fender finish during this procedure.

1. Remove the front fender as previously described.

2. Place the front fender in an arbor press with the outboard side facing up.

3. Use a suitable size tool, or socket, that matches the bearing outer race and is smaller in diameter than the fender bore.

4. Carefully press the bearing out of the fender bore.

5. Repeat for the bearing on the other side.

6. Place the fender on its side on the workbench.

7. Install the *new* bearing into the fender bore from the inboard surface.

8. Use the same tool setup used in Step 3 and carefully drive the new bearing into the fender bore.

9. Tap the new bearing in until it is flush with the outboard surface of the fender bore.

10. Repeat for the bearing on the other side.

11. Install the front fender as previously described.

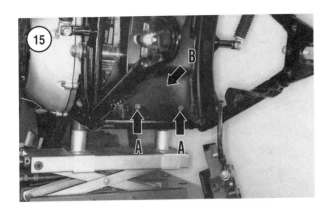

REAR FENDER INNER PANEL

Removal/Installation

1. Remove the rear wheel as described in Chapter Nine.
2. Remove the two bolts (A, **Figure 15**) securing the inner panel to the swing arm.
3. Lift the upper right side corner (B, **Figure 15**) and remove the inner panel from the swing arm and frame.
4. Inspect the inner panel (**Figure 16**) for cracks and deterioration. This component keeps out water and road debris from the electrical components located behind it.
5. Installation is the reverse of removal.

REAR FENDER

Removal/Installation
(FLSTS Models)

1. Support the motorcycle with the rear wheel off the ground. See *Motorcycle Stands* in Chapter Nine.
2. Remove the seat as described in this chapter.
3. Remove both saddlebags as described in this chapter.
4. Disconnect the battery negative lead as described in Chapter Eight.

5. Disconnect the rear wiring harness eight-pin electrical connector under the seat.
6. Disconnect both rear turn signals two-pin electrical connectors from the rear wiring harness.
7. Remove the ignition module and module tray as described in Chapter Eight.
8. Remove the bolts and threaded studs securing the fender mounting brackets on both sides. Remove the mounting brackets located on the inner surface of the rear fender.
9. Carefully lift the rear fender up and off the frame and remove it.
10. Installation is the reverse of removal. Note the following:
   a. Tighten the bolts and fender mounting bolts and threaded studs to 21-27 ft.-lbs. (29-37 N·m).
   b. Check the operation of the taillight/brake light and rear turn signals for proper operation.

Removal/Installation
(FXSTD Models)

1. Support the motorcycle with the rear wheel off the ground. See *Motorcycle Stands* in Chapter Nine.
2. Remove the seat as described in this chapter.
3. Disconnect the battery negative lead as described in Chapter Eight.
4. Working underneath the rear fender, remove the screws and washers securing the fender support on both sides.
5. At the front edge of the fender support, remove the screw, spacer and nut securing the fender support. Repeat for the fender support on the other side.
6. Remove the taillight/brake light assembly as described in Chapter Eight.
7. Disconnect both rear turn signals two-pin electrical connectors from the rear wiring harness.
8. Remove the ignition module and module tray as described in Chapter Eight.
9. Working underneath the rear fender, remove the nuts securing the fender to the fender mounting brackets on both sides.
10. Carefully lift the rear fender up and off the frame and remove it.
11. Installation is the reverse of removal. Note the following:
   a. Tighten the bolts and fender mounting bolts and threaded studs to 21-27 ft.-lbs. (29-37 N·m).
   b. Check the operation of the taillight/brake light and rear turn signals for proper operation.

14

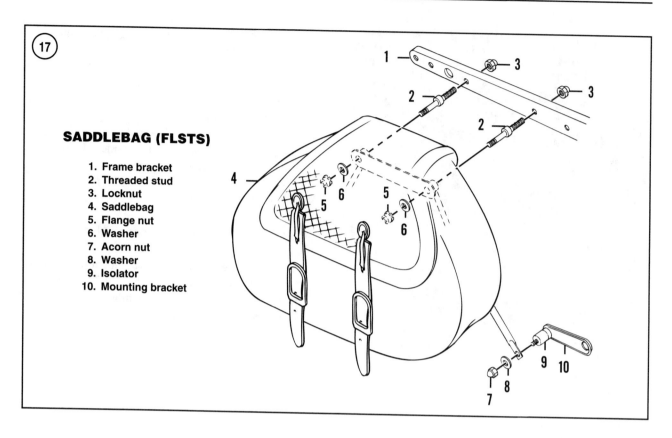

SADDLEBAG (FLSTS)

1. Frame bracket
2. Threaded stud
3. Locknut
4. Saddlebag
5. Flange nut
6. Washer
7. Acorn nut
8. Washer
9. Isolator
10. Mounting bracket

Removal/Installation
(All Models Except FLSTS and FXSTD)

1. Support the motorcycle with the rear wheel off the ground. See *Motorcycle Stands* in Chapter Nine.
2. Remove the seat as described in this chapter.
3. On FLSTC models, remove the sissy bar as described in this chapter.
4. On models so equipped, remove the saddlebags as described in this chapter.
5. Disconnect the battery negative lead as described in Chapter Eight.
6. Disconnect the rear wiring harness eight-pin electrical connector under the seat.
7. Disconnect both rear turn signals two-pin electrical connectors from the rear wiring harness.
8. Remove the ignition module and module tray as described in Chapter Eight.
9A. On FLSTC models, perform the following:
   a. Remove the bolts and saddlebag threaded studs securing the fender mounting brackets on both sides. Secure the sissy bar at this time
   b. Remove the mounting brackets located on the inner surface of the rear fender.
   c. Carefully lift the rear fender and sissy bar up and off the frame and remove it.

9B. On FLSTF models, perform the following:
   a. Remove the screws securing the fender mounting bracket to the mounting brackets and wiring retainer plate underneath the rear fender.
   b. Remove the mounting brackets and wiring retainer plates.
   c. Carefully lift the rear fender up and off the frame and remove it.
9C. On all other models, perform the following:
   a. At the front edge of the fender support, loosen but do not remove the two screws.
   b. Remove the remaining middle two fender support screws from the mounting bracket underneath the rear fender.
   c. Remove the rear screw from the mounting bracket underneath the rear fender.
   d. Remove the two screws at the front edge of the fender support.
   e. Repeat these steps for the other side.
   f. Remove both fender support brackets. Insert a long screwdriver or long rod through the frame and front fender holes to support the rear fender.
   g. Remove the locknuts and washers securing the rear fender to the fender mounting bracket.
   h. Remove the long screwdriver or long rod and remove the rear fender from the frame.

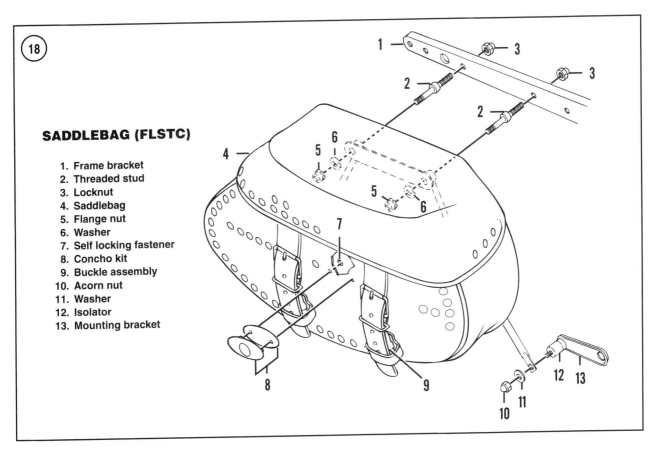

SADDLEBAG (FLSTC)

1. Frame bracket
2. Threaded stud
3. Locknut
4. Saddlebag
5. Flange nut
6. Washer
7. Self locking fastener
8. Concho kit
9. Buckle assembly
10. Acorn nut
11. Washer
12. Isolator
13. Mounting bracket

10. Installation is the reverse of removal. Note the following:

    a. Tighten the bolts and fender mounting bolts to 21-27 ft.-lbs. (29-37 N·m).

    b. Check the operation of the taillight/brake light and rear turn signals for proper operation.

WINDSHIELD

Removal/Installation

1. Place the motorcycle on level ground on the jiffy stand.

2. Use a finger to lift up on the wire form latch spring on each side of the windshield at the mounting brackets.

3. Straddle the front wheel and hold onto the windshield. Gently pull straight up on the top of the windshield until the upper notches on the side brackets are free of the upper grommets on the passing lamp support.

4. Continue to raise the windshield until the side brackets lower notches are free from the lower grommets and remove the windshield.

5. Installation is the reverse of removal. Note the following:

    a. Lower the windshield down until the latches are seated on the grommets.

    b. Push down on the wire form latch springs until they overhang the upper grommets.

    c. Make sure the windshield is securely in place prior to riding.

SADDLEBAGS

Removal/Installation

    Refer to **Figure 17** and **Figure 18**.

1. Place the motorcycle on level ground on the jiffy stand.

2. Remove the acorn nut and washer securing the saddlebag mounting bracket to the front lower support bracket.

3. Unhook the latches and open the saddlebag cover.

4. Within the saddlebag, remove the flange nuts and washers securing the saddle bag to the threaded studs.

5. Remove the saddlebag from the threaded studs.

6. Inspect the threaded studs for damage.

7. Installation is the reverse of removal.

14

19 **FLOORBOARDS AND FOOTRESTS**

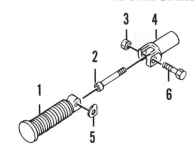
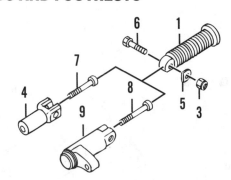
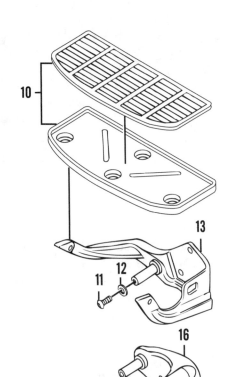
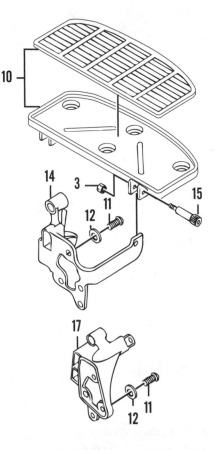

1. Footrest
2. Bolt
3. Locknut
4. Footrest bracket—passenger (right side)
5. Spring washer
6. Bolt
7. Bolt
8. Bolt
9. Footrest bracket—passenger (left side)
10. Floorboard and pad assembly
11. Screw

12. Washer
13. Mounting bracket (floorboard and brake pedal [FLST models])
14. Mounting bracket (floorboard and shifter pedal [FLST models])
15. Hinge bolt
16. Mounting bracket (floorboard and brake pedal [FXST models])
17. Mounting bracket (floorboard and shifter pedal [FXST models])

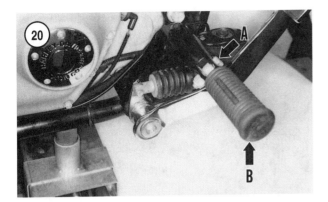

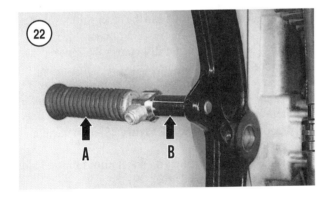

FOOTBOARDS AND FOOTRESTS

Floorboards
Removal/Installation

Refer to **Figure 19**.

1. Support the motorcycle with the front wheel off the ground. See *Motorcycle Stands* in Chapter Nine.

2. Remove the bolt and nut securing the floorboard to the mounting bracket. Remove the floorboard from the mounting bracket.

3. On the right side, perform the following to remove the mounting bracket:
   a. Remove the front brake pedal as described in Chapter Thirteen.
   b. Remove the rear master cylinder from the mounting bracket as described in Chapter Thirteen.
   c. Remove the bolts and washers securing the mounting bracket to the frame.
   d. Remove the mounting bracket.
4. On the left side, perform the following to remove the mounting bracket:
   a. Disconnect the shift rod from the inner shift lever.
   b. If necessary, remove the outer shift lever(s) from the inner shift lever shaft.
   c. Remove the bolts and washers securing the floorboard mounting bracket, jiffy stand and shift lever assembly to the frame.
   d. Remove the mounting bracket assembly from the frame.
5. If necessary, remove the rubber pad from the footboard and install a new one. Push the locating pins all the way through the footboard to secure the rubber pad in place.
6. Inspect the pivot bolts and nuts for damage. Replace them if necessary.
7. Inspect the footboard and the mounting brackets for damage and fractures. Replace as necessary.
8. Install the footboard(s) assembly onto the frame.
9. Apply a medium strength threadlocking compound to the bolt threads prior to installation.
10. Tighten the bolts to 25-30 ft.-lbs. (34-41 N·m).

Driver's Footrests
Removal/Installation

1. Place the motorcycle on level ground on the jiffy stand.
2. Remove the bolt, spring washer (models so equipped) and nut (A, **Figure 20**) securing the footrest to the mounting bracket. Remove the footrest (B, **Figure 20**).
3. Install by reversing these removal steps. Tighten the bolt and nut securely.

Passenger Footrests
Removal/Installation

1. Place the motorcycle on level ground on the jiffy stand.
2. Remove the bolt, spring washer (models so equipped) and nut (A, **Figure 21**) securing the footrest to the mounting bracket. Remove the footrest (B, **Figure 21**).
3. If necessary, remove the footrest (A, **Figure 22**), then remove the bolt securing the mounting bracket (B) to the frame and remove it.

14

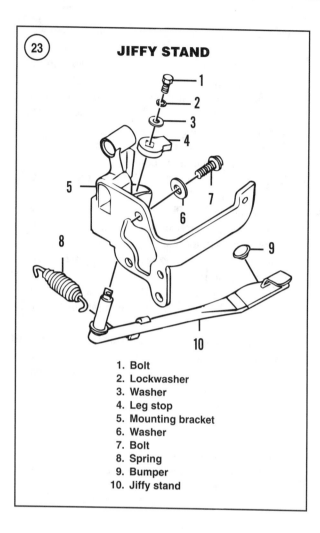

JIFFY STAND

1. Bolt
2. Lockwasher
3. Washer
4. Leg stop
5. Mounting bracket
6. Washer
7. Bolt
8. Spring
9. Bumper
10. Jiffy stand

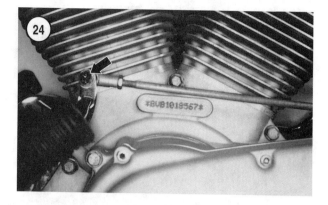

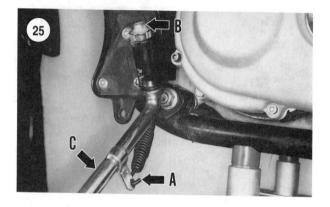

4. Install by reversing these removal steps. Tighten the bolt and nut securely.

JIFFY STAND

Refer to **Figure 23**.

1. Support the motorcycle with the front wheel off the ground. See *Motorcycle Stands* in Chapter Nine.

2. On models so equipped, remove the left side floorboard as described in this chapter.

3. Disconnect the shift rod from the inner shift lever (**Figure 24**).

4. Use Vise grip pliers and disconnect the return spring (A, **Figure 25**) from the frame tab.

5. Remove the bolt, lockwasher, washer and leg stop (B, **Figure 25**) securing the jiffy stand to the mounting bracket.

6. Remove the jiffy stand (C, **Figure 25**) from the mounting bracket.

7. Clean and lubricate the jiffy stand prior to installation as described in Chapter Three.

8. Installation is the reverse of removal. Note the following:

   a. Tighten the bolt securely.

   b. Ensure that the jiffy stand operates correctly in both positions prior to riding the motorcycle.

Index

15

15

15

NOTES

NOTES

NOTES

NOTES

2000 FLSTS AND FXSTD DOMESTIC AND HDI SOFTAIL MODELS

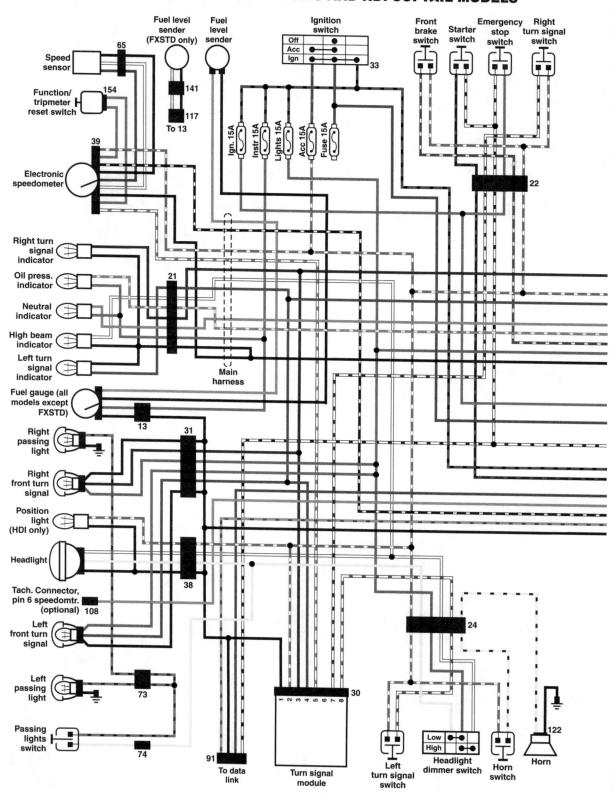

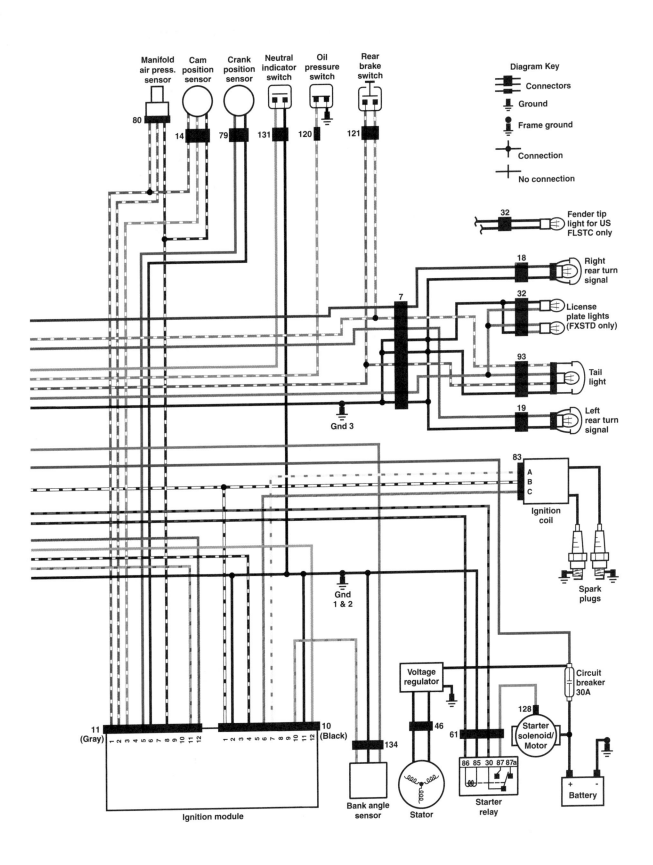

16

2000 ALL DOMESTIC AND HDI SOFTAIL MODELS EXCEPT FLSTC AND FXSTD

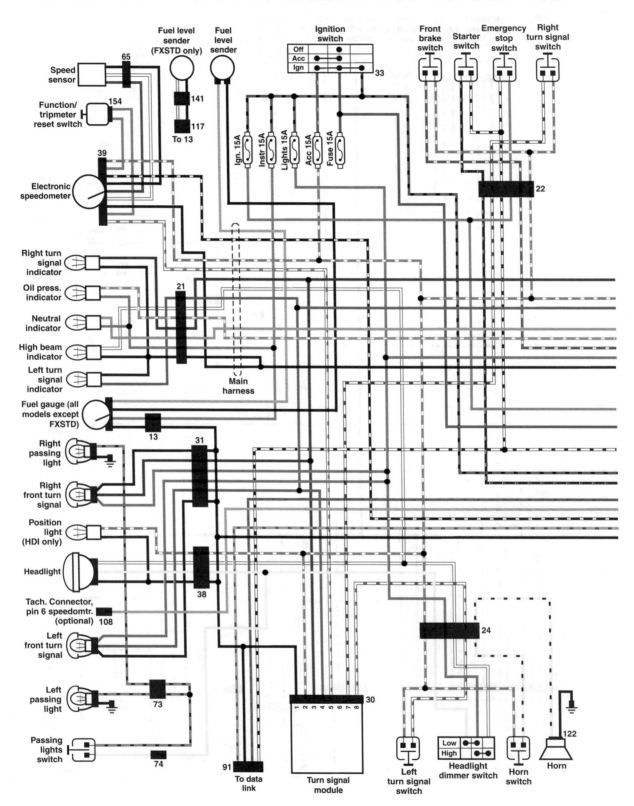

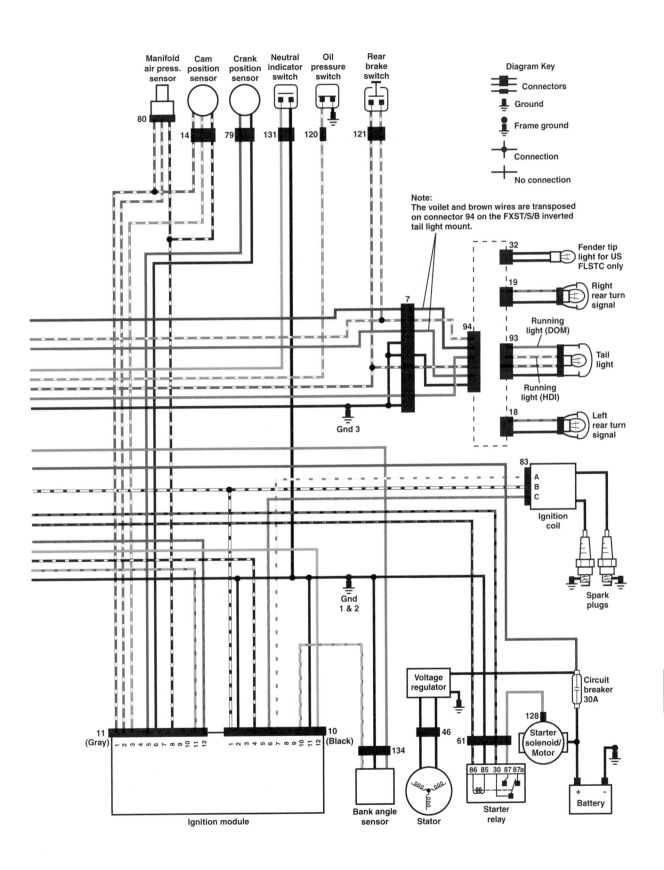

2001-2003 FLSTS AND FXSTD DOMESTIC AND HDI CARBURETED SOFTAIL MODELS

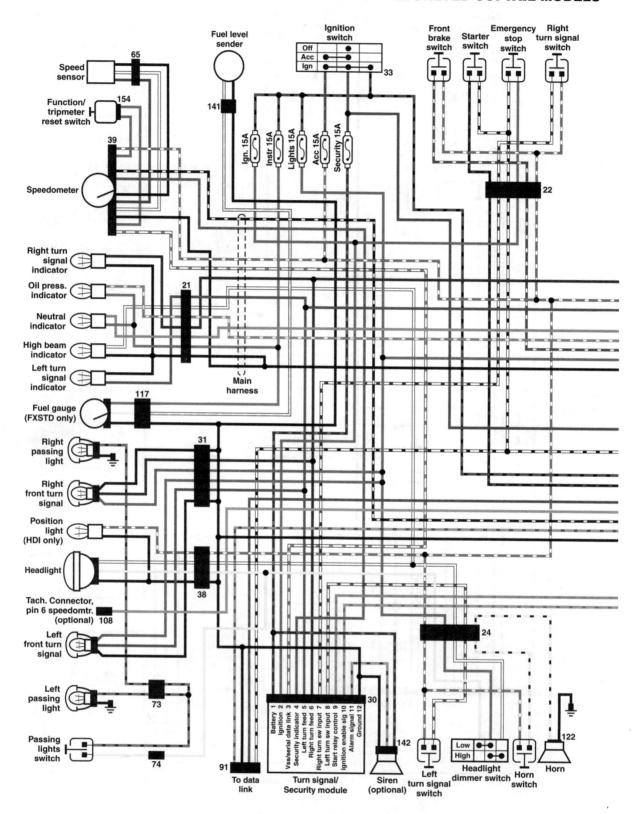

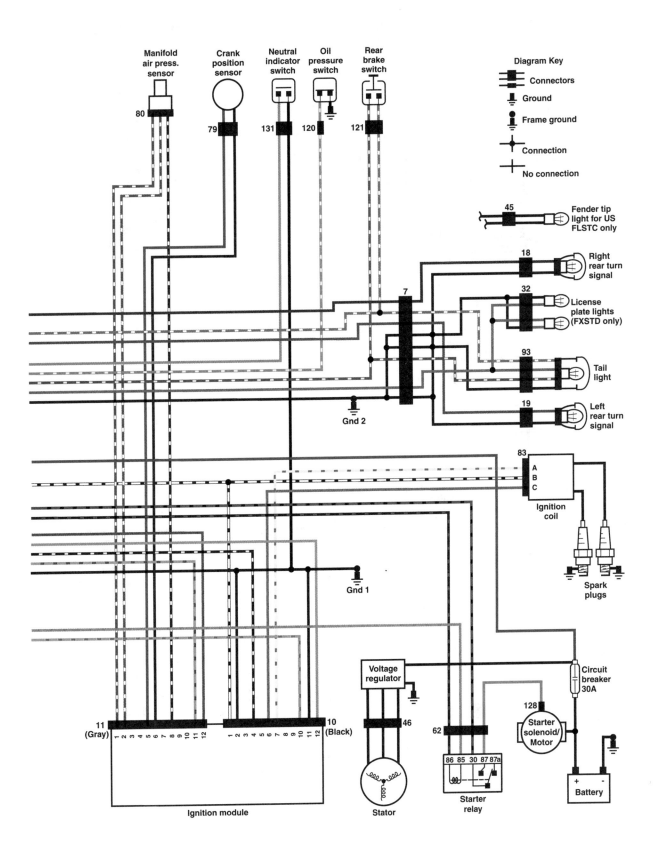

2001-2003 ALL DOMESTIC AND HDI CARBURETED SOFTAIL MODELS EXCEPT FLSTS AND FXSTD

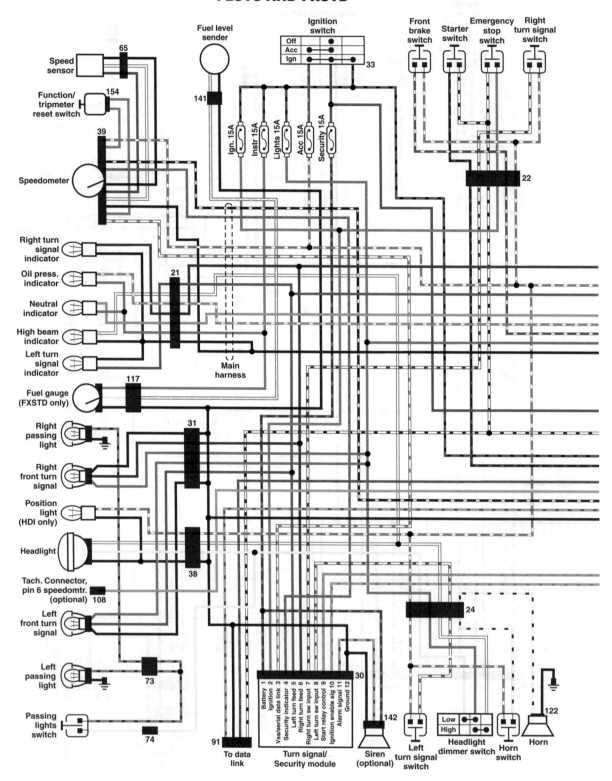

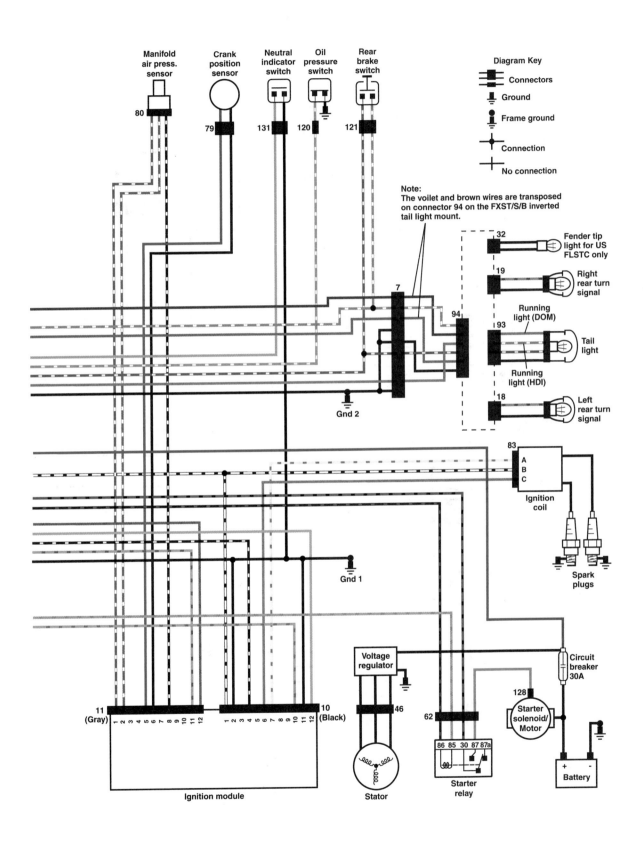

Manifold air press. sensor

Crank position sensor

Neutral indicator switch

Oil pressure switch

Rear brake switch

Diagram Key

Connectors

Ground

Frame ground

Connection

No connection

Note:
The voilet and brown wires are transposed on connector 94 on the FXST/S/B inverted tail light mount.

Fender tip light for US FLSTC only

Right rear turn signal

Running light (DOM)

Tail light

Running light (HDI)

Left rear turn signal

Gnd 2

Ignition coil

Spark plugs

Gnd 1

Voltage regulator

Circuit breaker 30A

11 (Gray)

10 (Black)

Starter solenoid/ Motor

Ignition module

Stator

Starter relay

Battery

16

2001-2003 FLSTS AND FXSTD DOMESTIC AND HDI EFI SOFTAIL MODELS

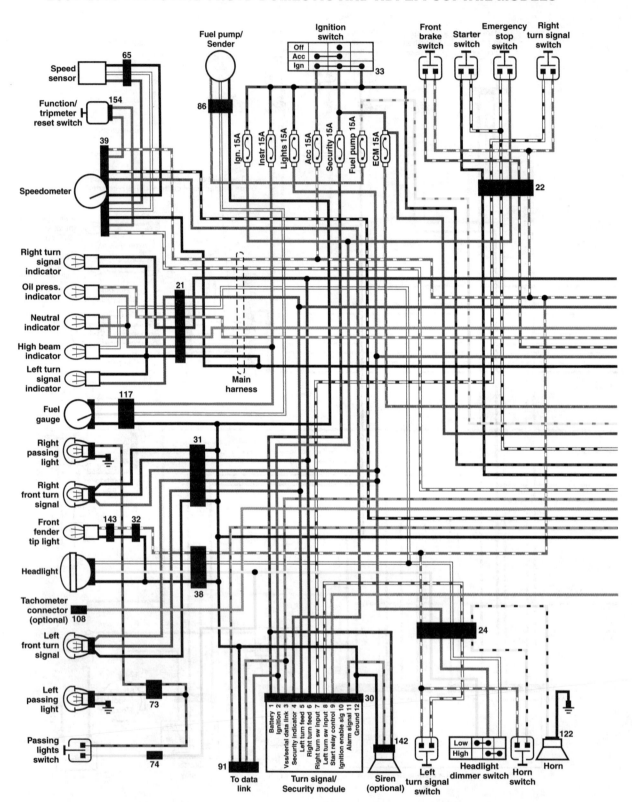

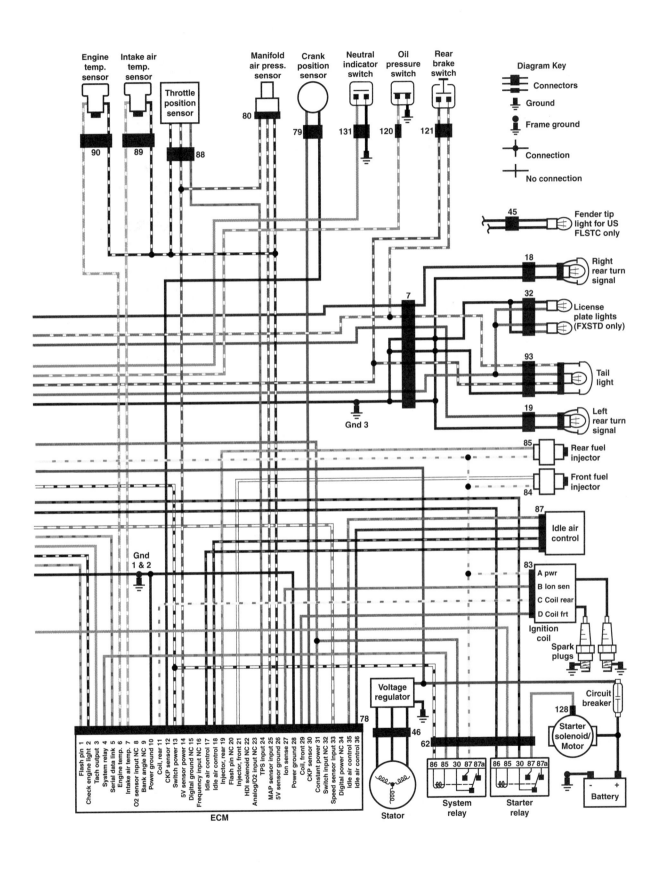

2001-2003 DOMESTIC AND HDI EFI SOFTAIL MODELS EXCEPT FLSTS AND FXSTD

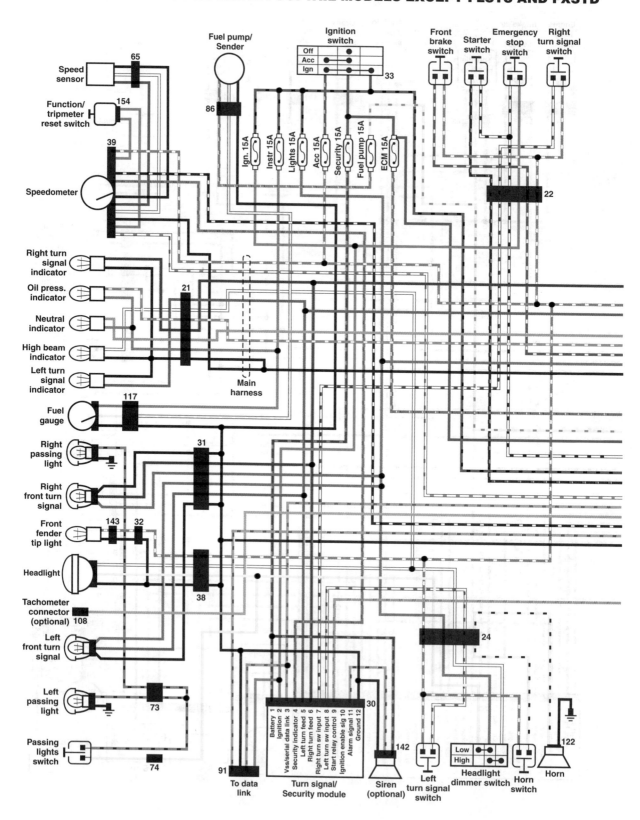

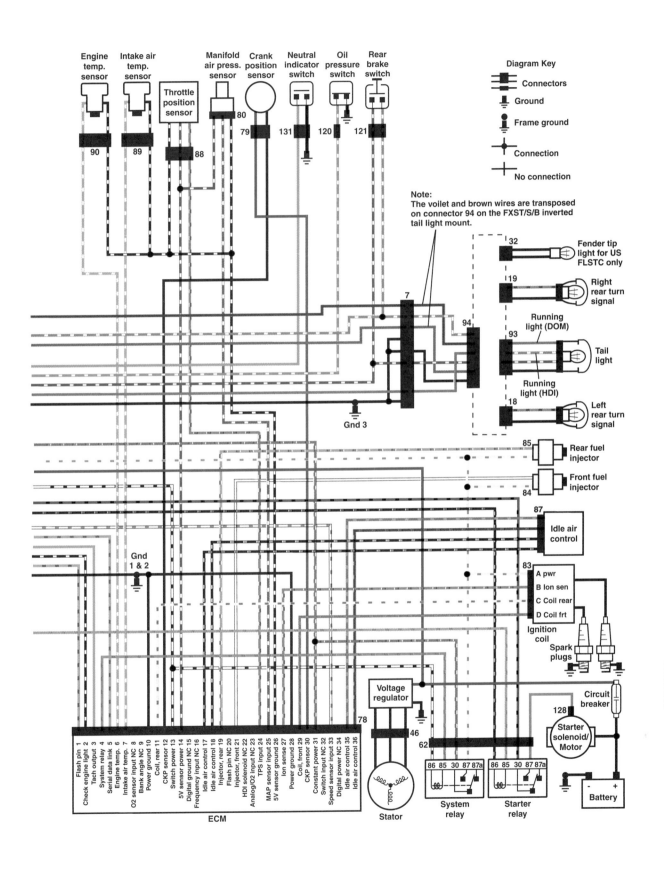

NOTES

MAINTENANCE LOG

Date	Miles	Type of Service